41: *Afro-American Poets Since 1955*, edited by Trudier Harris and Thadious M. Davis (19..)

42: *American Writers for Children Before 1900*, edited by Glenn E. Estes (1985)

43: *American Newspaper Journalists, 1690-1872*, edited by Perry J. Ashley (1986)

44: *American Screenwriters*, Second Series, edited by Randall Clark, Robert E. Morsberger, and Stephen O. Lesser (1986)

45: *American Poets, 1880-1945*, First Series, edited by Peter Quartermain (1986)

46: *American Literary Publishing Houses, 1900-1980: Trade and Paperback*, edited by Peter Dzwonkoski (1986)

47: *American Historians, 1866-1912*, edited by Clyde N. Wilson (1986)

48: *American Poets, 1880-1945*, Second Series, edited by Peter Quartermain (1986)

49: *American Literary Publishing Houses, 1638-1899*, 2 parts, edited by Peter Dzwonkoski (1986)

50: *Afro-American Writers Before the Harlem Renaissance*, edited by Trudier Harris (1986)

51: *Afro-American Writers from the Harlem Renaissance to 1940*, edited by Trudier Harris (1987)

52: *American Writers for Children Since 1960: Fiction*, edited by Glenn E. Estes (1986)

53: *Canadian Writers Since 1960*, First Series, edited by W. H. New (1986)

54: *American Poets, 1880-1945*, Third Series, 2 parts, edited by Peter Quartermain (1987)

55: *Victorian Prose Writers Before 1867*, edited by William B. Thesing (1987)

56: *German Fiction Writers, 1914-1945*, edited by James Hardin (1987)

57: *Victorian Prose Writers After 1867*, edited by William B. Thesing (1987)

58: *Jacobean and Caroline Dramatists*, edited by Fredson Bowers (1987)

59: *American Literary Critics and Scholars, 1800-1850*, edited by John W. Rathbun and Monica M. Grecu (1987)

60: *Canadian Writers Since 1960*, Second Series, edited by W. H. New (1987)

61: *American Writers for Children Since 1960: Poets, Illustrators, and Nonfiction Authors*, edited by Glenn E. Estes (1987)

62: *Elizabethan Dramatists*, edited by Fredson Bowers (1987)

63: *Modern American Critics, 1920-1955*, edited by Gregory S. Jay (1988)

64: *American Literary Critics and Scholars, 1850-1880*, edited by John W. Rathbun and Monica M. Grecu (1988)

65: *French Novelists, 1900-1930*, edited by Catharine Savage Brosman (1988)

66: *German Fiction Writers, 1885-1913*, 2 parts, edited by James Hardin (1988)

67: *Modern American Critics Since 1955*, edited by Gregory S. Jay (1988)

68: *Canadian Writers, 1920-1959*, First Series, edited by W. H. New (1988)

69: *Contemporary German Fiction Writers*, First Series, edited by Wolfgang D. Elfe and James Hardin (1988)

70: *British Mystery Writers, 1860-1919*, edited by Bernard Benstock and Thomas F. Staley (1988)

71: *American Literary Critics and Scholars, 1880-1900*, edited by John W. Rathbun and Monica M. Grecu (1988)

72: *French Novelists, 1930-1960*, edited by Catharine Savage Brosman (1988)

73: *American Magazine Journalists, 1741-1850*, edited by Sam G. Riley (1988)

74: *American Short-Story Writers Before 1880*, edited by Bobby Ellen Kimbel, with the assistance of William E. Grant (1988)

75: *Contemporary German Fiction Writers*, Second Series, edited by Wolfgang D. Elfe and James Hardin (1988)

76: *Afro-American Writers, 1940-1955*, edited by Trudier Harris (1988)

77: *British Mystery Writers, 1920-1939*, edited by Bernard Benstock and Thomas F. Staley (1988)

78: *American Short-Story Writers, 1880-1910*, edited by Bobby Ellen Kimbel, with the assistance of William E. Grant (1988)

79: *American Magazine Journalists, 1850-1900*, edited by Sam G. Riley (1988)

(Continued on back endsheets)

Dictionary of Literary Biography • Volume One Hundred Two

American Short-Story Writers, 1910-1945
Second Series

Dictionary of Literary Biography • Volume One Hundred Two

American Short-Story Writers, 1910-1945 Second Series

Edited by
Bobby Ellen Kimbel
Pennsylvania State University, Ogontz Campus

A Bruccoli Clark Layman Book
Gale Research Inc.
Detroit, London

Printed in the United States of America

Published simultaneously in the United Kingdom
by Gale Research International Limited
(An affiliated company of Gale Research Inc.)

The paper used in this publication meets the minimum requirements
of American National Standard for Information Sciences—Permanence
Paper for Printed Library Materials, ANSI Z39.48-1984. ∞™

ISBN 0-8103-4582-X
91-24164 CIP

For Philip, again,
in loving memory

Contents

Plan of the Series

The advisory board, the editors, and the publisher of the *Dictionary of Literary Biography* are joined in endorsing Mark Twain's declaration. The literature of a nation provides an inexhaustible resource of permanent worth. We intend to make literature and its creators better understood and more accessible to students and the reading public, while satisfying the standards of teachers and scholars.

To meet these requirements, *literary biography* has been construed in terms of the author's achievement. The most important thing about a writer is his writing. Accordingly, the entries in *DLB* are career biographies, tracing the development of the author's canon and the evolution of his reputation.

The purpose of *DLB* is not only to provide reliable information in a convenient format but also to place the figures in the larger perspective of literary history and to offer appraisals of their accomplishments by qualified scholars.

The publication plan for *DLB* resulted from two years of preparation. The project was proposed to Bruccoli Clark by Frederick G. Ruffner, president of the Gale Research Company, in November 1975. After specimen entries were prepared and typeset, an advisory board was formed to refine the entry format and develop the series rationale. In meetings held during 1976, the publisher, series editors, and advisory board approved the scheme for a comprehensive biographical dictionary of persons who contributed to North American literature. Editorial work on the first volume began in January 1977, and it was published in 1978. In order to make *DLB* more than a reference tool and to compile volumes that individually have claim to status as literary history, it was decided to organize volumes by topic, period, or genre. Each of these freestanding volumes provides a biographical-bibliographical guide and overview for a particular area of literature. We are convinced that this organization—as opposed to a single alphabet method—constitutes a valuable innovation in the presentation of reference material. The volume plan necessarily requires many decisions for the placement and treatment of authors who might properly be included in two or three volumes. In some instances a major figure will be included in separate volumes, but with different entries emphasizing the aspect of his career appropriate to each volume. Ernest Hemingway, for example, is represented in *American Writers in Paris, 1920-1939* by an entry focusing on his expatriate apprenticeship; he is also in *American Novelists, 1910-1945* with an entry surveying his entire career. Each volume includes a cumulative index of subject authors and articles. Comprehensive indexes to the entire series are planned.

With volume ten in 1982 it was decided to enlarge the scope of *DLB*. By the end of 1986 twenty-one volumes treating British literature had been published, and volumes for Commonwealth and Modern European literature were in progress. The series has been further augmented by the *DLB Yearbooks* (since 1981) which update published entries and add new entries to keep the *DLB* current with contemporary activity. There have also been *DLB Documentary Series* volumes which provide biographical and critical source materials for figures whose work is judged to have particular interest for students. One of these companion volumes is entirely devoted to Tennessee Williams.

We define literature as the *intellectual commerce of a nation:* not merely as belles lettres but as that ample and complex process by which ideas are generated, shaped, and transmitted. *DLB* entries are not limited to "creative writers" but extend to other figures who in their time and in their way influenced the mind of a people. Thus the series encompasses historians, journalists, publishers, and screenwriters. By this means readers of *DLB* may be aided to perceive literature not as cult scripture in the keeping of intellectual high priests but firmly positioned at the center of a nation's life.

DLB includes the major writers appropriate to each volume and those standing in the ranks immediately behind them. Scholarly and critical counsel has been sought in deciding which minor figures to include and how full their entries should be. Wherever possible, useful references are made to figures who do not warrant separate entries.

Each *DLB* volume has a volume editor responsible for planning the volume, selecting the figures for inclusion, and assigning the entries. Volume editors are also responsible for preparing, where appropriate, appendices surveying the major periodicals and literary and intellectual movements for their volumes, as well as lists of further readings. Work on the series as a whole is coordinated at the Bruccoli Clark Layman editorial center in Columbia, South Carolina, where the editorial staff is responsible for accuracy of the published volumes.

One feature that distinguishes *DLB* is the illustration policy–its concern with the iconography of literature. Just as an author is influenced by his surroundings, so is the reader's understanding of the author enhanced by a knowledge of his environment. Therefore *DLB* volumes include not only drawings, paintings, and photographs of authors, often depicting them at various stages in their careers, but also illustrations of their families and places where they lived. Title pages are regularly reproduced in facsimile along with dust jackets for modern authors. The dust jackets are a special feature of *DLB* because they often document better than anything else the way in which an author's work was perceived in its own time. Specimens of the writers' manuscripts are included when feasible.

Samuel Johnson rightly decreed that "The chief glory of every people arises from its authors." The purpose of the *Dictionary of Literary Biography* is to compile literary history in the surest way available to us–by accurate and comprehensive treatment of the lives and work of those who contributed to it.

The *DLB* Advisory Board

Foreword

The bleak and cheerless vision that we have come to associate with American literature in the first half of the twentieth century was not invented by the men and women who lived and wrote during the period. We find no greater affirmation in the poetry of Alfred Tennyson, A. E. Housman, and Edwin Arlington Robinson than in that of T. S. Eliot, Ezra Pound, and Robinson Jeffers and no greater claim for meaning or purpose in the world of human beings in the fiction of Thomas Hardy, Joseph Conrad, Hamlin Garland, and Henry James than in that of Theodore Dreiser, Ernest Hemingway, F. Scott Fitzgerald, and William Faulkner. Nineteenth-century science had abruptly and conclusively provided us with a world with nothingness at its center, a world in which the activities of men and women were, in Bertrand Russell's phrase, only "secular hurryings through space." And literary artists, reflecting as they invariably do the currents that define their own time and place, created poetry and fiction of despair: events, characters, and the natural world were depicted as clearly God-abandoned. But late-nineteenth-century writers had retained at least the externals of order; one finds in their works a continuity with established traditions of metrics and rhyme, of carefully structured plots, of trustworthy narrators, of consecutive chronologies. As the twentieth century advances, this adherence to rhetorical strategies of the past disappears, giving way to a new compression of material, a fragmentation of narrative, a break in rhythmic patterns, a dislocation of time, a freshness of language, a convolutedness and open-endedness of plot. The break with traditional forms becomes the hallmark of twentieth-century writings—compare even the look of a page of Tennyson's poetry with one of Eliot's—and nowhere is this shift more evident than in the American short story.

Gertrude Stein's *Three Lives* (1909) and Sherwood Anderson's *Winesburg, Ohio* (1919) are among the earliest examples of stories (both of these were written as collections) which exhibit marked departures from what had earlier been established as acceptable structure for the short-story form. Stein's accomplishment was in recording the process of consciousness itself: The effect is primitive, the technique extraordinarily sophisticated. The method she employed—careful limitation of vocabulary, absence of traditional punctuation, consistent use of present participles, repetition of simple words and phrases, distortion of syntax—allowed her to establish the unique personality of each of her characters and to suggest as well a mirroring of the mind as it perceives the world and experiences events. In the *Winesburg, Ohio* stories Anderson broke with those still obedient to the rhetorical strictures of the past. While many of his contemporaries were engaged in creating short fictions defined by Aristotelian plot structure, linear chronology, verisimilitude of character and event, and the assumption of available (if not often utilized) moral codes, Anderson created brief, intense moments in which his nearly always desperate characters are revealed in a sudden flash of illumination. The effect is epiphanic: often only a single gesture or bit of dialogue catches the complexity, the allusiveness of character or moment, and it remains uninterpreted, merely suggestive. His treatment of sexual longing as a defining characteristic of American loneliness in the industrial age is as much as anything else in Anderson shockingly new, and this, coupled with his use of those unusual linguistic cadences rooted in the American oral tradition, created possibilities for fiction writers not earlier available to them.

Anderson often acknowledged his debt to Stein; Hemingway acknowledged his to both of them (if only grudgingly to Anderson); all three are the stylistic children of Mark Twain, whose *Adventures of Huckleberry Finn* (1884) first brought to American literature a native idiom. The reaction against the "literary" (which is to say inflated, sentimentalized, rhetorically grand) style of the nineteenth century can be seen in the stories of George Ade, Ring Lardner, Stephen Crane, Gertrude Stein, Sherwood Anderson, and Ernest Hemingway, all of whom infused their works with the language of everyday speech—direct, colloquial, and in its effect, spontaneous.

The most famous exemplar of this increasingly characteristic prose idiom is Ernest Hemingway, whose 1925 collection of prose fiction, *In Our Time*, reveals his indebtedness to both Twain and Stein: "The kid came out and had to kill five bulls because you can't have more than three matadors, and the last bull he was so tired he couldn't get the sword in. He couldn't hardly lift his arm." The passage, like many in the collection, is in the American vernacular—deliberately loose, slangy, and ungrammatical. This flat, direct observation of experience, unmediated by any reflection upon its meaning, defines the Hemingway style. Critics are in general agreement that this distancing of event from response to it is a defence against feeling (articulated most convincingly in Philip Young's "would theory"). But it reveals as well Hemingway's background as a working journalist on the *Kansas City Star* and the *Toronto Star*.

It is a fact often remarked upon that many of the finest practitioners of the short-story form in the first half of the twentieth century began their writing careers as newspaper reporters. Jack London, Stephen Crane, Dreiser, Lardner, Damon Runyon, Anderson, Katherine Anne Porter, Hemingway, all served their apprenticeships in that intense, deadline-driven environment of the newsroom. Their awareness of the editor's blue-penciling developed an ear for transcribing the vitality of spoken language, an eye for recording the telling detail, and the ability to restructure the flabby and inchoate human scene into tightly organized and vivid tales. We know from the essays and memoirs of many of these men and women that some of their best-known short-fiction works had first lives as reported news events.

At the same time that newspapers provided a training ground for the sharpening of storytelling skills, American magazines, proliferating everywhere, became a source of income for struggling young writers and a forum which exposed their works to the public. Although by 1910, *Century*, *Harper's*, the *Atlantic*, and the *North American Review* were languishing (due in part to a misguided clinging to outworn editorial and advertising principles and in part to an increasingly literate but less discriminating populace), mass-circulation magazines flourished and under wise editorship continued to publish the works of America's literary artists. Throughout the next two decades stories by Edith Wharton, Ernest Hemingway, and Thomas Wolfe appeared with regularity in *Scribner's* magazine. In the 1930s the *Saturday Evening Post* featured the illustrations of Norman Rockwell on its cover, his stolid figures gazing benignly and reassuringly at the reader, while inside were printed many of the radically new, often unsettling fictions of F. Scott Fitzgerald and William Faulkner. (Fitzgerald received as much as four thousand dollars per story from the *Post* and in the combined years of 1928 and 1929 had an income of nearly fifty thousand dollars for the pieces the magazine published.) H. L. Mencken's *American Mercury*, although not, strictly speaking, a mass-circulation magazine, was influential, and writers as important as Sinclair Lewis, Dreiser, and Fitzgerald knew they had an appreciative audience when Mencken published their works. When Harold Ross's *New Yorker* first appeared in 1925 with Ross's celebrated admonition that its published works must make no concessions to "the little old lady from Dubuque," the most sophisticated, urbane of American magazines had arrived. The importance of this periodical for short-story writers of real talent cannot be overstated. In its nearly sixty-five years of publication, it has functioned, informally but incontrovertibly, as a *New Yorker* school of short-story writing, shaping its audience to expect and applaud the cool, allusive, frequently satiric, and usually brilliant works of such authors as Kay Boyle, John O'Hara, Irwin Shaw, Dorothy Parker, E. B. White, James Thurber, John Cheever, and John Updike.

For many serious readers and writers of short fiction, the little magazines provided the ideal medium for the publication of short fictions considered avant-garde at the time, but now regarded as indisputable classics of the canon. According to Frederick Hoffman, Charles Allen, and Carolyn Ulrich in their *The Little Magazines: A History and A Bibliography* (1947), since 1912 eighty percent of our most important writers (this includes critics as well as poets and fiction writers) and every significant literary movement found sponsorship in the little magazines. The function of these literary periodicals is described in this way:

> A little magazine is a magazine designed to print artistic work which for reasons of commercial expediency is not acceptable to the money-minded periodicals or presses. Acceptance or refusal by commercial publishers at times has nothing to do with the quality of the work. If the magazine can obtain artistic work from unknown or relatively unknown writers, the little magazine purpose is further accomplished. Little magazines are will-

ing to lose money, to court ridicule, to ignore public taste, willing to do almost anything—steal, beg, or undress in public—rather than sacrifice their right to print good material.

In general, then, the founding of the little magazine was an expression of revolt against the conservativism of both the general public and the editorial policies of commercial periodicals; indeed, the titles of several—*Blast*, the *Anvil*, the *Left* and *Masses*—reveal a political as well as a literary bias. But the risk of economic failure was great, and although there were as many as fifty new little magazines in the mid 1930s, relatively few of them survived in the war years.

Beginning in 1912 and for several years following, these literary journals acted as a forum for some of the country's most remarkable young writers. There were those publications designed exclusively for poetry: *Poetry: A Magazine of Verse; The Poetry Journal; Contemporary Verse; The Fugitive;* and *Others* are among the best known, and it is no exaggeration to say that for nearly every poet of note these small presses provided the first and often the only outlet for their work. For short-story writers whose fictions seemed unsuitable for and were therefore rejected by the mass-circulation magazines, publication in the little magazines frequently functioned to establish their careers. Hemingway's first six stories were printed in the little magazines; and the early works of Jean Toomer, Conrad Aiken, James Stephens, Sherwood Anderson, Kay Boyle, William Faulkner, Erskine Caldwell, and Katherine Anne Porter found a sophisticated and responsive readership in subscribers to such periodicals as *The Double Dealer, Hound and Horn, Broom, transition,* and *Story.*

Although two world wars and an economic boom and catastrophe have allowed literary and other historians of the twentieth century neatly to categorize the 1920s, 1930s, and 1940s, the forces at work in the first two decades were not as felicitously deployed. Until the beginning of the Great War in 1914 and most perceptibly in the disillusionment which followed it, American culture seemed of a piece with that of the late nineteenth century. To observe that throughout that complacent period of expansion and industrialization the very rich continued to become very much richer without the threat of taxation or of labor legislation; to note that at the same time, the number of immigrants arriving in the United States formed a huge underclass, the effects of

which was to keep millions unemployed or working for low wages in incredibly poor conditions; to remember that there coexisted, sometimes within only a few miles of each other, the squalor and misery of slums and the grandeur of palatial estates is but to recount the most obvious social data. The frontier and the midwestern plains, once glowing alternatives to life in the metropolitan East, no longer promised either the riches of gold or the welcoming smiles of farmers, who were now experiencing drought and foreclosures. The growth of industrial communities brought a gray unvarying pattern to the cityscape, and people of clashing nationalities, languages, and customs were daily thrown into uneasy alliances with each other. And America, which at least in the eyes of the privileged and the governing had seemed superior and inviolable, was slowly drifting toward involvement with other nations, and finally into the Great War.

Neither the dislocations undergirding the culture nor the rumblings of approaching disaster were reflected in the popular magazine stories of the time. Their subjects tended toward the sentimental and were treated in a cheerful, allusive way, and plots nearly always had a happy ending. They were, quite simply, false to experience, and the language in which they were written was, predictably, banal and lifeless. Philip Stevick, in his introduction to *The American Short Story, 1900-1945* (1984), observes that the magazine fiction of this period had an "obsessive adverbial quality," while works from that time that endured reveal a greater reliance on nouns and verbs to carry the burden of meaning. His examples, taken from one contemporary magazine story, make the point: "he said, indolently"; "nodding his head, sagaciously"; "he answered, gravely"; "replied Braithwaite, snappishly"; "he continued, ecstatically"; "he said, wearily." There is a tendency for such rhetoric to draw attention to itself as arch and knowing; at the same time, focus is shifted away from character and action, and the reader feels removed from the narrated events. The authors of such works were bound, or at least felt that they were, by the taboos of subject matter and language inherited from the past. And yet, those transitional figures—Willa Cather, Theodore Dreiser, Henry James, and Edith Wharton—remained resistant to the complacency around them and unfazed by the meretricious stories with which they had to compete for inclusion in many of the magazines of the day. They went on doing what they had to do, that is, writing with originality and conviction. Their short stories of this period (among them, James's "The Beast in the Jungle," Wharton's "Souls Belated," Dreiser's "Free," and Cather's "Paul's Case") reveal textures more tough and sinewy and truths much darker than the typical contemporary short fictions, but they are still read, taught, analyzed, anthologized, and emulated today, while the more esteemed writers of the period, courting popularity by maintain the tradition of the genteel and precious, have long since been forgotten.

The social upheavals of the postwar decade and the extraordinary fiction, poetry, and drama to which they gave birth have made the 1920s the most consistently scrutinized of any period in American literary history. Despite the bitterness of the young men and women returning from service overseas to a country untouched by the war and insensitive to its brutality, and the consequent expatriation of great numbers of artists to France and England, and despite the growing power of the Ku Klux Klan, gangsterism, prohibition, the increasing alienation and suspicion between the generations, and a tenacious Main Street repressiveness, the period evokes an unmistakable glamour. Women won the vote; the automobile, now available through mass production to enormous numbers of people (a Ford car sold for $290 in 1924), functioned as a means of escape from boredom and sexual restraint; jazz, formerly a subversive musical idiom played primarily by black performers, now defined the era; movies (attended by one hundred million people weekly by 1926) suggested a sensuous reality further reinforced by the popularization of Sigmund Freud's theories of the libido; new fashions in dancing and dress dictated social status and were taken up and cast off with equal impetuousness. It was, in Fitzgerald's words, "the greatest, gaudiest spree in history."

The American fiction writers of the 1920s who fled to Paris after the war in revolt against the nation of "philistines" remained curiously apolitical. Of those who either made Paris their home or traveled there often enough to be labeled "expatriates"—Gertrude Stein, Sherwood Anderson, F. Scott Fitzgerald, Ernest Hemingway, John Dos Passos, Kay Boyle—only Dos Passos and Boyle espoused specifically political views. Those authors most closely identified, then as now, with the modernist spirit of fiction works of the 1920s and the decade which followed—Hemingway, Fitzgerald, and Faulkner (who

served in the Canadian Royal Air Force during the war and then returned to his home in Oxford, Mississippi)—discovered methods of protest more rooted in the literary imagination. While the reputations of these three writers grow primarily out of their work in novelistic fiction, their steady output in the short-story form (even when dictated more by economic need than aesthetic impulse) reshaped and redefined its contours. Fitzgerald traced the psychic as well as the social history of the times (he is much more than the chronicler of that period, a debasing of his extraordinary talent still exercised today in some quarters), and his stories catch with superb irony the hysterical abandonment to youth, riches, glamour, and amusement that became both his subject and his personal fate. Hemingway, in his conviction that the past provides no source of value, the future no hope, focuses on the moral choices made from moment to moment as the only meaning available in human experience, and this theme and its variation throughout his stories are a powerful expression of American existentialism. And Faulkner's intricate weaving of southern myth and archetypal ritual, his stretching of American vocabulary and cadences to reveal complexities of chronology and consciousness, establish thematic and linguistic patterns undreamed of before his work appeared.

The years between 1910 and the end of World War II—the period covered by *DLB 86* and *DLB 102* (the third and fourth on American short-story writers in the *Dictionary of Literary Biography* series)—were dominated by fiction writing. Eugene O'Neill was the only genius writing for the American stage during this period; and although the poetry of such figures as Edwin Arlington Robinson, Ezra Pound, T. S. Eliot, Robert Frost, Hart Crane, and Wallace Stevens is extraordinary in its range of subjects and techniques and inevitably in its influence, the number of novels and stories published and avidly read by intellectuals and general readers alike make the first half of the twentieth century the era of American fiction. The increasing prominence of the short-story form is particularly apparent. In part, this is due to a new "packaging." In the 1920s two short-story annuals began publication, *The Best Short Stories* and *O. Henry Memorial Award: Prize Stories*. Thus, it was not unusual for stories of real artistic merit to find two forums—the first in a commercial magazine, the second in one of the two annuals whose inclusion in their titles of the lustrous and beckoning words, "best" and "prize," worked to insure a large readership. At the same time, a new format emerged for individual writers of the short story. Following the publication of Sherwood Anderson's *Winesburg, Ohio* in 1919, there appeared several collections, among them Willa Cather's *Youth and the Bright Medusa* (1920); F. Scott Fitzgerald's *Flappers and Philosophers* (1922); Jean Toomer's *Cane* (1923); Ernest Hemingway's *In Our Time* (1925); Ring Lardner's *The Love Nest* (1926); Richard Wright's *Uncle Tom's Children: Five Long Stories* (1938); and Eudora Welty's *A Curtain of Green* (1941).

But it was content even more than availability that created a continued demand for the short story. While the received ideas of Sigmund Freud, Carl Jung, Karl Marx, and G. S. Fraser (whose studies in cultural anthropology brought an awareness to the Western world of the cross-cultural pervasiveness and centrality of myths) are everywhere in evidence in the evolution of the form, the sources of its power are in native American material. Whether in the melancholy atmosphere of small towns (in the works, for exam-

ple of Anderson, Cather, Welty), the glamour and danger of the big city (as in O. Henry, Fitzgerald, James T. Farrell), or the capacity for violence, both potential and actual, lurking in the natural world (particularly in Hemingway, Faulkner, Katherine Anne Porter), our finest writers in the genre have found the means to make the regional universal. It is interesting to note how many of these authors lived on the fringes of the world about which they wrote so that they are themselves the "marginal figures," the members of a "submerged population group," about which Frank O'Connor (in his *The Lonely Voice*, 1963) speaks when he describes the solitary beings that populate the modern American short story. It may well be that the lonely wanderers who dominate these works are compelling precisely because they are the projected lives of their creators; in them the thoughtful readers of the nation and the world have been able to recognize themselves.

—*Bobby Ellen Kimbel*

Acknowledgments

This book was produced by Bruccoli Clark Layman, Inc. Karen L. Rood is senior editor for the *Dictionary of Literary Biography* series. Jack Turner was the in-house editor.

Production coordinator is James W. Hipp. Systems manager is Charles D. Brower. Photography editors are Susan Todd Brook and Edward Scott. Permissions editor is Jean W. Ross. Layout and graphics supervisor is Penney L. Haughton. Copyediting supervisor is Bill Adams. Typesetting supervisor is Kathleen M. Flanagan. Information systems analyst is George F. Dodge. Charles Lee Egleston is editorial associate. The production staff includes Rowena Betts, Polly Brown, Reginald A. Bullock, Teresa Chaney, Patricia Coate, Sarah A. Estes, Robert Fowler, Mary L. Goodwin, Ellen McCracken, Kathy Lawler Merlette, Laura Garren Moore, John Myrick, Pamela D. Norton, Cathy J. Reese, Laurrè Sinckler, Maxine K. Smalls, John C. Stone III, and Betsy L. Weinberg.

Walter W. Ross and Timothy D. Tebalt did the library research at the Thomas Cooper Library of the University of South Carolina with the assistance of the following librarians: Gwen Baxter, Daniel Boice, Faye Chadwell, Cathy Eckman, Gary Geer, Cathie Gottlieb, David L. Haggard, Jens Holley, Jackie Kinder, Thomas Marcil, Marcia Martin, Laurie Preston, Jean Rhyne, Carol Tobin, and Virginia Weathers.

Michael Kreyling, author of the Eudora Welty entry, acknowledges the help and support of the Mississippi Humanities Council.

Dictionary of Literary Biography • Volume One Hundred Two

American Short-Story Writers, 1910-1945
Second Series

Dictionary of Literary Biography

Conrad Aiken
(5 August 1889 - 17 August 1973)

Joseph Killorin

See also the Aiken entries in *DLB 9: American Novelists, 1910-1945* and *DLB 45: American Poets, 1880-1945*.

BOOKS: *Earth Triumphant and Other Tales in Verse* (New York: Macmillan, 1914; London: Macmillan, 1914);

Turns and Movies and Other Tales in Verse (Boston & New York: Houghton Mifflin, 1916; London: Constable / Boston & New York: Houghton Mifflin, 1916);

The Jig of Forslin: A Symphony (Boston: Four Seas, 1916; London: Secker, 1922);

Nocturne of Remembered Spring and Other Poems (Boston: Four Seas, 1917; London: Secker, 1922);

The Charnel Rose; Senlin: A Biography; and Other Poems (Boston: Four Seas, 1918; revised, 1922);

Scepticisms: Notes on Contemporary Poetry (New York: Knopf, 1919);

The House of Dust: A Symphony (Boston: Four Seas, 1920);

Punch: The Immortal Liar, Documents in His History (New York: Knopf, 1921; London: Secker, 1921);

Priapus and the Pool (Cambridge, Mass.: Dunster House, 1922);

The Pilgrimage of Festus (New York: Knopf, 1923; London: Secker, 1924);

Bring! Bring! (London: Secker, 1925); republished as *Bring! Bring! and Other Stories* (New York: Boni & Liveright, 1925);

Priapus and the Pool and Other Poems (New York: Boni & Liveright, 1925);

Conrad Aiken in his mid thirties (Collection of Clarissa Lorenz Aiken)

Blue Voyage (London: Howe, 1927; New York: Scribners, 1927);

Conrad Aiken, edited by Louis Untermeyer (New York: Simon & Schuster, 1928);

Dr. William Ford Aiken, Conrad's father, in 1888, the year he married Anna Potter (by permission of the Henry E. Huntington Library and Art Gallery)

Costumes by Eros (New York: Scribners, 1928; London: Cape, 1929);

Prelude (New York: Random House, 1929);

Selected Poems (New York & London: Scribners, 1929);

John Deth: A Metaphysical Legend, and Other Poems (New York: Scribners, 1930);

Gehenna (New York: Random House, 1930);

The Coming Forth by Day of Osiris Jones (New York: Scribners, 1931);

Preludes for Memnon (New York & London: Scribners, 1931);

Great Circle (New York: Scribners, 1933; London: Wishart, 1933);

Among the Lost People (New York: Scribners, 1934);

Landscape West of Eden (London: Dent, 1934; New York: Scribners, 1935);

King Coffin (New York: Scribners, 1935; London: Dent, 1935);

Time in the Rock: Preludes to Definition (New York: Scribners, 1936);

A Heart for the Gods of Mexico (London: Secker, 1939);

Conversation; or, Pilgrim's Progress (New York: Duell, Sloan & Pearce, 1940; London: Phillips & Green, 1948);

And In The Human Heart (New York: Duell, Sloan & Pearce, 1940; London: Staples, 1949);

Brownstone Eclogues and Other Poems (New York: Duell, Sloan & Pearce, 1942);

The Soldier: A Poem (Norfolk, Conn.: New Directions, 1944; London: Editions Poetry, 1946);

The Kid (New York: Duell, Sloan & Pearce, 1947; London: Lehmann, 1947);

Skylight One: Fifteen Poems (New York: Oxford University Press, 1949; London: Lehmann, 1951);

The Divine Pilgrim (Athens: University of Georgia Press, 1949);

The Short Stories of Conrad Aiken (New York: Duell, Sloan & Pearce, 1950); enlarged as *The Collected Short Stories of Conrad Aiken* (Cleveland & New York: World, 1960; London: Heinemann, 1966);

Ushant: An Essay (New York: Duell, Sloan & Pearce / Boston: Little, Brown, 1952; London: Allen, 1963);

Collected Poems (New York: Oxford University Press, 1953; enlarged, 1970);

A Letter from Li Po and Other Poems (New York: Oxford University Press, 1955);

Mr. Arcularis: A Play (Cambridge, Mass.: Harvard University Press, 1957; London: Oxford University Press, 1958);

Sheepfold Hill: Fifteen Poems (New York: Sagamore, 1958);

A Reviewer's ABC: Collected Criticism of Conrad Aiken from 1916 to the Present, edited by Rufus A. Blanshard (New York: Greenwich/Meridian, 1958; London: Allen, 1961); republished as *Collected Criticism* (London, Oxford & New York: Oxford University Press, 1968);

Selected Poems (New York: Oxford University Press, 1961; London, Oxford & New York: Oxford University Press, 1969);

The Morning Song of Lord Zero: Poems Old and New (New York: Oxford University Press, 1963; London: Oxford University Press, 1963);

A Seizure of Limericks (New York, Chicago & San
    Francisco: Holt, Rinehart & Winston, 1964;
    London: Allen, 1965);
Cats and Bats and Things with Wings (New York: Ath-
    eneum, 1965);
Tom, Sue and the Clock (New York: Collier / Lon-
    don: Collier-Macmillan, 1966);
Thee: A Poem (New York: Braziller, 1967; Lon-
    don: Inca, 1973);
The Clerk's Journal: Being the Diary of a Queer Man
    (New York: Eakins, 1971);
A Little Who's Zoo of Mild Animals (London: Cape,
    1977; New York: Cape/Atheneum, 1977).
Collections: *The Collected Novels of Conrad Aiken:*
    Blue Voyage, Great Circle, King Coffin, A Heart
    for the Gods of Mexico, Conversation (New
    York, Chicago & San Francisco: Holt, Rine-
    hart & Winston, 1964);
Preludes: Preludes for Memnon / Time in the Rock
    (New York: Oxford University Press, 1966,
    London: Oxford University Press, 1966).

Conrad Aiken's works—twenty-six volumes
of poetry, five novels, forty-one short stories, two
volumes of criticism, and one play—present a
range of achievement that made him "one of the
few genuine *men of letters* left in our world
today," as Allen Tate said, adding, when "sum-
ming up the total value of Conrad Aiken one
must give a very high place to his fiction."
Aiken's poetic achievement as a whole (see
Collected Poems—enlarged edition, 1970—1,049
pages) resists critical evaluation in its great variety and volume, but few would contest Harold
Bloom's judgment that Aiken—along with Edwin
Arlington Robinson, Robert Frost, Wallace Stevens, Ezra Pound, William Carlos Williams, and
T. S. Eliot—is one of "the strongest American
poets born in the last three decades of the nineteenth century."

Aiken's best novels and short stories come
from his psychologically intense middle period
(1922-1939). Various in design as they are, they
are all psychological dramas, and in this respect
they closely parallel Aiken's poems of this period.
Reading a story means entering the world of
someone's consciousness to follow with restless attention as that mind seeks illumination about
where it is going, or confronts some revelation of
beauty or terror. Aiken's work is of particular interest to those who value fiction that has a strong
psychological thrust. Graham Greene said that
the world of consciousness penetrated by Aiken's
fiction "was obviously the only real world, the

*Aiken in 1903, when he entered Middlesex School (by permis-
sion of the Henry E. Huntington Library and Art Gallery)*

only world worth describing. Henry James went
ahead, fearlessly, irretrievably, into the regions
where few are found who care to follow him.
Mr. Aiken is one of the few—which is only another way of saying that he is perhaps the most exciting, the most finally satisfying of living novelists" (*Spectator*, 8 November 1935). And Robert
Penn Warren introduces the 1982 republication
of Aiken's *Collected Short Stories* by emphasizing
that "these stories are not merely a collection.
They constitute a unity, a significant and haunting unity." That is, "the stories, by and large, are
about the moment when some piece of the ambiguous 'workings of our own minds or souls' is
made manifest. . . . A revelation may be seized or
pass unrecognized, but in either instance, a crisis
of awareness has come into being." Warren recognizes Aiken's weaknesses: "There are some [sto-

ries] that fail for all their skill ... but the very best here are superb and have the atmosphere of permanence; the good are very good indeed.... The stories remain freshly a testament of a complex, learned, and witty mind staring at the world and asking itself a question ... presented as a possibility [as in this excerpt from Aiken's soliloquy *Gehenna* (1930)]: 'I am myself a momentary sparkle on the swift surface of this preposterous stream. My awareness is only an accident and moreover my awareness is less truly myself than this stream which supports me, and out of which my sparkle of consciousness has for a moment been cast up.'" Plot in an Aiken story is, like that of Anton Chekhov and Katherine Mansfield, structured in the curve of the reader's discovery from moment to moment of what the story's interior journey reveals about the map of the human mind—this man's and every man's.

Conrad Potter Aiken was born in Savannah, Georgia, on 5 August 1889, the son of Anna Potter Aiken and Dr. William Ford Aiken, a physician. The young Aiken's education began in Savannah, but a tragic occurrence in 1901, when he was eleven, changed his life forever. On 27 February, Aiken's father shot and killed Aiken's mother, then killed himself with the same gun. After discovering their bodies, Aiken walked to the police station nearby and reported the situation. He subsequently began living with an uncle, William Tillinghast, in Cambridge, Massachusetts.

Aiken eventually became a student at Middlesex School in Concord and wrote for and edited the *Anvil*, the school's magazine, from 1904 to 1907, when he entered Harvard. His friends there included T. S. Eliot, and like him, Aiken soon began to write for the Harvard *Advocate*, later being elected its president and also being named class poet. After a trip to Europe, Aiken completed his degree in 1912. Two years later his first book, *Earth Triumphant and Other Tales in Verse*, was published, and it was followed by many others.

When Aiken wrote his first short story, "The Dark City" (*Dial*, April 1922; collected in *Bring! Bring!*, 1925), in December of 1921, he was thirty-two and felt that both his poetic career and his personal life had come to a crucial turning. He had married Jessie McDonald in 1912; they eventually had three children. The family had moved from Cape Cod to London, and after nine volumes of poetry Aiken was planning a novel. *Blue Voyage* (1927) was to be "as complete a

Jessie McDonald in 1911, the year before she married Aiken (Collection of Ruth Dadourian)

psychological statement of my own moral and social and aesthetic position as I could possibly make it": a calculated self-exposure, an "examination of consciousness," and his first step in a psychoanalysis of himself. But "The Dark City" was soon published, and Aiken decided to postpone his novel for a volume of short stories, which could bring in desperately needed cash and at the same time develop his prose skills.

"The Dark City" follows Andrew, a cheerfully domesticated man, in his daily twilight escape from the city to a suburban homecoming with his beloved wife and chattering children, through his ritual hour of gardening, his happily rowdy family dinner, and a brief walk alone in the country darkness, ending with a drowsy game of chess with his wife. But Andrew recognizes the suggestion of an uncertain horror beneath this benign landscape, beneath the high spirits of his interaction with his children. He dreads the ever-clearer revelation of this "Dark City," his vile secret that undermines the surface order and serenity of his life. On this night he casually describes to his wife a twilight vision of devouring maggots.

> Hilda stared at him.
> "Really, Andrew, I think you're going mad."
> "Going? I'm gone! My brain is maggotty."
> They laughed, and rattled the chessmen into their wooden box.

Of this story Warren comments: "We ask ourselves how much madness is in Andrew's comedy. And if he is going mad are we all held off from that fate by the skin of our teeth? As we regard the momentary beauty of the Dark City? . . . Perhaps the story is totally ambiguous, a comedy of ambiguity. . . ."

This ambiguity arises from Aiken's subtle union of a horrific dream (at last described with shocking precision, but at first only glimpsed) and the comforting perceptions of the ordinary. Aiken pits the real experience of the vile dream against the real experience of domestic peace, thus leaving unclear the reality of either. The rowdy peace of Andrew's home was modeled on the domestic life of Aiken's close friend, Robert Linscott. The dream vision—in precise detail—had been Aiken's own. His art lies in the ambiguous revelation that results from this union.

Next, in 1922, Aiken planned his first directly—and his only entirely—autobiographical story, published three years later. "Strange Moonlight" (*Dial*, March 1925; in *Bring! Bring!*) is Aiken's first experiment in recapturing, with elaborate exactness, some events, emotional tones, and sensory details of scenes from his Savannah childhood. The "plot" of the story again lies in the juxtaposing of contrasting experiences, this time presented in scenes of a boy's emotional awakening. The boy—about ten—reads Edgar Allan Poe's tales and has a dream seeming to lead him "towards a vast and beautiful or terrible conclusion," which nevertheless "always escaped him." During one particular week his experiences "seemed to unite, as if they were merely aspects of the same thing." First comes prize-day at school with an "ominous hushed gathering" that reduces him to a state of acute terror lest he be called on. He receives "a small black pasteboard box," which later, alone, he opens in an old graveyard and sees his gold medal. Later while playing soldiers in his back hall, he sees a goldfinch fly in

Clarissa Lorenz in 1927, three years before she became Aiken's second wife

from the rain, "beat wildly against a pane of glass," and then escape. The dream, the medal, and the goldfinch remind him of Caroline, a friend's young sister, whose voice pleased him and who showed him a gold piece he was tempted to steal.

Later he learns that this young girl has died, and he is incredulous, outraged. Next he overhears his father quarreling with his mother and then sees her sitting on his father's knee. Confused and offended, he retreats to bed and imagines a conversation with the dead girl, who tells him, "it's nicer than being alive. . . . You *understand* everything so easily!" The following day his father and mother abruptly decide on a family picnic at the beach: "the chief event of the afternoon was the burial of his father," who—like the young girl—would not stay buried. At night the family journeys sleepily home, to walk at last down "the long street, in the moonlight. . . . And their house, when at last they stopped before it, how strange it was! The moonlight, falling through the two tall swaying oaks, cast a moving pattern of shadow and light all over its face. . . . He stared up at this . . . feeling the ghostly vine of moonlight grow strangely over his face and hands. Was it in this, at last, that he would find the explanation of all that bewildered him?"

The plot lies in the gradual, subtle unfolding of emotions, in the tension the reader shares as the boy feels always closer to piercing the mystery of counterpointed terror and beauty. There could be no "resolution"; thus, Aiken was dissatisfied with his concluding emphasis: "he realized at last that Caroline was dead." The author omitted from this series of the boy's experiences the scene of his own parents' violent death—doubtless because that event was so horrific that it could not be presented as merely another moment of dawning consciousness.

In his struggle to comprehend his actual past Aiken wrote in the winter of 1922-1923 the first chapter of *Blue Voyage*, whose method expanded in scale the counterpointing of the lights and shadows of memory in "Strange Moonlight." Yet, at the same time, Aiken wrote short stories experimenting with other methods of presenting psychological drama: legend and parable or allegory.

In his long poems he had used the legendary Don Juan, Faust, and Punch to define psychological types. In the short story "The Disciple" (*Harper's*, December 1924; in *Bring! Bring!*) he used the legend of the Wandering Jew, who annually attempts to persuade Judas to hang himself again. It is a study of the megalomaniac fantasy of godlike power used sadistically, a theme that recurs in varying degrees, for example, in *King Coffin* (1935), in "The Letter" and "By My Troth, Nerissa"—two of the other stories in *Bring! Bring!* —and in "No, No Go Not to Lethe" (in *Among the Lost People*, 1934).

"Smith and Jones" (*Dial*, April 1923; in *Bring! Bring!*) is a parable, Aiken explained, of the struggle in the psyche among various forces: Smith is the instinctual, Jones the intellectual, and the erotic force is Gleason. Aiken suggested that the story mixed the macabre mental landscape of Poe with the dialectical plotting of James. Aiken wrote "Smith and Jones" while he was writing his long poem, *John Deth* (1930), which the story parallels in its allegory and in its tone of grim and subtle comedy. In both, Aiken anticipated the theme of Sigmund Freud's *Beyond the Pleasure Principle* (1922), which Aiken had not yet read. He said in a letter: "superficially, the par-

Aiken with his third wife, Mary Hoover Aiken, in 1938

able can be said to state that a great part of the effort of life is an effort to die; that consciousness is a disease of Matter, an abnormality, and that a part of consciousness knows this, and, like the Sibyl [in Eliot's *The Waste Land*, 1922], wishes to die, to return into unconsciousness."

In 1924 Aiken completed the collection *Bring! Bring!*, and he published it the following year. Edwin Muir in the *Criterion* called the stories "firm, economical, perfectly conscious, and informed with intelligence. These qualities make the volume one of the most remarkable that have appeared for some time." The reviewer for the *New York Times* doubted that Aiken wrote "veritable short stories according to academic canons," but praised "his insight into character, his feeling for the truly dramatic and intensely poetic."

By 1927 Aiken had completed *Blue Voyage*, left his family in England, and—having fallen in love with Clarissa Lorenz, who would become his second wife (in 1930)—moved to Cambridge, Massachusetts. Once more he began to write short stories and within a year completed fourteen for a volume he called *Costumes by Eros* (1928). All are drawn from Aiken's own erotic preoccupation at the time. Aiken's earlier stories tend to be dark toned and to focus on the painful pursuit of the se-

Aiken at Brewster, Massachusetts, in 1948

cret of one's "incomplete identification," whereas this volume presents a series of lighter-toned adventures, or "moments," in which sex performs a comic-pathetic mating dance—with the exception of the first story, that is (one of Aiken's most popular), "Your Obituary, Well Written" (*Scribner's*, November 1927). In this elegy for youth and love, the protagonist seeks "a woman who was, as it were, all sensibility—of a soul that was all of a tremulous awareness . . . [of an] ethereally delicate consciousness . . . [and a] burning intensity of spirit." It is a story of "the barest of encounters," which nevertheless reveals "the 'essence' of my life." The story is based on Aiken's own meetings in London with Katherine Mansfield in 1920.

"Spider, Spider" (*Scribner's*, February 1928) introduces Aiken's comedies about victims of Eros; in it the victim embraces the spider. But in "A Man Alone at Lunch" and "A Conversation," the reader can never be sure if the men are victims or if their devouring suspicion and jealousy are merely incipient paranoia. For his epigraph to *Costumes by Eros*, Aiken quotes Othello: "Excellent wretch! Perdition catch my soul / But I do love thee! and when I love thee not, / Chaos is come again."

Among the Lost People was Aiken's third collection of stories, these being written between 1929 and 1934. The title is from Dante's *Inferno* ("tra la gente perduta"), for like Dante's frozen souls in Cocytus, Aiken's characters, for the most part, discover themselves in that "infernal city"—of paralyzing and secret ice—of those who reject love. "The Night Before Prohibition" has the most power of all the stories, but the cruelty of rejected love is subtly varied in "The Fish Supper," "Pure as the Driven Snow," and "Thistledown." There are also stories of people who are lost in madness or thoughts of death. Nowhere is Aiken's portraiture, his observation of word and gesture, more exact or inevitable than in "Mr. Arcularis," his tenderly ironic study of a gentleman of Beacon Hill and Cambridge who is dying.

When they passed the Harvard Club Mr. Arcularis made a slow and somewhat painful effort to turn in his seat and look at it. . . .

"Goodbye to the old club," he said.

"The bar will miss you," said Harry smiling with friendly irony and looking straight ahead.

"But let there be no moaning," said Mr. Arcularis.

"What's *that* a quotation from?"

" 'The Odyssey.' "

Arcularis, a modestly adventurous brother, perhaps, of Aiken's character Senlin or Eliot's Prufrock, then voyages past the Harvard Club and Arcturus to stand at last, freezing, on the doorstep of the absolute. His mind, with its lifetime's furnishings, is finally seen dancing to the ether and the knife on an operating table.

"Silent Snow, Secret Snow" (*Virginia Quarterly*, October 1932) observes the mind of a boy of twelve moving farther and farther out into the blank cold of madness. So complete and precise is Aiken's observation of this withdrawal that the story has been cited by Peter A. Martin as a classic description of a disease in which a psychogenic visual disturbance, arising from excessive hostile impulses, appears to put layers of snow between the victim and the real world ("On Scierneuropsia," *Journal of the American Psychoanalytic Association*, January 1960). And yet, unlike most of Aiken's short stories, "Silent Snow" transcribes nothing from his own dreams or real experience. It is the most often anthologized of his stories and its genesis is of interest. He wrote to a teacher: "I'm pleased that you like Silent Snow, and to hear that it alarms your students! Well it might, it alarmed me to write it. Origin is simple, and not what you'd expect. I lived for some time in an English hill town, Rye, on a cobbled street. And from my bedroom window I used to amuse myself by listening to the clump-clump of the morning postman's feet coming nearer down the sidewalks, or crossing the cobbles. That started me off. But whether one day it snowed, and muffled the steps, or I simply *thought* of it snowing, and speculated on the effect it would have, I don't remember. That's all. The rest is pure invention." How imagination often invents works of fiction and poetry out of droplets of experience is itself the subject of "State of Mind" (*New Republic*, 6 July 1927; in *Costumes by Eros*) and, particularly, of "Life Isn't a Short Story" (*North American Review*, June 1934; in *The Short Stories*, 1950), one of only five short stories written after *Among the Lost People*.

In 1937 Aiken divorced Clarissa and married Mary Hoover. His later career centered on novels, poetry, and criticism, although his collected stories were also well received, and the anthology was enlarged in 1960.

Aiken's imagination throughout his stories usually speaks in a tone so quiet, so undramatic, that one must literally turn all one's attention to it in order to hear it. The voice is careful, circumspect even, like that of a spy, or voyeur, as if, though speaking with necessary patience, it is about to give away a secret, and perhaps one of uncertain importance, with implications disturbingly unclear. It is the voice of an imagination that heaps question upon question: Is this a matter for *terror*, or *hilarity*? Is this other a matter of star-crossed romance, or sadistic rejection? This confession—say, of cold indifference toward a proffered love, or of sexual exploitation—does it ask reproachful forgiveness or (amazingly, obscenely) grinning admiration? And above all, his stories ask: Who can one trust? Life is *not* a short story, Aiken seems to be saying, but let us invent a Procrustean bed with this short story in order to put life "to the question."

Letters:
Joseph Killorin, ed., *Selected Letters of Conrad Aiken* (New Haven & London: Yale University Press, 1978).

Interviews:
Andrew Sparks, "An Hour with Conrad Aiken," *Atlanta Journal and Constitution Magazine*, 5 May 1963, pp. 8, 46-47;

Ashley Brown, "An Interview with Conrad Aiken," *Shenandoah*, 15 (Autumn 1963): 477-488;

Patricia R. Willis, "Conrad Aiken: An Interview," *Rebel*, 8 (Winter 1965): 3-12;

Robert Hunter Wilbur, "The Art of Poetry IX: Conrad Aiken, an Interview," *Paris Review*, 11 (Winter-Spring 1968): 97-124.

Bibliographies:
R. W. Stallman, "Annotated Checklist on Conrad Aiken: A Critical Study," *Wake*, 11 (1952): 114-121;

F. W. Bonnell and F. C. Bonnell, *Conrad Aiken: A Bibliography (1902-1978)* (San Marino, Cal.: Huntington Library, 1982);

Catherine Harris, *Conrad Aiken: Critical Recognition, 1914-1981. A Bibliographic Guide* (New York & London: Garland, 1983).

Biography:
Clarissa Lorenz, *Lorelei Two: My Life with Conrad Aiken* (Athens: University of Georgia Press, 1983).

References:
Reuel Denney, *Conrad Aiken* (Minneapolis: University of Minnesota Press, 1964);

Frederick J. Hoffman, *Conrad Aiken* (New York: Twayne, 1962);

Jay Martin, *Conrad Aiken: A Life of His Art* (Princeton: Princeton University Press, 1962);

Steven Eric Olsen, "The Vascular Mind: Conrad Aiken's Early Poetry, 1910-1918," Ph.D. dissertation, Stanford University, 1981;

Houston Peterson, *The Melody of Chaos* (New York: Longmans, Green, 1931);

Douglas Robillard, "The Poetry of Conrad Aiken: A Critical Study," Ph.D. dissertation, Wayne State University, 1965;

Studies in the Literary Imagination, special Aiken issue, 13 (Fall 1980);

Wake, 11, special Aiken issue, edited by Seymour Lawrence (1952);

Robert Hunter Wilbur, "George Santayana and Three Modern Philosophical Poets: T. S. Eliot, Conrad Aiken and Wallace Stevens," Ph.D. dissertation, Columbia University, 1965.

Papers:

The major collections of Aiken's papers are at the Henry E. Huntington Library and Art Gallery in San Marino, California, and the Houghton Library, Harvard University.

Stephen Vincent Benét

(22 July 1898 - 13 March 1943)

Joel Roache
University of Maryland Eastern Shore

See also the Benét entries in *DLB 4: American Writers in Paris, 1920-1939* and *DLB 48: American Poets, 1880-1945.*

BOOKS: *Five Men and Pompey: A Series of Dramatic Portraits* (Boston: Four Seas, 1915);

The Drug Shop, or Endymion in Edmonstoun (New Haven: Yale University Press, 1917);

Young Adventure: A Book of Poems (New Haven: Yale University Press, 1918);

Tamburlaine the Great, adapted by Benét and Monty Woolley from Christopher Marlowe's play (New Haven: Yale University Press, 1919);

Heavens and Earth: A Book of Poems (New York: Holt, 1920);

The Beginning of Wisdom (New York: Holt, 1921; London & Sydney: Chapman & Dodd, 1922);

Young People's Pride: A Novel (New York: Holt, 1922);

King David (New York: Holt, 1923);

Jean Huguenot (New York: Holt, 1923; London: Methuen, 1925);

The Ballad of William Sycamore, 1790-1880 (New York & New Haven: Hackett/Brick Row Book Shop, 1923);

Tiger Joy: A Book of Poems (New York: Doran, 1925);

Spanish Bayonet (New York: Doran, 1926; London: Heinemann, 1926);

John Brown's Body (Garden City, N.Y.: Doubleday, Doran, 1928; London: Heinemann, 1928);

The Barefoot Saint (Garden City, N.Y.: Doubleday, Doran, 1929);

The Litter of the Rose Leaves (New York: Random House, 1930);

Ballads and Poems, 1915-1930 (Garden City, N.Y.: Doubleday, Doran, 1931; London: Heinemann, 1933);

A Book of Americans, by Benét and Rosemary Carr Benét (New York: Farrar & Rinehart, 1933);

James Shore's Daughter (Garden City, N.Y.: Doubleday, Doran, 1934; London: Heinemann, 1934);

Burning City: New Poems (New York: Farrar & Rinehart, 1936; London & Toronto: Heinemann, 1937);

The Magic of Poetry and the Poet's Art (Chicago: Compton, 1936);

Stephen Vincent Benét (Gale International Portrait Gallery)

The Devil and Daniel Webster (New York & Toronto: Farrar & Rinehart, 1937);

Thirteen O'Clock: Stories of Several Worlds (New York & Toronto: Farrar & Rinehart, 1937; London & Toronto: Heinemann, 1938);

The Headless Horseman, libretto by Benét and score by Douglas Moore (Boston: Schirmer, 1937);

Johnny Pye & the Fool-Killer (New York & Toronto: Farrar & Rinehart, 1938; London & Toronto: Heinemann, 1938);

The Ballad of the Duke's Mercy (New York: House of Books, 1939);

The Devil and Daniel Webster [opera], libretto by Benét and score by Moore (New York & Toronto: Farrar & Rinehart, 1939):

Tales Before Midnight (New York: Farrar & Rinehart, 1939; London & Toronto: Heinemann, 1940);

The Devil and Daniel Webster: Play in One Act (New York: Dramatists Play Service, 1939);

Nightmare at Noon (New York & Toronto: Farrar & Rinehart, 1940);

We Stand United: A Declaration (New York: Council for Democracy, 1940);

A Summons to the Free (New York & Toronto: Farrar & Rinehart, 1941; London: Oxford University Press, 1941);

Listen to the People (New York: Council for Democracy, 1941);

Tuesday, November 5th, 1940 (New York: House of Books, 1941);

They Burned the Books (New York & Toronto: Farrar & Rinehart, 1942);

A Child Is Born: A Modern Drama of the Nativity (Boston: Baker, 1942);

Western Star (New York & Toronto: Farrar & Rinehart, 1943; London: Oxford University Press, 1944);

America (New York & Toronto: Farrar & Rinehart, 1944; London & Toronto: Heinemann, 1945);

O'Halloran's Luck, and Other Short Stories (New York: Penguin, 1944);

Prayer. A Child Is Born (New York & Toronto: Farrar & Rinehart, 1944);

We Stand United, and Other Radio Scripts (New York & Toronto: Farrar & Rinehart, 1945);

The Last Circle: Stories and Poems (New York: Farrar, Straus, 1946; London & Toronto: Heinemann, 1948);

Stephen Vincent Benét on Writing, edited by George Abbe (Brattleboro, Vt.: Greene, 1964);

The Bishop's Beggar (Flemington, N.J.: St. Teresa's Press, 1968).

Collections: *Selected Works of Stephen Vincent Benét*, 2 volumes (New York: Farrar & Rinehart, 1942);

Selected Poetry and Prose, edited by Basil Davenport (New York: Rinehart, 1960).

PLAY PRODUCTIONS: *Nerves*, by Benét and John Farrar, New York, Comedy Theatre, 1 September 1924;

That Awful Mrs. Eaton, by Benét and Farrar, New York, Morosco Theatre, 29 September 1924;

The Devil and Daniel Webster [opera], libretto by Benét and score by Douglas Moore, New York, Martin Beck Theatre, 18 May 1939.

MOTION PICTURES: *Abraham Lincoln*, adaptation by Benét, continuity and dialogue by Benét and Gerrit Lloyd, United Artists, 1930;

Cheers for Miss Bishop, adaptation by Benét, based on Bess Streeter Aldrich's novel *Miss Bishop*, United Artists, 1941;

Benét at the age of four in the arsenal at Watervliet, New York, where his father, an army officer, was stationed from 1899 to 1904

All That Money Can Buy, screenplay by Benét and Dan Tothroth, based on Benét's story *The Devil and Daniel Webster*, RKO, 1941.

Born in Bethlehem, Pennsylvania, Stephen Vincent Benét was the son of James Walker Benét, a career military officer, and his wife, Frances Neill Rose Benét. The travels of the family during Benét's early life nurtured a broad and resilient national consciousness that is the basis of much of his most important work in poetry and the novel as well as in the short story. His parents also fostered a strong interest in history and encouraged the open-minded exploration of books and ideas, but against a background of firm professionalism. "I don't want any of my kids," the elder Benét once said, "to be amateurs." Thus it hardly seems surprising that from an early age Benét took his writing very seriously and published his first book at the age of seventeen, in the same year that he entered Yale University.

At Yale he made contacts who put him in touch with the New York literary world, and

henceforth (except for fellowships from Yale and from the Guggenheim Foundation) he earned his livelihood as a professional writer. By 26 November 1921 he could afford to marry Rosemary Carr, whom he had met in 1920 while on a Yale fellowship in Paris, and establish a home in Chicago; they later lived in Paris, Hollywood, and New York. According to his biographer, Charles A. Fenton, Benét "wrote short stories for money and poetry for love" throughout his career. Such production meant, of course, a perpetual struggle to meet the specifications of the mass-circulation magazines, which focused almost exclusively on simple-minded, saccharine romance. Benét spent the early 1920s wrestling with the formula and became predictably frustrated with the conflict among his own literary standards, the popular taste, and editorial prejudice, until he began to develop the kind of historical materials that would secure his reputation not only in fiction but in poetry.

In May 1926 he published "The Sobbin' Women" (in *Country Gentleman*; collected in *Thirteen O'Clock*, 1937), a farfetched but engaging tale of seven frontier brothers who literally kidnap

William Rose Benét's circa 1908 drawing of his younger brother, Stephen, then age ten (from Saturday Review of Literature, *27 March 1943)*

wives for themselves. Notwithstanding the echo of the legend of the Sabine women, the characters, tone, and setting of the story are thoroughly American, and Benét introduces here the "Oldest Inhabitant" narrator upon whom he would call repeatedly throughout his career. The story was the first of a series of historical tales written at the same time he was working on *John Brown's Body* (1928), which won the Pulitzer Prize for Poetry in 1929.

With the advent of the Great Depression he turned once more to prose to supplement his earnings, publishing his fifth novel, *James Shore's Daughter* (1934); many short stories, culminating in *The Devil and Daniel Webster* (*Saturday Evening Post*, 24 October 1936; separately published in 1937), which won the O. Henry Memorial Award; and two collections of personally selected tales, *Thirteen O'Clock* and *Tales Before Midnight* (1939). Some belletristically oriented reviewers worried over the marks of magazine money on the stories, but critical reception in general ranged from favorable to enthusiastic, and sales were respectable, resulting in part, no doubt, from the fame won by his epic 1928 poem. With the advent of World War II, however, he worked tirelessly and without remuneration on war propaganda until his death in 1943.

Benét has left us, then, with a substantial corpus of tales carefully crafted to reach a popular audience. Under these circumstances, and given Benét's own disposition, it is not surprising that he generally observed William Dean Howells's injunction to center on "the more smiling aspects" of American life. This is not to say, however, that he was blind to its more problematic aspects, and even if he comes down consistently on the side of conventional values, he is nonetheless sensitive to their inevitable erosion.

In "Too Early Spring" (*Delineator*, June 1933; in *Tales Before Midnight*), for example, he portrays the destruction of an adolescent romance by the narrow-mindedness of the people of Main Street, U.S.A. Benét avoids the bitterness of Sherwood Anderson or Sinclair Lewis, partly by concentrating on the love story and partly through the innocence of the first-person narrator, who ultimately (and perhaps shallowly) accepts the loss of his first love.

In "A Death in the Country" (*Harper's*, March 1932; in *Thirteen O'Clock*), on the other hand, a New York attorney, on a visit to his hometown, learns a lesson in the sustaining value of permanent roots when events and revelations surrounding a family funeral reveal an unremembered depth and complexity in relationships, pulling together the threads of his past to help him understand his present. He does not lose his perception of his family as "the jungle," or of the stifling, small-town culture of his youth, but he also carries valuable insight back to his current life. More than anything else, it is such recognition of both the bitter and the sweet that saves Benét's stories from banality.

A similar kind of recognition is the key to the tragicomic irony of "A Story by Angela Poe" (*Harper's Bazaar*, July 1935; in *Thirteen O'Clock*), wherein a young assistant editor forms a relationship with an elderly eccentric author of syrupy romances and her husband. As the narrator gradually becomes more interested in the couple, and moved by the husband's devotion, it emerges that Angela Poe probably murdered her previous husband and that her current spouse fears that he "may not really be indispensable to her." Notwithstanding the Lady Macbeth theme, however, the genuineness of the couple's love is unambiguous.

The human reality of both good and evil is also at the core of the story *The Devil and Daniel Webster*, in which the legendary orator pleads successfully for the soul of a Yankee farmer in a court full of sinister renegades and reprobates

Stephen and Rosemary Benét, 1934

from national history. At one level the power of the story derives from its folksy narrator and national hero. Old Scratch, the Devil, is described as having tiny, winged souls he carries casually wrapped in his handkerchief, in contrast to realistic, concrete details like Webster's "matched grays with one white forefoot. . . ." The orator/hero is gifted with a homespun, blustering wit and is humanized by a twinkle of manly mischief: "there's a jug on the table and a case in hand. And I never left a jug or a case half-finished in my life," he says.

With the climax of the story, Benét changes direction technically, and also reveals another, more important level of meaning. Webster's presentation for the defense is not given directly, but summarized in little more than a page. Recognizing "his own anger and horror" as being shared by the jury made up of the damned, he eschews the bombast of the politician or lawyer and instead talks quietly "about the things that make a country a country, and a man a man." He wins his case by allowing the jurors to see that they and the defendant are all part of "the

story and the failures and the endless journey of mankind."

The theme that surfaces here is foreshadowed earlier when the Devil points out that he was there "When the first wrong was done to the first Indian. . . . When the first slaver put out for the Congo. . . ." The same point is made by the American identity of the villainous jurors: that the nation, like the individual, like humanity itself, embodies both good and evil, and that "everybody has played a part . . . even the traitors." Thus Webster draws the jurors into an identification with his client, and Benét draws his readers into an identification with the nation and with the human family.

The story is virtually a showcase of the elements that Benét employed repeatedly in various proportions in his historical stories, at a time when the public desperately needed a sense of national identity. Sometimes folk elements dominate, as in *Johnny Pye & the Fool-Killer* (1938), and sometimes the focus is on the price that must be paid to forge one nation out of many, as in "Jacob and the Indians" (*Saturday Evening Post*, 14 May 1938; in *Selected Works*, volume 2, 1942).

THE BAREFOOT SAINT

By Stephen Vincent Benét

At Chezeray, the fertile, high-lying table-land between the Seine and the Eure, the whole town smells like a cider-press, in the Fall. They make good calvados in that neighborhood; they know how to cook and eat. They know the tricks of the rose, the horse and the spaniel, but they are not voluble people, and it takes a magician to cheat them in a bargain. They know how to keep their money warm, and they are hard to change. The priest rides a bicycle, with his black skirts tucked up to his knees; they radio at the Café Des-Sports gets the programs from the Eiffel Tower every night; but the striped fields beyond the town are the fields of generations of infinitely patient farmers, and the old mortar is still as hard as iron in the ruins of the old walls.

It is only a score of miles to the Deauville road, but Paris is another country, for all of that. This is France, or a stubborn part of it - the snail on the wall has his own house; the trees are knotted with bearing, but they continue to bear. The crypt of the little chapel goes back to Rome, and in the chapel itself you will find the statue of a saint who is not in any calendar - a small saint, carved from gray stone. Her smile is decided and courteous, her hand extended to bless, but she has no name and her feet have never worn shoes. Nevertheless, there is always a candle before her. They can pray to Ste. Thérèse at Lisieux or to Ste. Jeanne at Rouen, if they like, and as much as they like.

First page from Benét's typescript for his 1929 story that was separately published (by permission of Thomas C. Benét; courtesy of Princeton University Library)

One of the best of these stories, "The Captives" (*Atlantic Monthly*, February 1934; collected in *The Last Circle*, 1946), reinvigorates the perennial notion that Americans constitute virtually a new variety of human being. In the course of a prisoner exchange on the frontier in 1764, a Scottish officer encounters a young woman held by the Indians since childhood. The degree to which she has adopted her captors' culture is linked thematically with the (to the narrator) strange, egalitarian ways of the frontiersmen who are fighting the Indians for the land. When the captive finally, tearfully, remembers her European name as part of the lyric of a Scots ballad, and returns to the frontier with a new husband, the soldierly narrator dimly realizes the rich, complex potentiality of human nature, for "she had nations in her eyes." This sort of retrospective foreshadowing of a new, heterogeneous but unified people carried obvious ideological weight for a reading public on the eve of World War II, but "The Captives" is also a convincing portrayal of the transforming power of historical forces.

His ideological concerns are also explicit in some of the stories he himself designated (in *Selected Works*, volume 2) as "Fantasies and Prophecies," and these stories, too, are enriched by the underlying assumption that the human being is a blend of negative and positive potential. The imprisoned scientist of "The Blood of the Martyrs" (*Saturday Evening Post*, 12 December 1936) dies rather than subscribe to blatantly false scientific doctrines, but not before he has, almost obsequiously, agreed to support "the Dictator" publically in every other way possible. In "Into Egypt" (*Ladies Home Journal*, May 1939), on the other hand, the young soldier dutifully, even enthusiastically, supervises the forced exodus of an officially accursed people, but Benét also deftly portrays the kind of massive indoctrination that produces the enthusiasm; and in the end even the loyal storm trooper breaks the rules to allow the last family to bring their donkey with them. Like many of Benét's stories, "Into Egypt" is all but ruined by gratuitously tendentious allegory (the infant in his mother's arms, riding the donkey, even bears stigmata), but the realistic, sympathetic portrait of the ordinary human being qua fascist remains impressive.

The mixture of the human and the divine is the major theme in "By the Waters of Babylon" (originally published as "The Place of the Gods," *Saturday Evening Post*, 31 July 1937; in *Thirteen O'Clock*). Written almost a decade before Hiro-shima, this "prophecy" retains an eerie contemporaneity. A young priest of a tribe descended from the survivors of the last modern war enters the forbidden precincts of the ancient gods, the ruins of a modern city, and when he encounters the mummified corpse of an ancient master of modern technology, he realizes that the old gods were in fact human beings like himself. The story concludes then with his decision to return to his people with the knowledge of their creative, and destructive, power.

The subject matter and theme of "By the Waters of Babylon" are prophetic, but the technique is nonetheless quite familiar. As Parry Stroud has pointed out, Benét made no innovations in the form of the short story, for he deliberately shaped his gifts for a market rigidly inimical to experimentation. He did not, on the other hand, cynically crank out potboilers. In the first place, the record shows consistent, and often successful, resistance to editorial strictures, and Benét may have enjoyed more latitude after his reputation was fully established. Second, many of the major themes and materials of the short stories are at least consistent with those of the poetry and the novels, and if he took the latter more seriously, there is little to suggest that he falsified his perspective in order to sell his stories. At most, the short-story market dictated a slightly different, somewhat brighter emphasis.

It would be pointless to deny that this emphasis, along with Benét's relatively uncomplicated outlook on life, resulted in predictable weaknesses. The view of history in these stories is often naively patriotic, and Benét's politics are awash in facile, simple-minded liberalism. Similarly, his portrayal of interpersonal relationships is often embarrassingly sentimental. In addition, his techniques are unappealing to the refined, modernist sensibility of current literary criticism. There are no minutely detailed, suddenly determined absolutes of perception, and there are few archly understated epiphanies. Benét's gifts lay rather in the skillful characterization of familiar types, the evocation of engaging atmospheres, and in smooth, carefully paced summary, not in the depth and complexity of his analysis. He was the Frederick Remington or Norman Rockwell of the short story, not the Edouard Manet or Vincent Van Gogh.

It would be careless, on the other hand, to dismiss Benét's achievement as "mere" popularity, for his work embodies ideas and values that, despite their unfashionability in the academy,

Benét with publishers John Farrar and Stanley Rinehart. Benét is holding the 24 October 1936 issue of the Saturday Evening Post, *which includes* The Devil and Daniel Webster, *published as a book by Farrar and Rinehart in 1937.*

merit continuous reconsideration. The first and most obvious is that the artist creates for the community at large rather than for an elite of the initiated. Second, imbedded in the conventional simplicities of these stories is often a mature, realistic portrayal of traditional mores under the strain of social change, and if the conflicts are often too easily resolved, the portrayal remains nonetheless clear, honest, and useful.

Third and most important, Benét's love of country is not mindless chauvinism; it grows out of the familiar but often forgotten vision of America as a symbol and, at its best, an expression of the potentiality of the human species. Herein lies the primary problem with Benét's critical reputation. Modernist culture shares with religion a belief in the human potentiality for transcendence of the irreducible absurdity or evil of the concrete world. That potentiality is abstract, however; it is spiritual or imaginative. Benét, on the other hand, shared with popular culture a belief that absurdity is not irreducible, that humanity

can transcend its limitations within history and concrete experience. He saw human history, therefore, human experience, not as merely an endlessly irrational, cyclical burden, but as the richest available source of the knowledge and power that will allow the species, in William Faulkner's famous phrase, not merely to endure, but to prevail. And it is probably safe to say that that vision, and the considerable skill with which it is embodied, assures for Benét's short stories a modest but secure reputation for at least several more generations.

Letters:
Selected Letters of Stephen Vincent Benét, edited by Charles A. Fenton (New Haven: Yale University Press, 1960).

Bibliography:
Gladys L. Maddocks, "Stephen Vincent Benét: A Bibliography," *Bulletin of Bibliography and Dramatic Index*, 20 (September 1951): 142-146; (April 1952): 158-160.

Biography:

Charles A. Fenton, *Stephen Vincent Benét: The Life and Times of a Man of Letters, 1893-1943* (New Haven: Yale University Press, 1958).

Reference:

Parry Stroud, *Stephen Vincent Benét* (New York: Twayne, 1962).

Papers:

Benét's papers are in the Beinecke Library, Yale University.

Pearl S. Buck

(26 June 1892 - 6 March 1973)

Pat Salomon
Bowling Green State University

See also the Buck entry in *DLB 9: American Novelists, 1910-1945.*

BOOKS: *East Wind: West Wind* (New York: Day, 1930; London: Methuen, 1931);

The Good Earth (New York: Day, 1931; London: Methuen, 1931);

Sons (New York: Day, 1932; London: Methuen, 1932);

The Young Revolutionist (New York: Friendship, 1932; London: Methuen, 1932);

The First Wife and Other Stories (New York: Day, 1933; London: Methuen, 1933);

The Mother (New York: Day, 1934; London: Methuen, 1934);

A House Divided (New York: Reynal & Hitchcock, 1935; London: Methuen, 1935);

The Exile (New York: Reynal & Hitchcock, 1936; London: Methuen, 1936);

Fighting Angel: Portrait of a Soul (New York: Reynal & Hitchcock, 1936; London: Methuen, 1937);

This Proud Heart (New York: Reynal & Hitchcock, 1938; London: Methuen, 1938);

The Chinese Novel (New York: Day, 1939; London: Macmillan, 1939);

The Patriot (New York: Day, 1939; London: Methuen, 1939);

Other Gods: An American Legend (New York: Day, 1940; London: Macmillan, 1940);

Today and Forever: Stories of China (New York: Day, 1941; London: Macmillan, 1941);

Of Men and Women (New York: Day, 1941; London: Methuen, 1942);

American Unity and Asia (New York: Day, 1942); republished as *Asia and Democracy* (London: Macmillan, 1943);

China Sky (New York: Triangle, 1942);

The Chinese Children Next Door (New York: Day, 1942; London: Methuen, 1943);

Dragon Seed (New York: Day, 1942; London: Macmillan, 1942);

What America Means to Me (New York: Day, 1943; London: Methuen, 1944);

The Promise (New York: Day, 1943; London: Methuen, 1944);

The Dragon Fish (New York: Day, 1944; London: Methuen, 1946);

China Flight (Philadelphia: Triangle/Blakiston, 1945);

The Townsman, as John Sedges (New York: Day, 1945; London: Methuen, 1946);

Talk About Russia, by Buck and Masha Scott (New York: Day, 1945);

Portrait of a Marriage (New York: Day, 1945; London: Methuen, 1946);

Pavilion of Women (New York: Day, 1946; London: Methuen, 1947);

The Angry Wife, as Sedges (New York: Day, 1947; London: Methuen, 1948);

Far and Near: Stories of Japan, China, and America (New York: Day, 1947); republished as *Far and Near: Stories of East and West* (London: Methuen, 1949);

Pearl S. Buck, in Stockholm to receive the 1938 Nobel Prize for Literature (courtesy of Janice C. Walsh)

How It Happens: Talk About the German People, by Buck and Erna von Pustau (New York: Day, 1947);

Peony (New York: Day, 1948); republished as *The Bondmaid* (London: Methuen, 1949);

The Big Wave (New York: Day, 1948);

American Argument, by Buck and Eslanda Goode Robeson (New York: Day, 1949; London: Methuen, 1950);

Kinfolk (New York: Day, 1949; London: Methuen, 1950);

The Long Love, as Sedges (New York: Day, 1949; London: Methuen, 1950);

The Child Who Never Grew (New York: Day, 1950; London: Methuen, 1951);

One Bright Day (New York: Day, 1950); enlarged as *One Bright Day and Other Stories for Children* (London: Methuen, 1952);

God's Men (New York: Day, 1951; London: Methuen, 1951);

The Hidden Flower (New York: Day, 1952; London: Methuen, 1952);

Bright Procession, as Sedges (New York: Day, 1952; London: Methuen, 1952);

Come, My Beloved (New York: Day, 1953; London: Methuen, 1953);

The Man Who Changed China: The Story of Sun Yat-sen (New York: Random House, 1953; London: Methuen, 1955);

Voices in the House, as Sedges (New York: Day, 1953; London: Methuen, 1954);

My Several Worlds (New York: Day, 1954; London: Methuen, 1955);

The Beech Tree (New York: Day, 1954);

Imperial Woman (New York: Day, 1955; London: Methuen, 1956);

Letter from Peking (New York: Day, 1957; London: Methuen, 1957);

Friend to Friend, by Buck and Carlos Romulo (New York: Day, 1958);

Buck's parents, Absalom and Caroline Stulting Sydenstricker, in 1880 (courtesy of Janice C. Walsh)

Command the Morning (New York: Day, 1959; London: Methuen, 1959);

Fourteen Stories (New York: Day, 1961); republished as *With a Delicate Air and Other Stories* (London: Methuen, 1962);

A Bridge for Passing (New York: Day, 1962; London: Methuen, 1963);

Satan Never Sleeps (New York: Pocket Books, 1962);

The Living Reed (New York: Day, 1963; London: Methuen, 1963);

The Joy of Children (New York: Day, 1964);

Children for Adoption (New York: Random House, 1965);

Death in the Castle (New York: Day, 1965; London: Methuen, 1966);

The Gifts They Bring: Our Debt to the Mentally Retarded, by Buck and Gweneth T. Zarfoss (New York: Day, 1965);

For Spacious Skies: Journey in Dialogue, by Buck and Theodore F. Harris (New York: Day, 1966);

The People of Japan (New York: Simon & Schuster, 1966; London: Hale, 1968);

To My Daughters, With Love (New York: Day, 1967);

The Time Is Noon (New York: Day, 1967; London: Methuen, 1967);

The New Year (New York: Day, 1968; London: Methuen, 1968);

The Good Deed, and Other Stories of Asia, Past and Present (New York: Day, 1969; London: Methuen, 1970);

The Three Daughters of Madame Liang (New York: Day, 1969; London: Methuen, 1969);

Mandala (New York: Day, 1970; London: Methuen, 1971);

The Kennedy Women (New York: Cowles, 1970; London: Methuen, 1970);

China as I See It, edited by Theodore F. Harris (New York: Day, 1970; London: Methuen, 1971);

China Past and Present (New York: Day, 1972);

Once Upon a Christmas (New York: Day, 1972);

The Goddess Abides (New York: Day, 1972; London: Eyre Methuen, 1972);

All Under Heaven (New York: Day, 1973; London: Eyre Methuen, 1973);

The Rainbow (New York: Day, 1974; London: Eyre Methuen, 1976);

East and West (New York: Day, 1975);

Mrs. Stoner and the Sea, and Other Works (New York: Ace, 1976);

Secrets of the Heart (New York: Day, 1976);

The Lovers and Other Stories (New York: Day, 1977);

The Woman Who Was Changed, and Other Stories (New York: Crowell, 1979).

Pearl Buck's genius as a writer lay in her ability to portray her characters in a universal manner; their joys, sorrows, problems, and disillusionments transcend cultural barriers to become understandable to all readers. Buck's earlier works, most of them portrayals of Chinese characters and subjects, appropriately made her the bridge between the Eastern and Western worlds, China and America. She wrote more than sixty novels, several nonfiction essays and children's books, and numerous short stories. There are more than a hundred different books attributed to her. Buck's fame as a novelist has tended to draw attention away from her short stories, but to appreciate her art fully, one cannot ignore them; they capsulize themes that were often reworked in her novels.

Pearl Sydenstricker was born in Hillsboro, West Virginia, on 26 June 1892. Her parents, Absalom and Caroline Stulting Sydenstricker, were missionaries and took Pearl, at the age of three months, to live in Chinkiang on the Yangtze River in China. She did not return to America until 1910, at the age of seventeen, when she entered Randolph-Macon Woman's College in Lynchburg, Virginia. In her senior year she won two literary prizes, one for best short story. After graduation she received a teaching assistantship in the department of psychology and philosophy, but left two months later, at the close of 1914, to return to China to care for her ill mother, who later recovered.

On 30 May 1917 Pearl married John Lossing Buck, an American agricultural expert originally from upstate New York. He was employed by the Presbyterian Mission Board to teach American farming techniques to the Chinese. After their marriage the Bucks lived in remote northern China, where they often traveled, visiting the Chinese farmers and engaging them in conversation. In 1921 her only natural child, Carolyn, was born. (During her first marriage a second daughter, Janice, was adopted.)

The Bucks moved, later in 1921, to Nanking, where he taught rural economics and she taught literature part-time at the University of Nanking, Southeastern University, and Chung Yang University. In Nanking modern ideas from the West had already begun to infiltrate the old traditional Chinese customs and ways. The young Chinese felt trapped between these opposing forces; this situation would become one of Buck's major themes in her early writing.

In 1922 she began to write essays on her impressions of a country caught in the throes of change. Her first published article, entitled "In China, Too," appeared in the 23 January issue of *Atlantic Monthly*. She also wrote articles for *Forum* and *Nation*, began to write short stories, and planned her first novel.

In 1925 she brought Carolyn to the United States for medical treatment and discovered that her daughter would always be retarded. To distract herself, Buck enrolled at Cornell University in Ithaca, New York, for a master's degree in English. There she won the Laura Messinger Prize in history for her essay "China and the West"

Buck in 1900, with her younger sister, Grace (courtesy of Janice C. Walsh)

(later published in *Annals of the American Academy*, July 1933).

On the ship to America she had written the story that would become her first novel. It appeared as "A Chinese Woman Speaks" in *Asia* magazine (April-May 1926). Kwei-lan, a traditionalist, tells of her marriage, which is unhappy until she can accept the Western ideas of her modern Chinese husband. Buck was solicited by a publisher to expand the story into a full-length novel, but thinking the framework too slight and delicate, she suggested two shorter narratives in one volume. She was refused but found another publisher, the John Day Company. The story was published as *East Wind: West Wind* (1930), the first part concerning Kwei-lan, the second, her brother. In both parts the characters are caught in a dilemma between traditional and modern ideas.

In March 1927, having returned to China, Buck and her family, through the help of Chinese friends and servants, escaped Communist soldiers who had entered Nanking, looting and killing foreigners. Her observations on this and other scenes of revolution are portrayed in the group of stories that make up the second section of *The First Wife and Other Stories* (1933), her first collection.

The first section of the book, "The Old and the New," explores the clash between the traditions of the East and the modern ideas of the West. The title story ("The First Wife," *Asia*, December 1931, January 1932) tells of a traditional wife who is unable to change as her U.S.-educated husband has. He divorces her, takes a modern bride, and when he wants his first wife to leave his parents' household, she hangs herself. Another story in this section, "The Frill," communicates the idea of American exploitation of the East. Mrs. Lowe, a well-to-do American, browbeats her Chinese tailor. He works for hours making an elaborate frill for her dress, is underpaid for his efforts, then is refused further work, though he urgently needs the money. Mrs. Lowe is unconscious of her cruelty and callousness. The second section of the volume, "Revolution," includes the story "Wang Lung" (first published here), from which Buck took the title character and the looting scene and expanded them into her novel *The Good Earth*, for which she won the Pulitzer Prize in 1931. The last section of *The First Wife*, "The Flood," contains four stories centered on the tragic Yangtze flood of 1931.

The First Wife is probably the best collection of Buck's short stories. They are realistic and free of the sentimentalism and romanticism of her later work. The 9 August 1933 review in the *Christian Century* states, "Here one feels, are not only the deep realities about the soul of China, but some of the basic truths about nature regardless of race." This collection was also significant in Buck's attaining Nobel Prize status.

In 1934 Buck decided to settle permanently in the United States and purchased a home in Bucks County, Pennsylvania. Her marriage to John Buck ended in divorce on 11 June 1935. She married the president of the John Day Company, Richard J. Walsh, that very afternoon. During her marriage to Walsh, they adopted eight more children, some of them hard-to-place Amerasians. She became an American wife and mother, determined to continue her writing career and to explore American subject matter.

During the 1930s Buck's work flourished. She was awarded an honorary M.A. from Yale University in 1933; she received the William Dean Howells Medal for distinguished fiction in 1935; and she was elected to membership in the Na-

Pearl and John Lossing Buck on their wedding day, 30 May 1917 (courtesy of Janice C. Walsh)

tional Institute of Arts and Letters in 1936. In 1938 Buck became the third American to be honored with the Nobel Prize for Literature. The citation that accompanied the award read: "for rich and generous epic descriptions of Chinese peasant life and masterpieces of biography." The biographies referred to—*The Exile* and *Fighting Angel* (both 1936)—are of her missionary parents. Many critics assert that, although Buck had written some good stories, she received the Nobel Prize for humanitarian reasons rather than for her writing. Critics also agree that after she received the award, her work, for the most part, declined.

Buck's wartime activities included the writing of radio plays, some of which were written for the Office of War Information and broadcast to China, and the founding of the East and West Association, a nonprofit group dedicated to the promotion of greater understanding among the people of the world. These activities did not cur-

Buck with her second husband, Richard J. Walsh, in 1950 (Collection of William A. Smith); they were married on 11 June 1935, the day her divorce from John Buck became final.

tail her creative writing, and often she combined her interests, writing pro-Chinese, anti-Japanese propaganda novels and short stories. Buck's second collection of stories, *Today and Forever* (1941), resulted from this effort.

The stories in *Today and Forever* contain a special pattern of arrangement; the book begins with stories of old China, develops to stories illustrating the effect of new ways on the country, then follows China into the Sino-Japanese period. Buck states in the "Author's Note" that if she "at all portrayed . . . the tough, resistant, indominable quality of the Chinese people, then [she has] done what [she] wished to do." The intent is good, but because of the exaggerated Hollywood-style quality of most of the stories, this second collection is not as successful as her first. In "Tiger! Tiger!," for example (first published here), character and plot are both fantastic and incredible: a bored, American-educated Chinese girl falls in love with a warlord who is heavi-

ly taxing the area. She convinces him not to attack a neighboring bandit headquarters, but then he is captured by the bandit leader. He escapes, and afterward determines to lead his men against the Japanese.

The most effective story in this collection is "The Angel" (*Women's Home Companion*, April 1937), a portrait of an American missionary, Miss Barry, who, although dedicated to her work, despises the Chinese people: they are unclean, lazy, and never live up to her expectations. Out of frustration she commits suicide by leaping off a cliff. This story reveals a bleak realism in the same vein as "The First Wife."

Unlike Buck's first two collections, *Far and Near: Stories of Japan, China, and America* (1947) contains stories set in America. Though written in a cool, competent style, these American stories, except for one, are rather superficial. "The Truce" (first published here), concerning a woman who realizes there is no love in her marriage, reaches the quality of sophistication of Buck's Chinese stories. This theme of disharmony in family life, or variations of it, is contained in all the American stories here. The best works in this collection, however, are the Chinese stories, especially "The Tax Collector" and "A Few People" (both first published here); they contain the fundamental conflicts of Chinese village life. The *Times Book Review* (30 November 1947) summed it up: "Miss Buck's art thrives best on the Chinese scene; transplanted in America, it grows pale and artificial."

Much of the work in the next collection, *Fourteen Stories* (1961), is about love and marriage and is romantic in tone. The stories are easy to read and well written, yet they seem mechanical and too neatly worked out. Richard Sullivan, in his *New York Times* review, observed: "Everything always gets nicely, neatly, tidily resolved in these pages." "The Silver Butterfly" (*Saturday Evening Post*, 14 May 1960), however, is worth mentioning. The story is about an episode among members of a Chinese Communist commune. An aged woman gives a piece of family jewelry to one of the commune children. Since no one is supposed to own personal items, she is punished for this at a commune meeting. The story expresses the idea that, although many technological advances are being made in Communist China, the people still suffer; the intensity almost reaches that of her earlier Chinese stories, and the impact remains with the reader. There are several other collections, including those published posthumously: *East and West* (1975); *Secrets of the Heart* (1976); *The Lovers and Other Stories* (1977); and *The Woman Who Was Changed, and Other Stories* (1979). These focus on such contemporary topics as maintaining both a home and a career; marrying for security; illegal abortion; nuclear research; and racial prejudice.

Although her literary career had promise after she received the Nobel Prize, Buck's later works never fully reached the intensity of her earlier ones. As her humanitarian preoccupations increased, her literary reputation declined. In 1949

she helped establish Welcome House, an adoption agency for American-Asian children. In 1964 she founded the Pearl S. Buck Foundation, an agency established to care for half-American children who are forced to remain overseas. During this period she exchanged the objectivity and realism that had made her early works significant for didacticism, sentimentality, and romanticism. In addition to these weaknesses, critics object to her method of old-fashioned storytelling. Her conventional technique, lack of penetration into her characters, and the absence of myth and symbolism leave little for her readers to think about. Despite these drawbacks, Buck's best works reflect acute perceptions about humanity and remain, always, entertaining. Pearl S. Buck died of lung cancer on 6 March 1973 at her home in Danby, Vermont.

Bibliography:

Lucille S. Zinn, "The Works of Pearl S. Buck: A Bibliography," *Bulletin of Bibliography*, 36 (October-December 1979): 194-208.

Biographies:

Cornelia Spencer, *The Exile's Daughter: A Biography of Pearl S. Buck* (New York: Coward-McCann, 1944);

Theodore F. Harris, *Pearl S. Buck—A Biography*, 2 volumes (New York: Day, 1969, 1971);

Nora Stirling, *Pearl Buck: A Woman in Conflict* (Piscataway, N.J.: New Century, 1983).

References:

Phyllis Bentley, "The Art of Pearl S. Buck," *English Journal*, 24 (December 1935): 791-800;

George A. Cevasco, "Pearl Buck and the Chinese Novel," *Asian Studies*, 5 (December 1967): 437-450;

Paul A. Doyle, *Pearl S. Buck* (New York: Twayne, 1965; revised, 1980);

Doyle, "Pearl S. Buck's Short Stories: A Survey," *English Journal*, 55 (January 1966): 62-68.

John Cheever

(27 May 1912 - 18 June 1982)

James O'Hara
Pennsylvania State University

See also the Cheever entries in *DLB 2: American Novelists Since World War II, DLB Yearbook: 1980,* and *DLB Yearbook: 1982.*

BOOKS: *The Way Some People Live* (New York: Random House, 1943);

The Enormous Radio and Other Stories (New York: Funk & Wagnalls, 1953; London: Gollancz, 1953);

The Wapshot Chronicle (New York: Harper, 1957; London: Gollancz, 1957);

The Housebreaker of Shady Hill and Other Stories (New York: Harper, 1958; London: Gollancz, 1958 [i.e., 1959]);

Some People, Places, and Things That Will Not Appear in My Next Novel (New York: Harper, 1961; London: Gollancz, 1961);

The Brigadier and the Golf Widow (New York: Harper & Row, 1964; London: Gollancz, 1965);

The Wapshot Scandal (New York: Harper & Row, 1964; London: Gollancz, 1964);

Homage to Shakespeare (Stevenson, Conn.: Country Squire, 1968);

Bullet Park (New York: Knopf, 1969; London: Cape, 1969);

The World of Apples (New York: Knopf, 1973; London: Cape, 1974);

Falconer (New York: Knopf, 1977; London: Cape, 1977);

The Day the Pig Fell into the Well (Northridge, Cal.: Lord John, 1978);

The Stories of John Cheever (New York: Knopf, 1978; London: Cape, 1979);

The Leaves, the Lion-Fish and the Bear (Los Angeles: Sylvester & Orphanos, 1980);

Oh What a Paradise It Seems (New York: Knopf, 1982; London: Cape, 1982);

The National Pastime (Los Angeles: Sylvester & Orphanos, 1982);

Atlantic Crossing: Excerpts from the Journals of John Cheever (Cottondale, Ala.: Ex Ophidia, 1986).

SELECTED PERIODICAL PUBLICATIONS—UNCOLLECTED: "Why I Write Short Stories," *Newsweek,* 92 (30 October 1978): 24-25;

"Journals: From the Late Forties and Fifties," I and II, *New Yorker,* 66 (6 and 13 August 1990): 33-64; 29-61.

To outward appearances John Cheever was very much a child of the American twentieth century. Born just before World War I, he lived through the halcyon Jazz Age, suffered through the Depression, and served as a noncombatant in the army during World War II. Then in the middle decades he raised a family with his wife, Mary, as he pursued a thriving literary career in fiction. He experienced a personal decline of staggering proportions during the Vietnam era, but then finally, miraculously, managed to rehabilitate himself and his reputation before he died in 1982. It would be a disservice to Cheever and to American literature, however, to "locate" him so precisely. In his best short stories, he easily slips the bonds of time and place.

In a shaded corner of a Unitarian churchyard cemetery in the tiny Massachusetts village of Norwell, three small, black headstones mark the graves of the Cheever family. The first is for the husband and father, Frederick, and contains a line from William Shakespeare's *The Tempest*: "We are such stuff as dreams are made on." The second marker commemorates the passing of the wife and mother, Mary Liley Cheever, with the familiar prayer "Rest in Peace." The third grave bears no inscription other than the name John William Cheever and the dates of his life, 1912-1982. A brass star identifying the deceased as a military veteran stands in front of the headstone.

John Cheever's life as a child growing up in nearby Quincy probably appeared to be "normal"—if anyone's life can be so described. A second look at the headstones reveals that his father was forty-nine years old when John was born, but otherwise there was nothing in the circum-

John Cheever (Stanford University News Service)

stances of his family that would hint at anything but the most predictable standards of middle-class American life. Frederick Cheever had been successful in the shoe business (as a factory owner, according to John, but more probably as a salesman, according to biographer Scott Donaldson)—successful enough to move the family to the fashionable section of Quincy when John was eight. John shared the Cheevers' prosperity, but not his father's affection, with his older brother, Fred, ten years his senior. And sadly neither son had a claim on their mother's love. John had been conceived accidentally; further (and the most unsettling fact, assuming its veracity), his father had urged that he be aborted. Mr. Cheever had gone so far, John recalled his mother saying, as to invite the abortionist to dinner.

The good people of Quincy must have regarded Mrs. Cheever herself as a model mother. She not only had the time and energy to raise her two boys properly, but enough left over to invest in countless civic causes. A former head nurse at Massachusetts General Hospital, after her marriage she helped found Quincy Woman's Club and served in the fund-raising vanguard of religious, cultural, and educational projects. But all this activity belied the truth of the matter: as time and John Cheever's life wore on, his home situation became increasingly unhappy. His father's business started to turn sour in the early 1920s, as the New England shoe industry anticipated the eventual collapse of the national economy. A deeper problem lay at the root of the Cheevers' distress as a family, however. The exact causes of the collapse of the Cheevers' marriage into dry

Cheever with his older brother, Fred, and their father, Freder-ick Lincoln Cheever (Collection of Jane Cheever Carr)

respectability are a matter of speculation, but John's recollections of its failure were vivid and depressing. He remembered his mother as an incredibly cold woman, both to him and his father, and Frederick himself as a bemused, somewhat eccentric, and generally ineffectual man. Their characters, filtered through the prism of fiction, dominate much of their son's first novel, *The Wapshot Chronicle* (1957), where they appear at least partially responsible for the youthful confusions of the Wapshot boys, Coverly and Moses. Interestingly, the shortcomings of the fictional father in the novel, Leander, are softened into harmless eccentricities, while mother Sarah's are magnified. She is, in fact, only the most prominent in a small army of strong-willed, odious women created by Cheever in his fiction. Against them stands an even smaller legion of capable, loving females who can usually be identified by one important characteristic: they pose no serious threat to male happiness.

The tendency to find direct correspondence between John Cheever's fictional creations and people or events in his life is inescapable.

Cheever caught on to the game as soon as critics found him important enough to write about, and he objected strongly but unconvincingly to what he called the reading of his stories as "crypto-autobiography." Certainly a knowledge of the facts about Cheever and his relationships, family and otherwise, should not prevent an intelligent reader from appreciating his work on its own terms. If the narrative voices of his tales—especially those written during and after World War II—sound unusually distinctive, it is partially because the entire life experience informing them was so distinctive. Cheever, writing out of considerable psychic pain, found in his own luminous prose a way of penetrating and comprehending life's darkness.

Cheever's first published story, "Expelled" (*New Republic*, 1 October 1930), records the experience of a boy, on the verge of manhood, learning that the prep-school version of formal education in the United States can be a strange form of indoctrination: "The Governor will tell us what a magnificent country we have. He will tell us to beware of the Red menace. He will want to tell us that the goddam foreigners should have gone home a hell of a long time ago." Years later Cheever would tell interviewers that he was expelled from Thayer Academy for smoking, but "Expelled," besides demonstrating a remarkably advanced technical sense, reveals a social sensibility that must have made life in a private preparatory school almost unbearable. Cheever's father had almost certainly turned to drink for solace against the pain of business reverses and a difficult marriage while John attended Thayer, and John's academic record was shaky at best. The precise calculus of national, social, and personal factors that fed the rancor behind "Expelled" is now impossible to reconstruct, but it has more than historical interest for a close reader of Cheever's fiction. In addition to its tone of self-righteous anger, it features some impressive characters, like the history teacher Laura Driscoll, who almost transcends the follies that surround her: "She was the only teacher I have ever seen who was often ecstatical. She would stand by the boards and shout out her discoveries on the Egyptian cultures." Regrettably, the young storyteller adds, she didn't force-feed enough "facts" into her students to get enough of them into Harvard, so she was fired. But he also reports her profane valedictory to the headmaster at the last chapel meeting, as well as his own farewell: "It is strange to be so young and to have no place to report to at nine o'clock." In its disarming honesty and vigor, "Expelled" sounds a resonant keynote to Cheever's career; it introduces a writer who would have to find things out for himself.

Another demon that toyed with but never fully possessed the young Cheever was the alluring promise of communism. Several of his stories in the 1930s chronicle the failure, on a human level, of American capitalism prior to the heroic efforts of Franklin D. Roosevelt to revive it. An early example is the curious antistory "Fall River" (*The Left*, Autumn 1931), actually an impressionistic view of the Massachusetts mill town fallen on hard times. The narrator (who refers not to himself but "we," without further identification) paints a dark gray portrait of the town and its inhabitants, who are poised on the edge of economic chaos: "Our room was on the fourth floor of a high brick house. A great many people could not pay their rent and the landlady made the silence miserable with her complaints. There was a man on the third floor who had a job and who earned ten dollars a week. . . . The landlady would weep when she saw him and tell him she must eat and that he must pay his rent."

When Cheever finally broke into the charmed circle of *New Yorker* writers on 25 May 1935, it was with one of the most despairing pictures of city life in the Depression that he—or anyone—would ever paint. "Brooklyn Rooming House" records the gradual deterioration of one such building and its inhabitants, including the landlady, and represents a significant advance over the relative formlessness of "Fall River." Again the storyteller is one of the tenants, but he quickly fades into the shadows, and as a result the comings and goings of his fellow sufferers are rightly emphasized.

There is more than coincidental poignancy in all of this. During the 1930s Cheever corresponded with, and became a friend of, Elizabeth Ames, the director of a writers' and artists' retreat called Yaddo in Saratoga, New York. A lovely, secluded estate, Yaddo was then a haven for artists just beginning to gain attention (James Farrell and Muriel Rukeyser among them). In his letters to Ames, Cheever makes it painfully evident that he was barely able to subsist on his earnings as a writer and holder of various odd jobs in New York City, where he had moved from Boston in 1934. The move followed an apparently serious breach with his brother, Fred, over the affections of a young woman whom Fred subsequently married; although the brothers resumed

their friendship later, it would never again be as close as it had been. When John did find work—writing book synopses for MGM movie studios, for example—it was impossible at first to concentrate fully on his fiction.

Cheever's serious attempt at writing a novel would not bear fruit until *The Wapshot Chronicle* appeared in 1957. He continued to work on shorter fiction, although in a letter to Ames dated 22 April 1935, he complained that he did not feel encouraged, citing his "inability to sell," to "jolt" editors with his work. The same letter mentions acceptances by both the *New Yorker* and *New Republic*, however, and in retrospect 1935 marks a turning point—upward—in Cheever's career. In December of that year, *Story* magazine printed "Of Love: A Testimony," a much longer story than those accepted earlier by the *New Yorker*. When it later appeared in Cheever's first collection, *The Way Some People Live* (1943), it was singled out for praise by critics Struthers Burt and Weldon Kees. Kees's comment is a shrewd observation on one of Cheever's recurring problems as a writer: " 'Of Love: A Testimony' is an excellent commentary of what this writer is capable of doing when he is his own man, when he has room enough in which to work for something more than episodic notation and minor perceptive effects." Kees's larger point is that Cheever's style had been cramped by the insistence of the *New Yorker* on descriptive detail, what Kees calls "a patina of triviality" and "almost formulaic skill." In embryo this is a criticism that would haunt Cheever throughout his career and long after his heyday as a writer of short fiction: on the one hand he is regarded as a gifted writer constantly perfecting his skills; on the other hand he is scolded for selling out to the establishment by writing excessively polished narratives. (Ironically, when this criticism appeared in 1943, Cheever was well on his way to solving the problem of his identity as a writer. As an enlisted man in the army he had begun a series of stories that evinced a much more authoritative "voice," in spite of the fact that they are not combat stories. He continued to write while training with an infantry unit and gradually regained the assertiveness that had characterized "Expelled.")

The main character in "Of Love: A Testimony" is a young man named Morgan; his age and background are fairly close to Cheever's: "He was as good a representative of his class as you could find, born in a staid suburb, educated in mediocre schools, firmly grounded in the cyni-

Cheever and his wife, Mary, during World War II (Collection of the Cheever family)

cism of his class and education." Unlike his creator, however, he is a college graduate. His cynicism springs not so much from personal misfortune as "from a consciousness of his life's insignificance and lack of precedent." He is introduced to a young woman, Julia, by a slightly older acquaintance, a college tutor named Sears, who also happens to be Julia's former lover and a hypersensitive lost soul. Morgan falls in love with Julia, but her affections prove changeable. Cheever's characterization of Morgan as hopelessly vulnerable to Julia's whims is perhaps the best thing about the story; when she resumes her relationship with Sears, Morgan is devastated. A glaring weakness, however, is the failure to clarify her change of heart, suggesting a "feminine" flaw that borders on stereotyping. Later criticism that Cheever consciously or unconsciously displays misogyny in his fiction can find both supporting and contradictory examples in his early stories. Laura Driscoll, the heroine of "Expelled," stands as an instance of the latter.

In story after story from this period, Cheever recites the facts of each "case" with little

or no comment, since the facts themselves are meant to be sufficiently eloquent on the subject of economic hardship. In only one story is communism, an obvious alternative, fully explored with what looks like serious interest on the narrator's part. "In Passing" (*Atlantic Monthly*, March 1936) centers on the character and interests of a young man named Tom, in and around the racetrack town of what appears to be Saratoga, New York. (Cheever began his long association with Yaddo, located next to the Saratoga racetracks, at about this time.) At loose ends, Tom at first comes easily under the sway of a true subversive named Girsdansky, who has arrived in America in search of recruits for a communist uprising. The young New Englander listens as Girsdansky expounds his views to whoever seems disenchanted enough with the status quo to want to join the revolutionary ranks: "We depend upon your generation for a great deal, for if anyone has the right to ask revenge or justice it is the young men." Yet despite the crumbling of his own family's fortunes—the subject of the story's second half— Tom is unable to commit himself to a cause that ignores the dreamer in himself and most of his fellow countrymen. He realizes that much of their ambition is based on nothing more than greed, or hunger for a vaguely imagined "better life." But Girsdansky, for all his idealism, sounds more like a book than a human being. In the end Tom just walks away, presumably to pursue a dream yet to be dreamed. "In Passing," as the title suggests, is more concerned with transition than closure.

Cheever's stories from this apprenticeship phase of his career, for all their false starts and qualified successes, establish thematic lines of development that extend through the next four decades, a tumultuous time in American history and an incredibly diverse one for its literature. In all probability, future students of this period in America's national life will turn to Cheever's fiction (along with that of F. Scott Fitzgerald, Dorothy Parker, John O'Hara, and other socially sensitive writers) to get a clear sense of the era's moods, values, and social relations. In Cheever's case, however, they will notice an unusual disjunction between the fiction he created prior to World War II and the work he did after the war. In the first instance, following his first few intensely personal attempts Cheever's narrative tone is generally objective and naturalistic to a fault; he had discovered that the *New Yorker* and other magazines favored this style, and he sought the kind of success that "Expelled" had promised. It was only after a long run of acceptances, during the war and after an apparent surge in his self-confidence, that he would find the unique narrative voice so characteristic of his finest work. Part of that transition was an apparently calculated decision to distance the material of his fiction, insofar as that was possible, from the precise details of particular historical contexts—to make his characters and their situations more universal. As he later explained in a 15 July 1962 letter to Professor Frederick Bracher: "A sense of time that revolves around the sinking of ships and declarations of war seems to me a sense of time debased. We live at deeper levels than these and fiction should make this clear."

But in both phases of his career—indeed, throughout his life—Cheever's stories demonstrate an ongoing preoccupation with questions of public and private morality. When the main focus of his work moved from the city to the suburbs, and his art concentrated on the general trait more substantially than the particular detail

(his suburban "Shady Hill" and "Bullet Park" communities could just as easily lie outside Boston or Chicago as New York), his fiction still demonstrated an intense interest in the folly that results from personal and societal neglect of ethical issues, or from pursuing them too narrowly.

Between 1938 and 1940 Cheever wrote four stories that bring racetrack settings and characters into sharper focus than "In Passing" had required. His visits to Yaddo gave him the opportunity to make firsthand observations of those who thrive on horse racing; his own interest in the ethical and psychological problems associated with gambling as a vice took over from there. As a group these stories portray track "types" addicted to gambling, but neither as fools nor villains. They resemble alcoholics in their thirst for instant happiness, their subsequent desire to "kick the habit," and their inability to do so. Perhaps the most interesting story from this group is "His Young Wife" (*Collier's*, 1 January 1938). Here a moral point is driven home indirectly by the unraveling of events. The title character, Sue, is the May half of a May-September marriage to John, a quietly affectionate older man who is a gambler. With the appearance of a younger, flashier horseplayer named Rickey, the potential for trouble that John has long sensed in this union is realized. Over time Rickey gains Sue's affection, and although she appears blameless, the reader is made to understand that she does know what is happening. John patiently bides his time until, one day at the track, he is able to trick his rival into showing that his uncontrollable passion for playing the horses is greater than that for Sue's love. In the end she comprehends both his shallowness and her husband's depth, and the story ends happily. Considering the preponderance of unhappy or deeply troubled marriages in stories from Cheever's mature years, the appearance of a narrative like this during his early years (he was twenty-five when it was published) has some significance.

As the Depression decade wound down and political tensions in Europe heated up, Cheever's life as a writer, now very much at home in Greenwich Village, entered a new and happier phase. He met Mary Winternitz, the bright and attractive daughter of a prominent physician, in 1939; they were married on 22 March 1941. With the passage of time they were to discover antipathies and conflicting interests that eventually threatened to destroy their marriage. At the outset, however, they were happy despite their relative pov-

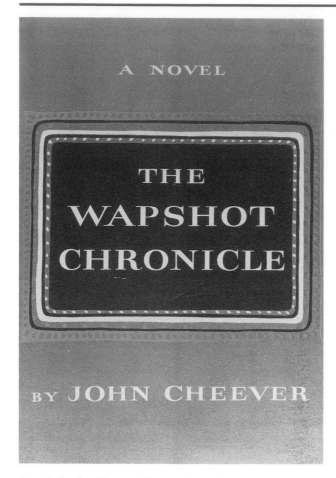

Dust jacket for Cheever's first novel (1957), the autobiographical saga of the Wapshot family, which was continued in The Wapshot Scandal *(1964)*

erty. Their love was only intensified by the experience of economic adversity they shared with most other young couples—a common theme in many of Cheever's narratives from these years—and, not surprisingly, his output during this period easily surpassed that of any other time in his career. From 1940 until he entered the army early in 1942, the *New Yorker* and other magazines accepted thirty-two of his stories.

Although Cheever was thirty years old, he enlisted in the army and trained as an infantryman in Georgia and South Carolina. But the army soon discovered two important facts: Cheever was not physically capable of becoming an effective combat soldier, and he was already a very good writer. He was reassigned to the Signal Corps in 1943 and became a scriptwriter for training films, a position he held for the remainder of the war.

Several of the dozen "army life" stories Cheever published during the war are unabashedly sentimental on such themes as soldierly cama-

raderie and virtue. The upbeat mood of these stories derives not so much from an intrusive narrator—Cheever was still trying to let his tales tell themselves at this point—as from the incidents the narrator chooses to describe. "Dear Lord, We Thank Thee for Thy Bounty" (*New Yorker*, 12 November 1943) is one such story; it uses the simple device of a Thanksgiving dinner in the field to bring together soldiers from all walks of life in a heartwarming symbol of the American fighting man preparing for combat. All of this is fairly predictable, even considering Cheever's earlier flirtations with radicalism, and several of Cheever's GIs are stereotypical. But there are some striking exceptions.

In its 13 March 1943 issue the *New Yorker* printed "Sergeant Limeburner," which confirms Cheever's credentials as a tough-minded realist, hearkening back to some of his best naturalistic writing of the 1930s. Its central character is a basic-training sergeant who earns the hatred of his men by bullying them into submission, before he is repaid in kind. It is Cheever's most caustic portrayal of military life. Limeburner, mentally deficient and psychologically suspect, pushes his trainees beyond the point of exhaustion. The story gains interest when he makes the mistake of trying to intimidate a soldier tougher than he is, an ex-convict named Brown. Following several confrontations, Brown takes it upon himself to beat the sergeant senseless, thus disgracing him in the eyes of his men. At this point the reader, as witness to Limeburner's brutality, may feel that a sort of moral balance has been achieved. Cheever, however, adds a thematic twist to the story, in a way that anticipates the ethical complexity of his best mature work. A corporal named Pacelli argues *against* a simplistic reading of Limeburner's character by his men: "Maybe you guys don't know it, but you can outshoot and outmarch any outfit in this battalion, and that's because he's given you good training. Only he wants everything to be too good. That's the trouble with him. You'll appreciate this training when you get into combat."

At the end of the story, when Limeburner has been reduced to a bloody mess by Brown, the men watch silently as he is led away: "The faces watching him walk toward his judgment were the lean, still faces of the soldiers he had destroyed himself to make. In the morning there was another sergeant to take his place." Having considered the implications of this ending, which straddles the line between pure objectivity and nar-

John and Mary Cheever at a picnic in Westchester County; they lived at Beechwood, a house in Scarborough, from 1951 to 1961 (Collection of the Cheever family).

rative commentary, the reader may know more than some of Limeburner's men (fictional or real) did. The closing affirms Pacelli's point and also implies that some terrible, inscrutable force has determined the events of the story. Men like Limeburner, it suggests, despite their fearsomeness, are little more than pawns in the larger scheme of things. This is a theme long familiar to readers of naturalistic prose, but the narrative viewpoint of "Sergeant Limeburner" sees beyond the mechanistic framework of the story material into the possibility of compassion for a repulsive antihero. Limeburner is weeping as he is carried away. A world at war demands strange sacrifices and wreaks its own forms of rough justice. Although he never saw combat himself, Cheever would see that truism played out on a larger scale at the end of the war. In 1945 he was briefly assigned to observe "mopping up" operations in the Philippines and apparently visited other islands recaptured from the Japanese.

Following his discharge from the service in late 1945, Cheever—like millions of other veterans—faced the problem of how to feed and

house his young family (a daughter, Susan, had been born in 1943) while contending with a housing shortage and the difficulties of resuming a peacetime career. His response, logically enough, was to write a series of six "Town House" stories (*New Yorker*, 21 April 1945 - 4 May 1946) about the tribulations of a group of former servicemen and their spouses living in a large but still overcrowded New York town house. Although the tales are somewhat circumscribed by the nature of their material, they are true to the awkward, transitory life-style they are based on and sufficient proof that Cheever was ready to return to his role as a voice for his generation. Marital strife emerges in the "Town House" series as a major preoccupation of that generation and of its increasingly self-assured spokesman in fiction.

Less than two years later, over a period of several months in 1947, the *New Yorker* published three stories that mark a great divide in Cheever's writing career. With some trepidation Cheever's *New Yorker* editor and friend William Maxwell first protested the change of artistic course, then decided to let Cheever shift stylistic gears out of straight naturalism and into a blend of realism and fantasy. "Roseheath" (6 August) is Cheever's first postwar, suburban tale; the other two landmark stories are "The Enormous Radio" (17 May) and the less well-known "Torch Song" (4 October), a Gothic tale, both collected in *The Enormous Radio and Other Stories* (1953).

"Torch Song" is notable as an example of Cheever's ability to construct a fairly elaborate plot in the service of a complex theme. Unfortunately his main character is a despicable woman who seeks out men on the skids with the apparent intention of enjoying—indeed deriving her vitality from—their death throes. The story barely avoids stereotyping, only to lapse into bizarre distortion. It comes as close to the nightmare visions of Franz Kafka as anything Cheever wrote and thus deserves some attention in any analysis of Cheever's evolution as a writer, but it also raises troubling questions about his recurring tendency to twist female psychology into something grotesque. Some critics have misread such characters as merely quaint eccentrics, just as others have failed to recognize Cheever's truly admirable women.

"The Enormous Radio" stands out as the premier story of this 1947 trio and perhaps the most imaginative story Cheever ever wrote. While its setting and characters are urban and urbane, its theme looks forward to the later suburban tales of young couples who, to all outward appearances, are normal, but who in fact are teetering on the brink of catastrophe. Jim and Irene Westcott live in a "typical" apartment building and are described as almost annoyingly "average," except for their mutual, intense love of classical music. When their radio fails, Jim buys a new one without consulting Irene. It turns out to be particularly ugly, and this failure of communication on Jim's part proves to be Cheever's sole clue to the story's outcome.

The fantastic premise of "The Enormous Radio," its spark of genius, is the idea that the radio can receive not only electronic signals but snatches of conversation and other sounds from all over the Westcotts' building. Their first reaction is bewilderment; their second, voyeuristic fascination: " 'Those must be the Fullers, in 11-E,' Irene said. 'I knew they were giving a party this afternoon. I saw her in the liquor store. Isn't this too divine? Try something else. See if you can get those people in 18-C.' " Once Cheever has the premise firmly established (and his narrative sleight of hand is truly impressive) the plot takes on its own momentum, and he gives full rein to his powers of characterization through realistic dialogue. He presents a sound panorama of vanity, perversity, selfishness, banality, and marital discord; all the skills he had so carefully honed during the difficult years of the Depression and the war are in full evidence in this story, as they are in "Roseheath" and "Torch Song," and as they would later be in the stories of his mature years.

The most compelling feature of "The Enormous Radio" is the effect of voyeurism on the Westcotts themselves (and perhaps, by extension, on the reader): "It was still mild when they walked home from the party, and Irene looked up at the spring stars. 'How far that little candle throws its beams,' she exclaimed. 'So shines a good deed in a naughty world.' She waited that night until Jim had fallen asleep, and then went into the living room and turned on the radio." At the story's end Jim and Irene face the fact that their own marriage has been skirting disaster. In "listening in" on the woes of others, they have merely been diverting themselves from honest confrontation with their own. When that self-examining process finally begins, Cheever quickly draws the curtain and leaves his readers to draw their own conclusions.

In 1951 the Cheevers (including a son, Benjamin, who had been born three years earlier) moved from New York City to nearby Scarborough. The change of scene would prove significant not only for them as a family but also for Cheever's work. They were part of the vast postwar migration from the cities to the countryside. The Cheevers brought hopes and ambitions with them to the suburbs—first to Scarborough and later (in 1961) to Ossining, farther north on the Hudson. Some of these dreams were to be realized, but the outward prosperity that followed this change of scene was deceiving.

Cheever had written his first suburban story several years before leaving New York. "Roseheath," another story that appeared in 1947, adopts a comic tone to mock the genteel aspirations of a young married couple living some distance from the city. The wife's ambition is simple: to resume a childhood love affair with Roseheath, a neighboring home and its grounds, where she had spent a large part of her girlhood. She and her husband seem close to realizing this dream when they strike up an acquaintance with the home's new owners, but their hopes—particularly hers—disintegrate in a scene that breaks new ground for Cheever. The young woman witnesses the spectacle of the owners, a family of zanies, stripping to the buff for a swim, without the slightest consideration for their guests. As comic as the moment is, Cheever seems more interested in the pathos of his heroine's sense of irreparable loss: "Ethel massaged her face, so that her smile would appear natural when she said goodbye to the Fields—goodbye and thank you and goodbye to Roseheath forever."

That note of wistful sadness, set perfectly against an absurd background, would in time become one of Cheever's hallmarks as a storyteller. He was by no means the inventor of the technique, but his unique way of yoking such tonally disparate elements reached a level of skill in the 1950s and 1960s that few writers, before or since, have attained. As he became more practiced in his craft, he experimented more often with the placement of such moments, shifting them to opening and middle sections of stories, and with their intensification through lyrical effects. The use of poetry in prose is not unique with Cheever; what sets him apart from other writers, however, is his way of using prose poetry to sound just the right note of sympathetic sadness in his depictions of suburban life. His stories, even as early as "Roseheath," strike an impressive balance between mockery and compassion, as if to say, "You are all fools—and so am I."

Photograph by Warren Inglese

JOHN CHEEVER

No. 0154P

SOME PEOPLE, PLACES, & THINGS THAT WILL NOT APPEAR IN MY NEXT NOVEL

A work of fiction by the author of THE WAPSHOT CHRONICLE

JOHN CHEEVER

Dust jacket for Cheever's 1961 collection of sketches and stories, most of which had appeared in the New Yorker

Several interesting urban-based stories followed "The Enormous Radio," but the shift in Cheever's main focus from city to suburbs became evident with the appearance of "O Youth and Beauty!" (*New Yorker*, 22 August 1953; collected in *The Housebreaker of Shady Hill and Other Stories*, 1958). This is the tragic story of Cash Bentley, a middle-aged former athlete domesticated in Shady Hill (a name that would soon become synonymous with Cheever's vision of suburbia), who persists in chasing his own dream of youthful glory: being a track star. Like many a Cheever nonhero, Cash's adult, professional life has been anything but successful. He has kept himself and his wife, Louise, afloat financially, but just barely; their greatest problem is his feeling out of place, trapped in nostalgia for a time when his prowess as a runner simplified his life and made it glorious. Cheever's twist, in this in-

stance, characteristically makes the narrative both more engaging and more realistic. Cash is made to undergo the closest thing to tragedy that Cheever ever attempted. First, Cash suffers the humiliation of a broken leg while attempting his favorite ritual of time-denial, an indoor hurdles race. One of the better examples of Cheever's growing confidence in himself and his ability to combine light and dark poetic effects is found tucked away in his rendition of the "quiet time" that follows in Cash's life, the prelude to the story's catastrophe: "The air [of Shady Hill] seems as fragrant as it is dark—it is a delicious element to walk through—and most of the windows on Alewives Lane are open to it. You can see Mr. and Mrs. Bearden, as you pass, looking at their television. Joe Lockwood, the young lawyer who lives on the corner, is practicing a speech to the jury before his wife.... Mrs. Carver—Harry

Farquarson's mother-in-law—glances up at the sky and asks, 'Where did all the stars come from?' She is old and foolish, and yet she is right: Last night's stars seem to have drawn to themselves a new range of galaxies, and the night sky is not dark at all, except where there is a tear in the membrane of light. In the unsold house lots near the track a hermit thrush is singing."

At such moments Cheever stops the main action of his narrative to redirect the reader's attention away from the particulars of the story and toward a larger thematic context. In "O Youth and Beauty!" what follows is a scene in which Cash, having recovered from his broken leg, is accidentally shot by his wife as he once again attempts to deny the inevitability of time and advancing age; she is "starting" him on another race over the furniture by firing a pistol he has forced upon her. It could be said, then, that the interlude's poetry is nothing more than an alternation in the larger rhythm of the story—and it is true that Cheever was fast becoming expert at the placement of these rhapsodies (the kind of lyricism that he had shunned as a younger writer). But an even stronger case can be made for another view: if it is true that Cheever, despite his well-earned success, was unsatisfied with his early work and had decided in mid-life to change his basic style, here is the most apparent manifestation of that change. No one had ever written quite like this before, and in all likelihood no one ever could again.

"The Country Husband" (*New Yorker*, 20 November 1954; in *The Housebreaker of Shady Hill*), like "The Enormous Radio," has become a favorite selection of short-story anthologizers; but unlike the earlier story, it falls into the category of Cheever tales that fail to explore their own implications. Francis Weed, its protagonist, survives a plane crash and returns home to Shady Hill, only to find a blank wall of indifference wherever he tries to describe his brush with death. Cheever then describes Mrs. Weed and the little Weeds (like the Cheevers, they live in a Dutch Colonial house) to underscore the point that they are all distinctly unlovable, thus setting the scene for Francis's brush with infidelity. He falls deeply and melodramatically in love with the babysitter, and the complications that arise from the mistake are full of seriocomic ambiguity. Francis daily grows less and less patient with the imbecilities of his life and work, and he is increasingly convinced that true, if illicit, love is his only recourse. He goes so far as to sabotage the job pros-

pects of a younger, more suitable rival for the sitter's affections, before settling into the realization that he has behaved like a fool: "He was in trouble. He had been lost once in his life, coming back from a trout stream in the north woods, and he had now the same bleak realization that no amount of cheerfulness or hopefulness or valor or perseverance could help him find, in the gathering dark, the path that he'd lost. He smelled the forest. The feeling of bleakness was intolerable, and he saw clearly that he had reached the point where he would have to make a choice." So he ponders a range of options, most of them unrealistic, before deciding to see a psychiatrist. While that choice looks more reasonable than most of the others (getting drunk, visiting a massage parlor), his subsequent decline into the solace of woodworking at the psychiatrist's urging will fail to satisfy many readers. Instead of an actual resolution, Cheever supplies a pathetic overview of Shady Hill winding down at the end of another day, panning from Francis in his basement, working on a coffee table, to various neighbors and household pets. "Then it is dark; it is a night where kings in golden suits ride elephants over the mountains."

The last line is often and justifiably quoted as an example of Cheever the enigmatic nonfinisher of otherwise highly polished stories. The image seems intended as a counterpoint to Francis Weed, anything but kinglike as he hunches over his woodworking project in his cellar, trying to "get his mind right" and forget his passion for the babysitter. And it is, in itself, a beautiful closing line, lifting the reader's gaze from the printed page into a shimmering vision of Shangri-la. It is also, unfortunately, a neat and easy way of ducking the problems of Francis's consciousness and future, and thus it indirectly calls attention both to the limitations of the short story as a narrative form and Cheever's own powers as a practitioner.

From late 1956 to late 1957 the Cheevers lived and prospered in Italy, where another son, Federico, was born in 1957. Before they left the United States *The Wapshot Chronicle* had been completed, in and of itself a major accomplishment as Cheever's first novel, and its friendly reception during their sabbatical made the family's European experience all the happier. Italy seems to have exerted an almost magnetic attraction for Cheever, and the resulting stories, which include "The Bella Lingua," "The Duchess," "Boy in Rome," "The World of Apples," and "Montraldo"

John and Mary Cheever at home in Ossining, New York, where they moved in 1961 (photograph copyright by David Gahr)

(all in *The Stories of John Cheever*, 1978), testify to his affection for the country and its people.

As a general rule ("The Duchess" is a striking exception), Cheever adopts the viewpoint of visitors like himself in these Italian tales, even though a pattern of great sympathy with—and considerable knowledge of—Italian culture emerges from the stories. His interest in the language is most evident in "The Bella Lingua" (*New Yorker*, 1 March 1958), another story that rebuts charges of Cheever's inability to portray women as either intelligent or admirable. Kate Dresser, a central character, is an American widow who supports herself and her son in Rome by dubbing films and teaching Italian to people such as Wilson Streeter, a divorced fellow American who works as a statistician.

Instead of pursuing the predictable romantic plot line, Cheever concentrates on the romance, and the antiromance, of the country itself: the story's main conflict is between Kate and her son, who is unhappy in Italy and has made his unhappiness known to his very American great-uncle. At Kate's behest Streeter agrees to act as moral support for her when the uncle arrives for a visit. Further complications result when the uncle is mugged while on a tour of the countryside, and also stem from the unvarnished

truth that Streeter himself has ambivalent feelings about living in Italy. Set against these tensions are the undeniable attractions of a country whose natural beauty belies its economic backwardness: "Nightingales sang in the trees, the double doors of the villa stood open, and in all the rooms there were bowls of roses and olivewood fires."

In the end, however, Kate's son and her uncle wear down her resistance, and she gives the boy up (allowing him to return to the United States with the uncle), realizing that he cannot adapt to the Italian ways and should not be forced to: "The boy laughed his owlish laugh. 'I'll miss the black hairs in my food,' he said. She didn't make a sound. She didn't even sigh. Then the boy went to her and began to cry. 'I'm sorry, Mummy,' he said. 'I'm sorry. That was a dumb thing to say. It's just an old joke.' " In the hands of a lesser writer the impulse to simplify this situation with a rosy ending (Streeter could marry Kate and return to America with her and the boy in tow) would be almost overwhelming. Cheever himself was not always capable of resisting the temptation, but for every such failure he made several sound artistic judgments, often transforming the most unlikely raw material into stories of considerable power.

The publication of *The Wapshot Chronicle* in 1957 heralded the onset of a new stage in Cheever's life. Despite some carping from the critics, he received a National Book Award the following year. Individual short stories had already won Benjamin Franklin and O. Henry awards, and by 1958 he had three published short-story collections to his credit. For the Cheevers, apparently, the American Dream had come true. Yet a close reading of Cheever's stories from these years and those that follow suggests that behind the outward success the demons were dancing all over suburbia.

Another suburban U.S. story, "The Death of Justina" (*Esquire*, November 1960; in *Some People, Places, and Things That Will Not Appear in My Next Novel*, 1961), stands out as a potential classic precisely because it combines solid material with a more decisive presentation than "The Country Husband" exhibits. This was also one of Cheever's own favorites; "I love it," he told Joshua Gilder in a 1982 interview: "I used to love giving readings of it . . . and if I were going to read a long story, something like 'The Swimmer,' I'd read 'The Death of Justina' just to find out what the audience was like, what the depth of their response was." The story begins on a contentious, almost breathless note—"So help me God it gets more and more preposterous, it corresponds less and less to what I remember and what I expect as if the force of life were centrifugal and threw one further and further away from one's purest memories and ambitions . . ."— and never lets up.

The problem, as the protagonist, a curmudgeon and writer of television commercials named Moses, sees it, lies in the unceasing onslaught of social chaos. More specifically, his nemesis is the growing insanity of contemporary American life as evidenced in two specific forms: his work and the aftermath of a relative's death. These are connected, chaotically enough, by his Scrooge-like boss's insistence that he stay on the job to write a commercial, even though he has just promised his wife to return home following the unexpected death of Justina, her elderly cousin. He fires off a parody of a television pitch: "Is your sense of smell fading, is your interest in gardening waning, is your fear of heights increasing, and are your sexual drives as ravening and intense as ever . . . ?" Then he leaves to catch the train for his home in Proxmire Manor.

In this version of suburban paradise, Moses is chagrined to discover, the zoning laws for his neighborhood permit neither death nor burial. The fact of Aunt Justina's death falls short of official reality; she cannot even be granted a death certificate. Moses tries to arrange for a zoning exception, but his plea to the mayor is turned down in a scene of brutal satiric force. Only when he threatens to dig a hole and bury Justina in his garden does the mayor relent, still complaining that the whole procedure is illegal. The burial takes place on the outskirts of Proxmire Manor, where the dead "are transported furtively as knaves and scoundrels and where they lie in an atmosphere of perfect neglect." Justina had been an "exemplary" person during her life, Moses observes, and the highly regulated stupidity surrounding her death merely mocks itself; "how can a people who do not mean to understand death hope to understand love, and who will sound the alarm?"

It would be comforting, perhaps, to invoke the logical separation of author and narrator in all such stories and note that Cheever never fully identified himself with the misanthropic teller of many of his tales. He is, in fact, on record (notably in an editorial in *Newsweek*, 30 October 1978) as a fairly satisfied, if occasionally bemused, admirer of many of the social behaviors he seems to ridicule in his fiction. On the other hand, both his detractors and admirers will find food for thought in his comments at a writers' conference held in 1960 in San Francisco (as reported by Robert Gutwillig in the *New York Times Book Review*, 13 November 1960). There he complained of the "abrasive and faulty surface of the United States" over the past quarter century and concluded that the "only possible position for a writer now is negation." Even granting some room for rhetorical overstatement, this is strong stuff from a writer often regarded as a lightweight, especially since its tenor has analogues in several of the stories written during and after this period. In fact some older members of the audience rose to criticize Cheever for his "deliberate obscurity" and anti-Americanism.

There are grounds, in short, for challenging the stereotype of Cheever as a quintessential *New Yorker* (read "safe," "sanitized," and "predictable") writer. If further proof that this view did not fit all the facts were needed, the point that Cheever and his work have become popular in the Soviet Union should also be made. Although Cheever himself interpreted this surprising development as due primarily to the poetic qualities of his writing, Soviet tests of literary acceptability in the 1960s and 1970s were essentially ideological,

Dust jacket for the 1978 collection that includes less than half of Cheever's previously published stories

and published criticism of his work in the Soviet Union reflects this orientation. Simply put, he was accepted and respected there, in large measure because his work reflects a deep-seated disaffection with American life as he saw it. Anyone who had been reading his stories closely after 1947 would probably have reached the same conclusion, but stereotypes, like "sound bites" in political reporting, are more easily digested.

Cheever brought the same kind of righteous anger that had sparked "The Death of Justina" to other stories in his mature years, among them "The Brigadier and the Golf Widow" (*New Yorker*, 11 November 1961; in the collection of the same name, 1964) and "The Fourth Alarm" (*Esquire*, April 1970; in *The World of Apples*, 1973). The former dissects the frenzied psychology that led some Americans of means to construct backyard survival shelters, as the cold war between the United States and the Soviet Union heated up. The brigadier of the title, Charlie Pastern, is one such extremist, eager to settle the issue by "nuking" any and all communist adversaries. The golf widow is his wife, and most of Charlie's fulminations are confined to his home

and the country club. His Achilles heel is a weakness for good whiskey and the charms of a woman whose husband spends too much time away from home on business; in the end Charlie is undone by his passion for her, and by hers for the key to his bomb shelter. Mrs. Pastern is alerted to the affair, and in the twinkling of an eye the deceptively well-ordered world these characters had inhabited comes unglued. Cheever's net of disdain for Charlie is wide enough to embrace anyone equally self-centered or mindless, including the Pasterns' bishop, marvelously dissected in a jewel of a scene in which Cheever also has vicious fun with Mrs. Pastern's obtuseness. In the end, however, he characteristically reserves some pity for one character. Charlie's paramour is seen walking forlornly to the train station after a last look at the bomb shelter; she has been abandoned by her husband.

The same all-encompassing sense of desolation in the midst of plenty informs "The Swimmer" (*New Yorker*, 18 July 1964; in *The Brigadier and the Golf Widow*). Here Shady Hill shades into its bleaker manifestation, Bullet Park, now become one vast backyard swimming pool; and the story's central character, Neddy Merrill, is a suburban Everyman swimming his way not toward salvation, but to a recognition that he is a lost soul: "Had you gone for a Sunday afternoon ride that day you might have seen him, close to naked, standing on the shoulders of Route 424, waiting for a chance to cross. You might have wondered if he was the victim of foul play, had his car broken down, or was he merely a fool. Standing barefoot in the deposits of the highway . . . exposed to all kinds of ridicule, he seemed pitiful."

The story struck a deep chord of recognition among its readers and was made into a feature film, with mixed results, in 1968. Like most if not all of Cheever's best tales, "The Swimmer" defies translation to film because of its frequent crossing of boundaries between reality and fantasy, darkness and light. Consider the central premise: Neddy, like Cash Bentley a middle-aged former athlete, decides one day to make his way home from a poolside gathering by using the swimming pools of other friends and acquaintances, creating "the Lucinda River," named for his wife, as he goes. The distance is great, the journey arduous; and the swimmer appears to traverse a whole lifetime before he arrives at the locked door to his home. Along the way he is met with a predictably diverse set of reactions, from boozy cheerfulness to puzzlement to outright hostility. His former mistress accuses him of showing up only to ask for money, and her disgust is one of several indications that something is seriously wrong with Neddy, that the Lucinda River is in reality a kind of Acheron. At one of his stops along the way, a well-intentioned neighbor accidentally hints at the nature of Neddy's difficulties, and thus indirectly presages the story's outcome:

"We've been *terribly* sorry to hear about all your misfortunes, Neddy."

"My misfortunes?" Ned asked. "I don't know what you mean."

"Why, we heard that you'd sold the house and that your poor children. . . ."

But Neddy interrupts to deny all of this and resumes his swim. Cheever can be faulted for being too elliptical on this and other points concerning Neddy's thoughts or emotional state; while he is drawing out his story's harshest implications, he is also skirting the issue of Neddy's full character.

In a 1976 interview with Annette Grant, Cheever revealed that "The Swimmer" had been

an extremely difficult story to write. The problem, he explained, was not so much with technique—although the story manages to sustain suspense and avoid confusion in masterful fashion—as with "imponderables." He failed to clarify the term, but added that he "felt dark and cold for some time" after completing the story. Readers searching for Cheever incarnations in his fiction will find the remark almost transparent, recalling that his alcoholism was well entrenched at this point (1964), and would continue for another dozen years.

Throughout the 1960s Cheever concentrated more heavily on writing novels than short stories, apparently encouraged by the success of *The Wapshot Chronicle*. The sequel, *The Wapshot Scandal* (1964), was only moderately successful, and *Bullet Park* (1969), a despairing look at the American mindscape that goes far beyond any of the social criticism he had built into his earlier short stories but then ends on an upbeat note, was given a critical thrashing from which it never recovered. The critical and popular success of *Falconer* (1977), a novel that dares to take middle-class values into prison (he taught writing classes at Sing Sing in the early 1970s), would later show that Cheever was capable of working out complex issues in extended fashion, but this triumph could not be foreseen as the 1960s drew to a clouded close. Despite his earlier reservations about the viability of the novel as an art form in modern times, he had made the decision (logical enough in economic terms) to move to the longer form; with the apparent failure of his second and third novels, the mood of cynicism that had become increasingly evident in his fiction after World War II deepened. What had been a history of fairly heavy drinking lapsed into the quicksand of alcoholism, and a variety of teaching positions became increasingly difficult to manage in the context of both personal dissolution and marital tensions stretched to the breaking point.

It is not surprising, then, that many of the "stories" he published in the late 1960s and throughout the 1970s are actually works in progress, excerpts from novels yet to be published, and mininarratives bundled into story "sets," rather than self-contained short stories. The quality of these later pieces is, also not surprisingly, uneven. Yet more than a few of them crackle with the inventive energy that had distinguished Cheever's earlier work. "Three Stories" (*Playboy*, 1973; in *The World of Apples*), for example, begins with a comic if somewhat acidic vignette reminis-

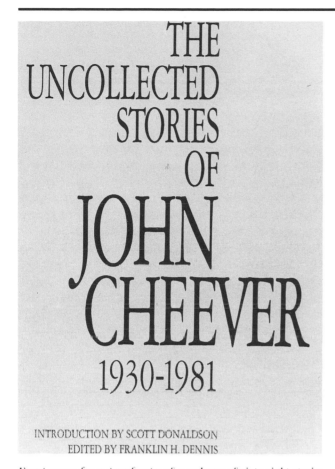

THE UNCOLLECTED STORIES OF JOHN CHEEVER
1930-1981

INTRODUCTION BY SCOTT DONALDSON
EDITED BY FRANKLIN H. DENNIS

Front cover for a proof copy of a volume of sixty-eight stories not included in Cheever's 1978 collection. Publication of this volume by Academy Chicago was blocked by the Cheever family in 1988.

cent of Jonathan Swift, narrated by the stomach of a dieter, in which the struggle between the two takes on heroic proportions (the stomach wins). The second piece is a brief report on the unsuccessful, and largely fantastic, campaign of a suburban woman to block the widening of a local highway death trap. Narrated by an unidentified sympathizer, this miniature demonstrates that, even in decline, Cheever's sense of moral outrage, so forcefully expressed in "The Death of Justina," could tolerate only so much in the way of folly before he decided to take up the weapon of satire: "The truck then rammed into a granite abutment . . . , fell on its side, and caught fire. The police and the fire department were there at once, but the freight was combustible and the fire was not extinguished until three in the morning. All traffic on Route 64 was rerouted. The women's auxiliary of the fire department served coffee."

In "Three Stories," this angry tone is balanced against the relative calm of the more senti-

mental final piece, a clever jeu d'esprit in which the narrator tells of an in-flight seduction of a mysterious, beautiful woman who turns out to be his wife. Like the much earlier "Of Love: A Testimony," this coda catches the reader off guard, but here the effect is heartwarming rather than depressing: "But look, look. Why does he point out her bag to the porter and why, when they both have their bags, does he follow her out to the cab stand, where he bargains with a driver for the trip into Rome? Why does he join her in the cab? Is he the undiscourageable masher that she dreaded? No, no. He is her husband, she is his wife, the mother of his children, and a woman he has worshiped passionately for nearly thirty years."

Within a few years Cheever got and lost a teaching job at Boston University and was forced to enter a clinic for alcoholics and addicts in New York. He emerged as both a reformed alcoholic and a better writer (*Falconer* was the most notable result of his drying out), but by 1976 he was an old man in decline. His victory over the demons in himself, however, should serve as an inspiration to those who believe in the resilience of both the human spirit and the artistic impulse. In the end, Cheever's life was perhaps his best story. He died in Ossining on 18 June 1982.

At present any assessment of John Cheever's place in the history of American fiction, and American short fiction in particular, must appear to be the critical equivalent of whistling in the dark. Most thoughtful readers of his work—currently a small minority of the American public—would probably accept the mistaken and damaging judgment of Cheever himself and his editors at Alfred A. Knopf, in assembling *The Stories of John Cheever*, that any of the short stories he wrote before or during World War II were mere exercises, or worse. The volume begins with postwar stories and includes nothing earlier. (But the volume is not truly selective even as a postwar collection; it essentially reprints all of Cheever's previously collected short stories from "The Enormous Radio" on, adding only five previously uncollected stories.) The implicit view that more than half of Cheever's published stories—mostly prewar—did not merit representation is little short of astounding, if that indeed was the judgment. It is just as likely, of course, that personal considerations yet to be revealed were a factor in the decision, but on the face of it this selection makes little sense. Cheever saw some 81 stories into print (out of a career total of 157 so far accounted for, excluding novel segments) prior to "The Enormous Radio," and many of these are quite good, even excellent, although none of them may ever attain the status of "The Swimmer," "The Country Husband," or "The Enormous Radio." Moreover, the commonsense notion that, following his earliest attempts at being different and then writing like the big sellers, Cheever gradually started to be more like himself as a writer, and that some of his Depression and prewar stories must have been good if they merited the attention of the *Atlantic Monthly* and the *New Yorker*, is certainly correct.

A volume titled "The Uncollected Stories of John Cheever: 1930-1981" was announced for 1988 publication by Academy Chicago and was to include sixty-eight stories, many of them written prior to World War II. However, even though she had signed a contract, Mary Cheever objected to the final selection on the grounds that too many of the stories were of low quality. Suits, countersuits, and appeals, focusing on contract and copyright issues, have since blocked publication indefinitely. Thus his earlier stories are not available in book form and remain virtually ignored, though some are examples of Cheever at his best, clearly indicating the promise of the career to come.

Letters:
"Cheever's Letters [to Elizabeth Ames]," *Vanity Fair*, 47 (May 1984): 62-65;
The Letters of John Cheever, edited by Benjamin Cheever (New York: Simon & Schuster, 1988).

Interviews:
Robert Gutwillig, "Dim Views Through Fog," *New York Times Book Review* (13 November 1960): 68-69;
Annette Grant, "John Cheever: The Art of Fiction LXII," *Paris Review*, 17 (Fall 1976): 39-66;
Scott Donaldson, ed., *Conversations with John Cheever* (Jackson: University Press of Mississippi, 1987).

Bibliographies:
Dennis Coates, "John Cheever: A Checklist, 1930-1978," *Bulletin of Bibliography*, 36 (January-March 1979): 1-13, 49;
Deno Trakas, "John Cheever: An Annotated Secondary Bibliography (1943-1978)," *Resources for American Literary Study*, 9 (1979): 181-199;
Francis J. Bosha, *John Cheever: A Reference Guide* (Boston: G. K. Hall, 1981);
Coates, "A Cheever Bibliographical Supplement, 1978-81," in *Critical Essays on John Cheever*, edited by R. G. Collins (Boston: G. K. Hall, 1982), pp. 279-285.

Biographies:
Susan Cheever, *Home Before Dark* (Boston: Houghton Mifflin, 1984);
Scott Donaldson, *John Cheever* (New York: Random House, 1988).

References:
Samuel Coale, *John Cheever* (New York: Ungar, 1977);
R. G. Collins, ed., *Critical Essays on John Cheever* (Boston: G. K. Hall, 1982);
George Hunt, *John Cheever: The Hobgoblin Company of Love* (Grand Rapids, Mich.: Eerdmans, 1983);
Lynne Waldeland, *John Cheever* (Boston: Twayne, 1979).

Papers:
Brandeis University has the typescripts of many of Cheever's short stories and books, including *The Wapshot Chronicle*.

Robert M. Coates

(6 April 1897 - 8 February 1973)

Richard Messer
Bowling Green State University

See also the Coates entries in *DLB 4: American Writers in Paris, 1920-1939* and *DLB 9: American Novelists, 1910-1945*.

BOOKS: *The Eater of Darkness* (Paris: Contact, 1926; New York: Macaulay, 1929);
The Outlaw Years: The History of the Land Pirates of the Natchez Trace (New York: Macaulay, 1930);
Yesterday's Burdens (New York: Macaulay, 1933);
All the Year Round: A Book of Stories (New York: Harcourt, Brace, 1943);
The Bitter Season (New York: Harcourt, Brace, 1946; London: Gollancz, 1949);
Wisteria Cottage (New York: Harcourt, Brace, 1948; London: Gollancz, 1949);
The Farther Shore (New York: Harcourt, Brace, 1955); republished as *The Darkness of the Day* (London: Gollancz, 1955);
The Hour After Westerly, and Other Stories (New York: Harcourt, Brace, 1957); republished as *Accident at the Inn and Other Stories* (London: Gollancz, 1957);
The View from Here (New York: Harcourt, Brace, 1960);
Beyond the Alps: A Summer in the Italian Hill Towns (New York: Sloane, 1961; London: Gollancz, 1962);
The Man Just Ahead of You (New York: Sloane, 1964; London: Gollancz, 1965);
South of Rome: A Spring and Summer in Southern Italy and Sicily (New York: Sloane, 1965).

TRANSLATION: André de Hevesy, *The Discoverer: A New Narrative of the Life and Hazardous Adventures of the Genoese, Christopher Columbus* (New York: Macaulay, 1928).

SELECTED PERIODICAL PUBLICATIONS—
UNCOLLECTED: "Us Ohio Boys, We Wander," *New Yorker*, 19 (27 March 1943): 16-18;
"I Don't Bother About Her," *New Yorker*, 19 (14 August 1943): 19-22;

Robert M. Coates (photograph by Erich Hartmann)

"Just an Ordinary Household," *New Yorker*, 19 (4 December 1943): 58;
"Proving Something," *New Yorker*, 19 (8 January 1944): 42;
"Sunday on Cranmore Mountain," *New Yorker*, 20 (14 August 1944): 20-23;
"When the Big Barn Burned," *New Yorker*, 20 (2 September 1944): 17-20;
"Summer Day," *New Yorker*, 21 (21 July 1945): 14-16;
"Evening in Springfield, Massachusetts," *New Yorker*, 21 (15 September 1945): 21-36;
"This is Where I Belong," *American Magazine*, 140 (September 1945): 30-31;

"Conversation at Midnight," *New Yorker*, 21 (8 December 1945): 32-34;

"Steps Going Down Stairs," *Collier's*, 116 (15 December 1945): 38;

"One of These Days," *New Yorker*, 22 (27 July 1946): 21-22;

"Downfall of Travis Penniman," *New Yorker*, 22 (7 December 1946): 38-41;

"Sense of Time," *New Yorker*, 23 (22 March 1947): 37-38;

"State of the Novel," *Yale Review*, 36 (June 1947): 604-610;

"Sail Before Dinner," *New Yorker*, 24 (10 July 1948): 21-23;

"Decline and Fall of Perry Whitman," *New Yorker*, 27 (18 August 1951): 26-30;

"Storm," *New Yorker*, 27 (2 January 1952): 25-28;

"Different Time, Different Place," *New Yorker*, 40 (26 September 1964): 40-45;

"Setting in of Winter," *New Yorker*, 43 (9 December 1967): 60-68.

Robert M. Coates's most popular works were *Wisteria Cottage* (1948)—a murder mystery—and *The Outlaw Years* (1930), a nonfiction book about the land pirates of the Natchez Trace between 1800 and 1835. His short stories, though superbly written and often anthologized in the 1940s, have not become standard fare. Still, despite the fact that he has not become as well known as some of his friends and contemporaries, such as Gertrude Stein and James Thurber, it is unfair and precipitous to pigeonhole him as a minor writer of the "lost generation." Generally his work has been undervalued, and in 1975 his novel *Yesterday's Burdens* (1933) was reprinted by Southern Illinois University Press as part of a series dedicated to reviving unrecognized masterworks.

Robert Myron Coates was born on 6 April 1897 in New Haven, Connecticut, to Frederick and Harriet Davidson Coates. His father was an itinerant machinist and tool designer, and Coates's loneliness as an only child must have been intensified as the family moved from town to town, coast to coast, throughout his early school years. The family settled in Rochester, New York, long enough for him to finish high school. He attended Yale and, after a brief stint as a cadet in naval aviation at the end of World War I, graduated in 1919. Going to New York, he stepped into the commercial world of publicity writing for a time, then into a bohemian life of penury and full-time poetry writing. There fol-

lowed a trip to France where he soon established himself among the expatriate literary crowd. It was in Paris that he came under the influences of Stein, Ernest Hemingway, and the Dadaists, especially Louis Aragon.

The Dada influence is clearly seen in Coates's first novel, *The Eater of Darkness* (1926). He finished this book in Giverny, a small village on the Seine, and Robert McAlmon (of Contact Editions) published it in a limited edition in Paris in 1926. It was republished three years later in New York. In a spare, highly controlled style, *The Eater of Darkness* mixes science fiction, fantasy, romance, violence, and an oddly non-sequitur plot into one of the most unusual literary concoctions of the period. One is reminded of *Nadja* (1928) by André Breton, and, indeed, Coates's book has often been proclaimed the first Dadaist or surrealist novel by an American.

Back in New York by 1927, Coates soon began working for the fledgling *New Yorker*, where he was to be an art reviewer until 1967. He also managed, between bouts of book reviewing and collaboration on the "Talk of the Town" column, to write many short stories and several books, including his most highly esteemed novel, *Yesterday's Burdens*. Malcolm Cowley, in his generous and insightful afterword to the 1975 edition, says it is "part of our heritage, not one of the major classics, but still a lasting book and . . . an essential one."

Cowley also believes that Coates's short fiction "should be reread and reissued; perhaps its time will come." Throughout his career Coates produced short fiction, and after the publication of his novel *The Farther Shore* in 1955 he turned almost exclusively to writing stories. He had had one collection, *All the Year Round*, favorably reviewed in 1943, and in 1957 a second, *The Hour After Westerly*, was also well received. Another collection, *The Man Just Ahead of You*, came out in 1964. At the end of his life, he was working on a last book of stories, one that promised to be his best, according to Cowley, but Coates died on 8 February 1973 before he could finish it. He was survived by his second wife, the former Astrid Peters; his son, Anthony (from his marriage to Elsa Kirpal, which had ended in divorce); and his stepdaughter, René Waldron.

All the Year Round contains twenty-eight stories, many of which first appeared in magazines ranging from the *New Yorker* and *Esquire* to the *Southern Review*. The collection's opening story is entitled "A Winter in the Country"; its final

The Yale Literary Magazine *editorial board, 1919: standing are Coates (at left) and Thornton Wilder (at right); seated in the center is Stephen Vincent Benét.*

story, "Winter Fishing." There is a loose thematic relationship between the arrangement of the stories and the cycle of the seasons. A central theme is the derangement of feeling among city dwellers and the dying out of a way of life in the country; the settings are divided almost equally between city and country scenes. The book is also given continuity by the fact that four of the stories deal with a couple named the Harrises, city folk who have a farm in Connecticut to which they retreat during the summer.

The stories are tersely written and often understated in the style of Hemingway's "Hills Like White Elephants." The treatment and subject matter of those dealing with city life also bring to mind James Joyce's stories of life in Dublin. In each of his stories Coates subordinates the importance of plot in order to emphasize setting, characterization, and above all mood. Even when the event around which a story pivots is sensational by its very nature—murder, for instance—the event itself is underplayed and the murderer's reactions are scrupulously recorded. The overall result of Coates's approach is a tense, highly polished story that leaves the reader ill at ease,

feeling that something dreadfully unspeakable lingers just beyond the story's last word. This "something" has to do with Coates's sense not only of a terrifying lack of feeling in modern life, but also the derangement of normal feelings and relationships.

The best stories from this collection often have been anthologized: "The Fury," "The Net," "Let's Not Talk About It Now," "Passing Through," and "A Winter In The Country." "The Fury" and "The Net," both selected as O. Henry Memorial Prize stories (1937 and 1940), are representative of Coates at his early best.

"The Fury" takes place in New York City and in quick flashes relates the last hour in the life of an exhibitionist, a man who walks the streets in an overcoat, searching for young girls. Caught trying to coax a child to come with him for ice cream, he flees into the subway, only to be killed by the train. The crucial element in this story is the voice within the man that goads him on and then rises to a crescendo of self-righteous fury at the treachery of the child and the "filth" of the world. Without melodrama or didacticism, the story makes its point about the relationship between puritanism and sexual maladjustment.

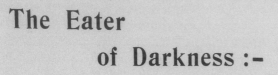

**The Eater
of Darkness :-**

Robert M. Coates

*Cover for Coates's first book (1926), often called the first
surrealist novel by an American*

In "The Net" the violence infusing all the stories is treated explicitly. A man strangles his estranged wife. As he leaves the scene, walking with a pretense of calm, he experiences the people along the street as parts of a net that is closing in on him. Finally he decides, knowing it will mean his apprehension, to visit the dead woman's brother. Again, it is the fine rendering of the character's mental state, of his sudden and utter alienation, that makes the story succeed. Starkly realistic and highly specific, both these stories demonstrate Coates's ability to create his effects through tone and sharply focused characterization.

The Hour After Westerly, Coates's second collection, is divided into three parts. The stories in each part are related by way of general subject and theme, but there seems to be no overall progression or development between parts. These stories differ in two ways from those of the earlier volume. First, they are not so strictly realistic in conception and technique; secondly, most are

in some way the working out of an idea about the nature of perception or epistemology. Thus, characterization and setting both tend to be sacrificed in order to make the plot work effectively along the lines of a fable or parable. One story is entitled "An Autumn Fable," another, "A Parable of Love." In most stories the allegorical quality is rendered more subtly.

In "In a Foreign City," the most often anthologized of the stories, the city in question is quite familiar to the main character at the outset of the story. He decides, however, to indulge in a practical joke that will alter his life forever. After a few drinks, he impulsively pretends to be a holdup man. The consequences of his little joke are enormous. Play becomes reality; the world he knew so well becomes hostile and alien.

The nature of reality as subject matter is further developed in another story anthologized from the collection, "Rendezvous," in which Coates works out an idea about solipsism and one's personal fate in the guise of a fable about the effects of art on life. Again a crime is committed: the perfect robbery. The hero commits the crime almost by way of demonstrating his cleverness, but afterward he finds that there are aspects of his fate that are beyond his control, even though he intellectually anticipates them.

The settings in *The Hour After Westerly* are not quite so pervasively grim as in Coates's earlier work, but the aura of the Great Depression still lingers. Coates's earlier interest in the effects of city life, modern life, on human values, however, has been recombined with his interest in Dadaism and Surrealism, and what emerges is a new spirit of play in his fiction. In a late preface to *The Eater of Darkness*, he says, "For me Dada always meant gaiety." The sense of play or gaiety in these stories always ends on a macabre or bizarrely ironic note. The dislocations of *All the Year Round* have taken on a deeper subjectivity, and now reality itself begins to look like a rather ominous hall of mirrors.

The Man Just Ahead of You contains thirteen stories. They depict people, mostly middle-aged, in moments of loneliness and isolation when their grasp of themselves and life is tentative. The intelligence and insight of the stories are of Coates's usual high quality, and in general the book was well reviewed. It did, however, receive tart comments from Weldon Kees and several others for an "overstudied casualness" and "occasional triviality" that these reviewers saw as typical of the *"New Yorker* fiction." By now Coates was identified as of a school: the *New Yorker* writers. The *New Yorker* fiction is known for its understated sophistication, its urbanity and adroitness, and charged by its critics with self-imitation and highbrow banality.

The variety of Coates's short fictions generally raises his work above such criticism, but there is no denying his sophistication. He once wrote that Sir Phillip Sidney's influence governed his writing; that he wrote under the influence of the aristocratic tradition. One feels, reading his autobiographical work, *The View from Here* (1960), that not only was he repelled by the idea of wide literary success, but that in fact the image of Sidney circulating his manuscripts only among a private circle of friends had a great influence on his own career. Malcolm Cowley pinpoints *Yesterday's Burdens* as the book which was for Coates "a sort of leavetaking, almost a symbolic suicide," a turning away from early dreams of literary fame.

Coates's aversion to the idea of becoming a famous writer may provide at least a partial explanation of why his short fiction, always admired by fellow writers and by magazine editors, never came into vogue, and why it has received so little critical notice. It may be that the reappraisal of Coates's work, begun in Cowley's article "Reconsideration," will gain momentum and give him the place he deserves in the best literature of the 1930s and 1940s. Coates's writing demonstrates a keen social intelligence, a true craftsman's love of form, and reflects the early beginnings of contemporary modes such as metafiction and fabulation.

References:

Malcolm Cowley, Afterword to *Yesterday's Burdens*, Lost American Fiction Series, edited by Matthew J. Bruccoli (Carbondale & Edwardsville: Southern Illinois University Press, 1975), pp. 257-273;

Cowley, "Reconsideration," *New Republic*, 171 (30 November 1974): 40-42;

Chester Eisinger, *Fiction of the Forties* (Chicago: University of Chicago Press, 1963);

C. Pierce, "Divinest Sense: Narrative Technique in Robert Coates's *Yesterday's Burdens*," *Critique*, 19 (1977): 44-52.

Theodore Dreiser

(27 August 1871 - 28 December 1945)

Paul A. Orlov
Pennsylvania State University

See also the Dreiser entries in *DLB 9: American Novelists, 1910-1945; DLB 12: American Realists and Naturalists;* and *DLB Documentary Series 1.*

BOOKS: *Sister Carrie* (New York: Doubleday, Page, 1900; abridged edition, London: Heinemann, 1901);

Jennie Gerhardt (New York & London: Harper, 1911);

The Financier (New York & London: Harper, 1912; revised edition, New York: Boni & Liveright, 1927; London: Constable, 1927);

A Traveler at Forty (New York: Century, 1913; London: Richards, 1914);

The Titan (New York: Lane / London: Lane/ Bodley Head, 1914);

The "Genius" (New York: Lane / London: Lane/ Bodley Head, 1915);

Plays of the Natural and the Supernatural (New York: Lane / London: Lane/Bodley Head, 1916); enlarged as *Plays, Natural and Supernatural* (London: Constable, 1930);

A Hoosier Holiday (New York: Lane / London: Lane/ Bodley Head, 1916);

Free and Other Stories (New York: Boni & Liveright, 1918);

The Hand of the Potter (New York: Boni & Liveright, 1918 [i.e., 1919]; revised, 1927);

Twelve Men (New York: Boni & Liveright, 1919; London: Constable, 1930);

Hey, Rub-a-Dub-Dub: A Book of the Mystery and Wonder and Terror of Life (New York: Boni & Liveright, 1920; London: Constable, 1931);

A Book About Myself (New York: Boni & Liveright, 1922; London: Constable, 1929; republished as *A History of Myself: Newspaper Days* (New York: Liveright, 1931);

The Color of a Great City (New York: Boni & Liveright, 1923; London: Constable, 1930);

An American Tragedy, 2 volumes (New York: Boni & Liveright, 1925; London: Constable, 1926);

Moods: Cadenced and Declaimed (New York: Boni & Liveright, 1926; enlarged, 1928; London:

Theodore Dreiser inscribed this photograph to Helen Patges Richardson, who became his second wife on 13 June 1944 (Van Pelt Library, University of Pennsylvania).

Constable, 1929); enlarged again as *Moods Philosophical and Emotional, Cadenced and Declaimed* (New York: Simon & Schuster, 1935);

Chains: Lesser Novels and Stories (New York: Boni & Liveright, 1927; London: Constable, 1928);

Dreiser Looks at Russia (New York: Liveright, 1928; London: Constable, 1929);

The Carnegie Works at Pittsburgh (Chelsea, N.Y.: Privately printed, 1929?);

A Gallery of Women, 2 volumes (New York: Liveright, 1929; London: Constable, 1930);

My City (New York: Liveright, 1929);

Epitaph (New York: Heron, 1930);

Fine Furniture (New York: Random House, 1930);

A History of Myself: Dawn (New York: Liveright, 1931; London: Constable, 1931);

Tragic America (New York: Liveright, 1931; London: Constable, 1932);

America Is Worth Saving (New York: Modern Age, 1941);

The Bulwark (Garden City, N.Y.: Doubleday, 1946; London: Constable, 1947);

The Stoic (Garden City, N.Y.: Doubleday, 1947);

Selected Poems, edited by Robert P. Saalbach (Jericho, N.Y.: Exposition, 1969);

Notes on Life, edited by Marguerite Tjader and John J. McAleer (Tuscaloosa: University of Alabama Press, 1974);

Theodore Dreiser: A Selection of Uncollected Prose, edited by Donald Pizer (Detroit: Wayne State University Press, 1977);

American Diaries, 1902-1926, edited by Thomas P. Riggio (Philadelphia: University of Pennsylvania Press, 1982);

Selected Magazine Articles of Theodore Dreiser, 2 volumes, edited by Yoshinobu Hakutani (London & Toronto: Associated University Presses, 1985, 1987).

Collections: *The Best Short Stories of Theodore Dreiser*, edited by Howard Fast (Cleveland: World, 1947);

Theodore Dreiser, edited by James T. Farrell (New York: Dell, 1962).

PLAY PRODUCTIONS: *The Girl in the Coffin*, New York, Comedy Theatre, 3 December 1917;

The Hand of the Potter, New York, Provincetown Playhouse, 5 December 1921.

OTHER: "The Tithe of the Lord," in *The Armchair Esquire*, edited by Arnold Gingrich and L. Rust Hills (New York: Putnam's, 1958).

Although Theodore Dreiser—generally considered the foremost writer in the tradition of American literary naturalism—is principally important as a novelist, he made a significant contribution to the development of short fiction. For while he needed a large canvas to achieve his best artistic effects, his stories and sketches, like his longer works, give uncompromisingly realistic pictures of human nature and social conditions, boldly defying the genteel tradition and defining a new honesty in American literature. Dreiser's fiction, powerful, though unevenly written, conveys his compassionate observations of individual lives

as they express the play of forces in nature and in the larger social world.

Theodore Dreiser was born on 27 August 1871 in Terre Haute, Indiana, and was one of ten children of John Paul Dreiser, an indigent and often unemployed German immigrant, and his wife, the former Sarah Maria Schänäb. Theodore's earliest years were marked by an exposure to family personalities and circumstances that significantly contributed to the worldview later expressed in his fiction. His father was a dogmatically religious Catholic, severely conservative in all matters of conduct, whose outlook on life was grim and pessimistic because of both spiritual conviction and material adversities. His mother, by contrast, was broadly tolerant and life-loving, a woman whose deep sympathies and gentle strength helped to anchor the unsteady family through many misfortunes, even as she was communicating to the future writer a disposition dreamily sensitive to life's beauty and wonder. The family's history, played out in various small towns in Indiana during Dreiser's childhood, featured not only the perennial struggle against poverty and its degradations but also an ongoing struggle between the father's rigid conventionalism and the older children's hedonism. Indeed, the deprivations imposed by poverty made all the children (like some of the characters Dreiser would later portray in his works) particularly resistant to restrictive moral doctrines and, in fact, involved them at times in scandalous behavior.

In 1887 Dreiser left home for Chicago, seeking freedom, pleasure, success, and a place in life for himself. After working at several menial jobs, he attended Indiana University at Bloomington for a year, as a result of the encouragement and generosity of Mildred Fielding, who had taught Dreiser in high school. But for Dreiser, as for virtually all the young individuals in his fiction, the city itself offered the most significant education. Living in Chicago in the heart of the "Gilded Age" gave him the chance to discover the whole range of human experience. And the opportunity for a worldly education was enlarged when Dreiser became a newspaper reporter assigned the task of observing the whole urban spectacle, first in Chicago, and subsequently in St. Louis and Pittsburgh.

Like several other major American writers of the late nineteenth and early twentieth centuries, Dreiser received his literary apprenticeship through the medium of newspaper work. While working as a newsman in three cities in the early

Dreiser in the late 1890s (Lilly Library, Indiana University) and his first wife, Sara White Dreiser, circa 1906 (Collection of Dr. Vera Dreiser)

1890s (and then as a magazine editor for several years in New York), Dreiser made the observations that shaped his awareness of the many moods of life, as manifested in the American cityscape. Studying the panorama, he began to conclude that life—as the subtitle of *Hey, Rub-a-Dub-Dub*, his book of philosophical essays of 1920 put it—is a thing of "mystery and wonder and terror." Around him he saw dramatic contrasts of wealth and poverty, beauty and squalor, triumphant individual self-assertion and tragic images of battered nonentity. Moreover, these contrasts seemed to reveal or result from the effects of chance, individual strength or weakness of temperament, instinctive human desires in conflict with conventional moral codes, and the poignant disparity between man's vast dreams and his limited capacities.

Influenced by his own early experiences, as well as by his reading of Honoré de Balzac's novels and Herbert Spencer's post-Darwinian evolutionary philosophy in *First Principles* (originally published in 1862 and extremely popular in America in the 1890s), Dreiser's philosophy developed and became a part of his first short stories (in the

summer of 1899), his first novel, *Sister Carrie* (1900), and all the other fictional and nonfictional works that occupied him for four and a half decades thereafter, until his death. These ideas inform his works with a quality of harsh realism or naturalism, given Dreiser's objective depiction of the way natural instincts and social circumstances largely control human destinies.

Dreiser's short fictional works generally involve one or more key themes: life as an expression of change and contrast; the city as a realm of wonder and terror; love as an always mysterious and frequently frustrating force shaping lives; the conflict between individual desires (especially those of powerful or "artistic" individuals) and social conventions; the hollowness of the materialistic American dream of success; and most fundamentally, the ironic discrepancy between initial dreams and ultimate realities. The technique Dreiser most relies upon to dramatize simultaneously his themes and his sympathetic engagement in the lives of his characters—a method used, for example, with consummate, compelling effect in his long masterpiece *An American Tragedy* (1925)—is the careful modulation of indirect discourse in narrative to mirror thoughts and feelings, while maintaining the sense of his authorial authority on the action under scrutiny.

Dreiser published only two collections of stories and two uncollected stories meriting attention. But many of the volumes in his canon include sketches; and some of those sketches add to Dreiser's distinctive contribution to American short fiction. For just as his best novels and stories derive their power partly from the critically compassionate observation of characters' experiences suggested by Dreiser's use of indirect discourse, so do his finest works in the sketch form become moving tales because of the shaping presence of the observer. Of particular interest are those sketches that offer vivid pictures of specific characters, as revealed through their actions, and produce essentially unified effects. Dreiser's best sketches (and stories) attain, in their way, epiphanies or revelations of character which James Joyce defined as the purpose of short stories—as do, in different ways, the stories in Joyce's *Dubliners* (1914) or in Sherwood Anderson's *Winesburg, Ohio* (1919).

The basic nature of Dreiser's "fictionalized" sketches is represented in a narrative sequence in the original manuscript of *A Traveler at Forty* (1913), his autobiographical account of his first trip to Europe. Unlike the rather impressionistic sketches of places and of anonymous or typical characters that abound in his explicitly autobiographical volumes—*A Hoosier Holiday* (1916), *A Book About Myself* (1922), *The Color of a Great City* (1923), and *A History of Myself: Dawn* (1931)—the story of Hanscha Jower vividly and movingly illuminates the essence of an individualized life rescued from obscurity by a sensitive observer. The story, excised from the work before publication by moral censors and published at last only in the special Dreiser issue of *Modern Fiction Studies* in autumn 1977, concerns a young German streetwalker whom the writer encountered in Berlin. Dreiser's narrative succeeds in revealing Hanscha's melancholy attitude toward her life, the sweet simplicity of her nature (untainted by her occupation), and the physical details of her humble room, suggesting her loneliness and material struggle. By questioning her and by imaginatively immersing himself in her experiences, Dreiser discovers her lost dreams and grim circumstances. The story's ending reflects a sad sense of Hanscha's waning prospects for any real future: "Two nights later, or perhaps the third . . . I walked in the swirling life of Leipzigerstrasse,

aglow with busy shops, crowded with well-dressed people, the windows displaying all those various components which make up homes, dresses, public appearances—the materials of a hopeful life. Somehow, before a great furniture store whose broad plateglass front was set with the details of one of those conventional middle-class diningrooms, 'parlors' and bedrooms—all bright, attractive sets—I thought of Hanscha and her possible man. Do you think I could resist the tears? Not me. To me the furniture, and all it represented of possible happiness, was not worth much—but to her! Why might not life have been kind to Hanscha Jower?"

The story conveys the Dreiserian themes of the city's lights and shadows and the mysteriousness of life—the inexplicable drama of the way circumstances shape lives. In the process, the sketch undercuts all conventional attitudes toward prostitution, expressing the artist's view of a gentle individual victimized by both the amoral currents of life and the stigma of appearances. Dreiser's treatment of his material here, as in his novel *Jennie Gerhardt* (1911), reveals the dignity and sad beauty in the life of a "fallen woman" otherwise ignored or scorned by society. More generally, this sketch typifies the method and impact of all Dreiser's best biographical sketches, simultaneously dramatizing the artist's compassionate insight and discovering the meaning in commonplace lives.

Free and Other Stories, Dreiser's first volume of short fiction, was published in 1918, collecting eleven stories, nine of which had earlier been published in monthly periodicals. Four of these stories, all written during the summer of 1899 and published in various magazines in 1901, demonstrate especially well some of the major techniques and themes that typify Dreiser's later fiction.

Nearly plotless, "When the Old Century Was New" (*Pearson's*, January 1901) relates the events in the life of young William Walton, member of a prestigious and wealthy New York family, on a spring day in 1801. During his leisurely stroll through town one day, Walton sees a man draw a crowd with his attempt to guide a steampowered boat, watches the unsuccessful effort of the city's poor fire-fighting equipment to save a burning mansion, enjoys the trees and stately residences of quietly fashionable Wall Street, and encounters such eminent citizens as Ben Franklin, John Jacob Astor, John Adams, and Thomas Jefferson. The high point of his day is Walton's suc-

Page from the manuscript for one of Dreiser's first short stories, written in 1899 (by permission of the Estate of Theodore Dreiser; courtesy of Van Pelt Library, University of Pennsylvania). It was published as "Butcher Rogaum's Door" in the 12 December 1901 issue of Reedy's Mirror *and collected as "Old Rogaum and His Theresa" in* Free and Other Stories *(1918).*

cessful marriage proposal to Beppie Cruger, daughter of a genteel family. References to the fashions of the time and to the political, financial, and commercial life of the early days of Manhattan are counterpointed throughout the narrative. At the story's close Walton walks in the Bowery region, contemplating its natural beauty and dreaming of a future mansion there in which happiness may unfold for himself and his future wife. Although this story's mode (historical romance) and language (a rather mannered, faintly archaic prose) are uncharacteristic of the later Dreiser, the piece is nonetheless interesting in its focus on his typical concerns. Despite the unfamiliar subject matter, the story deals with the familiar theme of the wonder and terror of the city. For as Walton muses upon the uncertain future of his dreams and the growing metropolis, one sees the implied ironies of time and change, technology's beneficial and baneful legacies, and the timelessness of youth's great expectations at the threshold of life: "He had no inkling, as he pondered, of what a century might bring forth. The crush and stress and wretchedness fast treading upon this path of loveliness he could not see."

"McEwen of the Shining Slave Makers" (*Ainslee's*, June 1901—as "The Shining Slave Makers") is a dream-vision story in which Dreiser dramatizes his idea (doubtless suggested by Spencer's concept of "the survival of the fittest") of life as an unending struggle. Escaping the heat of the summer sun and the "toil of the busy streets" on a day in August, a young man, Robert McEwen, enters a city park to soothe his body and spirit by sitting on a bench beneath a shady tree. There, after musing upon ants observed on the walk before him, he imaginatively enters their world, gaining a wholly new perspective on the physical realm and on his own existence. Hunting for food in a time of famine, he discovers in the other ants a cold attitude of self-centeredness and self-sufficiency that seems "at once surprising and yet familiar." Later, in battles against the fiercely aggressive red ants, McEwen, as a black ant, forms a friendship with another "shining slave maker," whose life he saves, and begins to feel an increasing lust for war. When he is mortally wounded in battle, he closes his eyes for death and reopens them to find himself restored to human shape with a new perspective on the world. Pondering the vision he has had and watching a war of ants at his feet, McEwen wonders if what he sees is "a revelation of the spirit and signif-

icance of a lesser life or of his own. . . ." Clearly conveyed through this speculation is the theme of life's forces and mysteries, and a post-Darwinian view of nature and man's part in it: McEwen understands his experience as an expression of "worlds within worlds, all apparently full of necessity, contention, binding emotions and unities—and all with sorrow. . . ."

Suggesting some of Dreiser's basic themes and even an implicit aesthetic for fiction, "Nigger Jeff" (*Ainslee's*, November 1901) is one of Dreiser's most powerful and most widely anthologized stories. The work, in part the record of Dreiser's own sudden growth into maturity, concerns a young midwestern newspaper reporter, Elmer Davies. A contentedly vain youth who holds a naive, simplistic view of life as well ordered and morally just, Davies is sent to a country town to investigate a report that a Negro has raped a young white woman. In the process of covering the story, the cub reporter learns lessons about the nature of the human drama that dramatically alter his philosophy of life. Against the ironic setting of a lovely spring day in the beautiful countryside of Pleasant Valley, the story follows Davies through experiences of horror and brutality. He sees Jeff Ingalls (the alleged rapist) captured by Sheriff Matthews to await trial, then being taken away from Matthews by a mob of white men led by Jake and Morgan Whitaker (the brother and father of nineteen-year-old Ada, the supposed victim), and finally hanged from a bridge over a tranquil moonlit stream. The old, convenient abstractions of "law and order" collapse in Davies's mind as he realizes how primitive instincts have driven both the criminal and the mob in their actions, and as he witnesses physical and psychological suffering that hauntingly individualizes the black youth's humanity. Seeing Mrs. Ingalls grieve over her son's twisted body and discovering that, ironically, Jeff had been caught because familial love had drawn him home for a farewell from his mother, Davies is quite moved by a new sense of human tragedy. The story's conclusion catches the injustices, the poignant drama, and the emotional complexities inherent in life—the "all" that the young reporter vows to "get . . . in" his writing.

The last of the four stories written in 1899 and first published in 1901 is "Old Rogaum and His Theresa" (*Reedy's Mirror*, 12 December—as "Butcher Rogaum's Door"), concerning a German butcher and his eighteen-year-old daughter in a New York immigrant working-class neigh-

Dreiser during his career as a magazine editor in New York (Lilly Library, Indiana University)

borhood. A sternly conservative disciplinarian, Rogaum grows increasingly angry at young Theresa's tendency to come in late each evening; despite his threats of punishment, she is too intoxicated by starry summer nights, bright city streets, and the romantic attentions of local young men to be at home by curfew. When he finally makes good his longtime threat to lock her out of the family flat (located above the butcher shop), she wanders away, uncertain of her alternatives. Theresa is finally found in a park, listening fearfully to a nineteen-year-old "masher's" slyly seductive urgings to put herself in his "protective care," and she is reunited with her parents at the police station. Dreiser makes clear that there can be no resolution to this family's problem: the girl, though glad to get home safely, will continue to feel desires causing a conflict with her father's ideas about proper conduct; for Rogaum, relieved and overjoyed at finding his Theresa alive, well, and morally uninjured, the drama portends an ongoing parental predicament. Mirroring the girl's thoughts and feelings through indirect discourse, the story vividly expresses her awakening desires for city lights, handsome youths, and the false promise of a glamorous life. The story dram-

atizes the Dreiserian themes of the lure of sex and beauty in the city, the conflict between freedom and responsibility, and the coexistence within the city of both splendor and terror.

Like some of the sketches in *Twelve Men* (1919), one of the stories collected in *Free*, "The Cruise of the 'Idlewild'" (*Bohemian*, October 1909), derives from the period (1901-1903) in which Dreiser suffered a physical and emotional collapse—and then slowly regained his health—after the infamous "suppression" of *Sister Carrie* (Frank Doubleday, the publisher, did not like the book, and though legally bound to publish it, did all in his power to discourage sales). Based on the writer's heavy, physical, rejuvenating work for the New York Central Railroad, the story is narrated by Henry, an employee in a railroad carpentry shop. Inspired by the shop's location (at a point where the Harlem and the Hudson rivers meet, with water on three sides of it) and by his longings for a pleasure boat belonging to the shop's engineer, the narrator conceives of the shop as a ship—the *Idlewild*—cruising each workday. The story recalls the experiences aboard the imaginary ship of Henry (as mate), John, the engineer (as captain), and other shop workers (as

Sister Carrie.

CHAPTER I.

The magnet attracting: a waif amid forces.

When Caroline Meeber boarded the afternoon train for Chicago, her total outfit consisted of a small trunk, ~~which was checked in the baggage car~~, a cheap imitation alligator skin satchel, ~~holding some minor details of the toilet~~, a small lunch in a paper box and a yellow leather snap purse, containing her ticket, a scrap of paper with her sister's address in Van Buren Street, and four dollars in money. It was in August, 1889. She was eighteen years of age, bright, timid and full of the illusions of ignorance and youth. Whatever touch of regret at parting characterized her thoughts, it was certainly not for advantages now being given up. A gush of tears at her mother's farewell kiss, a touch in the throat when the cars clacked by the flour mill where her father worked by the day, a pathetic sigh as the familiar green environs of the village passed in review, and the threads which bound her so lightly to girlhood and home were irretrievably broken.

To be sure, ~~she was not conscious of any of this. Any change, however great, might be remedied.~~ There was always the next station where one might descend and return. There was the great city bound more closely by these very trains which came up daily. Columbia City was not so very far away, even once she was in Chicago. What, pray, is a few hours - a hundred miles? ~~And then her sister was there.~~ She looked at the little slip bearing ~~the buttons~~ her sister's address and wondered. She gazed at the green landscape, now passing in swift review, until her swifter thoughts replaced its impression with vague conjectures of what Chicago might be, like.

Page from the typescript for Dreiser's first novel (by permission of the Estate of Theodore Dreiser; courtesy of the Van Pelt Library, University of Pennsylvania) lesser members of the crew). Initially, the *Idlewild* idea dramatizes the ability of the imagination to enhance drab, commonplace lives with a sense of bright excitement and importance. Yet the story finally becomes an oblique commentary on human nature within the special context of social power structures: the ship starts foundering and then "sinks" as the corrupt superiors mistreat those of humbler position, and as the captain and mate, the exploiters, themselves quarrel over priority and privileges. First Ike, a misshapen creature of sweet disposition, who has soured on the *Idlewild* experience because of "orders," ridicule, and harassment from the "officers," rebels and complains to the humorlessly unimaginative shop foreman; then a conflict between John and Henry destroys all potential for fellowship. But the story ends affirmatively and instructively, as the captain and the mate, chastened by experience and reduced in pride, succeed in raising the ship by significantly renaming it the *Harmony*—representing a new harmony of social justice.

"The Lost Phoebe," first published in the *Century* magazine in April 1916, has achieved over the years considerable popularity and even critical approval from scholars otherwise unimpressed by Dreiser's fiction. The story appears uncharacteristic in its setting and subject matter (the simple, "uneventful" lives of an old couple in a rural community), but it treats Dreiser's recurrent thematic interests, albeit in a unique way. Henry Reifsneider, a seventy-year-old mildly cantankerous, poor farmer, suffers the death of his wife, Phoebe, after forty-eight years of marriage. A few months after this loss, deranged by grief and loneliness, Henry begins to hallucinate that she has merely left him because of a quarrel and that she is beckoning him to follow her. Pursuing visions of his lost Phoebe at ever-greater distances from home in the countryside (over a period of several years), Henry, calling to and reaching toward an image of the beautiful young girl he had courted a lifetime ago, falls to his death off a cliff. The old farmer's increasingly homeless wanderings suggest the way in which all human lives ultimately return to the timeless embrace of nature; simultaneously, the basic rootedness of an older generation's lives (Henry had lived his whole life, before and during marriage, in the same little house) is set in contrast with a "modern" younger generation's mobility in pursuit of "better" lives (all the Reifsneider children had moved away once grown up, years before). The story conveys the major Dreiserian

themes of the power of love and the poignant drama of change in human experience, and achieves an almost mythic quality.

One of the most persistent themes in Dreiser's novels—the inability or unwillingness of the exceptional or "artistic" individual to conform to society's social and moral code—is central to two stories in the *Free* volume, "Married" (first published in *Cosmopolitan* in September 1917) and the title story (first published in the *Saturday Evening Post* on 16 March 1918). "Married," the story of an artistic midwesterner and his unsophisticated provincial bride, who has recently moved to New York, is reminiscent in its plot outline of both Dreiser's autobiographical novel *The "Genius"* (1915) and the novelist's own failed first marriage to Sara (known as Sallie or Jug) Osborne White (1898-1914; he lived with a distant cousin of his, Helen Richardson, beginning in 1919, and finally married her in 1944). Duer Wilde, a talented young pianist, has brought his bride of four months, Marjorie—fresh from the Iowa countryside—to the East to share New York's bohemian art world with him. But through a series of tellingly awkward attempts to introduce her into the circle of his unconventional artist friends, Duer realizes that he neither truly loves his wife nor considers her temperamentally suitable for him. Dreiser's use of indirect discourse emphasizes the story's themes by ironically contrasting the artistic protagonist's innermost thoughts and feelings with his unimaginative wife's ideas that she will "reform" him at her leisure while she holds him with her love.

Since the word *married* begins to sound in Duer's mind the death knell of all his creative freedom, the end of the story implies that with time, he will probably leave his wife and escape the confinement of a conventional relationship. "Free," which reads like a planned companion piece to "Married," suggests the ghastly consequences for a character similar to Duer Wilde who somehow never does escape the bonds of tradition and thus sacrifices his artistic nature. This title story concerns the memories and feelings of Rufus Haymaker, a sixty-year-old prosperously successful but passionately unfulfilled architect, as his wife, Ernestine, declines toward death through an extended illness, in their Central Park West apartment in New York. Expressed through all his past and present feelings is Haymaker's bitter awareness that his dreams of art and love have always been stifled by his wife—a woman utterly committed to the conventions of a materialistic

Dear H. L. M.
This is the way
I will look at
you if you
don't behave

Look who's here. Theodore Dreiser, whose power and force have placed him in the forefront of American novelists, and who has demonstrated that he can write a realistic novel with something real in it.

Caricature of Dreiser that he inscribed to his friend H. L. Mencken in 1916 (Astor, Lenox and Tilden Foundations, New York Public Library)

philistine society. Imprisoned in his marriage by social pressures, by the biological accident of parenthood (they have a son and a daughter), and by his sympathy for Ernestine, he has never had the freedom to fulfill himself romantically (with a beautiful woman of exciting passions) or creatively. Now, while her doctor tries to save her, Haymaker is torn between the secret desires for his wife's death and a genuine fondness for her. But when Ernestine does die, he sees the cruel irony that the "glorious dream of his youth was gone forever. It was a mirage, an ignis fatuus. His wife might just as well have lived as died," for now he is free at last, but only "free . . . to die!" The story (praised by H. L. Mencken and other com-

mentators since) poignantly conveys the mocking indifference of the universe to individual dreams, although it perhaps places too much burden upon telling rather than showing, unlike "Married," a technically superior work.

"The Second Choice" (*Cosmopolitan*, February 1918) is another exploration of social tradition, individual desires, and the mysterious force of love. Much of the story is revealed through flashbacks in the mind of Shirley, a young woman, as she holds a farewell letter from the dashingly exciting, elusive Arthur Bristow—a young man she loves too well, though not wisely. Over a year earlier, dazzled by the newcomer Arthur and the dream of a romantic life with him beyond the ordinary experience of her small town, she had forgotten the man she had previously planned on marrying—the stolidly dull, but kind and faithful Barton Williams, a railroad dispatcher. Now, in the wake of Arthur's departure and her magical dream's destruction, she finds Barton eager to forgive her and have her back again. Thus occurs an inner struggle whose outcome is ambiguous at the story's end: Shirley wonders if she should face an uncertain future of stigmatized spinsterhood, clinging to the hope of her adored one's return, or, surrendering to community pressures, wed her poor "second choice" for the sake of a loveless yet secure and conventionally approved domestic life. Counterpointing dramatized scenes and the indirect rendering of his heroine's feelings, Dreiser bases the narrative upon the ironic function of psychology in love: Shirley realizes sadly that she loves Arthur precisely as Barton loves her, with hopeless and slavish submissiveness; and as if to assure her own wretchedness, she is perversely drawn to one man because of his faithlessness and repelled by the other precisely because of his devotion and gentleness.

Unpublished previously in periodical form, the two remaining stories in the *Free* collection—"A Story of Stories" and "Will You Walk into My Parlor?"—are quite different from the rest in subject matter. Set in a western city along the Mississippi, the former story dramatizes the competition for "scoops" among newspapermen as a microcosm of the struggle for power and success in the larger world. The conflicts in the plot arise from the contrasting personalities of the two protagonists, key reporters on the city's two major newspapers. "Red" Collins of the *News* is crude but forceful and arrogant; only semiliterate and a poor writer, he is nonetheless very adept at gathering important news because of his cleverness and his friendly relationships with many local officials. Much better educated and a more talented writer, Augustus Binns of the *Star* is a rather artistically foppish transplanted easterner and is less forceful and self-confident—as well as less adaptable to his environment—than his rival. Formerly employed by the *News*, Binns had been assigned the task of ghostwriting articles from materials brought in by Collins, letting Collins get full credit for the stories. Resentment at this arrangement and the natural clash of their personalities caused Binns's move to the *Star* and the start of their intensely antagonistic rivalry. Dreiser's fast-paced narrative includes several inci-

dents in which Binns and Collins try to best each other, culminating in their race to report a "story of stories": the case of Lem Rollins, who had single-handedly held up a cargo train and stolen twenty thousand dollars. Like the train robber in his spectacularly daring deed, Collins uses cunning and ruthless force to gain a lead story with the first interview with and photograph of the just-captured Rollins. Not proving ruthless or determined enough at crucial moments, despite his hatred of Collins and wish to win, Binns is duped and even hypnotized by the iron will of his rival. The tale of their battle for news-reporting supremacy illustrates a frequent opposition in the drama of the social jungle: the man of forceful action and practical cunning opposed to the man of dreams and artistic instincts. Preoccupied by this conflict within his own character, Dreiser portrayed it in nearly all his novels, most strikingly in the stories of Frank Cowperwood (the hypnotic-eyed hero of *The Financier* [1912], *The Titan* [1914], and *The Stoic* [1947]) and Eugene Witla of *The "Genius."*

"Will You Walk into My Parlor?" is a story of intrigue and danger in the normally hidden world of corrupt political forces. Edward Gregory, a reform-minded newspaperman and investigator, is preparing to expose the graft and mismanagement of those ruling the city—rapacious millionaire Tilney and the powerful political ring of the mayor, his partner. During the summer months preceding the local election by which the reform party hopes to defeat and indict the crooked bosses, Gregory resides at a seaside resort while carrying on his investigation. There, protectively accompanied by his friend Frank Blount, he encounters several individuals soon suspected of working for Tilney: Mrs. Skelton, a voluble forty-year-old widow; Imogene Carle, a pretty young woman Skelton is presumably chaperoning; and Castleman, a rich youth. Despite Gregory's awareness that these foes will do anything necessary to stop him and his investigation, he is finally trapped by them. For after successfully eluding various attempts to injure him physically or morally, Gregory, cautious yet vulnerable to the lure of beauty, is tricked by the temptress Imogene into a kiss that is photographed. Months of effort are destroyed shortly before the election, as the criminal powerbrokers gain a means of blackmailing Gregory and discrediting his evidence.

Dreiser's uncompromisingly bold realism always proved costly to his efforts to sell material

"LOVE"

As Garrison left this last business conference in K----, where the tall buildings and the amazing crowds always seemed such a commentary on the power and force and wealth of America and the world, and was on his way to the railway station to take a train for G----, his home city, his thoughts turned with peculiar emphasis and hope, if not actually pleasure -- and yet it was a pleasure, of a sad, distressed kind -- to Idelle.   Where was she now?   What was she doing at this particular moment -- it was after four of a gray November afternoon; just the time, as he well knew, winter or summer, when she so much preferred to be glowing at an afternoon reception, a "thé dansant," or a hotel grill where there was dancing, and always, as he well knew, in company with those vivid young "sports" or pleasure-lovers of the town who were always following her.   Idelle, to do her no injustice, had about her that something, even after three years of marriage, that drew them, some of the worst or best -- mainly the worst, he thought at times -- of those who made his home city, the great far-flung G----, interesting and in the forefront socially and in every other way.

What a girl!   What a history!   And how strange that he should have been attracted to her at all, he with his forty-eight years, his superior (oh, very much!) social position, his conservative friends and equally conservative manners.   Idelle was so different, so hoyden, almost coarse, in her ways at times, actually gross and vulgar (derived from her French tanner father, no doubt, not her sweet, retiring Polish mother), and yet how attractive too, in so many ways, with that rich russet-brown-gold

Page from the typescript for a story first published in the 18 May 1919 issue of the New York Tribune *and collected as the title story in* Chains *(by permission of the Estate of Theodore Dreiser; courtesy of the Van Pelt Library, University of Pennsylvania)*

Helen Richardson, who began living with Dreiser in 1919 and married him the year before his death (Van Pelt Library, University of Pennsylvania)

to the popular monthly fiction magazines. Even though most contemporary reviews of the *Free* collection were moderately favorable, and even though sales were initially good (2,742 copies in the first three and a half months in late 1918), the stories generally had suffered several rejections before periodical publication and had sold for poor prices. Thus at a time when Sinclair Lewis, for example, earned up to eight thousand dollars per year for his stories, Dreiser's "The Lost Phoebe" (now critically praised and oft-reprinted) was repeatedly rejected before finally selling for a mere two hundred dollars. Subsequent critical reception of the volume has principally focused attention on the stories contemporary reviewers most liked—"Nigger Jeff," "Old Rogaum and His Theresa," "Free," and, of course, "The Lost Phoebe."

Dreiser's best short fiction (whether stories or sketches) derives its power from his close observation and compassionate revelation of individual character in the complex drama of Life, and *Twelve Men* illustrates this achievement. The dozen fictionalized biographical sketches in the volume (seven of which had been published in pe-

riodicals years before and most of which were based upon the author's experiences in the late 1890s and early 1900s), while nearly plotless, are memorably vivid pictures of characters captured in action. Despite almost uniformly enthusiastic reviews upon publication (even from those generally hostile to Dreiser) and despite continued praise from recent critics, the book sold rather poorly and has never received the readership it deserves. The set of sketches warrants more attention. Through a narrative weaving of selected major moments in a life, each sketch conveys the nature of a truly individual temperament—in most cases, the temperament of a man either artistically creative or unselfishly philanthropic. Especially worth reading are "My Brother Paul" (concerning the writer's brother Paul Dresser, a turn-of-the-century Broadway celebrity and famous songwriter), "A Doer of the Word" (about a simple man living a genuinely religious life), "Culhane, the Solid Man" (about a fiercely Spartan reformer of weak spirits and bodies), and "The Mighty Rourke" (a tale of a railroad foreman's relations with his work crew). Like most of the more fully developed stories, such sketches movingly convey the meaning of individual lives.

Dreiser's second volume of short stories, *Chains*, was published in 1927; the collection includes fifteen stories, of which all but two had been previously published in periodicals. Inscribed on the volume's cover and on an otherwise blank page as a "Foreword" is this statement: "The inevitabilities of our fate are: Love and hope, fear and death, interwoven with our lacks, inhibitions, jealousies and greeds." This assertion suggests the thematic thrust of the collection: almost all the stories either obviously or obliquely concern love, greed, or both.

Seven of the stories deal directly with the major Dreiserian theme of love as the most inscrutable and fate-shaping force in life. In their various ways these tales show what the title of both the book and one of its most important stories imply—that the passions of love often make prisoners of the lovers, placing them in invisible yet inescapable "chains."

The title story, published as "Love" by the *New York Tribune* on 18 May 1919, concerns the binding desire of Upham Garrison, a wealthy middle-aged businessman, for Idelle, his beautiful but faithless young wife. Interior monologue reveals the protagonist's troubled thoughts about Idelle throughout, as he returns home from a business trip. Though a commanding presence in the

Page from Dreiser's diary entry for the day he first met Helen Richardson (by permission of the Estate of Theodore Dreiser; courtesy of the Van Pelt Library, University of Pennsylvania) world of commerce, Garrison had always been weakly vulnerable to and unassertive before feminine beauty. Nothing that has happened in the three years of their marriage has given him the strength to repudiate her: he has continued helplessly loving Idelle despite discovery of her sordid and unrepented past, her selfishly callous nature, her lack of fidelity to him, her basic indifference to him, and her exploitation of his feelings and money. Having angrily resolved to leave her at last when she fails, despite a prior promise, to greet him at home, Garrison, placated by memories and a note from her, ends up remaining her slave: "There was something about sheer beauty, evil though it might be, which overcame moral prejudices or scruples. . . . Beauty, beauty, beauty! How could one gainsay the charm or avoid the lure of it?"

The ironically titled story "Fulfillment" (*Holland's*, February 1924) focuses on the thoughts and feelings of a young woman caught in a loveless marriage. Ulrica learns how unfulfilling wealth can be without love: having once been poor but happily in love with an artist who died of influenza before their life together could truly begin, she is now resigned to an existence of luxury with a much older man, for whom she feels at best grateful friendship, because he offered her a loving home at an hour of loneliness and grief. The story, technically weak in its excessive reliance upon summarizing, reveals, finally, the heroine's sense of life's mockery of one's most cherished dreams.

Both the ironies of human experience and the emptiness of material success are dramatized in "The Old Neighborhood" (*Metropolitan*, December 1918). The nameless protagonist, a prosperous and powerful inventor and industrialist, revisits the neighborhood where he had lived long ago with his first wife, Marie, and his children Peter and Frank. Failing to appreciate fully her sweetly loving nature and resenting the poverty and responsibilities that blocked pursuit of his youthful ambitions, he had selfishly left her following their sons' untimely deaths. Now, while possessing all the success he had once wanted and having built a new life, he bitterly regrets the loss of Marie's love and the pain he caused her. Haunted by nostalgia for what could have been, he feels that life is often "unconsciously cruel," as one follows the impulse and passions "driving one on and on like a harried steer up a narrow runway to one's fate." Although its effect is weakened through repetitiveness, the narrative con-

veys the poignant ironies created by time and change.

In "Marriage For One" (originally published in *Marriage: Short Stories of Married Life by American Writers*, 1923), Wray, a clerk who sees life as logically ordered and just, marries Bessie, a simple girl from a conservative, traditional family, planning to educate her to more liberal attitudes and to an appreciation of all the arts. Paradoxically, she becomes even more sophisticated and cultured than he is and rejects him as too conventional and narrow-minded. Yet long after she has abandoned him, Wray still desperately loves Bessie and feels married to her. As told by a nameless narrator, the tale reveals the strange workings of love.

While Dreiser's fiction generally shows love's overpowering resistance to restraints imposed on it by society, two stories in *Chains* are about characters who yield to the pressures of social convention by giving up passionate, unsanctioned relationships and remaining bound by loveless marriages. In "The Shadow" (*Harper's Bazaar*, August 1924—as "Jealousy"), increasingly attracted by artistic men more dynamic than her husband, Gilbert, Beryl Stoddard gives up a satisfying affair with the novelist Barclay and commits herself to a joyless marriage because a divorce might mean loss of her son, Gilbert, Jr. In "Convention" (*American Mercury*, December 1925), the odd story of Wallace Steele, a reporter, is retrospectively recounted by an artist with whom he had formerly worked at a midwestern newspaper. A few years before, Steele had enjoyed beauty and freedom in a relationship with a pretty young woman. But after a sensational exposure of the love triangle—caused by Mrs. Steele's attempt to kill herself and frame the mistress as a murderess by taking poisoned candy—Steele renounces his lover and returns soberly to his homely, older wife. At the story's end, after seeing the Steeles in the New York home to which they moved following the scandal, the narrator sadly contemplates all that Steele had repudiated by fearfully bowing to convention.

The last of the seven stories in *Chains* principally about love is "Typhoon" (*Hearst's International-Cosmopolitan*, October 1926—as "The Wages of Sin"). Ida Zobel, seventeen-year-old daughter of a strictly authoritarian, morally conservative German immigrant, having first been restricted too much, falls victim to a handsome but heartless seducer whom she loves; Edward Hauptwanger, spoiled son of a wealthy coal dealer,

Theodore Dreiser

While Dreiser clearly sees romantic love as thwarting individual fulfillment, he sees greed as the dominant driving passion working against relationships; thus he shapes three tales around man's hunger for money. Perhaps technically the weakest story in *Chains*, "The Victory" (*Jewish Daily Forward*, 24 April 1927) concerns the career of the wealthy industrialist J. H. Osterman. From an assortment of juxtaposed documents left by his associates after his death, the reader learns that Osterman's countless triumphs over others in his quest for wealth and power all led to an ironic ending: defeated by the ultimate "victor," death, Osterman has failed to sign a new will leaving his millions to homes for orphaned boys rather than to his coldly calculating wife, Nadia. "Phantom Gold" (*Live Stories*, February 1921) illustrates how avarice distorts human nature in its destruction of all communion even within the family unit. It is the story of what happens when the family of Bursay Queeder learns that its apparently worthless farm land contains valuable zinc deposits. Not content with the chance to rise up out of poverty, Queeder conspires with a prospector to cheat Queeder's wife and son of their share of the land's sale price, goes mad seeking wealth, and falls prey to his own vicious acquisitiveness. "The Hand" (*Munsey's*, May 1919) is about the death of a prospector and investor named Davidson. After they strike it rich together, he murders his partner, Mersereau, to avoid sharing the money; guilty fear soon makes the murderer feel that Mersereau's ghost seeks revenge. And as Davidson becomes increasingly obsessed with this idea over a four-year span, he declines in body and mind until he is found dead with the avenging hand he had feared would choke him—his *own* hand, a symbol of both greed and violence—clutching his throat.

From 1918 on Dreiser became increasingly interested in the new science of psychology through his developing relationship with Dr. A. A. Brill, a well-known American Freudian and a translator of Freud's works. This interest, evident in "The Hand" with the dramatization of the effects of guilt on the psyche, also underlies "The 'Mercy' of God" (*American Mercury*, August 1924). Here the story of Marguerite Ryan is framed by a narrative that is a cosmological debate between the narrator and his friend, a noted neurologist. Speculating about the indifference of nature, these two consider the case of Marguerite, a physically unattractive, painfully shy young woman whose lonely state becomes bearable by

spurns her as soon as he has had his pleasure. She becomes pregnant, and when she discovers that he will not marry her, Ida shoots Hauptwanger in a moment of crazed desperation; subsequently (though acquitted by a jury of criminal responsibility for his death) she drowns herself. With affinities to both "Old Rogaum and His Theresa" and Dreiser's 1925 novel *An American Tragedy*, "Typhoon" dramatizes his view of the potential tragedy in families whose members are estranged from one another by the communication gap between generations.

Painting of Dreiser by Boris Chaliapin (1939; from Dorothy Dudley, Dreiser and the Land of the Free, *1946)*

way of her delusion that she is irresistibly beautiful and constantly followed by men everywhere. At the close of the story, the narrator merely *wishes* he might believe in a beneficent, divine design of the kind the neurologist says the tale manifests.

The protagonists of two other stories in *Chains* express religious faith. Madeleine Kinsella in "Sanctuary" (*Smart Set*, October 1919) is, in her character and experiences, reminiscent of Stephen Crane's Maggie. A lovely flower born in "an ash-heap," Madeleine, long injured in every way but morally by a brutally squalid slum environment, escapes ruin by finding refuge in the calmly ordered world of a convent, the "House of the Good Shepherd." In "St. Columba and the River" (*Pictorial Review*, January 1925—as "Glory Be! McGlathery"), a devoutly Catholic Irish immi-

grant laborer, Dennis McGlathery, prays often to St. Columba (patron saint of those on water) while fearfully working on the project to build a tunnel beneath the Hudson River. After surviving several disastrous accidents on the job over a span of years, McGlathery is quite convinced that he owes his last escape from death to the saint and to God.

Both of the stories that were published initially in the *Chains* collection have settings strangely atypical of Dreiser's fiction—in the Middle East. Yet both involve the urban contrast between wealth and poverty frequently dramatized by Dreiser within an American context. "The Prince Who Was a Thief" is a story within a story. It tells of the plight of a poor, old taleteller, Gazzar-al-Din, and is set (in the narrative frame) against an Oriental romance of wealth and power. The adventures of the hero-prince are meant to amuse a circle of paying listeners. And in "Khat" an indigent beggar in the city of Hodeidah, old Ibn Abdullah, loses the will to live since he can no longer obtain the joy-inducing stimulant khat. He lies down in the desert, his head toward Mecca, awaiting death.

With the publication of *An American Tragedy* in 1925, Dreiser had attained for the first time financial success, popularity, and widespread critical acclaim as a writer. As a consequence, *Chains* received almost universally favorable reviews in 1927, and sold roughly twelve thousand copies in its first year (faring much better than *Free* had done nearly a decade before). Yet *Chains* has engaged less critical attention over the years than *Free* and represents a less important part of the Dreiser canon than the earlier volume. Only a few stories in the collection—perhaps "The Hand," "Chains," "St. Columba and the River," "Typhoon," and "Marriage for One"—emerge as examples of solid short fiction.

Similarly, only a few of the sketches in *A Gallery of Women*, published in 1929, help to shape a positive view of Dreiser's work in short fiction. For while it is ostensibly a companion to *Twelve Men*, this two-volume set of individual portraits lacks both the variety and the vigorous art of the earlier sketchbook. Among the causes for this decline may be the facts that unlike the dozen men depicted (who are nearly sexless and self-contained in finding paths to fulfillment), the women in *A Gallery* are mostly studies in frustration and are generally dependent on sexual relationships with men for meaningful lives. In any event a few sketches here—including "Olive Brand" (about an intellectually independent woman), "Ernita" (modeled after the anarchist/feminist Emma Goldman), and "Bridget Mullanphy" (about a colorful Irish scrubwoman)—are examples of Dreiser's success in developing fully realized characters.

Two of Dreiser's other published stories are also significant. *Fine Furniture* (published in 1930 in the Random House Prose Quarto series, in limited edition) is about the absurd efforts of a materialistic, social-climbing girl, Opal Feliss, to maintain an impressive home with fine furnishings in the Washington lumber camps where her husband Clem works. While the story is not very well written, it does effectively express a theme central to all Dreiser's novels—the way greed distorts or destroys human relationships. In "The Tithe of the Lord," first published in *Esquire* in

July 1938 (and then republished in *The Armchair Esquire* anthology in 1958), Dreiser uses a complex story about the rise and fall of a God-fearing businessman named Benziger to explore the psychological components of religious faith. Moreover, this little-known tale is interesting in relation to other works of Dreiser's last years—such as the posthumously published novels *The Bulwark* (1946) and *The Stoic* (1947)—conveying the writer's deepening concern with the relationship of the spiritual and the material in human experience. Having struggled to complete these books despite his failing health, Dreiser died in Hollywood on 28 December 1945.

Theodore Dreiser has always been viewed as a problematic figure in modern American literature: critics expound on his stylistic excesses, yet his work has been enjoyed and applauded by millions of readers; and scholars continue to explore his creativity, finding Dreiser has many strengths beyond his contribution to naturalism. Such recognition is overdue, for as Robert Penn Warren pointed out, only great art can account for Dreiser's power in depicting the feelings of individuals within the fabric of society. And while he has generally been regarded as a novelist with limited skill in the short story, Dreiser is in fact as powerful in his best short fiction as he is in his most memorable novels.

Letters:
Letters to Louise, edited by Louise Campbell (Philadelphia: University of Pennsylvania Press, 1959);
Letters of Theodore Dreiser, 3 volumes, edited by Robert H. Elias (Philadelphia: University of Pennsylvania Press, 1959).

Bibliography:
Donald Pizer, Richard W. Dowell, and Frederic E. Rusch, *Theodore Dreiser: A Primary and Secondary Bibliography* (Boston: G. K. Hall, 1975).

Biographies:
Dorothy Dudley, *Forgotten Frontiers: Dreiser and the Land of the Free* (New York: Harrison Smith, 1932);
Robert H. Elias, *Theodore Dreiser: Apostle of Nature* (New York: Knopf, 1949; revised edition, Ithaca, N.Y.: Cornell University Press, 1970);
Helen Dreiser, *My Life with Dreiser* (Cleveland: World, 1951);

Dreiser late in life (Van Pelt Library, University of Pennsylvania)

W. A. Swanberg, *Dreiser* (New York: Scribners, 1965);

Marguerite Tjader, *Theodore Dreiser: A New Dimension* (Norwalk, Conn.: Silvermine, 1965);

Vera Dreiser and Brett Howard, *My Uncle Theodore* (New York: Nash, 1976);

Richard Lingeman, *Theodore Dreiser*, 2 volumes: volume 1, *At the Gates of the City*; volume 2, *An American Journey* (New York: Putnam's 1986, 1990).

References:

Roger Asselineau, "Theodore Dreiser's Transcendentalism," in *English Studies Today*, edited by G. A. Bonnard (Bern: Francke, 1961), pp. 233-243;

David Brion Davis, "Dreiser and Naturalism Revisited," in *The Stature of Theodore Dreiser*, edited by Alfred Kazin and Charles Shapiro (Bloomington: Indiana University Press, 1955), pp. 225-236;

Blanche Gelfant, *The American City Novel* (Norman: University of Oklahoma Press, 1954), pp. 42-94;

Philip Gerber, *Theodore Dreiser* (New York: Twayne, 1964);

D. B. Graham, " 'The Cruise of the Idlewild': Dreiser's Revisions of a Rather Light Story," *American Literary Realism*, 8 (Winter 1975): 1-11;

Graham, "Dreiser's Ant Tragedy: The Revision of 'The Shining Slave Makers,' " *Studies in Short Fiction*, 14 (Winter 1977): 41-48;

Graham, "Psychological Veracity in 'The Lost Phoebe': Dreiser's Revisions," *Studies in American Fiction*, 6 (1978): 100-105;

Joseph Griffin, "Dreiser's Short Stories and the Dream of Success," *Etudes Anglaises*, 31 (1978): 294-302;

Helen and Theodore Dreiser in December 1945, several days before his death

Griffin, *The Small Canvas: An Introduction to Dreiser's Short Stories* (Rutherford, N.J.: Fairleigh Dickinson University Press, 1985);

Yoshinobu Hakutani, "The Making of Dreiser's Early Short Stories: The Philosopher and the Artist," *Studies in American Fiction*, 6 (Spring 1978): 47-63;

Hakutani, *Young Dreiser: A Critical Study* (Rutherford, N.J.: Fairleigh Dickinson University Press, 1980);

Lawrence E. Hussman, *Dreiser and His Fiction* (Philadelphia: University of Pennsylvania Press, 1983);

Alfred Kazin, *On Native Grounds* (New York: Harcourt, 1942), pp. 73-90;

Kazin and Charles Shapiro, eds., *The Stature of Theodore Dreiser: A Critical Survey of the Man and His Work* (Bloomington: Indiana University Press, 1955);

Ellen Kimbel, "The American Short Story: 1900-1920," in *The American Short Story 1900-1945: A Critical History*, edited by Philip Stevick (Boston: Twayne, 1984), pp. 33-69;

Richard Lehan, *Theodore Dreiser: His World and His Novels* (Carbondale: Southern Illinois University Press, 1969);

John Lydenberg, ed., *Dreiser: A Collection of Critical Essays* (Englewood Cliffs, N.J.: Prentice-Hall, 1971);

Kenneth Lynn, *The Dream of Success: A Study of the Modern American Imagination* (Boston: Little, Brown, 1955), pp. 13-74;

Jay Martin, *Harvests of Change: American Literature, 1865-1914* (Englewood Cliffs, N.J.: Prentice-Hall, 1967), pp. 252-263;

F. O. Matthiessen, *Theodore Dreiser* (New York: Sloane, 1951);

Dreiser's gravestone, in Forest Lawn Memorial Park, Glendale, California

John J. McAleer, *Theodore Dreiser: An Introduction and Interpretation* (New York: Holt, 1968);

Ellen Moers, *Two Dreisers* (New York: Viking, 1969);

T. D. Nostwich, "The Source of Dreiser's 'Nigger Jeff,' " *Resources for American Literary Study*, 8 (1978): 174-187;

Paul A. Orlov, "A Writer's Beginning in His 'End' " [review of Dreiser's *An Amateur Laborer*], *Old Northwest*, 10 (Summer 1984): 234-238;

William L. Phillips, "The Imagery of Dreiser's Novels," *PMLA*, 78 (December 1963): 572-585;

Donald Pizer, *The Novels of Theodore Dreiser: A Critical Study* (Minneapolis: University of Minnesota Press, 1976);

Pizer, "A Summer at Maumee: Theodore Dreiser Writes Four Stories," in *Essays Mostly on Periodical Publishing in America*, edited by James Woodress (Durham, N.C.: Duke University Press, 1973), pp. 193-204;

Pizer, "Theodore Dreiser's 'Nigger Jeff ': The Development of an Aesthetic," *American Literature*, 41 (November 1969): 331-341;

Pizer, ed., *Critical Essays on Theodore Dreiser* (Boston: G. K. Hall, 1981);

Jack Salzman, ed., "Special Issue: Theodore Dreiser," *Modern Fiction Studies*, 23 (Autumn 1977);

Salzman, ed., *Theodore Dreiser: The Critical Reception* (New York: Lewis, 1972);

Charles Shapiro, *Theodore Dreiser: Our Bitter Patriot* (Carbondale: Southern Illinois University Press, 1962);

Philip Stevick, ed., Introduction to *The American Short Story, 1900-1945: A Critical History* (Boston: Twayne, 1984), pp. 10-26;

J. D. Thomas, "Epimetheus Bound: Theodore Dreiser and the Novel of Thought," *Southern Humanities Review*, 3 (Fall 1969): 346-357;

Eliseo Vivas, "Dreiser, an Inconsistent Mechanist," *Ethics*, 48 (July 1938): 498-508; reprinted in his *Creation and Discovery: Essays in Criticism and Aesthetics* (New York: Noonday, 1955), pp. 3-13;

Arthur Voss, *The American Short Story: A Critical Survey* (Norman: University of Oklahoma Press, 1973), pp. 157-158, 178-182;

Charles Child Walcutt, "The Three Stages of Theodore Dreiser's Naturalism," *PMLA*, 55 (March 1940): 266-289; reprinted in his *American Literary Naturalism, a Divided Stream* (Minneapolis: University of Minnesota Press, 1956), pp. 180-221;

Robert Penn Warren, *Homage to Theodore Dreiser* (New York: Random House, 1971);

Ray B. West, Jr., *The Short Story in America, 1900-1950* (Chicago: Regnery, 1952), pp. 33-44.

Papers:

The Theodore Dreiser Collection of the University of Pennsylvania Library is the principal reposi-
tory. It contains manuscripts of published and un-published works, including drafts and notes; letters to and by Dreiser; and clippings and scrapbooks. Other important collections of Dreiser papers are in the Cornell University Library, the Lilly Library of Indiana University, the New York Public Library, the University of Texas Library, and the University of Virginia Library.

John Erskine

(5 October 1879 - 2 June 1951)

Leonard Mustazza
Pennsylvania State University

See also the Erskine entry in *DLB 9: American Novelists, 1910-1945.*

BOOKS: *The Elizabethan Lyric* (New York: Macmillan, 1903);

Actaeon, and Other Poems (New York: Lane, 1907);

Leading American Novelists (New York: Holt, 1910);

Written English: A Guide to the Rules of Composition, by Erskine and Helen Erskine (New York: Century, 1910; revised, 1913);

Great American Writers, by Erskine and W. P. Trent (New York: Holt, 1912; London: Williams & Norgate, 1912);

The Moral Obligation to Be Intelligent, and Other Essays (New York: Duffield, 1915; enlarged, 1921);

The Shadowed Hour (New York: Lyric, 1917);

Democracy and Ideals (New York: Doran, 1920);

Hearts Enduring: A Play in One Scene (New York: Duffield, 1920);

The Kinds of Poetry, and Other Essays (New York: Duffield, 1920; London: Nash & Grayson, 1927);

Collected Poems, 1907-1922 (New York: Duffield, 1922);

The Literary Discipline (New York: Duffield, 1923; London: Nash & Grayson, 1927);

The Private Life of Helen of Troy (Indianapolis: Bobbs-Merrill, 1925; London: Nash & Grayson, 1926);

Sonata, and Other Poems (New York: Duffield, 1925);

Galahad: Enough of His Life to Explain His Reputation (Indianapolis: Bobbs-Merrill, 1926; London: Nash & Grayson, 1926);

Adam and Eve: Though He Knew Better (Indianapolis: Bobbs-Merrill, 1927);

American Character, and Other Essays (Chautauqua, N.Y.: Chautauqua Press, 1927);

Prohibition and Christianity, and Other Paradoxes of the American Spirit (Indianapolis: Bobbs-Merrill, 1927; London: Nash & Grayson, 1927);

The Delight of Great Books (Indianapolis: Bobbs-Merrill, 1928; London: Nash & Grayson, 1928);

Penelope's Man: The Homing Instinct (Indianapolis: Bobbs-Merrill, 1928);

Sincerity: A Story of Our Time (Indianapolis: Bobbs-Merrill, 1929; London & New York: Putnam's, 1930);

Cinderella's Daughter, and Other Sequels and Consequences (Indianapolis: Bobbs-Merrill, 1930);

Uncle Sam in the Eyes of His Family (Indianapolis: Bobbs-Merrill, 1930);

John Erskine

Unfinished Business (Indianapolis: Bobbs-Merrill, 1931);

Tristan and Isolde: Restoring Palamede (Indianapolis: Bobbs-Merrill, 1932; London: Lane, 1933);

Bachelor—Of Arts (Indianapolis: Bobbs-Merrill, 1934);

Helen Retires: An Opera in Three Acts, libretto by Erskine and music by George Antheil (Indianapolis: Bobbs-Merrill, 1934);

Forget If You Can (Indianapolis & New York: Bobbs-Merrill, 1935);

Solomon, My Son! (Indianapolis & New York: Bobbs-Merrill, 1935);

The Influence of Women and Its Cure (Indianapolis & New York: Bobbs-Merrill, 1936);

Young Love: Variations on a Theme (Indianapolis & New York: Bobbs-Merrill, 1936);

The Brief Hour of François Villon (Indianapolis & New York: Bobbs-Merrill, 1937; London: Joseph, 1938);

The Start of the Road (New York: Stokes, 1938);

Give Me Liberty: The Story of an Innocent Bystander (New York: Stokes, 1940);

Casanova's Women: Eleven Moments of a Year (New York: Stokes, 1941);

Mrs. Doratt (New York & Toronto: Stokes, 1941);

Song Without Words: The Story of Felix Mendelssohn (New York: Messner, 1941);

The Complete Life (New York: Messner, 1943; London: Melrose, 1945);

The Philharmonic-Symphony Society of New York: Its First Hundred Years (New York: Macmillan, 1943);

The Voyage of Captain Bart (Philadelphia & New York: Lippincott, 1943);

What Is Music? (Philadelphia & New York: Lippincott, 1944);

The Human Life of Jesus (New York: Morrow, 1945);

The Memory of Certain Persons (Philadelphia & New York: Lippincott, 1947);

My Life as a Teacher (Philadelphia: Lippincott, 1948);

Venus, the Lonely Goddess (New York: Morrow, 1949; London: Wingate, 1950);

My Life in Music (New York: Morrow, 1950).

OTHER: *Selections from Spenser's The Faerie Queene*, edited, with notes and an introduction, by Erskine (New York: Longmans, Green, 1905);

Selections from Tennyson's Idylls of the King, edited by Erskine (New York: Holt, 1912);

Lafcadio Hearn, *Interpretations of Literature*, edited, with an introduction, by Erskine (New York: Dodd, Mead, 1915);

Hearn, *Appreciations of Poetry*, edited, with an introduction, by Erskine (New York: Dodd, Mead, 1916);

Hearn, *Life and Literature*, edited, with an introduction, by Erskine (New York: Dodd, Mead, 1917);

The Cambridge History of American Literature, 4 volumes, edited by Erskine, William Peterfield Trent, Stuart P. Sherman, and Carl Van Doren (New York: Putnam's, 1917-1921; Cambridge: Cambridge University Press, 1917-1921);

Hearn, *Talks to Writers*, edited, with an introduction, by Erskine (New York: Dodd, Mead, 1920);

Hearn, *Books and Habits*, edited, with an introduction, by Erskine (New York: Dodd, Mead, 1921);

Erskine in 1916, during his sixth year as an English professor at Columbia University, where he taught until his retirement in 1937

Hearn, *Pre-Raphaelite and Other Poets*, edited, with an introduction, by Erskine (New York: Dodd, Mead, 1922);

"Cannibal King," in *Second Mercury Story Book* (London: Longmans, Green, 1931), pp. 312-324;

A Musical Companion: A Guide to the Understanding and Enjoyment of Music, edited, with an introduction, by Erskine (New York: Knopf, 1935);

"Remember the Sabbath Day, to Keep It Holy," in *The Ten Commandments: Ten Short Novels of Hitler's War Against the Moral Code*, edited by Armin L. Robinson (New York: Simon & Schuster, 1943), pp. 146-180.

Although today John Erskine cannot be considered anything but a minor writer, one who exerted little lasting influence upon the short-story form itself, his fame in the first two quarters of the twentieth century was great indeed, based upon his distinguished accomplishments in several fields, fiction writing not the least of these. Many of Erskine's novels and short stories are realistic, usually satiric, treatments of fairy tales, myths, fables, and romantic legends. By either reexamining or, more frequently, continuing the stories of such familiar characters as Cinderella, Helen of Troy, and Lady Godiva, Erskine brought to bear upon these traditional stories a modern sensibility and a concern with the human condition that invariably belied the "happy-ever-after" optimism of the original materials. That his approach to fiction was well received is evidenced by the proliferation of his stories following the publication of his first commercially successful novel, *The Private Life of Helen of Troy*, in 1925. That novel, according to Erskine's obituary in the *New York Times* (3 June 1951), placed him in the "front ranks of writers about the revolt of youth," a reputation he held for some twenty years. As appealing as his approach proved to be, however, the reading public did eventually lose interest, and by the time of his death in 1951 his reputation as a writer had diminished considerably. Erskine's most lasting contribution to American arts and letters probably lies in his work as an educator and scholar.

John Erskine, the son of James Morrison Erskine, a textile merchant, and Eliza Jane Hollingsworth Erskine, was born and reared in New York City. Educated at Columbia College (B.A., 1900; M.A., 1901; Ph.D., 1903), he began his career as an English teacher at Amherst College (1903-1909) and then returned to Columbia, where he remained until his retirement as professor emeritus in 1937. Most of Erskine's published work prior to 1925 was of a scholarly or pedagogical nature. Yet, even within this limited field, his interests were eclectic, his productions including several volumes and numerous scholarly articles on British Renaissance poetry, two critical books on American novelists, several authorized editions of the works of Lafcadio Hearn, and some collections of essays on the value of humanistic study. In addition, and perhaps most significant, Professor Erskine was a contributing editor (along with William Peterfield Trent, Stuart Sherman, and Carl Van Doren) to the four-volume *Cambridge History of American Literature* (1917-1921), a landmark in American letters. To be sure, these and other scholarly accomplishments, along with his teaching, community work, and service on the executive boards of numerous learned societies, made for a career in themselves, but they were ap-

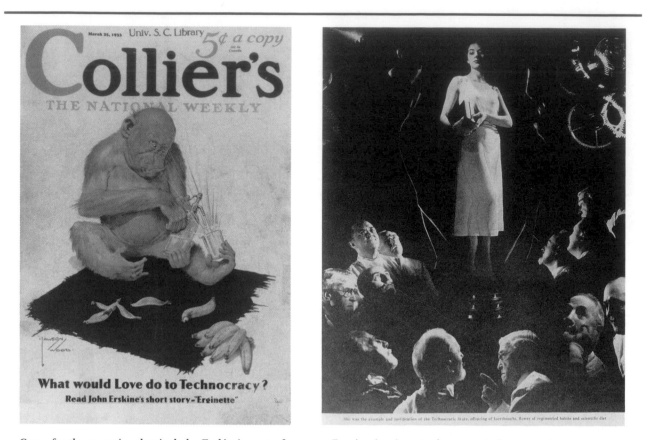

Cover for the magazine that includes Erskine's story of a young Russian immigrant who upsets technocratic American society with her poetry; and the illustration for the story

parently not enough for the ambitious and indefatigable Erskine. In 1925 he embarked on no fewer than two additional careers. Some twenty-two years earlier he had abandoned his plans to become a concert pianist, opting instead for a teaching career, but at the age of forty-six that early interest was rekindled. He returned to the piano with a vengeance and trained himself within a short period of time to such proficiency that he was invited to appear as a soloist with the New York Philharmonic. Moreover, his work in music also led to his receiving several honorary doctorates and his being appointed president of the Julliard School of Music in 1928 and director of the Metropolitan Opera Association in 1935. In 1925 he also entered the literary scene, where his popularity as a writer of satiric fictions soon became widespread.

Erskine's first short-story collection, *Cinderella's Daughter, and Other Sequels and Consequences* (1930), is very much in keeping with the techniques and thematic concerns of his novels. The opening lines of one of the stories, "Beauty and the Beast," perhaps best sum up his approach: "In our childhood they told us only the first part

of the fairy tale. A beautiful thing, as far as it went. But now, to a mature taste, it seems fantastic, unless we hear it all." By and large, this is precisely what Erskine does in the collection's eight stories—finishes the familiar tales in a realistic manner, thereby using them to address the concerns of a mature (and, for him, contemporary) taste.

In "Cinderella's Daughter," the title piece, Erskine sets the tone for what is to follow in the other stories, his primary interest being to question the static moral premises of all such tales. The story is about the lives of Cinderella and the Prince some seventeen years after their marriage. As seen here, the couple's "ever after" is far less than happy; indeed, they have proven to be intellectually mismatched: Cinderella is somewhat frivolous and excessively interested in fashionable pursuits; the Prince is conservative, decorous, and pensive. (In some ways, they remotely resemble Mr. and Mrs. Bennett in Jane Austen's *Pride and Prejudice*, 1813.) Their disparate attitudes toward life come into significant conflict over the rearing of their daughter, Cereus, a beautiful malcontent, who "looked like Cinderella and acted

Erskine, circa 1950 (from the Saturday Review of Literature, *25 November 1950)*

like the Prince." Observing this fusion of qualities but ignoring her individuality, both father and mother seek to remake the girl in their respective images, to contend for "possession of her soul." The result of their efforts, however, is not so much seen in the girl as in their marriage, which they have to work increasingly hard at preserving. Erskine's thematic concerns are fairly clear. Like Heraclitus, Erskine saw life as constantly in flux, and nothing—not moral codes or fairy-tale optimism—can escape change. In the end, though Cinderella and the Prince do effect a reconciliation of sorts, they are forced to acknowledge that it is the result of accommodation and love.

As for the other stories in the collection, they are moderately interesting, but as might be expected, the author's rather uniform approach does eventually grow tiresome. Such was the major objection raised by some book reviewers at the time of the collection's appearance.

Much more interesting is a story entitled "Cannibal King," which was published in the *Sec-*

ond Mercury Story Book (1931). In a marked departure from his usual approach, Erskine here tells the story of Adam Everson, a fictional professor of botany at the University of Delaware. A "pathetic, ineffectual creature," Everson displays, during a camping trip in Maine, a surprising proficiency at outdoor skills such as making campfires. The narrator asks where he picked up those skills, and Everson's lengthy response becomes the story's central narrative: on a university-sponsored trip to South America to do research, he is accidentally separated from his companions and eventually finds himself among cannibals in a jungle. Using his revolver, his only means of self-preservation, he is soon forced to kill one of the natives, an awe-inspiring feat that leads to his becoming the cannibals' king and master. He comes to enjoy this role so much that he willingly leaves aside his withdrawn self and becomes a brutal despot. Like the misguided Gulliver at the end of Jonathan Swift's tale, Everson eventually returns to civilized society, where, after he nearly takes the life of a companion, he abruptly recognizes what he has become. With this realization comes another: "I felt very small and very foolish, for I knew that I was only Adam Everson, the botanist." This story, perhaps Erskine's best, effectively sheds light on the contingencies of human behavior, the contexts in which it is formed. In some ways Everson's conclusion is a mistaken one, for he implies that who he is (his nature) should determine how he behaves. Rather, Erskine forcefully demonstrates in the story that nurture dominates human action and that certain contingencies can lead to frightening consequences.

In 1943 Armin L. Robinson edited a volume of original stories entitled *The Ten Commandments: Ten Short Novels of Hitler's War Against the Moral Code*. Robinson's professed goal in publishing the collection (stated in his introduction) was "to open the eyes of those who still do not recognize what Nazism really is." Specifically, of course, his target was Adolf Hitler, who, at about this time, had promised to liberate humanity from "the curse of Mount Sinai, the masochistic spirit of self-torment, the curse of so-called morals, idolized to protect the weak from the strong in the face of the immortal law of battle, the great law of divine nature." Robinson's stories, each named after one of the commandments, artistically militate against Hitler's claim by demonstrating the dehumanizing effects of living in a society without morals. The collection includes pieces by Thomas Mann, Rebecca West, and Bruno Frank; that Erskine, too, was asked to contribute testifies to his reputation as a writer at the time.

Erskine's contribution, "Remember the Sabbath Day, to Keep It Holy," is about German youths at the outbreak of World War I. Karl Ehrlich, the protagonist, is a farmer's son, a sensitive boy who cherishes the simple life of the farm, "the plowing, planting, reaping—cycles of work and love." In this regard he stands opposed to his best friend, Heinrich Braun, a self-styled "radical" who lives in a world of cynical ideas, which eventually lead him to suspect and then condemn the promises the Nazis make to a suffering Germany after the war. On the other hand, the sensitive Karl comes to lose faith in his simple ideals and to join with the Nazis, who give him a sense of purpose, a sense of belonging, and, ironically, who eventually murder him and Heinrich.

There are numerous thematic concerns in this subtle and evocative story, the most prominent being the destructive effects of a rigid and prejudiced ideology. The postwar nation that Erskine describes is not so much one in which no moral code prevails; rather, it is one where individual conscience and action have been replaced by a dehumanizing vision of perfection, the kind of vision that will just as soon destroy as preserve the lives it purports to ennoble.

In the last several years of his life, Erskine produced comparatively few fictions, short or extended, preferring to work instead on several autobiographical volumes. He died in New York on 2 June 1951, the result of a lengthy heart ailment, and at the time he was said to be working on two volumes, an autobiographical book (his fourth) and a version of Geoffrey Chaucer's *Canterbury Tales*. The *New York Times* obituary made note of all the roles Erskine had filled in his long, distinguished career: those of professor, author, translator, and musician.

References:

Ernest Boyd, "Reader and Writers," *Independent*, 115 (12 December 1925): 683;

Joyce Kilmer, "Literature in the Colleges," in his *Literature in the Making by Some of Its Makers* (New York: Harper, 1917), pp. 199-209;

William S. Knickerbocker, "John Erskine, Enough of His Mind to Explain His Art," *Sewanee Review*, 35 (April-June 1927): 155-174;

Annie R. Marble, "John Erskine," in her *A Study of the Modern Novel: British and American Since 1900* (New York: Appleton, 1928), pp. 290-292.

William Faulkner

(25 September 1897 - 6 July 1962)

Hans H. Skei
University of Oslo

See also the Faulkner entries in *DLB 9: American Novelists, 1910-1945; DLB 11: American Humorists, 1800-1950; DLB 44: American Screenwriters; DLB Documentary Series: 2;* and *DLB Yearbook: 1986.*

BOOKS: *The Marble Faun* (Boston: Four Seas, 1924);

Soldiers' Pay (New York: Boni & Liveright, 1926; London: Chatto & Windus, 1930);

Mosquitoes (New York: Boni & Liveright, 1927; London: Chatto & Windus, 1964);

Sartoris (New York: Harcourt, Brace, 1929; London: Chatto & Windus, 1932); original, uncut version, edited by Douglas Day as *Flags in the Dust* (New York: Random House, 1974);

The Sound and the Fury (New York: Cape & Smith, 1929; London: Chatto & Windus, 1931);

As I Lay Dying (New York: Cape & Smith, 1930; London: Chatto & Windus, 1935);

Sanctuary (New York: Cape & Smith, 1931; London: Chatto & Windus, 1931); unrevised version, edited by Noel Polk as *Sanctuary: The Original Text* (New York: Random House, 1981);

These 13 (New York: Cape & Smith, 1931; London: Chatto & Windus, 1933);

Idyll in the Desert (New York: Random House, 1931);

Miss Zilphia Gant (Dallas: Book Club of Texas, 1932);

Salmagundi (Milwaukee: Casanova, 1932);

Light in August (New York: Smith & Haas, 1932; London: Chatto & Windus, 1933);

A Green Bough (New York: Smith & Haas, 1933);

Doctor Martino and Other Stories (New York: Smith & Haas, 1934; London: Chatto & Windus, 1934);

Pylon (New York: Smith & Haas, 1935; London: Chatto & Windus, 1935);

Absalom, Absalom! (New York: Random House, 1936; London: Chatto & Windus, 1937);

The Unvanquished (New York: Random House,

William Faulkner, circa 1929 (photograph by J. R. Cofield)

1938; London: Chatto & Windus, 1938);

The Wild Palms (New York: Random House, 1939; London: Chatto & Windus, 1939);

The Hamlet (New York: Random House, 1940; London: Chatto & Windus, 1940; revised, New York: Random House, 1964);

Go Down, Moses and Other Stories (New York: Random House, 1942; London: Chatto & Windus, 1942);

Intruder in the Dust (New York: Random House, 1948; London: Chatto & Windus, 1949);

Knight's Gambit (New York: Random House, 1949; London: Chatto & Windus, 1951);

Collected Stories of William Faulkner (New York: Random House, 1950; London: Chatto & Windus, 1951);

Notes on a Horsethief (Greenville, Miss.: Levee, 1950 [i.e., 1951]);

Requiem for a Nun (New York: Random House, 1951; London: Chatto & Windus, 1953);

Mirrors of Chartres Street (Minneapolis: Faulkner Studies, 1953);

A Fable (New York: Random House, 1954; London: Chatto & Windus, 1955);

Big Woods (New York: Random House, 1955);

Faulkner's County: Tales of Yoknapatawpha County (London: Chatto & Windus, 1955);

Jealousy and Episode: Two Stories (Minneapolis: Faulkner Studies, 1955);

The Town (New York: Random House, 1957; London: Chatto & Windus, 1958);

New Orleans Sketches, edited by Carvel Collins (New Brunswick, N.J.: Rutgers University Press, 1958; London: Sidgwick & Jackson, 1959);

The Mansion (New York: Random House, 1959; London: Chatto & Windus, 1961);

The Reivers (New York: Random House, 1962; London: Chatto & Windus, 1962);

Early Prose and Poetry, edited by Collins (Boston: Little, Brown, 1962; London: Cape, 1963);

Faulkner's University Pieces, edited by Collins (Tokyo: Kenkyusha, 1962; Folcroft, Pa.: Folcroft, 1970);

Essays, Speeches & Public Letters, edited by James B. Meriwether (New York: Random House, 1966; London: Chatto & Windus, 1967);

The Wishing Tree (New York: Random House, 1967; London: Chatto & Windus, 1967);

The Big Sleep [screenplay], by Faulkner, Jules Furthman, and Leigh Brackett (New York: Irvington, 1971);

The Marionettes: A Play in One Act (Charlottesville: Bibliographical Society, University of Virginia, 1975);

Mayday (South Bend, Ind.: University of Notre Dame Press, 1976);

Mississippi Poems (Oxford, Miss.: Yoknapatawpha, 1979);

Uncollected Stories of William Faulkner, edited by Joseph Blotner (New York: Random House, 1979);

To Have and Have Not [screenplay], by Faulkner and Furthman (Madison: University of Wisconsin Press, 1980);

The Road to Glory [screenplay], by Faulkner and Joel Sayre (Carbondale & Edwardsville: Southern Illinois University Press, 1981);

Helen: A Courtship (Oxford, Miss.: Yoknapatawpha, 1981);

Faulkner's MGM Screenplays, edited by Bruce F. Kawin (Knoxville: University of Tennessee Press, 1982);

Elmer, edited by Dianne Cox (Northport, Ala.: Seajay, 1983);

A Sorority Pledge (Northport, Ala.: Seajay, 1983);

Father Abraham, edited by Meriwether (New York: Random House, 1984);

The DeGaulle Story [screenplay], edited by Louis Daniel Brodsky and Robert W. Hamblin (Jackson: University Press of Mississippi, 1984);

Vision in Spring, edited by Judith Sensibar (Austin: University of Texas Press, 1984);

Battle Cry [screenplay], edited by Brodsky and Hamblin (Jackson: University Press of Mississippi, 1985);

William Faulkner Manuscripts, 25 volumes, edited by Blotner, Thomas L. McHaney, Michael Millgate, and Noel Polk (New York & London: Garland, 1986-1987);

Country Lawyer and Other Stories for the Screen, edited by Brodsky and Hamblin (Jackson: University Press of Mississippi, 1987);

Stallion Road [screenplay], edited by Brodsky and Hamblin (Jackson: University Press of Mississippi, 1989).

Collections: *The Portable Faulkner*, edited by Malcolm Cowley (New York: Viking, 1946; revised and enlarged, 1967); republished as *The Essential Faulkner* (London: Chatto & Windus, 1967);

The Faulkner Reader (New York: Random House, 1954);

Snopes: A Trilogy, 3 volumes (New York: Random House, 1964)—comprises *The Hamlet* (revised edition), *The Town*, and *The Mansion*.

PLAY PRODUCTIONS: *Marionettes*, University, Miss., University of Mississippi, 4 March 1920;

Requiem for a Nun, London, Royal Court Theatre, 26 November 1957; New York, John Golden Theatre, 30 January 1959.

MOTION PICTURES: *Today We Live*, story and dialogue by Faulkner, M-G-M, 1933;

The Road to Glory, screenplay by Faulkner and Joel Sayre, 20th Century-Fox, 1936;

Slave Ship, story and additional dialogue by Faulkner, 20th Century-Fox, 1937;

To Have and Have Not, screenplay by Faulkner and Jules Furthman, Warner Bros., 1944;

William Faulkner
Oxford, Mississippi

MOONLIGHT

Approached from the rear, his uncle's
house lay blank and lightless under the August moon, because his uncle and aunt had been gone two days now, on their
summer vacation. He crossed the lane quartering, at once hurry-
ing and skulking, the bottle of corn whiskey jouncing and
burbling inside his shirt. On the opposite side of the lawn
(he could see it above the low roofline), stippled solid and
heavy and without depth on the sky) was a magnolia tree and
there was a mocking bird singing in it now, on the topmost
twig probably, high in the moon, as he lurked swiftly through
the gate and into the shadow of the trees. Now he could not be
seen as he went swiftly now across the dappled and dewdrenched
lawn on his rubber soles and reached the sanctuary of the
inky and vinescreened veranda. It was not some random and
casual passerby so much as a neighbor whom he feared, who
might be looking out a side window or even from another shadowed
porch---some women, some old woman who, representing the entire class and caste of mothers, parents, would be his mortal
foe by pure instinctive reflex.

But he gained the porch without having been
seen. Now there was no one to see him; now he began to believe, for the first time since he received the note, in his
own luck. There was a fatality in it---the empty house, the
fact that he had gained the veranda unseen. It was as though

1.

Page from the late-draft typescript for the story Faulkner called his first; written about 1920, it was first published in Uncollected Stories, *1979 (by permission of W. W. Norton and the Manuscripts Division, Special Collections Department, University
of Virginia Library; accession number 8172).*

The Big Sleep, screenplay by Faulkner, Furthman, and Leigh Brackett, Warner Bros., 1946;

Land of the Pharaohs, story and screenplay by Faulkner, Harry Kurnitz, and Harold Jack Bloom, Warner Bros., 1955.

TELEVISION: *The Graduation Dress*, teleplay by Faulkner and Joan Williams, CBS, 1960.

William Faulkner was first and foremost a novelist, and much of his achievement in the short-story form is closely related to his accomplishment as a novelist. This does not necessarily imply that his short stories are second to his novels in all respects, but it indicates how difficult it is to distinguish between Faulkner as novelist and as short-story writer. In the novel Faulkner was innovative, experimental, and influential, whereas his contribution to the short-story form is less significant. Yet one would do Faulkner's short fiction a serious injustice by regarding it as inferior. Compared to his novels the short stories may appear less impressive; compared to most other short-story writers, though, Faulkner is a major practitioner of the form.

William Cuthbert Falkner was born in New Albany, Mississippi, on 25 September 1897, the first child of Maud Butler Falkner and Murry Cuthbert Falkner (he added the "u" to his name in 1918). Shortly after his first birthday the family moved to Ripley, Mississippi, and four years later to Oxford, Mississippi, where Faulkner spent most of his life. His great-grandfather, Col. William Clark Falkner, had a literary reputation, based mainly on his novel *The White Rose of Memphis* (1881), and must be seen as a major influence on his descendant, not the least because of his active if not violent life, which Faulkner transformed and fictionalized as that of Col. John Sartoris. Growing up in an area of the United States that was just advancing from frontier land, Faulkner led an adventurous life as the oldest of four brothers, learning to handle guns and to hunt. His father had a livery stable for many years, and the boys lived among horses and dogs. Faulkner stopped attending Oxford High School midway through the 1914-1915 school year without completing the last grade. He returned the following fall, mostly to play football, but quit school at the end of the season. He had, however, been reading poetry with Phil Stone, an older friend who was important to Faulkner's development in these early years, and he had already begun showing his own poems to Stone.

Faulkner had several different jobs—ranging from bank clerk to postmaster at the university—during the long period before he established himself as a writer. In 1918, unable to meet height and weight requirements for the U.S. Army, he had instead joined the Canadian branch of the Royal Air Force and went into training in Toronto. World War I came to an end, though, before he could take part. He received a discharge in early December and returned to Oxford, where his girlfriend, Estelle Oldham, had married Cornell Franklin, a local lawyer.

In 1919-1920, while attending the University of Mississippi as a special student, Faulkner had his first poems and sketches published, and in the early 1920s—after officially withdrawing from the university in November 1920—he wrote numerous poems, a few sketches, and a verse play, *The Marionettes*, which was performed in 1920 but not published until 1975. He went to New York, where he worked briefly as a bookstore clerk in 1921, and his first book, *The Marble Faun*, a cycle of poems, was published in Boston in 1924. That same year he met Sherwood Anderson in New Orleans, and for the first half of 1925, Faulkner lived there with the Andersons. In this decisive year in Faulkner's career he made an almost complete transition from being a poet to becoming a fiction writer, publishing several pieces of experimental prose in the *New Orleans Times-Picayune* (most of them collected in *Mirrors of Chartres Street* in 1953; all of them in *New Orleans Sketches*, 1958).

Faulkner sailed for Europe aboard the *West Ivis* in July 1925 and traveled in Italy, Switzerland, France, and England before returning to the States in December. Some of his early stories are set in postwar Europe, and his travels also paid off in his later fiction. His first novel, *Soldiers' Pay*, was published in February 1926, apparently on Anderson's recommendation. In the same year he wrote *Mosquitoes* (1927) in addition to minor work, such as the novelette *Mayday* (1976) and poems for Helen Baird, whom he courted at this time, posthumously published as *Helen: A Courtship* (1981). In 1927, dividing his time between Oxford and Pascagoula, Mississippi, he wrote *Flags in the Dust*, which was accepted only after Faulkner's friend Ben Wasson cut it severely and was published as *Sartoris* in 1929 (the original version was published in 1974). As he struggled against reluctant publishers, bad reviews, and low sales, Faulkner discovered his own "postage stamp of native soil," the

Faulkner's father, Murry Cuthbert Falkner

Maud Butler, circa 1888, with Mary Holland Falkner Wilkins, her future sister-in-law

Faulkner in his RCAF uniform, circa 1918

basis for his fictional Yoknapatawpha County. With *The Sound and the Fury* (1929) a complete transition seems to have occurred. While his earlier novels are flawed by his almost narcissistic self-involvement and lack of distance from his characters, in *The Sound and the Fury* he has complete control of material and of narrative strategies. In his private life important events also took place: Estelle divorced her husband and married Faulkner on 20 June 1929. In 1930 they bought an old house, naming it Rowan Oak, and Faulkner began making money from the sale of short stories to the national magazines.

The years between 1928 and 1933 are in all respects the major years in Faulkner's career. In addition to *The Sound and the Fury*, he produced three more novels—*Sanctuary* (1931), *As I Lay Dying* (1930), and *Light in August* (1932)—and his short-story production was enormous. Safely established in the center of the world he chronicled, he was hard at work in Oxford for most of this period though he visited Charlottesville, Virginia, and New York in 1931.

Faulkner wrote short stories all through his literary career, but his greatest periods of short-story activity coincide with periods when he had

no new novels underway. Faulkner regarded the short story highly and deemed it the most demanding form after poetry. He worked consistently and conscientiously to perfect his stories—not to suit the needs of a particular market, but to satisfy his own artistic demands. This is demonstrated in his arduous work on his short-story collections, most notably *These 13* (1931) and *Collected Stories* (1950), in which he tried to superimpose a design or a structure upon the otherwise rather disparate short stories. He was a dedicated craftsman in all his work, and the seriousness of his short-story writing is demonstrated in the many different manuscripts and typescripts for individual stories, as well as in his correspondence with magazine editors and agents.

In a sense Faulkner's short stories are a novelist's short stories. Many of them may be regarded as a concentration of material later developed in novels. This does not imply that the short-story form was not the right one for the material. Faulkner's material—the immense array of strange local characters, hunting stories, and tall tales, and the southern legacy about the lost cause, slavery, and aristocratic families from which he drew—often seemed to require the longer form. Yet some of Faulkner's novels seem to have started in a single image, a central episode, material fit for a short story: Lena Grove, barefoot and pregnant, getting around in the world; Caddy Compson in the tree; the idiot Snopes and the cow in the long summer days of Yoknapatawpha. Faulkner's desire to penetrate as deeply as possible to see why and how people react, his unrelenting scrutiny and unflagging search for understanding, forced him to link episode to episode to see whether new evidence could be found, new insights achieved. Thus stories might grow into novels, or related stories might be combined into unified works of greater length; but short stories could also remain self-contained and independent, even in cases where they gain support from other stories and novels in the larger framework of Faulkner's Yoknapatawpha fiction.

The need that Faulkner apparently felt for supplying background information and adding atmosphere to many of his stories accounts for the length of some of them. One of his methods for creating suspense is to pause in his narration to provide capsule stories that include important information. Faulkner writes about his country and his village, about the South, and about the people living there: the Indians who originally owned the land, the blacks who slave on it, and the poor whites who barely eke out a living, as well as the well-to-do businessmen and plantation owners. Race relations is one of his subjects; war is another; and sex may well be said to be a third, although it is interlinked with other themes. In accordance with Faulkner's statements about the writer's proper material, his short stories deal with love, compassion, pride, pity, and sacrifice. The historical dimension cannot be overlooked. Broadly speaking the stories take place in three major periods: the past, which includes the early days of the Indian tribes, the Civil War, and the undisturbed and apparently changeless rural parts of Yoknapatawpha; the recent past—World War I and the years immediately following it; and the immediate past—Yoknapatawpha and the world beyond it in the 1920s, 1930s, and 1940s.

Faulkner published his first short story, a brief prose sketch called "Landing in Luck," in the *Mississippian*, the university's student paper, on 26 November 1919; it was collected in *Early Prose and Poetry* (1962). Drawing on Faulkner's experience during aviation training in Toronto in 1918, the story is about a young cadet's first solo flight. It displays humor and technical skill and has some interest as the author's first sketch about flyers and flying.

The second prose sketch to be published, "The Hill" (*Mississippian*, 10 March 1922, in *Early Prose and Poetry*), has been hailed by critics as Faulkner's most important early short story. It shows an author in complete control of his material and foreshadows many narrative techniques and themes in Faulkner's later fiction. "The Hill" is an artful prose version of a poem Faulkner had written earlier. A nameless figure climbs a hill after a day of hard work and remains immobile there, till he slowly descends again. Mostly a detailed description of the view from the hilltop, the story gives a succinct picture of man in his struggles and in his dreams.

In the early 1920s Faulkner also wrote intricate and overworked stories. "Moonlight" (first published in *Uncollected Stories*, 1979) and "Love" (in *William Faulkner Manuscripts*, 1986-1987) were probably written before "The Hill." Another story from these early years is "Adolescence." This story about young love misinterpreted by an adult world foreshadows Faulkner's later use of local backgrounds and exploits themes he would return to some years later. "Adolescence" was first published in *Uncollected Stories*.

Those five stories are apparently the only ones Faulkner wrote before his sojourn in New Orleans in 1925, with the possible exception of "Nympholepsy" (*Mississippi Quarterly*, Summer 1973; in *Uncollected Stories*)—an expansion of "The Hill." The young hill climber's dreams are of a more sexual nature in this story than in the earlier version.

The most important formative year in Faulkner's development as an artist was 1925. In this year Faulkner made the transition from poet to fiction writer. The so-called New Orleans Sketches, written just prior to and during his stay in New Orleans during the first half of 1925, represent Faulkner's first concentrated performance in fiction.

The sketches, influenced by Anderson and Faulkner's close contact with literary bohemia in New Orleans at that time, gave Faulkner useful practical experience, particularly in the handling of narrative and the presentation of character. The sketches are uneven, and the hand of the apprentice is clearly seen. They do not follow any fixed formula, but Faulkner seems to be most interested in character. He presents his characters from varying points of view, either through a character-narrator or with distinct detachment. "New Orleans" (*Double Dealer*, January-February 1925; in *New Orleans Sketches*) is a composite of eleven subnarratives. Most of the sketches Faulkner published in 1925 appeared in the Sunday magazine section of the *New Orleans Times-Picayune*. For some of the sketches the *Times-Picayune* used a running head to indicate that this was a series: "Another 'Mirror of Chartres Street.'" Not all the New Orleans sketches were published in 1925. Completed sketches that survived in typescript—"Peter," "Don Giovanni," and "The Priest"—were not published till much later. ("The Priest" appeared in the *Mississippi Quarterly*, Summer 1976, and was collected in *Uncollected Stories*; the two other texts were first published in *Uncollected Stories*.)

Closely related to the New Orleans material is also an untitled short story, an expansion of one of the subnarratives in "New Orleans." This rather competent story was published with the title "Frankie and Johnny" (*Mississippi Quarterly*, Summer 1978; in *Uncollected Stories*). In 1926 Faulkner revised "New Orleans," creating a handmade booklet, which he called "Royal Street" and gave to Estelle Oldham Franklin, his future wife.

Few of the New Orleans sketches are extended narratives, although "The Liar" and "Yo

<u>Love</u>

Page from a manuscript draft for a story written circa 1921 but unpublished until it was included in volume 25 of William Faulkner Manuscripts *in 1987 (by permission of W. W. Norton and the Manuscripts Division, Special Collections Department, University of Virginia Library; accession number 6074)*

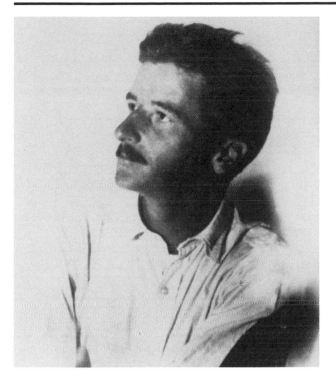

Faulkner in a 1924 publicity photograph for The Marble Faun *(Special Collections Department, University of Virginia Library)*

Ho and Two Bottles of Rum" may be considered short stories. The former is rooted in the back country of Yoknapatawpha; the latter has an international setting and cast of characters. Both texts point to two distinctly different types of stories that Faulkner would write in the near future.

Faulkner's experimentation in the New Orleans period seldom went further than an imitation of Joseph Conrad and Sherwood Anderson, but the variety of narrative methods anticipates the technical brilliance of *The Sound and the Fury*. Thematically these sketches may be said to emphasize the individual's alienation from a natural world but also his search for communal ties, participation, and sharing.

After Faulkner published *Soldiers' Pay*, he wrote several short stories in 1926 and 1927. Most of the stories from these years were later revised and appeared in print only after 1930. One story that found its final form in 1926 was *Mayday*, an allegorical tale about Sir Galwyn, who travels through life accompanied by the shadowy figures of Hunger and Pain and who finally finds peace in death by water. The hand-lettered, illustrated, and beautifully bound booklet that Faulkner made for Helen Baird in 1926 was not meant for publication, however, and was not published until 1976, when the University of Notre

Dame Press brought out a facsimile edition. *The Wishing Tree* (1967) is of a similar kind: Faulkner typed the story himself, binding at least one copy by hand as a present for one of Estelle Franklin's children in February 1927. Faulkner's only story for children, it employs the conventional framework of a fairy tale and gives comical treatment to numerous themes that occur in much of Faulkner's later writing. *Mayday* and *The Wishing Tree* were important steps toward Faulkner's conception of *The Sound and the Fury*. The unfinished "And Now What's To Do" (*Mississippi Quarterly*, Summer 1973) uses autobiographical elements to a degree not found in Faulkner's writing till a quarter of a century later, when he wrote "Mississippi" (*Holiday*, April 1954; in *Essays, Speeches & Public Letters*, 1966). For fun he also wrote a brief and humorous sketch, "Music—Sweeter Than the Angels Sing" (*Southern Review*, October 1976), while his long struggle with a novel called *Elmer* (published in fragmentary form in 1983), resulted in the short story "A Portrait of Elmer" (*Georgia Review*, Fall 1979; in *Uncollected Stories*). This complicated story about the artist as a young man was never successfully completed and is unrepresentative of Faulkner's capacity at the time he wrote it. "Two Dollar Wife" (*College Life*, January 1936; in *Uncollected Stories*) may be the same story as "The Devil Beats His Wife," written in 1926 and later revised as "Christmas Tree," which finally became "Two Dollar Wife," one of the worst stories Faulkner ever wrote. A much better and more ambitious story written in this period is *Father Abraham* (1984), the germ of the Snopes trilogy and Faulkner's first attempt with material that he would return to over and over again in the years ahead, till, in 1940, he brought the many loose ends together in *The Hamlet*.

Europe of the post-World War I years and Faulkner's own "lost generation" sentiments may have combined to strengthen his feeling of despair and certainly added colors and contours to his bleak picture of the world as a wasteland in many of the stories that he began in 1926 and 1927. These stories demonstrate the outrage of a potential believer; the criticism of a stale and stifling social life is harsh. Faulkner's narrators lament the loss of traditional values and criticize the materialistic, ephemeral values that replace them. Novel writing took most of his time in the late 1920s, but when he had finished typing *The Sound and the Fury* (in October 1928), he began his first serious effort to write and market short stories. His short-story activity reached a peak in the early 1930s. The record of his endeavors is a short-story sending schedule that Faulkner kept, as well as his correspondence with editors and agents. Within a four-year period, beginning in 1928 and ending in 1932, the months between January 1930 (when he finished *As I Lay Dying*) and August 1931 (when he began *Light in August*) were the most productive. On 20 January 1930 he recorded his first sale of a short story to a national magazine: *Forum* had bought "A Rose for Emily" (April 1930; in *These 13*), offering him encouragement to continue his short-story writing for the profitable American slick-magazine market of the 1930s. From the time of the acceptance of "A Rose for Emily" till he began work on *Light in August*, Faulkner submitted more than twenty different stories to various magazines. Altogether he made more than seventy submissions and resubmissions during this period. This productivity and the acceptances of stories by the better-paying magazines enabled Faulkner to buy Rowan Oak in April 1930; the family moved there in June. This transaction led to a chronic shortage of money, and in May 1932 Faulkner had to leave for Hollywood, to find a steady income. His short-story writing then came to a sudden halt, and only for brief intervals later in his career would he concentrate on short-story writing, never with more than moderate success. At home his first daughter, Alabama, had died a few days after her birth in 1931, and Jill was born in 1933.

The more than forty short stories that Faulkner wrote in the late 1920s and early 1930s are his most autonomous and "pure" short stories. With a few exceptions they do not stand in any close relationship to his novels, and only a few were reused in novels. Ten of these stories, published in the early 1930s or not published at all in Faulkner's lifetime, are known to have existed before 1930: "Ad Astra," from 1927; "Mistral," "Pennsylvania Station," "The Leg," "'Once Aboard the Lugger—'" (2 parts), "Spotted Horses," and *Miss Zilphia Gant* from 1928; and "Elly," "There Was a Queen," and "A Rose for Emily" from 1929. Some of the stories had different titles in their original versions, and some were so much revised as to become virtually new stories before they were published. Twenty-one new stories seem to have been written in 1930, including the separately published *Idyll in the Desert*. In 1931 five new stories were sent out. In addition, Faulkner used three short stories that he ap-

parently never submitted to magazines in *These 13*: "Victory," "Crevasse," and "Carcassonne." Only two stories can be dated to 1932: "Turn About" and, possibly, "With Caution and Dispatch."

During the spring of 1931 Faulkner put together his first short-story collection. He then had some forty stories from which to choose. One can only guess his motives for selecting the thirteen stories he included in the book, but the resulting volume presents a rather coherent and convincing picture of the world as wasteland filled with dust and dreams, hopes and frustrations, nonlife and death.

These 13 has three main sections. The first one includes four World War I stories: "Victory," "Ad Astra," "All the Dead Pilots," and "Crevasse." In section 2, six stories about Yoknapatawpha are grouped together: "Red Leaves," "A Rose for Emily," "A Justice," "Hair," "That Evening Sun," and "Dry September." The final section includes three stories: "Mistral," "Divorce in Naples," and "Carcassonne," all dealing with Americans abroad and with experiences far removed from Yoknapatawpha in all respects. Faulkner took great care in structuring this collection to achieve unity, moving toward one end, one finale.

"Victory" opens the collection. With its wide scope and long time span, it deals with World War I and its aftermath. A God-fearing young Scot, Alec Gray, is one of the many losers in the years of unemployment after the war. He has risen to the officer class through bravery, but his downfall after the war is as rapid as his rise. The generalizations in the other World War I stories, about the sad and undeserved fate of the soldiers who served their countries, are made concrete in the description of Gray's destiny. "Victory" is in some respects Faulkner's most successful World War I story, not the least because it is a long story and shows a development over time. "Ad Astra" (*American Caravan*, 1931), on the other hand, gives a concentrated, almost painful, image of loss and decay, and of the futility and waste of war. Soldiers drink, talk, quarrel, and fight on the night of Armistice Day in 1918, and an Indian subahdar voices the opinion that those who survive the war are also dead. Those who died in battle may in fact be better off. Rather vague "lost generation" sentiments slip into this story, as they also do in the companion piece, "All the Dead Pilots" (previously unpublished). A frame narrator looks back upon the war and describes

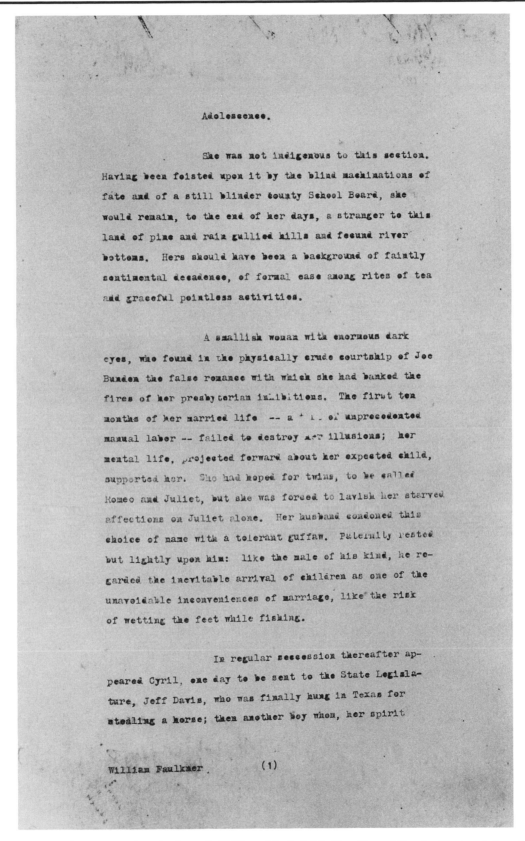

Adolescence.

She was not indigenous to this section.
Having been foisted upon it by the blind machinations of
fate and of a still blinder county School Board, she
would remain, to the end of her days, a stranger to this
land of pine and rain gullied hills and fecund river
bottoms. Hers should have been a background of faintly
sentimental decadence, of formal ease among rites of tea
and graceful pointless activities.

A smallish woman with enormous dark
eyes, who found in the physically crude courtship of Joe
Bunden the false romance with which she had banked the
fires of her presbyterian inhibitions. The first ten
months of her married life -- a t.l. of unprecedented
manual labor -- failed to destroy her illusions; her
mental life, projected forward about her expected child,
supported her. She had hoped for twins, to be called
Romeo and Juliet, but she was forced to lavish her starved
affections on Juliet alone. Her husband condoned this
choice of name with a tolerant guffaw. Paternity rested
but lightly upon him: like the male of his kind, he regarded the inevitable arrival of children as one of the
unavoidable inconveniences of marriage, like the risk
of wetting the feet while fishing.

In regular secession thereafter ap-
peared Cyril, one day to be sent to the State Legislature, Jeff Davis, who was finally hung in Texas for
stealing a horse; then another boy whom, her spirit

William Faulkner.   (1)

Page from the typescript for a story written in the early 1920s and included in Uncollected Stories *(by permission of W. W. Norton and the Manuscripts Division, Special Collections Department, University of Virginia Library; accession number 6074)*

the plights of the pilots who have had to live on after their short time of bravery and vitality. They are all "dead" now, because they survived the war and adjusted to a quiet, bourgeois life. The dreams of bravery and glory could only be realized by dying a hero's death. How heroic life on the battlefield might really be is then shown in "Crevasse" (originally a part of "Victory"), in which a small infantry patrol marching over a dead-looking and ominous landscape suddenly disappears when the earth begins to move. Trapped soldiers dig desperately to find a way out. War is here shown as demoralizing and brutalizing. "Crevasse" demonstrates what kind of reality the soldiers' dreams had to be tested against. Even though humor may be found in these war stories, the ultimate impression is one of darkness and despair.

"Red Leaves" (*Saturday Evening Post*, 25 October 1930), a story about the Indians of Yoknapatawpha County and one of Faulkner's three or four best stories, is placed first in section 2 of *These 13*. This story is structured around a burial ritual, which holds that the body servant of the dead Indian chief must die because tradition requires it. The black servant runs away, however, and must be hunted down before the corpse of the chief starts decomposing. The narrative focus shifts between the pursuing Indians and the desperately fleeing servant, who is eventually captured. Poetical in its symbolic richness and terrifying in its realistic descriptions, "Red Leaves" is also a story about the existential dilemma, a story about life and death. Images mingle and contrast throughout the story to give a final impression of man's ability to reconcile with his fate.

"A Rose for Emily," Faulkner's most widely read, criticized, and anthologized short story, begins with the announcement of the death of Miss Emily Grierson, who has lived so long she has become an anachronism. A "we" narrator recounts Emily's life—a life of loneliness and poverty because her father drove away her suitors and little was left for her when he died. Her one boyfriend, a northerner whom the town thought she would marry, disappeared suddenly, and a sealed upstairs room in Emily's house does not give away its terrible secret till Emily is buried. This Gothic story cleverly indicates that somehow Emily's gruesome acts are inevitable. She has grown out of touch with reality; she is unwilling to adjust to a world that has almost completely changed in her lifetime. Faulkner shows that Emily's solution—to destroy, not to be betrayed;

Faulkner in Paris, where he lived and wrote from August to December 1925

to conceal, not to be discovered; to withdraw to be alone with her memories—is not workable. Isolation helps her survive, but it drains her of vitality. Critics have found in "A Rose for Emily" a description of a whole society that lived with a dead but unburied past, and much energy has been expended in attempts to establish the chronology of events in the story. "A Rose for Emily" is not Faulkner's best story, but it may well be regarded as the central one in his short-story career.

Quentin Compson is the unreliable narrator of the second Indian story in *These 13*, "A Justice" (previously unpublished). An innocent child, he does not grasp what his story is really about. The story is amusing, but the Indians in "A Justice" are incapable of adjusting to new situations. In this story, which shows a development over a long period, important links between time past and time present in Yoknapatawpha are established.

"A Justice" is followed by "Hair" (*American Mercury*, May 1931), the weakest story in the collection. It is a story of stubborn patience, loyalty, and endurance beyond the grasp of the townspeople, told by a fallible narrator. Quentin takes over the narration again in the next story, "That Evening Sun" (*American Mercury*, March 1931), and the tragedy inherent in the story is seldom surpassed in Faulkner's short fiction. His accomplishment was perhaps equaled later, but hardly surpassed, in such small-scale masterpieces as "Barn Burning" (*Harper's*, June 1939; in *Collected Stories*), "Uncle Willy" (*American Mercury*, October 1935; in *Collected Stories*), and one or two of the short stories later revised for inclusion in *Go Down, Moses* (1942). One of the most inexhaustible of Faulkner's short stories, and a favorite among critics, "That Evening Sun" tells about the black servant Nancy and her irrational fear of being killed by her husband, Jesus. The white Compson household is juxtaposed with Nancy and her world, and Quentin tells the story some fifteen years after the events took place. By implication "That Evening Sun" becomes a story about the general human plight: despair, guilt, and lack of love. The uses of local history and racial injustice are combined with individual frustration and fear in a story with broad significance.

"Dry September" (*Scribner's*, January 1931), another of Faulkner's best stories, has been called classical in its tragic intensity and described as a ritualistic acting out of the scapegoat pattern to achieve redemption. The story is a superb example of how the description of landscape and climate can be used to set and to amplify tone. After many rainless days the men in town are restless, and Minnie Cooper, barren and dry in her empty life, initiates the action when she accuses a black man of rape. The brutal story of evil and injustice develops rapidly; the violent, tragic events have been interpreted differently by the many critics who have taken an active interest in this story. "Dry September" concludes the middle part of *These 13* on a note of stillness, death, and hostility.

The final group of stories is enigmatic. The three stories (all previously unpublished) are experimental departures from the rest of the volume. "Mistral" may be overwritten and too long, but its intricate presentation of passion and murder through the outsider experience of two young men who happen to travel by foreshadows narrative techniques Faulkner used later. "Divorce in Naples" tells about a homosexual "marriage" and divorce, and is in some respects more genuinely Faulknerian than "Mistral." The grim

but understanding humor, and the rich use of similes and metaphors in pure, lyrical passages leave Faulkner's stamp on this story. "Carcassonne" is one of the most abstract of Faulkner's stories. Its protagonist endures all his suffering because he has a dream of performing something, of negating death's ultimate effect, which is to make one lie still. "Carcassonne" also reflects Faulkner's own artistic beliefs in the sense that it shows the agony and fear an artist has to face in order to create.

Faulkner's first short-story collection received more laudatory reviews than any of his novels before 1931, although many critics complained that the volume was uneven. *These 13* still holds an important position in Faulkner's long career, although his major short-story collection, *Collected Stories*, may be said to have reduced the importance of this early volume of stories, since the stories reappear in a new context there.

Idyll in the Desert was published as a book in 1931, and in 1932 the Book Club of Texas published *Miss Zilphia Gant* (both collected in *Uncollected Stories*). *Miss Zilphia Gant* deals with overprotection and rebellion and is not too different from many other stories from this period in which females are shown as frustrated and deprived. *Idyll in the Desert* shows Faulkner's mastery of oral storytelling techniques and gives one version of his theme of endurance and love lasting beyond death.

Faulkner continued publishing numerous stories after 1932, although his writing of new stories declined drastically. By the time of *Doctor Martino and Other Stories* (1934) he had more stories than he needed for the book. Whereas *These 13* includes seven previously unpublished stories, *Doctor Martino* only includes two: "Black Music" and "The Leg." There seems to be no internal organization of the volume, and the stories do not form any discernible pattern.

There is a clear shift from the preoccupation with war, wilderness, and townspeople in *These 13* to a focus on sex, death, and loss in *Doctor Martino*. The title story (*Harper's*, November 1931) presents a love triangle of a peculiar kind, and usurpation and manipulation for private ends create an emotional parasitism. (This story reappears in the "Middle Ground" section of *Collected Stories*, a deliberately structured volume, together with five other stories from *Doctor Martino*: "Wash," "Honor," "Fox Hunt," "There Was a Queen," and "A Mountain Victory.") Although all the stories in *Doctor Martino* are compe-

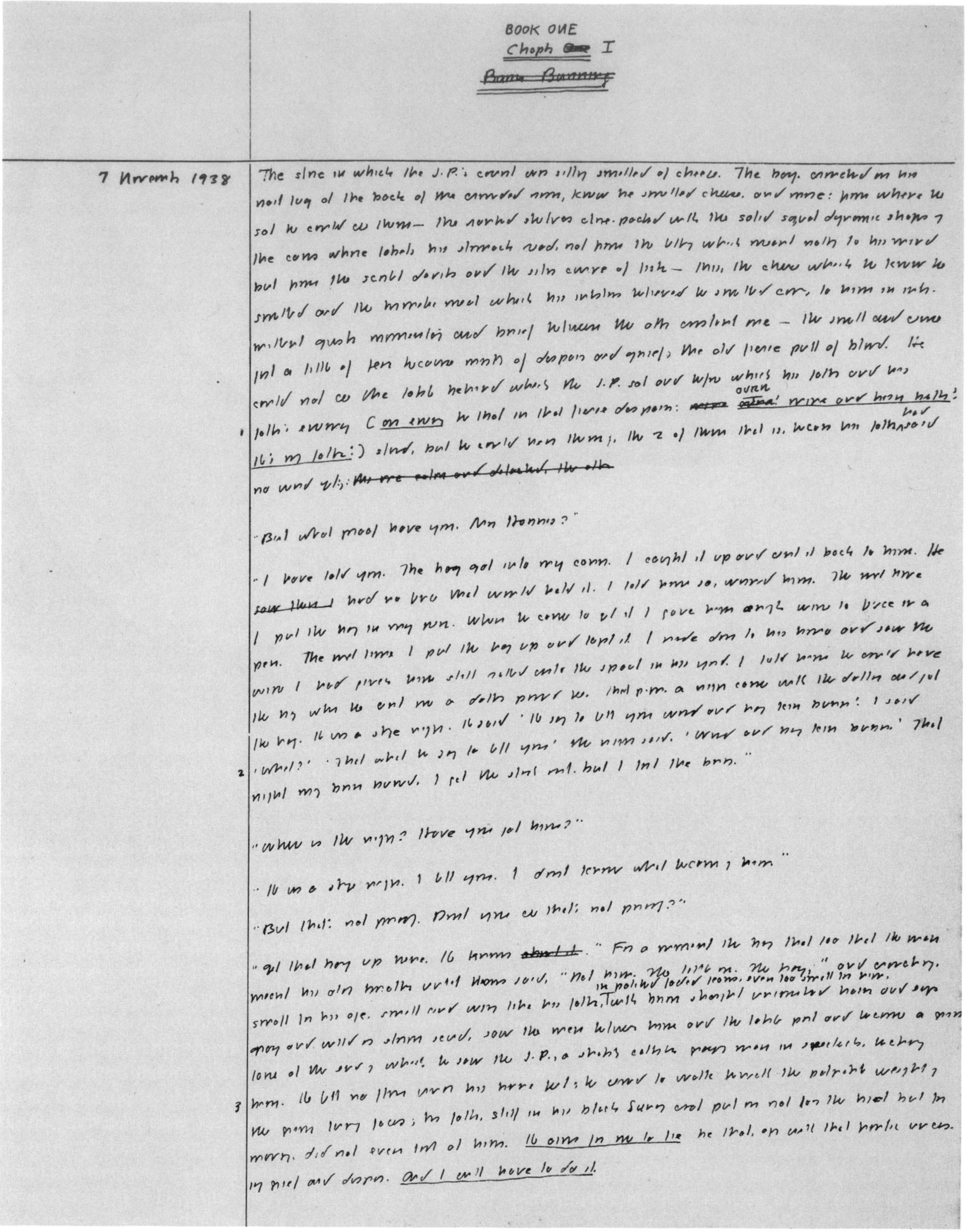
BOOK ONE

~~Chapter One~~ I

~~Barn Burning~~

7 November 1938

The store in which the J.P.'s court was sitting smelled of cheese.

Page from the manuscript for "Barn Burning," a story originally intended for the beginning of The Hamlet *(1940), Faulkner's first novel about the Snopes family (by permission of W. W. Norton and the Manuscripts Division, Special Collections Department, University of Virginia Library; accession number 6074)* tent, only "Wash" and "A Mountain Victory" show Faulkner at his best. "Wash" (*Harper's*, February 1934) is a taut and forceful narrative of almost apocalyptic horror, reused by Faulkner in *Absalom, Absalom!* (1936). "A Mountain Victory" (*Saturday Evening Post*, 3 December 1932), like "Wash," is set in the years after the Civil War. Here one sees the tragic development of a conflict, arising suddenly and inevitably from what should have been a normal encounter between strangers. The movement toward disaster is implacable, and brutal death comes at the end. A deeply felt humanity pervades this story, which should not be considered just another tale about the Civil War and its effects on people. The story clearly transcends this level of interpretation.

"Death Drag" (*Scribner's*, January 1932) and "Elly" (*Story*, February 1934) are the only two stories in *Doctor Martino* that are set in "the village." The young female title character in "Elly" resembles Miss Emily in her reaction against overprotection and conformity. "Death Drag" deals with stunt flying and wing walking, although the way people live and behave in the years after World War I is at the center of this story, as it is in "Honor" (*American Mercury*, July 1930). "Honor" is another of Faulkner's stories about a strange love triangle with a tragic outcome. "Turn About" (*Saturday Evening Post*, 5 March 1932) is the only full-fledged World War I story in the collection. It differs from earlier such stories in its being set in England and in its depiction of an unusual brand of courage. "The Hound" (*Harper's*, August 1931)—one of the strongest stories in the volume—was reused in the Mink Snopes section of *The Hamlet*, although it was not originally a Snopes story. "Smoke" (*Harper's*, April 1932) is Faulkner's first story of detection, but it is decidedly one of the weakest of his whodunits. It opens his 1949 collection of detective stories, *Knight's Gambit*.

The final three stories in *Doctor Martino* are all strange, so-called "Beyond" stories: tales of the supernatural or the fantastic. The story titled "Beyond" (*Harper's*, September 1933) was the only one of these that found periodical publication; "Black Music" and "The Leg" (called simply "Leg" in *Doctor Martino*) are the other two.

Doctor Martino elicited fewer reviews than *These 13*, and they were not quite in the same vein. The decline in quality of the individual stories and of the collection as a whole was too heavily stressed by most critics. Yet most Faulkner schol-

ars do consider *Doctor Martino* inferior to *These 13*.

In addition to the stories Faulkner either collected in his first two short-story collections or published as separate books, there are many stories that have other functions in his canon. "Spotted Horses" (*Scribner's*, June 1931) and "Lizards in Jamshyd's Courtyard" (*Saturday Evening Post*, 27 February 1932) were later reused in *The Hamlet*. Both are short stories in their own right, and together with "The Hound" and "Fool About a Horse" (*Scribner's*, August 1936), these "Snopes stories" are collected in *Uncollected Stories*. "Centaur in Brass" (*American Mercury*, February 1932) was reused in *The Town* (1957) but had by then already been collected in *Collected Stories*. Three more autonomous stories, all of which might easily have been included in one of the two early collections, remained uncollected till 1950, when they were included in the "Middle Ground" section of *Collected Stories*: "Artist at Home" (*Story*, August 1933), "The Brooch" (*Scribner's*, January 1936), and "Pennsylvania Station" (*American Mercury*, February 1934). Some stories from these years had their first book appearance in *Uncollected Stories*. They include "Thrift" (*Saturday Evening Post*, 6 September 1930)—a humorous World War I story about a proverbial Scotsman who makes a profit from his participation in somebody else's war, the first Faulkner story in the *Post* and hence a first encounter with this writer for thousands of readers—and " 'Once Aboard the Lugger' " (Part I, *Contempo*, February 1932), a story from the "prohibition industry," the second part of which first appeared in *Uncollected Stories*. Most of the previously unpublished stories from the early 1930s are included in *Uncollected Stories*. Finally, "Evangeline" (*Atlantic*, November 1979; in *Uncollected Stories*) deserves mention. "Evangeline" is a long story, closely related to the Sutpen family's life and mores, and it was absorbed into *Absalom, Absalom!*

With a few exceptions Faulkner's best short stories, and many of his good stories, were written in the early 1930s. More than before or after, they are short stories in their own right: conceived, executed, and published as such. Only in a few instances can they be seen as by-products of Faulkner's novels. The richness and diversity of themes and techniques were never to be surpassed in the years to come. Nevertheless, Faulkner continued to write short stories from time to time, and his apparent wish to write some series

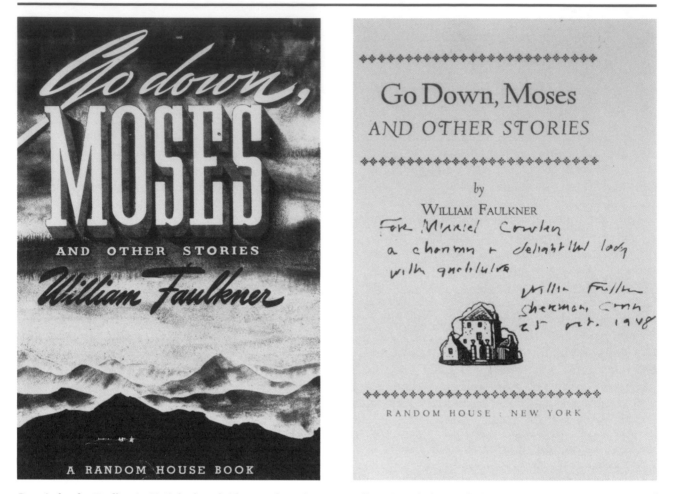

Dust jacket for Faulkner's 1942 book and title page from the copy Faulkner inscribed to Malcolm Cowley's wife, Muriel (auctioned by Sotheby Parke Bernet Inc., sale number 4035, 25 October 1977)

of stories led to the creation of many short stories in the late 1930s and early 1940s—some of them almost formulaic, others serious and of high literary merit.

Still, Faulkner's output of short fiction declined sharply after 1932, when financial problems forced him to go to Hollywood and write for the screen. Hollywood left him better off financially, and after 1933 he turned his attention almost exclusively to novel writing. Also, the Snopeses were beginning to occupy the author's mind, resulting in an occasional short story before he finally joined together material he had worked on for more than ten years in the episodic novel *The Hamlet*. In 1942 Faulkner made a short but concentrated attempt at short-story writing, with only moderate success, and near the end of that decade he started planning for publication of his collected stories, which finally resulted in two very different volumes: *Knight's Gambit* and *Collected Stories*.

The stories Faulkner wrote from 1933 until his last attempt to write short stories for a living in 1942 fall, roughly, into four major categories. Miscellaneous stories, some reused in novels, others collected in *Collected Stories*, make up the first group. The second category comprises the stories that were later considerably revised and used in *The Unvanquished* (1938). The stories for *Go Down, Moses* form a third group, and finally there are the detective stories collected in *Knight's Gambit*. In the first group, "Lo!" (*Story*, November 1934; in *Collected Stories*) was written in 1933 and is Faulkner's third Indian story, a wildly exaggerated and extremely funny tale about an Indian chief's visit to Washington. "Wash" (in *Collected Stories*) was also written in 1933, and so was "A Bear Hunt" (*Saturday Evening Post*, 10 February 1934; in *Collected Stories*). The latter is a story in the humorous vein and in the tradition of oral tales, relying on elements of superstition, exaggeration, and comic effects. "Mule in the Yard" (*Scrib-*

When me and Uncle Buck come back to the house from
finding out Tomey's Turl had run away again, the fox and the
dogs come out of the kitchen and crossed the dogtrot and went
into the dogs' room and we could hear them running out of the
dog room into Uncle Buck's room and then we seen them cross
the dogtrot again and go into Uncle Buddy's room and then we
heard them running out of Uncle Buddy's room into the kitchen
again and this time it sounded like the whole chimbley had done
got knocked down and Uncle Buddy hollering and cussing loud as
as a steamboat ^blowing and this time the fox and the dogs and three or
four sticks of firewood all come out of the kitchen together
with Uncle Buddy in the middle of them hitting at everything
in sight with another stick. It was a good race.

So me and Uncle Buck went into his room where the
fox had bayed on the mantel-shelf ^behind the clock, and Uncle Buck kicked the
dogs off anf lifted the fox down by the scruff of his neck
and put him back into his box under the bed, and we went into
the kitchen where Uncle Buddy was picking the breakfast up out
of the ashes, and told him that Tomey's Turl had done run away
again.

"Od dammit, Theophilus," Uncle Buddy said. "What
in tarnation hell did you mean by turning that dam fox out
with the dogs all loose in the house?"

"Never you mind about that," Uncle Buck said. "Get
me and Bayard some breakfast. We got to get started. He's riding Old Jake. We might just barely ketch him before he reaches
Prim's.@

Because we all knew where Tomey's Turl had went.

1.

First page of the typescript for "Was," one of the stories in Go Down, Moses *(by permission of W. W. Norton and the Manu-*
scripts Division, Special Collections Department, University of Virginia Library; accession number 6074)

ner's, August 1934; in *Collected Stories* and reused in *The Town*) is a Snopes story, hilarious and well worth its inclusion in the major short-story collection, despite its place in *The Town*. His work on the Snopes material also yielded "Barn Burning" (*Harper's*, June 1939; in *Collected Stories*). Many critics and readers hold this to be Faulkner's best short story. It was originally written as the opening chapter of *The Hamlet*, then excised from the typescript; only scattered minor fragments of the story can be found in the book. "Barn Burning" draws its interest, quality, and aura of deep personal suffering from its relationship with *The Hamlet*, which is a marvelous novel about the infestation of Yoknapatawpha by the Snopeses and about how myths are created. "Barn Burning" is a superb story in its own right; yet Faulkner was capable of fusing so many elements in this story because of his lasting interest in the Snopeses and because of the longer work in progress. The novel *Pylon* grew out of an unpublished, uncollected story, "This Kind of Courage," written in 1934 and revised when Faulkner began to expand it for the novel.

In 1934 Faulkner also wrote the first six stories in *The Unvanquished* series, and in December 1935 the first germ of *Go Down, Moses* was seen in the short story "Lion" (*Harper's*; in *Uncollected Stories*). In his second story of ratiocination, "Monk" (*Scribner's*, May 1937; in *Knight's Gambit*), Faulkner used the backwoods of Yoknapatawpha and his detective-lawyer Gavin Stevens. In 1939, 1940, and 1941 Faulkner wrote most of the short stories he later revised for use in *Go Down, Moses*, and he also wrote three more detective stories. During some hectic months from spring to autumn 1934 the first six "Bayard-Ringo" stories were written: "Ambuscade," "Retreat," "Raid," "The Unvanquished" (later titled "Riposte in Tertio"), "Vendée," and "Skirmish at Sartoris" (the "Drusilla" story). The first three stories were published in 1934, "Skirmish at Sartoris" in 1935, and the last two stories late in 1936. A seventh story, "An Odor of Verbena," was written in order to complete and finish the book, but Faulkner also made unsuccessful attempts to sell it as a short story. For *The Unvanquished*, Faulkner had to revise the stories, some of them substantially. He considered his Civil War stories, including these, "trash," and in a letter to Morton Goldman (August 1934) he stated that "As far as I am concerned, while I have to write trash, I don't care who buys it, as long as they pay the best price I can get." He felt that he sacrificed

more important work by writing his romanticized tales about heroic Southern action during the Civil War, but when he undertook the work of revising and transforming the stories into a unified book, more of his genuine concerns were included. The original magazine stories are now all available in *Uncollected Stories*, with the exception of "An Odor of Verbena," of which only the version printed in *The Unvanquished* exists. In his revision work Faulkner carefully brought the thematic content of the earliest stories in line with the serious direction of the later stories, adding a more mature narrator who could give a more clearly retrospective view of the incidents and cruelties of war. The issue of race became more significant, and Faulkner proved that he could make a unified and serious novel out of short fiction he had described as trash. *The Unvanquished* has a central position in Faulkner's career and in Faulkner scholarship, while the stories leading up to it are less important. *The Unvanquished* is certainly not a mere collection of short stories.

Like Faulkner's first six Civil War stories, the stories for *Go Down, Moses* were all written over a relatively short span of time, with almost no other short-story activity intervening. One may thus say that this continuous process resembles the writing of a novel, and it is commonplace today that *Go Down, Moses* is a novel and not a collection, although, by some editorial mistake, it was originally published as *Go Down, Moses and Other Stories*. Of course, the chapters of the book were written as short stories and, when accepted by magazines, published as short stories. "Lion" was greatly expanded and revised for chapter 5 of *Go Down, Moses*, the well-known long story "The Bear" (a version of which appeared in the *Saturday Evening Post*, 9 May 1942). "The Old People" was written in 1939, while "A Point of Law," "Gold Is Not Always," "The Fire on the Hearth," "Pantaloon in Black," "Was," "Go Down, Moses," and "Delta Autumn" were all composed in 1940. With the exception of "The Fire on the Hearth" and "Was" (of which only the version used in the book exists), *Uncollected Stories* includes all the original short-story material for *Go Down, Moses*. The *Post* version of "The Bear" is also included there.

Go Down, Moses is one of Faulkner's most convincing artistic creations, a unified volume with tremendous emotional impact far greater than that of any of the individual stories, though it is possible to discuss them independently. "Was" is the opening section of *Go Down, Moses*, while

Faulkner carving the Christmas turkey in 1948 at Rowan Oak, the house in Oxford, Mississippi, that he bought in 1930

three other stories form the second section, called "The Fire and the Hearth." Here a revised version of "A Point of Law" is used as the first chapter, while, extensively revised, "Gold Is Not Always" is incorporated as chapter 2 of section 2. The previously unpublished "The Fire on the Hearth" concludes this section, which, taken together, may be regarded as one of Faulkner's finest long stories. Centering on the scheming and cheating Lucas Beauchamp, it is a light, comic collection of anecdotes, including those about moonshining and "planted" gold coins. Lucas and his wife, Molly, appear as stereotyped blacks, but with "The Fire on the Hearth," people as well as tone are modified and softened. The central symbol of the fire burning on the hearth is strengthened, and Faulkner barely avoids melancholy and pathos in the descriptions of the old woman's plight. Molly becomes an embodiment of all the virtues cherished in her society.

"Pantaloon in Black" (*Harper's*, October 1940) is the story of a giant black man whose wife dies. He buries her and then goes on to do everything possible in an attempt to provoke his own lynching. His delicate feelings are contrasted

with the rude understanding that white characters show. In *Go Down, Moses* "Pantaloon in Black" intervenes between what may be regarded as the two main parts of the book: the story of Beauchamp and the story of Isaac McCaslin in "The Old People," "The Bear," and "Delta Autumn."

Isaac (Ike) becomes the central character in these stories little by little, whereas Quentin Compson was the central character in the early version of "The Old People" (*Harper's*, September 1940). The ritualistic hunt in that story points forward to "The Bear," and "The Old People" provides links with the past of Yoknapatawpha and with other stories, to an unusual degree. The revised story gives much space to the formative years in Ike's development, to explain where he got his knowledge of "the old people" and his deep respect for the untamed wilderness. Sam Fathers, an Indian of mixed ancestry, has been Ike's substitute father and mentor. Ike's renunciation of his inheritance later in life and most of his subsequent behavior may be considered acts of sacrifice and expiation, but they may also be viewed as acts of weakness and escape.

Most of the elements it takes to compound the believable fictional character Isaac McCaslin are found in "The Bear." The book version is often anthologized, frequently without the long fourth part (a practice begun by Malcolm Cowley in his *Portable Faulkner*, 1946). "The Bear" is one of the great hunting stories in world literature and one of the truly great stories in Faulkner's career.

Ike's three-part saga ends with "Delta Autumn" (*Story*, May-June 1942), set in the wilderness that is slowly being destroyed by civilization. "Delta Autumn" is a moving and penetrating story. Human beings in conflict with nature and with themselves are presented in a web of ideas and thoughts about race, history, morality, and love. The story provides the last view of Ike McCaslin, "uncle to half a county and father to no one."

The story "Go Down, Moses" (*Collier's*, January 1941) tells about Molly Beauchamp's struggle to get her dead grandson back home to be buried where he belongs. It opens onto a larger world beyond the plantation, beyond Yoknapatawpha, and is thus a fitting conclusion to *Go Down, Moses* as a novel.

In "Smoke," written circa 1930, Faulkner created Gavin Stevens, a detective with resources that could be put to use in the investigation of mysteries within the borders of Yoknapatawpha County. The second whodunit, "Monk," was not written till 1937. Stonewall Jackson "Monk" Odlethrop lives in an isolated area of the county, an area populated by clannish people who "made whiskey and shot at all strangers from behind log barns and snake fences." Monk is also mentally isolated. To a large degree the story is really his, and Gavin is only in the background, uncovering the truth about the deception of Monk by a fellow convict in prison. Gavin functions much more prominently as a detective in "Hand Upon the Waters" (*Saturday Evening Post*, 4 November 1939), perhaps because he shares so much with the story's central character, Louis Grenier Lonnie Grinnup. Gavin and Lonnie are the only surviving offspring from the three original founding fathers of the county. Still, the ratiocinative work, the solving of the murder of Grinnup, is more important here than the crime and its ramifications. Young Chick Mallison works with his Uncle Gavin in solving some crimes, and in "Tomorrow" (*Saturday Evening Post*, 23 November 1940) the ingenious detection work leads to insights into human nature so that Chick is taught

a moral lesson. "An Error in Chemistry," written in 1940, is the only story in *Knight's Gambit* that was originally published where it, so to speak, rightfully belonged, in a magazine devoted to the mystery genre. It appeared in the June 1946 issue of *Ellery Queen's Mystery Magazine*, having won second prize in a competition. The story is pure detection, but the detective work is so simple that even the boy narrator, Chick, draws the inevitable conclusion and finds out who the killer is. The last of Faulkner's detective stories, "Knight's Gambit," was written in 1942. Unable to sell the story, Faulkner expanded it into a novella with the same title, to make his collection of detective fiction large enough for publication in book form in 1949. The short, early version has never been published.

Knight's Gambit is closer in form to *The Unvanquished* and *Go Down, Moses* than to ordinary short-story collections, because it has a central figure and central themes: detection, justice, and the relation between outsiders and the community. Still, *Knight's Gambit* is less of a unified work; Faulkner simply collected his detective stories in the chronology of their periodical publication. The volume received little critical attention, although critics treated it with modest respect. *Knight's Gambit* still has a minor, perhaps even too-small, place in Faulkner's total oeuvre.

The short version of "Knight's Gambit" was the first work in Faulkner's 1942 outburst of short-story activity. He hoped to earn enough money on the sales of these stories to stay home from Hollywood. With the exception of "Knight's Gambit" and "Snow" (first published in *Uncollected Stories*), all the stories from this time are in *Collected Stories*. In "Two Soldiers" (*Saturday Evening Post*, 28 March 1942) a nine-year-old boy narrates a patriotic story about loyalty and endurance. In "Shall Not Perish" (*Story*, July-August 1943), a sequel to "Two Soldiers," the young narrator tells about receiving a message concerning his brother Pete's death and about the family's reaction. Another soldier, the son of wealthy parents, has also been killed in the war, and in the course of the narrative the boy slowly seems to grasp that he is part of a larger community and that if you love your country you may also die for it. "Shall Not Perish" is one of Faulkner's most emotional stories, but the personal grief and tragedy gain deeper significance, so that the story appears less sentimental than its companion piece, "Two Soldiers." Yet it is almost a relief when, in "Shingles for the Lord" (*Saturday Evening Post*, 13

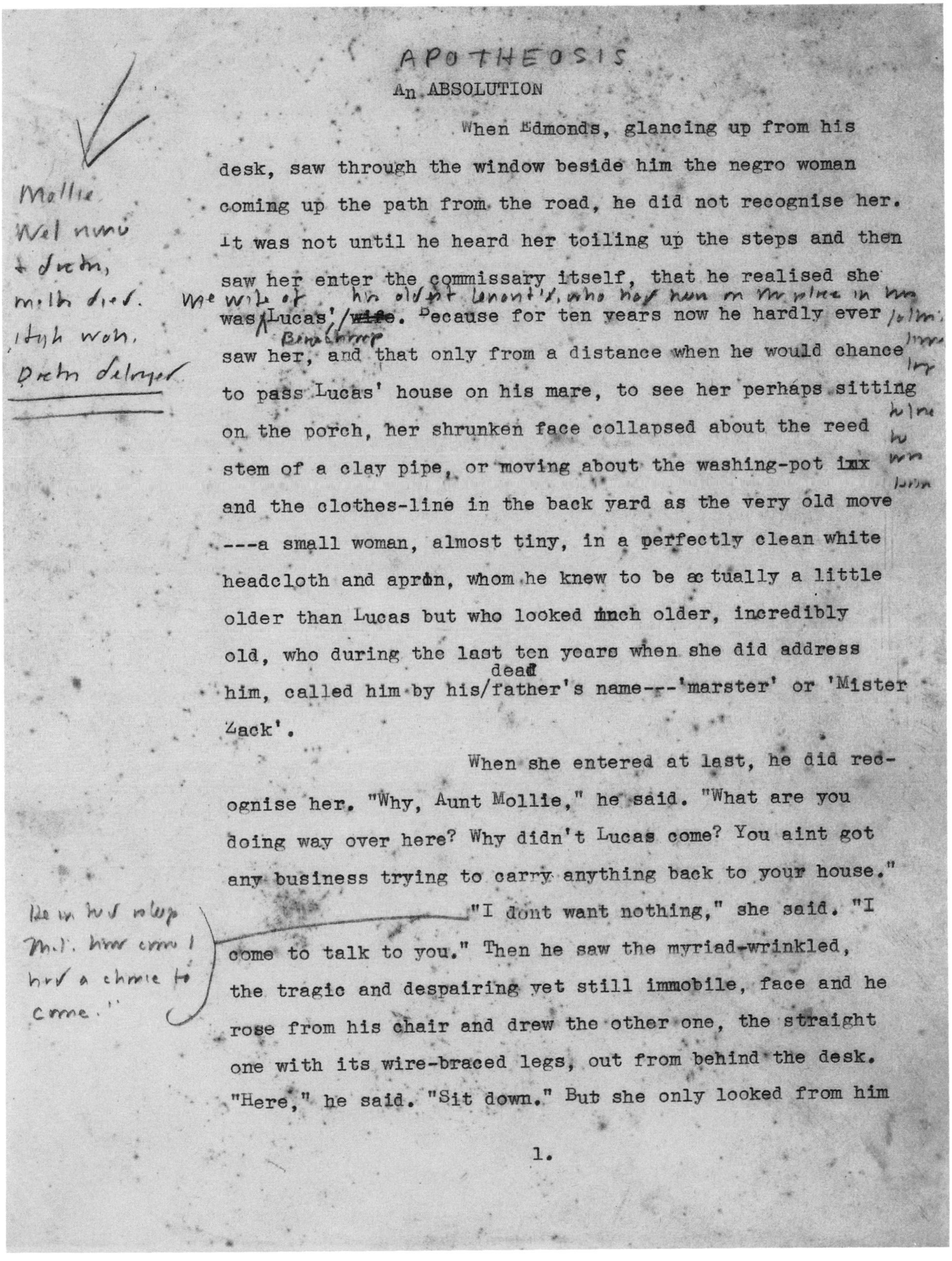

APOTHEOSIS

An ABSOLUTION

When Edmonds, glancing up from his
desk, saw through the window beside him the negro woman
coming up the path from the road, he did not recognise her.
It was not until he heard her toiling up the steps and then
saw her enter the commissary itself, that he realised she
was Lucas' wife. *Because for ten years now he hardly ever
saw her, and that only from a distance when he would chance
to pass Lucas' house on his mare, to see her perhaps sitting
on the porch, her shrunken face collapsed about the reed
stem of a clay pipe, or moving about the washing-pot
and the clothes-line in the back yard as the very old move
---a small woman, almost tiny, in a perfectly clean white
headcloth and apron, whom he knew to be actually a little
older than Lucas but who looked much older, incredibly
old, who during the last ten years when she did address
him, called him by his/father's name---'marster' or 'Mister
Zack'.

When she entered at last, he did rec-
ognise her. "Why, Aunt Mollie," he said. "What are you
doing way over here? Why didn't Lucas come? You aint got
any business trying to carry anything back to your house."
"I dont want nothing," she said. "I
come to talk to you." Then he saw the myriad-wrinkled,
the tragic and despairing yet still immobile, face and he
rose from his chair and drew the other one, the straight
one with its wire-braced legs, out from behind the desk.
"Here," he said. "Sit down." But she only looked from him

1.

Page from the typescript for the story that became "Fire on the Hearth," originally published in Go Down, Moses *(by permission of W. W. Norton and the Manuscripts Division, Special Collections Department, University of Virginia Library; accession number 6074)*

February 1943), readers meet members of the same stricken family again in a humorous, almost incredible story. "My Grandmother Millard and General Bedford Forrest and the Battle of Harrykin Creek" (*Story*, March-April 1943) is closely related to central elements in *The Unvanquished*, but the story is by no means serious: it was written with the sole purpose of evoking laughter and succeeds in doing so. Another funny story, "A Courtship" (*Sewanee Review*, October 1948), is about courtship and a competition between a white man and an Indian: David Hogganbeck and Ikkemotubbe. The competition is of marathon proportions, and Faulkner quotes from Homer as well as from Lord Byron in his description of the girl in the story.

With *Collected Stories* in 1950, Faulkner further solidified his reputation in the world of letters. The Nobel Prize for Literature in 1949, awarded to Faulkner in Stockholm in December 1950, was the ultimate proof of his success and achievement. *Collected Stories* is, of course, Faulkner's major short-story collection, a milestone marking the culmination of a long and varied short-story career and including almost all of Faulkner's previously published stories that do not stand in close relationship to his novels. Faulkner had suggested this new collection as early as 1939, but serious discussion did not begin till 1948. According to lists that Faulkner made, he planned to include only previously uncollected short stories, including the Gavin Stevens stories, in the new book. The decision to leave out the detective stories and publish a separate volume of them changed this plan, and it was decided to publish a volume of previously collected and uncollected stories. According to an 11 November 1948 letter to Robert K. Haas, Faulkner intended the volume to be "comprehensive of all my short pieces except those previously allotted to other complete volumes in future." Although *Collected Stories* is not really comprehensive, it may be said to include the forty-two stories Faulkner wanted to represent his achievement as a short-story writer. Even though the book contains most of Faulkner's independent short stories, it does not include all such stories, and most of the stories not collected here also deserve attention.

Twenty-five of the forty-two stories had been collected in *These 13* and *Doctor Martino* while seventeen stories had not been collected before. Some of them date back to 1930, and most of them were written before 1940. Planning his collection, Faulkner wrote to Malcolm Cowley on 1 November 1948 that "even to a collection of short stories, form, integration, is as important as to a novel—an entity of its own, single, set for one pitch, contrapuntal in integration, toward one end, one finale." He organized *Collected Stories* with such principles in mind, although the criteria for arrangement are often difficult to determine. There are six sections in the book. The first section, "The Country," includes six stories, none of them previously collected and all written between 1938 and 1942, beginning with "Barn Burning" and ending with "Two Soldiers" and "Shall Not Perish." These six stories deal with the people of the Yoknapatawpha countryside, black, white, and Indian, rich and poor, brave and foolish. The conflicts between black and white, and established families and foreigners to the region, are accompanied by broader conflicts inherent in loyalty and endurance, finding one's place in the world, and identity and self-assertion. "Barn Burning" establishes themes that recur throughout the volume. The first section has a high degree of unity, which is not true for all sections in the volume. Section 2, "The Village," includes ten stories, all written before 1935, with the four village stories from *These 13* at the core. These stories show a great variety in mood and narrative handling, although the community is central in all of them. Major themes in Faulkner's writing— individual versus community, isolation versus involvement, and escape versus endurance—are displayed here. The village itself, Jefferson, in Yoknapatawpha, comes to life in these narratives. The sense of place is strong, and the village functions also to measure the effects of change and progression, since the people of a town like this often struggle to keep up with improvements and changes in the larger, outside world.

Section 3, "The Wilderness," includes four Indian stories—two of them from *These 13*, together with the later "Lo!" and "A Courtship." Tragedy and comedy are thus found within the same section. In section 4, "The Wasteland," there is no place for humor or comedy. The four World War I stories from *These 13* make up this section, together with "Turn About" from *Doctor Martino*. It may be worth noting that Faulkner's war stories from the early part of his career are included in this section, while the war stories from the 1940s are included in the first section of the book. Antiwar sentiments seem to have been replaced by questions of loyalty, duty, and endurance in the more mature writer.

Faulkner receiving his Nobel Prize for Literature, 10 December 1950

Section 5, "The Middle Ground," comprises eleven stories, six of them from *Doctor Martino* and five previously uncollected stories from the first half of the 1930s. Bereavement, loss, suffering, symbolic death, and violent, physical death are central in them all. Rootless, searching characters try to find their place in life and ascertain their identity. In contrast to the country people, many of these characters are uprooted or alienated. Although this section includes quite a measure of criticism of the contemporary scene, some of the stories (such as "There Was a Queen" and "A Mountain Victory") deal with earlier events and with tradition, and the problems are more moral or aesthetic than social.

"Beyond," section 6 in *Collected Stories*, includes the three stories of the supernatural from *Doctor Martino* and, to conclude the whole volume, "Mistral," "Divorce in Naples," and "Carcassonne" (the stories that make up the final section of *These 13*). The collection thus moves from the cohesive and stable life in the countryside of Yoknapatawpha to an artist's dream of creation. In "Carcassonne" the artist goes "beyond" the bareness of his environment to live within the

world of the imagination. But to live within the walls of one's "Carcassonne" is not necessarily a dream come true: agony and anguish accompany the artist in his struggle "to create out of the materials of the human spirit something which did not exist before."

Collected Stories was reviewed widely, and not one reviewer was clearly hostile or negative. The critics stressed the practicality and usefulness of the volume as an introduction to Faulkner's rich fictional world. *Collected Stories* thus marked another important step forward in the general acknowledgment of Faulkner's total achievement. Many reviewers stated or implied that recognition of Faulkner as the leading American novelist of his generation would soon come, and they did this on the basis of the richness of *Collected Stories*. The collection was adopted by the Book-of-the-Month Club as an alternate fiction selection for September 1950, and it received the National Book Award for the most distinguished book of fiction by an American author published in 1950.

After the publication of *Collected Stories* Faulkner published few stories of importance. Those that were written relate in significant ways to his

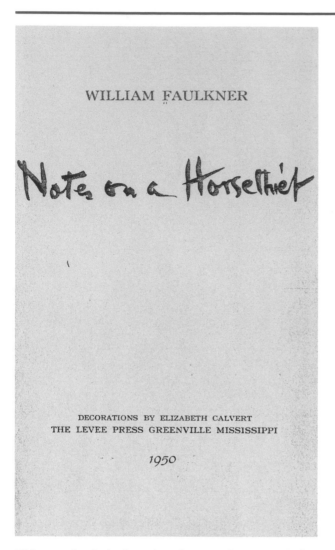

WILLIAM FAULKNER

Notes on a Horsethief

DECORATIONS BY ELIZABETH CALVERT
THE LEVEE PRESS GREENVILLE MISSISSIPPI

1950

*Title page for the book version of a story that was revised as
part of* A Fable *(1954)*

longer fiction, with few exceptions. *Notes on a Horsethief* (conceived as early as 1940, but not published until 1951) was an early precursor of Faulkner's *A Fable* (1954). It was revised before incorporation into the novel. The narrative prologue for act 1 of Faulkner's play *Requiem for a Nun* (1951) is a revised version of "A Name for the City," a story published in the October 1950 issue of *Harper's*. "By the People" (*Mademoiselle*, October 1955) is a lighthearted Snopes story about a political rally, and it went, quite naturally, into *The Mansion* (1959; chapter 13); whereas "Hog Pawn," which Faulkner tried to sell in 1955, remained unpublished as a short story until it appeared in *Uncollected Stories*. This is an early version of what later became chapter 14 of *The Mansion*, also known as the Meadowfill episode. The last short fiction to be published in

Faulkner's lifetime, "Hell Creek Crossing" (*Saturday Evening Post*, 31 March 1962), is hardly a short story in its own right, but rather an excerpt from *The Reivers* (1962).

In addition to these stories with their close relationship to novels, two independent short stories were written and published. "Race at Morning" (*Saturday Evening Post*, 5 March 1955) is Faulkner's most successful story from his later years. It is also his last hunting story, a tribute to the wilderness. A slightly revised version of this story was incorporated into *Big Woods* (1955) and reprinted in *Uncollected Stories*. The second independent short story is "Mr. Acarius" (written circa 1953, published in the *Saturday Evening Post*, 9 October 1965, and included in *Uncollected Stories*), a story about alcohol abuse and personal conflicts.

Preparations for the publication of Faulkner's hunting stories in *Big Woods* included revising and borrowing from previously published material and adding some text to link the various stories together. The volume is of a secondary nature and includes no new material of any special significance.

After receiving the Nobel Prize, Faulkner became a public figure and traveled widely on State Department missions. He spoke to his fellow southerners on racial issues, for the first time in his career publishing articles and essays more often than he published stories, and he responded to his incredible popularity in Japan by visiting there in 1955. Starting in 1957 he was writer in residence at the University of Virginia in Charlottesville, where he purchased a house and settled with his wife, Estelle (their daughter, Jill, had married in 1954). In 1957 and 1959 *The Town* and *The Mansion* were published, drawing heavily on material he had published before. This is also true for *The Reivers*.

In Charlottesville, Faulkner took up horseback riding on a regular basis and was injured in several falls. His final injury came in Oxford, Mississippi, however, on 17 June 1962; the connection between his injuries and the heart attack from which he died is by no means obvious, but he was taken to a sanatorium on 5 July and died the following day. He was buried in St. Peter's Cemetery, Oxford, near the graves of most of the Falkners.

The biographical facts of a writer's life and career cannot explain how the works were written or what made it possible to write them. Faulkner's craftsmanship came slowly, and he

Faulkner riding his horse, Tempy, at Rowan Oak, circa 1954 (from the Brodsky Collection, Southeast Missouri State University)

learned it through practice and stubborn dedication. He was willing to sacrifice most things to get his work done, and he was never in doubt as to the importance of the artist and his work. Faulkner was unwilling to compromise, and he had set a high standard for himself early on. Accordingly, his life never became simple or easy. His was a complex nature, so he had a complicated life. All his books have been examined thoroughly, but the man who wrote them is still an enigma.

Faulkner's best short stories are outstanding, and there are more than enough of them to secure him a place as a major writer in the genre. His stories do not completely follow any of the rules of the formula story, although they were influenced by their time and place and the market for which they were written. The narrative control in his stories varies significantly from text to text—from cold objectivity to heart-shattering closeness—but above and beneath it all is the controlling conscience of the craftsman and born storyteller, whose voice can be heard from time to time. Faulkner's lifelong interest, as he once stated in a discussion at the University of Virginia, was in "all man's behavior with no judg-ment whatever": "You write a story to tell about people, man in his constant struggle with his own heart, with the hearts of others, or with his environment. It's man in the ageless, eternal struggles which we inherit and we go through as though they'd never happened before, shown for a moment in a dramatic instant of the furious motion of being alive, that's all any story is. You catch the fluidity which is human life and you focus a light on it and you stop it long enough for people to be able to see it" (*Faulkner in the University*, 1959). To render man in his ageless struggle and to arrest motion for a moment, Faulkner explored the limits of storytelling techniques, but since the stories always have a solid kernel of substance, he succeeded in keeping the precarious balance between content and presentation. His searching curiosity and willingness to try over and over again to improve a story, to find the right angle to tell it from in order to catch the exact atmosphere, led to the creation of one of the most impressive bodies of short fiction in American literature.

Letters:

The Faulkner-Cowley File: Letters and Memories,

Faulkner in Tokyo, August 1955

1944-1962, edited by Malcolm Cowley (New York: Viking, 1966);

Selected Letters of William Faulkner, edited by Joseph L. Blotner (New York: Random House, 1976);

The Letters, volume 2 of *Faulkner: A Comprehensive Guide to the Brodsky Collection*, edited by Louis Daniel Brodsky and Robert W. Hamblin (Jackson: University Press of Mississippi, 1984).

Interviews:

Faulkner at Nagano, edited by Robert A. Jelliffe (Tokyo: Kenkyusha, 1956);

Faulkner in the University: Class Conferences at the University of Virginia, 1957-58, edited by Frederick L. Gwynn and Joseph L. Blotner (Charlottesville: University of Virginia Press, 1959);

Faulkner at West Point, edited by Joseph L. Fant III and Robert Ashley (New York: Random House, 1964);

Lion in the Garden: Interviews with William Faulkner, 1926-1962, edited by James B. Meriwether

and Michael Millgate (New York: Random House, 1968).

Bibliographies:

James B. Meriwether, *The Literary Career of William Faulkner: A Bibliographical Study* (Princeton: Princeton University Library, 1961; Columbia: University of South Carolina Press, 1971);

Linton R. Massey, *William Faulkner: "Man Working," 1919-1962, A Catalogue of the William Faulkner Collections at the University of Virginia* (Charlottesville: Bibliographical Society, University of Virginia, 1968);

Meriwether, "The Short Fiction of William Faulkner: A Bibliography," *Proof*, 1 (1971);

John E. Bassett, *William Faulkner: An Annotated Checklist of Criticism* (New York: Lewis, 1972);

Carl Petersen, *Each in Its Ordered Place: A Faulkner Collector's Notebook* (Ann Arbor, Mich.: Ardis, 1975);

Thomas L. McHaney, *William Faulkner: A Reference Guide* (Boston: G. K. Hall, 1975);

Louis Daniel Brodsky, *The Bibliography*, volume 1 of *Faulkner: A Comprehensive Guide to the Brodsky Collection* (Jackson: University Press of Mississippi, 1982).

Biographies:

Robert Coughlan, *The Private World of William Faulkner* (New York: Harper, 1954);

John Faulkner, *My Brother Bill: An Affectionate Reminiscence* (New York: Trident, 1963);

James W. Webb and A. Wigfall Green, eds., *William Faulkner of Oxford* (Baton Rouge: Louisiana State University Press, 1965);

Murry C. Faulkner, *The Falkners of Mississippi: A Memoir* (Baton Rouge: Louisiana State University Press, 1967);

Joseph L. Blotner, *Faulkner: A Biography*, 2 volumes (New York: Random House, 1974);

Meta Carpenter Wilde and Orin Borsten, *A Loving Gentleman* (New York: Simon & Schuster, 1976);

David Minter, *William Faulkner: His Life and Work* (Baltimore: Johns Hopkins University Press, 1980);

Michel Gresset, *A Faulkner Chronology*, translated by Arthur B. Scharff (Jackson: University Press of Mississippi, 1985);

Frederick R. Karl, *William Faulkner: American Writer* (New York: Weidenfeld & Nicolson, 1989).

Estelle and William Faulkner at Stewart Air Force Base, New York, 20 April 1962, after a visit to West Point
(photograph by Maj. R. W. Pinkston, USAF)

References:

Richard P. Adams, *Faulkner: Myth and Motion* (Princeton: Princeton University Press, 1968);

Warren Beck, *Faulkner: Essays* (Madison: University of Wisconsin Press, 1976);

Cleanth Brooks, *William Faulkner: The Yoknapatawpha Country* (New Haven & London: Yale University Press, 1963);

Brooks, *William Faulkner: Toward Yoknapatawpha and Beyond* (New Haven & London: Yale University Press, 1978);

James B. Carothers, *William Faulkner's Short Stories* (Ann Arbor: UMI Research Press, 1985);

Joanne V. Creighton, *William Faulkner's Craft of Revision: The Snopes Trilogy, "The Unvanquished" and "Go Down, Moses"* (Detroit: Wayne State University Press, 1977);

James Early, *The Making of Go Down, Moses* (Dallas: Southern Methodist University Press, 1972);

Edward M. Holmes, *Faulkner's Twice-Told Tales: His Re-Use of His Material* (The Hague: Mouton, 1966);

Irving Howe, *William Faulkner: A Critical Study*, third edition, revised and enlarged (Chicago: University of Chicago Press, 1975);

Elizabeth M. Kerr, *Yoknapatawpha: Faulkner's "Little Postage Stamp of Native Soil"* (New York: Fordham University Press, 1969);

Lewis Leary, *William Faulkner of Yoknapatawpha County* (New York: Crowell, 1973);

John L. Longley, *The Tragic Mask: A Study of Faulkner's Heroes* (Chapel Hill: University of North Carolina Press, 1963);

John Matthews, *The Play of Faulkner's Language* (Ithaca, N.Y.: Cornell University Press, 1982);

Michael Millgate, *The Achievement of William Faulkner* (New York: Vintage, 1966);

Joseph W. Reed, *Faulkner's Narrative* (New Haven: Yale University Press, 1973);

Stephen Ross, *Fiction's Inexhaustible Voice: Speech and Writing in Faulkner* (Athens: University of Georgia Press, 1989);

Estella Schoenberg, *Old Tales and Talking: Quentin Compson in Absalom, Absalom! and Related Works* (Jackson: University of Mississippi Press, 1977);

Hans H. Skei, *William Faulkner: The Novelist as

Short Story Writer (Oslo: Universitetsforlaget, 1985);

Skei, *William Faulkner: The Short Story Career* (Oslo: Universitetsforlaget, 1981);

Olga W. Vickery, *The Novels of William Faulkner: A Critical Interpretation*, revised edition (Baton Rouge: Louisiana State University Press, 1964);

Edmond L. Volpe, *A Reader's Guide to William Faulkner* (New York: Farrar, Straus & Giroux, 1964).

Papers:

The William Faulkner Collection at the University of Virginia Library, Charlottesville, is by far the most important repository of manuscripts and typescripts. Material related to Faulkner's short stories can also be found in the Henry W. and Albert A. Berg Collection, New York Public Library; the Harry Ransom Humanities Research Center, University of Texas at Austin; and the William Wisdom Collection, Tulane University.

Dorothy Canfield Fisher

(17 February 1879 - 9 November 1958)

J. P. Lovering
Canisius College

See also the Fisher entry in *DLB 9: American Novelists, 1910-1945.*

BOOKS: *Corneille and Racine in England* (New York: Macmillan, 1904);

Elementary Composition, by Fisher and George R. Carpenter (New York & London: Macmillan, 1906);

Gunhild: A Norwegian-American Episode (New York: Holt, 1907);

What Shall We Do Now?, by Fisher and others (New York: Stokes, 1907);

The Squirrel Cage (New York: Holt, 1912);

A Montessori Mother (New York: Holt, 1912; London: Constable, 1913);

The Montessori Manual (Chicago: Richardson, 1913);

Mothers and Children (New York: Holt, 1914);

The Bent Twig (New York: Holt, 1915);

Hillsboro People (New York: Holt, 1915);

Fellow Captains, by Fisher and Sarah N. Cleghorn (New York: Holt, 1916);

Self-Reliance (Indianapolis: Bobbs-Merrill, 1916);

The Real Motive (New York: Holt, 1916);

Understood Betsy (New York: Holt, 1917);

Home Fires in France (New York: Holt, 1918);

The Day of Glory (New York: Holt, 1919);

The Brimming Cup (New York: Harcourt, Brace, 1921; London: Cape, n.d.);

Rough-Hewn (New York: Harcourt, Brace, 1922);

Raw Material (New York: Harcourt, Brace, 1923);

The Home-Maker (New York: Harcourt, Brace, 1924);

Made-to-Order Stories (New York: Harcourt, Brace, 1925);

Her Son's Wife (New York: Harcourt, Brace, 1926; London & Toronto: Cape, 1932);

Why Stop Learning? (New York: Harcourt, Brace, 1927);

The Deepening Stream (New York: Harcourt, Brace, 1930);

Basque People (New York: Harcourt, Brace, 1931);

Bonfire (New York: Harcourt, Brace, 1933);

Tourists Accommodated (New York: Harcourt, Brace, 1934);

Fables for Parents (New York: Harcourt, Brace, 1937);

Seasoned Timber (New York: Harcourt, Brace, 1939);

Nothing Ever Happens and How It Does, by Fisher and Cleghorn (Boston: Beacon, 1940);

Dorothy Canfield Fisher, 1954

Liberty and Union, by Fisher and Cleghorn (New York: Book-of-the-Month Club, 1940);

Tell Me a Story (Lincoln, Neb.: University Publishing, 1940);

Our Young Folks (New York: Harcourt, Brace, 1943);

American Portraits (New York: Holt, 1946);

Four-Square (New York: Harcourt, Brace, 1949);

Something Old, Something New: Stories of People Who Are America (New York: Scott, 1949);

Our Independence and the Constitution (New York: Random House, 1950);

Paul Revere and the Minute Men (New York: Random House, 1950);

A Fair World for All: The Meaning of the Declaration of Human Rights (New York: Whittlesey House, 1952);

Vermont Tradition: The Biography of an Outlook on Life (Boston: Little, Brown, 1953);

A Harvest of Stories, from a Half Century of Writing (New York: Harcourt, Brace, 1956);

Memories of Arlington, Vermont (New York: Duell, Sloan & Pearce, 1957);

And Long Remember: Some Great Americans Who Have Helped Me (New York: Whittlesey House, 1959).

OTHER: "How 'Flint and Fire' Started and Grew," in *Americans All*, edited by B. A. Heydrick (New York: Harcourt, Brace, 1920), pp. 210-220;

Giovanni Papini, *Life of Christ*, translated by Fisher (New York: Harcourt, Brace, 1923).

SELECTED PERIODICAL PUBLICATIONS—
UNCOLLECTED: "Daughter of the Frontier," *New York Herald Tribune*, 28 May 1933, pp. 7-9;

"Mrs. Fisher Reads Professor Firebaugh," *Educational Forum*, 15 (March 1951): 291-298.

Dorothy Canfield Fisher (née Dorothea Frances Canfield) published her first collection of short stories, *Hillsboro People*, in 1915 and her last, *A Harvest of Stories, from a Half Century of Writing*, in 1956. Fisher used her maiden name, Dorothy Canfield, for her fiction writing. Her short stories were written and published when this literary form had already become an established genre and when some of its greatest practitioners, such as Ernest Hemingway and F. Scott Fitzgerald, were further developing the art. Fisher's contribution was not insignificant, though one can hardly say she was very much concerned with literature, per se. She wrote stories that centered on the lives of middle-class people, primarily people who were rooted in the smaller communities of Vermont, but she brought to the interpretation of these lives a rich and universal outlook born of a desire to share her wisdom and her educational psychology with as many people as she could. She was a writer with a natural gift for storytelling, and her strong desire to help others shows clearly in her writing.

Her forebears originally settled in the mountains of southern Vermont about two hundred years before her birth, near the town of Arlington, and this was Fisher's residence most of her life, though she was born in Lawrence, Kansas. Her father, James Hulme Canfield, was a professor and president of several midwestern universities in the early twentieth century and later was the first librarian of Columbia University. Her mother, Flavia Camp Canfield, was a painter, and the young Dorothy had the advantage of living in Paris, France, on occasion, where her mother had a studio. Dorothy went to college at the University of Nebraska (where her father was president), and there she met and became a lifelong friend of Willa Cather, who was slightly older than she.

On 9 May 1907 Dorothy married John R. Fisher and settled in Arlington on a farm she inherited from her Canfield grandfather. She went to France and Spain during World War I to assist her husband, who had become a volunteer member of the American Field Service. The Fishers' daughter, Sally (born in 1912), and son, James (born in 1914), were with them, and Mrs. Fisher became a part of the effort to assist the wounded, their families, and especially the children. Some of this vital work was performed in the Basque country at the foot of the Pyrenees.

After the war she returned home to Arlington with her family to turn her attention to the farm and her writing of fiction. Along with her steady production of both long and short fiction,

Dorothy Canfield in 1899, when she was a senior at the University of Nebraska

she always engaged herself in town life and in the affairs of the world community. She became the first woman member of the board of education of Vermont; she was a charter member and one of the prime movers behind the Book-of-the-Month Club, with which she continued to work until just after World War II. Her son, then Captain Fisher, a member of the U.S. Army Medical Corps, was killed in 1943 in the Philippines in an attempt to free some American prisoners. In spite of her grief, her work for others continued as she organized the Children's Crusade—a war-relief effort largely conducted by American children themselves. Fisher's educational and cultural interests and her humanitarian efforts often vied with and eventually eclipsed her writing. She died of a stroke on 9 November 1958.

Hillsboro People is a collection of eighteen stories that are structured simply. Their merit is in their human pulse beat, their earthy and folksy quality. Characters learn through life for better or for worse. "The Bedquilt" (*Harper's*, November 1906) is a story Fisher talked about in lectures regarding the genesis of her stories in her own experience with local people. Aunt Mehetabel, the chief character, is a poor relation living with the Elwells, a Hillsboro family. She is something like James Joyce's Maria in "Clay." "An old maid at twenty, [Mehetabel] at forty [was] everyone's servant, and at sixty [she] had gone through so much discipline that she could need no more in the next world," but Mehetabel's fortune changes. Good with the sewing needle, she directs her efforts mainly toward patching quilts. An idea for a great design comes to her. She draws the design, and for five years (at first secretly) she works to carry it out. At its completion the Elwells want her to exhibit it at the county fair. Mehetabel finally wins the blue ribbon, but it is her late flowering as a person that is so well brought out by the story's ending, as she sits in front of her quilt honestly admiring her own work.

Hillsboro is an old town, dating back to the American Revolution. It is set in its ways but not out of touch with the life of the cities. Its young folk leave fairly often but then return to bring some of the color of city ways. Life is grim and difficult and tragic at times, but Fisher is able to take the reader behind the grim masks and to discover some of the motives and ideals of the townspeople. These Vermonters may be a group apart, but they share common human traits.

The Real Motive (1916), Canfield's second volume of stories, contains fourteen in all, and most of these had previous magazine publication. This volume has more of a cosmopolitan flavor than *Hillsboro People*. There are some tales of World War I; some about the academic life at midwestern universities, which was also the subject of her novels *The Squirrel Cage* (1912) and *The Bent Twig* (1915); some concerning childhood; and some about old age. The title of the volume implies that sympathy for people depends in good measure upon a proper understanding of the real motives in others' behavioral patterns. This theme runs through many of Fisher's nonfiction works as well, as in *A Montessori Mother* (1912). More often than not there is an assumption that when one's actual purpose in a course of action is known, it will be found to be not as mischievous or evil as may be thought. Her mode of narrative in the volume is closely analytical of the characters.

"A Good Fight and the Faith Kept"—earlier published as "The Conqueror" (*American Maga-*

zine, March 1916)—is a study of inherited melancholia with a suicidal pattern. The main character is Elnathan Wardon, a member of a Hillsboro family that, although it had a long record of community achievement and financial success going back to colonial times, was clouded with suicides. The story follows the course of Elnathan's struggle for stability in the face of his sister Mary's melancholy. Elnathan eventually becomes a successful lawyer and comes to terms with the way the townspeople realize his family's past. It is an absorbing narrative.

"A Thread Without a Knot"—earlier published as "An Unframed Picture" (*Everybody's Magazine*, March 1910)—is another story that demonstrates Fisher's ability for strong characterization in a series of episodes. She was especially good at establishing and developing contrasts between Americans in Europe and their foreign friends, somewhat in the manner of Henry James. In this story Peter Harrison, a young American engaged to an American girl, is a graduate assistant in a history department and is in Paris doing work in the Bibliothèque Nationale for his doctorate. Fisher describes his naive and innocent acquaintance with an English student, Agatha Midland, who is researching in music. Peter senses that the English girl needs to have somebody help her get away from her strict British decorum, and he undertakes to do just that by having lunches and picnics with Agatha, as they discuss their different attitudes toward life. It is Peter's ingenuousness that catches the fancy of Agatha. She is of English nobility, and her parents are urging her to marry a nobleman just for the sake of getting married. Peter's absorption in his attempt to aid Agatha's coming out is carried on until a parting scene, by which time the reader has begun to sense the deeper, undeclared affection that the British girl has for the American. Most of Fisher's short fiction is not written with the detachment one is accustomed to in modern writing, and the reader can usually sense her desire to bring home with emphasis the moral implications of the story.

In 1916 Fisher joined her husband, who was then working with the French Ambulance Corps, in Europe. She, with her two children, plunged into war-relief work just behind the Allied lines in France and, later, Spain. It seems astonishing, in the light of all her duties, that she was able to turn out a volume of stories, *Home Fires in France* (1918). The volume does not measure up to the earlier books, because it seems

Dorothy and John R. Fisher; they were married on 9 May 1907.

aimed primarily at acquainting the reader with conditions at the front and in the homes of the French. The material of the stories, along with Fisher's preface, confirms the idea that she was depending heavily on describing actual experience and was not working these stories through the prism of the imagination. Much the same can be said of *The Day of Glory* (1919), a smaller group of war stories.

All the stories from *Home Fires in France* do not deal with the suffering of the war. One exception, for example, is called "A Fair Exchange." It concerns an American dealer in toiletry who is in France just after the war to make his fortune, but who is not without his own notions of helping the French. He perceives quickly what he thinks is wrong with French business methods—their conservatism and their lack of the enterprising spirit—and he sees the chance for a little missionary work. He tries to set straight a village pharmacist on modern improvements in the manufacture of cold cream. It must be done by mass production rather than the slower family methods. The Frenchman quietly refuses, thinking that his precious formula being mass-produced would destroy his whole way of life. Each character is left with some doubts, but each will never

be the same thereafter because of their exchange. This theme of the interaction of one culture with another is one that Fisher used often. In her novel *Gunhild* (1907), for instance, she had portrayed a group of Americans in Norway.

Two novels, *The Brimming Cup* (1921) and *Rough-Hewn* (1922), continued the author's mode of experiential realism, the development of character through everyday experiences. Through such writings she was gaining a wide audience both in England and her own country.

Raw Material (1923) is a volume of sketches of Vermont people whom the author found interesting. The book might be cited as further evidence of the idea that to Fisher life was more fascinating than fiction. In a prefatory essay she invites the reader (in Emersonian fashion) to help create the stories for themselves. Fisher was quite forthright on this point, even truculent: "Personally I do not believe the foundations of the world would move by a hair if novels ceased altogether."

"Old Man Warner" (*Outlook*, 11 January 1922) is typical of the stories in *Raw Material*. Fisher starts off by saying that, probably, if the reader or some of the reader's folks are not from Vermont, then the reader will not appreciate this

"She was looking so far, so far away"

Illustration by Mary M. Ludlum for "The Cage," in the December 1924 issue of the Bookman. *The story was collected in*
Fables for Parents *(1937).*

character. But the tale is really universal in its appeal. Warner has settled into the Vermont hillside just after the Civil War, along with his wife and two sons, who had fought with him. The boys eventually move out West and prosper. When Old Man Warner is seventy-one, he sees no reason (even though the town wants to buy up his place for right of roadway) to go live with his sons. Twenty-two more years go by, and not even the cruel Vermont winters or the urgings of the one granddaughter who still communicates with him can bring old Warner down from his mountain home. He owes no one and lives off raising small livestock and growing vegetables. However, the selectmen still try in various ways to badger him down from his hillside. He holds out. The manner of his death, though not surprising, is more triumphant than not. At the age of ninety-three Warner dies and is found in his kitchen, his face composed and serene. Even if these sketches (at least semifictional in terms of narration) may not, for one reason or another, sat-

isfy the formal critic, they leave the reader with rewards of another sort. The book is significant when viewed in relation to the author's overall attitude toward her fictional art. She was trying very hard to take the reader deeper into life.

In 1925 Fisher began an important new venture. She became a charter member of the selection committee of the Book-of-the-Month Club, along with William Allen White, Henry S. Canby, Christopher Morley, and Heywood Broun. She relished the opportunity to promote good reading and remained a valued member of this group until her eyes began to weaken, near the end of World War II.

Made-to-Order Stories, a children's book, was published in 1925. Fisher's next collection for adults, *Basque People*, was not published until 1931; the author was, however, drawing on earlier experiences. She had, of course, done war-relief work in the remote Basque country before it had become a sightseeing attraction. The eight stories in this collection are narrated by a fictional schoolteacher—based on a friend of Fisher who was, according to the author, "a fiery-hearted Basque, hotly, almost amusingly proud, of her race." Curiously the tales remind one of her first volume, *Hillsboro People*, and it was probably no accident that Fisher used this independent race to show the same resourcefulness she admired in the inhabitants of Vermont. At any rate she succeeded in presenting the manners and customs of Basques—a small group of people of obscure origins who have stayed in the same place for centuries.

These stories appear to have been derived from the Basques themselves and their history. "Ancestral Home" (*Delineator*, September 1931) tells of an American schoolteacher, thirty-seven, who has inherited some letters written in the Basque language from her great-grandfather but was never able to decipher them. Gradually these letters take on an aura of romance for her, and she goes to the Basque country and discovers her great-aunt still living there. She is welcomed as a family member who has been living in America. Here among the Basques she comes to experience a feeling of family, of kinship, and ownership as well. A cave with primitive drawings on its walls, discovered on the kin's land, symbolizes the American woman's transformation, as she yields to the spell of the hardy, self-reliant Basque elements within herself. She convinces her impoverished relatives not to sell the land with the cave but to retain it and care for it, just as they do their heritage.

Fables for Parents, Fisher's next collection, was published in 1937; it is a collection of seventeen stories, all quite diversified but all reflecting an interest in educational themes. Edward Wagenknecht called them "really for the most part a group of sketches." In some stories the moral or didactic stress eclipses the narrative art. Some of the fables are illustrative of childhood problems, especially the lack of parental understanding of the child's motivations and behavioral patterns. The stories are perhaps too neat in their patterning and in their outcome, in comparison with the author's best short fiction. A *New York Herald Tribune* reviewer, Margaret Culkin Banning, put it well: Fisher "has apparently never seen any need for the separation between the artist and the teacher. She is a greatly respected writer but the devotion of the citizen and the student of child life can be read between the lines of nearly everything she writes. Perhaps the penalty of her conscientious attitude to the world she

lives in is that her work will be dated. . . . It may not be what is called stark reality (which is suitable because most of [her] characters would not be stark if they could help it) but it is reality just the same" (12 September 1937).

One story from this collection is an excellent exception. It has a powerful sense of small-town community life in the New England of the 1930s. "The Murder on Jefferson Street" (*Story*, June 1935) is a study of the breakdown of Francis Tuttle, a poetically tempered young clerk whose fragile psyche seems largely held together by his devoted wife, who understands and supports him in most matters, but who fails to perceive his hidden animosity toward his brother, a much more successful man, working for the same electric company. Francis lives in dread that someone will discover his secret malice, which he tries desperately to hide from everyone. This situation is complicated by a coarser neighbor who bullies and goads Francis about his personality at every turn, bringing on a fatal climax to this story that depicts very successfully the substratum of psychic conflicts in a small Yankee community, which does not yet have much of an idea about the causes of its human frustrations.

Four-Square (1949) was the first of three final collections of stories by Fisher; it republished seventeen pieces chosen from all of her earlier writing. She undertook careful revisions of all the stories, as she also did for those in *Something Old, Something New*, also published in 1949. In 1956 she supervised the publication of a last collection of her short fiction: *A Harvest of Stories*, comprising twenty-seven selections under three headings—"Vermont Memories," "Men, Women and Children," and "War." Eight of the stories in this volume were repeated from *Four-Square*. One of these is "Sex Education," which is a good, representative Fisher story. It first appeared in the *Yale Review* of December 1945, after being originally turned down by *Good Housekeeping*, and eventually was included in the *O. Henry Memorial Prize Stories of 1946*.

"Sex Education" centers on the narrator's Aunt Minnie, who tells her niece and her lady friends three different versions of a traumatic episode in her life. It occurred when she was fifteen and had been sent from her New England home to recuperate from an illness in the home of her relatives in the Midwest. While taking a shortcut through the cornfield one evening, Minnie lost her way and began to race frantically down the field. She began to scream and ran headlong to-

The Fishers at their home in Arlington, Vermont

ward a man with a scarred face, who began to paw her and tear her dress. Minnie was then quieted down by her relatives, who were friends of the young minister with the burn scars on his face, and the matter was dispensed with by Minnie's being sent home to New England. This first version is told by Minnie when she is thirty. Her niece is a young teenager whom Minnie wants to warn of the possible danger for young girls of sleeping out in backyard tents.

Some years later, in middle age, Minnie gives another version of the episode to the same listeners. This time she diminishes the size of the cornfield, calls herself a "well-grown" girl of sixteen, and believes the whole thing was probably her own fault for clutching the minister without any warning, and with her hair tumbling down and her dress half unbuttoned. Aunt Minnie warns her sewing-circle listeners that common sense has to be used about this business of teaching the facts of life to young girls.

Finally, when telling her third version, Minnie is nearly eighty and has spent a good part of her life trying to straighten out her rather worthless son, who has been involved in "women trouble." Once more Minnie's social cir-

cle has gathered around her, and she is rocking away, her eyes fixed on the hills beyond. She has forgotten her previous accounts. This time when she comes to the meeting in the cornfield, she frankly admits she had been "kind of interested" right along in the young minister with the scars. She says she hugged the minister for dear life, and had she been taught a little more about sex "she might have come out of that cornfield halfway engaged to marry him."

"Sex Education" in several ways is one of Fisher's best stories. In it she subordinates the didactic impulse to the dramatic and the narrative impulses, which fuse inextricably together (as they do in all good stories) until the story itself is the moral. There is not any grafting on of instructional pointers. And the motif of losing one's way is well established, with its counter-motif of the need for the soft human touch, along with the mellowness that time alone can bring.

Dorothy Fisher's main achievement in short fiction is that she used her natural gift for narrative to share her deep convictions about the spiritual significance of life. She eschews the niceties of the well-made story in favor of probing the roots of human situations. Her continued popular-

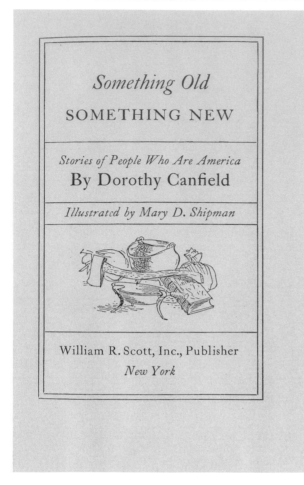

Title page for one of Fisher's last collections (1949); the book comprises nine stories dating from 1915 to 1946.

times catches enough of ageless and timeless human nature to make her stories still worth reading.

ity during her long creative period indicates to a large extent her success in doing what she set out to do: to transmit to the reader her notions about the human character and how it always learns through the experiential situation to come to terms with itself. One criticism of her story handling could well be that it lacks scale and pace. In many of her stories, she might better have highlighted certain scenes or actions and diminished others. Details tend to become burdensome. But the experienced reader will understand that this stylistic fault follows from her psychological and educational theories. She felt that life, too, was like that, complex and entangled. The stories often give the feeling that they are more observed experiences than invented narratives. By and large her themes concern the lives of quiet villagers, and in the handling of these, she some-

Biographies:
Elizabeth Yates, *Pebble in a Pool: The Widening Circles of Dorothy Canfield Fisher's Life* (New York: Dutton, 1958);
Ida H. Washington, *Dorothy C. Fisher: A Biography* (Shelburne, Vt.: New England Press, 1982).

References:
Percy H. Boynton, "Two New England Regionalists," *College English*, 1 (January 1940): 291-299;
Joseph J. Firebaugh, "Dorothy Canfield and the Moral Bent," *Educational Forum*, 15 (March 1951): 283-294;
Joseph P. Lovering, "The Friendship of Willa Cather and Dorothy Canfield," *Vermont History*, 48 (Summer 1980): 144-154;
Dorothea Lawrance Mann, "Dorothy Canfield: The Little Vermonter," *Bookman*, 65 (August 1927): 695-701;
William Lyon Phelps, "Dorothy Canfield Fisher," *English Journal*, 22 (January 1933): 1-8;
Edward A. Post, "Neo-Puritanism of D. C. Fisher," *Christian Register* (17 August 1933): 531-532;
Frederick A. Pottle, "Catharsis," *Yale Review*, 40 (January 1951): 621-641;
Bradford Smith, "Dorothy Canfield Fisher," *Atlantic*, 203 (August 1959): 73-77;
Smith, "Dorothy Canfield Fisher: A Presence Among Us," *Saturday Review*, 41 (29 November 1958): 13-14;
Edward Wagenknecht, *Cavalcade of the American Novel* (New York: Holt, 1952), pp. 294-299;
Blanche Colton Williams, *Our Short Story Writers* (New York: Moffat, Yard, 1920), pp. 41-54;
Elizabeth Wyckoff, "Dorothy Canfield; A Neglected Best Seller," *Bookman*, 74, no. 1 (1931): 40-44.

Papers:
The Bailey Howe Library of the University of Vermont in Burlington houses the important Dorothy Canfield Fisher papers in its Wilbur Collection.

Rudolph Fisher

(9 May 1897 - 26 December 1934)

Vilma Raskin Potter
California State University, Los Angeles

See also the Fisher entry in *DLB 51: Afro-American Writers from the Harlem Renaissance to 1940*.

BOOKS: *The Walls of Jericho* (New York & London: Knopf, 1928);
The Conjure-Man Dies: A Mystery Tale of Dark Harlem (New York: Covici, Friede, 1932);
The City of Refuge: The Collected Stories, edited by John McCluskey, Jr. (Columbia: University of Missouri Press, 1987).

PLAY PRODUCTION: *Conjur' Man Dies*, adapted by Fisher from his novel, New York, Lafayette Theatre, 11 March 1936.

SELECTED PERIODICAL PUBLICATION—
UNCOLLECTED:
"The Caucasian Storms Harlem" [essay], *American Mercury*, 11 (August 1927): 393-398.

Rudolph Fisher began writing fiction as a medical student in Washington, D.C. When he came to New York he found his real subject: the lives and experiences of poor, urban blacks. Between 1925 and 1934 he wrote medical articles, critical articles, two novels, a play, two juvenile pieces, and several short stories. His stories show a doctor's eye for detail and what lies beneath. Surfaces, like symptoms, signify the less visible. Fisher's love of music also appears in subject and form (he arranged music and sang with Paul Robeson). He had a fine ear for the varieties of black speech and considerable skill as a formal storyteller. His tone is an ironic combination of comedy and seriousness.

Fisher usually opens with vivid, peopled panoramas of city life, at dances, barbershops, and so on. The male rivals (for power, prestige, or women) in his stories are distinguished by anatomy: he admires very dark, stocky, strong men, as opposed to lighter-colored, weaker ones. He attributes physical alertness, good humor, generosity of spirit, and moral superiority to the darker

Rudolph Fisher

men. They deserve the women, according to Fisher—and usually win them. His stories illuminate conflicts of temperament, experience, and ethnicity in Harlem. His characters are Harlem's strugglers, survivors, and failures. He reports and interprets conflicts between religious immigrants from the rural South and urban black predators, between black Americans and West Indians, and between the light black people and dark ones. Fisher's stories are often deeply pessimistic, but his characters are always animated and vivid, clothed in the raiment of their hope. From such painful contrasts comes Fisher's irony.

Rudolph John Chauncey Fisher was the son of John Wesley Fisher, a clergyman, and Glendora Williamson Fisher. He was born on 9 May 1897 in the nation's capital, but at an early age

62 Carrington Ave.,
Providence, R. I.,
July 3, '24.

Dear Mr. Locke,

The last week or two has been such a precipitate upheaval that I want to make sure my more important connections didn't fall short. I sent an awful looking typescript to the Survey which was intended to meet you there Saturday. You see I did not realize summer school had started already and was disappointed in learning Friday morning that you would not be back in New York till Saturday. I had hoped to get your reaction to it before turning it in. (The MSS — not summer school.)

Page from a letter to Alain Locke in which Fisher discusses a story that is probably "The South Lingers On," which appeared in the March 1925 issue of Survey Graphic *and was abridged as "Vestiges" for publication in Locke's* New Negro *later in 1925 (Alain Locke Papers, Moorland-Spingarn Research Center, Howard University)* moved with his family to New York City and later to Providence, Rhode Island, receiving his education in the public schools of those cities. Attending Brown University on a scholarship, he soon changed his major from English to biology and earned his B.A. in 1919. After a year of intensive study he received his M.A. there and went on to Howard University Medical School, graduating with highest honors in 1924. Later that year he married Jane Ryder, a schoolteacher; the marriage was to produce one child, Hugh.

In 1925 the Fishers moved to New York, where Rudolph had a fellowship at Columbia University. He later set up a private medical practice in the city. Even before his in-person contacts with the literati of the Harlem Renaissance, Fisher's writing career had begun in Washington with a few early publications, including three stories.

"The City of Refuge," his first published work (*Atlantic Monthly*, February 1925; collected in *The City of Refuge: The Collected Stories*, 1987), earned important recognition for the young writer. It is a bleak story given vitality by a strong sense of character and voice. King Solomon Gillis has fled the South to Harlem for rights, privileges, and money. He emerges from the belly of the subway like Jonah into a black city. Gillis will discover—and forgive—the fact that a black city is like any other, only a place where innocence is always at risk, and a place that always provides temptation to predators. Uggams, the black antagonist, betrays Gillis to protect himself. In an ironic ending Gillis surrenders to a black policeman. It matters to Gillis that the policeman is black. Fisher, however, makes it clear that he thinks black policemen are fragments of the larger white authority, which is corrupt and which rewards black corruption. Later, Fisher modified his severe judgment of black policemen.

In March 1925 Fisher published "The South Lingers On" (in *Survey Graphic*; collected in *The City of Refuge*). Its five individual narratives are like notebook entries for later development. The total effect is an impression of lives in conflict: those of a displaced preacher, a desperate grandmother, anxious parents, two young bootleggers, and a cook. Almost without exception, Fisher suggests unreconcilable differences between old-time rural values and Harlem, the "great noisy heartless crowded place where you lived under the same roof with a hundred people you never knew."

"Ringtail" (*Atlantic Monthly*, May 1925; in *The City of Refuge*) opens with a vignette of place:

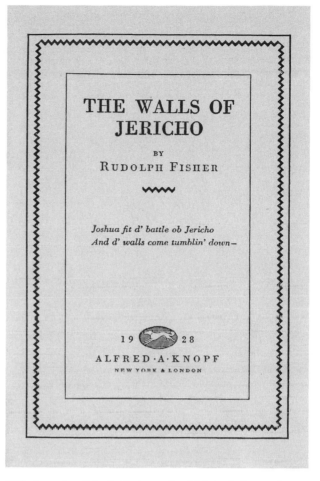

Title page for Fisher's first novel, which includes a glossary of "Harlemese"

Sunday spring crowds of Harlemites "like music full of exotic disharmonies." Ringtail (Cyril Best) is a young West Indian adventurer who despises male black Americans because they lack his own virtues: "self-esteem, craftiness, contentiousness, acquisitiveness." The hostility between West Indians and native-born American blacks is the matrix of this tale of ambition, self-love, and brutal revenge. Both groups have passages of discourse in parallel quartets. An American accuses his fellow cardplayers of black prejudice no better than that of whites. The West Indians argue about Marcus Garvey's dream of Liberia and the future of Harlem. All the characters seem displaced.

Toward the end of 1925, Fisher's "High Yaller" won the *Crisis* short-story prize (appearing in two parts in that journal in October and November; it was later collected in *The City of Refuge*). It is a long, complex narrative on a familiar and controversial theme: given a choice, why should one remain black? The opening is characteristically panoramic: a rushing impression of light, color, and music at a post-football-game dance. Fisher creates crowds of attractive and variously shaded black dancers, a sensation of social pressure, and a theme song that will fix the story's point of view, "Yaller Gal's Gone Outa Style." At the heart of this story lies a mix of love and self-hate, of fear and desire that clings to those like Evelyn Brown who could "pass." Blacks, says Fisher, find it hard to believe that "pinks" do not want to be white. Three duets are at the center of the story: Jay argues with his alter ego, which warns him against Evelyn; Evelyn cringes before her mirror image, which reminds her that only the care of her brown mother keeps Evelyn from passing as white; and Jay and his light-colored friend Jim voice their fears and desires about the consequences of being seen as white. Fisher uses an operatic style. At the end, when Evelyn has made her choice (to try to pass as white), the "Yaller Gal" song flashes up to indict her. There is greater emphasis upon feeling in this story than upon action. But Fisher shows how in the Harlem environment the idea of being white negates black self-images and directs black choices. The price of "passing" is the loss of family, love, friends, and community.

During 1927 Fisher published several stories about Harlem tensions and antagonisms. "The Promised Land" (January) and "Blades of Steel" (August), both in *Atlantic Monthly* (collected in *The City of Refuge*), were on Edward O'Brien's "Roll of Honor" of American short stories in 1927 and 1928, respectively. In "The Backslider" (*McClure's*, August 1927; in *The City of Refuge*) a simple-hearted innocent is expelled from his church fellowship after he is reported leaving a cabaret and being drunk. The secular/sacred division of Harlem life is both comic and serious in the tale. Young Eben Grimes, the innocent, is betrayed both by the hypocritical northern preacher and the yellow-skinned sinner Spider Webb. But Fisher obviously loves the common, black Eben, who is as unsuccessful a sinner as he is a saint.

"The Promised Land" will be discussed later. "Blades of Steel" describes the confrontation between Dirty Cozzens and Eight-Ball, antagonists who are physically and morally different. Eight-Ball is black, smooth-skinned, small, well-built, and sturdy. Cozzens is unevenly pigmented, ugly, vicious, and cowardly. Their mythic confrontation is described with the care of a choreographer, their physical appearance with the

care of a doctor. Fisher records the Harlemite love of discourse, a part of which is the love of stylish naming. The story of Eight-Ball's triumph is set in a barbershop and a ballroom—which gives Fisher yet another opportunity to write expressively about music.

Published at the end of 1927, "Fire By Night" (*McClure's*, December; in *The City of Refuge*) emphasizes a pathology of place: Lenox Avenue is a "spine, wounded . . . [with] pallor . . . grayness . . . lividity. . . ." The story, however, expresses the triumph of traditional ethical values over new secular ones. Young Rusty Pride may say there is little difference between prancing in his dad's church and prancing in a dance hall, but his moral education helps him see the spiritual ugliness of the dance hall's owners. Rusty's return to his community is in the spirit of optimism that colors Fisher's last works.

Fisher wrote at least two overtly moral tales: "Common Meter" (*New York News*, 8 and 15 February 1930; in *The City of Refuge*) and "Dust" (*Opportunity*, February 1931; also in *The City of Refuge*). The latter was on O'Brien's "Roll of Honor" for 1931. "Common Meter" is a romantic story of simplicity triumphing over trickery, as embodied in the musical styles of the rivals. The story is saturated with musical detail, clearly showing Fisher's understanding of music history, composition, and performance. Like solo and small groups of instruments taking improvisational turns, voices speak out in lively episodes. Bus, the dark man who offers marriage, makes "honest" music that echoes the experience of the black community. The light-colored trickster, Fess, is a "tonalist." Fisher declares the superiority of the former's blues, with the strong beat that binds new music to the old "shout." There is tradition behind that sound, says Fisher. It goes back to slave songs in America and deeper to the antecedent chant. The blues reaches the soul's depth. "Common Meter" is the obverse of "City of Refuge" in its optimism. In "City of Refuge" trickery triumphs over simplicity. In "Common Meter" simple virtues are victorious when they confront trickery.

"Dust" is the clever story of a car race with an unexpected ending: believing he is racing his expensive car against a white driver, Pard, the protagonist, discovers that he has run a black man off the road. The economical narrative is enriched by Pard's almost constant anger. Black success, he believes, arouses white envy and rage. The car, he says, is his safety valve; its speed lets him "out-hate" them.

OPPORTUNITY
JOURNAL OF NEGRO LIFE

L. HOLLINGSWORTH WOOD
Chairman

EUGENE KINCKLE JONES
Executive Secretary

CHARLES S. JOHNSON
Contributing Editor

Published Monthly by
NATIONAL URBAN LEAGUE
1133 BROADWAY, NEW YORK CITY
Telephone: Chelsea 3-1838

ELMER ANDERSON CARTER
Editor

WILLIAM H. BALDWIN
Secretary

LLOYD GARRISON
Treasurer

NOAH D. THOMPSON
Business Manager

VOLUME IX.   FEBRUARY, 1931   No. 2.

Contents

You are invited to attend the Annual Meeting of the National Urban League, which will be held at the office at 3 o'clock on Wednesday afternoon, February 11, 1931.

The agenda will include a report of the 1930 accomplishments, plans for 1931 and the audited treasurer's report.

Allen T. Burns, director of the Association of Community Chests and Councils, will be the guest speaker.

Single Copies, Fifteen Cents—Yearly Subscription, One Dollar and a Half, Foreign, $1.75.
Entered as second-class matter, Oct. 30, 1923, at the Post Office at New York, N. Y., under the act of March 3, 1879.

Contents page for the issue of Opportunity *that includes "Dust," the story of a car race motivated by hatred and anger*

Fisher's three most important stories, like some of his others, set traditional ethics and folkways against the ways of the new, urban world. Fisher acknowledges that traditional people are the least powerful and that love of family and community is not always a shield against urban danger. His folk figures in these tales are angry but not inflexible; they despair, but they endure. Three old women—one in each story—exemplify what Houston Baker, Jr., calls the "celebration of survival values."

Published in 1927, "The Promised Land" is the most despairing of the three. Separated by a tenement airshaft are a solitary old woman singing an unheeded spiritual and a bunch of raucous people, including her two grandsons, at a party. She is not an ignorant, old-time moralist. She blames decadent Harlem, though, for her grandsons' new enmity. To stop their impending violence over a frivolous girl, she hurls her Bible at them across the airshaft and through the opposite window. But it is a gesture of violent impotence, much like their own gestures. Harlem has not proven the promised land of money, work, and freedom she had dreamt it would. This story is a deep glimpse into darkness. It begins and ends at the airshaft and with the brutal spectacle of corrupted young lives, in this place where the young curse the old, where Cain slays Abel, and where one's residence is not one's true home.

But Fisher turns away from despair in his two other major stories. He affirms that rural experiences have created tough, wise, adaptable people. They are not impotent but quick and resourceful. Although uneasy in the city, they do not condemn utterly the new secular ways. Fisher seems to have concluded that the best of the new ways are derived from folk experience.

"Guardian of the Law" (*Opportunity*, March 1933; in *The City of Refuge*) contains the familiar sexual rivalry of the earlier stories. As in "The Promised Land" the rivals are closely observed by an old woman. Her handsome grandson, a policeman, is tied to the old values; the con artist, his rival for a woman, has "too much Harlem in him." The rival uses the woman to snare the policeman. The grandmother watches the plot unfold from her window, rushes out to intervene, calling upon her reserves of boldness, strength, and anger that she remembers from her youth. At the end she declines credit for the capture of the wicked con man Beasely and spins out a homey fantasy crediting her grandson Sam in the presence of his white superior officers. Why the lie, the deception? She is old but not a fool. She knows young Sam is a rookie on probation; she knows that the white boss can drop him for any reason. Therefore, how could Sam admit his grandmother had helped him capture two lawbreakers? "Twasn't no time for the truth," she says. "When y'all get old as I is, y'all can lie too." In her person, both honor and courage triumph.

The comic spirit of "Miss Cynthie" (*Story*, June 1933; in *The City of Refuge*) floods the narrative with joy. Carrying her umbrella like a weapon against snakes, Miss Cynthie arrives in Harlem to join her grandson. She is seventy, "bewildered but unafraid." The porter tells her there are no snakes in New York. She answers with tart black certainty: "There's snakes everywhere, chile." Her response to Harlem is intense. Fisher says it is not architecture, not the surface that is exciting, but that the atmosphere is at once dark and bright: pedestrian life, color, sound, "the tireless carnival to which Harlem's life quickens in the summer." The old woman is wary but cheerful. Her song motif is not spiritual but secular: "Oh I danced with the gal with the hole in her stockin. . . ." Her grandson takes her to see the show he is in at the Lafayette Theatre. She is horrified by the huge passionate audience and the half-naked dancers, her grandson among them, singing and tap dancing for a "sin-sick, flesh-hungry mob of lost souls." But her grandson salutes her from the stage with a dance improvisation based on her favorite song, and the response of the audience is now more subdued, while cheering them both. Because she wants to love her grandson, she sees all the audience as children "who didn mean nothin," and she accepts the tribute that includes black contemporary modes in harmony with black traditional modes of music.

Dust jacket for the 1987 book that includes all Fisher's published stories

This story of reconciliation is the most widely anthologized in Fisher's canon. But Fisher died at thirty-seven, after chronic intestinal problems, and reconciliation may have been only a tentative theme.

Sterling Brown, writing within three years of Fisher's death, believed that Fisher's "jaunty realism" emphasized a spirit of underlying "racial unity." But Fisher also explores the effects of racial disunity. Over ten years later Hugh Gloster noted Fisher's objectivity and independence, and declared that Fisher was less preoccupied with race than with humanity. Recent critics, such as Margaret Perry, emphasize Fisher's craftsmanship. Addison Gayle, Jr., looking back to the 1920s, places Fisher among those black American writers engaged in the struggle to control the public images of blacks.

The characters of Rudolph Fisher's tales search for meaning in ghetto life. Their desperate situation has often made them one another's enemies; they could as easily have become one another's support. The best of these men and women bear their lives with fortitude. Gayle calls them the forerunners of modern black men and women in fiction, "the brick and mortar of a new literary tradition."

References:

Doris E. Abramson, *Negro Playwrights in the American Theatre, 1925-1959* (New York: Columbia University Press, 1969), pp. 59-63;

Houston Baker, Jr., *Long Black Song* (Charlottesville: University of Virginia Press, 1972), p. 107;

Sterling Brown, *The Negro in American Fiction* (Washington, D.C.: Associates in Negro Folk Education, 1937), pp. 135-136;

Arthur P. Davis, *From the Dark Tower* (Washington, D.C.: Howard University Press, 1974), pp. 98-103;

James A. Emanuel and Theodore Gross, eds., *Dark Symphony* (New York: Free Press/Macmillan, 1968), pp. 110-111;

Addison Gayle, Jr., *The Way of the New World* (New York: Anchor, 1976), pp. 135-140;

Hugh M. Gloster, *Negro Voices in American Fiction* (Chapel Hill: University of North Carolina Press, 1948), pp. 174-177;

John McCluskey, Jr., "Healing Songs: Secular Music in the Short Fiction of Rudolph Fisher," *C.L.A. Journal*, 26 (December 1982): 191-203;

Margaret Perry, "A Fisher of Black Life: Short Stories of Rudolph Fisher," in *The Harlem Renaissance Re-examined*, edited by Victor Kramer (New York: AMS, 1987), pp. 253-263;

Perry, *Silence to the Drums* (Westport, Conn.: Greenwood, 1976), pp. 64-68, 112-116;

Eleanor C. Queen, "A Study of Rudolph Fisher's Prose Fiction," M.A. thesis, Howard University, 1961;

Saunders Redding, *To Make a Poet Black* (Chapel Hill: University of North Carolina Press, 1939), pp. 108, 112, 118.

Papers:

Four unpublished stories and a modified version of a published story are in the Brown University Archives, Providence, Rhode Island. Letters written to Carl Van Vechten are at Yale University's Beinecke Rare Book and Manuscript Library. See also the Rudolph Fisher folder at the New York Public Library, Schomburg Collection.

Caroline Gordon
(6 October 1895 - 11 April 1981)

Robert H. Brinkmeyer, Jr.
University of Mississippi

See also the Gordon entries in *DLB 4: American Writers in Paris, 1920-1939; DLB 9: American Novelists, 1910-1945;* and *DLB Yearbook: 1981.*

BOOKS: *Penhally* (New York: Scribners, 1931);

Aleck Maury, Sportsman (New York: Scribners, 1934); republished as *The Pastimes of Aleck Maury: The Life of a True Sportsman* (London: Dickson & Thompson, 1935);

None Shall Look Back (New York: Scribners, 1937); republished as *None Shall Look Back: A Story of the American Civil War* (London: Constable, 1937);

The Garden of Adonis (New York: Scribners, 1937);

Green Centuries (New York: Scribners, 1941);

The Women on the Porch (New York: Scribners, 1944);

The Forest of the South (New York: Scribners, 1945);

The Strange Children (New York: Scribners, 1951; London: Routledge & Kegan Paul, 1952);

The Malefactors (New York: Harcourt, Brace, 1956);

How to Read a Novel (New York: Viking, 1957);

A Good Soldier: A Key to the Novels of Ford Madox Ford (Davis: University of California Library, 1963);

Old Red, and Other Stories (New York: Scribners, 1963);

The Glory of Hera (Garden City, N.Y.: Doubleday, 1972);

The Collected Stories of Caroline Gordon (New York: Farrar, Straus & Giroux, 1981).

OTHER: *The House of Fiction: An Anthology of the Short Story, with Commentary,* edited by Gordon and Allen Tate (New York: Scribners, 1950; revised, 1960).

SELECTED PERIODICAL PUBLICATIONS— UNCOLLECTED:

"A Morning's Favor," *Southern Review,* 1 (Autumn 1935): 271-280;

Caroline Gordon, circa 1938 (courtesy of Nancy Tate Wood)

"The Women on the Battlefield," *Southern Review,* 2 (Winter 1936-1937): 515-524;

"Frankie and Thomas and Bud Asbury," *Southern Review,* 4 (Spring 1939): 696-712;

"Mr. Faulkner's Southern Saga," review of *The Portable Faulkner, New York Times Book Review,* 5 May 1946, pp. 1, 45;

"Notes on Faulkner and Flaubert," *Hudson Review,* 1 (Spring 1948): 222-231;

"Notes on Hemingway and Kafka," *Sewanee Review,* 57 (Spring 1949): 215-226;

"Stephen Crane," *Accent*, 9 (Spring 1949): 153-157;

"Notes on Chekhov and Maugham," *Sewanee Review*, 57 (Summer 1949): 401-410;

"The Art and Mystery of Faith," *Newman Annual* (1953): 55-61;

"Some Readings and Misreadings," *Sewanee Review*, 61 (Summer 1953): 384-407;

"The Feast of St. Eustace," *Kenyon Review*, 16 (Spring 1954): 234-256;

Mr. Verver, Our National Hero," *Sewanee Review*, 63 (Winter 1955): 29-47;

"How I Learned to Write Novels," *Books on Trial*, 15 (November 1956): 111-112, 160-163;

"Flannery O'Connor's *Wise Blood*," *Critique*, 2 (Fall 1958): 3-10;

"The Novels of Brainard Cheney," *Sewanee Review*, 67 (Spring 1959): 322-330;

"A Narrow Heart: The Portrait of a Woman," *Transatlantic Review*, new series 3 (Spring 1960): 7-19;

"The Dragon's Teeth," *Shenandoah*, 13 (Autumn 1961): 22-34;

"On Learning to Write," *Four Quarters*, 12 (January 1963): 8-15;

"Flannery O'Connor: A Tribute," *Esprit*, 8 (Winter 1964): 28;

"Letters to a Monk," *Ramparts*, 3 (December 1964): 4-10;

"Cock-Crow," *Southern Review*, new series 1 (Summer 1965): 856-871;

"The Elephant," *Sewanee Review*, 74 (Autumn 1966): 856-871;

"Heresy in Dixie," *Sewanee Review*, 76 (Spring 1968): 263-297;

"Cloud Nine," *Sewanee Review*, 77 (Autumn 1969): 591-629;

"Always Summer," *Southern Review*, new series 7 (Spring 1971): 430-446;

"Rebels and Revolutionaries: The New American Scene," *Flannery O'Connor Bulletin*, 3 (1974): 40-56;

"The Strangest Day in the Life of Captain Meriwether Lewis As Told to His Eighth Cousin, Once Removed," *Southern Review*, new series 12 (Spring 1976): 387-397.

Although Caroline Gordon was far more productive as a novelist than as a short-story writer (she published nine novels and two story collections—not including her *Collected Stories* [1981]—plus a smattering of other stories), her critical reputation now rests, with the exception of a novel or two, primarily on her stories. Ironi-

cally, she saw herself first as a novelist and only secondarily as a short-story writer; stories, she frequently complained, were minor achievements, distractions from her more important, long projects. "I wasn't cut out to write short stories," she said in a 1971 interview, and to Josephine Herbst she wrote (6 October 1929) that she loathed stories, adding that "they are all just a trick, and they simply drive me mad." After completing in 1937 "The Brilliant Leaves," one of her most accomplished stories (*Harper's Bazaar*, November 1937; collected in *The Forest of the South*, 1945), she told Robert Penn Warren that she was through with short fiction: "I am quite seriously determined never to try my hand at another. I can face a lifetime of incessant toil writing novels but each short story takes as much out of you—me, anyhow, as a novel and then you have to start all over again" (as quoted by Ann Waldron, her first biographer).

Gordon, it turns out, continued to write stories, though not with the regularity or the enthusiasm she had for her novels. Rose Ann C. Fraistat has pointed out, however, that Gordon's imaginative vision was more sympathetic to short fiction than Gordon would have it; she frequently conceived her novels, for instance, in smaller sections of story length and, indeed, first published as stories several of what became chapters in her novels. And whatever her personal feelings about the genre, Gordon clearly was its master. She strongly admired Gustave Flaubert and Henry James, and like them she approached her art with meticulous precision, carefully constructing tightly knit stories that rely as much on detail, image, and point of view as on plot. Her stories, particularly those from the late 1930s and afterward, were also profoundly influenced by New Critical thinking (she was married to Allen Tate and was close personally and artistically to other New Critics, particularly those from the South, including Warren, Cleanth Brooks, and John Crowe Ransom). The theory emphasized structure, tension, and irony. In *The House of Fiction* (1950), an anthology coedited by Gordon and Tate (though Gordon wrote most of the commentary), she and Tate endorsed what they called "symbolic naturalism"—the technique of presenting objective details necessary for the story's literal action that also, with symbolic resonance, fused the story's deeper levels of significance. Such is what they found in James Joyce's "The Dead" (in *Dubliners*, 1914): "If the art of naturalism consists mainly in making *active* those ele-

Gordon's parents, James Morris Gordon and Nancy Meriwether Gordon (courtesy of Princeton University Library [left] and Nancy Tate Wood [right])

ments which had hitherto remained *inert*, that is description and expository summary, the further push given the method by Joyce consists in manipulating what at first sight seems to be mere physical detail into dramatic symbolism." Such, too, is what Gordon strove for in her own short fiction.

The second of three children of James Maury Morris Gordon and Nancy Meriwether Gordon, Caroline Gordon was born on 6 October 1895 on one of her mother's family's farms, Merry Mont, in Trenton County, Kentucky, near the Tennessee border. She spent her first seven years at the farm, where life was peaceful but rarely dull. Gordon delighted in the farm routines, the woods, and all the people—extended family, friends, and servants—who always were around. "When I think of my childhood," Gordon later wrote in "Always Summer" (*Southern Review*, Spring 1971), a memoir, "my first impression is of a rounded whole, of a world that was so self-contained, yet so fully peopled and so firmly rooted in time and space that today when its name [Merry Mont] is pronounced I feel a stir-

ring of the heart which no other name can evoke." Perhaps deriving from the essentially religious view of humanity underpinning the traditional southern life on the farm, Gordon also, she claims, became aware of the evils and sufferings of the perilous human journey through life. "I, myself," she wrote in another memoir ("Cock-Crow," *Southern Review*, Summer 1965), "cannot remember a time when I was not aware that life was a desperate affair, at best, and lying awake at night or early in the morning, I used to ponder the way it indubitably was." This piercing tension between idyllic community life and the troubled existential struggles of individuals proved to be crucial in the development of Gordon's mature vision and art.

In 1902 Gordon left Merry Mont to live in Clarksville, Tennessee, where her father had opened a preparatory school. Here began her lifelong love of the classics, a love that she later admitted probably had more to do in shaping her critical positions than anything else. When Mr. Gordon decided to devote himself full-time to the min-

Gordon at ten (courtesy of Nancy Tate Wood)

istry of the Church of Christ, the family moved to Wilmington, Ohio, the beginning of a series of moves that included stays at Lynchburg, Virginia; Princeton, Kentucky; and Poplar Bluff, Kentucky. Gordon attended Bethany College from 1912 to 1916 and, after graduating, first taught high school in Clarksville, Tennessee, and then worked for a while at the *Chattanooga News*. In 1924, while visiting her family in Guthrie, Kentucky, she met Tate, who was visiting his friend Robert Penn Warren. By this time Gordon was an aspiring writer, and like Tate she moved to New York to be in the thick of the literary world. Gordon and Tate were married in New York on 15 May 1925, and their only child, Nancy, was born in September.

The late 1920s were trying times for Tate and Gordon. The lack of a steady income was an ongoing problem as both struggled with their writing, Tate more successfully than Gordon. In 1927 Gordon began working as a secretary-typist for Ford Madox Ford and quickly came under his influence as he encouraged her with her own work. This influence grew after Tate and Gor-

don went to Europe in 1928 (Tate had won a Guggenheim Fellowship) and Gordon for a while went back to work for Ford. Ford's encouragement and discipline came at a crucial time for Gordon, who was torn by doubt about her writing. "Ford took me by the scruff of the neck . . . ," she wrote to Sally Wood on 21 January 1930, "set me down in his apartment every morning at eleven o'clock and forced me to dictate at least five thousand words, not all in one morning, of my novel [*Penhally*] to him. If I complained it was hard work with everything so hurried and Christmas presents to buy, he observed 'You have no passion for your art. It is unfortunate,' in such a sinister way that I would reel forth sentences in a sort of a panic. Never did I see such a passion for the novel as that man has." In large part through Ford's inspiration and guidance, Gordon went on to finish *Penhally*, a novel about the decline of a southern planter's family through several generations, and it was published in 1931.

Gordon had already published several stories by that time. Her first two stories, "Summer Dust" (*Gyroscope*, November 1929; collected in *The Forest of the South*) and "The Long Day" (*Gyroscope*, February 1930; also in *The Forest of the South*), both explore the experiences of two children who have startling moments of recognition concerning the terrors and cruelties life can hold. Both children retreat from such recognition, the young girl in the former story into the world of imagination and fairy tale, and the young boy in the latter back to the safety of his ordered home. Together "Summer Dust" and "The Long Day" point to the theme Gordon would explore in almost all her fiction of the 1930s: the hero's struggle to affirm order and meaning in a world shadowed by death and disintegration.

All of Gordon's fiction from the 1930s to the early 1940s—numerous stories and her five novels *Penhally*; *Aleck Maury, Sportsman* (1934); *None Shall Look Back* (1937); *The Garden of Adonis* (1937); and *Green Centuries* (1941)—is set in the South, the backdrop usually being a traditional southern society under stress and challenge from a new modern order, or perhaps a new modern disorder. Amidst and against this decline and confusion, Gordon's heroes take their solitary stands, inevitably being either crushed by forces beyond their control or, at the very least, brought to see their impending doom. These heroes are not ivory-tower intellectuals or artists who think and write passionately but people who literally *act* bravely—in doing battle, discovering new lands, tilling the soil, or hunting prey.

For most of this period, Tate and Gordon were living in the South, struggling, as always, to make ends meet. In 1930 they had returned from Europe and—after a brief stay in New York—moved to a farm outside Clarksville, Tennessee; their place, Benfolly, quickly became a gathering place for writers, at least one of whom was in residence almost all the time. Tate and Gordon then spent almost a year in Europe (1932-1933); upon returning, they lived at their Tennessee farm, then later in Memphis and Greensboro, when teaching appointments came along. In 1939, after Tate received an appointment at Princeton, they left the South, almost for good; except for two brief stays in Tennessee during the 1940s and six years in Dallas during the 1970s, Gordon would live outside the region that had so profoundly shaped her.

Particularly noteworthy, in terms of her achievement with short fiction during the 1930s, are her stories about Aleck Maury—"The Burning Eyes," "Old Red," "One More Time," "To Thy Chamber Window Sweet," and "The Last Day in the Field." Maury, also the hero of the novel bearing his name, is based on Gordon's father and is her most memorable character: a great southern sportsman, forever searching for the perfect stream to fish and woods and fields to hunt. Despite being a schoolteacher and a man with a family, Maury bristles against the demands of home, job, and society (particularly female society) and instead looks for order and meaning in the hunting rituals he so assiduously upholds. In "The Burning Eyes" (which became the first chapter of *Aleck Maury, Sportsman* and was collected in *The Forest of the South*) the young Maury is taken on his first possum hunt; at the end, he stands transfixed before the treed possum, joined in a mystical bond between hunter and prey that will mark all his future excursions. In the other stories from this period Maury is an old man who deftly avoids the attempts of family and women to domesticate him; with zest and glee he is forever leaving them behind and lighting out for the wilderness, an elderly version of Mark Twain's Huck Finn. But as Maury comes to see, his primary antagonist is less the people seeking to inhibit his sport than it is time itself which is progressively ravaging his body and will ultimately claim him in death. In "One More Time" (*Scribner's*, December 1935; in *The Forest of the South*) Maury learns of the suicide of one of his old fish-

Gordon, circa 1912-1916, when she was a student at Bethany College in West Virginia

ing buddies, who had been suffering from cancer and had decided he would rather drown in the river than be prevented from fishing it. And in "The Last Day in the Field" (*Scribner's*, March 1935; in *The Forest of the South*) Maury embarks on his last bird shoot, hobbled by a bad leg and poor health. After taking his last shots of the day, he watches the dove fall: "I saw it there for a second; its wings spread, it came whirling down, like an autumn leaf, like the leaves that were everywhere about us, all over the ground." He knows that someday soon he, too, will follow the fallen dove and autumn leaves. Despite his growing enfeeblement, Maury never foregoes his heroic struggle, living each moment as intensely as possible. Time for most people may seem a heavy gray blanket that smothers and confines, but for Maury, as described in "Old Red" (*Scribner's*, December 1933; in *The Forest of the South*), it is a challenge to seize the day, which is "a banner that whipped before him always in the wind! He stood on tiptoe to catch at the bright folds, to strain them to his bosom."

Few other of Gordon's characters achieve the stature and dignity of Aleck Maury. Other characters in the stories and novels who possess something like Maury's fire for life frequently are depicted as restless wanderers who disrupt rather than enhance life. An epigraph to one section of *Green Centuries* is a quote from Thucydides that underscores masculine roving: "and as they thought that they might anywhere obtain their necessary daily sustenance, they made little difficulty of removing: and for this cause they were not strong, either in greatness of cities or other resources." This statement embodies the failures of these characters. Failure also surfaces often in Gordon's early stories that focus on love between men and women. Veronica A. Makowsky, in her 1989 biography of Gordon, has argued persuasively that in her fiction men and women have such hopelessly different aspirations that lasting and meaningful relationships are rare if not impossible. In Makowsky's discussion of Gordon's first collection of stories, *The Forest of the South*, she suggests that "the forest of the South becomes more than a geographical setting; it is Caroline's dark metaphor for the human condition. Like the couples in *A Midsummer Night's Dream*, Caroline's lovers are separated and lost in the forest but for them there are no happy reconciliations."

In the mid 1940s Gordon's work entered a new phase, embodied most tellingly in her novel *The Women on the Porch* (1944) and her story "The Olive Garden" (*Sewanee Review*, Autumn 1945; in *The Collected Stories*). In these works Gordon began exploring the possibility of renewal and transcendence in the face of life's dark forces. In the novel, she tentatively suggests the transforming power of Christian faith, in the story, the sustaining structure of ancient Western tradition and mythology. In "The Olive Garden" a rootless and emotionally fatigued university professor regains vitality and purpose on a trip to the Mediterranean coast. There he comes under the spell of the landscape and the stories of the ancient heroes who once wandered there, realizing through their examples the possibility of honor and renewal through heroic struggle. As he walks back from the shore all seems different in his new vision: "The garden no longer seemed deserted. He did not now wish that he might meet somebody on its paths. Far below, in the rocky caves, that would always furnish refuge, that could, if

Gordon, Allen Tate, and their friend Sally Wood in Toulon, France, 1932 (Papers of Caroline Gordon, Princeton University Library)

they were needed, bring forth a new race of men, he could hear the heroes murmuring to each other."

Gordon's positing of a larger order for structure and meaning may have reflected her own needs during these turbulent times. The world was deep into war and her marriage to Tate was coming undone. In 1945 they separated and in 1946 were divorced. Although they remarried three months later, their marriage continued to be troubled. During the late 1940s Tate and Gordon lived in New York, Chicago, and Princeton, teaching, writing, and coping with their relationship.

In a step that dramatically changed the shape of her imaginative vision and her fiction, Gordon joined the Catholic Church in 1947. As Waldron has noted, Gordon gave herself to her new faith with an all-embracing fervor. In Gor-

Illustration for "Old Red," one of Gordon's stories about sportsman Aleck Maury (Scribner's, December 1933).
Based on Gordon's father, Maury is also the title character in her 1934 novel.

don's essay "The Art and Mystery of Faith (*Newman Annual*, 1953) she wrote that finding belief had "revolutionized my life" and that "it is, to me, a little as if I had all my life been engaged in the writing of a novel and had only recently discovered that the plot is entirely different from what I thought it was!" Gordon's understanding of her life changed with her conversion, and so did her fiction, which now became explicitly Catholic. "I was nearly fifty years old," Gordon wrote in the same essay, "before I discovered that art is the handmaiden of faith."

Two stories written after her conversion suggest the new thrust of her fiction: "The Presence" (*Harper's Bazaar*, October 1948; in *Old Red, and Other Stories*, 1963) and "Emmanuele! Emmanuele!" (*Sewanee Review*, Spring 1954; also in *Old Red, and Other Stories*). In "The Presence" Gordon returns to Aleck Maury, now too enfeebled for any sport. Maury's despair about his severely limited life and his approaching death intensifies when the landlady at his boardinghouse plans to sell out and move away. Whatever comfort and order Maury now has will be gone with her departure; and in his anguish he thinks back to his childhood when, under the spell of an aunt who was Catholic, he had learned the Catholic liturgy and had been present when his aunt had a divine vision. Now a man facing life's ultimate questions, he turns to prayer for Mary's guidance: "Holy Mary, Mother of God, pray for us sinners, now and at the *hour* . . . of our death." Here Gordon suggests the Catholic answer to the dilemma of death and dissolution that has haunted Maury as an old man—the answer that now became central to all her fiction.

"Emmanuele! Emmanuele!," inspired in part by the correspondence of André Gide and Paul Clandel, which Gordon had read upon Walker Percy's suggestion, explores the nature of the artist and artistic creation from Gordon's Christian perspective. Her character Guillaume Fay, who writes only before a mirror, is an artist entirely consumed by self-absorption. Opposed to him is another writer, Raoul Pleyol, who understands that the artist must devote himself to God and his creation. "An artist's first duty," he tells Robert Heyward, Fay's secretary and the central consciousness of the story, "is the same as any other man's—to serve, praise, and worship God." At the end, when Fay discovers that his wife has destroyed his letters to her, his whimpering collapse underscores the selfish pride—rather than his concern for others or for God—that drives his life and art.

Whatever structure and stability Gordon's Catholic faith gave her, her marriage with Tate during the 1950s continued to be anything but settled. As in the past they moved about following teaching careers—to Minneapolis and Princeton for example—and they had an extended stay in Rome from 1953 to 1954. In part because of her troubles with Tate and her concern about his heavy drinking, Gordon, while in Rome, began seeing a psychotherapist, and she quickly became entranced with Jungian analysis. Despite efforts at reconciliation, particularly hers, their second marriage ended in 1959 in divorce. By all accounts she was devastated and never recovered fully. "The divorce," Walker Percy later commented, "was the tragedy of her life" (as quoted by Waldron).

Gordon's interest in Jungian thought profoundly affected her fiction from the late 1950s until her death in 1981. Drawing on Carl Jung's theories of archetypes and Jacques Maritain's ideas about literary creation, Gordon developed a definition of Christian art that focused on archetypal patterns rather than literal subject matter. Gordon had gotten to know Maritain during her stays at Princeton; particularly influential to her thinking was his *Creative Intuition in Art and Poetry* (1953). From her new perspective, she argued, in "On Learning to Write" (*Four Quarters*, January 1963), that great literature "comes into being when one of those timeless patterns reveals itself in time and conflict in which human beings are involved." Works of literature structured on some deep level by archetypal patterns, she added, could be understood finally as being Christian, since archetypes embodied the full range of human experience and thus ultimately led to Christian mysteries.

During this last phase of her writing, Gordon focused much of her energy on completing a double novel that would embody her theories of art. Describing her plans for this ambitiously conceived project, she said (as reported by Donald E. Stanford in 1971) that the work's "lower pattern" "deals with the archetypal world which the present day Jungians and the archaic Greek inform us lies at the very bottom of every human consciousness." The "upper pattern," she explained, "purports to be my own autobiography but is actually the history of the lives of certain members of my family who have been associated, to some extent, with public figures (Dr. John Hunter, Thomas Jefferson, Meriwether Lewis, Sir Walter Scott, et al.)." As she made clear, Gordon hoped to reveal with her novel's structure the ongoing reverberations throughout history of archetypal action, with a particular focus on heroic endeavor against misfortune.

Gordon never finished her double novel, although in 1972 she did publish separately the "lower pattern," a novel of the exploits of Heracles called *The Glory of Hera*. She also published some stories that apparently were to be parts of the "upper pattern," but these were never brought together as planned. Perhaps the best of these stories is "One Against Thebes" (originally published as "The Dragon's Teeth," *Shenandoah*, Autumn 1961; in *Old Red, and Other Stories*), a rewritten version of her first published story, "Summer Dust." Unlike the young girl in the original story, who retreats from disturbing knowledge into the unrealistic world of fairy tales, the young heroine in the rewritten story looks to Heracles' adventures as a model for her battle with the evil forces in life. As the title suggests, she comes to resemble in her struggles the ancient heroes who battled the forces of destruction at Thebes.

During the 1960s Gordon made her home in Princeton, but also spent several years teaching creative writing at Purdue, the University of California at Davis, and Emory. Her second collection of stories, *Old Red, and Other Stories*, was published in 1963, and *The Collected Stories*, with an introduction by Robert Penn Warren, came out in 1981. From 1973 until 1978 she taught at the University of Dallas, a Catholic school that stressed the teaching of Western culture and tradition. In 1978 she moved to San Cristóbal, Mexico, to live with her daughter and son-in-law, Nancy and Percy Wood, Jr. She died there on 11 April 1981.

Perhaps Gordon's most noteworthy achievement as a writer of short fiction, as *The Collected Stories* makes so evident, is the consistently high quality of that fiction in a career that spanned more than five decades and passed through several stages of development that profoundly altered Gordon's thought and artistic vision. Only very late in her career did her fiction begin showing signs of seriously falling off, possibly in part because of the sometimes strained efforts to work through her complex ideas of archetypes and Christianity in her fiction. But overall Gordon's mistakes were few, and she has left many finely crafted stories representing the best of the southern literary renascence. Warren said of her short fiction in his introduction to *The Collected Stories*: "They are dramatic examples of man in contact with man, and man in contact with nature; of living sympathy; of a disciplined style as unpretentious and clear as running water, but shot through with glints of wit, humor, and poetry.

Gordon at San Cristóbal de las Casas, Mexico, circa 1980 (courtesy of Nancy Tate Wood)

Caroline Gordon belongs in that group of Southern women who have been enriching our literature uniquely in this century—all so different in spirit, attitude, and method, but all with the rare gift of the teller of the tale."

Interview:
Catherine B. Baum and Floyd C. Watkins, "Caroline Gordon and 'The Captive': An Interview," *Southern Review,* new series 7 (Spring 1971): 447-462.

Letters:
The Southern Mandarins: Letters of Caroline Gordon to Sally Wood 1924-1937, edited by Sally Wood (Baton Rouge & London: Louisiana State University Press, 1984).

Bibliographies:
Joan Griscom, "Bibliography of Caroline Gordon," *Critique,* 1 (Winter 1956): 74-78;

M. E. Bradford, "Caroline Gordon: A Working Bibliography, 1957-1972," in *The Short Fiction of Caroline Gordon: A Critical Symposium,* edited by Thomas H. Landess (Irving: University of Dallas Press, 1972), pp. 130-133;
Robert E. Golden and Mary C. Sullivan, *Flannery O'Connor and Caroline Gordon: A Reference Guide* (Boston: G. K. Hall, 1977).

Biographies:
Ann Waldron, *Close Connections: Caroline Gordon and the Southern Renaissance* (New York: Putnam's, 1987);
Veronica A. Makowsky, *Caroline Gordon: A Biography* (New York & Oxford: Oxford University Press, 1989).

References:
Robert H. Brinkmeyer, Jr., "The Key to the Puzzle: The Literary Career of Caroline Gordon," in his *Three Catholic Writers of the Mod-*

ern South (Jackson: University Press of Mississippi, 1985), pp. 73-118;

Ashley Brown, "Caroline Gordon's Short Fiction," *Sewanee Review*, 81 (Spring 1973): 365-370;

Brainard Cheney, "Caroline Gordon's Ontological Quest," *Renascence*, 16 (Fall 1963): 3-12;

Rose Ann C. Fraistat, *Caroline Gordon as Novelist and Woman of Letters* (Baton Rouge & London: Louisiana State University Press, 1984);

Thomas H. Landess, ed., *The Short Fiction of Caroline Gordon: A Critical Symposium* (Irving, Tex.: University of Dallas Press, 1984);

Andrew Lytle, "Caroline Gordon and the Historic Image," *Sewanee Review*, 57 (Fall 1949): 560-586;

James E. Rocks, "The Mind and Art of Caroline Gordon," *Mississippi Quarterly*, 21 (Winter 1967-1968): 1-16;

Donald E. Stanford, "Caroline Gordon: From *Penhally* to *A Narrow Heart*," *Southern Review*, new series 7 (Spring 1971): xv-xx;

William J. Stuckey, *Caroline Gordon* (New York: Twayne, 1972);

Williard Thorp, "The Way Back and the Way Up: The Novels of Caroline Gordon," *Bucknell Review*, 6 (December 1956): 1-15.

Papers:

The repository of Caroline Gordon's papers is the Firestone Library at Princeton University.

Ernest Hemingway

(21 July 1899 - 2 July 1961)

Susan F. Beegel

See also the Hemingway entries in *DLB 4: American Writers in Paris, 1920-1939; DLB 9: American Novelists, 1910-1945; Documentary Series 1;* and *DLB Yearbooks: 1981, 1985,* and *1987.*

BOOKS: *Three Stories and Ten Poems* (Paris: Contact, 1923; Bloomfield Hills, Mich.: Bruccoli Clark, 1977);

in our time (Paris: Three Mountains Press, 1924; London: Jackson, 1924; Bloomfield Hills, Mich.: Bruccoli Clark, 1977);

In Our Time (New York: Boni & Liveright, 1925; London: Cape, 1926; revised edition, New York: Scribners, 1930);

The Torrents of Spring (New York: Scribners, 1926; London: Cape, 1933);

Today Is Friday (Englewood, N.J.: As Stable, 1926);

The Sun Also Rises (New York: Scribners, 1926); republished as *Fiesta* (London: Cape, 1927);

Men Without Women (New York: Scribners, 1927; London: Cape, 1928);

A Farewell to Arms (New York: Scribners, 1929; London: Cape, 1929);

Death in the Afternoon (New York & London: Scribners, 1932; London: Cape, 1932);

God Rest You Merry Gentlemen (New York: House of Books, 1933);

Winner Take Nothing (New York & London: Scribners, 1933; London: Cape, 1934);

Green Hills of Africa (New York & London: Scribners, 1935; London: Cape, 1936);

To Have and Have Not (New York: Scribners, 1937; London: Cape, 1937);

The Spanish Earth (Cleveland: Savage, 1938);

The Fifth Column and the First Forty-Nine Stories (New York: Scribners, 1938; London: Cape, 1939); republished as *The Short Stories of Ernest Hemingway* (New York: Scribners, 1954);

The Fifth Column: A Play in Three Acts (New York: Scribners, 1940; London: Cape, 1968);

For Whom the Bell Tolls (New York: Scribners, 1940; London: Cape, 1941);

Ernest Hemingway at Princeton, October 1931 (Hemingway Collection, John F. Kennedy Library)

Across the River and Into the Trees (London: Cape, 1950; New York: Scribners, 1950);

The Old Man and the Sea (New York: Scribners, 1952; London: Cape, 1952);

The Collected Poems, unauthorized edition (San Francisco, 1960);

Hemingway: The Wild Years, edited by Gene Z. Hanrahan (New York: Dell, 1962);

A Moveable Feast (New York: Scribners, 1964; London: Cape, 1964);

By-Line: Ernest Hemingway, edited by William White (New York: Scribners, 1967; London: Collins, 1968);

The Fifth Column and Four Stories of the Spanish Civil War (New York: Scribners, 1969);

Ernest Hemingway, Cub Reporter, edited by Matthew J. Bruccoli (Pittsburgh: University of Pittsburgh Press, 1970);

Islands in the Stream (New York: Scribners, 1970; London: Collins, 1970);

Ernest Hemingway's Apprenticeship, edited by Bruccoli (Washington, D.C.: Bruccoli Clark/NCR Microcard Editions, 1971);

The Nick Adams Stories (New York: Scribners, 1972);

88 Poems, edited by Nicholas Gerogiannis (New York & London: Harcourt Brace Jovanovich/ Bruccoli Clark, 1979); enlarged as *Complete Poems* (Lincoln & London: University of Nebraska Press, 1983);

Hemingway on Writing, edited by Larry W. Phillips (New York: Scribners, 1984, London: Granada, 1985);

The Dangerous Summer (New York: Scribners, 1985; London: Hamilton, 1985);

Dateline: Toronto, edited by White (New York: Scribners, 1985);

The Garden of Eden (New York: Scribners, 1986; London: Hamilton, 1987);

The Complete Short Stories of Ernest Hemingway (New York: Scribners, 1987).

Collections: *Hemingway*, edited by Malcolm Cowley (New York: Viking, 1944); abridged as *The Essential Hemingway* (London: Cape, 1947);

The Hemingway Reader, edited by Charles Poore (New York: Scribners, 1953);

The Enduring Hemingway, edited by Charles Scribner, Jr. (New York: Scribners, 1974).

PLAY PRODUCTION: *The Fifth Column*, adapted by Benjamin Glazer, New York, Alvin Theater, 6 March 1940.

MOTION PICTURES: *The Spanish Earth*, commentary written and spoken by Hemingway, Contemporary Historians, 1937;

The Old Man and the Sea, screenplay supervision and technical advice by Hemingway, Warner Bros., 1958;

Hemingway's Adventures of a Young Man, some narration written by Hemingway, Twentieth Century-Fox, 1962.

OTHER: *Men at War*, edited, with an introduction, by Hemingway (New York: Crown, 1942; London & Glasgow: Collins, 1946).

SELECTED PERIODICAL PUBLICATIONS—
UNCOLLECTED:
FICTION
"A Divine Gesture," *Double Dealer*, 3 (May 1922): 267-268;

"The Young Hemingway: Three Unpublished Short Stories," edited by Peter Griffin, *New York Times Sunday Magazine*, 18 August 1985, pp. 14-23, 59, 61;

Clarence (Ed) and Grace Hemingway with their children Ursula, Ernest, and Marcelline, October 1903

"[Philip Haines Was a Writer . . .]," edited by Donald Junkins, *Hemingway Review*, 9 (Spring 1990): 2-9;

"A Lack of Passion," edited by Susan F. Beegel, *Hemingway Review*, 9 (Spring 1990): 57-68.

NONFICTION

"Homage to Ezra," *This Quarter*, 1 (Spring 1925): 221-225;

"Bullfighting, Sport and Industry," *Fortune*, 1 (March 1930): 83-88, 139-146, 150;

"The Farm," *Cahiers d'Art*, 9 (1934): 28-29;

"Who Murdered the Vets?," *New Masses*, 16 (17 September 1935): 9-10;

"On the American Dead in Spain," *New Masses*, 30 (14 February 1939): 3;

"Safari," *Look*, 18 (26 January 1954): 19-34;

"The Nobel Prize Speech," *Mark Twain Journal*, 11 (Summer 1962): 10;

"African Journal," *Sports Illustrated*, 35 (20 December 1971): 5, 40-52, 57-66; 36 (3 January 1972): 26-46; 37 (10 January 1972): 22-30;

"The Art of the Short Story," *Paris Review*, 79 (Spring 1981): 85-102;

"Hemingway's Spanish Civil War Dispatches," edited by William Braasch Watson, *Hemingway Review*, 7 (Spring 1988): 4-92.

"Any man's life, told truly," Ernest Hemingway wrote in *Death in the Afternoon* (1932), "is a novel," and he strove to lead a life "better than any picaresque novel you ever read." The mention of his name conjures up a host of images—a cub reporter chasing mayhem in Kansas City; a Red Cross ambulance driver wounded in World War I; a traumatized veteran trout fishing in the Michigan wilderness; a bereted young writer rubbing elbows with Ezra Pound, Gertrude Stein, F. Scott Fitzgerald, and James Joyce in 1920s Paris; a drunken fiesta hero running with the bulls in Pamplona; a deep-sea fisherman battling the Gulf Stream's giant marlin; a big-game hunter stalking lions in Africa's long grass; a war correspondent braving Fascist bullets in the Spanish Civil War; a World War II reporter liberating the Ritz bar; a bearded Nobel Prize winner who survived two plane crashes and lived to read his own obituaries. Hemingway is well known as a man of prodigious appetites—for food, alcohol, travel, celebrity, rage, and most of all for beautiful, intelligent, exciting women. Hemingway married four times and sired three sons. As well as his love for his wives—amateur pianist Hadley Richardson, *Vogue* reporter and heiress Pauline Pfeiffer, war correspondent and novelist Martha Gellhorn, and journalist Mary Welsh—he had emotional entanglements with Red Cross nurse Agnes von Kurowsky, artist Jane Mason, and Venetian aristocrat Adriana Ivancich. Not since Lord Byron has a man of letters led so romantic an existence.

The exciting truths of Hemingway's life make it easy to forget that his most vital achievement involved the very quiet business of setting pen to paper. Hemingway's contribution to American literature was substantial, and today he is best remembered for four novels, *The Sun Also Rises* (1926), *A Farewell to Arms* (1929), *For Whom the Bell Tolls* (1940), and *The Old Man and the Sea* (1952), and for the short stories collected in *The Fifth Column and the First Forty-Nine Stories* (1938). Of these, "Big Two-Hearted River," "The Killers," "A Clean, Well-Lighted Place," "The Snows of Kilimanjaro," and "The Short Happy Life of Francis Macomber" are among the most read, taught, and criticized stories in the English language. Hemingway was a distinguished writer of nonfiction, too. *Death in the Afternoon*, his treatise on bullfighting, is perhaps the best book in English on that subject, as well as an important modernist aesthetic manifesto. *Green Hills of Africa* (1935) is an early experiment with the nonfiction novel, and Hemingway's posthumously published memoir, *A Moveable Feast* (1964), is the fully ripened fruit of that experimentation. *The Garden of Eden* (1986), an unfinished novel published in abridged form some twenty-five years after the author's death, is notable for its daring treatment of sexual metamorphoses. Hemingway's minor works—a satire, a play, a sizable amount of feature journalism, two little-regarded novels, and reams of interesting letters—give testimony to his versatility as a writer.

His most important contribution to American literature, however, is not any given work of fiction or nonfiction, but the celebrated Hemingway style, at its best in the opening paragraph of *A Farewell to Arms*:

> In the late summer of that year we lived in a house in a village that looked across the river and the plain to the mountains. In the bed of the river there were pebbles and boulders, dry and white in the sun, and the water was clear and swiftly moving and blue in the channels. Troops went by the house and down the road and the dust they raised powdered the leaves of the trees. The trunks of the trees too were dusty and the leaves fell early that year and we saw the troops marching along the road and the dust ris-

ing and leaves, stirred by the breeze, falling and the soldiers marching and afterward the road bare and white except for the leaves.

Hemingway wrote in simple and compound sentences, seldom subordinating one idea to another, but instead augmenting his meaning through a skillfully orchestrated counterpoint of repetitions. He imitated the rhythms of life—striving, for example, to recreate the march of troops with the repeated *and-and-and-and* of the passage above. He chose concrete words of Anglo-Saxon origin, avoiding abstract and Latinate diction, thereby endowing his prose with an almost biblical dignity. He avoided adjectives, but let nouns and verbs, objects and actions, carry the emotion, as in the sentences above, where the rising of the dust, the falling of the leaves, and the bareness of the road after the soldiers have passed may make the reader feel the men have gone to their deaths. Hemingway's style dealt the florid prose of the Victorian era a death blow and permanently changed the way Americans write.

More than a stylist, Hemingway also possessed a gift for storytelling. The adventures of his boxers, soldiers, bullfighters, expatriates, fishermen, femmes fatales, and mountain guerrillas have enormous popular appeal. Despite his often grim existentialist message, Hemingway's common touch, his universality, resides in the quality of adventure that permeates his work. As Ford Madox Ford describes it in his introduction to the Modern Library edition of the novel (1932): "I experienced a singular sensation on reading the first sentence of *A Farewell to Arms* . . . it was just excitement. Like waiting at the side of a coppice, when foxhunting, for the hounds to break cover. One was going on a long chase in dry clear weather, one did not know in what direction or over what country." And that is why in approaching Hemingway's life and work, one can be grateful that he did not, like Emily Dickinson, shun both marriage and travel. For wherever Hemingway and his characters are going, the reader is going, too.

Ernest Hemingway was born on 21 July 1899 in the prosperous Chicago suburb of Oak Park, Illinois. His childhood and young manhood provided subject matter for much of his best fiction and permanently molded his personality; this period, therefore, claims a disproportionate amount of attention in any study of his life. The second child of Dr. Clarence Hemingway

Hemingway at Horton Creek, near Horton Bay, Michigan, July 1904. His family's summer cottage on Walloon Lake was nearby.

and Grace Hall Hemingway, he was one of six children and the only son until he was nearly sixteen, when his mother gave birth to Leicester, her last child. Hemingway grew up in a female-dominated household, used to quarreling and competing with his older sister, Marcelline, and showing off for three admiring younger sisters.

Hemingway's parents possessed powerful personalities that left indelible marks on their sensitive son. His mother was an ardent suffragette and advocate of women's rights. She studied voice and music and made an opera debut in her youth; after her marriage she pursued a career in teaching voice, giving recitals, composing and publishing popular songs, and directing a church choir. Grace earned more money than her husband and employed servants to look after their home and children. Hemingway inherited his mother's charismatic stage presence and love of the arts, a love she cultivated in her children by filling their home with music, books, and magazines.

Mother and son were perhaps too much alike, however, their relationship one of dueling egos and clashing artistic temperaments. If he yearned for a conventional, warmly maternal mother, Grace disappointed him. When he went off to World War I, she did not worry that he

would be killed so much as she envied him the ocean voyage, the adventure, and the opportunity to see Paris and hear opera at La Scala. When he was wounded in Italy, Grace basked in the role of hero's mother, showered with roses by sympathetic neighbors. Limping theatrically up and down Oak Park streets in an Italian officer's cape, he resented sharing the stage. When he sent his mother a book he had published, she sent him news of an exhibition where her paintings had appeared. When he wanted uncritical acceptance, she told him instead exactly what she thought. When the world greeted *The Sun Also Rises* with a storm of critical acclaim, Grace inquired how it felt to have written "one of the filthiest books of the year." Hemingway made his resentment manifest in short stories such as "Now I Lay Me," "The Doctor and the Doctor's Wife," and "Soldier's Home," where mothers appear as selfish, emasculating women.

Hemingway's father was a harried doctor with a small but busy general practice and a specialty in obstetrics. Like his wife, he was a committed professional, designing surgical instruments and prosthetic devices in addition to experimenting with infant nutrition. Dr. Hemingway also helped manage his large household, overseeing the servants and doing the cooking from time to

Staff of the Trapeze, *the Oak Park High School newspaper, 1916; Hemingway is second from the right on the bottom row. His first byline appeared in the January 1916 issue of the* Trapeze.

time. A pillar of the local Congregational church, he had a piety that was sometimes indistinguishable from intolerance, and his opposition to smoking, drinking, dancing, and cardplaying left his children socially isolated. He was a strict and even harsh disciplinarian: when young Hemingway shot a porcupine that had injured a neighbor's dog, his father lectured him on killing harmless animals and forced him to cook and eat the porcupine. Dr. Hemingway's greatest gifts to his son were an abiding love of natural history, hunting, and fishing. He helped the boy search out wild plants and animals for identification and study, and taught him the arts of wing shooting and fly-fishing. The observant habits of a naturalist would stand Hemingway in good stead as a writer, as would the sportsman's respect for craft.

Tragically, Clarence Hemingway also bequeathed to his son a legacy of mental illness. Dr. Hemingway suffered from a depressive disorder that worsened as he aged, leaving him increasingly more anxious and withdrawn, subject to profound depression and to outbursts of paranoia and irrational rage that distressed and confused

his wife and children. In 1928, at the age of fifty-seven, he shot himself, and three of his six children, including Ernest, would also eventually commit suicide. In short stories such as "Indian Camp," "The Doctor and the Doctor's Wife," and "Fathers and Sons," Hemingway would present his father with a mixture of contempt and compassion.

Young Hemingway's parents formed two poles of his existence, and so did two places. Oak Park, with its tree-lined streets, handsome Victorian homes, and upper-middle-class values was a well-to-do and homogenous white community, heavily influenced by evangelical Protestantism. Even the mildest dangers to public morality were controlled by legislation within its sheltered bounds. Although Hemingway's adult exposure to the heady ethnicity of Catholic Europe and to the Roaring Twenties' drinking and sexual experimentation would cause him to reject Oak Park as a community of "broad lawns and narrow minds" (as he is popularly supposed to have called it), one part of him would remain a detached and critical observer of contemporary mores, even while participating in their excesses.

Hemingway's high-school graduation picture (1917), inscribed, with the pseudonym Jack Boyd, to his fishing buddy Lewis Clarahan

Every summer Hemingway's parents took their children to a primitive cabin on Walloon Lake in Michigan. There the young Hemingway swam, hunted, fished, hiked, explored, and consorted with Ojibway Indians. Michigan then "was a country of forests, lakes and streams and small farms with hills and pastures," as he recalled it in manuscripts for *Death in the Afternoon*. For Hemingway it was "The Last Good Country," wellspring of such fine Nick Adams stories as "The Battler," "Big Two-Hearted River," and "Indian Camp," stories linking him to American literature's wilderness tradition. Like James Fenimore Cooper, Nathaniel Hawthorne, Herman Melville, and Mark Twain, he needed unspoiled country to mirror the American soul, and when urban sprawl from Detroit destroyed the Michigan of his boyhood, Hemingway passionately sought its equivalents in Spain, Kenya, Key West, Cuba, and Idaho.

The United States entered World War I on 4 April 1917, just two months before Hemingway graduated from high school. He wanted to enlist in the army, but his father forbade it, and his poor eyesight made acceptance unlikely anyway. His parents hoped he would attend Oberlin Col-

lege, but instead he chose a job as cub reporter for the *Kansas City Star*, covering the police station and the city hospital and interviewing victims of accidents and violent crimes. The work was excellent training for an aspiring writer. Hemingway learned a reporter's spare, objective style and garnered material for later use in stories such as "God Rest You Merry, Gentlemen" and the *in our time* vignettes (1924). After six months at the *Star* he found a way to get to the war despite his poor eyesight, applying to the American Red Cross for work as an ambulance driver. After persuading his father to drop his objections, Hemingway sailed for France in March 1918.

Three days after his arrival in Paris, which was under bombardment from German long-range guns, Hemingway was sent to an ambulance unit in Italy. Here he collected fragmented bodies after a munitions factory explosion in Milan and drove an old Fiat ambulance on the dangerously steep and curving roads of Monte Pasubio. Hemingway's real baptism of fire, however, came when he was sent to Fossalta di Piave, where a major Austrian offensive was underway.

There, shortly after midnight on 8 July 1918, he was delivering cigarettes, chocolate, and postcards to Italian soldiers when an Austrian shell hit their trench. Hemingway received 227 pieces of shrapnel in his legs but was able to get up and help a wounded Italian soldier back toward the command post. Before reaching safety, he was hit again, this time by machine-gun fire. One bullet lodged in his right knee and another in his right foot. Stretcher-bearers carried him down a road that was "having the entrails shelled out of it" (letter to his family, 21 July 1918) and left him to await evacuation in a roofless stable. After being sent to a distributing station for morphine and tetanus shots and thence to a field hospital for a five-day stay, he was taken by hospital train to Milan.

Here he was the first patient in a newly established American Red Cross hospital, a converted villa that resembled a country club. A staff of attractive nurses mixed cocktails for patients, played the mandolin for them in the evenings, necked with them at night in wicker armchairs on shadowy balconies, and accompanied them, when they were well enough, to dinner, the opera, and San Siro racetrack. A series of operations to remove the shrapnel and bullets from his legs kept Hemingway hospitalized for three months, long enough to fall seriously in love with Agnes von Kurowsky. Tall, with chestnut hair, gray eyes, and a wicked, dimpled smile, Kurowsky was strikingly good-looking and enjoyed her impact on men. Trained at New York City's Bellevue hospital, she was also a highly competent and committed nurse. Kurowsky was adventurous and fearless, using her free hours to explore wartime Italy, volunteering to nurse in a dangerous influenza epidemic in Florence, and traveling after the war to care for tubercular children in Rumania and train native nurses in Haiti. In short she was exactly the sort of woman who would appeal to Hemingway, and undaunted by the difference in their ages (Agnes was twenty-six while he was nineteen), he set out to take her affections by storm.

Kurowsky's diary reveals how confusing she found his advances: "Ernest Hemingway is getting earnest . . . he is adorable & we are very congenial in every way." Another passage reads, "All I know is 'Ernie' is far too fond of me, & speaks in such a desperate way every time I am cool, that I dare not dampen his ardor as long as he is here in the Hospital." Flattered by Hemingway's attentions and attracted by his charm, Kurowsky never-

Hemingway in Milan, late 1918, wearing his tailored uniform

theless realized that she ought to discourage the affair. Yet even a nurse who had worked Bellevue's psychiatric and alcoholic wards could be manipulated by his desperate behavior, which included binging on liquor, creating public scenes, and threatening to do something rash. Inexorably, Hemingway wrung from Agnes a promise to marry him, perhaps more with his "champion love-letter[s]" (as she called them in a 1 December 1918 love letter to him) than with anything he could say or do in person.

In pain, in love, and confined for months to a hospital bed, Hemingway seems to have made up his mind to become a writer, a resolve that may have formed earlier when he chose the *Star* instead of Oberlin College. In an 11 December 1918 letter to his parents, he asserted that he was "made for to be one of those beastly writing chaps." At least two stories written during this Milan period survive in manuscript form at the John F. Kennedy Library—one about a maimed soldier committing suicide, and another about a wounded soldier afraid to kiss his nurse-lover, who has tried to resuscitate a patient dying of

Agnes von Kurowsky in 1920 (Hemingway Collection, John F. Kennedy Library)

influenza. The latter, juxtaposing as it does a woman brave in the defense of life and a soldier cowardly in the expression of love, is an insightful tale for a nineteen-year-old to have written.

When Hemingway's convalescence ended, he returned to the United States at Agnes's urging, expecting her to follow and marry him. However, as soon as the Atlantic was between them, her letters gradually cooled and finally ended with a "Dear John" letter announcing that she was engaged to someone else (an engagement never fulfilled). Interviewed by Michael Reynolds when in her eighties, Kurowsky insisted that she never had any firm intention of marrying Hemingway but had simply wanted to get him out of Europe (*Hemingway's First War*, 1976). Back home in Oak Park, this rejection of his first deeply felt love devastated him. "When you get the damned hurt, use it," he would later admonish F. Scott Fitzgerald in a 28 May 1934 letter. Hemingway used his wounding on the Italian front in "A Natural History of the Dead" and the Nick Adams stories "In Another Country," "Now I Lay Me," and "A

Way You'll Never Be"; his jilting by Agnes can be seen in "A Very Short Story" and "Snows of Kilimanjaro"; and both sources of pain are in *A Farewell to Arms*. The senseless slaughter that was World War I and his own near death also helped form his distinctive style by endowing him with the true modernist's distrust of "abstract words, such as honor, glory, courage" (*A Farewell to Arms*).

For months after his return home in January 1919, Hemingway hung around his parents' home and cottage drinking and smoking clandestinely, hunting and fishing with friends, swimming and boating with the local girls, telling tall tales about his wartime adventures, and displaying his shrapnel-riddled breeches to the Ladies' Aid Society. Dr. and Mrs. Hemingway urged him either to get a job or go to college, but he had other ideas. In his Oak Park bedroom, at the Walloon Lake cabin, and wherever else he could find privacy, Hemingway worked at writing short stories and submitting them (in vain) to popular magazines such as the *Saturday Evening Post*. The writing continued when, in January 1920, he went to Canada to be a live-in companion for a rich man's lame son, and also found part-time work doing articles for the *Toronto Star*. However, when warm weather came, Hemingway returned once more to his family's Michigan cottage for a summer idyll. His parents were upset by his coming home again to be "a sponger." Quarrels were frequent and vitriolic, and when, a few days after his twenty-first birthday, he kept two younger sisters and a neighbor girl out until 3 A.M., Grace Hemingway's patience with her son snapped. She wrote a letter asking him to leave home that he never forgot or forgave.

That fall (1920) he moved to Chicago to share an apartment with his friend Bill Smith and found work writing ads and copy for the *Cooperative Commonwealth*, a slick-paper magazine. Sherwood Anderson, author of *Winesburg, Ohio* (1919), was Hemingway's next-door neighbor and a frequent visitor, often talking of the artistic revolution then taking place in Paris. Another visitor to the Chicago apartment, Hadley Richardson, would become Hemingway's first wife. "The moment she came into the room," he would later tell his brother, Leicester, "I knew she was the girl I was going to marry."

In the autumn of 1920, Hadley was twenty-eight, a tall young woman with bobbed auburn hair. Like Agnes she was seven years older than Hemingway, but unlike Agnes she was shy and inexperienced. Hadley's life had been filled with personal tragedy. As a child, she had injured her back severely in a fall that kept her bedridden for months and made her overprotective mother, Florence, deny her normal childhood excursions ever afterward. When Hadley was eleven, her father, James Richardson, committed suicide. She was accepted at Bryn Mawr College but, at her mother's urging, withdrew after a single year. Hadley found self-expression in music and flung herself into studying the piano, but her teacher's coldness discouraged her from pursuing a career as a concert artist. Her older sister Dorothea was badly burned in a fire and died after giving birth to a stillborn child, and when Hadley's mother developed Bright's disease, Hadley nursed her through months of agonizing decline until her death in summer 1920.

Hemingway must have seemed the gallant prince Hadley needed to rescue her from long imprisonment in a tower of misery. "Yes," she wrote to him on 27 December 1921, "I think you are the nicest lover a person ever had.... I feel snatched up and appreciated and taken care of the way I did the night I rolled so scaredly down the sand dunes in the dark and you whirled me up and kissed me." To Hemingway, still smarting from Agnes's and his mother's rejections, Hadley offered unqualified devotion and a willingness to be shielded and led. Warmly maternal, she was willing to listen, admire, and soothe his considerable ego. Both lovers found intellectual satisfaction in each other—discussions of books and music, and of her piano playing and his writing fill their letters. She bought him a Corona typewriter and declared herself willing to move with him to Paris. On 3 September 1921 they were married in a country church, filled with swamp lilies and goldenrod, at Horton Bay, Michigan.

All during the unsettled time between his return from the war and his marriage to Hadley, Hemingway had been struggling to write fiction. Five of the thirteen surviving manuscripts from this period have been published in Peter Griffin's biography, *Along with Youth* (1985). "The Ash Heel's Tendon" features a hard-boiled detective and a hit man with a fatal passion for opera, while "The Mercenaries" describes the badinage of soldiers for hire. More sentimental, "The Current" focuses on a rich boy who wins the hand of Dorothy Hadley by taking a boxing title, while in "Portrait of the Idealist in Love" Hemingway appears to have framed some unsuspecting person's letter with an introduction and conclusion

of his own. "Crossroads—An Anthology" collects brief sketches of people from Horton Bay. Only one short story written in this period, the bizarre fable "A Divine Gesture" (*Double Dealer*, May 1922), was published during Hemingway's lifetime, and to date no scholar has unlocked its incomprehensible allegory. Of the other stories, Hemingway would recall that "The Saturday Post did not buy them nor did any other magazine and I doubt if worse stories were ever written" (John F. Kennedy Library manuscript number 820).

The stories themselves bear out Hemingway's judgment. They are sometimes extravagantly plotted and sometimes cloyingly sentimental. When they strive to be humorous, they collapse into what Fitzgerald would label "elephantine facetiousness." They swagger and pontificate like a cocksure young man; they are juvenilia. But they are also a beginning. "Crossroads—An Anthology" shows Hemingway starting to hone a keen observation of character and voice, and the use of a borrowed letter in "Portrait of the Idealist in Love" presages the technique of "One Reader Writes." In a satirical portion of "The Mercenaries," a game of wordplay performed with patriotic slogans foreshadows the "*nada* prayer" of one of his most famous stories, "A Clean, Well-Lighted Place."

With Hadley at his side and letters of introduction from Anderson in his pocket, Hemingway embarked for Paris and a literary education that would discipline his uncontrolled talent and channel his considerable ambition. Paris in the 1920s teemed with artists and writers. French postwar inflation so strengthened the dollar's purchasing power that the Hemingways, like many other Americans flocking to Paris, could live comfortably on her small trust fund and his meager earnings from sending foreign dispatches to the *Toronto Star*. They rented a primitive fourth-floor apartment in the Latin Quarter, and he settled to write.

Anderson's letters of introduction played a vital role in Hemingway's education as an artist. One was to Gertrude Stein, a Jewish-American expatriate whose Paris atelier was the center of a "charmed circle" of writers and artists. Stein's philosophy of language, based on the psychological theories of William James and the new artistic school of cubism, was intensely experimental. Believing that it was "the business of art" to "live in the complete actual present," Stein abandoned conventional plot structure, grammar, and punc-

Ernest and Hadley Richardson Hemingway on their wedding day, 3 September 1921, with Ursula, Grace, and Leicester Hemingway

tuation and used repetition, color, and sound to achieve a sense of immediacy. For a time, Hemingway was her eager protégé, and Stein was an accomplished critic of his early work, able to give him such tart advice as "Begin over again and concentrate." Another Anderson letter was to poet and critic Ezra Pound, a founder of the imagist movement in poetry, a school preoccupied with economy of language and brevity of treatment. The imagists sought to create an intuitive insight in the reader through the presentation of an object. A series of sketches titled "Paris 1922" (published in Carlos Baker's 1969 biography) shows Hemingway having absorbed Pound's tutelage and creating imagist moments like this: "I have watched two Senegalese soldiers in the dim light of the snake house of the Jardin des Plantes teasing the King Cobra who swayed and tightened in tense erect rage as one of the little brown men crouched and feinted with his fez."

The Paris years were among the most exciting and productive of Hemingway's career. In July 1923, little more than a year after his arrival, Hemingway published *Three Stories and Ten*

Poems with a small Parisian press (Contact). Critical consensus regards the ten poems as negligible, but the three stories are still seen today as "vintage Hemingway." "Up in Michigan" treats the first sexual stirrings of a young Horton Bay waitress named Liz Coates. Jim, a local blacksmith, makes Liz "feel funny," and she idealizes her feelings into love. Her romantic illusions are shattered when Jim, drunk after a hunting party, rapes her on the "hard and splintery and cold" planks of a Michigan dock. Although written in the third person, "Up in Michigan" is sensitively told from Liz's point of view. "My Old Man" is narrated by a boy named Joe Butler, whose father, an aging and seemingly crooked steeplechase jockey, breaks his neck in a race. "My Old Man" is strongly indebted to Anderson, but its own achievements—the authenticity of Joe's voice, the poignance of the theme, and the complex irony of the narrative perspective—are considerable. The third story, "Out of Season," describes a quarreling American couple's abortive fishing trip after they are led by a drunken Italian guide to a murky trout stream near Cortina d'Ampezzo.

Critics of the story have been confused by Hemingway's statement to Fitzgerald that it is "an almost literal transcription" of a fight with Hadley and by his insistence in *A Moveable Feast* that the "real end" of the story was the old guide's suicide. Nevertheless, the ambiguities in "Out of Season" fascinate both those who read it as a comedy of manners and those who perceive it as a tragedy of spiritual alienation.

In March 1924 William Bird of Three Mountains Press published a slender collection of eighteen Hemingway vignettes evoking images of contemporary violence—scenes from World War I and the Greco-Turkish war, firing squads and executions, gorings and manic celebrations drawn from the Spanish bullfight—concluding with the image of a deposed king pruning roses in his prison garden. Hemingway took his collection's ironic title, *in our time*, from a prayer: "Give peace in our time, O Lord." He used small letters after the fashion of e. e. cummings to emphasize his departure from outmoded literary conventions.

The culmination of Hemingway's Paris apprenticeship came in autumn 1925, when the New York firm of Boni & Liveright published his first major trade publication, a collection called *In Our Time*. The volume gathers fifteen full-length short stories, interleaving them with the vignettes from *in our time*. Seven stories treat the experiences of a young man named Nick Adams; eight treat other characters in varying situations. Like Anderson's *Winesburg, Ohio* and James Joyce's *Dubliners* (1914), *In Our Time* is arranged so that the stories develop and inform one another and constitute, in their way, a bildungsroman of a young man's struggle to achieve a coherent identity, even as modern existence conspires against him. *In Our Time* can be read as a cubist novel that, like a Pablo Picasso painting, recreates the frightening chaos of modernity by rendering a single picture from numerous fragmentary and dissonant perspectives.

The volume opens with "Indian Camp" (*Transatlantic Review*, April 1924—as "Work in Progress"), a story of sexual and racial conflict and of a child's introduction to horror and despair. At its conclusion, Nick, a young boy who has watched his father perform a cesarean with a jackknife on a screaming, struggling, biting Indian woman and who has seen her suicidal husband's slit throat by lantern light, is still able to feel "in the early morning on the lake sitting in the stern of the boat with his father rowing . . .

quite sure that he [Nick] would never die." In the second story, "The Doctor and the Doctor's Wife" (*Transatlantic Review*, December 1924), Nick's father submits to insult and humiliation by two Ojibway Indians and endures the nagging and platitudes of a hypochondriacal Christian Scientist wife. Nick's sympathies are with his father in this crisis of masculine identity, and the two escape into the cool hemlock woods to look for black squirrels.

"The End of Something" (previously unpublished) treats the beginning of Nick's adult sexuality by describing the end of an early relationship. Feeling as if "everything was gone to hell inside of me," Nick breaks off a romantic moonlight fishing trip with a girl named Marjorie, ending their relationship. The story's conclusion reveals that he had prearranged the break-up with a friend named Bill, who materializes at Nick's fire as soon as Marjorie has left. Another previously unpublished story, "The Three Day Blow," finds Nick seeking solace for Marjorie's loss in drinking, joking, and hunting with Bill. He is relieved to have escaped matrimony but wants to be in love again, so that his state of loss need not be permanent.

In "The Battler" (also previously unpublished) Nick is thrown from a train passing through the Michigan woods, and there, by a flickering campfire, meets one of the oddest and most sinister couples in American literature: Ad, an ex-boxer, beaten into deformity, who has been made insane by publicity about his marriage to his sister, and Bugs, a madly servile black ex-convict who "cares" for Ad with a blackjack. Like the atmosphere of "Indian Camp" that of "The Battler" is tainted with sexual and racial tensions, dark with inexplicable insanity. "A Very Short Story" (from *in our time*) is a bitter little piece recounting an unnamed protagonist's rejection by a nurse named Luz, who has cared for his war wounds and promised to marry him. Luz in her turn is rejected by the Italian major who has promised to marry her, and the protagonist contracts "gonorrhea from a sales girl in a loop department store while riding in a taxicab through Lincoln Park."

"Soldier's Home" (first published in the *Contact Collection of Contemporary Writers*, 1925) treats a veteran of Belleau Wood, Soissons, the Champagne, St. Mihiel, and the Argonne who returns home to find he must ask permission to borrow the family car. War has permanently alienated Krebs from the ice-cream-parlor wholesomeness

Title page for Hemingway's first book (1923), inscribed to his friend Philip Jordan

of American life, his father's pursuit of the dollar, and his mother's saccharine religion. With "The Revolutionist" (from *in our time*) Hemingway moves from postwar America to postwar Europe. The protagonist is a young Hungarian Communist traveling through Italy who, despite the failure of the revolution in his own country and his torture by the victors, still believes unreservedly in world revolution, even while he is surrounded by Italy's climate of gathering Fascism. His dislike of Andrea Mantegna's realistic crucifixions is proof of his naïveté, and at the story's conclusion he is unwittingly hiking into Switzerland toward his own imprisonment.

The four stories that follow are often referred to as "the marriage group" and treat a different kind of imprisonment. "Mr. and Mrs. Elliot" (*Little Review*, Autumn-Winter 1924-1925) describes the ménage à trois of a sexually and artistically impotent writer, his barren and neurotic wife, and her lesbian lover. Prefiguring Hemingway's late unfinished novel, *The Garden of Eden*, "Mr. and Mrs. Elliot" both satirizes and pays homage to the influences of Gertrude Stein and T. S. Eliot. "Cat in the Rain" (previously unpublished) is a sympathetic portrayal of a young wife's domestic yearnings, cut off by her husband's selfish insistence on a rootless life. "Out of Season," from *Three Stories and Ten Poems*, provides another version of the quarrelling expatriate couple, while the final story in this group, "Cross-Country Snow" (*Transatlantic Review*, January 1925), reverses the point of view in "Cat in the Rain" with a portrait of a young husband whose wanderlust is thwarted by the impending birth of his first child. According to these stories, marriage is a trap for both men and women.

After the marriage group, Hemingway inserted "My Old Man," a story that undermines the reliability of paternal authority, and then concluded *In Our Time* with the best story he had written to date: "Big Two-Hearted River" (*This Quarter*, May 1925). After the feverish parental, sexual, racial, political, marital, and martial strife

Note to Dr. Don Carlos Guffey on the front flyleaf of a copy of Three Stories and Ten Poems *(auctioned by Swann Galleries, sale number 1509, 19 October 1989). Guffey, a Kansas City obstetrician, delivered Hemingway's two sons by his second wife, Pauline Pfeiffer Hemingway.*

that characterizes the volume, "Big Two-Hearted River" offers cool relief and therapy. Little happens in the story. Nick travels alone into the Michigan woods, where he pitches his tent, cooks dinner, sleeps, makes breakfast, catches and rigs bait, and fishes for trout. Refusing to think about an unspecified something that is troubling him, Nick focuses instead on observing his wilderness surroundings clearly and well: "Nick looked down into the clear, brown water, colored from the pebbly bottom, and watched the trout keeping themselves steady in the current with wavering fins. As he watched them they changed their positions by quick angles, only to hold steady in the fast water again. Nick watched them a long time." Nick also devotes considerable attention to performing with care the tasks that make him self-reliant in the woods. His reward is an almost sexual satisfaction in successful fishing—"The reel ratcheted into a mechanical shriek as the line went out in a rush ... his heart feeling stopped with the excitement, leaning back against the current that mounted icily his thighs, Nick thumbed the reel hard with his left hand"—and he gives himself a temporary reprieve from the necessity of "fishing the swamp," of confronting the anxieties clamoring for his attention.

"Big Two-Hearted River" is a story by and about a young writer who has achieved the fullness of his powers, who has learned to observe intently, to work with consummate craft, to discipline his tendency to self-indulgence, to rely upon his own judgment of what is right and good, and to harness the disturbing forces of memory and experience to his own ends. Like the masterwork a medieval apprentice prepared to earn his professional independence, it is a fitting conclusion to the period from 1921 to 1925, years that made Hemingway the artist he longed to become.

This period was not entirely spent scratching out stories in a Latin Quarter garret and discussing writing in Left Bank cafés. The Hemingways traveled extensively, skiing in Switzerland and Austria, trout fishing in the Italian Dolomites, hiking in Germany's Black Forest, and attending Spanish fiestas and bullfights. Hemingway's job as foreign correspondent took him to the international peace conference in Lausanne, got him an interview with Benito Mussolini, and sent him to Constantinople to cover the Greco-Turkish war. Each new journey enriched the fund of material Hemingway could draw on as a writer. In 1923 the couple returned briefly to Toronto for the birth of a son, John Hadley Nicanor, nicknamed Bumby. Hemingway was made restless by this forced absence from Paris, and the little family went back in just a few months to continue the Bohemian life in a larger apartment in a more pleasant neighborhood. Gertrude Stein and Alice B. Toklas were godmothers to the child, and poet William Carlos Williams, an M.D., dropped by to advise Hadley about the baby's feedings.

There were, however, tensions in the Hemingway marriage. Fate had driven one wedge between the couple in 1922, when Hadley, traveling to meet her husband in Switzerland, decided to surprise him by bringing his manuscripts—all the fiction and poetry she could find in their apartment, carbons included—and the valise containing them was stolen from her train compartment.

Only "Up in Michigan," stuffed in the back of a drawer, and "My Old Man," sent out for publication, escaped. If the stories lost were as good as the stories spared, the loss was tragic. As Hemingway recalled in *A Moveable Feast*, Hadley "cried and cried," and he, too, was as hurt by the loss as by "death and unbearable suffering." The relationship was never entirely the same.

Hadley's ambivalence about his career may have precipitated the accident. Years of enforced poverty as Hemingway pursued his dream and weeks of enforced solitude as he chased stories for the *Star* eroded Hadley's willingness to suppress her strongly domestic needs and desires. Bumby's arrival, as both "Cat in the Rain" and "Cross-Country Snow" suggest, widened the rift. Finally, the difference in their ages began to tell as well. By 1925 Hemingway was an ambitious twenty-six-year-old still ripe for adventure and full of his burgeoning talent; Hadley, a matronly thirty-three, was ready to settle down. Hemingway's awakening interest in other women manifested itself at the 1925 Fiesta of San Fermín in Pamplona, when he joined the circle of admiring men hovering around the racy Lady Duff Twysden. The sexual tensions of that particular fiesta provided the plot for *The Sun Also Rises*, Lady Duff being a model for the novel's heroine, Brett Ashley.

Real trouble, however, came when Hemingway met Pauline Pfeiffer, a chic heiress working at the Paris offices of *Vogue* magazine. A dark, petite woman with a stylish haircut and a fur coat, Pauline ran with a crowd of wealthy American writers that Hemingway found equally irresistible—John Dos Passos, Archibald and Ada MacLeish, F. Scott and Zelda Fitzgerald—as well as artist Gerald Murphy and his wife, Sara, whose villa on the French Riviera was famous for its hospitality to the talented. There was a quality of rich-girl ruthlessness about Pauline's pursuit of Hemingway. "I'm going to get a bicycle and ride the bois," she wrote to Hadley on 15 July 1926. "I am going to get a saddle, too. I am going to get everything I want." She wanted Hemingway, with his good looks, charisma, and talent. Despite her devout Catholicism, Pauline was willing to detach a man from wife and child. He wanted her small-breasted modern beauty, her flattering desire, her savoir faire within the circle of financially successful writers he longed to join, and perhaps her substantial trust fund.

Despite this emotional turmoil, by the time *In Our Time* was published on 5 October 1925

Frontispiece and title page for Hemingway's second book, a collection of vignettes that were intercalated with stories in the 1925 collection In Our Time

Hemingway had finished a rough draft of his first novel, *The Sun Also Rises*. When reviews of *In Our Time* claimed that Hemingway's first novel might rock the country, prestigious publishers came courting. Hemingway favored Charles Scribner's Sons, recommended by his new friend Fitzgerald, but his contract with Boni & Liveright gave them right of refusal over his next book. Undaunted, Hemingway sat down and swiftly penned a vicious satire of Sherwood Anderson titled *The Torrents of Spring* (1926). Boni & Liveright, Anderson's publisher, could not possibly accept it. Their refusal freed Hemingway to give Scribners both *The Torrents of Spring* and the eagerly sought *The Sun Also Rises*. Hadley, Dos Passos, and Stein were all appalled by the callousness of this career move—only Pauline applauded.

In August 1926, two months before his first novel's publication, Hemingway and Hadley separated. Both he and Pauline felt guilty. "I went through hell," Pauline wrote to him on 29 October 1926. "Ernest and Pfeiffer, who tried to be so swell ... didn't give Hadley a chance." And Hemingway's own remorse was lifelong. *A Moveable Feast* contains his stricken farewell to Hadley: "When I saw my wife again standing by the

tracks as the train came in by the piled logs at the station, I wished I had died before I ever loved anyone but her." Nevertheless, he and Pauline were married in a nuptial mass in Paris on 10 May 1927.

The Sun Also Rises was an immediate success, establishing Hemingway as a young writer of the first rank, a spokesman for the Lost Generation that the novel's epigraph by Stein made immortal. Scribners chose to capitalize on that success by following the novel with a volume of short stories, and Hemingway's second major collection, *Men Without Women*, was published in October 1927. As with *In Our Time* Hemingway took care that the stories complemented one another, and he perceived them as bound together by the absence of "the softening feminine influence, through training, death, or other causes."

In the volume's first story, "The Undefeated" (*This Quarter*, Autumn-Winter 1925-1926), an aging and incompetent matador named Manuel Garcia clumsily fights and kills a difficult bull, refusing to abandon the arena even when he is fatally gored. Manuel dies in existentialist triumph, having upheld his masculine dignity and professional honor in the face of death. The second story provides another profile in existential-

EDWARD J.
O'BRIEN

"I regard this volume of short stories as a permanent contribution to the American literature of our time—a brave book not only for us but for posterity."

SHERWOOD ANDERSON

"Mr. Hemingway is young, strong, full of laughter, and he can write. His people flash suddenly up into those odd elusive moments of glowing reality, the clear putting down of which has always made good writing so good."

GILBERT SELDES

"Extraordinary in its vividness and its brutality, it is, for the most part, deliberately unliterary, in the modern style. I can see it being warmly admired as I admire it, and violently disliked as I dislike some of it. But it has too much character, too much vital energy and passion to leave anyone indifferent. To me that is a high recommendation."

IN OUR TIME
BY ERNEST HEMINGWAY

DONALD OGDEN STEWART

"After trying to make a meal out of the literary lettuce sandwiches which are being fed to this country, it is rather nice to discover that one of your own countrymen has opened a shop where you can really get something to eat."

WALDO FRANK

"Not in a long time have I been so impressed by the work of a new American author. Mr. Hemingway can write. His stories are hard, passionate bits of life."

FORD MADOX FORD

"The best writer in America at this moment (though for the moment he happens to be in Paris), the most conscientious, the most master of his craft, the most consummate, is Ernest Hemingway."

Dust jacket for Hemingway's first short-story collection, his first book published in the United States

ist courage. A wounded World War I veteran undergoing physical therapy in a Milan hospital narrates "In Another Country" (*Scribner's*, April 1927). An Italian major with a shrivelled hand shares his ordeal, as the two sit at machines that mechanically exercise their damaged bodies. The unnamed narrator may be Nick Adams or an early version of Frederic Henry of *A Farewell to Arms*, but the story centers on the major's coming to terms with his young wife's sudden death. "A man must not marry," he angrily advises the narrator. "If he is to lose everything, he should not place himself in a position to lose that." Yet by biting his lips and choking down his sobs, the major learns to bear his desolation with "straight and soldierly dignity."

"Fifty Grand" (*Atlantic*, July 1927) is an ironic story of masculine courage at the service of sordid ends. Aging boxer Jack Brennan ac-

cepts fifty thousand dollars to lose a fight against the heavy favorite, a young fighter named Walcott. Walcott, however, double-crosses Brennan, attempting to lose the fight himself by fouling Brennan with a devastating blow below the belt. It requires all of Brennan's physical courage to refuse the foul, remain on his feet, and save his money by losing the fight with a foul blow of his own that Walcott cannot endure. *Today is Friday* (separately published in 1926) suggests a religious analogue for the volume's preoccupation with male courage. The one-act play features three Roman soldiers discussing Christ's crucifixion. Their language is the crudest Chicago-American—"Hey, what you put in that, camel chips?" one inquires of a wineseller—but illuminates the volume's masculine ethos of stoic behavior, as the first Roman soldier admires Christ's physical courage under torture and his refusal to come down off the cross.

A Nick Adams story, "The Killers" (*Scribner's*, March 1927) explores a more passive acceptance of fate's cruelty. Two hit men in search of a prizefighter named Ole Andreson enter a lunchroom where Nick is dining and tie up him and the cook in the kitchen. Andreson fails to show up for his supper, and his would-be executioners leave. Released from his bonds, Nick runs to Andreson's boardinghouse to warn him and finds the old man lying on his bed staring at the wall. Andreson has accepted his death as inevitable and refuses young Nick's suggestions to run, call the police, or try to fix things with the gangsters. Nick "can't stand to think about him waiting in the room and knowing he's going to get it" and decides to leave town himself. Andreson's limpness in the face of death aligns him with William Campbell in the previously unpublished story "A Pursuit Race." An advance man for a burlesque show, Campbell abandons his job, climbs into bed, and takes to alcohol and heroin. Shrouded in a sheet, he carries on a tragicomic conversation with the show's manager, William Turner, who wants him to seek treatment and fight out his addiction. But Campbell is "in love with" his sheet, preferring, like Ole Andreson, to wait passively for the end. When he falls asleep, Turner, who understands the value of oblivion, steals away.

Some stories in *Men Without Women* treat the anguish of human sexual relations. "Hills Like White Elephants" (*transition*, August 1927) is perhaps Hemingway's finest "puzzle story," its interpretation hinging on an unarticulated word. A man and a woman share drinks at a Spanish train station. He urges her to have "an awfully simple operation" and assures her that afterward they will be "all right" and "happy" and "just like [they] were before." Jig, wiser and more imaginative than the man, knows that there is nothing "perfectly simple" about it and that their love is already gone. Confronting her partner's insensitivity and her own no-win situation with brave realism, Jig is among Hemingway's most interesting women characters, and his refusal to use the word "abortion" outright gives this exploration of sexual politics the understated power of the best imagist poetry. "A Simple Enquiry" (previously unpublished) is also a puzzle story, its unarticulated word "homosexuality." A major calls a soldier named Pinin into his bunkroom/office, questions him about his sexuality, and cannot decide whether Pinin has lied. An adjutant in the outer room snickers when Pinin departs. That is all that happens, but this far-from-simple story leaves a host of questions behind. Is Pinin a homosexual? Is the major a homosexual? Whatever the major's sexual preferences, what are his motives for questioning Pinin? Is the adjutant a homosexual? Why does he smile at Pinin's discomfiture? The story's "point" seems to be the inscrutability of human nature. In "Ten Indians" (also previously unpublished) Nick Adams confronts an equally baffling sexual problem. Returning home from a Fourth of July picnic he has shared with the warm and jovial Garner family, Nick is given a cold supper and some unpleasant news by his father, who informs Nick that his Indian girlfriend, Prudie, has been "threshing around" in the woods with Frank Washburn. The story raises unanswered questions about the father's apparently single state, his motives for betraying Prudie's infidelity to Nick, and the nature of Prudie's "happiness" with Frank. Nick believes that his heart is broken, but his feelings, too, are called into question when it takes him a long time the next morning to remember his grief.

Two other stories imply grave problems with the married state. In "A Canary for One" (*Scribner's*, April 1927) an American couple returning to Paris to "set up separate residences" meets a woman who has broken up her daughter's love affair with a Swiss engineering student. "I took her away, of course," says the mother. "No foreigner can make an American girl a good husband." She is taking her inconsolable daughter a caged canary as a gift. The juxtaposition of the daughter's plight with the couple's is ironic—neither the sheltered nor the experienced have escaped the grief of a broken relationship. "An Alpine Idyll" (first published in the anthology *American Caravan*, 1927) is a story of emotional attrition recounted by a young American skiing in Austria. When a peasant's wife dies during the long mountain winter, he lays her out on a woodpile in his shed to await spring burial. Although he later asserts that he "loved her fine," as the winter progresses and the peasant requires wood from his wife's resting place, he props her frozen body against the wall and hangs a lantern from her jaw to light his chores. The American narrator feels an unexplained affinity with the peasant's experience of love's perishability.

In "Che Ti Dice La Patria?" (*New Republic*, 18 May 1927—as "Italy, 1927"), the title being Italian for "What do you hear from the Fatherland?," an American narrator and his companion, Guy, motor through Fascist Italy, finding the

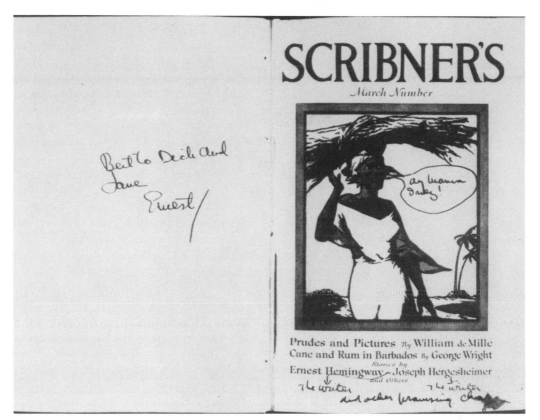

The copy of the March 1927 Scribner's—*which includes* "The Killers"—*that Hemingway inscribed to Dick and Jane
Armstrong (Clifton Waller Barrett Library, University of Virginia)*

country's wine embittered by alum and the people made hard and suspicious by Mussolini's regime. Armed police extort fines for imaginary offenses, and restaurants are brothels that officially do not exist. Critics often dismiss the story as a straightforward account of an actual trip Hemingway took with Guy Hickok in March 1927, but the hypermacho posturings of the Fascists and the prostitution of their women make "Che Ti Dice La Patria?" an interesting political commentary on the collection's masculine theme. Another apparently anomalous piece, "Banal Story" (*Little Review*, Spring-Summer 1926), is Hemingway's clearest statement of the effect he was striving to achieve with seemingly plotless stories that broke all the rules of contemporary magazine fiction. A piece of metafiction, a story that reflects self-consciously on its own artifice, "Banal Story" depicts a young writer reading an advertisement for a popular magazine called the *Forum*. He jibes at the magazine's notions of "life" and "romance," at its sentimental and formulaic distortions of reality. A harshly realistic sketch, beginning "And meanwhile, stretched flat on a bed in a darkened room in his house in Triana, Manuel Garcia

Maera lay with a tube in each lung, drowning with pneumonia," then interrupts the narrative of "Banal Story." Here, at last, is life—at least as Hemingway saw it.

The volume concludes with a previously unpublished Nick Adams story, "Now I Lay Me," that hearkens back to "Big Two-Hearted River." Nick, a lieutenant stationed in World War I Italy, is suffering from insomnia and trying to sleep on a straw-covered floor. He has been wounded in the past, will likely be wounded in the future, and is kept awake not only by his knowledge that "If ever I shut my eyes in the dark and let myself go, my soul would go out of my body," but by the relentless chewing of silk worms in the trees outside his window. On his best nights, Nick occupies himself by fishing imaginary and remembered trout streams, but on nights when he is "cold-awake" he prays for all the people he has ever known and tries to remember everything that has ever happened to him. One memory in particular haunts him, a Freudian nightmare of his smiling mother burning his father's preserved snakes and Indian weapons on the lawn. Nick tries thinking of all the girls he has known and

Pauline and Ernest Hemingway in San Sebastian, soon after their 10 May 1927 marriage

traveling from Michigan to Paris with his revolutionist father. A freak accident interrupted the book. Fumbling for a toilet pull chain in the night, Hemingway grabbed a skylight cord instead and pulled the entire window down on his head. The resulting concussion made it difficult to concentrate, and he abandoned the book when it had reached forty-five thousand words. Two chapters, "The Train Trip" and "The Porter," appear as stories in the posthumously published *Complete Short Stories of Ernest Hemingway* (1987).

By March 1928 Pauline was several months pregnant, and Ernest had settled to work on a different novel. Set in wartime Italy and concerning a wounded ambulance driver's love affair with his nurse, this manuscript would become *A Farewell to Arms*. Pauline's pregnancy, however, dictated a return to the United States for the baby's birth. This time Hemingway was enthusiastic about leaving Europe, for he wanted to visit Key West. There he and Pauline found an apartment, and Hemingway quickly established a schedule of writing, fishing, and visiting bars. This tropical idyll was interrupted by a visit to Pauline's parents in Piggott, Arkansas, and by the birth of a son, Patrick, in a Kansas City hospital. Pauline was in labor for eighteen hours, and the baby was finally delivered by cesarean section. Hemingway was well along on *A Farewell to Arms* by this time, and the character Catherine's death in childbirth surely reflects his worst fears during his wife's ordeal. Yet as soon as Pauline and the baby were able to travel, he returned them to Piggott and lit out to Wyoming for a regimen of cool mountain air, trout fishing, and work on the novel. By August's end he had finished the first draft of *A Farewell to Arms*, and he and Pauline returned to Key West for the winter.

In December 1928 Hemingway's father committed suicide, shooting himself behind the ear with a Smith and Wesson revolver. Dr. Hemingway had been worrying about money invested in worthless Florida real estate, suffering mentally from depression and paranoia, and ailing physically from diabetes and angina. Ernest channeled grief, guilt, and a disturbing empathy with his father into his work. On 22 January 1929, after a six-week burst of concentrated revision, he finished *A Farewell to Arms*. Despite controversy over the novel's illicit sex and soldierly language—its serialization in *Scribner's* magazine was banned in Boston—*A Farewell to Arms* was blessed with both critical and popular acclaim. "First reviews splen-

wondering what kind of wives they would make, but that kills trout fishing and interferes with his prayers. He has no faith in his orderly's assertion that marriage will "fix up everything." Though the fishing rituals of "Big Two-Hearted River" brought relief and therapy at the conclusion of *In Our Time*, by the end of *Men Without Women* they no longer have the power to bring Nick peace from fear or heal his emotional wounds.

Ernest and Pauline Hemingway spent the months after their wedding traveling in France and Spain and skiing in Switzerland. Back in their Paris apartment Hemingway worked on a novel he hoped would be a modern *Tom Jones*, tentatively titled "Jimmy Breen" or "A New Slain Knight," about the adventures of a young man did," cabled editor Maxwell Perkins, "Prospects bright."

In another sense, however, Hemingway's prospects had already begun to dim. Autumns in Wyoming, winters in Key West, summers in France and Spain—the wealthy lifestyle made possible by Pauline's trust fund and his own success was unsettled. The need to care for his widowed mother's household as well as for Bumby, the child of his first marriage, further complicated his domestic arrangements. Financial independence eroded discipline by creating a conflict between writing and sport. An established career and international celebrity also involved Hemingway in manifold distractions. The drinking he had begun during World War I, when a fellow patient saw and later recalled Hemingway's closet full of empty bottles, was becoming problematic. Alcohol-related accidents, quarrels, and mornings he was too hung over for work had increased after his divorce from Hadley and further increased after his father's suicide. From *Three Stories and Ten Poems*, published in 1923, until *Men Without Women*, published in 1927, Hemingway had managed at least a book a year. *A Farewell to Arms* had taken two years but had achieved classic status. In the Depression years of the 1930s the distance between his books would lengthen, while their quality became erratic. Things were no longer the same as they had been in Paris, when Hemingway and Hadley "were very poor and very happy" (*A Moveable Feast*).

In 1932, not long after the birth of his third son, Gregory, and three years after the birth of his second novel, *A Farewell to Arms*, Hemingway published *Death in the Afternoon*, a nonfiction book about bullfighting. *Death in the Afternoon* displays a knowledge of this uniquely Spanish ritual truly remarkable for an American writer, as well as containing some of Hemingway's most important critical writing about his aesthetic theories. The book also marks the emergence of the Hemingway persona, the author confident in his own wisdom and celebrity, pronouncing his beliefs ex cathedra. *Death in the Afternoon* was not a popular success. The American public, never enthusiastic about bullfighting at the best of times, did not rush out to buy a book about it in the midst of the Depression.

In October 1933 Hemingway published a collection of short stories written over the last five years, *Winner Take Nothing*. The volume opens with "After the Storm" (*Cosmopolitan*, May 1932), based on the true story of the Spanish passenger

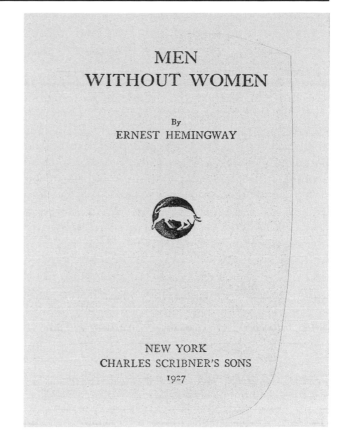

MEN
WITHOUT WOMEN

By
ERNEST HEMINGWAY

NEW YORK
CHARLES SCRIBNER'S SONS
1927

Title page for Hemingway's second collection of short stories

liner *Valbanera*, lost with all hands in a 1919 Key West hurricane. The story's narrator, a sponge fisherman, encounters the wrecked vessel when he flees the storm-torn town after a barroom brawl. He tries repeatedly to break into the ship and sees through a porthole a drowned woman whose hands are covered with rings, but the water's depth thwarts his attempts. Finally, Greek fisherman use dynamite to penetrate the ship and claim its riches. A Depression-era story of predatory have-nots only temporarily stopped from plundering the corpses of the rich, "After the Storm" presents an ironic contrast between the ship's emotion-laden tragedy and the narrator's chillingly indifferent voice.

Other stories explore the hollowness of religious consolation. In "A Clean, Well-Lighted Place" (*Scribner's*, March 1933) two waiters working late in a Madrid café attend their last customer, a drunken but dignified old man known to have attempted suicide. The younger waiter is impatient to go home to his wife's embraces and wishes the old man would leave. The older waiter identifies with his suicidal old customer's need for a clean, well-lighted place as a defense against the night. When the younger waiter succeeds in driving the old man away and departs for home, the older waiter delivers the *nada* prayer, perhaps the best-known statement of existential dread in American literature: "Our nada who art in nada, nada be thy name thy kingdom nada thy will be nada in nada as it is in nada. Give us this nada our daily nada and nada us our nada as we nada our nada and nada us not into nada but deliver us from nada; pues nada. Hail nothing full of nothing, nothing is with thee." In "The Light of the World" (previously unpublished) Nick Adams and a friend encounter a peroxide-blonde whore who tells a long and sentimental story about famous boxer Steve Ketchel's undying love for her. Ketchel, murdered by his father, is the story's Christ figure. Peroxide's proud claim that she once belonged to Ketchel body and soul is debunked by a huge whore named Alice, who claims to speak the truth: that Ketchel once called Alice, not Peroxide, "a lovely piece." Alice then replaces Peroxide's fictitious "true, wonderful memories" with a brutal recital of a whore's probable memories. The story's title—taken from John 8:12, in which Jesus says, "I am the light of the world: he that followeth me shall not walk in darkness"—emphasizes Alice's role as teacher, introducing the boys to the emptiness of Christian doctrine and the sordidness of human sexual relations.

"God Rest You Merry, Gentlemen" (separately published earlier in 1933—in slightly different form) is an even more graphic treatment of the clash between Christianity and sexuality. Two Kansas City doctors tell the story's narrator about a young boy so disturbed by his awakening sexual desires that he seeks castration. His turgid adolescent penis seems to him "a sin against our Lord and Saviour," and when the doctors refuse to castrate him, he amputates his penis with a razor blade on Christmas Day. Ironically, instead of escaping the torture of unfulfillable desire that drives him to self-mutilation, the boy unwittingly makes his predicament permanent, dramatizing the age-old conflict between acquired morality and natural impulse. "The Sea Change" (*This Quarter*, December 1931) offers the contrasting plight of a sophisticated man named Phil, grappling not with the puritanical attitudes of Kansas City but the sexual permissiveness of Paris. Phil's lover, a beautiful young woman, is leaving him for a lesbian affair and seeks his understanding and forgiveness. Outraged and humiliated, he at first resists her pleas, calling lesbianism a "vice" and a "perversion," but when she argues that "we're made up of all sorts of things," he gives her the permission she is seeking. After her departure Phil sees himself in the mirror as "a different man." His confrontation with his lesbian lover has forced him to recognize his own homosexuality.

Nick Adams reappears in "A Way You'll Never Be" (previously unpublished), this time as a shell-shocked soldier wandering a devastated portion of the Italian front. He is suffering from a head wound that was never properly trepanned and has a recurring hallucination about a long, yellow house by a bend in the river, a vision more terrifying than shell fire or his memories of helmets full of brains. When taken by his madness, he babbles about the grasshoppers he has once used for fishing. "Gentlemen, either you must govern—or you must be governed," he proclaims to an audience of worried Italian officers. This may be the Nick who once fished in "Big Two-Hearted River" with such control and tried to lay his fears to rest with fishing memories in "Now I Lay Me." If so, he is no longer able to govern his incipient madness with real or imagined fishing. Rather, his fears govern him, and his identification now is with the grasshopper impaled on the hook, wings disintegrating in the water, waiting to be swallowed.

Two more stories raise unanswerable questions. Roger, former manager of a second-rate and apparently homosexual bullfighter, narrates "The Mother of a Queen" (previously unpublished), fulminating bitchily about how the matador had refused to pay the rent on his (the matador's) mother's funeral plot, so that finally her corpse was dug up and cast on the public bone heap. Roger also holds a grudge against his former employer for refusing to pay him six hundred pesos he is owed. The story ends with Roger's asking about the matador, "What kind of blood is it that makes a man like that?" But like "A Simple Enquiry" the story raises many other questions. Is Roger himself a homosexual? Why does the matador allow his mother's grave to be despoiled? What really motivates Roger's rage and the matador's decision to fire him? "One Reader Writes" (also previously unpublished), based on an actual letter shown to Hemingway by Dr. Logan Clendening, presents a woman trapped in a biological no-win situation. Her husband has contracted syphilis while with the armed forces in Shanghai, and she is writing to a medical-advice columnist to ask whether it will ever be safe for her to live with him again. In effect, she is begging the doctor to deny what she knows to be true—that if she sleeps with her husband she will be infected, that his disease has ended their marriage. The story closes with her despairing "I don't know why he had to get a malady," raising a question even "Dear Doctor" cannot answer.

"Homage to Switzerland" (*Scribner's*, April 1933) features three different protagonists waiting for the Simplon-Orient Express at three different train stations at the same moment. At one station a homosexual counterfeits virility by harassing a waitress. At another a newly divorced man discusses his personal life with three porters, while at a third a Mr. Harris, whose father has committed suicide, encounters an eccentric member of the National Geographic Society. "Homage to Switzerland" destroys the absolute values of manly behavior, the sanctity of marriage, and parental authority, as it envisions the human cost of moral rootlessness. The previously unpublished story that follows, "A Day's Wait," treats a divorced father's effort to nurture his son. The little boy, Schatz, has the flu and, mistaking his temperature in degrees Fahrenheit for Centigrade, believes that he is going to die. Imitating the masculine virtues promulgated by boys' fiction, he confronts his death with stoic silence. Not until the story's end does the father discover Schatz's mistake and end his terrified vigil. Critical of the male taciturnity that prohibits father and son from exchanging love, confidence, and reassurance, "A Day's Wait" challenges values Hemingway is popularly believed to promulgate.

Like "Banal Story" before it, "A Natural History of the Dead" (a revised version of chapter 12 in *Death in the Afternoon*) is half satire and half fiction. Its opening section, a pseudoscientific examination of bloated corpses decaying on the battlefield, attacks humanist critics who found the less graphic treatment of war in *A Farewell to Arms* "disgusting." The narrative that follows concerns a hysterical lieutenant who wishes to silence an unconscious and dying soldier whose breathing disturbs him. The lieutenant quarrels with and finally threatens to shoot a dressing-station doctor who refuses to overdose the dying man, but the doctor quells the lieutenant by flinging a saucer of iodine in his eyes. Hemingway's richest example of metafiction, "A Natural History of the Dead" forces the reluctant reader to confront both the horrors of war and his or her own mortality.

Two period pieces follow. "Wine of Wyoming" (*Scribner's*, August 1930) indicts the hypocrisy and bigotry of prohibition-era America, where in 1928 the Catholic Al Smith ran a hopeless presidential campaign on an antiprohibition platform. The Fontans, a French Catholic couple making wine illegally in Wyoming, represent the European values of good food and drink, cleanliness and order, and friendship and communion, contrasting with Americans who eat canned beans, drink only to get drunk, vomit on the table, and reject friendship and spiritual communion to whir along in cars on concrete roads, shooting at hapless prairie dogs. The story's conclusion intimates that America's lust for progress will destroy the Fontans and all they represent, that the old couple will last no longer in the teeth of modernity than Wyoming's game-rich sagebrush country. Hemingway wrote "The Gambler, the Nun, and the Radio" (*Scribner's*, May 1933) in 1931-1932 when, as he put it in a 14 October letter to Guy Hickok, two hundred thousand American homeless were "on the road like the wild kids in Russia," and the country seemed on the verge of revolution. The story involves the hospital stay of a writer named Frazer and examines various "opiates of the people." All through the night, Frazer finds surcease from psychological and physical pain by listening to the radio, tuning in to stations farther and farther west as they sign off one after the other. He admires the cheerful Sister Cecilia, a nun whose opiates are religious faith and baseball, and Cayetano Ruiz, a poor Mexican worker who seeks relief in gambling, after being shot twice in the stomach for drinking coffee with a Russian beet worker. Inspired by Cayetano's friends, who play for him the Mexican revolutionary tune "La Cucaracha," Frazer has a flash of insight: "Revolution . . . is no opium. Revolution is a catharsis; an ecstasy which can only be prolonged by tyranny." But when the Mexicans leave and "take the Cucaracha with them," he turns once more to his alcohol and radio.

Like *In Our Time* and *Men Without Women* before it, *Winner Take Nothing* concludes with a Nick Adams story. In the previously unpublished "Fathers and Sons" Nick drives through quail-hunting country, his young son asleep on the seat beside him. As he drives, Nick remembers his own father, the keenness of his eyesight, the soundness of his passion for fishing and shooting, the unsoundness of his ideas about sex, his suicide—"the handsome job the undertaker had

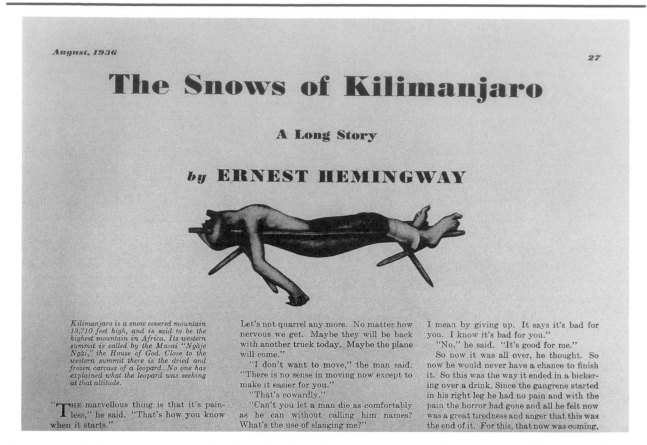

August, 1936 27

The Snows of Kilimanjaro

A Long Story

by ERNEST HEMINGWAY

Kilimanjaro is a snow covered mountain 19,710 feet high, and is said to be the highest mountain in Africa. Its western summit is called by the Masai "Ngàje Ngài," the House of God. Close to the western summit there is the dried and frozen carcass of a leopard. No one has explained what the leopard was seeking at that altitude.

"The marvellous thing is that it's painless," he said. "That's how you know when it starts."

Let's not quarrel any more. No matter how nervous we get. Maybe they will be back with another truck today. Maybe the plane will come."

"I don't want to move," the man said. "There is no sense in moving now except to make it easier for you."

"That's cowardly."

"Can't you let a man die as comfortably as he can without calling him names? What's the use of slanging me?"

I mean by giving up. It says it's bad for you. I know it's bad for you."

"No," he said. "It's good for me."

So now it was all over, he thought. So now he would never have a chance to finish it. So this was the way it ended in a bickering over a drink. Since the gangrene started in his right leg he had no pain and with the pain the horror had gone and all he felt now was a great tiredness and anger that this was the end of it. For this, that now was coming,

Illustration for the Esquire *magazine publication of Hemingway's story about a writer dying of gangrene. The story was later collected in* The Fifth Column and the First Forty-Nine Stories *(1938).*

done on his father's face had not blurred in his mind." No summary can capture the lyrical quality Hemingway's prose gives to Nick's memories, nor how imbued they are with the intense ambivalence of filial love: "His father came back to him in the fall of the year, or in the early spring when there had been jacksnipe on the prairie, or when he saw shocks of corn, or when he saw a lake, or if ever he saw a horse and buggy, or when he saw, or heard, wild geese, or in a duck blind; remembering the time an eagle dropped through the snow to strike a canvas covered decoy, rising, his wings beating, the talons caught in the canvas."

Then Nick's own son stirs and wakes, and as if he has been in telepathic communication with his father, begins asking about his grandfather and Nick's childhood in Michigan. Nick's answers, carefully censored for his son, have little to do with his memories. Grandfather is "hard to describe . . . a great hunter and fisherman." Nor is Nick much better than his father at teaching his son about sex. He cannot tell the boy about Trudy, who "did first what no one has ever done

better" and cannot "mention plump brown legs, flat belly, hard little breasts, well holding arms, quick searching tongue. . . ." Hemingway's last Nick Adams story, "Fathers and Sons" reminds readers that each generation must repeat fundamental human experiences, that life cannot be transmitted verbally, it can only be lived. The child's innocent desire to visit the tomb of his grandfather is a desire to know himself through his family's past. Nick, older and wiser, with a past of his own and a father's suicide to contemplate, knows that tomb to be a Pandora's box that life will open for his son all too soon, a box whose tumultuous metaphorical contents cannot be restrained by prayer. Nor can the visit be avoided. "We'll have to go," Nick says. "I can see we'll have to go."

The Depression years were prosperous ones for Hemingway. The movie rights to *A Farewell to Arms,* for instance, brought eighty thousand dollars in an era when hamburger cost five cents a pound. He and Pauline bought a house in Key West with high ceilings, airy rooms, French windows, wrought-iron balconies, a patio, and a swimming pool. In the winter of 1933-1934, with assistance from Pauline's millionaire uncle, Gus, they embarked upon an African safari, traveling to Kenya and Tanganyika to hunt big game. On their return to Key West, Hemingway purchased a thirty-eight-foot cabin cruiser named *Pilar* with advance money received for a series of *Esquire* articles. Comfortable and seaworthy, the *Pilar* was to gratify her owner's passion for deep-sea fishing, taking him to Dry Tortugas, Bimini, and Cuba, as well as into the Gulf Stream to hunt for marlin.

Hemingway's observations of Depression-era life in Key West spawned two short stories that, after revisions, became parts of *To Have and Have Not* (1937), a novel about a down-on-his-luck charterboat captain named Harry Morgan. In "One Trip Across" (*Cosmopolitan*, April 1934) Harry displays his dog-eat-dog business ethic. After accepting money to smuggle Chinese immigrants from Cuba to Key West, he murders them in cold blood and double-crosses his clients to avoid compromising himself with customs authorities, while making "a good stake . . . for the summer." Harry is so ruthless that pragmatic reasons alone keep him from silencing his helpless rummy "pal" Eddy with a .38. Harry himself narrates "One Trip Across," but "The Tradesman's Return" (*Esquire*, February 1936) is told in the third person. Harry heads into Key West with a boatload of Cuban rum, his boat shot up, his arm smashed by a bullet, and his sole companion a badly wounded and whining black man named Wesley. A fishing party of wealthy Washington bureaucrats spots Harry dumping his cargo, an encounter between haves and have-nots that may cost him his boat. However, the rich men's charter captain, angry with the price-fixing in Washington that forces fishermen to risk their lives at smuggling, feels enough solidarity with Harry to take his party out to sea and give the rumrunner time to escape.

In 1935 Hemingway published *Green Hills of Africa*, a nonfiction account of his safari, to see whether "if truly presented . . . the shape of a country and the pattern of a month's action [could] . . . compete with a work of imagination." As far as the critics were concerned, it could not. Appearing in a year when millions of Americans were unemployed and Germany's Adolf Hitler was consolidating his power, Hemingway's account of his rich-man's holiday, however literary, seemed a species of fiddling while Rome burned. Later in 1936 the safari bore finer fruit—two of

the best short stories he ever wrote—"The Short Happy Life of Francis Macomber" and "The Snows of Kilimanjaro," both later collected in *The Fifth Column and the First Forty-Nine Stories.*

"The Short Happy Life of Francis Macomber" (*Cosmopolitan*, September 1936) is the story of Macomber and his wife, Margot, a rich American couple on safari with their British white hunter, Robert Wilson. When the story opens, Macomber is in disgrace for gut-shooting a lion, lacking the courage to track the wounded animal in the brush, and then "bolting like a rabbit" when the lion charges. Humiliated by her husband's cowardice, Margot exacerbates his disgrace by alternately sobbing and taunting him, and finally by cuckolding him with Wilson, who has a double cot in his safari tent in case of "windfalls." This armed and volatile sexual triangle continues the hunt, this time seeking Cape buffalo for Macomber's "bag." After holding his ground and killing one buffalo, Macomber finds his courage and achieves his "happy life" when he is able to stand and fire repeatedly into the charge of a second, dangerously wounded bull. Margot shortens that happy life. Ostensibly firing at the buffalo, she accidentally, or deliberately, kills her husband by blowing the back of his head off in his moment of triumph. The fact that "The Short Happy Life of Francis Macomber" is Hemingway's most-criticized short story, with a bibliography some seventy articles long, suggests its complex ambiguities. Is Wilson an exemplar of courage or a lecherous brute? Is Macomber's "short happy life" an ascension to honorable manhood or merely to the ability to leave his wife? Is Margot a bitch "enamelled in cruelty" or is she simply a woman striving to maintain control in a world dominated by male violence? Does she shoot to save her newly courageous husband or to rid herself of him? And what about the lion? What are we to make of this spoiled rich couple and their manipulative hireling wreaking havoc on the unspoiled African landscape? There are as many answers to these questions as there are readers of this multifaceted story.

"The Snows of Kilimanjaro" (*Esquire*, August 1936) is made up of the lucid moments, memories, and delirious imaginings of a dying writer named Harry. On safari with a rich wife, Harry has contracted gangrene from an infected scratch and, his leg rotting, lies on a camp cot in view of Africa's zebra and gazelle-strewn plains. Harry knows that he is dying and passes the time by verbally abusing his solicitous wife, by watching the

Hemingway with journalist Martha Gellhorn in New York during the late 1930s; they were married on 21 November 1940 (Hemingway Collection, John F. Kennedy Library).

vultures gather around their camp, and by remembering all the stories he has wanted to write and has not written. The gangrene rotting Harry alive echoes his corruption as a writer. Delirious, he sees death as a hyena crouching at the foot of his cot and breathing the foulness of decay. Finally, however, death comes for Harry as a dream of an airplane flight to the snowcapped peak of Mt. Kilimanjaro, a clean, well-lighted escape from quarreling, corruption, and guilt: "and there, ahead, all he could see, as wide as all the world, great, high, and unbelievably white in the sun, was the square white top of Kilimanjaro. And then he knew that was where he was going." The second most-discussed short story in the Hemingway canon, "The Snows of Kilimanjaro" can be read as autobiography, symbolist fiction, or metafiction. Arguments rage back and forth over the story's antecedents in Hemingway's life, the meanings of the hyena and the snows, the ways in which the "unwritten" stories comment on the text proper. The story's success resides in its complexity, containing something to puzzle and attract many different kinds of readers.

In June 1936 Hemingway published in *Esquire* magazine a short story called "The Horns of the Bull," later retitled "The Capital of the World" and included in *The Fifth Column and the First Forty-Nine Stories*. The story concerns a boy named Paco, fatally gored by the taped-on carving-knife horns of a kitchen-chair "bull" while playing at matador. The child's death is a short, unhappy initiation into manhood, the nature of fear, and the necessity of facing death alone. But Hemingway needed a novel to sustain the critical reputation he had won in the 1920s and had published none since 1929. Under considerable pressure he produced a graceless novel, *To Have and Have Not*, for publication in 1937. The book recycles his two previously published Harry Morgan stories—"One Trip Across" and "The Tradesman's Return"—and adds Harry's death after a gun battle with escaping bank robbers. Other new chapters treat the "haves"—the predatory Helene Bradley and her impotent husband, Tommy; the drunken and ineffectual writer Philip Gordon, who is Helene's prize; his childless and embittered wife, Helen; and her bemused lover, Professor MacWalsey—and contrast with the Morgan stories. The yachting set's sordid doings make Harry's criminal activities seem cleancut by comparison. Yet coming from the author of *The Sun Also Rises* and *A Farewell to Arms*, the pastiche called *To Have and Have Not* gravely disappointed both critics and the general public.

The uneven quality, erratic frequency, and troubled content of Hemingway's fiction during the late 1930s suggests that his marriage to Pauline was growing increasingly troubled, and that, like Harry in "The Snows of Kilimanjaro," he may have come to regard his wife as "this rich bitch, this kindly caretaker and destroyer of his talent." It is possible, too, that Pauline's Catholicism created some sexual coolness between the couple, preventing her from practicing birth control, even though her difficult pregnancies and cesarean sections understandably made her wish to avoid a third conception. From 1931 until 1935 Hemingway carried on an intermittent affair with a beautiful young married woman named Jane Mason, a strawberry blonde with a talent for painting, drinking, and disaster. Their relationship survived such incidents as Jane's drunkenly rolling a car with two of Hemingway's children as passengers and her suicide leap from a second-story window that broke her back and sent her to a mental hospital for months. However, the affair cooled in 1935 when her psychiatrist, Dr. Lawrence Kubie, threatened to publish an article in the *Saturday Review* exposing Hemingway's neuroticism and his hostility toward women. Hemingway took his revenge for Jane's perceived betrayal in *To Have and Have Not*, shocking *Esquire* editor Arnold Gingrich by libeling Jane "up to the eyebrows" in the character of Helene Bradley.

The outbreak of civil war in Spain, the much-loved country where for many summers Hemingway had followed the bulls, offered him an escape from a dying marriage and a destructive affair. On one side were the Loyalists or Republicans, Spaniards loyal to the Popular Front government of President Manuel Azaña y Díaz. On the other were the Fascists, also known as Falangists or Nationalists, led by Gen. Francisco Franco. The Soviet Union sent aid to the Loyalists, some of whom were Communists, while Nazi Germany and Fascist Italy supported Franco. A vocal minority of American citizens of either pro-Communist or anti-Fascist sympathies favored the Loyalist cause, and when the U.S. government refused to intervene, three thousand American volunteers traveled to Spain to fight in the Abraham Lincoln Brigade.

Like many American writers, Hemingway supported the Loyalists, not as a Communist sympathizer, but as a confirmed anti-Fascist. In 1937 he traveled to the Spanish Civil War as a correspondent for the North American Newspaper Alliance, commenting on the fighting in and around Madrid, helping director Joris Ivens make a propaganda film called *The Spanish Earth* (1937; Hemingway's commentary for the film was published in 1938), and staying at the Hotel Florida under bombardment by Franco's artillery. Not coincidentally, the Hotel Florida also housed a young woman Hemingway had recently met in Key West: blonde, blue-eyed Martha Gellhorn, then a journalist and the author of two novels, including a critically acclaimed work on the Depression—*The Trouble I've Seen* (1936). Despite her Bryn Mawr education and Junior League background, there was nothing "soft" about Martha, who was fearless under fire, strongly committed to her writing, and unswervingly anti-Fascist. While Pauline stayed at home with the children, Martha unflinchingly dodged machine-gun bullets with Hemingway during the day and slept with him in besieged Madrid at night. She thought him most attractive, with his sense of self-importance lost in his deep concern for Spain, and she was anxious to learn the war correspondent's trade from a master who could instruct her on such subjects as the different sounds of gunfire.

During 1937 Hemingway made several trips to the United States to raise money for the Loyalist cause. Late in the year he completed a play called *The Fifth Column* (separately published in 1940), in which the bombings, espionage, and assassinations of the war swirl around the love affair of Dorothy Bridges—a war correspondent the text variously labels a "bored Vassar bitch" and a "handsome commodity"—and Philip Rawlings, a spy for the International Brigades who shares some traits of the Hemingway hero (insomnia, nighttime "horrors," and superstitious behavior) but whom Edmund Wilson labeled "besotted and maudlin" (*Nation*, 10 December 1938). Adapted for the stage by Benjamin Glazer, the play ran less than three months (6 March - 18 May 1940) in New York. Again Hemingway would have better luck with a short story: "Old Man at the Bridge" (*Ken*, 19 May 1938), a vignette drawn from field notes he made during the Loyalist retreat across the Ebro River to Barcelona. A brief sketch about an old man too exhausted to keep up with the retreat but worried

Hemingway with Col. Charles T. (Buck) Lanham on the Siegfried Line, 18 September 1944

only about the fate of the cat, goats, and pigeons he has left behind, "Old Man at the Bridge" effectively captures both the dignity of the human spirit and the horror of war conducted against civilians.

In 1938 Hemingway published the last collection of short stories to appear in his lifetime, *The Fifth Column and the First Forty-Nine Stories*. The volume includes the contents of *In Our Time, Men Without Women*, and *Winner Take Nothing*, as well as four additional stories: "The Short Happy Life of Francis Macomber," "The Capital of the World," "The Snows of Kilimanjaro," and "Old Man at the Bridge." In one sense the collection marks the true end of Hemingway's career as a short-story writer. Throughout his life, he preserved a sharp distinction between stories worthy of permanent preservation in hardcover collections and stories good enough only for ephemeral appearances in magazines. Although in his preface to *The First Forty-Nine* Hemingway expressed hope that he would live long enough to write twenty-five more stories, never again would he create another he considered worthy of inclusion in a book. Perhaps, like Harry in "The Snows of Kilimanjaro," he "destroyed his talent by not using it, by betrayals of himself and what he believed in, by drinking so much that he blunted the edge of his perceptions, by laziness, by sloth, and by snobbery, by pride and by preju-

dice, by hook and by crook." Or perhaps it is simply true that short stories are a young writer's form.

Nevertheless, more stories of the Spanish Civil War followed "Old Man at the Bridge" in 1938, as Hemingway toured various sites in the Loyalist zone, and in early 1939, as Franco's troops pressed toward victory. Stories narrated by war correspondent Henry Emmunds are collected in the posthumous anthology *The Fifth Column and Four Stories of the Spanish Civil War* (1969). In "The Denunciation" (*Esquire*, November 1938) a waiter at Chicote's bar betrays a Fascist flyer, Luis Delgado, to the authorities. A former friend of Delgado's, Emmunds takes responsibility for the denunciation because he does not want Delgado to be "disillusioned or bitter about the waiters" at Chicote's before he dies. In "The Butterfly and the Tank" (*Esquire*, December 1938) Emmunds witnesses a young practical joker murdered by a grim soldier for squirting people with a perfume-filled flit gun. "Night Before Battle" (*Esquire*, February 1939) studies the psychology of men confronting almost certain death; "Under the Ridge" (*Cosmopolitan*, October 1939) focuses on the execution of a frightened boy named Paco, who has shot himself in the hand to escape the war. Scribners gathered two additional Spanish Civil War works in the posthumously published *Complete Short Stories of Ernest Hemingway*.

In "Nobody Ever Dies" (*Cosmopolitan*, March 1939) a Spanish Loyalist is gunned down in Cuba, and a girl named Maria, dragged to her execution, frightens superstitious locals by emulating Joan of Arc. "Landscape with Figures" (previously unpublished) is thinly disguised autobiography and treats a writer named Edwin Henry's introduction of a young woman to war. All these stories concern themselves with human behavior—considered and irrational, manic and murderous, saintly and cynical—under the extreme stress of war.

The Spanish Civil War stories proved to be dress rehearsals for Hemingway's most ambitious novel, *For Whom the Bell Tolls*. Robert Jordan, an American professor sympathetic to the Loyalist cause, joins a band of Spanish mountain guerrillas in their hideaway and endeavors to organize them for a special mission: blowing up a strategic bridge to assist a Loyalist advance. Jordan falls passionately in love with Maria, a girl who has been raped and has seen her parents murdered by the Fascists. The guerilla leader Pilar, an earthy character Hemingway modeled on Gertrude Stein and the Loyalist orator La Pasionaria, abets both Jordan's mission and his love affair. Internal treachery and the stupidity of Communist bureaucrats doom the Loyalist advance to failure, but Jordan nevertheless blows the bridge, even though he is left too badly wounded to escape from the approaching Fascists. Written in 1938 and 1939, as Spain was falling to Franco's forces, and published in 1940 as the United States mobilized for war with Germany, *For Whom the Bell Tolls* was not only a sweeping historical novel of the Spanish Civil War but a compelling indictment of America's failure to halt the Fascist advance in Europe. Despite grumbling from leftists who resented Hemingway's criticism of Communist conduct in Spain, the novel was a smashing success, restoring its author to a popular acclaim he had not enjoyed since *A Farewell to Arms*.

Hemingway's wartime affair with Gellhorn had finished his marriage to Pauline. They separated in 1938, Ernest shunning their Key West home to work on his novel at the L-Bar-T Ranch in Wyoming and the Ambos Mundos Hotel in Havana, while Martha was away covering the war in Finland. On her return to Cuba, in the spring of 1939, they rented an old estate called Finca Vigía (Watchtower Farm), some fifteen miles from Havana, and moved in together. When Cuba's torrid summers and autumn hurricanes proved too much for them, they sought relief at a resort

hotel in Sun Valley, Idaho. Both were writing. In March 1940 Martha published a novel about the Nazi invasion of Czechoslovakia, *A Stricken Field*, dedicated to Hemingway, and in October *For Whom the Bell Tolls* appeared with its dedication to Martha. One month later Hemingway's divorce from Pauline became final. He and Martha were married on 21 November in a civil ceremony in Cheyenne, Wyoming, and as a Christmas gift to himself and Martha, Hemingway bought Finca Vigía. The bride's idea of a honeymoon, however, was a trip to Burma and China to cover the developing Sino-Japanese war. Hemingway let himself be badgered into accompanying her, but when Martha insisted on going on to Java, he returned to the United States without her.

The couple was reunited in New York, but the separation was an augury of trouble to come. In 1941 Hemingway was forty-two years old, drained perhaps by the effort of producing *For Whom the Bell Tolls* and content to enjoy his celebrity and deep-sea fishing in Cuba's Gulf Stream. He wanted a wife to "recognize," as he put it in a mock contract Martha signed on 19 January 1940, "that a very fine and sensitive writer cannot be left alone," and he wanted her to admit that "he and his business are what matter to [her] in this life." Martha, an ambitious thirty-four, had no intention of subordinating her career to anyone else's. She had expected a marriage of two mutually supportive professionals, sharing the hazards of war together as they had done in Spain, and working at their fiction side by side, as they had done with *A Stricken Field* and *For Whom the Bell Tolls*. Upon her return from Asia, Martha immediately set to work on another novel, *Liana*, and not long after the United States entered World War II on 7 December 1941, she set off alone into the Caribbean for six weeks to report the effects of submarine warfare on Allied shipping. Yet Martha regarded this as a mere "sideshow" compared to what was happening in Europe, and she chafed at Hemingway's refusal to accompany her there. Instead he preferred to cruise Cuban waters in the *Pilar*, ostensibly searching for submarines, and producing no work except an anthology of other men's writing, *Men at War*, published in 1942. Gradually Martha lost respect for her husband, and in the fall of 1943, after seeing *Liana* into print, she departed for England without him. Still she sent him pleading letters—"You will feel deprived as a writer if this is all over and you have not had a share in it. . . .

*Ernest and Mary Welsh Hemingway in Venice, October 1948; they were married on 14 March 1946
(Hemingway Collection, John F. Kennedy Library).*

I hate not sharing it with you . . . " (12 December 1943)—and Ernest responded with angry telegrams such as this: "Are you a war correspondent or wife in my bed?"

Intensely lonely, Hemingway remained in Cuba, brooding long and drinking hard. In March 1944 Martha returned home to pry him loose, arranging with the British Embassy to give him priority air passage if he would undertake to report the heroic activities of the R.A.F. This Hemingway agreed to do, but not before vengefully depriving Martha of her credentials as a major war correspondent by volunteering to write for *Collier's*, her employer (she was demoted to second correspondent and restricted to rear areas). Undaunted, Martha returned to England as the sole passenger onboard a cargo ship loaded with dynamite, while Hemingway lingered in New York eating caviar, drinking Scotch, and waiting for a plane. After his flight came through, Ernest arrived in London well before Martha, who was still traversing the submarine-infested Atlantic. There he began almost immediately to court Mary Welsh, a petite blonde reporter for London's Time-Life Bureau. Her husband was away on assignment and her tastes ran more toward dancing, gold earrings, and pie baking than Martha's. A drunken car crash after an all-night party gave Hemingway a concussion that left him hospitalized for four days, but it did not slow his destructive drinking. When Martha arrived, she was disgusted with his behavior and told him so, while he inflamed her wrath by playing abusive pranks and flaunting his affair with Mary. Husband and wife went their separate ways.

Hemingway had recovered sufficiently from his head injury to attend the D-day invasion, which he watched through binoculars from the attack transport *Dorothea Dix*. Undeterred by his usurpation of her front-line credentials, Martha hid onboard a hospital ship and helped to carry wounded soldiers through the barbed wire and mine fields of Normandy Beach. Both stories went to *Collier's*; Hemingway's was featured. Martha went to cover the Italian front; Hemingway stayed at London's Dorchester hotel, flying missions with the R.A.F., writing war dispatches, and sending poetry to Mary. In July 1944 he returned to France for the march on Paris, joining the 22nd Regiment and becoming close friends with its commander, Col. Buck Lanham. Lanham allowed Hemingway special privileges, including a captured Mercedes-Benz convertible, a private driver, and a little squad of irregular troops for reconnaissance missions.

In August Hemingway joined Col. David Bruce for the liberation of Paris and lingered for several days at the Ritz Hotel to drink champagne, enjoy a reunion with Mary, and revisit old haunts. Then he rejoined Lanham in Belgium for the drive into Germany and the assault on the Westwall. His adventures were interrupted by a summons to be court-martialed for bearing arms as a war correspondent, but perjury and influential friends got him off. He returned to the Ritz for a six-week stay, hobnobbing with Marlene Dietrich, Janet Flanner, and Paul Valéry; writing more poetry to Mary; worrying about his 21-year-old son, Bumby, now an O.S.S. officer missing in action behind enemy lines; and considering Martha's demands for a divorce. Early in November he returned to Lanham's side for the terrible battle of Hürtgen Forest—in eighteen days, the 22nd regiment sustained 2,678 casualties. After a brief trip to Luxembourg, too late to witness the Von Runstedt offensive, Hemingway left the war for good and returned to Paris.

Mary, who had asked her husband for a divorce in order to marry Hemingway, was waiting for him there. Her resolve wavered momentarily when, in a moment of drunken exhibitionism, he mounted a photograph of her husband on a toilet seat in the Ritz Hotel's men's room and machine-gunned it, blowing the toilet to bits, flooding the floor, and creating a scene by climbing atop the bidet to deliver a speech. Somehow she forgave him. Cheerful and plucky, calling herself "the short, happy wife of Mr. McPappa," Mary proved able to excuse more inexcusable behavior than any of Hemingway's previous wives, and her love of entertaining, travel, mink coats, and Cartier diamonds helped her find contentment in the role of celebrity's wife. After his experience with Martha, Hemingway must have been

relieved by the prospect of marriage to a woman who sent hamburger recipes to *Woman's Day* rather than dispatches from the Battle of the Bulge. He returned to the Finca Vigía in the early spring of 1945 to await Mary's arrival. There he sought medical treatment for the still-lingering effects of his London concussion, struggled to control his alcoholism with moderate success, and swam, sunned, played tennis, and sorted bookshelves to get in shape for Mary.

They were married in Havana on 14 March 1946. Shortly thereafter Hemingway began work on a novel he called *The Garden of Eden* (1986), a work about the out-of-control life of a writer named David Bourne and his androgynous metamorphoses at the whims of his mad wife, Catherine, with whom he shares a lover, Marita. The story of a young painter and his wife, Nick and Barbara Sheldon, is juxtaposed with that of the Bournes. Daring in its treatment of bisexuality, *The Garden of Eden* seems an attempt to treat at novelistic length the kinds of relationships merely glimpsed in early short stories such as "Mr. and Mrs. Elliott" and "The Sea Change." The manuscript soon swelled to more than one thousand pages, but it, too, was out of control. Although Hemingway would return to the novel again in the 1950s, he was never able to complete it. The posthumously published version of *The Garden of Eden* is heavily edited, representing little more than a third of the tangled mass of manuscripts Hemingway finally abandoned.

The closing years of the 1940s were marked by two triumphs—Bumby returned safely from a German prisoner-of-war camp; Hemingway was awarded a Bronze Star for his conduct as a war correspondent—and many disasters. Mary nearly bled to death from an ectopic pregnancy, and the only thing that saved her life was Hemingway's insistence that an intern who had given her up try again to find a vein for a transfusion. Another car accident gave Hemingway another concussion, and his son Patrick was also involved in a car crash and shortly afterward was diagnosed as a paranoid schizophrenic. He was given shock treatments that apparently "cured" the problem, which may have resulted from an untreated head injury. Mary broke her ankle skiing, and Hemingway began to suffer from dangerously high blood pressure. The heavy drinking continued, and the writing suffered. The Hemingways alternated between the Finca Vigía in Cuba and the Sun Valley Inn in Idaho.

FINCA VIGIA. SAN FRANCISCO DE PAULA. CUBA

17/8/55

My Dear Senator.

Thanks for the letter. I have no glossary of my written works and so if you want to use the quotation I would slug it " in conversation." It might be in "Death In The afternoon" but consider this letter as conversation. Not privileged and quote as you wish.

This part is privileged: I sweated out your back last winter and prayed for you whenever the pain of mine was un-bearable. I hope yours is better. Mine is fine now. But if I ever learned anything it is that it is better, on that thing, not to let them operate. (This may be wrong.) Naturally they are all different. But surgeons are awfully ambitious. I do not know politics where you come from but if it is OK give my best to Chris Herter.

Closing with the pious hope that there is nothing wrong with the Jr. Senator from Wisconsin that a .577 solid would not cure although this alleviation should never be applied except by a registered physician duly tested and authorized by the parties of the second part hereunder known as the Producer or PRODUCER or the Distributor or DISTRIBUTOR. No one (Have you to read several hundred pages of contract on the aforementioned sea and I has out double-talked until so without further impediment I am yrs. very truly) and wishing you all luck, [sic]

and I hope the back is OK.

Ernest Hemingway.

You don't have to answer.
EH.

Letter to Senator John F. Kennedy, giving him permission to use the phrase "grace under pressure" in his Profiles in Courage *(1956). Hemingway also expresses his dislike for Senator Joseph McCarthy of Wisconsin (auctioned by Sotheby's, New York, sale number 5660, 23 October 1987).*

A 1948 trip to Italy to revisit the site of his World War I wounding and to hunt ducks in the salt marshes of Venice gave Hemingway material for his first viable fiction since *For Whom the Bell Tolls*. At an Italian count's villa after a partridge shoot, he met nineteen-year-old Adriana Ivancich, a dark beauty drying her wet and tangled hair before an open fire. Smitten, Hemingway broke his comb in two and gave her half. They developed an abiding affection, Hemingway calling her "daughter" and encouraging her to write poetry, but the relationship remained platonic, their meetings chaperoned by Adriana's mother, Dora, and brother, Gianfranco, a young tank officer who had fought at El Alamein. As always, a fresh love interest seemed to stir Hemingway's creative juices, and the result was a brief novel, *Across the River and Into the Trees* (1950), about an aging American colonel's love affair with a beautiful young Venetian woman named Renata.

Except for a handful of dispatches and the anthology *Men at War*, *Across the River* was the sole published fruit of the years 1940-1950, Hemingway's middle age, years that are the prime of most men's lives but which instead had brought him two divorces, a fourth marriage, war, repeated head injuries, confirmed alcoholism, and general ill health. And now that sole fruit ended the decade with critical disaster, for *Across the River* could not compete with *The Sun Also Rises, A Farewell to Arms*, or *For Whom the Bell Tolls* on any level. While a few critics lauded the book for its tenderness, the majority saw it as "Hemingway's worst novel," "trash," full of the "pettiest, most irrelevant opinions," exuding "self-pity and egotism," filling the reader with "a continuous sense of embarrassment." "Hemingway is finished" seemed to be the critical consensus. Some critics even went so far as to suggest that former estimates of Hemingway's talent should be drastically revised, and for awhile it seemed possible that *Across the River* might even erase Hemingway's earlier achievements from the literary record.

Not surprisingly such reviews threw him into a profound depression, but again Adriana proved a muse of sorts when she visited the Finca with her mother and brother. He found her "fresh as a young pine tree in the mountain snow" (6 July 1951 letter to her), and he settled to work on a series of three books about the sea: "The Sea When Young," "The Sea When Absent," and "The Sea in Being." These fragmen-

tary works, published posthumously as *Islands in the Stream* by Scribners in 1970, concern a painter named Thomas Hudson, his wartime patrols for submarines off Cuba, his loneliness and depression augmented by drinking, his perverse yearnings for his first wife, and his surviving the deaths of his three sons only to be killed himself before fulfilling his talent as an artist. While the "Sea" books were somewhat more coherent than *The Garden of Eden*, Hemingway was once more at work on a project he could neither control nor complete. Yet the writing may have helped him work through his 1940s struggles—with war, divorce, depression, and alcohol—and his fears that those unproductive years and the abortive *Across the River* may have destroyed his chance for literary immortality.

Hudson's dying question "We didn't do so good, did we?" might have served as an epitaph for Hemingway's career if his efforts on *Islands in the Stream* had not prepared him for writing *The Old Man and the Sea* (1952), a work that was to rescue his reputation and permanently enshrine him in the literary hall of fame. Limbered and restored to confidence by his work on the "Sea" books, cheered by a lovely Christmas, and with his Venetian muse still in attendance, Hemingway began, on a cool winter morning at the Finca, to write his story of an old Cuban fisherman's battle with a giant marlin. Working with speed and ease, he finished the book in just six weeks and returned to the Thomas Hudson project he would never finish. Yet despite its completion in February 1951, *The Old Man and the Sea* would not see print for more than a year and a half, as Hemingway was overtaken by a series of emotional shocks. Hemingway's mother died at the age of seventy-nine, Fulgencio Batista seized power in Cuba, and Hemingway's old friend and publisher, Charles Scribner, died suddenly. Biographers Carlos Baker, Charles Fenton, and Philip Young began to pressure Hemingway for information, exacerbating his growing sense of his own mortality. Worst of all, his youngest son, Gregory, was arrested in Los Angeles, and Hemingway's former wife Pauline died suddenly of a heart attack after a violent telephone quarrel with him about Gregory's behavior. Father and son each accused the other of responsibility for her death, causing irreparable damage to their relationship, and Hemingway penned a vengeful short story: "I Guess Everything Reminds You of Something" exposes an act of plagiarism Gregory committed in school. "Great News from the Main-

The Cross Roads – 7

German prisoners who had been taken by ~~the~~ irregulars

were often as cooperative as head waiters or minor diplomats. *Sometimes*

~~general we regarded the Germans as perverted Boy Scouts.~~ This is

~~Sometimes They regarded them less tenderly~~

~~another way of saying they were splendid soldiers.~~ ~~We were~~ *not*

~~splendid soldiers.~~ ~~We were~~ specialists in a dirty trade. In French

~~we said,~~ "un metier tres sale."

~~We~~ knew, from repeated questionings, that all Germans

coming through on this escape route were making for Aachen and ~~I~~

knew that all ~~w~~ killed now we would not have to fight in Aachen

nor behind the West Wall. ~~We, in the Division, were racing them~~ *This was simple.*

~~He knew this trade.~~ ~~Their present trade was a duty~~

~~to the West Wall and we ranged ahead of the Division and fought on~~

~~He wanted to kill as many of them as they could,~~

~~a personal basis every day.~~

~~I was pleased when anything was real simple,~~

~~he Germans~~ ~~that we~~ *we* saw coming now were on bicycles.

~~T~~here were four of them and they were in a hurry too but they were

very tired. They were not cyclist troops. They were just Germans

on stolen bicycles. The leading rider saw the fresh blood on the

road and then he turned his head and saw the vehicle and he put his

weight hard down on his right pedal with his right boot and we

opened on him and on the others. A man shot off a bicycle is always

a sad thing to see, although not as sad as a horse shot with a

Typescript page for one of Hemingway's last stories, "Black Ass at the Crossroads," written in 1956 but not published until its inclusion in The Complete Short Stories *in 1987 (auctioned by Charles Hamilton Galleries, sale number 19, 24 May 1967)*

land," written near the same time, is about Patrick's incarceration in a mental hospital for electroshock treatment. Hemingway probably never contemplated publishing either one, but Scribners included them in *The Complete Short Stories*.

In September 1952 *The Old Man and the Sea* was published at last, appearing in a single issue of *Life* magazine. More than six million copies were sold virtually overnight. The simplicity of the novella's style, its exhalation of symbols and allegories, its exquisite descriptions of the Gulf Stream, and its affirmative assertion that "a man may be destroyed but not defeated" saw *The Old Man and the Sea* critically acclaimed as a masterpiece, while Santiago's Christ-like ordeal and his painful struggle to kill and bring in the giant marlin, only to have his achievement devoured by sharks, won the sympathies of readers worldwide. The public was perhaps equally moved by Hemingway's own triumphant comeback. Everywhere he went, strangers came pressing up to wring his hand.

The following summer Hemingway and Mary set off on his second and last safari, after a stop in Spain for bullfights and visits to the Prado, Hemingway's first trip there since Franco had won the Civil War. In Kenya they shot gnu, gerenuk, rhino, lion, and leopard. Hemingway was appointed an honorary game warden for the Kimana Swamp region during the Mau-Mau Emergency and took a keen interest in the uprising. But once again bad luck was waiting. A pilot friend, Roy Marsh, offered the Hemingways an airborne sightseeing tour. As they were circling Victoria Falls taking pictures, a flight of ibis caused Marsh to dive suddenly and accidentally strike a telegraph wire stretched across the gorge. Badly damaged, the plane crashed into the African scrub. None of the three was badly injured, but their radio messages for help went unheeded, and they spent the night camped by the Nile, watching the hippos and elephants come down to drink. Late the next afternoon they waved down a chartered sightseeing boat, which delivered them to another pilot willing to fly them to Uganda. The plane crashed on takeoff. This time matters were more serious, for the plane burst into flames. Marsh kicked out a window, and he, Mary, and the pilot escaped through it. Hemingway bashed his way through a jammed door and emerged with another concussion, cerebral fluid seeping from one ear. Meanwhile, would-be rescuers had been searching the African bush for the wreckage of the first plane.

The Hemingways were reported dead, and when they eventually arrived in Nairobi, Hemingway had the unusual experience of reading his own obituaries, clipped from newspapers around the globe. Yet despite blinding headaches, back pain, and kidney trouble, Hemingway continued his travels, anesthetizing himself with alcohol, writing an article for *Look* magazine on the crashes, and going on to visit with the Ivancichs in Venice and attend the San Isidro bullfights in Madrid.

Back home in Cuba in the autumn of 1954, he worked on recording his experiences in a nonfiction African book intended to be a kind of *Green Hills of Africa* revisited. The manuscript reached eight hundred typed pages before it was interrupted forever by the news that he had won the Nobel Prize. The news seemed to bring the entire world, unannounced and uninvited, to Hemingway's doorstep. Everyone from Portuguese consuls-general to Princeton sophomores on holiday showed up at the Finca, and the Hemingways were besieged by the media. Hemingway felt "like an elephant in the zoo." "I don't want to win a prize if it means losing a book," he told a *Time* reporter (for a 17 November 1954 cover story), but there is little doubt that the Nobel Prize caused the miscarriage of his African book. *Sports Illustrated* published excerpts from it ("African Journal," 20 December 1971 - 10 January 1972) after his death.

Still more precious writing time was squandered on helping to film fishing sequences for a movie version of *The Old Man and the Sea* (released in 1958). Not until the summer of 1956 did Hemingway return to his desk. There he turned out in rapid succession four stories about his World War II experiences: "A Room on the Garden Side," about life in the Ritz Hotel after the liberation of Paris; "The Monument" and "Indian Country and the White Army," about the fighting in Belgium; and "Black Ass at the Cross Roads," an account of irregular troops ambushing Germans fleeing on the road to Aachen. Hemingway did not see fit to publish any of these stories; Scribners published only "Black Ass at the Cross Roads" in *The Complete Short Stories*. That story *is* the best of the lot, the narrator exploring the emotions of men at war who have accidentally killed a friendly local and deliberately killed a young enemy. This same period in 1956 also saw the composition of "A Man of the World," a story about how a grotesque bum came to have his eyes gouged out in a fight. Not one of Hemingway's finer moments, it was paired in *At-

lantic (November 1957) with a more promising story titled "Get a Seeing-Eyed Dog" (both are in *The Complete Short Stories*). A fine depiction of the changes wrought in a relationship by one partner's new dependence, it treats a blind American writer's unmanning by the unfamiliar necessity of his wife's taking care of him.

"Get a Seeing-Eyed Dog" may reflect Hemingway's anxieties about his own deteriorating health, as he struggled with high blood pressure, liver disease, depression, and the lingering effects of his African injuries, all the while alternating between alcoholic binges and abstention. Feeling his mortality closing in, he was inspired to begin writing his memoirs in the spring of 1957, when *Atlantic* invited him to write about his early association with Fitzgerald for a centennial issue. Through the fall of 1957 and the spring of 1958 he worked steadily at the book that would be published posthumously as *A Moveable Feast*. A tightly patterned nonfiction novel about Hemingway's Paris years, it is filled with nostalgia and regret, a story of the making and marring of writers during a remarkably exciting period of literary history. In revisiting his youth, Hemingway recaptured qualities of prose—both viciously satirical and lyrically beautiful—that he had not been able to command for a long time. He was also inspired to return to the abandoned manuscript of *The Garden of Eden*, adding to it an interpolated short story of an elephant hunt and a young boy's initiation into the sordid realities of adult life and of disillusionment with his father. Collected in *The Complete Short Stories* as "African Story," it is a strongly written tale of love betrayed and nature violated. The quality of Hemingway's work at this time belied his growing anxiety about the deteriorating political situation in Cuba as Fidel Castro challenged the Batista regime.

The summer of 1959 marked Hemingway's sixtieth birthday. While he and Mary were away in Idaho, revolution erupted in Cuba, and Batista's secret police murdered a dozen young men from villages near the Finca. Worried about losing his home of twenty years, with his books, paintings, and memorabilia, his beloved boat *Pilar*, the tennis court, and the swimming pool so essential to his health, Hemingway bought a tiny two-bedroom chalet in Ketchum, made tolerable by seventeen acres of land and spectacular views of the Sawtooth Mountains and the Big Wood River. He and Mary then departed for Spain to follow a series of *mano a mano* bullfights between

two superb young matadors, Antonio Ordoñez and Luis Miguel Dominguín. Criss-crossing the country to attend more than twenty corridas in the heat of a Spanish summer, Hemingway began to show signs of a mental breakdown like his father's. Friends were astonished by his verbal abuse of Mary, his obscenity, his paranoid bursts of rage, and his weeping apologies. Back in Cuba for the last time, in the summer of 1960, his attempt to write a short account of the Ordoñez-Dominguín rivalry for *Life* magazine spiraled out of control. They had asked for 10,000 words; he produced 120,000. But he felt himself too confused to discipline the material, and for the first time in his life asked another writer, Aaron Hotchner, to help him cut the manuscript. Still, they could only remove 50,000 words between them, and the resulting product, *The Dangerous Summer*, appeared in *Life* in three installments (5-19 September 1960; enlarged, revised, and published as a book in 1985).

Exhausted by his behavior, Mary fled to an apartment in New York, and Hemingway returned to Spain to stay with his friends Bill and Annie Davis. They were appalled by the change in him: Hemingway was suffering from severe depression, insomnia, memory failure, and paranoia. They tried to cope with the situation for a time, but when Hemingway accused Bill of trying to kill him, they grew alarmed at his condition and put him on a plane back to New York. Mary got him to the house in Ketchum, but his paranoid delusions of being followed by the F.B.I. and persecuted by tax men, his wildly fluctuating blood pressure, his growing physical frailty, and his inability even to speak in coherent sentences convinced her that he required hospitalization. In November 1960 he was sent to the Mayo Clinic and diagnosed as suffering from diabetes, cirrhosis of the liver, and depression so severe that his psychiatrist prescribed electroshock treatments.

In January 1961 Hemingway was discharged to his home in Ketchum, where he tried to arrange the sketches of *A Moveable Feast* in the best possible order, and he wept with shame and grief that the writing would not come any more. Mary was unnerved by his long silences and vacant stare, and when on an April morning she found him gazing out the window with a shotgun in his hands, she coaxed him to hand it over, taking him to the Sun Valley Hospital to be placed under heavy sedation. Mary arranged his readmission to the Mayo clinic, but when he returned home to pack, he managed to seize and load a shot-gun, relinquishing it only after a ferocious struggle with family friend Don Anderson. At the airport Hemingway tried to walk into the whirring propellers of a taxiing plane. Once he was safe in a locked wing of the clinic, his doctors resumed shock treatments, and soon he was well enough to write letters. Late in June his psychiatrist felt he was well enough to be discharged, despite Mary's misgivings.

"The masters of the short story," Hemingway had written in a 1959 essay, "come to no good end" ("The Art of the Short Story," first published in the *Paris Review*, Spring 1981). He slept two nights at home, and then, before Mary was awake, on Sunday morning, 2 July 1961, he crept downstairs to take the keys to the basement from the kitchen windowsill. He unlocked the basement storage room, chose a double-barrelled Boss shotgun, took it upstairs to the coffinlike oak-lined foyer of the Ketchum house, and, like his father before him, blew his brains out. "Longevity, gentlemen," he had lectured students in "The Art of the Short Story," "is not an end. It is a prolongation. . . . Shuck it off, Jack."

Interviews:

Lillian Ross, "How Do You Like It Now, Gentlemen?," *New Yorker*, 26 (13 May 1950): 40-51;

George Plimpton, "An Interview with Ernest Hemingway," *Paris Review*, 18 (Spring 1958): 85-108;

Seymour Betsky and Leslie Fiedler, "An Almost Imaginary Interview: Hemingway in Ketchum," *Partisan Review*, 29 (Summer 1962): 395-405;

Matthew J. Bruccoli, ed., *Conversations with Ernest Hemingway* (Jackson: University Press of Mississippi, 1986).

Letters:

Ernest Hemingway: Selected Letters, 1917-1961, edited by Carlos Baker (New York: Scribners, 1981);

Hemingway in Love and War: The Lost Diary of Agnes von Kurowsky, Her Letters, and Correspondence of Ernest Hemingway, edited by Henry S. Villard and James Nagel (Boston: Northeastern University Press, 1989).

Bibliographies:

Audre Hanneman, *Ernest Hemingway: A Comprehensive Bibliography* (Princeton: Princeton University Press, 1967);

Philip Young and Charles W. Mann, *The Hemingway Manuscripts: An Inventory* (University Park: Pennsylvania State University Press, 1969);

Jackson J. Benson, "A Comprehensive Checklist of Hemingway Short Fiction Criticism, Explication and Commentary," in *The Short Stories of Ernest Hemingway: Critical Essays*, edited by Benson (Durham, N.C.: Duke University Press, 1975) pp. 312-375;

Hanneman, *Supplement to Ernest Hemingway: A Comprehensive Bibliography* (Princeton: Princeton University Press, 1975);

William White, "Hemingway Checklist," *Fitzgerald/Hemingway Annual* (1975): 351-368; (1976): 260-272; (1977): 255-266; (1978); 449-463; (1979): 463-483;

Linda Welshimer Wagner, *Ernest Hemingway: A Reference Guide* (Boston: G. K. Hall, 1977);

White, "Hemingway: A Current Bibliography," *Hemingway Notes*, 5 (Fall 1979): 34-35; (Spring 1980): 38-40; 6 (Fall 1980): 39-40; (Spring 1981): 39-40;

White, "Current Bibliography," *Hemingway Review*, 1 (Fall 1981): 64-68; 2 (Fall 1982): 90-94; (Spring 1983): 63-65; 3 (Fall 1983): 73-76; (Spring 1984): 57-60; 4 (Fall 1984): 61-64; (Spring 1985): 61-63; 5 (Fall 1985): 60-64; (Spring 1986): 57-61; 6 (Fall 1986): 118-120; (Spring 1987): 58-60;

Jo August, *Catalog of the Ernest Hemingway Collection at the John F. Kennedy Library*, 2 volumes (Boston: G. K. Hall, 1982);

Al DeFazio, "Hemingway Bibliography," *Hemingway Review*, 8 (Fall 1988): 68-77; (Spring 1988): 55-65; 9 (Fall 1989): 104-112; (Spring 1990): 188-201.

Biographies:

Leicester Hemingway, *My Brother, Ernest Hemingway* (Cleveland: World, 1961);

Marcelline Hemingway Sanford, *At the Hemingways: A Family Portrait* (Boston: Atlantic/Little, Brown, 1962);

A. E. Hotchner, *Papa Hemingway: A Personal Memoir* (New York: Random House, 1966);

Constance Cappel Montgomery, *Hemingway in Michigan* (New York: Fleet, 1966);

Carlos Baker, *Ernest Hemingway: A Life Story* (New York: Scribners, 1969);

James McLendon, *Papa: Hemingway in Key West* (Miami: Seeman, 1972);

Madelaine Hemingway Miller, *Ernie: Hemingway's Sister "Sunny" Remembers* (New York: Crown, 1975);

Gregory H. Hemingway, *Papa: A Personal Memoir* (Boston: Houghton Mifflin, 1976);

Mary Welsh Hemingway, *How It Was* (New York: Knopf, 1976);

Scott Donaldson, *By Force of Will: The Life and Art of Ernest Hemingway* (New York: Viking, 1977);

Bernice Kert, *The Hemingway Women* (New York: Norton, 1983);

Norberto Fuentes, *Hemingway in Cuba*, translated by Consuelo Corwin (Secaucus, N.J.: Stuart, 1984);

Peter Griffin, *Along with Youth: Hemingway, The Early Years* (New York: Oxford University Press, 1985);

Jeffrey Meyers, *Hemingway: A Biography* (New York: Harper & Row, 1985);

Michael Reynolds, "Hemingway's Home: Depression and Suicide," *American Literature*, 57 (December 1985): 600-610;

Reynolds, *The Young Hemingway* (Oxford: Blackwell, 1986);

Kenneth S. Lynn, *Hemingway* (New York: Simon & Schuster, 1987);

Denis Brian, *The True Gen: An Intimate Portrait of Hemingway by Those Who Knew Him* (New York: Grove, 1988);

Hotchner, *Hemingway and His World* (New York: Vendome, 1989);

Reynolds, *Hemingway: The Paris Years* (Oxford: Blackwell, 1989).

References:

Richard Astro and Jackson J. Benson, eds., *Hemingway in Our Time* (Corvallis: Oregon State University Press, 1974);

Carlos Baker, *Hemingway: The Writer as Artist* (Princeton: Princeton University Press, 1952);

Sheridan Baker, *Ernest Hemingway: An Introduction and Interpretation* (New York: Holt, Rinehart & Winston, 1967);

Susan F. Beegel, *Hemingway's Craft of Omission: Four Manuscript Examples* (Ann Arbor: U.M.I. Research Press, 1988);

Beegel, ed., *Hemingway's Neglected Short Fiction: New Perspectives* (Ann Arbor: U.M.I. Research Press, 1989);

Jackson J. Benson, *Hemingway: The Writer's Art of Self-Defense* (Minneapolis: University of Minnesota Press, 1969);

Benson, ed., *The Short Stories of Ernest Hemingway: Critical Essays* (Durham, N.C.: Duke University Press, 1975);

James D. Brasch and Joseph Sigman, comps., *Hemingway's Library: A Composite Record* (New York: Garland, 1981);

Matthew J. Bruccoli and C. E. Frazer Clark, Jr., comps., *Hemingway at Auction, 1930-1973* (Detroit: Gale, 1973);

Joseph DeFalco, *The Hero in Hemingway's Short Stories* (Pittsburgh: University of Pittsburgh Press, 1963);

Charles A. Fenton, *The Apprenticeship of Ernest Hemingway* (New York: Farrar, Straus, & Young, 1954);

Joseph M. Flora, *Ernest Hemingway: A Study of the Short Fiction* (Boston: Twayne, 1989);

Flora, *Hemingway's Nick Adams* (Baton Rouge: Louisiana State University Press, 1982);

Sheldon Norman Grebstein, *Hemingway's Craft* (Carbondale: Southern Illinois University Press, 1973);

Leo Gurko, *Ernest Hemingway and the Pursuit of Heroism* (New York: Crowell, 1968);

Richard B. Hovey, *Hemingway: The Inward Terrain* (Seattle: University of Washington Press, 1968);

John M. Howell, ed., *Hemingway's African Stories: The Stories, Their Sources, Their Critics* (New York: Scribners, 1969);

Kenneth G. Johnston, *The Tip of the Iceberg: Hemingway and the Short Story* (Greenwood, Fla.: Penkevill, 1987);

Nicholas Joost, *Ernest Hemingway and the Little Magazines: The Paris Years* (Barre, Mass.: Barre Publishers, 1968);

John Killinger, *Hemingway and the Dead Gods: A Study in Existentialism* (Lexington: University Press of Kentucky, 1960);

Jeffrey Meyers, ed., *Hemingway: The Critical Heritage* (London: Routledge & Kegan Paul, 1982);

Michael Reynolds, *Hemingway's First War: The Making of A Farewell to Arms* (Princeton: Princeton University Press, 1976);

Reynolds, comp., *Hemingway's Reading, 1910-1940* (Princeton: Princeton University Press, 1981);

Reynolds, ed., *Critical Essays on Ernest Hemingway's In Our Time* (Boston: G. K. Hall, 1983);

Earl Rovit and Gerry Brenner, *Ernest Hemingway* (Boston: Twayne, 1986);

Paul Smith, *A Reader's Guide to the Short Stories of Ernest Hemingway* (Boston: G. K. Hall, 1989);

Linda Welshimer Wagner, ed., *Ernest Hemingway: Five Decades of Criticism* (East Lansing: Michigan State University Press, 1974);

Wagner, ed., *Ernest Hemingway: Six Decades of Criticism* (East Lansing: Michigan State University Press, 1987);

Arthur Waldhorn, *A Reader's Guide to Ernest Hemingway* (New York: Farrar, Straus & Giroux, 1972);

Robert P. Weeks, ed., *Hemingway: A Collection of Critical Essays* (Englewood Cliffs, N.J.: Prentice-Hall, 1962);

Philip Young, *Ernest Hemingway: A Reconsideration* (University Park: Pennsylvania State University Press, 1966).

Joseph Hergesheimer

(15 February 1880 - 25 April 1954)

Richard Messer
Bowling Green State University

See also the Hergesheimer entry in *DLB 9: American Novelists, 1910-1945*.

BOOKS: *The Lay Anthony* (New York & London: Kennerley, 1914; revised edition, New York: Knopf, 1919; London: Heinemann, 1922);

Mountain Blood (New York & London: Kennerley, 1915; revised edition, New York: Knopf, 1919; London: Knopf, 1929);

The Three Black Pennys (New York: Knopf, 1917; London: Heinemann, 1918);

Gold and Iron (New York: Knopf, 1918; London: Heinemann, 1919);

The Happy End (New York: Knopf, 1919; London: Heinemann, 1920);

Hugh Walpole: An Appreciation (New York: Doran, 1919);

Java Head (New York: Knopf, 1919; London: Heinemann, 1919);

Linda Condon (New York: Knopf, 1919; London: Heinemann, 1919);

San Cristóbal de la Habana (New York: Knopf, 1920; London: Heinemann, 1921);

The Bright Shawl (New York: Knopf, 1922; London: Heinemann, 1923);

Cytherea (New York: Knopf, 1922; London: Heinemann, 1922);

Wild Oranges (New York: Knopf, 1922);

Tubal Cain (New York: Knopf, 1922);

The Dark Fleece (New York: Knopf, 1922);

Tol'able David (New York: Knopf, 1923);

The Presbyterian Child (New York: Knopf, 1923; London: Heinemann, 1924);

Balisand (New York: Knopf, 1924; London: Heinemann, 1924);

From an Old House (New York: Knopf, 1925; London: Heinemann, 1926);

Tampico (New York: Knopf, 1926; London: Heinemann, 1927);

Quiet Cities (New York & London: Knopf, 1928);

Swords and Roses (New York & London: Knopf, 1929);

Triall by Armes (London: Mathews & Marrot, 1929);

The Party Dress (New York & London: Knopf, 1930);

The Limestone Tree (New York: Knopf, 1931; London: Heinemann, 1931);

Sheridan: A Military Narrative (Boston & New York: Houghton Mifflin, 1931);

Berlin (New York: Knopf, 1932; London: Cassell, 1933);

Love in the United States, and The Big Shot (New York: Knopf, 1932; London: Benn, 1932);

Tropical Winter (New York: Knopf, 1933; London: Cassell, 1933);

The Foolscap Rose (New York: Knopf, 1934; London: Cassell, 1934).

SELECTED PERIODICAL PUBLICATIONS—
UNCOLLECTED: "The Feminine Nuisance in American Literature," *Yale Review*, 10 (July 1921): 716-725;

"The Lamentable Trade of Letters," *American Mercury*, 25 (March 1932): 262-268.

Of Joseph Hergesheimer's many books of fiction, seven are short-story collections. Each of the seven was well received. Several of his stories were adapted into films that became box-office hits, and critics such as Carl Van Doren and,

later, Alfred Kazin spoke of him in the same breath with such writers as F. Scott Fitzgerald, John Galsworthy, and Henry James. However, Hergesheimer's fame has dwindled until he is now known mainly by literary historians, who have relegated him to a small but solid niche as a highly skilled popular author of the 1920s and 1930s.

Joseph Hergesheimer was born on 15 February 1880 in Philadelphia, the son of Joseph and Helen MacKellar Hergesheimer; he grew up in a stable, middle-class, suburban family. His father, a cartographer, worked with the U.S. Coast and Geodetic Survey. After studying art at the Pennsylvania Academy of Fine Arts, the young Hergesheimer traveled to Europe. He studied and painted in Florence and Venice, and lived very well on money inherited from his grandfather. Returning to America in 1907, he married Dorothy Hemphill. By then he had focused his artistic interests on fiction writing. Years of apprenticeship were finally rewarded in 1913 when the *Forum* magazine published his sketch "The City of Pleasure"; then in 1914 his first novel, *The Lay Anthony*, was published. Still, it was not until the release of his third novel, *The Three Black Pennys* (1917), that Hergesheimer attained public and financial success.

Success, when it came, was good to Hergesheimer. The year 1919 saw four of his books published. *Java Head*, which had been serialized the year before by the *Saturday Evening Post*, sold especially well and was soon adapted into a successful movie. He began to move among celebrities, some of whom, such as H. L. Mencken, James Branch Cabell, and Sinclair Lewis, became his lifelong friends. Quite clearly, Hergesheimer's skillful blending of history, foreign settings, and romance held a special appeal for the people of the glamour-loving 1920s.

Through the harsh realities of the 1930s and early 1940s, his work remained popular. However, after the publication of his novel *The Foolscap Rose* in 1934, he wrote only magazine fiction. The last twenty years of his life seem to have been spent mainly in genteel seclusion. He died on 25 April 1954 in Sea Isle, New Jersey.

The trend in Hergesheimer's short fiction toward escapist entertainment is undeniable, but this is less true of his early stories than of the later ones. In general, the themes of his short works have lasting significance. The stories are well written, and their popularity reflects a great deal about a young, industrial America in which

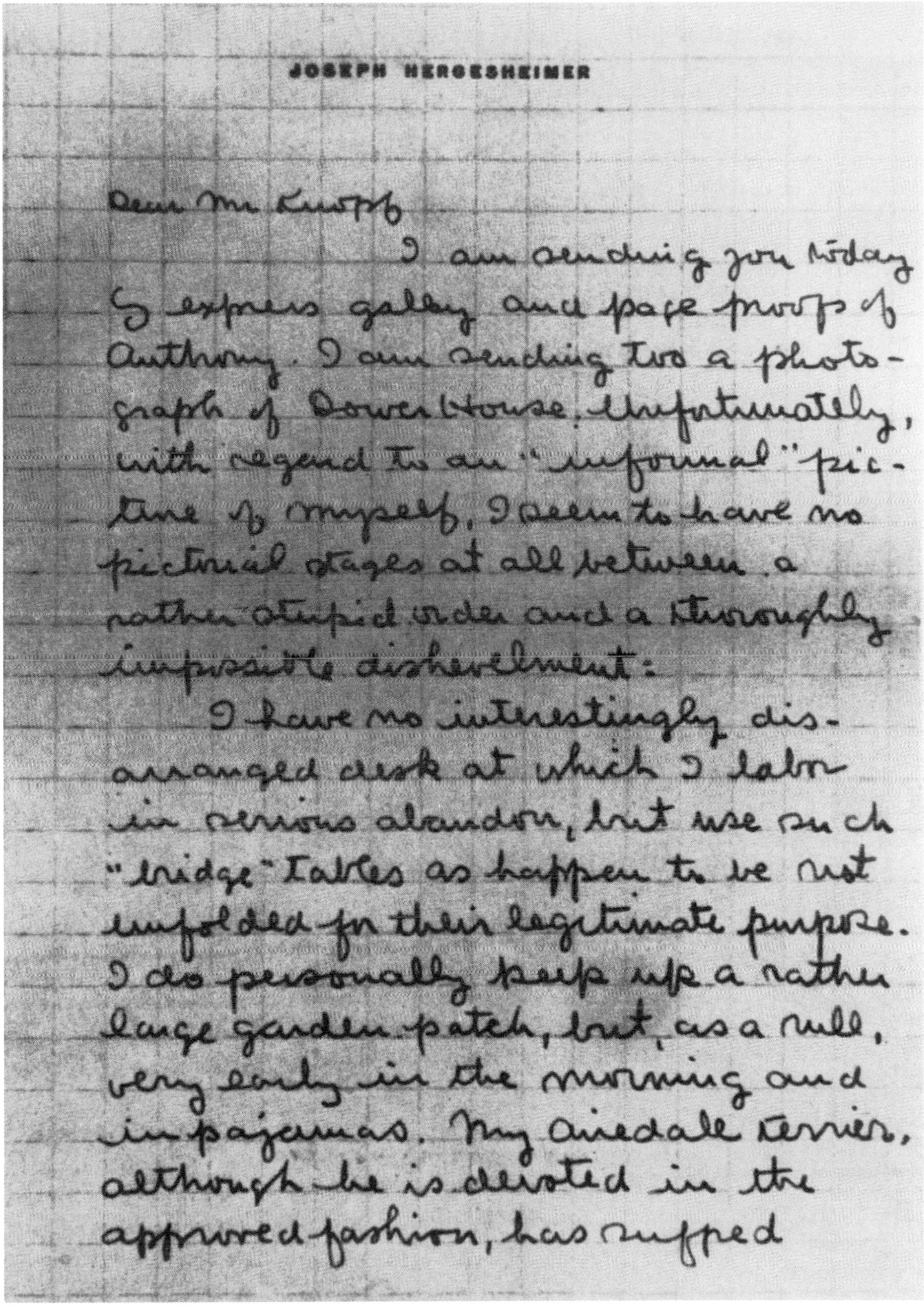

JOSEPH HERGESHEIMER

Dear Mr Knopf,

I am sending you today by express galley and page proofs of Anthony. I am sending too a photograph of Dower House. Unfortunately, with regard to an "informal" picture of myself, I seem to have no pictorial stages at all between a rather stupid order and a thoroughly impossible dishevelment:

I have no interestingly disarranged desk at which I labor in serious abandon, but use such "bridge" tables as happen to be not unfolded for their legitimate purpose. I do personally keep up a rather large garden patch, but, as a rule, very early in the morning and in pajamas. My airedale terrier, although he is devoted in the approved fashion, has supped

Page from an 8 July 1914 letter to Alfred Knopf, who published a revised edition of The Lay Anthony *in 1919 (from Herb Stappenbeck,* A Catalogue of the Joseph Hergesheimer Collection at the University of Texas at Austin, *1974)*

people at every social level were grappling with ideals that had come to seem like broken promises. Hergesheimer was always, as Ronald E. Martin says, "fascinated by the shifting surface of society and the flow of time around places and people," and was able adroitly to manipulate point of view and narrative structure in his stories so the present could be viewed in terms of the complexity of its relationship to the past. In confronting one generation with another in his works, he dramatized the nervous unrest, the search for distraction, and the sense of ineffectuality felt in the 1920s. This dramatization, however, often verges on the melodramatic. The world of spirit and the world of flesh are neatly opposed. Women appear time and again as temptations that test a man's will. Worldly failure serves to open the way to higher ideals and inspired gestures. The past is too clearly a time of simple, straightforward ways that encourage direct, confident action as opposed to a modern age in which men descended from empire builders struggle against their self-doubt and sense of lost glory.

Hergesheimer's historical interests and technical virtuosities were evident early on. *Gold and Iron* (1918) comprises three long stories, each separately published later (all in 1922) as novellas. Each narrative is set far enough back in the misty nineteenth century that characters and actions can loom larger than life with no problems of credibility arising. *Tubal Cain*, for example, tells the Horatio Alger type story of Alexander Hullings, a steelworker who rises to prominence in that burgeoning industry. Hergesheimer himself worked in Pennsylvania steel mills to get the story's atmosphere and setting exactly right. In *The Dark Fleece*, a California gold rush adventurer, appropriately named Jason, returns to his native New England. Rejected by a traditional young woman and her staunch family—because of his checkered, questionable past—Jason finds love and acceptance with an aristocratic woman named Honora. Hergesheimer was proud of the story, and it was well received.

Wild Oranges is set in Georgia and is the best of the three; it was often anthologized in the 1930s. Like the other two stories in the volume, its main protagonist is caught in a mid-life crisis through which he must struggle in order to reestablish a meaningful sense of life. John Woolfolk, a widower, renounces human society when his young bride is killed, and goes to live on a yacht with his friend Halvord, who is a self-exacting seaman of the old school. Woolfolk's growing involvement with the Stopes family, particularly with the daughter, Millie, leads to a series of conflicts that ends with Halvord's sacrifice of his life for Woolfolk. The power of the story derives from the deft handling of atmosphere and characterization.

The seven stories of Hergesheimer's next book, *The Happy End* (1919), were written, the author affirms in his introduction, "with one purpose: to give pleasure." The pleasure they give is that of the rousing tale well told. "Tol'able David" (*Saturday Evening Post* 14 July 1917; published separately in 1923), a Hatfield-and-McCoy story and the most popular of the collection, gives evidence of Hergesheimer's ability to handle fast-paced action and create convincing backwoods scenes and characters. Reviewers praised the technique in the stories, the mastery of appearance, gesture, form, and color.

Quiet Cities (1928) and *Tropical Winter* (1933) are ambitious volumes in which Hergesheimer develops a series of stories with an overall theme and effect in mind. The stories of *Quiet Cities* recreate the atmosphere of different cities at differing stages of the American past from colonial to Civil War days. The typical conflict in the stories is between one generation and the next. In the tenth story, for instance, the owner of a shipping company in Boston during the 1840s must meet the crisis arising when his son decides to abandon the ways of commerce, move to Brook Farm, and marry the daughter of a philosopher. *Quiet Cities* met with uneven reviews. Many critics praised the technical skill of the works. Others felt the pieces were too hazy and romantic.

Tropical Winter is a series of ten long stories that all have to do with the idle rich wintering at Palm Beach. In each story the boredom and superficiality of the socialites' lives are contrasted in various ways with the energy and idealism that went into the founding of America's wealthy dynasties. The third story is about a man, Charles, who has dreamed for years of again meeting an early love whom he lost for lack of money and social position. A widower now, he is invited to the winter colony, where his dream comes true. His former love says to him, "You do look young and so handsome. It's the life you've led. The true life. Life with an ideal!" Ultimately, Charles sees through her and the shallow values she represents. But he is not much happier for his insight. This story is representative of most in the collection. Details of place, dress, etiquette, and scenery are carefully built up and readers become thoroughly fa-

Caricature of Hergesheimer by William Gropper (from the Bookman, *May 1922)*

miliar with Palm Beach and the social scene there, but quickly the characters become interchangeable. The book sold well despite critical disparagement of its rigid structure and mannerism.

Late in his career Hergesheimer published almost exclusively in the high-paying, mass-circulation magazines of the day, such as the *Saturday Evening Post*. In his 1921 article for the *Yale Review*, "The Feminine Nuisance in American Literature," he bemoans the low quality of commercial short stories, blaming this on the audience: "The ladies want a flattering plot." He seems to have made a clear distinction between his serious fiction, the earlier stories and novels, and the work he did for magazines. These stories are uniformly adroit and formulaic. "Anyone," said Hergesheimer in an interview with Robert Van Gelder, "who thinks writing magazine fiction is difficult is simple-minded or a liar." In general the stories contain Hergesheimer's typical

themes, but they are played out superficially.

The general consensus of critical opinion is that Hergesheimer's early works are his best. He was a good craftsman and his stories, though long by modern standards, still have popular appeal. His themes are central to American fiction but generally find better expression in works by Fitzgerald and others. J. B. Priestley's comment in *Bookman* (May 1926) speaks most tellingly to this point: "There is a curious suggestion in this fiction of an adolescent daydreaming, very cleverly disguised and decorated in most places, but still there as a basis, or perhaps better, a starting point." The extensive critical interest in Hergesheimer's work during the 1920s and 1930s was often based on the implicit assumption that he would one day transcend this starting point to write major works. He did not, but what he did write is well honed and richly evocative of his era and of the American past.

Interview:

Robert Van Gelder, "The Curious Retirement of Mr. Hergesheimer," in his *Writers and Writing* (New York: Scribners, 1946).

Bibliographies:

Herbert Swire, *A Bibliography of the Work of Joseph Hergesheimer* (Philadelphia, 1922);

James J. Napier, "Joseph Hergesheimer: A Selected Bibliography, 1913-1945," *Bulletin of Bibliography*, 24 (September-December 1963): 46-48; (January-April 1964): 54, 69-70.

Biographies:

Llewellyn Jones, *Joseph Hergesheimer: The Man and His Books* (New York: Knopf, 1920);

Carl Van Vechten, "How I Remember Joseph Hergesheimer," *Yale University Library Gazette*, 22 (January 1948): 87-92.

References:

James Branch Cabell, *Joseph Hergesheimer: An Essay in Interpretation* (New York: Bookfellows, 1921);

Padraic Colum and Margaret Freeman Cabell, eds., *Between Friends: Letters of James Branch Cabell and Others* (New York: Harcourt, Brace & World, 1962);

John Tyree Fain, "Hergesheimer's Use of Historical Sources," *Journal of Southern History*, 18 (November 1952): 497-504;

Victor E. Gimmestad, *Joseph Hergesheimer* (Boston: Twayne, 1984);

Sara Haardt, "Joseph Hergesheimer's Methods," *Bookman*, 67 (June 1929): 398-403;

James H. Justus, "Joseph Hergesheimer's Germany: A Radical Art of Surfaces," *Journal of American Studies*, 7 (Spring 1973): 47-66;

Leon Kelley, "America and Mr. Hergesheimer," *Sewanee Review*, 40 (June 1932): 171-193;

Alfred A. Knopf, "Reminiscences of Hergesheimer, Van Vechten, and Mencken," *Yale University Literary Gazette*, 24 (April 1950): 145-164;

Gerald Langford, ed., *Ingénue Among the Lions: The Letters of Emily Clark to Joseph Hergesheimer* (Austin: University of Texas Press, 1965);

Ronald E. Martin, *The Fiction of Joseph Hergesheimer* (Philadelphia: University of Pennsylvania Press, 1965);

J. B. Priestley, "Joseph Hergesheimer, an English View," *Bookman*, 63 (May 1926): 272-280;

Geoffrey West, "Joseph Hergesheimer," *Virginia Quarterly Review*, 8 (January 1932): 95-108.

Papers:

The University of Texas has the largest collection of manuscripts, letters and other documents, memorabilia, and first editions. See Joseph Evans Slate, "The Joseph Hergesheimer Collection," *Library Chronicle of the University of Texas*, 7, no. 1 (1961): 24-31; and Herb Stappenbeck, *A Catalogue of the Joseph Hergesheimer Collection at the University of Texas* (Austin: Humanities Research Center, 1974). Manuscripts are also held at the Harvard, Princeton, and New York Public Libraries.

Paul Horgan

(1 August 1903 -   )

Robert W. Morrison
Montana State University

See also the Horgan entry in *DLB Yearbook: 1985*.

BOOKS: *Men of Arms* (Philadelphia: McKay, 1931);
The Fault of Angels (New York & London: Harper, 1933);
No Quarter Given (New York & London: Harper, 1935; London: Constable, 1935);
From the Royal City of the Holy Faith of St. Francis of Assisi (Santa Fe: Rydal, 1936);
The Return of the Weed (New York & London: Harper, 1936); republished as *Lingering Walls* (London: Constable, 1936);
Main Line West (New York & London: Harper, 1936; London: Constable, 1936);
A Lamp on the Plains (New York & London: Harper, 1937; London: Constable, 1937);
Far From Cibola (New York & London: Harper, 1938; London: Constable, 1938);
The Habit of Empire (Santa Fe: Rydal, 1939; New York & London: Harper, 1939);
Figures in a Landscape (New York & London: Harper, 1940);
The Common Heart (New York & London: Harper, 1942);
A Tree on the Plains: A Music Play for Americans, by Horgan and Ernest Bacon (New York: Williams, 1942);
The Devil in the Desert (New York: Longmans, Green, 1952);
One Red Rose for Christmas (New York: Longmans, Green, 1952);
Humble Powers (London: Macmillan, 1954; Garden City, N.Y.: Image Books, 1955);
Great River: The Rio Grande in North American History, 2 volumes (New York: Rinehart, 1954);
The Saintmaker's Christmas Eve (New York: Farrar, Straus & Cudahy, 1955; London: Macmillan, 1956);
The Centuries of Santa Fe (New York: Dutton, 1956; London: Macmillan, 1957);
Give Me Possession (New York: Farrar, Straus & Cudahy, 1957; London: Macmillan, 1958);
Rome Eternal (New York: Farrar, Straus & Cudahy, 1959);

A Distant Trumpet (New York: Farrar, Straus & Cudahy, 1960; London: Macmillan, 1960);
One of the Quietest Things (Los Angeles: University of California School of Library Service, 1960);
Citizen of New Salem (New York: Farrar, Straus & Cudahy, 1961); republished as *Abraham Lincoln, Citizen of New Salem* (London: Macmillan, 1961);
Conquistadors in North American History (New York: Farrar, Straus, 1963); republished as *Conquistadors in North America* (London: Macmillan, 1963);
Toby and the Nighttime (New York: Farrar, Straus, 1963; London: Macmillan, 1963);
Things As They Are (New York: Farrar, Straus, 1964; London: Bodley Head, 1965);
Peter Hurd: A Portrait Sketch From Life (Austin: University of Texas Press, 1965);
Songs After Lincoln (New York: Farrar, Straus & Giroux, 1965);
Memories of the Future (New York: Farrar, Straus & Giroux, 1966; London: Bodley Head, 1966);
The Peach Stone: Stories From Four Decades (New York: Farrar, Straus & Giroux, 1967; London: Bodley Head, 1967);
Everything to Live For (New York: Farrar, Straus & Giroux, 1968; London: Bodley Head, 1969);
Maurice Baring Reconsidered (Middletown, Conn.: Wesleyan University Press, 1969);
The Heroic Triad: Essays in the Social Energies of Three Southwestern Cultures (New York: Holt, Rinehart & Winston, 1970; London: Heinemann, 1971);
Whitewater (New York: Farrar, Straus & Giroux, 1970; London: Bodley Head, 1971);
Encounters With Stravinsky: A Personal Record (New York: Farrar, Straus & Giroux, 1972; London: Bodley Head, 1972);
Approaches to Writing (New York: Farrar, Straus & Giroux, 1973; London: Bodley Head, 1974);

Paul Horgan (photograph by Walt Odets)

Lamy of Santa Fe: His Life and Times (New York: Farrar, Straus & Giroux, 1975);

The Thin Mountain Air (New York: Farrar, Straus & Giroux, 1977; London: Bodley Head, 1978);

Josiah Gregg and His Vision of the Early West (New York: Farrar, Straus & Giroux, 1979);

Henriette Wyeth (Chadds Ford, Pa.: Brandywine River Museum, 1980);

On the Climate of Books (Middletown, Conn.: Wesleyan University Press, 1981);

Mexico Bay (New York: Farrar, Straus & Giroux, 1982; Henley on Thames, U.K.: Ellis, 1982);

Of America: East & West (New York: Farrar, Straus & Giroux, 1984);

The Clerihews of Paul Horgan (Middletown, Conn.: Wesleyan University Press, 1985);

Under the Sangre de Cristo (Santa Fe: Rydal, 1985);

A Certain Climate (Middletown, Conn.: Wesleyan University Press, 1988);

A Writer's Eye (New York: Abrams, 1988).

Collection: *Mountain Standard Time* (New York: Farrar, Straus & Cudahy, 1962; London: Macmillan, 1962)—comprises *Main Line West, Far From Cibola*, and *The Common Heart*.

PLAY PRODUCTION: *Yours, A. Lincoln*, New York, Schubert Theatre, 9 July 1942.

RECORDING: *Paul Horgan Reads Paul Horgan [The Devil in the Desert]*, Chicago, Thomas More Association, 1976.

OTHER: Witter Bynner, *Selected Poems*, preface by Horgan (New York: Knopf, 1936);

New Mexico's Own Chronicle: Three Races in the Writings of Four Hundred Years, adapted and edited by Horgan and Maurice Garland Fulton (Dallas: Upshaw, 1937);

Maurice Baring Restored: Selections from His Work, edited by Horgan (New York: Farrar, Straus & Giroux, 1970; London: Heinemann, 1970).

Paul Horgan's early writing is primarily short fiction and is significant for its sharp characterization and luminous style. As John Barkham indicated in the *New York Post* (29 September 1970): "Time, place, and character are all recalled by an acutely sensitive mind. His sensibilities are those of a generation that valued elegance, symmetry, and morality." Some of his short stories are still among the finest in American letters, as they exceed their southwestern settings to become universal in appeal.

His major themes are as versatile as his style. Although he is a Catholic writer and southwestern regionalist, the themes of human relationships often in conflict with each other are expressions of deep emotional feeling that far exceed the confinements of any one religion or region. Perhaps his most memorable stories are those which, though not focused on death as a theme, revolve around death and the effects it has on the human emotions of those it touches. Horgan's characters are questing for dignity and sometimes must work through the cruelty and deceit that make up many human relationships in order to find a level of acceptable balance for themselves and others. To accomplish this goal, his fictional characters are as real and believable as the real-life figures of his histories and biographies. They are truly "figures in a landscape," as his 1940 collection of short stories is entitled.

Paul Horgan was born in Buffalo, New York, on 1 August 1903 to Edward and Rose Marie Rohr Horgan. Because his father was in failing health, the family moved to Albuquerque, New Mexico, in 1915. New Mexico would well serve Horgan over five decades of writing as the setting for most of his work. Because New Mexico had only joined the Union three years before the author's arrival, the low person-to-land ratio, the strong Spanish-Catholic influence, and the isolated rural setting all contributed to his view of New Mexico as "tierra encantada," the land of enchantment. For young Paul Horgan this area became his "new world of land," and his writings abound with references to its huge vistas: mountains, plains, and mesas.

Horgan attended Albuquerque public elementary schools, and his secondary education (1920-1923) was received at the New Mexico Military Institute in Roswell, New Mexico, where he was active in dramatics, music, and art, and as the editor of the school literary journal. While attending the institute, he worked briefly as a reporter and music critic for the *Albuquerque Jour-*

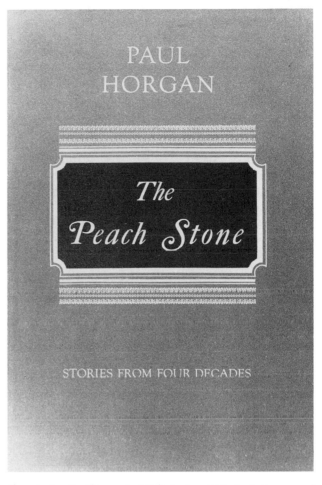

Dust jacket for Horgan's 1967 book, which includes several stories from earlier collections as well as previously uncollected stories

nal. In 1921 his father died, and in 1923 Horgan moved back east to study for three years in voice training at the Eastman School of Music in Rochester, New York, where he also worked with the school's theater department as an actor and backstage assistant.

In 1926 he returned to the New Mexico Military Institute as its librarian, a post he held until 1942. It was at this time that he began to channel his many artistic talents toward a writing career. The late 1920s became a period of development that led to his first historical work, *Men of Arms* (1931), a publication for juveniles that he also illustrated. His diverse writing career was launched, and over the next six decades his writing would include short stories, novels, poetry, biographies, essays, and histories.

Horgan's first major collection of short fiction was *The Return of the Weed* (1936). This collection of six stories, five of them previously unpublished, follows a motif of growth and decay. As

Horgan states in the introduction, "We can learn from the past by thinking about its lingering walls, built by men along their way through wilderness. The men are taken away by life or death, and their houses stay until the weather and the weed render dust."

Growth and decay in *The Return of the Weed* are reflections of the power of nature on the efforts of man through time from the 1650s until 1930. Nature is unrelenting and, in all but the last story, "The Star," not only destroys the edifices but also the humans who built them. The priest in the first story, "The Mission," dedicates thirty years to administering to the Indians only to be "rewarded" with their killing him. In "The Brothers," a large cattle ranch reverts to dust when false accusations by jealous neighbors destroy the one brother and force the other to escape. The land developer who builds the luxurious house in "The Mansion" is ruined by faulty speculation and dies, leaving his eighty-year-old widow, now poverty-stricken, to die alone in their mansion. In "The Tank," a struggling young farmer is deserted by his socialite El Paso wife, who cannot stand the New Mexico isolation. He lets the farm go to ruin and moves on to be a mere ranch hand; the water tank left crumbling and deserted is all that remains of his efforts. The Spanish influence in the Southwest is represented in "The Hacienda" (*Yale Review*, March 1936). The grandeur and wealth of generations disintegrates as members of a family scatter or die and only one Don Elizario remains, as a drunken boarder in the local Elks Club, living in the past and ridiculed in the present. In "The Star" a former star high-school athlete is relegated to building, owning, and running a service station in an isolated New Mexico setting. In this optimistic concluding story, the buildings revert to the New Mexico dust, but unlike all the other major characters of this collection, the former athlete is able to shake loose from the unrelenting force of nature and move on to a successful life. *The Return of the Weed* is a montage in condensed form of those elements of nature and humankind that still dot the landscape of the western United States.

Horgan's next collection of short fiction, *Figures in a Landscape*, brings together thirty stories written between 1931 and 1940. His distinct craftsmanship in storytelling once more dramatizes the people and landscape of the Southwest. Each story is a vignette of the past, its people, and their environment.

Four of these stories sharply exemplify his progress in the short-story genre since his earlier volume. In one of these, his 1935 story "Tribute" (*Scribner's*, October), Horgan creates a typical western bank-robber hero, Honeyboy Benton, and then proceeds to examine in fiction the process by which western oral legends and ballads of socially negative figures are enhanced.

In "The Surgeon and the Nun" (*Harper's Bazaar*, December 1936) Horgan moves back in time to 1905. A young doctor, going by rail to establish his new practice in New Mexico, and a Catholic nun are faced with performing an appendectomy on a Mexican railroad section hand under threat of their lives if he should die. In this story Horgan carefully contrasts his central characters and juxtaposes them with the harsh figures and harsher landscape of the settled but not fully civilized western scene.

Earlier figures in the historical New Mexican landscape are two Mexican boys, Julio (thirteen) and Luis (sixteen), who in the 1880s go through a maturation ritual in "To The Mountains" (*Atlantic*, January 1938), when they journey home to prove themselves to their family. Julio meets and overcomes the harsh environment of the mountains and saves his brother's life; both become more mature and more responsible figures who survive and grow in the harsh landscape of the plains.

A more contemporary story, "In Summer's Name," written in 1940 and previously unpublished, ironically portrays the dilemma of a pregnant, unmarried high-school girl, Trillie Dee Spelzer, and the son of a rich, successful banker in small-town America. She leaves the community and becomes a movie star, while he marries a local girl and becomes the town bum. As Horgan reveals, "Trillie Dee has seized life, and condemned them to existence."

These four stories exemplify Horgan's progress in character revelation: characters are finely honed, and his polished style reveals them as bright spots in a changing world. The collection blends these characters into a montage of advances and regressions that is typical of a rural, nineteenth-century society moving into a more hectic and urban twentieth century. Each story is an example of this changing process. In the later stories of the collection especially, one feels that Horgan's attitude is one of regret—regret for losing the old ways, the more sedate manners, and most of all the simple feeling of one human being for another.

Horgan circa 1979 (photograph by William Van Saun)

Two years after the publication of *Figures in a Landscape*, in 1942, Horgan entered the army and worked with its information branch at the Pentagon during World War II. After the war he returned to Roswell, New Mexico, to resume his writing career. In 1960 he began a long association with Wesleyan University in Middletown, Connecticut, as teacher and administrator, thus leaving his beloved Southwest to become a resident of the East.

Horgan's major collection of stories, *The Peach Stone* (1967), republishes several stories from earlier collections and adds several more that were previously uncollected. This collection varies from earlier ones in that the twenty stories are ordered under headings of childhood, youth, maturity, and age. The setting is no longer exclusively New Mexico, although most of the stories occur in the West. Once more Horgan brings his talent to bear on the delineation of realistic rather than romantic themes and reveals his characters at moments of time in an ever-changing America. These stories, selected by Horgan, constitute what he and most readers have found to be his best collection.

One of the earliest stories here, "The Other Side of the Street" (*Yale Review*, December 1930), is included in the works reflecting maturity. Dreams found in romantic novels replace the reality of a yearned-for affair, as a married woman, Mrs. Schluzer, thinks of the exciting world of the other side of Elmer Avenue with its boardinghouse, Italian bootlegger, and doctor's office. In the boardinghouse a young photographer dreams of his imaginary unfulfilled romance with Mrs. Schluzer. For both characters, thinking of the other side of the street serves as a brief hiatus in their rather sedate, if not boring, lives. The reality of everyday life in small-town American is succinctly and delicately captured as each character escapes from their only meeting back into the safe world of dreams.

Perhaps the most outstanding of Horgan's short stories is the title story, "The Peach Stone" (*Yale Review*, June 1942). A two-year-old girl has been incinerated by burning tumbleweeds, and the parents, Jodey and Cleotha Powers, with their nine-year-old son, Buddy, are taking the body on a four-hour drive to Weed, New Mexico, for burial. They are accompanied by Miss Arlene

Latcher, the boy's schoolteacher, who feels that she can help and comfort them but not give way to emotions. The symbolic force of the peach stone representing Arlene—hard, dry, and wrinkled on the outside, but still possessing the seed of life within—is well handled. Ironically Arlene becomes the recipient of Cleotha's tenderness. Horgan's combination of succinct character portrayal and symbolism makes this one of his most powerful short stories, and it met with considerable critical acclaim. Often anthologized, "The Peach Stone" is a revelation of the spirit and tenacity of human beings.

The Devil in the Desert (*Saturday Evening Post*, 30 March 1950; published separately in 1952) may not have achieved the critical reputation of "The Peach Stone," but its presentation is just as striking. This outstanding story of a simple man existing in harsh desert conditions is notable for its revelation of the character Father Louis Bellefontaine. He is spellbound by his hallucination of the Devil as a speaking serpent. The story is one of Horgan's most effective portrayals of the deep faith that was so much a part of traditional southwestern American character.

One of Horgan's last major stories in *The Peach Stone* is "Black Snowflakes" (a section of his 1964 novel *Things As They Are*; the story originally appeared in the *Saturday Evening Post*, 30 March 1963). Horgan is able to retain a youthful perspective while relating the feelings of a nine-year-old boy who is facing his initial contact with death, as his sickly grandfather (Grosspa) returns to Germany to die. This story is a fitting example of Horgan's storytelling strength as he closes the circle of life represented by the young boy and his old grandfather. As are most of Horgan's char-

acters, they are realistic representations of the human spirit in movement. (According to Robert Gish, Grosspa is likely a fictional embodiment of Horgan's grandfather Matthias Rohr.)

Paul Horgan has had a long, diversified writing career, including the production of many short stories, novels, histories, and biographies. His work encompasses some extensive projects, such as his major two-volume history *Great River: The Rio Grande in North American History* (1954), which was awarded the 1955 Pulitzer Prize in history as well as the Bancroft Prize. Central to all his work are those formative and developing years in New Mexico, and it is his strong regional sense of character that enhances the universal themes that make his writings a valuable contribution to American letters.

Bibliography:

James Kraft, "A Provisional Bibliography," in Horgan's *Approaches to Writing* (New York: Farrar, Straus & Giroux, 1973), pp. 237-332.

References:

James Day, *Paul Horgan* (Austin: Steck-Vaughn, 1967);

Robert Gish, "Calliope and Clio: Paul Horgan's River Muses," *Southwest Review*, 69 (Winter 1984): 2-15;

Gish, *Paul Horgan* (Boston: Twayne, 1983);

Terry L. Hansen, "The Experience of Paul Horgan's *The Peach Stone*," *South Dakota Review*, 22 (Summer 1984): 71-85;

David McCullough, "Historian, Novelist, and Much, Much More," *New York Times Book Review*, 8 April 1984, VII: 3, 22.

MacKinlay Kantor

(4 February 1904 - 11 October 1977)

Laura M. Zaidman
University of South Carolina—Sumter

See also the Kantor entry in *DLB 9: American Novelists, 1910-1945.*

BOOKS: *Diversey* (New York: Coward-McCann, 1928);

El Goes South (New York: Coward-McCann, 1930);

The Jaybird (New York: Coward-McCann, 1932);

Long Remember (New York: Coward-McCann, 1934, London: Selwyn & Blount, 1934);

Turkey in the Straw (New York: Coward-McCann, 1935);

The Voice of Bugle Ann (New York: Coward-McCann, 1935; London: Selwyn & Blount, 1935);

Arouse and Beware (New York: Coward-McCann, 1936; London: Gollancz, 1937);

The Romance of Rosy Ridge (New York: Coward-McCann, 1937);

The Boy in the Dark (Webster Groves, Mo.: International Mark Twain Society, 1937);

The Noise of Their Wings (New York: Coward-McCann, 1938; London: Hale, 1939);

Here Lies Holly Springs (New York: Pynson, 1938);

Valedictory (New York: Coward-McCann, 1939);

Cuba Libre (New York: Coward-McCann, 1940);

Gentle Annie: A Western Novel (New York: Coward-McCann, 1942; London: Hale, 1951);

Angleworms on Toast (New York: Coward-McCann, 1942);

Happy Land (New York: Coward-McCann, 1943);

Author's Choice (New York: Coward-McCann, 1944);

Glory for Me (New York: Coward-McCann, 1945);

But Look, the Morn: The Story of a Childhood (New York: Coward-McCann, 1947; London: Falcon, 1950 [i.e., 1951]);

Midnight Lace (New York: Random House, 1948; London: Falcon, 1949);

Wicked Water: An American Primitive (New York: Random House, 1948; London: Falcon, 1950);

The Good Family (New York: Coward-McCann, 1949);

One Wild Oat (New York: Fawcett, 1950; London: Allen, 1952);

Signal Thirty-Two (New York: Random House, 1950);

Lee and Grant at Appomattox (New York: Random House, 1950);

Don't Touch Me (New York: Random House, 1951; London: Allen, 1952);

Gettysburg (New York: Random House, 1952);

Warwhoop: Two Short Novels of the Frontier (New York: Random House, 1952);

The Daughter of Bugle Ann (New York: Random House, 1953);

God and My Country (Cleveland: World, 1954);

Andersonville (Cleveland: World, 1955; abridged edition, London: Allen, 1956);

Lobo (Cleveland: World, 1957; London: Allen, 1958);

Silent Grow the Guns, and Other Tales of the American Civil War (New York: New American Library, 1958);

The Work of St. Francis (Cleveland: World, 1958); republished as *The Unseen Witness* (London: Allen, 1959);

Frontier: Tales of the American Adventure (New York: New American Library, 1959);

It's About Crime (New York: New American Library, 1960);

If the South Had Won the Civil War (New York: Bantam, 1961);

Spirit Lake (Cleveland: World, 1961; London: Allen, 1962);

The Gun-Toter, and Other Stories of the Missouri Hills (New York: New American Library, 1963);

Mission with LeMay: My Story, by Kantor and Curtis E. LeMay (Garden City, N.Y.: Doubleday, 1965);

Story Teller (Garden City, N.Y.: Doubleday, 1967);

Beauty Beast (New York: Putnam's, 1968);

The Day I Met a Lion (Garden City, N.Y.: Doubleday, 1968);

Missouri Bittersweet (Garden City, N.Y.: Doubleday, 1969; London: Hale, 1970);

Hamilton County (New York: Macmillan, 1970);

MacKinlay Kantor in 1935 (photograph by George W. Vassar)

I Love You, Irene (Garden City, N.Y.: Doubleday, 1972; London: Allen, 1973);

The Children Sing (New York: Hawthorne, 1973; London: Hale, 1974);

Valley Forge (New York: Evans, 1975).

Collection: *Three: Happy Land, Lobo, Cuba Libre* (New York: Paperback Library, 1962).

Best known for his historical novels, especially the winner of the 1956 Pulitzer Prize, *Andersonville* (1955), MacKinlay Kantor wrote many books and hundreds of short stories. When he is remembered in the literary annals of American short fiction, it will be for his entertaining tales appealing to pre-World War II readers' tastes for wholesome and uplifting narratives.

MacKinlay Kantor was born in Webster City, Iowa, on 4 February 1904. His autobiography *But Look, the Morn* (1947) describes the disastrous marriage (1899-1904) of his parents, Effie Rachel McKinlay Kantor and John Martin Kantor. His father lost many jobs, failed to support his family, and even spent time in jail; consequently, the couple separated before Kantor's birth and divorced soon thereafter. His birth certificate reads "Benjamin McKinlay Kantor," but

he shed his "uncouth" first name in his youth, taking instead the original Highland Scottish form of his mother's maiden name (adding the "a" to McKinlay). Encouraged to write by his newspaper-editor mother, after his public-school education was complete, Kantor worked with her as a *Webster City Daily News* reporter from 1921 to 1925. His winning a short-story contest sponsored by the *Des Moines Register* spurred his decision to become a writer of fiction. He began sending out stories, having no initial success; it took almost six years to receive another check for his writing. When the newspaper failed in 1925, he moved to Chicago, suffering "several weeks of semi-starvation in a grim room" and beating his "mauled head against newspaper office doors with no fortune."

But his fortune changed. While a member of the Graeme Players theater company, he met Florence Irene Layne, a commercial artist, whom he married on 2 July 1926. Kantor tells about the first twenty-eight months of their lifelong romance in *I Love You, Irene* (1972). They had two children: their daughter, Layne Kantor Shroder, became a novelist; and their son, Thomas (Tim) MacKinlay Kantor, a professional photographer (he provided the pictures for his father's *Hamilton County*, 1970). In their early married years, the Kantors were plagued by poverty until MacKinlay became a successful writer. Losing his job as a *Cedar Rapids Republican* reporter when the paper was sold in 1927, he continued to work both on short stories for one cent a word and his first novel, *Diversey* (1928), about Chicago gang wars in the 1920s. *Diversey* received good reviews in major newspapers and magazines. His career was launched. Ironically, a scathing remark may have helped him, in terms of public recognition, when Senator Coleman Blease of South Carolina denounced *Diversey* in the U.S. Senate as "the dirtiest thing I have ever read."

While writing his next two novels, Kantor worked as a columnist for the *Des Moines Tribune* (1930-1931). His first historical novel, *Long Remember* (1934), about Gettysburg, won popular and critical acclaim. In the depths of the Depression one winter he did not have an overcoat; the next winter *Long Remember* was a Literary Guild choice, and he had a Hollywood contract. Even so, Kantor also wrote many short stories during the late 1930s. His best-known screenplay, for Samuel Goldwyn's *The Best Years of Our Lives*, winner of thirteen Academy Awards, was adapted from Kantor's verse novel, *Glory for Me* (1945). It was inspired by his World War II experiences with the British Royal Air Force as a war correspondent, and with the U.S. Air Force as a B-17 gunner on eleven missions. In 1950 he served as a war correspondent in Korea. That same year he published *Signal Thirty-Two*, detailing his year as a New York City policeman, a job he took to write a screenplay for a police movie never produced. In the 1950s Kantor published thirteen books and numerous stories, but not as many as two decades before. He republished his best stories, primarily those of the 1930s, in collections: for example, twelve in *Silent Grow the Guns, and Other Tales of the American Civil War* (1958) and nine in *The Gun-Toter, and Other Stories of the Missouri Hills* (1963).

Kantor's 1944 anthology, *Author's Choice*—subtitled *40 Stories . . . With copious Notes, Explanations, Digressions, and Elucidations; the Author telling frankly why he selected these Stories, why they were written, how much Money he received for them, and of his thrilling Adventures with wild Editors in their native Haunts*—offers a sampling of stories written from 1921 to 1944 and shows his development as a writer. In the introduction, publisher Thomas Coward acknowledges Kantor's purpose to enter-

tain, perhaps an admission of these stories' transitory popularity. Even Kantor admits to some unsuccessful tales. Among the interesting insights are Kantor's comments on the shifts in popular magazines' tastes over twenty-five years. His remarks appear between the stories.

The collection begins with his first published story, "Purple," which he wrote under a pen name (Sheridan Rhodes, after his Sheridan Road, Chicago, address) as required for the *Des Moines Register* short-story contest; it won the first prize of fifty dollars and was published in the 26 February 1922 issue. "Purple" opens with a chauffeur-driven foreign car stopping at the rural Hamilton County, Iowa, farmhouse of John Jones. The passenger, Paul Floireaux, a well-known artist, admires the rich purples, blues, and lavenders of the flower-covered hills and begins to photograph them. He has just completed a series of landscapes by finding the perfect expression for his image of "Purple." Ironically, months later, farmer Jones spends a large amount in Des Moines to own the famous Floireaux portrait. "Purple!" Mrs. Jones exclaims in "rapt adoration": "My, that's too pretty to be real. . . . Somewhere in this world, there are places like that; maybe I can never see them, but I can have this to look at every day." Thus, Kantor's first published story ends with the ironic twist of coincidence that concludes many of his stories.

His next story ("a very bad one" and not in the collection) was published without payment: "The Pasture of the Blessed" appeared in 1924 in *Outdoor America*, the Izaak Walton League's publication. "Joth Countryman Retires" (the story after "Purple" in *Author's Choice*) was published in 1925 in the *Iowa Magazine*, which went bankrupt before Kantor could get paid; the story is noteworthy as the first of more than fifty Civil War stories he had written by 1944. "Joth Countryman Retires" depicts an old man's recollections of the battle of Shiloh. In an ironic note after the story Kantor displays some of his cantankerousness in admitting that one part may have been "lifted" unintentionally from elsewhere, making him "guilty of a little subconscious poaching"; if so, he says he will gladly pay the author (or heirs) a share of his royalties, which were to date, "exactly nothing."

"The Biggest Liar in Eagle Falls" (*McClure's Magazine*, 1928), another early story—the second one for which Kantor was paid—shows his fondness for the surprise ending (a "snapper"), using

First two pages of a story by Kantor in the September 1935 issue of American Magazine. *The story was later collected in* Frontier *(1959).*

the dramatic revelation of a famous person, in this case Buffalo Bill. Other stories showing his affection for historical figures are "Then Came the Legions" (U. S. Grant), "Lemonade for Lance" (Stonewall Jackson), "Highway Number One" (George Washington), "Old Man Begins to Cry" (Kaiser Wilhelm II), and "Hester Burns the Horses" (Abraham Lincoln)—only the first of which is in *Author's Choice*. Kantor called these stories accurate, effective pictures of the period, despite "simple and threadbare" plots. They show his early penchant for the Civil War period as well as his fascination with the frontier West.

Kantor's first successful market was the pulps, the popular "cheap little magazines with lurid covers" read avidly by millions of Americans. In his essay "Pulp Stuff" (in *Author's Choice*) he classifies writers who contribute to pulps: first, the professional writers who amazingly "manufacture stories at a sweat-shop pace"; second, young writers on their way up to better magazines such as *Saturday Evening Post* and *Cosmopolitan*; and finally, the dismal unfortunates who slide back

from slick magazines into the pulps. While Kantor did not categorize himself, one assumes he identified with the second group, although in the 1930s he produced enough to rival the first group. Kantor published in the pulp *Real Detective Tales* in Chicago from 1928 to 1930, his first payment being thirty-six dollars for two short stories at the rate of one cent per word. He appeared often in this magazine, along with another frequent contributor, Erle Stanley Gardner. Kantor learned a great deal about editorial censorship during these days; for instance, Christ's name was never permitted, so "God A'mighty" replaced "Jesus Christ" as the sole expletive allowed. The relationship with *Real Detective Tales* ended when the editor, having raised Kantor's rate to two cents, demoted him back to one cent for his five-thousand-word "bang-bang-cops-and-robbers" stories.

Kantor also sold stories to the literary supplement of the *Chicago Daily News*, whose editor offered him a feature reporter job; Kantor chose instead to eke out a living writing stories, dreaming

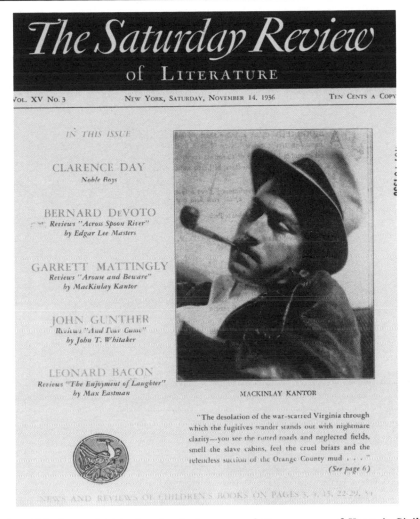

Cover of the magazine in which Garrett Mattingly refers to Arouse and Beware, *one of Kantor's Civil War novels, as "first rate entertainment at the hands of an accomplished craftsman"*

of being a top fiction writer. Some typical stories written in the late 1920s deal with poverty, opulent dreams, hungry men being fed, and starving clerks discovering great wads of money in old luggage or clothes hampers—topics Kantor groups in *Author's Choice* under "the eternal seeking after comfort and security—even the most flickering and temporary prosperity—which plagues the dreams of the poor." One story about poverty and discomfort, "The Woman on the Roof " (*Chicago Daily News*, 1929), describes how a man is moved to buy an electric fan for a poor woman and her children whom he sees as he passes on a train.

Kantor realized he could secure a maximum profit for a minimum of time and labor with short stories; he frequently wrote two-and-a-half-page stories in an hour or two and made up to five hundred dollars. Profitable and fun to write,

these entertaining stories have no literary value, as he admitted. Kantor could produce many stories quickly by recalling isolated incidents from his past and embellishing them; he often chose reflections of small-town America from his youth in Iowa. An example in *Author's Choice* is "Neither Hand Nor Foot" (*Detective Fiction Weekly*, 1932), a "far-fetched melodrama" inspired by his desperate economic situation in the midst of the Depression, when he had an income of barely more than thirty dollars for five months. The story derives its title from the repeated description of Old Scott Simson, who can move "neither hand nor foot" because of injuries sustained when his house burned down. Dave McCloud has returned home from three years in prison intent on revenge against Simson, whom he blames for his father's murder and his own jail sentence for operating a still. Simson, immobile in bed, convinces McCloud that his father drew a gun first; moreover, Simson betrayed McCloud to the authorities to save him from being a murderer—or murdered. After the appeased McCloud leaves, Simson reveals from beneath the comforter a double-barreled sawed-off shotgun aimed at the chair where McCloud sat. A typical Kantor story with little action, it ends happily with a sudden recognition of some truth, often with an ironic twist. When he wrote the story, Kantor felt just like Simson, "bandaged, hog-tied and helpless" financially. Fortunately, "Neither Hand Nor Foot" led to orders for other detective stories, chasing away "a whole pack of extremely carnivorous wolves" from his door.

While he worked on *Long Remember*, he supported his family with stories such as "Mamma Is So Proud" (*Redbook*, 1933), which earned $250. It describes how a mother fools a group of story-hungry reporters by never admitting she knows her famous actress-daughter has been arrested for murdering a boyfriend. By 1934 Kantor was contributing frequently to *Detective Fiction Weekly* with murder mysteries that challenged his imagination to come up with new ideas. Once when he parked his car on a quiet road to work out a plot, policemen with drawn guns surrounded him, demanding to know why he was there; Kantor replied, "Trying to think up a unique way of murdering a man." He had a lot of explaining to do.

After his mystery stories came more Civil War tales in the mid 1930s and thereafter. One notable short one is "Then Came the Legions" (*Redbook*, 1934), which marked the beginning of his success in selling Civil War stories. He says they "became the sound gangplank on which I walked across from pulps into the realm of slick paper." This particular story has a "trick" ending: the town drunkard who drills the home guard is U. S. Grant. Another, "Mountain Music" (*Cosmopolitan*, 1932), was his first thousand-dollar story; by the early 1940s he was receiving two thousand a story.

His best-known Civil War tale, "Silent Grow the Guns" (*Redbook*, 1935), won the 1935 O. Henry Memorial Award. It tells of a seven-year-old Virginian, Roverton (Rover) Appleby, whose father has died at Mechanicsville. Rover just happens to be playing with his neighborhood friend Nellie McLean the day Gen. Robert E. Lee surrenders at the McLean home in Appomattox. Rover has gone to the McLeans' house to share the special brandied peaches a soldier gave his mother. The children fall asleep elsewhere in the house

Kantor in 1937 (photograph by Robert Disraeli)

as the truce is signed, unaware of the historic event. As Rover runs home through a field, he trips over something in the thorny path: "A man in tattered butternut coat and pants lay there, staring at the sky. His eyes were like great marbles, and his face was a solid chalky purple, and one shoulder was drenched with a brown stain." Safe in his mother's arms, Rover notices a sudden silence of the guns. Shouting "We licked them damnyankees," he learns, instead, that Lee has surrendered. In the romanticized ending, his mother, Lucia Appleby, is courted by the Yankee sergeant who had been so generous in giving them food.

Other war stories include "A Long Line of Soldiers" (*Harper's*, October 1935), about Arlington National Cemetery and the successful generations of Clarks in every American war. Kantor felt that the magazines with the largest audiences, such as the *Saturday Evening Post*, rejected it because it had little love interest and action. Another Civil War story, "Spoils of War" (*American Magazine*, February 1936), raised a storm of criticism because it referred to Johnson's Island, an Ohio prison—similar to the infamous Andersonville, Georgia, prison—where many soldiers died due to insufficient or bad food and unsanitary conditions. Counterattacking the "valiant ladies of the Daughters of Union Veterans" who protested with cancelled magazine subscriptions, Kantor fired his own ammunition at these "hot-tempered and sharp-tongued females" by quoting from unbiased historians to support the accuracy of his story and noting that he himself was a member of the Sons of Union Veterans.

Kantor did battle with editors as well as readers. He labeled some editors "Simon Legrees" because the slightest deviation from their expectations resulted in "violent disapproval and a rapid-fire rejection" unless he made revisions. Consequently, to sell his stories he had to be willing to change plots, often cheapening the stories with melodramatic climaxes. Moreover, he had to accept new titles, some of which, he admits, were superior to his; for instance, his title "Here Lies Holly Springs" (for the story separately published in 1938) had been changed to "Drummer Boy" when published in the *American Legion Monthly* in February 1937.

But a more serious form of editorial censorship came with taboos, such as avoiding stories about the mentally ill, Jews, or blacks. An example is his story "I Will Do My Best" (*Saturday Evening Post*, 11 February 1939), which incidentally made him a "high priest of Scouting" and put him on the National Council of the Boy Scouts of America. The original version had to be changed because the scoutmaster was a minister and the boy yearning to be a scout was Jewish. In the revision, the boy is black. Of course, more problems arose from readers who criticized his use of *nigger* and *darky*; Kantor responded with scathing remarks about the "nuts" and "ignoramuses" who failed to understand that the pejorative terms were used by ignorant, insensitive characters and did not reflect his own views. Just as he was criticized for being racist in "I Will Do My Best," Kantor came under fire for his humorous story "The Darkies Are Gay" (*Country Gentleman*, 1938). He explains in *Author's Choice* that he saw signs, just as in the story, along a road near Darien, Georgia: "Stop and See Famous Slave," "Oldest Slave in These Parts," "Only One Mile to Only Man Slave Existing in This World," and "See Slave 105 Years Old." He was fascinated by the signs (but did not stop), and thus evolved this "cartoon story," never intended to libel blacks. Even though many years of publishing toughened Kantor's hide, he was thin-skinned and irascible enough to be annoyed by criticism he considered stupid, and he fired back equally hostile letters.

Based on the success of his 1958 anthology *Silent Grow the Guns, and Other Tales of the American Civil War*, Kantor collected eight stories in *Frontier: Tales of the American Adventure* (1959), again relying primarily on his 1930s work. These stories of frontier men and women are described on the dust jacket in epic terms: "BIG as the sweeping plains, the towering mountains, the endless swamps." The only story not about pioneers who "tamed the West" is "King Giant," and the *Frontier* cover boasts that Kantor captures "the spirit of a growing America and the heart of the men and women who made the legends, braved the badlands, built the West."

In "Not Cloudy All Day" (*American Magazine*, September 1935), thirteen-year-old Adelaide Mendenhall's dreams of her brother Joe's marriage to Telitha Countryman die when news comes of Joe's death. What is even worse is the sworn testimony of Bradgate Dodge that Joe murdered an officer at the Battle of Nashville in December 1864. But the officer and Joe miraculously return (they are still alive) to reveal the lies of Brad, who is himself anxious to marry Telitha; thus, Addie's dreams of Joe's marriage come true.

In the sequel, "This Little Wife Stayed Home" (*American Magazine*, March 1936), the happy two-month marriage of Telitha (Litha) and Joe is threatened when flirtatious Charlotte Bayard, daughter of Joe's commanding officer, Major Bayard, visits with her father. Litha is convinced she will lose Joe when he suddenly leaves with Charlotte and Bayard on "pretty serious business" and fails to return as expected. When men come with a dispossession notice for the Mendenhalls' mill, Litha defends their property with a double-barreled shotgun, slightly wounding one man's hand. Just then Joe appears with legal papers refuting the intruders' land claim, thanks to Major Bayard. When Joe confesses relief to be rid of the annoying Bayard girl, Litha, guilty of doubting her husband, runs to the stove to make corn cakes, fried pork, cream gravy, and gooseberry cobbler, just as a good "little wife" should.

In the longest story (thirty-five pages) in *Frontier*, "King Giant" (*Saturday Evening Post*, 1953), a giant former slave is freed after saving the baby daughter of a plantation overseer from a panther attack. Establishing his home deep in the Florida swamps, guarded by a hundred crocodiles and hired killers, he swears death to all white intrud-

Kantor, circa 1975 (photograph by Tim Kantor)

ers. One day a fifteen-year-old white boy, Cyrus Gabeson, and Melvina Hendry, the girl Cy scorns but who has a crush on him, beg Giant to save the settlers against an Indian attack, led by Seminole Billy Bowlegs. The huge black man agrees to come with his army. He saves the whites only because Melly asks him—she is the girl he rescued as a baby. Three years later Giant reemerges from his swamp domain to attend Cy and Melly's wedding.

Similar to these frontier stories are those recalling early days in the Missouri hills. In 1937 Kantor wrote his first Rosy Ridge story, expanded and published as *The Romance of Rosy Ridge*, a short novel, later that year (the original story was published in the *Saturday Evening Post*, 5 June 1937); it began a series about a mythical Missouri region. The stories reached millions of readers in the *Post* and led to other novellas, such as *Happy Land* (1943). Soon thereafter he began a series about Prickly Orange Hill, Missouri, for *Country Gentleman*. He managed to keep the two Ozark areas separate with their numerous charac-

ters and places; the Prickly Orange people of Sabine and Winstone he depicted as more humorous than the Rosy Ridge inhabitants of Delight and Billingsgate. His attempts at humor, as seen in the Prickly Orange story "The Darkies Are Gay," often backfired. Eight stories about Rosy Ridge and Prickly Orange appear in *The Gun-Toter, and Other Stories of the Missouri Hills*; six had been published from 1937 to 1940, the other two in 1953 and 1958.

"The Purple Moccasin" (*Saturday Evening Post*, 21 August 1937), the second in the series, is narrated by twelve-year-old Jesse Bowen, the storyteller in several Rosy Ridge stories. He runs away from home to join Jesse James's gang after a whipping from his father. Instead of finding the outlaws, he meets botanist Dr. Samuel Sickles and his twelve-year-old daughter, Flora Katherine, who risk their lives to dig up a gorgeous rare plant, the purple moccasin, on Ben Travis's property. Travis, believing the trespassers are after buried Confederate gold, nearly shoots them, but the sheriff—Jesse's father—and Jesse's uncle save them just in time. Before riding home, Jesse gives the pretty little girl a quick kiss goodbye.

In "The Woman with Kind Hands" (*Saturday Evening Post*, 12 March 1938), Jesse tells of his friendship with Moses Applejohn and the story behind the huge scar along Moses's skull. Riding with Col. John Mosby's Partisan Rangers in the days of the "Lost Cause," Moses carries on him his share of pirated fortune; however, he is nearly killed by Yankee robbers. Left blind and seriously wounded, he is nursed by a woman with angelic, gentle hands. He regains his sight after the war, and years later he feels those same hands again touch his face, during a Bowens get-together. Thus Jesse's "old maid" aunt Mary May ("well past thirty") falls in love with and marries Moses, and Jesse acquires his best friend for an uncle.

Jesse's next tale, "The Gun-Toter" (*Saturday Evening Post*, 12 November 1938), begins shortly after that marriage with the visit of Tipton Tadlock, the Billy the Kid of Barbary County, Missouri. Tip impresses Jesse, who is at the right age ("squirming up into" his teens) to be fascinated by someone who killed five men before seventeen; Tip is "hard and mean and quick" to his enemies but "upright and friendly" to his friends. He soon falls in love and elopes with the beautiful Cordelia Dane; her father dislikes the "heathenish" gun-toter, but she and others understand he is not an outlaw—circumstances have caused him to kill. The reconciliation between father and daughter, plotted by Jesse's mother, occurs at a box social with Mr. Dane outbidding Tip for Cordelia's box dinner for a hundred dollars in gold. Mr. Dane embraces Cordelia, her now-respectable husband (wearing no revolvers), and the family's newest grandchild, who lies in that dinner box.

A similarly formulaic story of a romance that succeeds despite barriers is "The Witch Doctor" (*Saturday Evening Post*, 1958). Seventeen-year-old Jimmy Blackshears, raised by his grandmother, befriends twelve-year-old Adela Mercer, daughter of the town doctor. Several years later, while Doc Mercer is in Kentucky with his dying brother, Adela becomes deathly ill, and Granny Blackshears is summoned. Some believe Granny is a witch who has a pact with the Devil, for she can cure the sick with home remedies. Because she is tending to another sick person, Jimmy comes to Adela's side with his cures: wormwood, sumac roots, and smartweed, all boiled down with lard and turpentine; he also uses pigs' knuck-

les, dried potatoes, and crawdad claws. When Letcher Billins, Adela's boyfriend, fears the witch doctor (Jimmy) will "magic away" Adela, he rallies his gang of friends to attack Jimmy, but they are soundly beaten. Doc Mercer arrives in time to bandage the bloodied boys, announce Adela's miraculous improvement, and offer Jimmy the opportunity to join him on house calls, thus ending the tale of how Jimmy became a certified doctor and married Adela.

Prickly Orange stories, like the above Rosy Ridge tale, are usually first-person narratives about colorful Missouri hills characters. "The Star of Prickly Orange" (*Country Gentleman*, 1938) began the series. The day after "Bible-roaring" Joe Lackey, as "stiff-necked and sour-mouthed" as an Old Testament prophet, prays for a thunderbolt to smite his no-good, slothful son-in-law, Tanner Hale, a flaming meteor crashes into Tanner's land. When a museum offers money for the meteor, called "Jehovah's artillery," Joe claims ownership because he invoked God's wrath; however, the judge (a comical figure who mutters in Latin phrases) declares the rightful owner to be Tanner, who later makes peace with his father-in-law. The young narrator confesses that he and the other boys got a little chunk off "God's cannonball" before it was shipped to the museum.

"The Circus Cat of Prickly Orange" (*Country Gentleman*, 1938) appeared next. Joe Lackey's son Phelps stops dead in his tracks one day as he sees a cat dressed in a coat with brass buttons and a little soldier cap. But what interests him more is the owner, a beautiful young French woman, now the widow of Odell Hooper, who had left Prickly Orange to travel with a circus. Hooper had gone to bed drunk with an elephant—"the elephant turned over in the night but Odell Hooper didn't." Mrs. Hooper calls the cat "John," with a z and y French sound. Phelps and his cantankerous father, Joe, think a cat dressed like a man and strutting so pridefully is unnatural. So do Phelps's cat, Tige, and dog, Choctaw, known far and wide as a cat killer. When Choctaw meets John, instead of wanton cat murder there ensues a different sight: "That dog defied all laws of nature. He walked in the air. He flopped backwards about ten flops, and then his hindquarters hit the ground, and he bounced. His nose had been slit from between his eyes down to the top of his muzzle, and the cat was kind of leaning on one elbow a-watching him." Nevertheless, Phelps, charmed by the widow and having once risked his life saving her from horse thieves, again comes to her rescue to search for John when he disappears. They find the cat with six kittens that resemble Phelps's Tige; thus, Phelps learns that "John" is actually "Jan," and he continues courting Mrs. Hooper.

A related story, "The Heathen of Prickly Orange" (*Country Gentleman*, 1940), focuses on Phelps's father, Joe, whose sternness about religion contrasts with the lackadaisical attitude of most Prickly Orangers, who do not worry much about original sin, caring more that their "chicken gravy still flowed and potato pie tasted tolerable." When Joe's wife dies, he begins at age eighty to soften up and devotes his time and money to the spiritual miseries of heathens in uncivilized parts of the world, having given up on converting his neighbors. With his children pressuring him to abandon his pigsty home, he decides that one of the people he has supported with money, clothes, and Bibles could show appreciation by becoming his housekeeper. In response to his letter to some St. Louis missionaries, a young man arrives—"so fat that he must have fed on only the tenderest missionaries." The tag attached to his shirt button reads, "ONE HEATHEN TO JOSEPH LACKEY, ESQ., SABINE, MISSOURI. TREAT KINDLY." Joe, naming him Esau, after the shaggy Biblical hunter, is amazed how rapidly the heathen acquires the language; in fact, Esau suggests that, with enough money, he can save all the miserable souls he left behind. Pocketing some Prickly Orangers' savings, Esau almost succeeds in boarding the train, but he is stopped by detectives who reveal that he is actually a U.S. mail clerk who intercepted Joe's letter with the wad of money; this charlatan, Ellwood Gramson, let his hair grow long, applied skin stain, put a string of bones around his neck, and headed for Sabine to get rich.

In contrast to the irreverent humor in these Prickly Orange stories, "Forever Walking Free" (*Good Housekeeping*, July 1944), also in *The Gun-Toter*, shows a different side of Kantor—his fascination with the supernatural. He believed he had lived on "time borrowed from humanity in general" ever since 1943, when a teletype error prevented him from being sent on a fatal B-17 mission that no one else survived; the men were buried at Brookwood Cemetery in Surrey, England. The story, written hastily in four and a half hours, opens with Joan Warrock running from bombs exploding in the Bloomsbury section of London; then she sees in the night's darkness the brightness of "a thousand lightning flashes

rolled into one" and imagines being on a balcony at a theater, seeing herself run to safety. Under an archway she falls but is helped up by an American soldier, Sgt. J. A. ("Buster") Menton, who has flown eleven missions as a gunner. After a romantic evening, Joan suddenly realizes a policeman has walked right between them on the street, never touching them—as if they were air. Only then does she realize that Buster's base, Brookwood, is a military cemetery, that she is dead, too, and that their spirits are forever free.

If indeed Kantor was living on "borrowed time," he certainly made the most of it. While many of his stories have superficial plots relying on trick endings or ironic twists for resolution, and his orchestrated "boy-gets-girl" stories can be formulaic and predictable, even sexist, readers enjoyed the sudden revelation of a famous historic person or the romantic pairing of a handsome, resolute young man and a beautiful, resourceful young woman for happily-ever-after endings. Thought-provoking themes interested Kantor less than entertaining stories to amuse the average reader of popular magazines.

From his first published story in 1922 to his last book in 1975, Kantor's novelettes (as he called his short novels), biographies, autobiographies, poetry, children's fiction, and stories portray many interesting characters and situations. His depiction of America's history has been compared to Walt Disney's nostalgic films and Norman Rockwell's sentimental portraits. He could entertain with an O. Henry-type story, but, of course, *Andersonville* became his claim to fame. He received honorary doctorates from several colleges (1957-1961), and he was a Library of Congress consultant (1967-1973), member of the National Council of Boy Scouts of America, and recipient of the Medal of Freedom.

In 1976 he told a *Writer's Digest* interviewer (Marcia Corbino), "I hope to make it to 50 books before I lay down my typewriter, or pen, or Dictaphone piece. . . . When I don't feel able to write any more, I don't want to live." His forty-fifth and last novel, *Valley Forge* (1975), written for the bicentennial, capped nearly half a century of publishing books. He died of a heart attack on 11 October 1977 in Sarasota, Florida, his home since 1936.

Kantor's hundreds of short stories were published in the worst and the best magazines in America. Even he readily acknowledged his lack of consistent literary quality. Some critics may discredit his historical scholarship or find his subjects too sentimental, his plots too formulaic, his style too unsophisticated, and his writing too unpolished. Perhaps quantity too often overcame quality.

The fact remains, though, that because readers liked his stories about America's past, Kantor became a popular teller of legends and dreams of greatness. While MacKinlay Kantor's stories may not rank as masterpieces, they appealed to a wide audience in their day. Even today some of his better tales, particularly those about the Civil War and frontier adventures, are still worth reading.

Interviews:

John F. Baker, "PW Interviews: MacKinlay Kantor," *Publishers Weekly*, 208 (17 November 1975): 6-7;

Marcia Corbino, "MacKinlay Kantor Is Resting on His Laurels. Hah!," *Writer's Digest*, 56 (August 1976): 20-21.

Biography:

Tim Kantor, *My Father's Voice* (New York: McGraw-Hill, 1988).

References:

William B. Hesseltine, "*Andersonville* Revisited," *Georgia Review*, 10 (Spring 1956): 92-100;

"MacKinlay Kantor," *Wilson Bulletin for Librarians*, 7 (September 1932): 82, 86;

Stanley Kaufman, "O Dear God, O Dear All," *New Republic*, 145 (30 October 1961): 15-16;

Earl Schenck Miers, "A Literary Fort Knox," *Saturday Review*, 38 (29 October 1955): 13;

Frank Paluka, *Iowa Authors* (Iowa City: Friends of the University of Iowa Libraries, 1967), pp. 180-186;

William Van O'Connor, "Go West, Young Man . . . to the Massacre," *Saturday Review*, 44 (21 October 1961): 23, 38.

Papers:

Most of Kantor's papers and manuscripts are held by the Library of Congress. The University of Iowa Library has papers relating to *Andersonville* and to *God and My Country*.

Sinclair Lewis

(7 February 1885 - 10 January 1951)

Victor Lasseter
California State University, Bakersfield

See also the Lewis entries in *DLB 9: American Novelists, 1910-1945* and *DLB Documentary Series 1*.

BOOKS: *Hike and the Aeroplane*, as Tom Graham (New York: Stokes, 1912);

Our Mr. Wrenn: The Romantic Adventures of a Gentle Man (New York & London: Harper, 1914; London: Cape, 1923);

The Trail of the Hawk: A Comedy of the Seriousness of Life (New York & London: Harper, 1915; London: Cape, 1923);

The Job: An American Novel (New York & London: Harper, 1917; London: Cape, 1926);

The Innocents: A Story for Lovers (New York & London: Harper, 1917);

Free Air (New York: Harcourt, Brace & Howe, 1919; London: Cape, 1924);

Main Street: The Story of Carol Kennicott (New York: Harcourt, Brace & Howe, 1920; London: Hodder & Stoughton, 1920);

Babbitt (New York: Harcourt, Brace, 1922; London: Cape, 1922);

Arrowsmith (New York: Harcourt, Brace, 1925); republished as *Martin Arrowsmith* (London: Cape, 1925);

Mantrap (New York: Harcourt, Brace, 1926; London: Cape, 1926);

Elmer Gantry (New York: Harcourt, Brace, 1927; London: Cape, 1927);

The Man Who Knew Coolidge; Being the Soul of Lowell Schmaltz (New York: Harcourt, Brace, 1928; London: Cape, 1928);

Dodsworth (New York: Harcourt, Brace, 1929; London: Cape, 1929);

Speech Accepting the Nobel Prize (Girard, Kans.: Haldeman-Julius, 1931?);

Ann Vickers (Garden City, N.Y.: Doubleday, Doran, 1933; London: Cape, 1933);

Work of Art (Garden City, N.Y.: Doubleday, Doran, 1934; London: Cape, 1934);

Jayhawker: A Play in Three Acts, by Lewis and Lloyd Lewis (Garden City, N.Y.: Doubleday, Doran, 1935; London: Cape, 1935);

It Can't Happen Here (Garden City, N.Y.: Doubleday, Doran, 1935; London: Cape, 1935);

Selected Short Stories (Garden City, N.Y.: Doubleday, Doran, 1935);

It Can't Happen Here [play], by Lewis and John C. Moffitt (New York: Dramatists Play Service, 1938);

The Prodigal Parents (Garden City, N.Y.: Doubleday, Doran, 1938; London: Cape, 1938);

Bethel Merriday (New York: Doubleday, Doran, 1940; London: Cape, 1940);

Gideon Planish (New York: Random House, 1943; London: Cape, 1943);

Cass Timberlane: A Novel of Husbands and Wives (New York: Random House, 1945; London: Cape, 1946);

Kingsblood Royal (New York: Random House, 1947; London: Cape, 1948);

The God-Seeker (New York: Random House, 1949; London: Heinemann, 1949);

World So Wide (New York: Random House, 1951; London: Heinemann, 1951);

The Man from Main Street; A Sinclair Lewis Reader: Selected Essays and Other Writings, edited by Harry E. Maule and Melville H. Cane (New York: Random House, 1953; London: Heinemann, 1954);

I'm a Stranger Here Myself, and Other Stories, edited by Mark Schorer (New York: Dell, 1962);

Storm in the West, by Lewis and Dore Schary (New York: Stein & Day, 1963; London: Sidgwick & Jackson, 1964).

Collection: *Lewis at Zenith; A Three-Novel Omnibus: Main Street. Babbit. Arrowsmith* (New York: Harcourt, Brace & World, 1961).

PLAY PRODUCTIONS: *Hobohemia*, New York, Greenwich Village Theatre, 8 February 1919;

Jayhawker, by Lewis and Lloyd Lewis, New York, Cort Theatre, 5 November 1934;

It Can't Happen Here, by Lewis and John C. Moffitt, New York, Adelphi Theatre, 27 October 1936;

Sinclair Lewis (George Arents Research Library for Special Collections at Syracuse University)

Angela Is Twenty-Two, by Lewis and Fay Wray, Columbus, Ohio, Hartman Theatre, 30 December 1938.

The literary reputation of Sinclair Lewis rests on his best novels, which depict and often penetrate the confusion caused by America's change from a rural to an urban, industrial culture. Lewis's 125 short stories, however, seldom transcend the tastes of the popular magazine market for which they were written. When they do, though, they are good examples of American writing in the first half of the twentieth century.

Harry Sinclair Lewis was born on 7 February 1885 in the prairie village of Sauk Centre, Minnesota, to Dr. Edwin J. Lewis and Emma Kermott Lewis. A rather awkward and lonely

boy, he read Charles Dickens, Sir Walter Scott, and Arthurian romances, though later his tastes would include H. G. Wells, H. L. Mencken, and Theodore Dreiser. Lewis began writing poetry and decided at the age of eleven to become a writer of short stories. He was, of course, to become a famous novelist instead.

In 1903 Lewis entered Yale, where he wrote essays, romantic fiction, and Tennysonian poetry for campus publications; some of these pieces are collected in *The Man from Main Street* (1953). After delaying his graduation by some wanderings in England and Panama, Lewis graduated in 1908, having already sold his first short story, "Matsu-No-Kata: A Romance of Old Japan," to *Pacific Monthly* in 1905. It appeared in the December issue and was collected in *Selected Short Stories* (1935).

HUGO WOULD STAND
IN A DREAM.

HE LOVED HIS COUNTRY

by Sinclair Lewis

Author of "Our Mr. Wrenn," "The Trail of the Hawk," etc.

ILLUSTRATIONS BY CHARLES S. CHAPMAN

HE WANTED TO SPEND EVERY MOMENT OF WHAT MIGHT BE HIS LAST
SPRINGTIME WITH THE FIELDS.

Illustrations for a story by Lewis that appeared in the October 1916 issue of Everybody's Magazine *and was collected by Mark Schorer in* I'm a Stranger Here Myself, and Other Stories *(1962). The main character is a German-American who experiences conflicting loyalties during World War I.*

He continued his literary apprenticeship by selling a few short stories and holding various journalism and publishing jobs in Iowa, New York, California, and Washington, D.C. In 1912 Lewis published his first novel, *Hike and the Aeroplane*, a pseudonymous boy's book. Two years later (on 15 April 1914) he married Grace Livingstone Hegger, whom he had met in New York City; they had a son, Wells, in 1917. *Our Mr. Wrenn: The Romantic Adventures of a Gentle Man*, published in 1914, establishes a familiar pattern in Lewis's novels and stories: an idealistic protagonist becomes dissatisfied, rebels, then adjusts to his discontent.

In general Lewis's publication of short stories declined as his novels sold. From 1909 to 1915 he published three novels and fourteen stories; from 1916 to 1919, three more novels and forty-four stories. From 1920 to 1930, when he published his critically and commercially successful novels, he wrote seven novels but only twenty stories, or about two a year. He wrote with relief to his publisher after the success of *Babbitt* (1922): "I don't believe I shall ever again be the facile [*Saturday Evening*] *Post* trickster I by God was." But from 1930 to his death in 1951, Lewis continued to produce short fiction sporadically: sometimes he did not publish a story for two or three years; he wrote no more than four a year at the most.

Significantly, Lewis's literary talents flourished in the decade of complacent prosperity before the stock market crash of 1929. The telephone, automobile, radio, skyscraper, and mass-circulation magazine seemed to point to an era of progress and contentment, symbolized by the calm assurance of Warren G. Harding and Calvin Coolidge; but America's provincial smugness was an inviting target for Lewis's satire.

Lewis joined the so-called revolt from the village by denying the myth of the happy, traditional but progressive small town, and later he would reject the notion of the industrialized but enlightened city. Lewis popularized the revolt in the best-seller *Main Street* (1920), satirized a tired business culture in *Babbitt*, explored the thwarted idealism of a scientist in *Arrowsmith* (1925), exposed the hypocrisy and commercialism of evangelical religion in *Elmer Gantry* (1927), and depicted the confused values of an American businessman in Europe in *Dodsworth* (1929). With the possible exception of *It Can't Happen Here* (1935), none of his later novels and very few of his short stories equal these confrontations with American culture.

In 1928 Lewis divorced Grace Hegger on 16 April and married the journalist Dorothy Thompson on 14 May; they were to have one child, Michael. In 1930, the year of Michael's birth, Lewis became the first American to win the Nobel Prize for Literature. (He had rejected the Pulitzer Prize for *Arrowsmith* in 1926 because he had not been awarded one in 1921 for *Main Street*; the trustees had overruled the selection committee.)

The only collection of Lewis's short stories published during his lifetime was *Selected Short Stories*. It sold poorly and attracted little critical attention. Lewis's introduction makes the obvious admission that he is a better novelist than short-fiction writer. In particular he criticizes his pre-1930 stories as sharing the naive optimism of the 1920s. Actually the later stories tend to be no less sentimental or optimistic. And one story that Lewis calls "fairly good," "Let's Play King" (*Cosmopolitan*, January-March 1931), is a long, tedious fantasy on the prince-and-pauper theme. Lewis, however, is perceptive in admitting that in his short fiction he is "a romantic medievalist of the most incurable sort." His short stories, in other words, rely heavily on romance and sentiment instead of the realistic detail and satire of *Main Street* or *Babbitt*.

The satire that made Lewis notable as a novelist competes with sentimentality in *Selected Short Stories*. Biographer Mark Schorer notes that Lewis's method in writing short fiction was to use notes taken on his travels, but then to impose a melodramatic or sentimental situation on these observations of American life. Although Lewis laughs at boosterism and aristocratic pretensions in "Let's Play King," at expatriates and bohemians in "Young Man, Go East" (*Cosmopolitan*, December 1930), and at American acquisitiveness and snobbery in "Things" (*Saturday Evening Post*, 22 February 1919), most of the stories cater to the sentimental tastes of the popular magazines. Idealistic and yearning characters dominate these stories, which dwell on Lewis's theme of "the fallacy of elsewhere" (the idea that a change of place can repair lives), on the superiority of the country over the city, and on the triumph of the simple folk over the sophisticated.

One problem with the stories is that any situational irony is usually both perfunctory and conspicuous. In "The Hack Driver" (*Nation*, 29 August 1923), for instance, a city slicker is tricked by a Vermonter; in "Land" (*Saturday Evening Post*, 12 September 1931), a young man whose father wants him to be a dentist yearns instead to be a simple farmer; and in "The Willow Walk" (*Saturday Evening Post*, 10 August 1918), a bank employee embezzles his bank, only to lose the money to a robber. "Young Man Axelbrod" (*Century Magazine*, June 1917) is considered one of the best stories but depends on the improbability of an aging, self-educated farmer enrolling at Yale and then dropping out because of the college's intellectual and spiritual stupor.

The years after 1935 (when *Selected Short Stories* came out) are marked by Lewis's restlessness, by his abuse of alcohol, and by a deterioration of his literary talents. In 1942 he divorced Dorothy Thompson but did not remarry, though he continued his affair with Marcella Powers, a young actress, which had begun in 1938 and lasted until 1946. Wells Lewis, his son from his first marriage, was killed in World War II. After frequent traveling, Lewis eventually moved to Italy, where he died in Rome of heart disease on 10 January 1951. (His ashes are buried in Sauk Centre.) His last novel, *World So Wide*, was published later that year.

In 1962 Schorer published the second and more discriminating collection of Lewis's stories, *I'm a Stranger Here Myself*. Schorer dropped seven weak stories and added seven that show Lewis's realism, but even these new selections are often diluted by sentimentality and improbable plots. "He Loved His Country" (*Everybody's Magazine*, October 1916), for instance, realistically depicts the divided patriotism of a German-American farmer in World War I, but ends mawkishly: the audience at a pro-German rally spontaneously bursts into "God Bless America" after the farmer steps forward to prevent the speaker's desecration of a U.S. flag.

In "A Woman by Candle-light" (*Saturday Evening Post*, 28 July 1917), a young traveling salesman chooses an older, wiser woman over a young, superficial woman. Lewis realistically describes the town Gopher Prairie's Main Street with its "rows of two-story brick stores running off into straggling frame houses," and he documents his tale with newspaper advertisements and colloquial speech. Sentimental romance, however, is the story's focus, typified by such flat symbols as violin music, honeysuckle, and morning sunlight.

Other stories are more convincing. In "He Had a Brother" (*Cosmopolitan*, May 1929), Lewis

Lewis's first wife, Grace Hegger Lewis, with their only child, Wells, born 26 July 1917

depicts the alcoholism of a successful attorney. The truthful treatment of the alcoholic's self-justification is weakened, however, by a trick ending in which a friend pretends to be sick in order to distract the attorney from alcohol. "The Man Who Cheated Time" (*Good Housekeeping*, March 1941) tells of a man who sees the stadium clock at a football game as a symbol of his mortality and predicts the exact time of his death. His friend, the narrator, gives him a sleeping pill so he will sleep through the appointed time, a plausible turn of events because the narrator is a physician.

The title story, published in *Smart Set*, August 1916, anticipates Lewis's satirical novels of the 1920s. A midwestern couple travel on the Eastern Seaboard but cannot leave their provinciality at home; they visit Florida towns such as New Chicago and associate only with tourists from their own state. Lewis's irony is banal ("How wondrous 'tis to travel in unfamiliar climes!"), but he turns the apologetic phrase "I'm a stranger here myself" into a comment on lazy ignorance that unifies the story.

Both the Lewis and the Schorer collections passed over what may be Lewis's finest short story, "The Man Who Knew Coolidge" (*American Mercury*, January 1928; enlarged and published as a novel later in 1928). This dramatic monologue grew out of Lewis's improvised monologue on a newspaper article about a midwesterner who had met the president; Mencken liked the improvisation so much that he urged Lewis to expand it into a short story. When later expanded into a novel, the story lost focus, but its brevity as short fiction is the ideal medium for Lewis's mimicry. And since his purpose is to let the narrator, Lowell Schmaltz, satirize himself, the limited point of view prevents the author from sentimental intrusion.

As in Ring Lardner's "Haircut" (1925) and Mark Twain's "Celebrated Jumping Frog of Calaveras County" (1865), considerable appeal comes from Schmaltz's apparent unawareness of the tedious effect he has on his audience. In a train's club car, he discourses manically about politics, religion, progress, the family, and service clubs. He is breathlessly beginning to start another editorial as the story ends. What he does not realize is that he and his family have been kept away from President Coolidge by a White House aide. With Schmaltz's uncritical, enthusiastic embrace of "progress" (filling stations, filing cabinets, advertising, and electric refrigerators) and with his grossly insensitive hypocrisy and bigotry, "The Man Who Knew Coolidge" is Lewis's response to the complacency of the Harding and Coolidge years.

Lewis wrote his short stories during the period that produced such significant collections as Sherwood Anderson's *Triumph of the Egg* (1921), F. Scott Fitzgerald's *Tales of the Jazz Age* (1922), Ernest Hemingway's *In Our Time* (1925), Katherine Anne Porter's *Flowering Judas* (1930), and William Faulkner's *These Thirteen* (1931). In his best-selling novels, Lewis had room to let his satiric imagination work on his carefully researched documentation. But in his short fiction, popular-fiction formulas and bad prose blur Lewis's observations on American life in a period of transition. His stories satirize attitudes such as bigotry, smugness, and provincialism, but they seldom go deeper to examine the causes or effects of these attitudes. Nevertheless they show some of the talent and concerns that made him an important writer.

Letters:

From Main Street to Stockholm: Letters of Sinclair Lewis, 1919-1930, edited by Harrison Smith (New York: Harcourt, Brace, 1952).

Interviews:

Frederick Manfred, "Sinclair Lewis: A Portrait," *American Scholar*, 23 (Spring 1954): 162-184;

Betty Stevens, "A Village Radical Goes Home," *Venture*, 2 (Summer 1956): 17-26;

Stevens, "A Village Radical: His Last American Home," *Venture*, 2 (Winter 1957): 35-48;

Allen Austin, "An Interview with Sinclair Lewis," *University Review*, 24 (March 1958): 199-210.

Biographies:

Mark Schorer, *Sinclair Lewis: An American Life* (New York, Toronto & London: McGraw-Hill, 1961);

Vincent Sheean, *Dorothy and Red* (Boston: Houghton Mifflin, 1963).

References:

Warren Beck, "How Good Is Sinclair Lewis?," *College English*, 9 (January 1948): 173-180;

Robert Cantwell, "Sinclair Lewis, in *After the Genteel Tradition*, edited by Malcolm Cowley (Carbondale: Southern Illinois University Press, 1964), pp. 92-102;

Stephen S. Conroy, "Sinclair Lewis's Sociological Imagination," *American Literature*, 42 (November 1970): 348-362;

Howell Daniels, "Sinclair Lewis and the Drama of Dissociation," in *The American Novel and the Nineteen Twenties*, edited by Malcolm Bradbury and David Palmer (London: Arnold, 1971), pp. 85-105;

Jack L. Davis, "Mark Schorer's Sinclair Lewis," *Sinclair Lewis Newsletter*, 3 (1971): 3-9;

D. J. Dooley, *The Art of Sinclair Lewis* (Lincoln: University of Nebraska Press, 1967);

George H. Douglas, "*Babbitt* at Fifty—The Truth Still Hurts," *Nation*, 214 (22 May 1972): 661-662;

Douglas, "*Main Street* After Fifty Years," *Prairie Schooner*, 44 (Winter 1970): 338-348;

John T. Flanagan, "A Long Way to Gopher Prairie: Sinclair Lewis's Apprenticeship," *Southwest Review*, 32 (Autumn 1947): 403-413;

Robert E. Fleming and Esther Fleming, *Sinclair Lewis: A Reference Guide* (Boston: G. K. Hall, 1980);

Maxwell Geismar, "Diarist of a Middle Class Mind" and "A Postscript," in his *American Moderns: From Rebellion to Conformity* (New York: Hill & Wang, 1958), pp. 107-118;

Geismar, "Sinclair Lewis: The Cosmic Bourjoyce," in his *The Last of the Provincials: The Ameri-*

Lewis with his second wife, Dorothy Thompson Lewis, and Hugh Walpole in 1928 at Brackenburn, Walpole's country home in Cumberland, England (George Arents Research Library for Special Collections at Syracuse University)

can Novel, 1915-1925 (Boston: Houghton Mifflin, 1947), pp. 69-150;

Sheldon N. Grebstein, *Sinclair Lewis* (New York: Twayne, 1962);

Anthony C. Hilfer, "Caricaturist of the Village Mind" and "Elmer Gantry and That Old Time Religion," in his *The Revolt from the Village* (Chapel Hill: University of North Carolina Press, 1969), pp. 158-192;

Hugh C. Holman, "Anodyne for the Village Virus," in *The Comic Imagination in American Literature*, edited by Louis D. Rubin, Jr. (New Brunswick, N.J.: Rutgers University Press, 1973), pp. 247-258;

Alfred Kazin, "The New Realism: Sherwood Anderson and Sinclair Lewis," in his *On Native Grounds* (New York: Reynal & Hitchcock, 1942), pp. 217-226;

Grace H. Lewis, *With Love from Gracie: Sinclair Lewis, 1912-1925* (New York: Harcourt, Brace, 1955);

Robert W. Lewis, "Babbitt and the Dream of Romance," *North Dakota Quarterly*, 40 (1972): 7-14;

Martin Light, "H. G. Wells and Sinclair Lewis: Friendship, Literary Influence, and Letters," *English Literature in Transition*, 5 (1962): 1-20;

Light, *The Quixotic Vision of Sinclair Lewis* (W. Lafayette, Ind.: Purdue University Press, 1975);

Jack London, *Letters from Jack London; Containing an Unpublished Correspondence Between London and Sinclair Lewis* (New York: Odyssey, 1965; London: MacGibbon & Kee, 1966);

Glen A. Love, "New Pioneering on the Prairies: Nature, Progress and the Individual in the

Novels of Sinclair Lewis," *American Quarterly*, 25 (December 1973): 558-577;

James Lundquist, *Sinclair Lewis* (New York: Ungar, 1973);

Perry Miller, "The Incorruptible Sinclair Lewis," *Atlantic Monthly*, 187 (April 1951): 30-34;

Geoffrey Moore, "Sinclair Lewis: A Lost Romantic," in *The Young Rebel in American Literature*, edited by Carl Bode (London: Heinemann, 1959), pp. 51-76;

Mark Schorer, "Sinclair Lewis and the Method of Half-Truths," in *Society and Self in the Novel: English Institute Essays*, edited by Schorer (New York: Columbia University Press, 1956), pp. 117-144;

Schorer, ed., *Sinclair Lewis: A Collection of Critical Essays* (Englewood Cliffs, N.J.: Prentice-Hall, 1962);

Dorothy Thompson, "The Boy and Man from Sauk Centre," *Atlantic Monthly*, 206 (November 1960): 39-48;

James W. Tuttleton, "Sinclair Lewis: The Romantic Comedian as Realist Mimic," in his *The Novel of Manners in America* (Chapel Hill: University of North Carolina Press, 1972), pp. 141-161;

Thomas K. Whipple, "Sinclair Lewis," in his *Spokesmen* (Berkeley: University of California Press, 1963), pp. 208-229;

Hiroshige Yoshida, *A Sinclair Lewis Lexicon: With a Critical Study of His Style and Methods* (Tokyo: Hoyu, 1976).

Papers:

Most of Lewis's manuscripts and letters are at Yale University; an additional important collection is at the University of Texas at Austin.

Ludwig Lewisohn

(30 May 1882 - 31 December 1955)

Bernard F. Engel
Michigan State University

See also the Lewisohn entries in *DLB 4: American Writers in Paris, 1920-1939*; *DLB 9: American Novelists, 1910-1945*; and *DLB 28: Twentieth-Century American-Jewish Fiction Writers.*

BOOKS: *The Broken Snare* (New York: Dodge, 1908; London: Paul, 1908);

German Style: An Introduction to the Study of German Prose (New York: Holt, 1910);

The Modern Drama: An Essay in Interpretation (New York: Huebsch, 1915; London: Secker, 1916);

The Spirit of Modern German Literature (New York: Huebsch, 1916);

The Poets of Modern France (New York: Huebsch, 1918; London: Kennikat, 1970);

The Drama and the Stage (New York: Harcourt, Brace, 1922);

Up Stream: An American Chronicle (New York: Boni & Liveright, 1922; London: Richards, 1923);

Don Juan (New York: Boni & Liveright, 1923);

The Creative Life (New York: Boni & Liveright, 1924);

Israel (New York: Boni & Liveright, 1925; London: Benn, 1926);

The Case of Mr. Crump (Paris: Black Manikin Press, 1926; New York: Henderson, 1930; London: Bodley Head, 1948); republished as *The Tyranny of Sex: The Case of Mr. Crump* (New York: Penguin, 1947; London: Sphere, 1969);

Holy Land: A Story (New York: Harper, 1926);

Roman Summer (New York & London: Harper, 1927; London: Butterworth, 1929);

Cities and Men (New York & London: Harper, 1927; London: Butterworth, 1929);

The Defeated (London: Butterworth, 1927); republished as *The Island Within* (New York & London: Harper, 1928);

Adam: A Dramatic History (New York & London: Harper, 1929);

Mid-Channel: An American Chronicle (New York & London: Harper, 1929; London: Butterworth, 1929);

Stephen Escott (New York & London: Harper, 1930); republished as *The Memories of Stephen Escott* (London: Butterworth, 1930); republished again as *The Vehement Flame: The Story of Stephen Escott* (New York: Farrar, Straus, 1948);

The Golden Vase (New York & London: Harper, 1931);

A Jew Speaks: An Anthology from Ludwig Lewisohn, edited by James Waterman Wise (New York & London: Harper, 1931);

The Last Days of Shylock (New York & London: Harper, 1931; London: Butterworth, 1931);

The Romantic: A Contemporary Legend (Paris: Black Manikin Press, 1931);

Expression in America (New York & London: Harper, 1932; London: Butterworth, 1932); republished as *The Story of American Literature* (New York & London: Harper, 1937);

This People (New York & London: Harper, 1933);

An Altar in the Fields (New York & London: Harper, 1934; London: Hamilton, 1934);

The Permanent Horizon: A New Search for Old Truths (New York & London: Harper, 1934);

Trumpet of Jubilee (New York & London: Harper, 1937);

The Answer: The Jew and the World: Past, Present and Future (New York: Liveright, 1939);

For Ever Wilt Thou Love (New York: Dial, 1939);

Haven, by Lewisohn and Edna Lewisohn (New York: Dial, 1940);

Renegade (New York: Dial, 1942);

Breathe Upon These (Indianapolis & New York: Bobbs-Merrill, 1944);

Anniversary (New York: Farrar, Straus, 1948);

Among the Nations (New York: Farrar, Straus, 1948);

The Magic Word: Studies in the Nature of Poetry (New York: Farrar, Straus, 1950);

The American Jew: Character and Destiny (New York: Farrar, Straus, 1950);

What Is This Jewish Heritage? (New York: B'nai B'rith Hillel Foundations, 1954; revised edition, New York: Schocken, 1964);

In a Summer Season (New York: Farrar, Straus, 1955).

OTHER: J. Hector St. John de Crèvecoeur, *Letters from an American Farmer*, introduction by Lewisohn (New York: Fox, Duffield, 1904);

The Dramatic Works of Gerhart Hauptmann, 9 volumes, edited by Lewisohn (New York: Huebsch, 1912-1916);

A Modern Book of Criticism, edited by Lewisohn (New York: Boni & Liveright, 1919);

Rebirth: A Book of Modern Jewish Thought, edited by Lewisohn (New York & London: Harper, 1935);

Among the Nations: Three Tales and a Play About Jews, edited by Lewisohn (New York: Farrar, Straus, 1948).

TRANSLATIONS: Hermann Suderman, *The Indian Lily, and Other Stories* (New York: Huebsch, 1911);

David Pinski, *The Treasure: A Drama in Four Acts* (New York: Huebsch, 1915);

Georg Hirschfeld, *The Mothers*, with an introduction by Lewisohn (Garden City, N.Y.: Doubleday, Page, 1916);

Jakob Wassermann, *The World's Illusion*, 2 volumes (New York: Harcourt, Brace, 1920);

Wassermann, *Wedlock* (New York: Boni & Liveright, 1926);

Hanns Heinz Ewers, *The Sorcerer's Apprentice* (New York: Day, 1927);

Bernhard Guttmann, *Ambition* (New York: Harper, 1930);

Franz Werfel, *The Eternal Road: A Drama in Four Acts* (New York: Viking, 1936);

Werfel, *The Song of Bernadette* (New York: Viking, 1942; London: Hamilton, 1942);

Selma Stern, *The Spirit Returneth* (Philadelphia: Jewish Publication Society of America, 1946);

Goethe: The Story of a Man, translated and edited, with an introduction, by Lewisohn (New York: Farrar, Straus, 1949).

Ludwig Lewisohn spent his career arguing for what he saw as the need for cultural traditions that would support the development of firm individual identities. He held that people of other backgrounds should develop their traditions with the same imaginative and ethical determination that he urged for his fellow American Jews. The advocating of his sociopolitical views in his short fiction sometimes limited its effect as literary art, but he considered the ideas desperately important.

Some of this insistence on tradition may have been a reaction against the indifference of his parents to their Jewish ancestry. Born on 30 May 1882, he was the only child of Jacques and Minna Eloegger Lewisohn. In *Up Stream* (1922), the first volume of his autobiography, Lewisohn tells how at the age of seven he was brought from his birthplace in Berlin, Germany, to South Carolina, and how his upbringing in Charleston left him so unaware of the religion he was born into that he thought of himself as an ardent Christian. He began to question his position in American life when, after graduate work at Columbia University (M.A. 1903), he found it impossible to obtain an appointment to teach English literature, a rejection he attributed to his Jewishness. After several years as a free-lance writer, he won

Lewisohn circa 1900, in Charleston, South Carolina (photograph by Dowling)

an appointment to teach German at the University of Wisconsin in 1910. In 1911 he became a teacher of German at Ohio State University.

He was also building a reputation as a critic and might have followed an academic career (late in life he reentered teaching, at Brandeis University) if the suspicions directed at professors of German during World War I had not impelled him to take a leave of absence for the 1917-1918 academic year; he did not return to Ohio State. Until the rise of Adolf Hitler, Lewisohn spoke of American participation in World War I as the result of hysteria, and he blamed the political disarray in Germany on Allied revenge. After World War II, however, Lewisohn wrote in the introduction to *Goethe: The Story of a Man* (1949) that the Germans had destroyed their own humanity.

In 1919 Lewisohn went to work in New York City as drama editor and article writer for the *Nation*, and in the next several years he published hundreds of pieces in newspapers and magazines. Most of these are on literary topics. Still disturbed, however, by his early difficulties in

obtaining academic appointments, he also began to assert the need for Jews to develop ethnic solidarity instead of being assimilated. A second concern in his work was the problems associated with sex and marriage. At the age of twenty-three Lewisohn had married Mary Arnold Child Crocker, an English grandmother twenty years his senior. The marriage was unhappy, but because of the rigidity of New York's divorce laws it lasted until 1937.

Lewisohn's early short fiction includes two pieces crafted in the manner of the "well-made" story. Even in these, however, he advances sociophilosophical views. He insisted that the editors of *The Smart Set Anthology* (1934) append to their reprinting of "The Story Ashland Told at Dinner" (*Smart Set*, February 1919; collected in *This People*, 1933) a note saying the piece is an example of "a period of style and point of view" that he had outgrown. Most of this story's impact comes from the revelation in the climax that a married woman who had had an affair with a married man continues to love him even after his death. The story suggests that the woman and her own husband are maintaining, at great cost to themselves, the appearance of a loving marriage. Moral, legal, and social restrictions leave no way out of their entrapment. Lewisohn's note indicates that he had come to dislike the use of clever but unrealistic endings and also believed that in failing to attack the couple's situation directly the story implicitly supports "Puritan" emphasis on keeping up the semblance of supposed virtues no matter what damage this does to the people involved.

Lewisohn shows in *Holy Land* (*Harper's*, October 1925; published separately in 1926), another well-made story, his belief that a path to rational behavior could be found by emphasizing one's cultural identity. The narrator, an American-Jewish businessman, meets a midwestern couple on their way to visit biblical scenes. He observes the woman's disenchantment as she finds that the actual Holy Land of roughly cobbled streets, clamoring merchants, possessive religious sects, and an exotic population has little resemblance to the land of Sunday-school images. The reader might expect a "Puritan-baiter"—Lewisohn used this term to describe himself—to exploit the situation for satire. But the narrator listens attentively as the woman says that, upon returning home, she will seek her religious ideal in the small-town church of her childhood. He agrees with her feeling that she will find the center of her emotional life in her own community.

In the 1920s America imposed its first serious limits on immigration, a move that was accompanied by debate among immigrants over whether or not to merge into the general culture. Lewisohn argued vigorously for the maintenance of a Jewish identity. Associated with this affirmation was his debunking attack on genteel restrictions on thought and behavior. To Lewisohn conventional morality represented the unfair imposition of Protestant values. The issue was heightened for him by his continuing imprisonment, as he saw it, in his marriage. Unwilling to enter a prolonged court battle for a divorce, Lewisohn in 1924 began a ten-year residence in Europe with Thelma Spear, twenty-three, a singer. His best novel, *The Case of Mr. Crump* (1926), is an autobiographical work that is convincingly authentic in its portrait of a destructive wife. The book was first published in Paris; the then-prevailing American disapproval of divorce, together with the danger of libel suits (criticism of Mrs. Lewisohn was obvious), delayed appearance of a U.S. edition until 1930. In 1933 Lewisohn's only child, James Elias, was born to him and Spear. Finally divorcing Crocker in 1937, Lewisohn sought to marry Spear, but she refused. He then engaged in a lengthy court battle with her over custody of their son; custody finally was awarded to her in 1941. In 1940 Lewisohn married Edna Manley. But after a brief period of happiness, this relation, too, ended in divorce. In 1944 he married his third and last wife, Louise Wolk. The battles and discouragements of these relationships furnished material for much of his writing, both fiction and nonfiction.

Lewisohn put the case for a sustaining ethnic heritage in most of the works of his last thirty years, including the sketches appearing in *Adam: A Dramatic History* (1929), the Freudian literary history *Expression in America* (1932), and the short stories in *This People*. He continued to give ideas priority, digressing as necessary to argue for them and to instruct the reader on how to feel about characters and situations related to these ideas. *Adam* is presented as a play, but opens with a nine-page prologue giving a debate among three rabbis in the second century A.D. They argue over whether Jews should resist the oppressions of the Roman Empire by peaceful means or by the sword; each man decides to follow his own ideas. This discussion is followed by a sketch reporting the conversation of a present-day Brit-

ish couple. The husband is willing to obtain capital for investment from a somewhat mysterious newcomer to London, Adam Elhar, but the wife doubts that they should associate with the man, no matter how wealthy he is, because she suspects that he is Jewish. The following six sketches are similarly static conversations, acceptable in fiction but quite undramatic. Adam, said to be an assimilated Jewish citizen of Great Britain, is discussed in all the scenes presented as taking place in the twentieth century, but he never actually appears as a character; in the end, the reader learns that Adam has committed suicide.

Adam's difficulty is that, though he has made millions, as a Jew he has no "earth, home, speech, inner oneness, inner security" in British society. In *Mid-Channel* (1929), the second volume of his autobiography, Lewisohn suggests that the desired fulfillment might be made possible by a reconciliation of Christians and Jews, a goal to be accomplished by developing a synthesis of Hellenism and Hebraism. He again took up the theme of the need for a fulfilling culture in *Expression in America*, one of his best-known books. The argument here is that American culture does not allow people of any ethnic heritage to fulfill themselves. Although this book purports to be a Freudian study of American writing, it has much Puritan baiting and little Freudian doctrine.

Lewisohn returned to the topic of Jewish homelessness in some of his last ventures in short fiction, the stories in *This People*, most of which were previously unpublished. The first of these, "The Saint," shows a father who, like Lewisohn's own father, reads Herbert Spencer and Ernst Haeckel, believes in America and science, and does not associate with poor Jews who cling to what he sees as religious superstition. His son, shown as superior, prefers to marry a rabbi's daughter and become a counselor to the poverty-stricken. The story is heavy with the argument that wealthy Americanized Jews lead emotionally impoverished lives, that the communism some took up is an inadequate substitute for an ethical heritage, and that the ideal course for young Jews is to prepare by study and consecration to enter life in Palestine.

Jan, the central character in "Bolshevik," is more firmly envisioned, though the organization of the story is less disciplined. The narrative is told in flashbacks as Jan's mistress in Berlin hears of his endeavors as a hard-bitten inciter of riots. Jan hates the middle class and believes the revolutionary should have no possessions, no pieties, no

Page from the manuscript for Mid-Channel *(1929), Lewisohn's second volume of autobiography (Lilly Library, Indiana University)*

Ludwig Lewisohn

country, no pride in race, and no compassion: he is as stonyhearted, as much the despiser of his fellowman, as Nathaniel Hawthorne's Ethan Brand. Like Brand, Jan expresses an absolute individualism that is distinctively American. But Lewisohn presents Jan's ideology as a projection of a self-hatred that causes him to want to tear down all sanctity and order. Radical positions were always, to Lewisohn, a result of psychological difficulties.

In *The Romantic* (separately published in 1931; also in *This People*) Lewisohn seems almost to approve of the feeling of a man of Jewish ancestry who sees that the people who execute him as a supposed traitor act out of a bone-deep identification with their nation ("the Carpathian State"), a homogeneity that he can never know, even though his family has lived there for three generations and his father had him baptized a Catholic. The story is perhaps best understood as a meditation on the relationship between one's nation and his selfhood; Lewisohn's position comes close to that of race theorists from Josiah Strong to Alfred Rosenberg: the argument that one can have a true identity only in a culture that is his or hers

by centuries-old inheritance. "Writ of Divorcement: An Anonymous Document" exhibits somewhat contradictory attitudes. Two characters believe that puritanical restrictions on contraceptives are unfair because, they say, traditional Jewish views allow use of such devices. Others in the story, however, argue that Jews who drink and "pet" are as vulgar as Gentiles, and that a girl of Jewish ancestry who marries an Englishman is engaging in "falsification and escape."

This People concludes with "By the Waters of Babylon," the tale of Mordechai, a well-to-do, middle-aged Jew living in Susa in the Babylonian empire around the year 500 B.C., two generations after the Babylonian captivity. Mordechai holds to his religion and therefore succeeds in modifying the king's hostility toward Jews. The moral again is that Jews who surrender to pressure and circumstance will live unhappily, but those who remain loyal to their heritage will succeed spiritually. Although Lewisohn appended a glossary to *This People*, the stories make such heavy use of Yiddish and Hebrew expressions, and the narrators so often use "we," that it is apparent the intended audience was Jewish readers. In his last novel, *In a Summer Season* (1955), perhaps influenced by the Holocaust, Lewisohn modified his position, dropping the idea of cultural separatism and suggesting that Christians and Jews develop a mutual approach to a discovery of valid religious faith.

Critics have tended to respond to the arguments rather than to the aesthetics of Lewisohn's short stories and other fiction. Because in the 1920s and 1930s he denied the myth of the melting pot, he was attacked by Jewish critics as well as others for, as they saw it, feeling sorry for himself and adopting an un-American stance. Lewisohn's counterattacks were equally assertive. In all his writing, indeed, Lewisohn's aim was primarily polemic. He insisted on the need for a coherent identity that can be developed only within a tradition broad enough to allow individual variation but disciplined enough to provide direction and profound enough to allow full expression of imaginative and emotional life.

Except for a shrill period in the late 1920s and early 1930s, when he assumed the posture of one defending against all comers what he saw as the Jewish heritage (he never saw that heritage as flowing in more than one channel), he argued for an America hospitable to many ethnic and cultural traditions, and he came eventually to the vision of a merging of interests in a united religiophilosophical search. This vision, rather than his modest accomplishments as a literary artist, gives Lewisohn's work interest for those who hope to develop a society that can maintain unity while encouraging continuation of diverse humane traditions.

References:

Ernest Sutherland Bates, "Lewisohn into Crump," *American Mercury*, 31 (April 1934): 441-450;

Louis J. Bragman, "The Case of Ludwig Lewisohn," *American Journal of Psychiatry*, 11 (1931): 319-331;

Stanley F. Chyet, "Lewisohn and Crèvecoeur," *Chicago Jewish Forum*, 22 (Winter 1963-1964): 130-136;

Chyet, "Ludwig Lewisohn in Charleston (1892-1903)," *American Jewish Historical Quarterly*, 54 (1964-1965): 296-322;

Chyet, "Ludwig Lewisohn: The Years of Becoming," *American Jewish Archives*, 11 (1959): 125-147;

Adolph Gillis, *Ludwig Lewisohn: The Artist and His Message* (New York: Duffield & Green, 1933);

Milton Hindus, Introduction to Lewisohn's *What Is This Jewish Heritage?*, revised edition (New York: Schocken, 1964), pp. 1-8;

Hindus, "Ludwig Lewisohn: From Assimilation to Zionism," *Jewish Frontier*, 31 (February 1964): 22-30;

Jerrold Hirsch, "Ludwig Lewisohn: Can He Still Help Us? A Reconsideration of *Expression in America*," in *Seasonal Authors for a New Season: New Standards in Popular Writing*, edited by Lewis Filler (Bowling Green, Ohio: Bowling Green University Popular Press, 1988), pp. 98-116;

Seymour Lainoff, *Ludwig Lewisohn* (Boston: Twayne, 1982);

Arthur J. Lelyveld, "Ludwig Lewisohn: In Memoriam," *American Jewish Archives*, 17 (1965): 109-113;

F. A. Levy, "Ludwig Lewisohn, 1882-1955," *Jewish Book Annual*, 14 (1956-1957): 46-55;

James Lewisohn, "My Father, Ludwig Lewisohn," *Midstream*, 12 (November 1966): 48-50;

Norton Mezvinsky, "The Jewish Thought of Ludwig Lewisohn," *Chicago Jewish Forum*, 16 (Winter 1958-1959): 77-82;

Harold Ribalow, "Ludwig Lewisohn's 'The Island Within,'" *Jewish Heritage*, 5 (Fall 1963): 44-48;

David F. Singer, "Ludwig Lewisohn and Freud: The Zionist Therapeutics," *Psychological Review*, 58 (Summer-Fall 1971): 169-182;

Singer, "Ludwig Lewisohn: A Paradigm of American-Jewish Return," *Judaism*, 14 (1965): 319-329;

Singer, "Ludwig Lewisohn: The Making of an Anti-Communist," *American Quarterly*, 23 (December 1971): 738-751;

Lionel Trilling, "Flawed Instruments," in his *Speaking of Literature and Society* (New York: Harcourt Brace Jovanovich, 1988), pp. 21-26.

Papers:

There is no complete collection of Lewisohn's manuscripts, letters, and other papers. The most useful assemblage is in the library of Columbia University. Other collections are at Hebrew Union College in Cincinnati, in the Goldfarb Library at Brandeis University, and in the College of Charleston library.

Albert Maltz

(28 October 1908 - 26 April 1985)

Kenneth A. Robb
Bowling Green State University

BOOKS: *Peace on Earth* (New York, Los Angeles & London: French, 1934);

Black Pit (New York: Putnam's, 1935);

The Way Things Are and Other Stories (New York: International, 1938);

The Underground Stream: An Historical Novel of a Moment in the American Winter (Boston: Little, Brown, 1940);

The Cross and the Arrow (Boston: Little, Brown, 1944; London: Harrap, 1946);

The Journey of Simon McKeever (Boston: Little, Brown, 1949; London: Gollancz, 1949);

The Citizen Writer: Essays in Defense of American Culture (New York: International, 1950);

A Long Day in a Short Life (New York: International, 1957; London: Calder, 1957);

Abseits von Broadway/Off-Broadway, as Julian Silva (Berlin: Aufbau, 1960);

A Tale of One January (London: Calder & Boyars, 1966 [i.e., 1967]);

Afternoon in the Jungle: The Selected Short Stories of Albert Maltz (New York: Liveright, 1970);

The Naked City: A Screenplay, by Maltz and Malvin Wald, edited by Matthew J. Bruccoli (Carbondale: Southern Illinois University Press/ London: Feffer & Simons, 1979).

PLAY PRODUCTIONS: *Merry Go Round*, by Maltz and George Sklar, Provincetown, R.I., Provincetown Playhouse, 22 April 1932;

Peace on Earth, by Maltz and Sklar, New York, Civic Repertory Theatre, 29 November 1933;

Black Pit, New York, Civic Repertory Theatre, 20 March 1935.

MOTION PICTURES: *This Gun for Hire*, screenplay by Maltz and W. R. Burnett, Paramount, 1941;

Moscow Strikes Back, commentary by Maltz, Republic, 1942;

Destination Tokyo, screenplay by Maltz and Delmar Daves, Warner Bros., 1943;

The House I Live In, screenplay by Maltz, RKO, 1945;

The Pride of the Marines, screenplay by Maltz, Warner Bros., 1945;

Cloak and Dagger, screenplay by Maltz and Ring Lardner, Jr., Warner Bros., 1946;

The Naked City, screenplay by Maltz and Malvin Wald, Universal, 1948;

Two Mules for Sister Sara, screenplay by Maltz, Universal, 1970.

OTHER: "Red Headed Baker," in *One Hundred Non-Royalty Radio Plays*, edited by William Kozlenko (New York: Greenberg, 1941).

SELECTED PERIODICAL PUBLICATIONS— UNCOLLECTED: "Private Hicks," *New Theatre*, 2 (November 1935): 20-25;

"Rehearsal," *One Act Play Magazine*, 1 (March 1938): 994-1020;

"What Shall We Ask of Writers?," *New Masses*, 58 (12 February 1946): 19-22;

"Moving Forward," *New Masses*, 59 (9 April 1946): 8-10, 21;

"The Spoils of War," *Saturday Evening Post*, 241 (5 October 1968): 65-66, 70-72.

Albert Maltz began his varied, prolific writing career in the early 1930s. Some of Maltz's first stories are among the best representatives of the proletarian literature of their time. The experience gained in writing proletarian dramas and, later, screenplays can be discerned in his stories and novels, which are often highly visual and dramatic. Several major works are set in literal prisons or prisonlike environments, but other forms of repression—economic, racial, or political—can be seen as metaphorical prisons from which the individual struggles to free himself, often unsuccessfully.

Maltz was born on 28 October 1908 in Brooklyn, New York, to Bernard Maltz, a builder, and Lena Sherry Maltz. He graduated, Phi Beta Kappa, with an A.B. from Columbia College in

Albert Maltz (Gale International Portrait Gallery)

1930. The following two years were spent studying at Yale University's School of Drama, where he met George Sklar, with whom he wrote two proletarian dramas. In 1935, the same year in which he joined the Communist party, Maltz's drama *Black Pit* was produced by the Theatre Union (and published later that year). About this time, Maltz began selling short stories successfully, and with two previously unpublished stories they were collected in *The Way Things Are* (1938). In 1937 Maltz married Margaret Larkin; they were to have a son and daughter—Peter and Katharine. Soon after publication of his first novel, *The Underground Stream* (1940), Maltz moved with his family to Los Angeles, spending the war years writing screenplays and the novel *The Cross and the Arrow* (1944).

Maltz received Academy Awards for writing the commentary for the documentary *Moscow Strikes Back* (1942) and for the screenplay of a short, *The House I Live In* (1945), but his screen-

play for *The Pride of the Marines* (1945) is widely considered his best, and according to Bernard F. Dick, it is "a World War II movie still capable of moving an audience." Further, Dick makes clear that in 1945-1946 Maltz wrote the original screenplay for *The Robe* (Fox, 1953) but never received any credit for it because of his being blacklisted in 1947.

As one of "The Hollywood Ten," Maltz appeared before the House Committee on Un-American Activities in 1947 and was cited for contempt of Congress, convicted, and sentenced to a year in prison (he served time from June 1950 to April 1951). As his case progressed through the courts, his third novel, *The Journey of Simon McKeever* (1949), was published, a fine character study of a retired pipe fitter who escapes from an old folk's home to seek a cure for his arthritis.

Maltz, after completing his prison sentence, went immediately to live in Cuernavaca, Mexico, where he continued to write in several genres, sometimes under the name Julian Silva. A collection of stories titled *Abseits von Broadway/Off-Broadway* (1960) was published in East Germany. After returning to Los Angeles in 1962, Maltz wrote the screenplay of *Two Mules for Sister Sara* (1970) and published in England a fifth novel, arguably his best, *A Tale of One January* (1967). In addition, several short stories and the collection *Afternoon in the Jungle* (1970) were published. Maltz's stories were first published in a wide variety of periodicals, including *New Masses*, *Scribner's*, *Southwest Review*, *Story*, *Masses & Mainstream*, the *New Yorker*, and the *Saturday Evening Post*.

Even though his career gave him satisfaction and success, Maltz's personal life was often troubled. He divorced his first wife, Margaret, in 1963 and married Rosemary Wylde the following year. She died in 1968. Maltz married Esther Engelberg in 1969. (Only his first marriage produced children.) As was the case in the late 1940s, Maltz's outspoken political views also caused him problems throughout his life.

In many of his stories Maltz focuses on individuals trapped in the mechanisms of a capitalist society. His first published story, "Man on a Road" (*New Masses*, 8 January 1935; collected in *The Way Things Are*), has been frequently reprinted, notably in *The Best Short Stories of 1936*. The narrator's bewilderment at the preoccupied behavior of a miner, to whom he gives a ride on a rainy night in West Virginia, is resolved when the miner, Jack Pickett, asks the narrator to re-copy a letter to Pickett's wife, whom he has left. Pickett tells her he has contracted silicosis and is dying; the company has failed to provide the workers proper ventilation and masks. Through the simple plot, understated style, and excellent characterization of Pickett, Maltz effectively conveys the theme, which is explicitly stated by the narrator toward the end: "In me there was only mute emotion—pity and love for him, and a cold, deep hatred for what had killed him." Two other stories, "Good-By" (1936; collected in *The Way Things Are*) and "The Drop-Forge Man" (first published in *The Way Things Are*), portray somewhat less effectively other individuals victimized by a capitalistic, industrial society.

In "The Game" (*Scribner's*, December 1936; in *The Way Things Are*) Maltz uses a dramatic approach, depending on dialogue between father and son, and the father's interior monologue, to convey a grim theme. As he teaches his son to steal a bottle of milk, the father rebukes the boy for seeing theft as a game, acknowledges that

theft conflicts with his own moral code, and fears his son will grow up to be a criminal; but poverty has made the father desperate. When the theft is successful and the boy reassures his father that he wants only to grow up to be like him, the father looks at the undersized, malnourished boy and wonders if he will live to grow up at all.

The first-prize winner in the O. Henry Memorial Awards for 1938, "The Happiest Man" (*Harper's*, June 1938; collected in *Afternoon in the Jungle*), belongs in this group of stories; it was favorably received by critics and has been frequently reprinted. The story vividly portrays the desperate straits to which the victims of the Depression were reduced, as Jesse Fulton begs his brother-in-law, Tom Brackett, for a job driving a truck. Jesse, a linotype operator out of work for six years, has left his family in Kansas City and walked to Tulsa in search of the high wages Tom's company pays truck drivers. Tom himself has lost his hardware store to the Depression and views Jesse's plight with empathy, mixed with love for his sister, Jesse's wife, and admiration for Jesse, but Tom knows the fatality rate for drivers of trucks carrying nitroglycerin to the oil fields. However, he is unable to dissuade Jesse and at last hires him. Jesse leaves the office, "the happiest man on earth," while Tom faces the prospect of Jesse's death at any moment. Maltz presents the story dramatically, irony emerging naturally from the situation.

When using groups rather than individuals to present the need for the proletariat to unite, Maltz tended to produce sketches or scenes rather than short stories, as in "Incident on a Street Corner" (1937; in *The Way Things Are*), "Letter from the Country" (1937; also in *The Way Things Are*), and the ironic "Sunday Morning on Twentieth Street" (1940; in *Afternoon in the Jungle*), in which the proletariat does *not* unite. "Season of Celebration" (in *The Way Things Are*; originally published as "Hotel Raleigh, the Bowery" in *Story*, September 1937) is more effective. Most of the action is set in the dormitory of a Bowery hotel and occurs within three hours on New Year's Eve; the ten main characters are individualized but united in their abject, Depression-caused poverty—they are "underdogs." (Philip Stevenson dramatized the story as *Transit* in 1937.) Throughout, Jimmy O'Shaughnessy lies dying while a variety of men drifts in for the night, and at the climax of the story, each man's fear of death is actualized in Jimmy's death. The theme is made explicit by a man named Benson: "Me.

Illustration by Victor Candell for Maltz's "The Game" (Scribner's, December 1936; collected in The Way Things Are, *1938*),
a story about a poor man who teaches his son to steal in order to survive

... That's me! ... I'm the best goddam harvester mechanic in the whole United States.... But they turned me into a bum.... An' I let 'em. *I let 'em.*" By midnight Jimmy's body has been removed, and most of the men are asleep, but in the toilet Reynolds, a union man, talks intently to a Russian, Zets, probably about the need for the proletariat to unite. Maltz tellingly evokes the atmosphere of the Depression and portrays its victims, men apparently sentenced for life to a Bowery flophouse dormitory.

According to Victor S. Navasky, Maltz, as early as his college years, had become alert to racial discrimination and aspired to use it as a theme in his writing. "The Way Things Are" (first published in the collection of that name) burns with the kind of indignation that leads to caricature and simplification, as Maltz tells of the suicide of a young black worker whom a drunken southern sheriff tricks into thinking he is about to be lynched. Others have handled the theme better. Maltz also portrayed racial discrimination in

the novel *A Long Day in a Short Life* (1957) and the story "With Laughter" (*Southwest Review*, Spring 1960, as Julian Silva; in *Afternoon in the Jungle*), in which Tom Fennel, a Korean war veteran, must aid his wife at childbirth; she clings to the bars of the railing outside a private hospital that has denied them admittance because of their race. The story is skillfully told, a reminder of the blatantly explicit barriers of the 1950s.

"The Way Things Are," "Man on a Road," and "The Happiest Man" are reprinted in *Afternoon in the Jungle*; in addition, five stories published since 1938 and one new story appear. The conflict in the title story (*New Yorker*, 11 January 1941) is between Charlie, a small boy trying to retrieve a fifty-cent piece that has rolled into a subway grille, and a man who depends on such treasure-hunting for a living and arrives with tools more effective for the job than Charlie's string with gum on the end. Charlie will not yield and, by throwing snow and ice at the man, brings the issue to a standstill, showing no sympa-

Cover for Maltz's last collection of stories (1970)

thy for the man's desperation. The story is simply told, suggesting but not stating several economic implications and ironies. Similarly "Circus Come to Town" (*Masses & Mainstream,* July 1950; in *Afternoon in the Jungle*) suggests but does not underline the exploitation of a group of boys by Pusher, the man responsible for raising the tents. Eager as they are to see the circus, Eddie and Alan work to the limits of their strength, only to fall asleep when they have finally earned their admission.

Maltz's attitudes toward informers, betrayers, and corrupt authorities, expressed in his House Un-American Activities Committee testimony and in earlier works, tempt one to give an allegorical reading to "The Farmer's Dog" (*Saturday Evening Post,* 13 July 1968—as "The Prisoner's Dog"; in *Afternoon in the Jungle*) and "The Cop" (first published in *Afternoon in the Jungle*). In the former, the dog Pani is taken from his master, Antek, during World War II, trained to be an SS

guard dog, and appears not to recognize his former master when Antek is imprisoned by the SS at the same camp where Pani is. But when Antek makes an attempt to escape, Pani insures his success by attacking the dogs and guard that pursue him. A dog will not inform against or betray a friend, Maltz seems to say—why does man? In "The Cop," Enzo, an Italian policeman during World War II, tells a writer how he cooperated with the Germans until he attempted to save the life of a young girl working for the partisans. Ironically, when he escaped to the hills with the girl and the German commissar as hostage in a German staff car, the partisans opened fire with grenades and a tommy gun. Only Enzo survives, having lost his legs. His character is given depth by his recognition of his mistakes and of how his bravery in rescuing the girl was mixed with desire for her.

A onetime friend of Maltz, as quoted by Navasky, once said of him, "Albert's a very rigid man, and yet he has the most extraordinary compassion." Indeed, Chester E. Eisinger, in "Character and Self in Fiction on the Left" (1968), finds Maltz's compassion for his characters—his concern for the individual—often at odds with the ideology he propounds, and Maltz said of himself, as reported by Navasky, "I'm not really a sound theoretical person." Maltz often allows character and dialogue to convey his theme, and he shows great powers of characterization in his early stories and later novels. Sometimes—but not always—he underlines the theme explicitly, but does not often seem overly intrusive.

Few other writers convey so well the despair felt by underdogs and victims of the Depression, or depict so well the convergence of external and internal forces that make life hardly bearable. As his career progressed, Maltz seemed increasingly concerned with aesthetics and tended to submerge ideology, but his gift for irony is everywhere abundant. He died on 26 April 1985 in New York.

In the 1930s Maltz earned the respect of establishment critics—the jurors for the O. Henry Memorial Awards for 1938, for example—and Alfred Kazin reviewed *The Underground Stream* under the title "Here is a Left-Wing Writer Who Can Write" (*New York Herald Tribune Books,* 30 June 1940). Today Maltz's work is often viewed favorably, but not without qualifications, by students of proletarian literature. It deserves a wider audience.

References:

Bernard F. Dick, *Radical Innocence: A Critical Study of the Hollywood Ten* (Lexington: University Press of Kentucky, 1989);

Chester E. Eisinger, "Character and Self in Fiction on the Left," in *Proletarian Writers of the Thirties*, edited by David Madden (Carbondale: Southern Illinois University Press, 1968), pp. 158-183;

Eisinger, *Fiction of the Forties* (Chicago: University of Chicago Press, 1963);

Victor S. Navasky, *Naming Names* (New York: Viking, 1980);

Jack Salzman, *Albert Maltz* (Boston: G. K. Hall/ Twayne, 1978).

Papers:

The Albert Maltz Papers at the Wisconsin Center for Theatre Research include the typescript of *Merry Go Round* (1932) and materials relating to the Theatre Union. Letters and other material are in the Albert Maltz Collection, State Historical Society of Wisconsin. The library of Columbia University has source material for Maltz's *A Tale of One January*. Other papers are in the Department of Special Collections, Research Library, UCLA, and in the Archives of Performing Arts, University of Southern California.

John P. Marquand

(10 November 1893 - 16 July 1960)

Paul H. Carlton
Converse College

See also the Marquand entry in *DLB 9: American Novelists, 1910-1945*.

BOOKS: *Prince and Boatswain: Sea Tales from the Recollection of Rear-Admiral Charles E. Clark*, by Marquand and James Morris Morgan (Greenfield, Mass.: Hall, 1915);

The Unspeakable Gentleman (New York: Scribners, 1922; London: Hodder & Stoughton, 1922);

Four of a Kind (New York: Scribners, 1923);

The Black Cargo (New York: Scribners, 1925; London: Hodder & Stoughton, 1925);

Lord Timothy Dexter of Newburyport, Mass. (New York: Minton, Balch, 1925; London: Unwin, 1926);

Do Tell Me, Doctor Johnson (Cleveland: Rowfant Club, 1928);

Warning Hill (Boston: Little, Brown, 1930; London: Hale, 1939);

Haven's End (Boston: Little, Brown, 1933; London: Hale, 1938);

Ming Yellow (Boston: Little, Brown, 1935; London: Dickson & Thompson, 1935);

No Hero (Boston: Little, Brown, 1935); republished as *Mr. Moto Takes a Hand* (London: Hale, 1940);

Thank You, Mr. Moto (Boston: Little, Brown, 1936; London: Jenkins, 1937);

The Late George Apley (Boston: Little, Brown, 1937; London: Hale, 1937);

Think Fast, Mr. Moto (Boston: Little, Brown, 1937; London: Hale, 1938);

Mr. Moto Is So Sorry (Boston: Little, Brown, 1939 [i.e., 1938]; London: Hale, 1939);

Wickford Point (Boston: Little, Brown, 1939; London: Hale, 1939);

Don't Ask Questions (London: Hale, 1941);

H. M. Pulham, Esquire (Boston: Little, Brown, 1941; London: Hale, 1942);

Last Laugh, Mr. Moto (Boston: Little, Brown, 1942; London: Hale, 1943);

So Little Time (Boston: Little, Brown, 1943; London: Hale, 1944);

Repent in Haste (Boston: Little, Brown, 1945; London: Hale, 1949);

The Late George Apley: A Play, by Marquand and George S. Kaufman (New York: Dramatists Play Service, 1946);

B. F.'s Daughter (Boston: Little, Brown, 1946); republished as *Polly Fulton* (London: Hale, 1947);

John P. Marquand

Point of No Return (Boston: Little, Brown, 1949;
London: Hale, 1949);

It's Loaded, Mr. Bauer (London: Hale, 1949);

Sun, Sea, and Sand (New York: Dell, 1950);

Melville Goodwin, USA (Boston: Little, Brown,
1951; London: Hale, 1952);

Thirty Years (Boston & Toronto: Little, Brown,
1954; London: Hale, 1955);

Sincerely, Willis Wayde (Boston & Toronto: Little,
Brown, 1955; London: Hale, 1955);

Stopover: Tokyo (Boston & Toronto: Little, Brown,
1957; London: Collins, 1957);

Life at Happy Knoll (Boston & Toronto: Little,
Brown, 1957; London: Collins, 1958);

Women and Thomas Harrow (Boston & Toronto: Little, Brown, 1958; London: Collins, 1959);

Timothy Dexter Revisited (Boston & Toronto: Little,
Brown, 1960);

The Last of Mr. Moto (New York: Berkley, 1963).

Collections: *Mr. Moto's Three Aces* (Boston &
Toronto: Little, Brown, 1956)—comprises
Thank You, Mr. Moto; Think Fast, Mr. Moto;
and *Mr. Moto Is So Sorry*;

*North of Grand Central: Three Novels of New En-
gland* (Boston & Toronto: Little, Brown,
1956)—comprises *The Late George Apley; Wickford Point*; and *H. M. Pulham, Esquire*; with
new prefaces by Marquand.

PLAY PRODUCTION: *The Late George Apley*, by
Marquand and George S. Kaufman, New
York, Lyceum Theatre, 21 November 1944.

John P. Marquand is best remembered as a
highly accomplished novelist of manners, whose
ironic portraits of the foibles and burdens of the
privileged classes enjoyed enormous popularity
during the 1940s and 1950s. Though his critical
reputation has declined significantly since his
death, during his most productive years he was
among the most widely read and admired writers
of his generation. As a satirist he is frequently compared to Sinclair Lewis, with whom he shared mutual respect, though as Granville Hicks once remarked, "his eye is as good as Sinclair Lewis at
his best, and his ear more dependable than Lewis
ever was" (*Harper's Magazine*, April 1950). Nor
was such praise isolated. At the height of his
fame, at mid century, Marquand's work received
important attention from many of the most respected critics and reviewers then passing judgment on American literature—including Alfred
Kazin, Arthur Mizener, and Malcolm Cowley.

As popular and influential as he proved to
be with such novels as *The Late George Apley*
(1937), *Wickford Point* (1939), *H. M. Pulham,
Esquire* (1941), and *Point of No Return* (1949), in
the fifteen years prior to his recognition as a serious writer in 1938 (when *The Late George Apley*
won the Pulitzer Prize), he had already gained
the admiration of the mass reading public as the
creator of dozens of entertaining and thoughtful
stories for popular magazines—particularly the
Saturday Evening Post. Indeed, as biographer
Millicent Bell has noted, because Marquand was
so recognized as a "front cover" name during the
years between the wars, he "was one of the makers of the *Post* . . . as much responsible for the
character of its pages" as its fabled editor,
George Horace Lorimer. Although his efforts for
mass-circulation magazines are perhaps limited
by their conformity to audience expectations for
light and diverting fiction, they demonstrate
Marquand's devotion to the highest standards of
his craft and are among the best of their type. Furthermore, many of these stories deserve attention
on their individual merits and as introductions to

The young Marquand in Newburyport, Massachusetts

the themes more expansively treated in his best novels: the effects of success, money, and social class on character; the demand for and the emotional price of conformity; and the continuing influence of the past upon the present.

John Phillips Marquand's interest in the personal and historical past was the direct result of an upbringing steeped in the tradition and lost glories of his New England heritage. Although born in Wilmington, Delaware (on 10 November 1893), he came from old New England stock, a family that had been prominent in and around Newburyport, Massachusetts, since the middle of the eighteenth century. As a young child he enjoyed a privileged upbringing, shuffling between New York, Boston, and Newburyport as his father, Philip Marquand, a Harvard-trained engineer, tried to build on the fortune of his own father, an influential New England financier. John's great-aunt, for whom his mother was named, was Margaret Fuller, the famous nineteenth-century feminist and friend to Ralph Waldo Emerson and Henry David Thoreau. Another great-aunt had been a brief resident at the transcendental community at Brook Farm, and

Marquand was also connected by family to many other New England luminaries.

Always a speculator, Philip Marquand lost his share of the family fortune in the panic of 1907, forcing him to seek work as an engineer on the Panama Canal. Just a teenager, John was packed off to live with three maiden aunts at Curzon's Mill (near Newburyport), the once-splendid family estate. Having attended nothing but private schools, Marquand initially felt socially alienated at Newburyport High School, a sensibility that permeates much of his work. Newburyport was to be fictionally re-created in much of his work.

Despite straitened family circumstances, Marquand was able to enter Harvard in 1911, but only as a scholarship student, which increased his sense of social insecurity. As a condition of his funding he was forced to study science (majoring in chemistry), though as a student he developed a keen interest in literature and writing. Although he never was invited to join any of the exclusive clubs or societies catering to literary-minded students, his ready wit and devastating talent for parody earned him a spot on the staff of the *Harvard Lampoon*, to which he regularly contributed humorous articles for a couple of years. Eager to earn a living, Marquand completed his course of study for the A.B. in three years, leaving Harvard in 1914 to join the staff of the *Boston Evening Transcript* as a reporter. He saw brief service with the National Guard along the Mexican border during the 1916 border dispute, and in the following year was commissioned a lieutenant in the army artillery. In France, Marquand witnessed and participated in some of the heaviest fighting of World War I, an experience by which he was profoundly affected. Military types and war veterans frequently appear in both his short and long fiction, though such characters often exhibit a kind of curious detachment—even bemusement—toward their experiences.

Like many of his contemporaries, Marquand returned from the war restless and eager to make his way in the boisterous days of what F. Scott Fitzgerald would christen the "Jazz Age." Marquand was drawn to New York, where he worked for a year on the Sunday magazine of the *New York Tribune* (1919-1920), contributing humorous pieces about modern life. At the suggestion of Robert Benchley, a colleague from his *Harvard Lampoon* days, Marquand left newspaper work for advertising. Although the money proved better, he found the work tedious, his satiric sense of the ridiculous provoked by the excesses of commercial promotion, and left shortly afterward.

By late 1920 Marquand had decided to pursue a career as a professional writer, and with modest savings he returned to Curzon's Mill, where he produced his first long piece of fiction, a historical romance largely set in Federalist Newburyport, titled *The Unspeakable Gentleman*. The novel was eventually serialized in *Ladies' Home Journal* in February, March, and May 1922, and when published by Scribners that spring, it was politely received, selling respectably well for a first book.

However, even while the manuscript was making the rounds, Marquand had already broken into the ranks of the popular magazines with his first commercially published short story, "The Right That Failed." Published by the *Saturday Evening Post* (23 July 1921), the story revolves around the kind of love interest typical to commercial fiction of the day, but with an unusual angle. A young prizefighter meets and falls in love with a beautiful society girl, who accepts him as a social peer, not realizing his profession. After a predictable complication, she eventually accepts him for his innate charm over a more socially appropriate suitor. The story was eventually collected in *Four of a Kind* (1923), one of the few story collections Marquand was to publish in his long career. The plot of this story—as well as much of the other work Marquand contributed to the slick magazines—is summed up by the title of a later (uncollected) story, "The Cinderella Motif" (*Saturday Evening Post*, 5 March 1927). In such stories the hero or heroine is able to rise in society by capturing the heart of someone of higher station, thus satisfying the kind of wish-fulfillment mentality common to popular fiction of the day. While few of these efforts barely rise above the strict limits of their formula, they afforded Marquand the opportunity to sharpen his storytelling skills and develop what has come to be characterized—usually derisively—as his smooth, honeyed style.

Other efforts by Marquand during the 1920s are less bound by the conventions of the mass audience, resembling the more studied investigations into character and social manners for which he became famous two decades later. As early as 1923 in "The Ship" (*Scribner's Magazine*, January; uncollected), he explored a loss of purpose in the last descendant of an old and once prosperous New England family. The main character goes mad and is eventually driven to self-destruction waiting for a phantom ship, which he

feels will restore his wealth and dignity, like those that once brought riches to his forefathers in the golden days of the great Yankee traders. The story is also notable for its narrative structure, employing a Conradian distanced narrator, himself only marginally invested in the action but profoundly affected by the events he relates. This technique would reach its zenith in American fiction three years later in Fitzgerald's *The Great Gatsby*, itself a study in character and social values, and was a technique Marquand would frequently use in much of his other short and long fiction.

While "The Ship" demonstrated Marquand's potential, it hardly satisfied his need for money. Its price hardly approached the twenty-five hundred dollars Marquand was consistently receiving from the *Saturday Evening Post* by the mid 1920s. His marriage on 8 September 1922 to Christina Sedgwick, daughter of a prominent Stockbridge, Massachusetts, family, the young couple's establishing themselves in proper Boston society, and the eventual birth of a son and daughter (John and Christine, known as Tina) placed financial demands on Marquand that, he felt, bound him to the story mill. As a result he tended to disparage most of the work he did for the popular magazines, collecting little of it. Nonetheless, as his popularity and influence with editors grew, he continued to develop as a writer. Indeed, one of his best-known stories, "Good Morning, Major," was published in the *Saturday Evening Post* on 11 December 1926. The story is an inquiry into the nature of the military mind, in this case that of a crusty old cavalry officer who finds himself in a modern war in command of dilettantish staff officers (one of whom narrates the story). While these young officers taunt him behind his back for his crude and abrupt manner, he eventually earns their sympathy and respect, but at the cost of his own son's life, whom he sends out as a messenger into withering artillery fire. Like all of Marquand's work, the story demonstrates a strong, stoic strain, even puritanical in its insistence on suppressing emotion in the adherence to duty.

"Good Morning, Major" was one of the first of Marquand's short stories to find recognition beyond the readers of the *Post*, being chosen the following year for inclusion in Edward J. O'Brien's *Fifty Best Short Stories for 1927*. It was regularly anthologized for years as a representative story of the World War I experience and was one of the short works from the early years that Marquand

Marquand in 1927 at home in Boston with his first wife, Christina Sedgwick Marquand, their children, Johnny and Tina, and their dog, Prince

later collected in *Thirty Years* (1954), commenting in a headnote that if the story remained readable it was "because some values remain constant in a changing world. War is still war. Boys will be boys, and generals are still (essentially) generals."

Marquand was also working on several series for the *Post* late in the 1920s. One of these series, including "The Cinderella Motif," is built around the misadventures of Beverly Witherspoon, a young man who is socially superior but inept as a Harvard undergraduate. Despite his inability to meet the world realistically, Beverly somehow manages to muddle through, his anachronistic values intact. Aside from representing a deliciously satirical portrait of exaggerated social manners, the Witherspoon character is a prototype for George Apley. As in the case of Apley, the reader feels both contempt and warmth toward him—making the character more complex and, therefore, more believable than the two-dimensional stereotype of second-rate satire.

Another series Marquand developed in the

Post during the late 1920s, and into the early 1930s, shows a continuing passion of his: the New England past. These stories chronicle, through three centuries, the contentious relationships between the Scarlets and the Swales, two proud New England families—the former explosively emotional, the latter stiffly rational. Collected in 1933 as *Haven's End*, the tales represent Marquand's most ambitious efforts in short fiction centered in the body of material he felt particularly his own. In artifice and subject matter they more closely resemble Nathaniel Hawthorne's fiction (even self-consciously so) than the work of a twentieth-century mannerist, though they are characteristically Marquandian with their ironically distanced narrators. Referred to by Elmer Davis in the *Saturday Review* (26 August 1933) as "an admirable and living history," the collection was not successful, and its failure to find a broader audience depressed Marquand. The weaknesses of the volume are clearly apparent:

its heavily symbolic quality (not a Marquand strong point) and its air of artificiality. As the years passed, he became increasingly skeptical of the legitimacy of writing about historical subject matter as though it were the chronicle of a current event.

Nonetheless, Marquand's interest in historical subjects was further evidenced by much of the work he published in the early 1930s. One series features a Confederate cavalry officer, Scott Mattaye of Deer Bottom, Virginia; as an elderly veteran sitting comfortably in his drawing room sipping bourbon, he recalls his youth as a scout for J. E. B. Stuart's cavalry. Civil War fiction was a staple of the popular magazines in the 1930s—full of distortions and exaggerations, to which the Mattaye stories sometimes descend. But they remain particularly readable because of Marquand's talent for creating a convincing picture of great men, great events, and the great confusion of those caught up in a moment of history. For instance, in the uncollected story "High Tide" (*Saturday Evening Post*, 8 October 1932), perhaps the best of the series, Mattaye recalls his impressions of a harrowing night before Gettysburg, of "armies moving like blind monsters, each groping toward the other." Though obviously written for their entertainment value, the Mattaye stories frequently achieve a sense of reality not common to historical romance and are a testament to Marquand's ability to extend the limits of the medium.

Around 1935 Marquand's work in short fiction began to decline as he devoted more attention to new projects, particularly his very popular serials featuring the inscrutable Japanese detective Mr. Moto. Marquand's marriage, which had always been shaky, also ended that year, thus closing a major chapter in his life. More important, however, the magazine market for popular fiction was undergoing changes as well, beginning its long decline as the audience was being drawn away increasingly to radio and movies.

Nevertheless, Marquand continued to publish short fiction between his major projects, though his contributions were fewer and more selective. Perhaps his finest short story from the later 1930s, and one reflecting his new attitude, is "Pull, Pull, Together" (*Saturday Evening Post*, 24 July 1937; uncollected). A middle-aged New England father ponders the value of his own upbringing on the occasion of enrolling his adolescent son in the same prestigious prep school he himself attended as a youth. Not questioning the traditional values such institutions represent, he cannot help but wonder if such places actually fail to prepare young people for a world in which those values have become seemingly irrelevant. Characteristically for Marquand, the rebellion ends there; the father enrolls his son, partly as an obligation to class—but the point that is subtly wrought, and frequently missed in discussions of Marquand's work, is that, like all his heroes, the father realizes that everyone is the product of his environment, and that conformity—despite its emotional price—is the only rational alternative in maintaining a sense of stasis in a world undergoing alarming change. Published the same year as *The Late George Apley*, "Pull, Pull, Together" helps explain the novel's complexity of characterization, and also offers a useful key to all the later novels.

During the 1940s Marquand's attention went almost entirely to his major novels, which appeared like clockwork every two or three years to generally approving audiences and critics. Furthermore, his work for the War Department as a civilian analyst, and later as a correspondent for *Harper's* in the Pacific, cut into his writing time, limiting his short fiction to barely a trickle. Having remarried on 16 April 1937 to Adelaide Hooker, an eccentric New York socialite, Marquand was also distracted by his rapidly growing family; three more children of his were born during the war years (Blanche, Timothy, and Elon).

Two stories that came out of those years, both from Marquand's direct observations, are good examples of his continuing experiments in examining character. The first, "The End Game" (*Good Housekeeping*, March 1944; in *Thirty Years*), explores generational conflict within a family of career military officers. Although the story relies on an appalling trick ending, it still manages to be an absorbing account of character, the consequences of rebellion, and the continuity of family values despite the willfulness of individual members.

"Lunch at Honolulu" (*Harper's*, August 1945; also in *Thirty Years*) uses the locale of wartime Hawaii as a backdrop for a study in the psychological effects of combat on the consciousness of a young naval officer. At a polite luncheon the young man, just in port following a desperate battle at sea, makes himself obnoxious to his civilian host and several staff officers. Unable to integrate his recent harrowing experience into the staid surroundings, the young man drinks too much, talks too much, and abruptly leaves. Like

Illustration for one of Marquand's many stories in the Saturday Evening Post. *This story, first published in the 8 April 1939 issue, was collected with two others under the heading "School and College" in* Thirty Years *(1954).*

all of Marquand's fiction involving men at war—and there is much of it—the focus is not on action or the intensity of the individual's experience but rather on the enormity of the vast enterprise itself and its profound effects on the social order. Called "superb" by Granville Hicks in a 31 October 1954 review of *Thirty Years*, "Lunch at Honolulu" is perhaps Marquand's finest piece of short fiction, blending many of his concerns into a single, unified work.

Not all of Marquand's later short stories are probing studies into military character. Indeed, in the 1950s, the final decade of his life, he returned to the medium many feel is his true métier: light social satire. Like much of the work he had done in the heyday of his *Saturday Evening Post* era, these stories were created as series for popular magazines, their primary objective being entertainment. The most successful are "Sun, Sea, and Sand" (*Cosmopolitan*, May 1950;

published separately later that year) and "King of the Sea" (*McCall's*, November 1952); Marquand included them in *Thirty Years*. Both revolve around the antics of several members of the Mulligatawny Club, a closed community located at a Caribbean resort. Although generally humorous in their intent, both stories are also strident critiques of a self-satisfied leisure class whose only purpose seems to be the performance of an endless round of adolescent high jinks.

Similar to the Mulligatawny stories is a series of sketches Marquand developed for *Sports Illustrated* in 1956. Collected as *Life at Happy Knoll* (1957), these tales present the hypocrisy and social pretentiousness of the country-club set, a growing feature of the cult of suburban America in the 1950s. Although clever in their structure (presented as a series of letters between members) and clinically accurate in their descriptions of social types, the sketches are not as satisfying

Marquand and his second wife, Adelaide Hooker Marquand, at their home on Kent's Island, near Newburyport, 1951

as the satires Marquand had more deftly created in his earlier career. Of course, the 1950s were declining years for him. A heart attack in 1953 had slowed him considerably, and his second marriage was undergoing considerable strain, ending in divorce in 1958. Nonetheless, he continued writing and publishing until his death on 16 July 1960 at his Kent's Island home near Newburyport.

Critics have had a hard time ascribing value to both Marquand's short and long fiction. What little discussion he has attracted continues to dwell on his important novels. Literary criticism has always tended to focus on innovation, and Marquand's few experiments in the genre of the short story were more within the context of his own themes and style and not with the form itself. After all, Marquand began his career by writing in the form defined by O. Henry and not as it was later transformed by Ernest Hemingway (whose work he admired). Nor was he a brilliant stylist like his other contemporary Fitzgerald. John P. Marquand was instead a craftsman who viewed writing as a profession that only produces art when the result reflects an experience with which the reader can identify.

Interviews:

Robert Van Gelder, *Writers and Writing* (New York: Scribners, 1946), pp. 38-41;

Van Gelder, "An Interview with a Best-Selling Author: John P. Marquand," *Cosmopolitan*, 122 (March 1947): 18, 150-152;

Harvey Breit, "An Interview with J. P. Marquand," *New York Times Book Review*, 24 April 1949, p. 35;

Frederick Houghton and Richard Whitman "J. P. Marquand Speaking," *Cosmopolitan*, 147 (August 1959): 46-50.

Bibliography:

William White, "John P. Marquand: A Preliminary Checklist," *Bulletin of Bibliography*, 19 (September-December 1949): 268-271; updated in *The Late John Marquand: A Biography*, by Stephen Birmingham (Philadelphia & New York: Lippincott, 1972), pp. 243-247.

Biographies:

Stephen Birmingham, *The Late John Marquand: A Biography* (Philadelphia & New York: Lippincott, 1972);

Millicent Bell, *Marquand: An American Life* (Boston & Toronto: Little, Brown, 1979).

References:

John W. Aldridge, "Not Too Pro for Posterity," *Saturday Review*, 34 (17 June 1972): 63-71;

Louis Auchincloss, *Reflections of a Jacobite* (Boston: Houghton Mifflin, 1961);

Roger Butterfield, "John P. Marquand: America's Most Famous Novelist of Manners," *Life*, 17 (31 July 1944): 64-73;

Elmer Davis, "Living History," *Saturday Review*, 10 (26 August 1933): 66;

Clifton Fadiman, "Party of One: Introduction to J. P. Marquand's *Thirty Years*," *Holiday*, 16 (October 1954): 6-9;

John L. Gross, *John P. Marquand* (New York: Twayne, 1963);

Philip Hamburger, *J. P. Marquand, Esquire* (Boston: Houghton Mifflin, 1952);

Hamburger, "Profiles: There's No Place," *New Yorker*, 28 (29 March, 5 April, 12 April 1952): 37-57, 43-67, 39-64;

Harlan Hatcher, "John Phillips Marquand," *College English*, 1 (November 1939): 107-118;

Granville Hicks, "Marquand of Newburyport," *Harper's Magazine*, 200 (April 1950): 101-108;

Hicks, "Marquand's Journey," *New York Times Book Review*, 31 October 1954, p. 5;

C. Hugh Holman, *John P. Marquand* (Minneapolis: University of Minnesota Press, 1965);

James W. Tuttleton, "Stasis and Change," in his *The American Novel of Manners* (Chapel Hill: University of North Carolina Press, 1972);

Edward Weeks, "John P. Marquand," *Atlantic Monthly*, 206 (October 1960): 74-76.

Papers:

Most of Marquand's private and business correspondence is located at the Harvard University Library. His manuscripts are at Yale.

Edison Marshall
(29 August 1894 - 29 October 1967)

Joseph S. Tedesco
St. Bonaventure University

BOOKS: *The Voice of the Pack* (Boston: Little, Brown, 1920; London: Hodder & Stoughton, 1920);

The Snowshoe Trail (Boston: Little, Brown, 1921; London: Hodder & Stoughton, 1921);

The Strength of the Pines (Boston: Little, Brown, 1921; London: Hodder & Stoughton, 1921);

The Heart of Little Shikara, and Other Stories (Boston: Little, Brown, 1922; London: Hodder & Stoughton, 1924);

Shepherds of the Wild (Boston: Little, Brown, 1922; London: Hodder & Stoughton, 1922);

The Sky Line of Spruce (Boston: Little, Brown, 1922; London: Hodder & Stoughton, 1922);

The Isle of Retribution (Boston: Little, Brown, 1923; London: Hodder & Stoughton, 1923);

The Land of Forgotten Men (Boston: Little, Brown, 1923; London: Hodder & Stoughton, 1924);

The Death Bell (Garden City, N.Y.: Garden City Publishing, 1924);

Seward's Folly (Boston: Little, Brown, 1924; London: Hodder & Stoughton, 1924);

Ocean Gold (New York & London: Harper, 1925);

The Sleeper of Moonlit Ranges (New York: Cosmopolitan, 1925; London: Hodder & Stoughton, 1925);

Campfire Courage: The Woodsmoke Boys in the Canadian Rockies (New York & London: Harper, 1926);

Child of the Wild: A Story of Alaska (New York: Cosmopolitan, 1926; London: Hodder & Stoughton, 1926);

The Deadfall (New York: Cosmopolitan, 1927; London: Hodder & Stoughton, 1927);

The Far Call (New York: Cosmopolitan, 1928; London: Hodder & Stoughton, 1928);

The Fish Hawk (New York: Cosmopolitan, 1929; London: Hodder & Stoughton, 1929); republished as *Singing Arrows* (London: Hodder & Stoughton, 1929);

Vernon Gould

The Missionary (New York: Cosmopolitan, 1930; London: Hodder & Stoughton, 1930);

The Doctor of Lonesome River (New York: Cosmopolitan, 1931; London: Hodder & Stoughton, 1931);

The Deputy at Snow Mountain (New York: Kinsey, 1932; London: Hodder & Stoughton, 1932);

Forlorn Island (New York: Kinsey, 1932; London: Hodder & Stoughton, 1932);

The Light in the Jungle (New York: Kinsey, 1933); republished as *Victory in the Jungle* (London: Hodder & Stoughton, 1933);

Ogden's Strange Story (New York: Kinsey, 1934);

The Splendid Quest (New York: Kinsey, 1934);

Dian of the Lost Land (New York: Kinsey, 1935; London: Hodder & Stoughton, 1935);

Sam Campbell, Gentleman (New York: Kinsey, 1935; London: Hodder & Stoughton, 1936);

The Stolen God (New York: Kinsey, 1936; London: Hodder & Stoughton, 1937);

Darzee, Girl of India (New York: Kinsey, 1937); republished as *The Flower Dancer* (London: Hodder & Stoughton, 1937);

The White Brigand (New York: Kinsey, 1937; London: Hodder & Stoughton, 1938);

The Jewel of Malabar (New York: Kinsey, 1938; London: Hodder & Stoughton, 1938);

Benjamin Blake (New York: Farrar & Rinehart, 1941);

Great Smith (New York: Farrar & Rinehart, 1943; London: Aldor, 1947);

The Upstart (New York: Farrar & Rinehart, 1945; London: World, 1959);

Shikar and Safari (New York: Farrar, Straus, 1947; London: Museum Press, 1950);

Yankee Pasha: The Adventures of Jason Starbuck (New York: Farrar, Straus, 1947; London & Sydney: Huston, 1950);

Castle in the Swamp: A Tale of Old Carolina (New York: Farrar, Straus, 1948; London: Muller, 1949);

Gypsy Sixpence (New York: Farrar, Straus, 1949; London: Muller, 1950);

The Infinite Woman (New York: Farrar, Straus, 1950; London: Muller, 1951);

Love Stories of India (New York: Farrar, Straus, 1950);

The Viking (New York: Farrar, Straus & Young, 1951; London: Muller, 1952);

The Bengal Tiger: A Tale of India, as Hall Hunter (Garden City, N.Y.: Doubleday, 1952);

Caravan to Xanadu: A Novel of Marco Polo (New York: Farrar, Straus & Young, 1953; London: Muller, 1953);

American Captain (New York: Farrar, Straus & Young, 1954); republished as *Captain's Saga* (London: Muller, 1955);

The Gentleman (New York: Farrar, Straus & Cudahy, 1956; London: Muller, 1956);

The Heart of the Hunter (New York: McGraw-Hill, 1956; London: Muller, 1957);

The Inevitable Hour: A Novel of Martinique (New York: Putnam's, 1957; London: Muller, 1958);

Princess Sophia: A Novel of Alaska (Garden City, N.Y.: Doubleday, 1958; London: Muller, 1959);

The Pagan King (Garden City, N.Y.: Doubleday, 1959; London: Muller, 1960);

Earth Giant (Garden City, N.Y.: Doubleday, 1960; London: Muller, 1961);

West with the Vikings (Garden City, N.Y.: Doubleday, 1961);

The Conquerer (Garden City, N.Y.: Doubleday, 1962);

Cortez and Marina (Garden City, N.Y.: Doubleday, 1963);

The Lost Colony (Garden City, N.Y.: Doubleday, 1964).

The majority of Edison Marshall's literary work consists of historical novels, ranging from fictionalized biographies of historical figures to fictionalized heroes in actual historical settings. His short stories, while representing a relatively small portion of the literary works produced early in his career, constitute a microcosm of his artistic skills at storytelling.

The son of Lille Bartoo Marshall and George Edward Marshall, who was an editor and publisher of a small newspaper, Marshall was born on 29 August 1894 in Rensselaer, Indiana, but grew up after the age of thirteen in Eugene, Oregon, where he attended the state university from 1913 to 1916. He later served in the U.S. Army and attained the rank of second lieutenant. After his marriage, on 4 January 1920, to Agnes Sharp Flythe (with whom he later had two children—Edison and Nancy), he began a permanent residence in the Augusta area of Georgia. Drawn by an avid interest in hunting and the outdoor life, he traveled extensively throughout three continents—North America, Africa, and Eurasia—where his experiences provided the source material for much of his writing.

His literary career began with publishing stories in pulp magazines, which featured fiction about hunting, animals, and nature. His first major success was receiving the O. Henry Memorial Award in 1921 for his short story "The Heart of Little Shikara" (*Everybody's Magazine*, January 1921), which was collected a year later under that title with other adventure stories about hunting and the outdoors. For the next two decades he continued this kind of writing but published with greater frequency in slick magazines, where many of his short stories and novels in serial form appeared and revealed his interest in historical characters and settings.

His most critically successful era began with the publication of the novel *Benjamin Blake* in

1941 and lasted until his death in 1967. During this period he produced twenty novels, a collection of short stories, and two memoirs of his hunting experiences. His novels were regularly translated in nine European languages, and several of them were the bases of films.

His novels between 1941 and 1967 generally follow two basic patterns: in the first, Marshall develops a fictional narrative based on a historical figure but with a limited amount of historical evidence. Examples of these are *Caravan to Xanadu: A Novel of Marco Polo* (1953); *The Pagan King* (1959—about King Arthur); *The Conqueror* (1962—concerning Alexander the Great); and *Cortez and Marina* (1963). In other novels he focuses on the local color of an area, as in *Castle in the Swamp: A Tale of Old Carolina* (1948); *The Bengal Tiger: A Tale of India* (1952); *The Inevitable Hour: A Novel of Martinique* (1957); *Princess Sophia: A Novel of Alaska* (1958); and *The Lost Colony* (1964—about the colonizing of Roanoke Island in 1587).

Among the many films based on his novels, the most prominent was *Son of Fury* (1942), based on *Benjamin Blake* and starring Tyrone Power. In 1952 the film *Treasure of the Golden Condor* was produced from the same novel; it was a less successful adaptation.

The best of his short stories are contained in two collections published twenty-eight years apart. *The Heart of Little Shikara, and Other Stories*, the first, represents his first decade as a writer and includes "The Elephant Remembers," another O. Henry Memorial Award story (*Everybody's Magazine*, October 1919), which has been widely anthologized in high-school textbooks. *Love Stories of India*, published in 1950, collects stories written beginning in 1933 and reflects not only a departure from the outdoor world of animals and hunters but a new maturity and sophistication as a writer.

Even though he had not yet embarked on much of his worldwide travel by the time he published his first collection, Marshall wrote with a knowledge and intimacy about animals and the outdoors that is compelling. In "The Heart of Little Shikara" a young boy, named after a hunter hawk called a shikara, idolizes a white hunter, Warwick Sahib, whose reputation is godlike throughout the area. On a tiger hunt Warwick is wounded and rendered defenseless against Nahara, a preying tigress in the nearby jungle. When he does not return, the villagers suspect he is dead and are reluctant to search for him

for fear of the dreadful tigress. Little Shikara, without his parents' knowledge, sneaks into the jungle where his hero is incapacitated and about to be attacked by Nahara. With directions from Warwick, he slays the tigress and becomes a legendary hero like his idol.

"The Elephant Remembers," which appears in both collections, is a story about animal memory. Muztagh, an elephant of the superior Kumirian breed, is befriended by a low-caste hill man, Langur Dass, who works for the owner of an elephant herd in captivity. During Muztagh's early years, Langur feeds and cares for this prince of the herd in such a manner that he makes a lasting impression on the elephant's instinctive nature. The young elephant eventually escapes captivity and roams the jungle unfettered, soon becoming a legendary monarch renowned as White-Skin throughout the area and much pursued by a white hunter. Meanwhile, Langur fades into the nondescript existence of an elephant catcher, often ignored and sometimes despised by the others. The elephant and the man meet once again when Langur frustrates a plan to catch White-Skin by warning the elephant, who instinctively "remembers" the sounds of the man who fed and cared for him when he was young; the two escape to live in freedom in the jungle.

The other stories in the 1922 collection, which take place in the forests of Oregon, are equal in quality to the two major pieces. Especially powerful is the closing piece, "Brother Bill the Elk," another story about animal memory. Marshall demonstrates in these stories an unusual ability to portray life in the wilderness, to capture the sounds, smells, moods, and mystery. The stories' authenticity is a testimony to his acute powers of observation. Even more skillful is Marshall's ability to recreate animal consciousness. He consistently depicts animal response in terms of instincts and sensibilities not rooted in human equivalents—a discipline in his work that enhances his credibility.

Love Stories of India represents for Marshall a complete change of direction in subject matter. The stories in this volume, as Marshall says in the introduction, "deal with strange, romantic events and adventures rather than everyday life . . . and sexual love is the motif of most of them." The setting for all the stories is the Far East, with its implied mysticism and rigid formality. Despite the oriental ethos that pervades the world of these stories, the point of view is that of

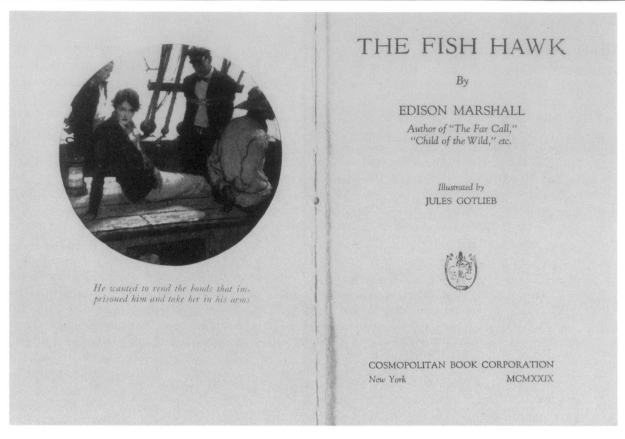

THE FISH HAWK

By

EDISON MARSHALL

*Author of "The Far Call,"
"Child of the Wild," etc.*

Illustrated by
JULES GOTLIEB

COSMOPOLITAN BOOK CORPORATION
New York   *MCMXXIX*

He wanted to rend the bonds that imprisoned him and take her in his arms

Frontispiece and title page for one of Marshall's many adventure novels

the Western observer with Judeo-Christian morality. In different degrees the stories reflect the engagement of the two worlds.

Of the fifteen stories at least four are outstanding in that they represent perceptive and sophisticated storytelling. The rest, though less successful, are convincing, and they vary in mood and in the intensity of narrative fluency and focus.

"The Closed Trophy Room," one of the best stories, has at its center a man who is married to a shallow, hen-pecking woman, whose true personality was not apparent to him before marriage. In addition to restraining his living habits and confining them to her view of life, she belittles his success and accomplishments, particularly his love of big-game hunting and the trophies he has collected, which she banishes to the attic. With a quiet defiance, he embarks on a hunting trip to India, where he not only kills two royal Bengal tigers and escapes an attack by wild tribesmen but also experiences genuine warmth and affection from a young native girl, who saves his life and profoundly influences his personality. When he returns home, his new outlook permits him to re-

sist his wife's nagging criticism for the remaining years of their life together. In his dying moments, he reveals his idyllic romance with the native girl—a "trophy" his wife cannot demean. While the surface plot and secondary characterizations are drawn with conventional techniques, the relationship between the man and the native girl is delicately portrayed, especially in its dual-world context.

"The Unturned Card," though set for the most part in India, centers on characters from the sophisticated American society of the 1930s. A young woman, Grace, marries Roger, a somewhat immature friend from her social set, even though she has admitted her love for Graham, a more mature and stable man who is not only a friend of the couple but adores the young woman himself.

Grace chooses her immature husband because, as she says, "I need you, Graham . . . but Roger needs me more." Some years later she meets Graham in India, where she seeks his help in finding her missing husband, supposedly the victim of a boating accident. As Graham consents to help her search, he inquires about her feelings toward him, and she responds gently but firmly by "putting her cards on the table" (a frequently used metaphor in their relationship), stating that she loves him, but if he finds Roger, nothing will change and there will be no chance for them. After an exhaustive search, which includes finding Roger's ring on an unidentified body, Grace and Graham marry. The unturned card is a telegram they receive from a hired searcher a few hours after they marry, which they do not open until the next morning. The story ends with the assurance that their new life will survive regardless of the content of the telegram—which is left to the reader's imagination.

While the characterization emerges by way of an omniscient narrator, the symbol of the unturned card not only creates a delicate ambiguity at the end of the story but, more significantly, presents Grace as reaching a new awareness about her world, and effects a resolution of two competing demands within herself—her romantic love for Graham and her maternal love for Roger.

Contrary to the usual portrayal of British aristocracy in India throughout the stories, "Matter of Honor" (*Cosmopolitan*, May 1938) makes a pukka Sahib the villain of the piece. Arthur Millbank is a genuine aristocrat right down to the pedigree of the horses in his stables and the dogs in his kennels. Maintaining the purity of his family lineage by always acting in good form is the highest priority in his life. When his wife, whom he treats as one of his tastefully acquired possessions, gets pregnant by a neighboring writer from a lower social class, he murders her lover, arranges for the blame to be placed on a housemaid who conveniently flees the area, and diverts any suspicion of scandal away from his wife by giving the illegitimate child an appearance and name that indicate the boy is his own son.

Although the boy, who is raised according to strict family tradition, is deprived of affection, as his mother was, he manages to maintain a humane attitude toward others. He discovers that the murdered man is his father from a portrait, found by a childhood sweetheart, which reveals the uncanny resemblance of the young man to his true father. The story ends with a confrontation between the young man and his stepfather in the presence of his mother and sweetheart. The result is the vindication of his real father's name, the freedom of his mother from the enslaving threat by her husband to disinherit him, and his marriage to his girlfriend, a virtual com-

moner. All this is effected by the young man's manipulation of the stepfather's fear of scandal.

The strength of this story lies in Marshall's characterization of the villain: his punctilious attention to matters of form, the subordination of any humane attitude toward others because of the necessity of maintaining the facade of respectability, and the impenetrable social mask, which finally collapses at the end of the story.

"Besides the Shalimar," the last story in the collection—a place of honor according to Marshall—represents his most skillful portrayal of a major theme throughout all the stories: the meeting of East and West. Jim Carpenter, from the fraternity-pin world of Kansas, and Princess Lira, "the fruit of thirty centuries of beauty-breeding by the kings of India," meet on an Italian liner bound for Bombay. Their clandestine romance, the first for both, is presented as idyllic despite a slight suggestion of adolescent comedy, stemming from the secrecy that is necessitated by the threat of the dark, swift justice of the East if they are caught. The voyage ends without such incidence, but Lira does warn Carpenter that he is not to seek her presence or to reveal ever meeting or speaking to her, particularly while he is in India, where she is scheduled to marry a fifty-year-old rich and powerful king chosen for her by her father. Her fiancé, a gentle and kind maharaja schooled in the West, has divorced three previous wives for failure to give birth to a son.

Almost a year later, while traveling through this king's realm, Carpenter is involuntarily removed from his train and brought before the maharaja, where he is told that the king's wife, Lira, expects a child momentarily and that there is reason to believe that it is not the maharaja's child. The ruler also has proof that the princess visited Carpenter's stateroom during her voyage to Bombay. Carpenter is offered his freedom if he confesses to the fact, or death if he does not. Carpenter refuses, admitting no acquaintance or communication with Lira. He undergoes several days of torture and is to be executed because he still refuses to confess. He is led in secret by an old native woman to see Lira and her newly born child. The former lovers meet and act as strangers to each other. The story ends with the king stepping in and explaining that this meeting was staged and that Carpenter had been on trial and was now acquitted of the charge. It is important that the king have a son; otherwise a degenerate cousin would assume the throne upon his death. "It may be that the child is your son," says the king, "but if so, he is the son of a true sahib who has shown that he can keep his secret sacred at all costs."

The artistry of this story lies in its plot development. Marshall does not simply depend upon a surprise ending but begins with a simple episode of love between two adolescents from the different worlds of the Orient and the West, and with a few brief strokes, he resolves a conflict between the universal power of the mating instinct and the mystical world of oriental values. Consequently, his manipulation of plot is not simply structuring events toward an unexpected ending but developing them from a simple arrangement into a context that leads the reader into the deeper implications of the story's action.

Edison Marshall's stories exist outside any clearly defined literary tradition, since by his own admission he read little or no contemporary fic-

tion for fear of being influenced by it. His exceptional narrative skill is evident throughout his major short stories, particularly because they demonstrate his ability to create a fictional world: in the hunting narratives, the reader sees and hears the life of the jungle or forest and senses the instinctive consciousness of the animals, which is never reduced to mere personification; in the later collection of romantic tales, the cultural world of Marshall's characters is not only sensitively portrayed but is also made a dominating force in the story's development. Marshall's artistry is centered in the dynamics of storytelling. In his words: "I suspect that I am an anachronism, and my career is *contre tempes*. I write ... precisely what I want to write with no thought of the audience. My first obligation is to tell an exciting story, and if I can instruct and inspire as well, all to the good."

Katherine Anne Porter

(15 May 1890 - 18 September 1980)

Joan Givner
University of Regina

See also the Porter entries in *DLB 4: American Writers in Paris, 1920-1939; DLB 9: American Novelists, 1910-1945;* and *DLB Yearbook: 1980.*

BOOKS: *My Chinese Marriage*, as M. T. F. (New York: Duffield, 1921);

Outline of Mexican Popular Arts and Crafts (Los Angeles: Young & McCallister, 1922);

Flowering Judas (New York: Harcourt, Brace, 1930); enlarged as *Flowering Judas and Other Stories* (New York: Harcourt, Brace, 1935; London: Cape, 1936);

Hacienda (New York: Harrison of Paris, 1934);

Noon Wine (Detroit: Schuman's, 1937);

Pale Horse, Pale Rider: Three Short Novels (New York: Harcourt, Brace, 1939); republished as *Pale Horse, Pale Rider and Other Stories* (London: Cape, 1939);

The Leaning Tower, and Other Stories (New York: Harcourt, Brace, 1944; London: Cape, 1945);

The Days Before (New York: Harcourt, Brace, 1952; London: Secker & Warburg, 1953);

A Defense of Circe (New York: Harcourt, Brace, 1955);

The Old Order: Stories of the South (New York: Harcourt, Brace, 1955);

A Christmas Story (limited edition, New York: Mademoiselle, 1955; trade edition, New York: Seymour Lawrence, 1967);

Ship of Fools (Boston & Toronto: Atlantic Monthly/ Little, Brown, 1962; London: Secker & Warburg, 1962);

Collected Stories (London: Cape, 1964; New York: Harcourt, Brace, 1965; enlarged edition, London: Cape, 1967);

The Collected Essays and Occasional Writings of Katherine Anne Porter (New York: Delacorte, 1970);

The Never-Ending Wrong (Boston: Little, Brown, 1977; London: Secker & Warburg, 1977).

TRANSLATIONS: *Katherine Anne Porter's French Song-Book* (Paris: Harrison of Paris, 1933);

Jose Joaquin Fernandez de Lizárdi, *The Itching Parrot*, translated, with an introduction, by Porter (Garden City, N.Y.: Doubleday, 1942).

Katherine Anne Porter's literary reputation rests on the twenty-seven stories in her *Collected Stories* (1964) rather than on the best-selling novel *Ship of Fools* (1962), on which she worked intermittently for thirty years. She was one of the most brilliant practitioners of the art of the short story, and, because of her style (personal as well as literary), she was an important influence on the generation of writers that followed her, which included William Humphrey, William Goyen, Tillie Olsen, Carson McCullers, Flannery O'Connor, and Eudora Welty. During Porter's lifetime, critical response was skewed by her flamboyant personality and by the distortions in her biographical record. She was seen as an aristocratic daughter of the Old South whose depictions of the Plain People were excursions into foreign territory. Critics treated her in a manner befitting an exquisite southern belle, vying in their praises. She was subjected to little rigorous criticism, but not surprisingly—since her friends were the leading exponents of New Criticism in the United States—her work was the focus of close readings, which led to minor shifts in emphasis in the interpretations of her stories.

Two years after her death the publication of *Katherine Anne Porter: A Life* (1982) made long-needed corrections in the biographical record. Coincidentally, the growing volume and sophistication of feminist criticism was providing new insights into women writers and their works. A climate had been created in which an understanding of the art and life of Katherine Anne Porter could finally be achieved.

Born Callie Russell Porter in a small log house on a dirt farm in the central Texas community of Indian Creek, she was the fourth of five children of Mary Alice Jones Porter and Harrison Boone Porter. Her mother died before she was two, and the four surviving children (Porter,

Courtesy of Paul Porter

Katherine Anne Porter

two sisters, and a brother) were raised by their paternal grandmother, Catherine Anne Porter, in Kyle, Texas. This household, dominated by a strong-willed woman, with Porter's ineffective father reduced to the role of an elder child, shaped her attitude toward gender roles and greatly influenced her aspirations, unusual in a woman of her time, for a career.

Notable among Porter's childhood experiences was the beginning of a lifelong friendship with a neighborhood child whom she perceived as an alter ego. The same age as Porter and, like her, one of four children, Erna Schlemmer belonged to an affluent family of German immigrants. From this early association Porter developed the interest in Germans that recurs in her stories and in her novel. The Schlemmers were remarkable in the small town for their cultural interests and for their trips back to Germany, when they took the children to the great European art galleries. Porter recorded her earliest memories of the family in her story "The Leaning Tower" (*Southern Review*, 1941; collected in *The Leaning Tower, and Other Stories*, 1944).

The death of Porter's grandmother in 1901

left the family emotionally and financially destitute because Harrison Porter, since his wife's death, had been incapable of caring for his family. During a period of dislocation after the grandmother's death, he left Porter with some cousins while he tried to resettle the family in San Antonio. These cousins (the Thompsons), their dairy farm, and their hired man provided rich material, which Porter used more than thirty years later for the story *Noon Wine* (*Story*, June 1937; separately published later that year).

In San Antonio, Porter enjoyed, for two years at the most, the only effective education she ever had. Aspiring to be an actress, she persuaded her father to let her enter a school which would provide training in the dramatic arts. He borrowed money so she and her older sister, Annie Gay (called Gay), could attend the Thomas School, an excellent private girls' school run by a Methodist principal. Equipped with the training she had there, Porter and her sister subsequently supported themselves and their father by running a little school of elocution, singing, and dramatic arts in a rented room in Victoria, Texas,

Porter's parents, Harrison Boone Porter and Mary Alice Jones Porter (Estate of Katherine Anne Porter)

where they had moved from San Antonio.

The necessity of earning a living was removed when Porter, a month after her sixteenth birthday, married John Henry Koontz on 20 June 1906. Her twenty-one-year-old husband worked as a railway clerk in Louisiana and was a member of a prominent ranching family in the town of Inez, not far from Victoria. The Koontzes were of German-Swiss descent and Catholic, and Porter (who had changed her name to Katherine Russell and liked to be called K. R.) was attracted to the rituals of their church. She converted to Catholicism when she was twenty and in later years said that she was raised a Catholic. Her experiences at this time in two heavily patriarchal institutions—the Koontz family and the Catholic church—were later to inform the story

"Holiday" (*Atlantic Monthly*, December 1960; in *Collected Stories*), which describes the sojourn of a young woman amid a German farming family in rural Texas.

In spite of Porter's conversion to her husband's faith, the marriage had been troubled from the beginning. She longed for a child and for an outlet for her artistic aspirations. She also resented her husband's limited job prospects and small income. When his job as railway clerk was terminated, he found work as a traveling salesman for a wholesale grocery firm in Houston. From there the Koontzes moved to a small apartment in Corpus Christi, and Porter was reunited with her old friend Erna Schlemmer, now Mrs. Glover Johns. Once again Erna's life provided a dramatic contrast with Porter's. Her husband was a successful businessman, and she was a contented wife and mother. The two spent a cheerful summer with daily visits together to the beach, and Erna was shocked when Porter decided to leave her husband and try for a career as a movie actress. To this end, Porter left Koontz in the spring of 1914 for Chicago, where there were several large movie studios. The nine-year marriage ended in divorce in 1915, and Porter at that time assumed the name Katherine Anne Porter.

The movie work turned out to be far more strenuous than she had anticipated, and in the fall of 1914 she went to Gibsland, Louisiana, to help Gay, who had been deserted by her husband and was undergoing a difficult pregnancy. In order to support her sister and the child, Porter made herself a costume and performed a song-and-dance routine on the Lyceum circuit in small towns in Louisiana. Eventually Gay regained her health, her husband returned, and Porter set out once more hoping to start a new life, this time in Dallas. She was there only a short time when she contracted tuberculosis. A friend of the Koontz family who saw her at the time was told that she did not expect to live much longer.

Porter had thought often about the experience of death and rebirth, being preconditioned to the experience of being "born again" at the revivalist meetings of her childhood. She told interviewer Barbara Thompson in 1963, "I knew what death was, and had almost experienced it. I had what the Christians call the 'beatific vision,' and the Greeks called the 'happy day,' the happy vision just before death. Now if you have had that, and survived it, come back from it, you are no longer like other people." In her fictional and autobiographical accounts, she indicates that this experience happened during the plague of influenza which swept the United States at the end of World War I. It is true that she nearly died of influenza in Denver, in the fall of 1918. Her family had already made arrangements for her burial, and the newspaper had prepared her obituary, when a shot of strychnine administered by an intern brought her back to life. But that was a brief incident. In fact, her long bout with tuberculosis and her incarceration in various hospitals were the turning points in her life.

When she first fell ill in 1915, since she had no means of support, she was sent to a grim "pesthouse" for the indigent in Dallas. Then in spring 1916 her brother managed to find the money to send her to Carlsbad Sanatorium near San Angelo in west Texas, a pleasant hospital sometimes described as having the atmosphere of a college campus. It was here that the fear of death, the long period (perhaps as long as two years) of inactivity, the time for reflection, and the close camaraderie of a group of intelligent and interesting young women caused her to reassess her life and redefine her goals. Among her fellow sufferers was Kitty Barry Crawford, one of the first women journalists in Texas and a committed career woman. Through this friendship Porter learned of Kitty's old school friend, Jane Anderson, a journalist and fiction writer who sent letters from England of her life there and her friendship with Joseph Conrad.

When she left her husband, Porter had already rejected the traditional life of a wife and mother and aspired to the most likely career for a woman of beauty and grace—that of a stage performer. After Carlsbad, however, she no longer thought of the performing arts as the only outlet for female expression; she thought of writing. Kitty and her husband ran a Fort Worth newspaper. When the two women were released from Carlsbad, they went to Fort Worth together, and Porter began to work on the paper. Later when Kitty's slow recovery made the move to a more healthful climate necessary, Porter accompanied her to Denver and shared a house not only with Kitty and her daughter but with the glamorous Jane Anderson, recently returned from Europe. Porter also began work on the *Rocky Mountain News*. There she did the work usually assigned to female reporters, covering the social events and the entertainment news. Yet the paper was a prestigious one, her position a step up from the *Fort*

John Henry Koontz, Porter's first husband, whom she married a month after her sixteenth birthday (Collection of Mary Koontz Lowery)

Worth Critic, and soon she had the title of dramatic editor.

Jane was not the encouraging mentor that Kitty was to Porter. Rather, she looked down on her as provincial, inexperienced and uneducated, and the two disliked each other. Yet Jane's experiences and her published stories gave Porter an idea of what she wanted to do next. Also, through Jane she met the musicologist Deems Taylor, who had come to Denver for a summer music festival. When he told her to go to New York, she readily took his advice and in the early fall of 1919 headed east by train for Greenwich Village.

There she did publicity work for a movie company and continued the kind of work she had done in Denver—adapting some myths and legends for a children's magazine and undertaking to ghostwrite *My Chinese Marriage* (1921), the story of a Michigan woman who had married a Chinese student and lived briefly as his wife in China. The most important influence on the future direction of her career, however, was her

*Porter in 1913, during a visit with her lifelong friend Erna Schlemmer Johns in Corpus Christi (Estate of
Katherine Anne Porter)*

meeting with an interesting group of young Mexican artists and revolutionaries—among them Adolpho Best-Maugard. Inspired by their accounts of Mexico, armed with introductory letters to their friends, and with contracts for some journalistic work to provide her support, Porter in late 1919 headed south by train and arrived in Mexico City just in time to witness Alvaro Obregón's inauguration as president.

By this time her writing ambitions had formed very clearly in her mind. She had vowed in a letter to her sister when she headed for New York that she intended one day to write as well as anyone in the United States. Eventually she made good that vow, but it was another ten years before she won recognition. As she entered her third decade she was only too conscious of her lack of qualifications for her chosen career. When she compared herself with Kitty Crawford, Jane Anderson, and the talented women she met in New York, such as Ernestine Evans, Genevieve

Taggard, and Elinor Wylie, or even with Erna, who had no career ambitions, she could not help being conscious of her educational deficiencies. She had left school when she was fourteen and had never traveled abroad, learned a second language, or been outside Texas for less than a year. The excursion to Mexico promised to make up some of her deficiencies in education and at the same time provide the wider range of experience that she deemed the proper stuff of fiction.

Her first six months in Mexico City during a time of political turmoil could hardly have been more eventful. Her friends included foreigners such as Joseph Retinger and Robert and Thorberg Haberman; revolutionaries such as Felipe Carillo, governor of the Yucatán, who was subsequently murdered; and artists such as David Siqueiros and Diego Rivera. Through her friends she was drawn into political intrigue and was forced to flee the country. Leaving by train, she found a haven once again with Kitty in Fort

Worth. She lived with the Crawfords, did some journalistic chores for them, and, most importantly, started to turn her recent experiences into short stories. Ever restless, she left after a few months, packing up her drafts of stories and heading for Greenwich Village. There she finished "María Concepción" and published it in *Century* magazine in December 1922. (It was collected in *Flowering Judas* in 1930.)

Nothing betrays so clearly Porter's lack of ease with her role as professional writer as her need to fantasize about her own creative process. Once her work was published, the problem disappeared because she could slip into the role of performer. In that guise she loved reading her stories on platforms and stages across the country (preferably under a single spotlight), elegantly coiffed and gowned, sometimes with a corsage (by her own account as big as a cabbage), and sometimes (according to Flannery O'Connor, in a 14 April 1958 letter to Cecil Dawkins) with long evening gloves which impeded her turning of the pages. But the actual writing presented difficulties. Typically, she described herself as going into self-imposed confinement with her muse. She loved telling the stories of these retreats—adumbrating the items in her spare but nutritious diet—as if speaking of pregnancies. She said "María Concepción" had a gestation period of seventeen days and seventeen nights in a rooming house in Washington Square. And although a 1922 letter from Mary Doherty indicates that Porter had intended for some time to place a story in *Century* magazine, she often told interviewers that a friend took the story to the editor of *Century* and that she was amazed to discover not only that it was accepted but that she was to be paid for it.

The story "María Concepción," which she designated as her first, was told to her by an archaeologist friend in Mexico City, and it resembles the three children's stories she had already published in its depiction of a strong woman character who triumphs over her weak husband, takes control of her own life, and sets her world in order. Her second story, "The Martyr," was based on her observations of Diego Rivera. It also appeared in *Century* magazine (July 1923; in *Collected Stories*), as did some of her essays about Mexico. She might have remained in New York for some time to mine this rich vein of material, but the political situation in Mexico changed again, and she was invited back by her artist friends to write the catalog for a proposed travel-

ing exhibition of Mexican folk art (which was published in 1922). Always prey to distractions and new adventures, she set aside her fiction writing and departed in spring 1922 for six months in Mexico.

When she returned from her second visit to Mexico, she was completely disillusioned with the country, the government there, and her friends. The exhibition for which she had written the catalog ran into problems and never reached the United States. Although Porter continued to be regarded as an expert on Mexico and was often asked to review books about the country for the New York papers, her interest had been transferred to the eastern seaboard—Connecticut, Massachusetts, and, most often, New York City—where she spent the next several years.

Porter continued to gain strength as a short-story writer, moving away from Mexico in her settings but developing the same themes. The output of these years is sometimes misunderstood by critics because of Porter's habit of setting aside stories, sometimes for decades, and publishing them much later. Of the stories written during the mid 1920s, "Holiday" is paradigmatic. She wrote Genevieve Taggard on 14 November 1924 that she had finished the story in a bath of sweat. That verdict was overly optimistic for, in fact, she could not decide on the ending. She set the story aside, finishing and publishing it only in 1960—a protracted struggle even for a writer noted for procrastination and for the inability to complete works in progress. Yet, in her envoi to *Collected Stories* she diagnosed her problem accurately. She wrote that the story reflected "one of my prolonged struggles, not with questions of form or style, but my own moral and emotional collision with a human situation I was too young to cope with at the time it occurred."

The story, written in the first person, describes the brief stay of the nameless narrator in the home of some Germans in rural Texas. The young woman by choice takes an attic room, where she hopes to write letters and read nineteenth-century romantic novels left by a previous guest. The Muller family's nationality indicates Porter's usual association of the German and the patriarchal. The family could hardly be more patriarchal in its structure—the men and children sit at different sides of the table, the women standing behind the men to serve them. The narrator's anomalous position at the table points to the theme of the story: the exploration of the place in a patriarchal community of the

Drawing by Ross Santee of the title character in "María Concepción," an illustration for the December 1922 Century *magazine publication of the story, which was later collected in* Flowering Judas *(1930)*

woman who does not fill the traditional roles of wife and mother. At the climax of the story the narrator is left behind by the family as they attend the burial of the mother, who has died suddenly and unexpectedly. Also left behind is the crippled, uncoordinated, mute servant girl Ottilie. The narrator, hearing her howling like a member of a subhuman species, learns that she is actually a daughter of the family, grieving for her mother. The two have a brief outing together and share a moment of camaraderie in the spring sunshine. In the outcast, speechless girl, the narrator recognizes briefly an image of herself, an alter ego. If the resolution of the story eluded Porter, it was because she never managed to resolve her own ambivalent feelings toward patriarchal society. She never managed to belong, but she never reconciled herself to not belonging, and the idea of being an outcast (bringing back memories of her deprived childhood) frightened her. She was particularly alarmed by the idea of developing strong bonds with women, a fear which accounted for her lifelong panic in the face of female sexual overtures. In "Holiday" her feelings about aligning herself with women

find expression in the narrator's brief outing with the grotesque figure of Ottilie. At one point, as she tries to grasp the servant girl, the narrator's "fingers slipped between her clothes and bare flesh." The narrator crosses "the shallow ditch where the small road divided from the main travelled one," but such deviations and byways are not for her, and she quickly returns to the main thoroughfare.

"The Cracked Looking Glass," also written in the mid 1920s, was successfully finished and published in May 1932 (in *Scribner's Magazine*; collected in the enlarged edition of *Flowering Judas*, 1935). Its theme is a variation of that of "Holiday," in that it describes the adventures of an anomalous woman. Nominally, Rosaleen is a dutiful daughter of the patriarchy, a married woman. Actually, she is cut off from the roles of wife and mother because of her elderly husband's impotence. The frustration is extreme for a woman caught in the double bind of being married to an ineffective man and at the same time prevented from using her own energies. Nevertheless, Rosaleen tries to find expression for her creative energy in nontraditional ways. She forms liaisons with young men, and, through her storytelling, she mesmerizes anyone who will listen. When her frustrations become unbearable, she takes a holiday from her married life on the pretext of a reunion with her sister. Unfortunately, a chance encounter with a young man turns nasty, and fearing disgrace she returns thankfully to the safety of the domestic hearth and to the fragmented image of herself that she finds in her cracked mirror. The dream she has had at the beginning of the story, that of a prowling cat who ends up in a trap, has proved prophetic.

While the resolutions to these two stories, which touched her own life deeply, evaded Porter and delayed their publication, other works were brought to completion. "Virgin Violeta," the last of the early Mexican stories, published in *Century* in December 1924 (in *Collected Stories*), is based on Porter's shocked reaction to the Nicaraguan poet Saloman de la Selva's account of the seduction of a young girl. In the story, young Violeta watches the mannered courting gestures of her older sister and her male cousin, Carlos. These take place under the half-alert eyes of a chaperone and under a framed picture of the Virgin and St. Ignatius Loyola. Violeta, spontaneous and natural like a wild creature, resists being "framed." She leaves herself open to the illicit sexual advances of the cousin, and the story ends

Porter outside her apartment on Gay Street in Greenwich Village, circa 1923 (Estate of Katherine Anne Porter)

with her terror, her hysteria, and, finally, her reduction to the status of a child protected by her parents. Her fright is caused not only by what she unleashed in Carlos but in herself: "He was loathsome. She saw herself before him, almost as if his face were a mirror. Her mouth was too large; her face was simply a moon; her hair was ugly in the tight convent braids."

In another successfully completed story, "Magic" (*transition*, Summer 1928; in *Flowering Judas*), a woman is "framed," her image reflected in a mirror as her storytelling maid brushes her hair. The woman is riveted by a story of the violent abuse of a prostitute in a New Orleans brothel. The prostitute runs away, but as in so many of Porter's stories of escape from the degrading or menial life of patriarchal institutions, her flight turns out to be only a brief "holiday." She is brought back by a "magic" spell, is welcomed

by the madam and the male clients, and settles down happily in what she now recognizes as her home. What connection the respectable listener makes between her own life and her maid's story can only be guessed at, as she stares at her reflection and sniffs her perfume.

During this period of residence in New England and New York, Porter made many literary friends who influenced her work in various ways. Some were women, such as the glamorous poets Genevieve Taggard, Elinor Wylie, and, most important, Josephine Herbst, who became a friend of very long standing. As always there was also an endless stream of lovers, even another husband, Ernest Stock, with whom Porter lived briefly in 1925. A Chilean lover, Francisco Aguilera, echoing Shelley's poem "From Ariel to Miranda," gave her the name "Miranda," which she later used for the name of her fictional representative. She often said that her story "Rope" (*The Second American Caravan*, 1928; in *Flowering Judas*)—a vivid account of marital discord—was based on the quarrels of friends and their husbands, but it seems most likely that it was based on her own relationship with Stock.

She also met at this time a group of sophisticated southerners who became lifelong friends: Allen Tate, Caroline Gordon, Andrew Lytle, and Robert Penn Warren. Some of them were working on biographies, and following their example, Porter decided to try her hand at the genre. Her choice of subject—the New England theologian Cotton Mather—seems at first glance a surprising departure from her usual themes, but in fact she had always been interested in witchcraft, witches, and religious fanaticism. It was Mather's role in the Salem witch trials that drew her to him, and in order to do the research at the Essex Institute she spent several months in 1927 in Salem. From there, in the summer of 1927, she made the short journey into Boston to join many of her friends who were involved in the protest movement surrounding the execution of Nicola Sacco and Bartolomeo Vanzetti.

Her time in Salem did not lead to the completion of her biography, but it did have another unexpected result. The dark atmosphere of the town evoked memories of her early life and the stark poverty and moral rectitude of her grandmother's house. Setting aside the biography, she wrote "The Jilting of Granny Weatherall" (*transition*, February 1929; in *Flowering Judas*), the story of a strong matriarchal figure based on her own grandmother. This was an important turning

Porter's second husband, Ernest Stock, in his Royal Flying Corps uniform (Collection of Marian L. Burroughs). The couple married in 1925 but soon separated.

point because it signaled her discovery of the rich lode of material to be found in her Texas roots, and it provided the subject matter and setting of most of her subsequent stories. In retrospect it seems clear that Porter's art was moving steadily and surely toward maturity. Yet as she approached forty, struggling with the (for her) impossible Cotton Mather project and publishing at most two stories a year, she felt that she was making little progress. In addition her personal life was always tormented. The series of lovers at once reflected and reinforced her own uncertainties about herself. They were all different, each one assigning her to a different, unsatisfactory role, and each one doomed to fail. Aguilera, serenading her as Miranda, saw her as a beautiful work of art and muse, but had no intention of marrying her; Sumner Williams wanted to make her his wife, to support and protect her in a traditional marriage, but she knew that would not work; Ernest Stock did marry her, but she found the confinement of marriage unbearable; Matthew Josephson, happy with his own wife and children, wanted her for his mistress while he acted as her literary mentor. It was this last relation-

ship which, more than any other, disappointed her and pushed her toward the breakdown in health she suffered in 1928.

Some of the anguish of that relationship and the discomfort with herself is expressed in one of her best stories, "Theft" (*Gyroscope*, November 1929; in the 1935 edition of *Flowering Judas*), in which a nameless woman comes to see that her own passivity and failure to assert herself sours all her relationships and encourages unscrupulous people to exploit her. The final revelation of the story is that the woman is not only causing her own losses but is responsible for the moral decline of those around her.

It may have been true that Porter allowed her lovers to take advantage of her, but she did have many loyal friends who frequently offered to help her. Herbst once complained that she herself was perceived as a strong, self-sufficient woman and that no one felt protective toward her as they did toward the apparently vulnerable and charming Porter. Herbst's comment is well illustrated by the events of 1928 when, in the wake of Porter's ill health, her New York friends rallied to send her to Bermuda to rest, recover, and work on the biography of Mather.

The five months Porter spent in Bermuda were some of the most productive of her life, but not in the way she or her friends anticipated. The biography was not finished, but instead many of her future successful stories began to take shape. Unexpectedly she found in her new surroundings an atmosphere conducive to the development of her Texas stories. In the stories she told to her friends, she had already shed the deprivations of her childhood and presented her early life as one of aristocratic elegance. In Bermuda, renting the gracious home of an affluent local family, she found the physical details of the ancestral home she had always wanted. There "Old Mortality" (in *Pale Horse, Pale Rider*, 1939), the stories of "The Old Order" sequence (in *The Leaning Tower*), and "The Fig Tree" (lost until 1961; in *Collected Stories*) began to form in her mind.

Years later she acknowledged the five months on Bermuda as a period of great creativity, but when she returned to New York the problems that had caused her physical decline were still there. The relationship with Josephson was as hopeless as ever, and, combined with her inability to finish the biography, it gave her a sense of failure and sterility. Once again, she began to think of Mexico as a place to which she might escape. In this mood in December 1929 she picked up some notes she had made during her first visit to Mexico and had intended to work into a novel, and pulled together a story she called "Flowering Judas." She mailed it to the journal the *Hound and Horn*, and when it appeared there in the spring of 1930, it made her literary reputation. Soon afterward Harcourt, Brace published her first short-story collection, *Flowering Judas*, in a limited run of six hundred copies.

Porter based "Flowering Judas" on two episodes which had happened in Mexico City ten years earlier. One was her experience with a fat revolutionary whose unwelcome attentions had made one of Porter's friends, Mary Doherty, ask Porter to act as chaperone while he serenaded her on his guitar. The other was a story Mary told about a young revolutionary in prison who had persuaded her to let him have more than the usual harmless number of sleeping pills she normally carried to him in jail. When Mary returned the next day, she discovered that the young man had killed himself. She told Porter about a terrible dream she had in which the young man appeared and accused her of killing him.

Porter named the obese revolutionary Braggioni and made him, like all her villains, a complete caricature. He looms in the story like a huge purple-and-yellow Easter egg. With a cat's eyes and a pig's paunch, he is the hideous embodiment of the seven deadly sins. In contrast to Braggioni is the young, innocent prisoner, Eugenio. Yet the focus is on neither of these characters but on the supposedly innocent girl, Laura. Like the protagonist of "Theft," she turns out, through her passivity, to be responsible for the abuses that go on around her. She promotes Braggioni's wickedness by not resisting him and is, therefore, guilty for his moral decline and his neglect of his wife as well as for the death of Eugenio. The implication is that if Braggioni is a self-serving, self-indulgent villain, he has not always been so. Once he was a young idealist in both politics and love. It is Laura, the main character, and those like her who caused him to change from idealist to opportunist. In turn, Laura's own indifference and alienation are explored. They are caused by her own sense of uncertainty about herself, her loss of the religious faith of her childhood, and her anomalous position as an independent woman living outside the family structure.

Porter's strength was not in showing growth and change in her characters, and in any event such a method was more appropriate to the novel than the short story. But she made a spontaneous discovery of a method of suggesting all the ramifications of the situation. As the story was nearing completion a pattern of symbolism appeared to her, not imposed upon the story but implicit in it, an extended use of the symbolic naturalism she had used in "Theft." As she told interviewer Barbara Thompson in 1963, she remembered the Judas tree in the little Mexican patio where Mary Doherty lived, and it suggested to her the betrayal of Jesus by Judas Iscariot. The tree suggested lines in T. S. Eliot's poem "Gerontion" (1920), a description of spiritual aridity and betrayal:

. . . In the juvescence of the year
Came Christ the tiger

In depraved May, dogwood and chestnut, flowering
    judas,
To be eaten, to be divided, to be drunk
Among whispers. . . .

She also thought of the epigraph Eliot used for his poem, from William Shakespeare's *Measure for Measure*, a play also closely related to her theme: "Thou hast nor youth nor age / But as it were an after dinner sleep / Dreaming of both."

Above all, she thought about the source of Eliot's description of the dogwood and flowering Judas in Henry Adams's account of the eastern springtime. It had been just over a year since she read and discussed Adams's autobiography, *The Education of Henry Adams* (written in 1905; commercially published in 1918), with Josephson, and she remembered "The Dynamo and the Virgin," in which Adams compares his feelings on seeing the forty-foot dynamo with those of an early Christian contemplating the cross. The chapter suddenly seemed highly relevant to Laura's sense of being stranded between the lost religion of her childhood and her inadequate faith in machines. With her title Porter brought Eliot's and Adams's works to bear on her theme, and the rich superstructure of symbolism lifted the story onto a new plane and marked a great step forward in her art.

When the story appeared in the spring of 1930, Porter was already on a boat to Mexico for her longest period of residence in that country. She had barely recovered from the pain of her association with Josephson and might have been expected to avoid further amorous entanglements and devote herself to the Mexican novel she in-

Eugene Dove Pressly, whom Porter married on 11 March 1933 (Estate of Katherine Anne Porter). Pressly was the model for the character David Scott in Ship of Fools (1962).

tended to finish. But she was simply incapable of imagining her life without a relationship with a man. Her frame of mind at this time is indicated by a letter she wrote to Herbst from the S.S. Havana. She said she was on deck in the moonlight, listening to the orchestra playing, and wondering why it was that, at such moments when the scene was set for a romantic encounter, she was alone. She did not remain alone for long; soon after she arrived in Mexico, she met Eugene Dove Pressly, a young man thirteen years her junior, who became her companion for the next few years and her third husband.

Pressly, who worked as a secretary for the Crane Foundation in Mexico City, was an attractive man who, by all accounts, had a surly, withdrawn personality. Most of Porter's old friends disliked him, interpreting his silence (perhaps correctly) as hostility. All agreed that he lacked the stature of Porter, who was already beginning to assume the role of grande dame. Always ready to mock her own garrulousness, Porter said that he had no need to talk because she talked so much. No doubt his subdued nature was largely responsi-

ble for the relative success of this relationship, which lasted longer than any other in her life. If he seemed to outsiders dull and ineffective beside his forceful partner, that situation was one which, to her, was a familiar repetition of her childhood home. Pressly provided the traditional heterosexual relationship she needed and at the same time allowed her a certain amount of autonomy within that relationship.

Since the union with Pressly encouraged the side of her that yearned for a traditional domestic life, she at once threw herself into the role of chatelaine. She rented a large house in Mixcoac, spent much time acquiring furniture and tending the garden, collected a menagerie of small animals, entertained a great deal, and had a stream of house guests, including Hart Crane, Malcolm and Peggy Cowley, and other Americans. Not surprisingly, she made little progress on the Mexican novel, which was destined like the Cotton Mather project never to be finished.

The time in Mexico did, however, yield one important work. In Mexico City she had met the Russian director Sergei Eisenstein, who was making the film Que Viva Mexico (unfinished, but later edited by Marie Seton and released as Time in the Sun, 1939). Through her old friend Adolpho Best-Maugard, she was invited to spend some days at the film set and possibly work on the film as a scriptwriter. The visit was not a success, and she quickly rejected the idea of working on the film, but the experience provided the material for Hacienda, which was published in the October 1932 issue of the Virginia Quarterly Review before its separate publication in 1934. The long story is a roman à clef which provides a vivid portrait of Eisenstein, his entourage, and various Mexican actors and assistants, including Best-Maugard. It also expresses Porter's own feelings about Mexico, as she prepared to leave it for the last time. Thoroughly disillusioned with the political and social atmosphere, she returned subsequently only for brief visits as an invited guest, and then only decades later. Of course, Porter's restlessness and desire to move was only partly related to the country itself. Her unresolved personal conflicts made her prey to dissatisfaction with all locations and, feeling alienated everywhere, she always hoped that she might feel at home in some other, distant, future place. In August 1931 her desire to move was encouraged by the Guggenheim Foundation, which had awarded her a fellowship as a result of the success of her book *Flowering Judas*. She decided to go, as she had long wished, to Europe.

For the journey to Europe with Pressly, Porter chose the cheapest means of travel she could find, the S.S. *Werra*, which she called a tramp steamer disguised as a passenger ship. The *Werra* left from Veracruz on the Yucatán peninsula and called along the way at various ports, including Havana and Tenerife. The passengers were of all nationalities, including Germans returning thankfully to their homeland after long periods of "exile" in Mexico. Since she was not married to Pressly, Porter was assigned to a cabin with two other women, and, gregarious by temperament, she got to know many of the passengers. She took detailed notes on the journey and immediately saw in it the possibility for a story, which she tentatively called "The Promised Land." It eventually grew into *Ship of Fools*.

She said later that, when she set out on her first trip to Europe, her destination was France and that she landed in Germany only because she chose a German ship bound for Bremen as the cheapest available transportation. Yet the interest in that country sparked by her association with German families in Texas (she did, in fact, tell Erna Schlemmer that she went to Germany on her account) drew her to the country and kept her in Berlin for six months after arrival.

She was, as usual, feeling frustrated because so few of her planned fictions ever got finished. Most of her friends published far more than she did, and she began to despair of ever accomplishing what she knew she was capable of. Once in Berlin, she tried to cut down on the distractions and live in isolation and write. Pressly went off as planned to Spain, where his knowledge of the language qualified him for a secretarial job at the American Embassy. Porter, who had encouraged him to go because she longed for some time alone, remained behind in a pension. Pressly's absence did not, of course, guarantee for Porter a cloistered productive time. Almost immediately she made contact with the American community and was being escorted around Berlin by Herbert Klein, a young journalist, and attending soirees at the home of Sigrid Schultz, the head of the *Chicago Tribune* bureau. At one of the dinner parties in Berlin she attracted the attention of Hermann Goering and was escorted by him (accompanied by his bodyguard) on at least one outing to a nightclub. Once again, her active life and lively, gregarious personality were exposing her to experiences that provided the material for fic-

tions, if she could only find the time and concentration to finish them. In one sense, she was working on future fictions, because in Berlin, as on the S.S. *Werra*, she kept detailed accounts of everything that happened. Not only did she write up her impressions for future use, but her loneliness and sense of isolation made her a copious letter writer. Her letters to such friends as Malcolm Cowley and Caroline Gordon and her daily outpourings to Pressly were almost as long as stories. Without realizing what she was doing, she was writing draft after draft of "The Leaning Tower," sharpening and refining her observations and expressions in preparation for the time when she would write the final version.

In the early months of 1932, disappointed that Goering had quickly lost interest in her, and knowing that the long projects would never be completed, she decided to go to Spain and marry Pressly. A stopover in Paris, however, and a fling around the city with a new beau made her change her mind, and after a short visit with Pressly in Madrid she returned to Paris. She valued the stability of Pressly's devotion but said she had fallen in love with Paris and the city was his only rival. Yet when he was transferred to Geneva, she followed him. Hoping for a compromise between his constant distracting presence and the solitary life, she chose to move to a small hotel in Basel, where he could easily visit her on the weekends. During his weekday absences, she did manage to work, and stories began to appear more quickly than before. But one of the most important results of her months in Basel was that the place sparked memories of her early dark years in Texas, just as her time in Salem, Massachusetts, had done years before. In the chill fall, her mind went back to the period after her grandmother's death when she had been left with her relatives Ellen and Gene Thompson on their small farm outside Buda, Texas. She wrote the first draft of *Noon Wine*, the story which, more than any other, captures the atmosphere of her native state. The story describes the effect on a failing dairy farm of a mysterious stranger from another region—a hired man—who proves to be the salvation of the little farm. The harmony caused by his presence is abruptly shattered when an unscrupulous character comes from the North, announcing that the hired man is an escaped criminal and seeking to return him to prison. In a moment of rage the hired man kills the bounty hunter and, finally, after many vain efforts to convince his neighbors that he is not a mur-

Porter in her Paris apartment, 1934 (Estate of Katherine Anne Porter). She never learned to play the piano, but liked to have one in her home.

derer, kills himself. The title of the story suggests the rough wine of a southern region, well expressing Porter's consciousness that she was mythologizing and capturing the essence of her own region. In an essay, "Noon Wine: The Sources" (*Yale Review*, September 1956), she purports to explain the origin of the story. She deliberately dissociates herself from firsthand knowledge of common people like the Thompsons, saying she never knew them, but she does accurately describe the effect of her European travels on her own understanding of Texas: "My time in Mexico and Europe served me in a way I had not dreamed of, even, besides its own charm and goodness: it gave me back my past and my own house and my own people—the native land of the heart."

The story, begun in Basel, was not finished there because once again she moved. The reason this time was that Pressly was posted to the American Embassy in Paris, where both of them longed to live. When they were settled exactly where they wished to be and with a steady income, there seemed no reason not to marry. On 11 March 1933 Porter married for the third time, in a small ceremony attended by Ford Madox Ford and his companion Janet Biala.

The next three years, in which she was Mrs. Eugene Pressly, living first in a small apartment overlooking a convent on the boulevard Montparnasse and later in a pleasant studio apartment on rue Notre Dame des Champs, were perhaps the happiest of her life. Since Pressly was at work all day, she had time to work. She developed a pleasant group of friends, and the café society of

Paris curbed to some extent her hospitality and prevented another lapse into domesticity on a large scale. She met Matthew Josephson again, as well as her old friend Josephine Herbst, and made new friends who were to be lifelong supporters—Glenway Wescott, Barbara Harrison (who later married Wescott's brother Lloyd), and Monroe Wheeler.

Porter often wondered why Paris should have cast such a spell on her and caused such a flowering of her art. She said she did not love the cold drizzling gray city for all the obvious reasons—the American bar life, the pretty clothes, the people, the theaters, the art shows, and the music. Perhaps the best account of the coming together of external circumstances with her internal development, producing her full maturity as a writer, is given in her 29 April 1945 letter to Josephine Herbst:

> I didn't begin to feel contemporary, or as if I had come into my proper time of life until just a few years ago. I think after I went to Europe— Europe was the place for me, somehow, Paris the city, France the country. From there, I got a perspective and somehow without struggle my point of view fell into clear focus, right for *me*, at any rate; and what other rightness is there for the individual.

Perhaps the crucial factor was the geographical and cultural distance of Paris from Texas. No place can have been more antithetical to Texas than Paris, and it gave her a new perspective on her early years. She was able to contemplate her childhood in an atmosphere that revived no painful memories of poverty, death, and strict fundamentalist morality. In Paris she started for the first time to research her family's roots because, she said, she did not want to feel like an exile. Yet for all the so-called research, the family past she reconstructed was based more on her imagination than on historical records, and the result was not factual but fictional. In a speech she gave at the urging of Sylvia Beach to the American Women's Club in Paris in 1934, she spoke of a novel-in-progress about her family, the first section of which was called "Legend and Memory." Predictably, the novel was never finished, but the material appeared in the form of stories. It was used in "Old Mortality" and the sequence of eight stories eventually collected under the title *The Old Order* (1955), which began to appear at this time.

During Porter's three years in Paris, while many works were started only to be abandoned, others did actually come to fruition, were sent out, and published. Porter had always relied on the assistance of friends in placing her work. Herbst had been instrumental in placing two early stories in *transition*, and Josephson had promoted the 1930 publication of *Flowering Judas*. Now, once again, friends helped to usher her work into print. Barbara Harrison and Monroe Wheeler ran a small press called Harrison of Paris, which published fine editions. They brought out *Katherine Anne Porter's French Song-Book* in 1933 and *Hacienda* in 1934. Adding to her sense of accomplishment, Harcourt, Brace in 1935 republished the *Flowering Judas* collection, adding "Theft" and "That Tree" along with two new stories: "The Cracked Looking-Glass" and "Hacienda." Other friends back in the United States were now associated with important literary magazines—Allen Tate with the *Virginia Quarterly* and Robert Penn Warren with the *Southern Review*. Her stories were quickly published in these journals.

Two stories, both published in 1935, are remarkable treatments of a subject which had appeared in "Virgin Violetta"—sexual terror. The difference is that, whereas in the early version of the theme she had distanced herself from her subject, she now moved courageously into her own autobiographical experience. In "The Grave" (*Virginia Quarterly Review*, April 1935; in *The Leaning Tower*), through her fictional representative Miranda Gay, Porter describes an incident which had happened about the time her grandmother died in 1901. Porter was accompanying her brother on a rabbit-shooting expedition when he shot and eviscerated a female rabbit carrying young. In the story Miranda is just experiencing the first stirrings of her female destiny. She is growing tired of being a tomboy and yearns for the trappings of femininity: pretty clothes, jewelry, and perfumes. The knowledge thrust upon her so crudely and abruptly when her brother lays open the womb of the dead rabbit is a shock. Yet this knowledge of the other, more dangerous, side of female destiny seems something she has really known all along (Miranda's mother, like Porter's own, had died as a result of childbearing).

The rabbit incident is powerful enough to stand alone as a complete story, but Porter adds another dimension by placing it in the context of Miranda's whole life, showing that the effects of this small event are neither trivial nor transient and that the past is not easily sloughed off. She tells of Miranda years later walking through the marketplace of a strange city in a strange country; a Mexican-Indian vendor shows her a tray of dyed sugar sweets. Suddenly the sights and sounds converge to bring back to her mind, from where it has long lain buried, the memory of her brother and the rabbit. The memory horrifies her, reinforcing the frightening nature of the incident and showing the capacity of past experiences to lie dormant and make an unexpected ambush.

The story is one of Porter's finest and most popular, frequently anthologized and endlessly explicated. Students of her work have commented on the grave image, which links the episodes and underscores the connection of life and love and death. They have continued to explore the suggestion of such objects as the coffin screw, shaped like the dove of Venus (symbol of earthly love), and the womb-grave of the dead rabbit. Like "Flowering Judas," this story is one of the great achievements of her art as a short-story writer. Yet, when it was accepted for publication by Tate, Porter was surprised because she had regarded it as a fragment of a novel.

"The Circus" (*Southern Review*, 1935; in *The Leaning Tower*) is an almost equally powerful treatment of the same theme. Here Miranda has her first experience of a family excursion. She is taken to the circus in the company of her older cousin who is also named Miranda Gay, the family beauty, and young Miranda wishes to be "exactly like her" when she grows up. She is still a child, however, and does not understand why little boys stand under the bleachers looking under the skirts of the women and grinning without friendliness. The sinister grins of the boys are replicated by one of the circus clowns, who dangles apparently out of control from the high wire. His head turns from side to side like a seal, and he blows "sneering kisses from his cruel mouth." At the sight of the man's face, Miranda is overwhelmed with fear and is carried out, screaming hysterically. As in "The Grave" the terror of the moment comes back to haunt her as a nightmare. Thus, Porter, having transformed her family's outward appearance to one of elegant southern gentility, was able to bear witness unflinchingly to her own deepest inner terrors.

Having through time, geographical distance, and fictional shaping reassembled her own past and achieved success as a writer, it was perhaps natural that she should wish to reinforce

her newly achieved sense of wholeness by returning to her family and to the scenes of her childhood. To this end, she left Pressly in Paris in 1936 and made the trip to the United States. In New York she visited the friends recently returned from Paris who had already become very important to her—Monroe Wheeler, Glenway Wescott, and Barbara Harrison, who had just married Glenway's brother. But the most important part of her trip was her visit to Houston, where her father, sisters, and brother now lived. Greeted as a returning celebrity, she made acquaintance with the next generation of the family—her sister Gay's daughter, Ann, and her brother's son, Paul. For the rest of Porter's life and in spite of temporary quarrels, Ann and Paul became her protégés and surrogate children. With her father and sister, Porter made the pilgrimage back to Indian Creek, where she was born and where her mother was buried. It was an important scene of reconciliation with her past, and she celebrated it in a poem ("Anniversary in a Country Cemetery"), recalled it often, and ever afterward thought of Indian Creek as her home.

She had hoped that her teenage niece, Ann, who was interested in ballet, would join her in Paris, but when Porter returned, her situation there began to deteriorate. Sometimes she later explained her quick return to the United States as being due to the European political situation. In fact, her relationship with Pressly was coming to an end, her creativity was at its peak, and once again she needed a change of surroundings.

In the fall of 1936 Porter and Pressly left Paris and, on arrival in New York, went their separate ways. Porter went into a period of seclusion in an inn in Pennsylvania, choosing that location in part because it was near to Erwinna, the home of Herbst.

Porter's difficulties with the final drafts of stories which were almost complete in her mind had, as we have seen, various causes. She was always prey to distractions and to affairs of the heart; she had developed in her best stories the techniques of probing painfully repressed experiences, and this process, as she aptly expressed it herself, was as painful as tapping spinal fluid. But there was another compelling reason for her difficulty in completing projects. This was her difficulty in reconciling herself to the activity of being a professional writer, not associated in her mind with femininity. This difficulty was shared by many of her writer friends and literary admir-

Porter with her fourth husband, Albert Erskine (standing), and Monroe Wheeler (photograph by George Platt Lynes). Erskine and Porter were married on 19 April 1938.

ers, who, captivated by her delicacy and beauty, related to her as suitors rather than as fellow professionals. Wescott, for instance, described her fancifully as looking like Marie Antoinette Porter playing her typewriter as if it were a spinet. The poet-priest Raymond Roseliep wrote many poems praising her beauty, depicting her in her library with volumes of Cotton Mather, Laurence Sterne, and Voltaire, resting her hand beside them "moonflower pale / light as a mussel shell." The descriptions are charming, but they were highly destructive as she waged her own constant struggle between being an artist and being a desirable woman.

She could best cope with the tensions generated by that struggle by going into seclusion. Of the many retreats she made during her life, none was more productive than the period she spent in the Doylestown Inn. There she finished the two long stories *Noon Wine* and "Old Mortality" and was well into a third—"Pale Horse, Pale Rider"—before the pleading of Eugene Pressly

drew her back in early 1937 to live with him in New York.

In the early months of 1937 there was a brief attempt to patch up the marriage, painfully complicated by his reluctance to admit that the relationship was over and by her desire to be free. When he finally left New York for a posting to South America, Porter decided to leave the city, too, so she would be far away if he decided to return. Some of her southern friends had been urging her to visit, and she set out that summer for Clarksville, Tennessee, to visit Tate and Gordon at their home, Benfolly. She was not the only writer visiting the hospitable Tates; Robert Lowell, eager to learn from Tate, had set up a tent in the garden, and Albert Erskine, the business editor of the *Southern Review*, was also a guest. Erskine had fallen in love with Porter's stories that had been published in the review, and now the young man fell in love with their glamorous silver-haired author. When the two sat up talking long into the night, Tate lay awake listening to them, incredulous that, despite the twenty-year age gap between them, they should be lovers.

When the visit ended in September, Porter settled in an apartment in New Orleans, and Erskine made regular weekend visits from Baton Rouge (he was a graduate student at Louisiana State University) to be with her. During those weeks, she tried to maintain the momentum in her writing that she had established in the previous fall. But inevitably, the excitement of the affair slowed down the progress on the third long story, and perhaps for that reason, when she visited her family for Christmas, she decided to remain in Houston for the next few months. She told Erskine she had developed bronchial troubles and had to stay near her family doctor, but her health seems to have been the excuse rather than the reason for her decision to find an apartment in Houston.

In the comparative calm of Houston, where her only distractions were visits with family members, she managed to finish "Pale Horse, Pale Rider" (*Southern Review*, 1938; in the collection of the same name). This long story was based on her experiences twenty years earlier when she nearly died of influenza in Denver. The details of her life and work in the story, when compared with the columns she wrote in the *Rocky Mountain News*, are so accurate that it seems likely that she was working from a draft written close to the time of the actual events. Yet when she created the character of Adam, Miranda Gay's boyfriend, she drew on her own most recent lover—Erskine. The story became Porter's portrait of the artist as a young woman, the story of an aspiring writer struggling to survive the many forces threatening her existence. Miranda is sickened by the anti-German propaganda, the trumped-up patriotism, and the exploitation and materialism of the patriarchal figures in authority, in the military, and on the paper for which she works. Her lover dies, and she almost dies, but ultimately she emerges, alive but much changed by her experiences. With that ambitious story successfully completed, Porter again took up "The Promised Land," the story based on the journey she had made in 1931 from Vera Cruz to Bremerhaven, Germany.

During the weeks of work on "Pale Horse, Pale Rider," she had been exchanging daily letters with Erskine. Many of these dealt with his urging her to marry him and with her resistance. Finally she gave in and decided that what he wished was what she also wished. Her divorce

Dust jacket for Porter's 1939 collection, which comprises her major fiction of 1936-1938

from Pressly was finalized on 9 April 1938; on 16 April Erskine came to Houston to drive her back to Louisiana. She carefully prevented his meeting her family (so embarrassingly at odds with her descriptions of them) and went with him to Baton Rouge, where the two were married, with Robert Penn Warren acting as best man, on 19 April.

The marriage was doomed almost from the moment the vows were taken. In the first place, Erskine, who was in his mid twenties, learned only during the actual wedding ceremony that Porter was approaching fifty. His shock deeply humiliated Porter. In addition, he turned out to be much more assertive than the taciturn Pressly. He resented his wife's attendance at conferences and the time she spent on her work. Apart from his objections to her activities, he was the constant distraction that any partner would have been for her. She once more played the housewifely role, making a home, cooking on a grand scale, entertaining, and socializing. In her 1938

Christmas letter to Erna Schlemmer Johns she wrote almost boastfully of her marital happiness, clearly sensing that it was this aspect of her life rather than her literary achievements that represented status in Erna's eyes. Her letter could not have been more false, because the truth of her situation during the next few years was that personal unhappiness and literary success went hand in hand. In 1939 she published *Pale Horse, Pale Rider*, a collection of three of her best long stories—the title story, *Noon Wine*, and "Old Mortality". She was the heroine of the hour, and when she attended a literary conference in Olivet, Michigan, the audience applauded spontaneously when she entered the room.

On the literary horizon there was only one cloud. The Texas Institute of Letters, the chief literary body in her native state, had just established a prestigious award. When she was told that she was certain to win, she was jubilant at the thought of gaining honor in her own state, and the medal promised to put the final touch on her reconciliation with her roots. But the medal went instead to J. Frank Dobie for his book *Apache Gold and Yacqui Silver* (1939), the decision being justified by the "indigenous nature of his subject matter" and his long residence in Texas. Porter was outraged, and all the recent goodwill toward her native state collapsed in an instant. Over the years, the attempted rapprochement between Porter and Texas was repeated. She thought that the University of Texas was going to name a library for her; she planned to return to live where she had grown up on the outskirts of Austin; the University of Texas thought that she would give her papers to its library. But nothing ever came of these plans. Porter yearned always to be accepted as the first and most distinguished Texas writer—which she was—but that honor and all the attendant honors went instead to Dobie. It was he who had a room set up in his honor, a literary fellowship named for him, and eventually a university chair named for him. Although writers such as William Humphrey and William Goyen have acknowledged that they were inspired by Porter, the apparently virile image of Dobie as literary forebear seems to have been more acceptable to Texans.

The end of her fifth decade should have been the happiest time of Porter's life, because she was at the peak of success, but disappointments came crowding in. She and Erskine decided to separate in spring 1940, and she traveled north to Yaddo, the artist's colony in upstate New York. Once again her recent achievements caused her to be received almost with reverence, and the unofficial title "Queen of Yaddo" was given to her. She mourned the fall of France, her failed marriage, and the conclusion that she would never be a wife, and she despaired over her homelessness (reinforced by her estrangement from Texas), worried about her state of financial insolvency, and tried to write.

As she listened to the radio accounts of events in Europe, her thoughts turned to her months in Berlin in 1931, and it was the story of that time, "The Leaning Tower," which claimed her attention. She saw that, from her present perspective, she could finish it. By doing so she hoped to solve several of her problems. She would feel that she had rallied her creative energies once more, and she hoped she could sell the story for a good price. And there was another factor. She had been worrying a great deal about what the artist should do in time of war and, with her strong moral sense, had wondered if her own kind of writing, based on her own personal inner life, was not somehow irrelevant in a time of global disaster. The Berlin story was not narrowly personal, and since it dealt with the menace of the Nazi party, she felt that it was a contribution to the war effort.

In her final version she drew on experiences of a widely disparate kind. For the first and only time she made her fictional representative male, a choice which possibly reflects her identification with Pressly during the Berlin period. For protagonist Charles Upton's childhood friend Kuno Hillentafel, whose German background and German holidays had first stimulated his interest in Germany, she drew on her own memories of Erna Schlemmer:

> He and Kuno did not remember when they had not known each other. Their first recollection was of standing next to each other in a row of children like themselves, singing, or some such nonsense—it must have been kindergarten. . . .
>
> Mr. Hillentafel took his family back to Germany for a few months every two years, and Kuno's post cards, with their foreign stamps, coming from far-off places like Bremen and Wiesbaden and Mannheim and Heidelberg and Berlin, had brought the great world across the sea, the blue silent deep world of Europe, straight to Charles' door.

In depicting the boarders of Rosa Reichl's pension, where she had stayed in Berlin, Porter did not change the names but modified the characters, often grafting onto them traits of people she had known elsewhere. Rosa, whom she had really liked, she turned into an unpleasant character. She suppressed Rosa's anti-Semitism but heightened other offensive characteristics, making the landlady barely able to mask her hatred for the American Upton, whose rich country she believes responsible for the poverty of her own.

Herr Bussen, a young Dalmatian student, is the closest to the original of her characters, and she used a melancholy conversation she had with him in the hall about Rosa's insults to him and another male boarder. For the military boarder she had not actually seen, she used the character of Hermann Goering, but she suppressed what Goering had told her about Jews, that they were the ruin of Germany and that, once the Hitler regime was established, there would not be a Jew left in Germany with any political or cultural or economic power. She did, however, use Goering's Nietzschean views.

For the Polish boarder, Tadeusz Mey, she used the appearance, mannerisms, and even whole speeches of Joseph Retinger which she had recorded twenty years earlier in Mexico City. She even gave her character the family name of Retinger's guardian, Zamoyski (spelled differently). When Mey is introduced he says: "Tadeusz Mey. Polish in spite of the misleading name. Indiscreet grandmother married an Austrian. The rest of my family have names like Zamoisky, lucky devils." And her notes for the story show that she used the memories of another Pole, Janice Tworkov Biala, the companion of Ford Madox Ford: "The Polish Jews also believe that a Jew must not pass a Catholic Church at midnight, for at that moment the souls of all members of the congregation who have died that year will rush out in the shape of swine and drown him (told to me by Biala, Polish Jewish painter as told from her grandmother)."

In this story she uses again the symbolic method which had proven so effective in "Flowering Judas." Here the symbolic structure developed from a cheap souvenir of the Leaning Tower of Pisa, which Pressly had crumpled in his hand as they looked at pensions in Berlin.

On its simplest level it is a tawdry tourist souvenir, as fragile and insubstantial as the dreams of the characters. The original, built in the fourteenth century as a bell tower, is an ornate and impressive structure in sturdy white marble. Yet a weakness in the foundations caused it to settle and lean, so that it cannot be used as a bell tower and must receive injections of cement to prevent its collapse. Thus it suggests the Germany that Porter saw, so apparently solid and substantial, and yet undermined by a basic flaw in its foundations.

The Leaning Tower of Pisa, furthermore, has sinister overtones from its association with Canto XXXIII of *The Inferno*, in which Dante meets the traitors to their own country. Dante's central figure here is Ugolino of Pisa, who conspired with an enemy party of that city to defeat a rival faction within his own Guelph party. His treachery merely served to weaken his own party, so that he found himself at the mercy of the very enemy with whom he had conspired. He was imprisoned with his children and grandchildren in a tower (not the Leaning Tower, although Dante's story is closely connected with Pisa through Ugolino's imprecation against that city), and the keys were thrown away, so that he was forced to watch his children and grandchildren die of hunger before he himself starved to death. Although critics disagree about the meaning of Ugolino's statement that, after the death of his children, hunger had more power than grief, a frequent conclusion has been that Ugolino resorted to cannibalism. Even if the historical facts behind Dante's story do not entirely justify this interpretation, the fact that Ugolino in hell is feeding upon the skull of his enemy suggests that Dante saw such activity as the appropriate fate for those who hope to advance themselves by destroying their own kind and kin.

The account of the chance-gathered occupants of Rosa Reichl's pension, all wanderers or defectors from their native lands, is full of images from the Ugolino story. The claustrophobic atmosphere of the house in which they are all shut up, waiting for disaster and with no means of escape (only for Upton is a ship coming from America), is conveyed in images of imprisonment, starvation, cannibalism, death, and hell.

The Leaning Tower of Pisa has always been associated with Galileo because of his birth in that city, and according to legend he once dropped weights from the tower to test his theory of the velocity of falling bodies. Since the life story of Galileo evokes and dramatizes the dilemma of the clear-sighted man in a misguided society, it is relevant to the predicament of the man of vision in Nazi Germany. When Porter was asked about the responsibility of writers in time of war she replied, "The responsibility of the artist toward society is the plain and simple responsibility of any other human being, for I refuse to separate the artist from the human race: his prime responsibility 'when and if war comes' is not to go mad" ("Three Statements about Writing," in *The Collected Essays*, 1970).

A more detailed answer to the question is contained in "The Leaning Tower." While one cynical artist retreats into the romantic music of Frédéric Chopin, Upton does not see his art as a refuge or a retreat. He sees very clearly what is going on around him, does not deceive himself, and records the ghastly caricatures of human beings that he sees.

It seems possible that if Porter had settled down quietly at Yaddo and kept on working, the flow of creativity which produced the fine "Leaning Tower" might have been sustained. Instead of doing so, however, she found another major distraction. She decided to solve her problem of homelessness by buying a house in the Saratoga Springs area.

Not only did the purchasing of the house, the arranging for renovations, and the choosing of furniture prove to be a major distraction, but it also plunged her into financial difficulties. First of all, the projected sale of "The Leaning Tower" for a large sum of money to *Harper's Bazaar* had fallen through. She had sent in the story, and, as she wrote in a 21 January 1941 letter to Glenway Wescott, it had been returned to her "most expertly disemboweled" by one of the editors. Porter realized that the story was very long, but she had understood it was to run in two installments. Furious, Porter demanded that the story be returned rather than have it appear in a shortened form. She then sold it to the *Southern Review* for a mere three hundred dollars. Then, in an effort to raise money for her house, she signed several contracts for works that she could not possibly finish on time. These included a novel then called "No Safe Harbor," which was to be an extended version of "The Promised Land," based on her journey to Germany ten years earlier. The contracts and deadlines, as they always did, set up a sense of panic, which in turn led to creative paralysis.

She was fifty years old, lonely, unhappy, financially insolvent, and, after she moved into her house, geographically isolated. Most discouraging of all was her sense that her creative powers were failing. And the cap sheaf of her misery was that in spring 1942 she had to undertake alone the dreary journey to Reno, Nevada, to get the quick

divorce Erskine was now urging on her because he wanted to remarry. Perhaps her desperation alone can account for the shabbiest episode of her life, which took place during her period of residence in Reno.

In any life there are shameful incidents. Porter shared with many writers of her generation the anti-Semitism rife in America before World War II. To that she added her own personal feelings of racism. She came out publicly against integration in 1958, and she filled the margins of her books with slurs against blacks and Jews. Her doing so conflicts dramatically with the high moral tone she adopted toward Nazi Germany and with the political acumen she claimed as a result of her firsthand experience of events in Mexico and in Germany. Like her attitudes to feminism, her attitudes to politics were ambivalent and confused, as might be expected given her confusions about her own position as a woman in a patriarchy. Confusion, however, hardly excuses the episode in Reno, when she was interviewed by FBI agents on the subject of Josephine Herbst and gave testimony so damaging that Herbst was subsequently unable to find work. Herbst knew that someone had informed against her but never guessed the identity of the informant, and the friendship between the two women continued.

At this time Porter's publishers optimistically expected the novel. Instead, they were besieged by constant requests for money—further advances on works-in-progress, pleas for new contracts, and instructions to sell parts of unfinished works to well-paying magazines. Finally, they realized that finished projects, least of all a full-length novel, were not forthcoming. In 1944, therefore, Harcourt, Brace published her third and last volume of previously uncollected stories—*The Leaning Tower, and Other Stories*. Only two of the stories had been finished in the last eight years, and most of the volume consisted of stories written and published during her years in Paris. The book was deservedly praised, but the publishers were correct in assuming that Porter's chief period of creativity was over.

She continued to work at her writing, occasionally publishing stories and essays, working intermittently on the novel, in which the interest of publishers and readers never abated. And her own life continued to be as eventful as ever. In 1943 she moved to Washington, D.C., where Tate, who held the first Chair of Poetry at the Library of Congress, recommended that she be

HOLIDAY

BY KATHERINE ANNE PORTER

In FLOWERING JUDAS, *her first and memorable collection of short stories, and in* PALE HORSE, PALE RIDER, KATHERINE ANNE PORTER *evoked some beautiful impressions of the Southwest, a region which she knew as a girl and which is very dear to her. To it she returns in this new and exceptional narrative.*

Illustration by Thomas W. Nason for the December 1960 Atlantic Monthly *publication of a story that was later included in* Collected Stories *(1964)*

asked to fill out John Peale Bishop's uncompleted term as consultant. After that she went to Hollywood and worked for two brief terms as a scriptwriter; she stayed on in California to write for a while, then moved back east. She taught in a series of universities—including Stanford, Michigan, and Washington and Lee—and she was a Fulbright Fellow at the University of Liege in Belgium. Finally, after all her peregrinations, she settled once again in Georgetown and, to everyone's surprise, finished the novel, now called *Ship of Fools*.

Ship of Fools was published on 1 April 1962. Not surprisingly, for a work that had been so long anticipated, it achieved instant bestsellerdom. In addition, the movie rights were sold soon after publication, and the film, directed by Stanley Kramer, had a brilliant cast that included Vivien Leigh, Simone Signoret, Lee Marvin, Jose Ferrer, Jose Greco, and Oskar Werner. As a result, Porter achieved in her mid seventies the financial security that had eluded her for most of her life. Henceforth, as long as her strength lasted, she was able to travel, buy designer clothes and expensive jewelry, and live in

the style she had always craved. And she could boast that she had earned it all herself.

After the immediate excitement had subsided, more sober critical judgments were made. It was generally agreed that her reputation would rest not on the novel—which upon reflection appeared to have some major flaws—but on her short stories. This consensus was evident when the *Collected Stories*, published in 1964, won both a National Book Award and a Pulitzer Prize.

When in 1940, at the time of the fall of France, she had written an introduction to the Modern Library edition of *Flowering Judas and Other Stories*, Porter said that her aim in all her work had been "to understand the logic of his majestic and terrible failure of the life of man in the Western World." *Ship of Fools* was clearly her final and most ambitious attempt to achieve her aim. As on her own journey, her fictional ship was headed toward a Germany in which Hitler was just beginning his rise to power. The ship *Vera* was presented as a microcosm of Europe in 1931, written with the immediacy of observations made at the time and finished decades later with the benefit of hindsight. She summed up her theme in a September 1961 talk she gave to students at the University of Wichita in Kansas (in *Katherine Anne Porter: Conversations*, 1987):

> I had seen these criminals—these *clowns*—like Hitler, and was stricken by an idea: if people like this could take over the world! Of course there were all the good people who didn't believe in the clowns but they still let them, the clowns, commit the crimes good worthy people would commit if only they had the nerve. How else would you account for the collusion in evil that enables a creature like Mussolini, or Hitler, or Huey Long, or McCarthy . . . to get hold of things. . . . The tragedy of our times is not an accident but a total consent.

It was a simplistic assessment of a situation she lacked the historical knowledge and political acumen fully to understand. Oddly enough, the movie version of the novel, by making one small change, illustrated how dangerously near to melodrama her vision was. The film transformation of Herr Rieber, her obnoxious caricature of a Jew, into a benign character made the good/evil conflict apparent. An anonymous reviewer in the *Times Literary Supplement* (2 November 1962) well expressed the final verdict on the novel: "One cannot help wondering whether she *knows* enough—of German history, of the sources of modern anti-Semitism, of European middle-class speech and values—or whether that knowledge has penetrated the exquisite, but very special range of her feelings."

For all that, *Ship of Fools* presented the culmination of the theme which had run through her work as a powerful undertow since the beginning—the plight of women trying to live and express themselves in a patriarchal society. She had written in "Holiday," the story which had for so long resisted resolution, "I felt divided into many fragments, having left or lost a part of myself in every place I had travelled, in every life mine had touched, above all, in every death of someone near to me that had carried into the grave some part of my living cells."

If Porter was not equipped for the ambitious scope of the theme she articulated in numerous interviews, she was more sure than ever before in her treatment of the powerful concern which had always informed her work—the destiny of the woman who refuses to be confined by the limited roles allotted to her under patriarchy. Her German boat under a German captain, as-

Porter, circa 1962, when Ship of Fools *was published (photograph by Arthur B. Long)*

sisted by a German doctor, becomes in her hands, once again, a representative patriarchal institution. When she traveled to Germany in 1931, she was struggling with the work of Virginia Woolf, and *Ship of Fools*, like *The Voyage Out* (1915), includes all the possible female roles. There are wives and widows, prostitutes, virgins, and a bride. Yet three characters seem closely related as Porter's own fictional representatives, a fact noted by critic Daniel Curley, who found three Mirandas in *Ship of Fools*, and by Stanley Kramer. These characters are the young artist Jenny Brown, the middle-aged divorcée Mary Tread-well, and the aristocratic political activist La Condesa, now in her advanced years and still a brave soul in spite of her drug addiction and predilection for young men.

At first glance the ending of the novel might seem to be as unresolved as the endings of "Holiday" and "The Cracked Looking Glass." The joy which many of the characters feel at the end of the voyage, when they see their fatherland, is undercut by the knowledge of the political morass into which they are headed. At the same time, the three women characters closely associated with Porter's point of view make strong gestures of independence and defiance. They are not drawn back into traps, domestic and otherwise, as were so many of the characters in the earlier stories—such as Violeta, Rosaleen, the narrator in "Holiday," and the prostitute in "Magic." La Condesa refuses the conciliatory gestures of Dr. Schumann and leaves him to face the knowledge of his shameful exploitation of her. Mary Treadwell strikes back at the drunken oaf who insults her and all women. It is true that she is lonely as she sails away from the *Vera*, but she is also self-sufficient and knows where she is headed. Above all, Jenny Brown, locked in a destructive relationship with her lover, determines that "this business" is not going to throw her off track as an artist. And she realizes that there is going to be something more important in her life than David Scott or any other man.

Porter had eighteen more years in which to enjoy the material rewards of her novel, to celebrate the collections of her stories and essays, and even to produce a new work. *The Never-Ending Wrong* (1977), an account of her participation in the Sacco-Vanzetti affair, was published three years before her death, to coincide with the fiftieth anniversary of the execution. It was an ill-advised book which added no luster to her literary reputation and illustrated once more her tenuous grasp of political situations.

Perhaps the most important event of her last years for students of her work was the setting up of the Katherine Anne Porter Room in the McKeldin Library at the University of Maryland. The room houses her extensive personal archive of manuscripts and letters, her collection of books, photographs, furniture, and other items of personal memorabilia.

The geographical separation of her literary and physical remains was indicative of a lifelong ambivalence on many subjects, most of all her relationship with her native state. After her death, her ashes were, at her request, taken back to Texas, to the cemetery in Indian Creek where her mother was buried.

Interviews:
Barbara Thompson, "The Art of Fiction XXIX—Katherine Anne Porter: An Interview," *Paris Review*, no. 29 (Winter-Spring 1963): 87-114;

Enrique Hank Lopez, *Conversations with Katherine Anne Porter: Refugee from Indian Creek* (Boston: Little, Brown, 1981);

Katherine Anne Porter: Conversations, edited by Joan Givner (Jackson & London: University Press of Mississippi, 1987).

Bibliographies:
William A. Sylvester, "A Selected and Critical Bibliography of the Uncollected Works of Katherine Anne Porter," *Bulletin of Bibliography*, 19 (January 1947): 36;

Edward Schwartz, *Katherine Anne Porter: A Critical Bibliography* (New York: New York Public Library, 1953);

Louise Waldrip and Shirley Ann Bauer, *A Bibliography of the Works of Katherine Anne Porter and A Bibliography of the Criticism of the Works of Katherine Anne Porter* (Metuchen, N.J.: Scarecrow Press, 1969);

Robert F. Kiernan, *Katherine Anne Porter and Carson McCullers: A Reference Guide* (Boston: G. K. Hall, 1976);

Joan Givner, Jane DeMouy, and Ruth M. Alvarez, "Katherine Anne Porter," in *American Women Writers: A Critical Reference Guide from Colonial Times to the Present*, edited by Lina Mainiero (New York: Ungar, 1979);

George Bixby, "Katherine Anne Porter: A Bibliographical Checklist," *American Book Collector*, 1 (November-December 1980): 19-33.

Biography:
Joan Givner, *Katherine Anne Porter: A Life* (New York: Simon & Schuster, 1982; London: Cape, 1983).

References:
Charles A. Allen, "Katherine Anne Porter: Psychology as Art," *Southwest Review*, 41 (Summer 1956): 223-230;

Allen, "The Nouvelles of Katherine Anne Porter," *University of Kansas City Review*, 29 (December 1962): 87-93;

Harold Bloom, ed., *Katherine Anne Porter*, Modern Critical Views Series (New York, New Haven & Philadelphia: Chelsea House, 1986);

George Core, "The Best Residuum of Truth," *Georgia Review*, 20 (Fall 1966): 278-291;

Daniel Curley, "Katherine Anne Porter: The Larger Plan," *Kenyon Review*, 25 (Autumn 1963): 671-695;

Jane DeMouy, *Katherine Anne Porter's Women: The Eye of Her Fiction* (Austin: University of Texas Press, 1983);

Winfred S. Emmons, *Katherine Anne Porter: The Regional Stories* (Austin: Steck-Vaughn, 1967);

Joan Givner, "The Genesis of *Ship of Fools*," *Southern Literary Journal*, 10 (Fall 1977): 14-30;

Givner, "Her Great Art Her Sober Craft: Katherine Anne Porter's Creative Process," *Southwest Review*, 62 (Summer 1977): 217-230;

Givner, "Katherine Anne Porter and the Art of Caricature," *Genre*, 5 (March 1972): 51-61;

Givner, "Katherine Anne Porter, Eudora Welty and *Ethan Brand*," *International Fiction Review*, 1 (January 1974): 32-38;

Givner, "Katherine Anne Porter: Journalist," *Southwest Review*, 64 (Autumn 1979): 309-321;

Givner, "The Plantation of This Isle: Katherine Anne Porter's Bermuda Base," *Southwest Review*, 63 (Autumn 1978): 339-351;

Givner, "Porter's Subsidiary Art," *Southwest Review*, 59 (Summer 1974): 265-276;

Givner, "A Re-reading of Katherine Anne Porter's *Theft*," *Studies in Short Fiction*, 6 (Summer 1969): 463-465;

Givner, "Two Leaning Towers: Viewpoints by Katherine Anne Porter and Virginia Woolf in 1940," *Virginia Woolf Quarterly*, 3 (June 1977): 85-90;

Caroline Gordon, "Katherine Anne Porter and the ICM," *Harper's*, 229 (November 1964): 146-148;

Lodwick Hartley, "Katherine Anne Porter," *Sewanee Review*, 48 (April 1940): 206-216;

Hartley, "The Lady and the Temple," *College English*, 14 (April 1953): 386-391;

Hartley and George Core, eds., *Katherine Anne Porter: A Critical Symposium* (Athens: University of Georgia Press, 1969);

Willene Hendrick and George Hendrick, *Katherine Anne Porter*, revised edition (Boston: Twayne, 1988);

James William Johnson, "Another Look at Katherine Anne Porter," *Virginia Quarterly Review*, 36 (Autumn 1960): 598-613;

S. Joselyn, "Animal Imagery in Katherine Anne Porter's Fiction," in *Myth and Symbol*, edited by Bernice Slote (Lincoln: University of Nebraska Press, 1963), pp. 101-115;

M. G. Krishnamurthi, *Katherine Anne Porter: A Study* (Mysore, India: Rao & Raghavan, 1971);

M. M. Liberman, *Katherine Anne Porter's Fiction* (Detroit: Wayne State University Press, 1971);

Harry John Mooney, Jr., *The Fiction and Criticism of Katherine Anne Porter* (Pittsburgh: University of Pittsburgh Press, 1957; revised, 1962);

William L. Nance, *Katherine Anne Porter and the Art of Rejection* (Chapel Hill: University of North Carolina Press, 1964);

Robert L. Perry, "Porter's 'Hacienda' and the Theme of Change," *Midwest Quarterly*, 6 (Summer 1965): 403-415;

Leonard Prager, "Getting and Spending: Porter's 'Theft,'" *Perspective*, 11 (Winter 1960): 230-234;

Marjorie Ryan, "*Dubliners* and the Stories of Katherine Anne Porter," *American Literature*, 31 (January 1960): 464-473;

Edward Greenfield Schwartz, "The Fictions of Memory," *Southwest Review*, 45 (Summer 1960): 204-215;

Schwartz, "The Way of Dissent: Katherine Anne Porter's Critical Position," *Western Humanities Review*, 8 (Spring 1954): 119-130;

William Bysshe Stein, "'Theft': Porter's Politics of Modern Love," *Perspective*, 11 (Winter 1960): 223-228;

Darlene Harbour Unrue, *Truth and Vision in Katherine Anne Porter's Fiction* (Athens: University of Georgia Press, 1985);

Thomas F. Walsh, "Deep Similarities in 'Noon Wine,'" *Mosaic*, 9 (Fall 1975): 83-91;

Walsh, "The Dream Self in 'Pale Horse, Pale Rider,'" *Wascana Review*, 2 (Fall 1979): 61-79; reprinted in *Katherine Anne Porter*, edited by Harold Bloom;

Walsh, "Identifying a Sketch by Katherine Anne Porter," *Journal of Modern Literature*, 7 (September 1979): 555-561;

Walsh, "The Making of 'Flowering Judas,'" *Journal of Modern Literature*, 12 (March 1985): 109-130;

Walsh, "Xochitl: Katherine Anne Porter's Changing Goddess," *American Literature*, 52 (May 1980): 183-193;

Robert Penn Warren, Introduction to *Katherine Anne Porter: A Collection of Critical Essays*, edited by Warren (Englewood Cliffs, N.J.: Prentice-Hall, 1979);

Warren, Introduction to *Katherine Anne Porter: A Critical Bibliography*, by Edward Schwartz (New York: New York Public Library, 1953);

Warren, "Katherine Anne Porter (Irony with a Center)," *Kenyon Review*, 4 (Winter 1942): 29-42;

Glenway Wescott, "Katherine Anne Porter Personally," in his *Images of Truth* (New York: Harper & Row, 1962), pp. 25-58;

Ray B. West, Jr., *Katherine Anne Porter* (Minneapolis: University of Minnesota Press, 1963);

West, "Katherine Anne Porter: Symbol and Theme in 'Flowering Judas,'" *Accent*, 7 (Spring 1947): 182-187;

Joseph Wiesenfarth, "Illusion and Allusion: Reflections in 'The Cracked Looking-Glass,'" *Four Quarters*, 12 (1962): 30-37;

Wiesenfarth, "Internal Opposition in Porter's 'Granny Weatherall,'" *Critique*, 11, no. 2 (1969): 47-55;

Wiesenfarth, "Negatives of Hope: A Reading of Katherine Anne Porter," *Renascence*, 25 (Winter 1973): 85-94;

Wiesenfarth, "The Structure of Katherine Anne Porter's 'Theft,'" *Cithara*, 10 (May 1971): 64-71;

Edmund Wilson, "Katherine Anne Porter," *New Yorker*, 20 (30 September 1944): 64-66; republished in his *Classics and Commercials: A Literary Chronicle of the Forties* (New York: Farrar, Straus, 1950), pp. 219-223.

Papers:

The Katherine Anne Porter Room at the McKeldin Library, University of Maryland, is the chief repository of Porter material, containing most of her manuscripts, papers, correspondence, personal library, books, phonograph records, photographs, furniture, and assorted memorabilia. Other libraries have small collections of Porter material. After the McKeldin Library, the Beinecke Rare Book and Manuscript Library of Yale University is the largest repository of Porter material. It contains, for example, her important correspondence with George Platt Lynes, Robert Penn Warren, Matthew Josephson, and Josephine Herbst.

Marjorie Kinnan Rawlings

(8 August 1896 - 14 December 1953)

Victor Lasseter
California State University, Bakersfield

See also the Rawlings entries in *DLB 9: American Novelists, 1910-1945* and *DLB 22: American Writers for Children, 1900-1960.*

BOOKS: *South Moon Under* (New York & London: Scribners, 1933; London: Faber & Faber, 1933);

Golden Apples (New York: Scribners, 1935; London: Heinemann, 1939);

The Yearling (New York: Scribners, 1938; London & Toronto: Heinemann, 1938);

When the Whippoorwill— (New York: Scribners, 1940; London & Toronto: Heinemann, 1940);

Cross Creek (New York: Scribners, 1942; London & Toronto: Heinemann, 1943);

Cross Creek Cookery (New York: Scribners, 1942); republished as *The Marjorie Rawlings Cookbook: Cross Creek Cookery* (London: Hammond, Hammond, 1960);

Jacob's Ladder (Coral Gables, Fla.: University of Miami Press, 1950);

The Sojourner (New York: Scribners, 1953; London: Heinemann, 1953);

The Secret River (New York: Scribners, 1955);

The Marjorie Rawlings Reader, edited by Julia Scribner Bigham (New York: Scribners, 1956).

SELECTED PERIODICAL PUBLICATIONS—
UNCOLLECTED:

FICTION

"Cracker Chidlings," *Scribner's*, 89 (February 1931): 127-134;

"In the Heart," *Collier's*, 105 (3 February 1940): 19, 39;

"The Provider," *Woman's Home Companion*, 68 (June 1941): 20 ff.;

"Black Secret," *New Yorker*, 21 (8 September 1945): 20-23;

"The Friendship," *Saturday Evening Post*, 221 (1 January 1949): 14, 44;

Mountain Prelude [novel], *Saturday Evening Post*, 26 April - 31 May 1947.

NONFICTION

"Hyacinth Drift," *Scribner's*, 94 (September 1933): 169-173;

"Regional Literature of the South," *College English*, 1 (February 1940): 381-389;

"Here is Home," *Atlantic*, 169 (March 1942): 277-285;

"Who Owns Cross Creek?," *Atlantic*, 169 (April 1942): 439-450.

Although Marjorie Kinnan Rawlings is best known as the author of *The Yearling* (1938) and thus—inaccurately—as a writer of children's books, her other novels deserve consideration as serious fiction. So do her short stories, eleven of which were collected in *When the Whippoorwill—* (1940). Three others were included by Julia Scribner Bigham in *The Marjorie Rawlings Reader* (1956). Still others, also worth reading, remain uncollected.

Marjorie Kinnan was born on 8 August 1896 in Washington, D.C., where her father, Arthur, worked for the Patent Office. She did not become a writer by accident. As a child, she read Sir Walter Scott and Charles Dickens and also liked to tell stories to other children; by the age of six she was writing for the children's pages of area newspapers. At age eleven she won a two-dollar prize for a story, which was published in the *Washington Post*, and at fifteen a seventy-five dollar second prize in the *McCall's* Child Authorship Contest for a story called "The Reincarnation of Miss Hetty" (published in the magazine in August 1912).

A year after her father died in 1913 and Marjorie had finished high school, her mother, Ida May Traphagen Kinnan, moved with Marjorie and her younger brother, Arthur, to Madison, Wisconsin. There Marjorie majored in English at the university, was active in campus literary life and dramatics, made Phi Beta Kappa her junior year, and graduated in 1918.

In May 1919 she married the writer Charles A. (Chuck) Rawlings, Jr., whom she had known at Wisconsin, and moved with him to Rochester, New York. From 1919 to 1928, she wrote newspaper features, advertising copy, and, starting in 1926, a daily syndicated column for the *Rochester Times-Union* called "Songs of the Housewife," which consisted of sentimental poetry and was eventually syndicated to fifty other papers. She also tried, unsuccessfully, to publish fiction.

In 1928 the couple made a decision that would revive Marjorie's stalled career as a fiction writer: shortly after vacationing in Florida in 1928, they bought a farm with an orange grove in Cross Creek, near Gainesville, Florida. (Her husband's brothers were already living nearby.) Marjorie greatly preferred rural to city life, and both her marriage and her writing needed revitalizing.

Like Henry David Thoreau's move to Walden Pond, Rawlings's move allowed a literary concentration she might not have found in the city.

"Let's sell everything and move South," she had exclaimed to her husband. "How we could write!" (as quoted by biographer Elizabeth Silverthorne). Now, instead of writing for newspapers, she tended the orange groves and cows, largely abandoned the romantic and melodramatic tendencies of her apprentice fiction, and instead wrote about the new, tangible matter of the Florida backcountry, which she called "the invisible Florida."

The relatively undeveloped land of north-central Florida provided a rich vein for fiction and changed her publishing fortunes. In 1930 she sold the first Florida piece she submitted to *Scribner's* for $150: "Cracker Chidlings," subtitled "Real Tales from the Florida Interior" (published in February 1931). These eight sketches about Florida Crackers (poor whites) attracted the attention of Scribners editor Maxwell Perkins, who urged Rawlings, as Sherwood Anderson urged William Faulkner, to write about the undiscovered region she lived in. Rawlings followed her first success with *Jacob's Ladder* (*Scribner's*, April 1931; separately published in 1950), which she also sold in 1930, this time for $750. "Gal Young Un," published by *Harper's* in June and July 1932, won the 1933 O. Henry Memorial Award and was later collected in *When the Whippoorwill—*.

In 1933 she immersed herself deeper in rural Florida by staying for several months with a Cracker family in the scrub country. This experience resulted in her first novel, *South Moon Under* (1933), the story of a young Cracker who becomes a moonshiner and kills the cousin who betrays him. The novel was a Book-of-the-Month Club selection and a critical success. Her private life, though, was troubled; in the same year, her divorce from Chuck Rawlings became final. The marriage had produced no children.

Golden Apples (1935) is an uneven second novel about an Englishman exiled in nineteenth-century Florida. Rawlings's greatest book, of course, is *The Yearling*, a novel about a young boy in the nineteenth-century Florida wilderness who has to kill his pet deer because it destroys the family's meager crops. This story of Jody Baxter's initiation into manhood became a best-seller, won Rawlings a Pulitzer Prize, was made into a popular movie, and made her a national celebrity.

For commercial reasons, Scribners usually followed a successful novel with a collection of short stories. Rawlings's only collection of short fic-

Illustration for the December 1936 Scribner's Magazine *publication of a story Rawlings included in her first collection,*
When the Whippoorwill— *(1940)*

tion to appear in her lifetime, *When the Whippoorwill—*, was published in 1940, two years after *The Yearling*. Thematically the eleven stories fall into two groups: affirmative, comic tales and stark tales of disappointment and betrayal. The comic stories belong to the tradition of local color. Their chief appeal is the revelation of regional customs, speech, and character; their greatest limitation is the frequent failure to transcend the anecdotal.

Three of these stories are narrated by Quincey Dover, a large, talkative Wife-of-Bath character, whose tales constitute a "marriage group." In "Cocks Must Crow" (*Saturday Evening Post*, 25 November 1939), she admits that age has made her more tolerant of her husband's pleasures, in this case his fondness for cockfighting. Her view of marriage, however—that a "man worth his salt can't be helt [*sic*] to heel like a bird dog"—is too oversimplified to create a story with lasting interest.

Quincey's narration of "Benny and the Bird Dogs" (*Scribner's*, October 1933) continues the theme that a wife must hold a husband by a very long rope. Rawlings's real purpose, however, is not so much to explore the complex relationship between husband and wife as to relate the eccentric escapades of Uncle Benny Mathers and his ubiquitous bird dogs. His wife, old Hen, is almost incidental to the story; his true wife seems to be his Ford, which is "trained" to take him home drunk.

Quincey tells of another kind of partnership in "Varmints" (*Scribner's*, December 1936), this time that of two rivals, Luty Higgenbotham and Jim Lee, who unwisely buy a mule together. Luty encourages the mule to chew tobacco and drink rum, increasing the tension between the partners. The tall tale ends in a legal snarl, when the drunken mule dies in Quincey's sweet-potato bed, and she takes the owners to court for damages.

"Alligators" (*Saturday Evening Post*, 23 September 1933) is a series of loosely related anecdotes (originally told to Rawlings by a Cross Creek neighbor, Fred Tompkins) full of alligator lore and highlighted by the narrator's tall tale about riding an alligator "like a halter-broke mule." Another local-color story is "Plumb Clare Conscience" (*Scribner's*, December 1931), in which a moonshiner amusingly tells how he fooled prohibition agents by outwaiting them in the mosquito-infested palmetto scrub; the plot has too little conflict, however, to develop a compelling theme.

The comic stories, in short, amuse as they faithfully reproduce local customs, dialect, and character. They are not, however, as the Quincey Dover stories have been called, a major literary accomplishment. In contrast to comic masterpieces such as Faulkner's "Spotted Horses" (1931) or Eudora Welty's "Petrified Man" (1939), which humorously and imaginatively explore the contradictions of human behavior, these comic pieces primarily entertain.

The other stories in *When the Whippoorwill—* explore some of the deeper themes encountered in Rawlings's novels: the value of being close to nature, the inevitability of being betrayed by others, and the integrity of persevering in the face of misfortune. "A Crop of Beans" (*Scribner's*, May 1932) pits a young dirt farmer and his wife against the frost. As Rawlings once did, the Gentrys save their bean crop from a hard frost that kills the other local crops. They make a substantial profit for the first time, but the bank in which they grudgingly deposit their money fails, and they must plant again. "The Pardon" (*Scribner's*, August 1934) is another story of waiting. A man just released after years in prison returns home to find a child he has not fathered. He senses an affinity between himself and the child, however, and seems patiently determined to start again.

"The Enemy" (*Saturday Evening Post*, 20 January 1940) tells of poor cattlemen whose cattle are endangered when a wealthy outsider from the North buys rangeland and fences off the water supply. An irrascible old man, Doney Milford, wants to fight the newcomer, but the old cattleman's son determines to settle the issue without violence and ends up working for the newcomer. The real enemy, Rawlings suggests, is not the Yankee or the fence but life itself.

The only story in the collection without a Florida setting is "A Mother in Mannville" (*Saturday Evening Post*, 12 December 1936), about a writer vacationing in the North Carolina mountains (where Rawlings wrote part of *The Yearling*). At a local orphanage she befriends a young boy who tells her of his mother in town. Just before the writer leaves, however, she learns that the mother does not exist.

"Gal Young Un" emits some of the gray terror of Faulkner's *Sanctuary* (1931). Trax Colton, an arrogant young drifter, stalks a widow for her money and her farm, both of which he wants for his moonshining business. Because Mattie Syles is lonely and eager for a man, she marries Colton and submits to him, quickly becoming unhappy when he mistreats her. When he brings home a young girl, Mattie endures the outrage for a while but then burns his still and his new automobile. Colton runs away without the helpless young girl, whom the widow befriends.

One of Rawlings's deeper stories is *Jacob's Ladder*, a tale inspired by an impoverished young couple who once camped under a tree in Cross Creek. In the story Florry and Mart are poor and illiterate, and decide after meeting at a square dance to run away together from their bleak lives. When Florry leaves her drunken father, the young couple begins an odyssey that is confined to a narrow part of Florida but takes on a cosmic quality as a struggle against the elements, bad luck, human greed, and dishonesty. Mart earns a marginal living as a trapper, fisherman, and grove tender but enjoys a primal relationship to nature; after a series of misfortunes, however, the two retreat to their home county. The title expresses this burden of life. The characters, as Samuel I. Bellman has complained, are somewhat colorless, but their dignified struggle for subsistence takes on a universality, and the contrast between Florry's rise and Mart's temporary decline adds a subtley to the characterization. The structure is episodic, but not as loose as Gordon E. Bigelow claims. The power of place felt by Mart and Florry and the many seasonal references, including hurricanes at the beginning and end, give the story a cyclical unity.

Cross Creek (1942) is Rawlings's *Walden* (1854)—her book a nonfiction account of how she adapted to the heat, frosts, mosquitoes, and people of rural Florida. Its publication marked the end of her continuous residence in the Florida backwoods, and she began to shift away from backwoods subject matter. On 27 October 1941 she had married Norton Sanford Baskin, a hotel and restaurant manager, and begun to spend time at his hotel in St. Augustine and at a beach cottage she bought nearby. In 1948 after losing a

With unspeakable effort Jock dragged him to clear ground as the fire enveloped the cockpit.

Mountain Prelude *By MARJORIE KINNAN RAWLINGS*

THE SKY HAD ROBBED HELEN JACKSON OF EVERYTHING SHE LOVED. COULD THE EARTH EVER GIVE HER PEACE AGAIN, ANY REASON FOR LIVING? BEGINNING A POWERFUL, POIGNANT NOVEL BY THE AUTHOR OF THE YEARLING,

First page of the serialization (26 April - 31 May 1947) of the novel Rawlings based on her story "Mother in Mannville," which had also been published in the Saturday Evening Post *(12 December 1936)*

lawsuit brought by Zelma Cason, one of her former Cross Creek friends, for invasion of privacy, she moved to Van Hornesville, New York, to work on what turned out to be her last novel, spending winters in St. Augustine with her husband. Even though she only had to pay Cason just over a thousand dollars (including a token sum of one dollar and court costs), her total expenditure on the case was around eighteen thousand, and the case had been long and emotionally difficult, a bitter experience for her.

Her fiction soon moved away from the rich local detail of her earlier novels and stories. "Black Secret" (8 September 1945), one of five stories she published in the *New Yorker* during the war years, has a southern setting. But the characters are middle class and the setting is vague. Surprisingly, Rawlings's subject is miscegenation. She does not penetrate this topic, however, relying instead on a boy's accidental discovery of his respectable uncle's interracial romance to create simple pathos. Rawlings creates a fine scene between the young boy and a black barber, but it is difficult to understand why this conventional story won the 1946 O. Henry Memorial Award.

Her last novel, *The Sojourner* (1953), continued the move from Cross Creek. Her only book with a northern setting, *The Sojourner* is the allegorical story of a Michigan farm family.

Compared to her Cross Creek years, Rawlings's last years were unhappy. She suffered through glaucoma, several automobile accidents, several operations, deep depression, and heavy drinking. In her last year, Rawlings was working on a biography of the writer Ellen Glasgow, a friend of hers. On 14 December 1953, while at home at her cottage in Crescent Beach, Florida, she died after a cerebral hemorrhage. She is buried in Island Grove, a few miles from Cross Creek. Her last children's book, *The Secret River*, was published posthumously in 1955.

Marjorie Kinnan Rawlings is more than a children's writer and more than a regionalist, although her best writing is her Florida fiction. Stories such as "A Crop of Beans" and *Jacob's Ladder* begin with local fact but suggest the universal. She thus belongs to the tradition of such writers as John Steinbeck, Eudora Welty, and William Faulkner. Her short fiction cannot equal theirs, but it is obviously the work of a writer with significant talent.

Letters:
Selected Letters of Marjorie Kinnan Rawlings, edited by Gordon E. Bigelow and Laura V. Monti

(Gainesville: University of Florida Press, 1983).

Biography:
Elizabeth Silverthorne, *Marjorie Kinnan Rawlings: Sojourner at Cross Creek* (Woodstock, N.Y.: Overlook, 1988).

References:
Samuel I. Bellman, *Marjorie Kinnan Rawlings* (New York: Twayne, 1974);

Gordon E. Bigelow, *Frontier Eden: The Literary Career of Marjorie Kinnan Rawlings* (Gainesville: University of Florida Press, 1966);

Papers:
The major collection of Rawlings's manuscripts and papers is at the University of Florida.

Elizabeth Madox Roberts
(30 October 1881 - 13 March 1941)

Wade Hall
Bellarmine College

See also the Roberts entries in *DLB 9: American Novelists, 1910-1945* and *DLB 54: American Poets, 1880-1945, Third Series.*

BOOKS: *In the Great Steep's Garden: Poems* (Colorado Springs: Gowdy-Simmons, 1915);

Under the Tree (New York: Huebsch, 1922; London: Cape, 1928; enlarged edition, New York: Viking, 1930);

The Time of Man (New York: Viking, 1926; London: Cape, 1927);

My Heart and My Flesh (New York: Viking, 1927; London: Cape, 1928);

Jingling in the Wind (New York: Viking, 1928; London: Cape, 1929);

The Great Meadow (New York: Viking, 1930; London: Cape, 1930);

A Buried Treasure (New York: Viking, 1931; London: Cape, 1932);

The Haunted Mirror: Stories (New York: Viking, 1932; London: Cape, 1933);

He Sent Forth A Raven (New York: Viking, 1935; London & Toronto: Cape, 1935);

Black Is My Truelove's Hair (New York: Viking, 1938; London: Hale, 1939);

Song in the Meadow: Poems (New York: Viking, 1940);

Not By Strange Gods: Stories (New York: Viking, 1941).

Elizabeth Madox Roberts's first collection of stories, *The Haunted Mirror* (1932), was reviewed ecstatically in the *New York Times* by J. Donald Adams (20 November 1932): "In that remarkable galaxy of talent and genius formed by writers of the contemporary South, no star is more brilliantly ascendant than that of Elizabeth Madox Roberts. She is an artist in whom there is an extraordinary blending of delicacy and power that is nowhere more clearly exhibited than in this collection of her short stories." Indeed, by 1932 she was placed by most critics in the front rank of American fiction writers. Although the most lavish praise was directed at her novels, particularly *The Time of Man* (1926) and *The Great Meadow* (1930), her short stories were admired by readers of the *American Caravan, Harper's Magazine*, and

Elizabeth Madox Roberts (photograph by Jay Te Winburn)

the *American Mercury*. Roberts published only thirteen stories, all of them available in her two collections: seven in *The Haunted Mirror* and six in *Not By Strange Gods* (1941). Nevertheless, in several of her stories she demonstrates mastery of the form.

Born 30 October 1881 near Perryville, Kentucky, Roberts grew up a few miles away in Springfield, which she called home the rest of her life. She was the second of eight children in the family of Mary Elizabeth Brent Roberts and Simpson Roberts, who was a surveyor, farmer, and schoolteacher. Because of ill health she was unable to complete a college degree until 1921, when she graduated from the University of Chicago. As a student she joined the University Poetry Club and became friends with such student writers as Glenway Wescott, Monroe Wheeler, Janet Lewis, and Yvor Winters. She was also acquainted with *Poetry* editor Harriet Monroe. While Roberts's Chi-

cago years liberated her artistically, they also made her more acutely aware of the rich reservoir of literary materials back home in Kentucky, and she returned to Springfield, where, despite continuing health problems, she wrote seven novels, two more collections of poetry (an earlier collection had been published in 1915), and her short stories.

Following her death (of Hodgkin's disease) in 1941, her reputation suffered an almost total eclipse. Although editions of *The Great Meadow* and *The Time of Man* were issued in 1961 and 1962, most of her works stayed out of print. Except for several master's and doctoral theses, for almost fifteen years she was neglected by critics. In 1956 Harry Modean Campbell and Ruel E. Foster published their *Elizabeth Madox Roberts: American Novelist*, which, in spite of its sometimes uncritical adulation of Roberts, served to call renewed attention to an almost forgotten writer. They concluded that eleven of her thirteen stories are "excellent" and that "even the two relative failures—'Record at Oak Hill' and 'Love by the Highway'—reveal careful craftsmanship."

Her reputation was considerably enhanced with the publication of Frederick P. W. McDowell's objective reappraisal, *Elizabeth Madox Roberts*, in the Twayne Series (1963). While placing her with the twenty most important American novelists of the twentieth century, he judged her as "an accomplished but not an outstanding" writer of short stories. In fact, she had her own reservations about the genre—or at least her ability to use it. In a letter to her friend Marshall A. Best in the early 1930s she wrote: "I do not think that the 'short story' is a satisfactory form or that anything very good can be done with it." The novel may have afforded her the broad canvas and open spaces for her particular epic genius; nevertheless, in her best short stories she exhibited her remarkable skill in using poetic prose to create believable landscapes, placing in them rounded characters facing moments of psychological crisis. Even though it is hardly possible to assert a major reputation in short fiction based on a mere thirteen stories, among them are stories that deserve to stand with the best American stories of the twentieth century.

In her stories (some of them approaching novella length) she was able to create large worlds teeming with people who do significant things. Although most of them are set in her fictional Pigeon River country (supposedly a four-county area surrounding the real Washington County in central Kentucky), she managed to draw a considerable range in character types, subjects, tone, and even setting.

Much of the excellence of her stories can be attributed to their vivid sense of place. Here is a part of Kentucky on the fringes of the fabled Bluegrass region, where the good life is orderly, where roads lead somewhere important, and where fields are carefully marked off by wire or stone fences, and boundary lines are clear. In her only story with a mountain setting, "On the Mountainside" (*American Mercury*, August 1927; in *The Haunted Mirror*), she describes Pigeon River country through the eyes of Newt Reddix, a mountain lad who has heard of the flatlands from his teacher, Lester Hunter, and wants to go there: "Lester had come from one of the low counties of the rolling plain where the curving creeks of the Pigeon River spread slowly, winding broadly to gather up many little rills. . . . There the fields rolled out smoothly and the soil was deep. The grass of any roadside was bluegrass mingled, perhaps, with rich weeds. Fat cattle, fine beasts, ate in the mythical pastures. Smooth roads ran between the farms." Despite anxieties raised by the warnings of an old man he meets on his way down the mountainside—that the level country is no paradise—the young man continues toward the unknown life awaiting him, as the story ends.

If Roberts's other stories are any indication of what Newt Reddix might experience, it is a mixed life of joy and sorrow; psychological and religious crisis; adjustment to the rigors of farm work; living with intimate friends and enemies; love and fear of love; traumas that lead to maturation; death and its terrors; and the land and the love of it. For example, in "The Shepherd's Interval" (*Harper's Magazine*, November 1932; in *The Haunted Mirror*) Flynn Thompson is freed from the county jail after serving four months for making and selling moonshine whiskey, but first, in jail, he pictures his farm: "Fourteen miles down in a westerly way—south by west, rather—over into the Bearwallow country but back again in a southerly slant, lay his own fifty-five acres of hill land. The house, tall in front and one story behind, stands beside the barns, before a cornfield. A long crook scythe hangs against the meathouse wall and four large flat stones bring one from the kitchen door to the iron pump. Down in the hollow, behind the house, deep in a thicket of hackberry and sassafras, was the still until the government agents wrecked it with axes." Flynn

serves his time and walks joyously, fearfully, expectantly toward his home, arriving in time—as he has prayed—to shear the sheep and to see his daughter married. This story is typical of the ones in which Roberts creates a kind of choral persona ("they"), which sees and speaks for the community: " 'Don't name the place where he's been,' they said."

Taken together, her stories compose a social history of Roberts's region. Some of the characters are, in fact, based on family members, friends, and neighbors. The narration often sounds the rhythms of a folk song or a Greek chorus, and the characters speak a folk language distilled sensitively from the sometimes rough but eloquent speech handed down from Anglo-Saxon forebears. Even when the character is semiliterate and crude, his language is expressive. "Children of the Earth" (*Harper's Magazine*, November 1928; in *The Haunted Mirror*) displays Roberts's version of southern "poor-white trash." Dovie Green berates her "cockroach" husband, Eli, for being a sorry provider. In turn he reminds her that he has protected her when she stole and butchered a neighbor's hog: "I already lied enough for you, Dovie Green, to go to perdition three times over. I even lied in court the day Jake NcNab lost the gilt, swore in the magistrate's house with my hand in the air, 'S'elp me God' we never seen a sign of hit, and hit salted down in our cellar hole under the house then, and your insides full of tripe and hog-meat hash that very minute. If the court had 'a' given you a vomit right then, it would 'a' seen a sight, would 'a' seen Jake NcNab's hogmeat run outen your mouth." In a letter to Harriet Monroe, Roberts once commented that "My people here are close to the soil and their talk is talk out of the clods."

In many of Roberts's stories there is a significant psychological dimension, usually focused on a young person facing a crisis. The central character is often a young girl who is reaching out to know the world and reaching in to know herself. In "I Love My Bonny Bride" (in *Not By Strange Gods*), for example, a girl named Lena grows inwardly and outwardly as she anticipates her aunt Patty's marriage.

In one of Roberts's most successful stories, "The Sacrifice of the Maidens" (in *The Haunted Mirror*), the consciousness of an adolescent boy, Felix Barbour, is the battleground for the conflicting claims of flesh and spirit. While Felix waits in a small convent chapel to see his sister Anne become Sister Magdalen, his memories of her

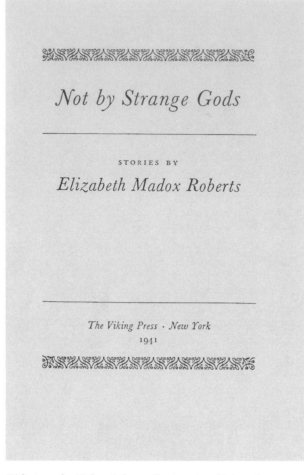

Not by Strange Gods

STORIES BY

Elizabeth Madox Roberts

The Viking Press · New York
1941

Title page for Roberts's last collection, in which each story, according to reviewer Gladys Graham Bates, has "an almost mystical significance" (Saturday Review, 22 November 1941)

young life at home are rich in sensual imagery: "Summer and winter and Anne, they were running down the channel of the year. The year spread widely then, as if it flowed abroad to fill a wide field with corn. There was sweetness in the high blades of the corn and abundance in the full shucks as he tore each ear from the ripe stem." The new nun's renunciation of the world's natural fertility is, Roberts implies, a sacrifice. Whether it is justified by the higher claim of the spiritual life is left open to question. The story won second prize in the O. Henry Memorial Award contest for 1932. In this story, as elsewhere, in asserting a rural Catholic presence, Roberts reflects accurately the actual milieu that served as the basis for her fiction. Although Catholic churches, convents, and monasteries are rare in most of the rural South, in central Kentucky they have been in existence since the 1790s, when pioneers from Maryland founded Catholic settlements alongside Protestant communities.

Roberts's interest in abnormal psychology is demonstrated in "The Scarecrow" (*Harper's Magazine*, September 1932; in *The Haunted Mirror*), the story of a frigid young woman who cannot accept the sexual intimacies of marriage. Like the scarecrow she has made to keep the crows out of her father's cornfield, she is unable to respond physically to another person. In a moment of weakness, which follows a dream in the cornfield, she agrees to marry Tony Wright. On her wedding night she becomes terrified of her husband, slips a knife into the bosom of her dress and hides until near daylight, when she flees to her parents.

Another effective story about emotional and sexual maturation is "Death at Bearwallow" (*American Caravan*, 1927; in *The Haunted Mirror*), which focuses on Dave Nally, a boy who is prevented by a swollen creek from returning home one night from a visit to his grandmother. He finds refuge in a lighted farmhouse, where two gamblers keep a strange vigil over a dying man. Several years later Dave attends the wake for Valery, a woman he had loved who had been engaged to another man, and he remembers the night the old dying man had whispered the name of his beloved, "Kate." Suddenly he realizes that both people—the old man and the young girl—had reached a fulfillment he does not yet know.

"The Betrothed" (*Harper's Magazine*, August 1933; in *Not By Strange Gods*) contains one of the strongest scenes in Roberts's fiction. It shows the repulsion that Rhody, a young girl facing marriage, feels for a while about physical relationships. While Kirk Brown, her husband-to-be, is away in another part of the state helping his brother build a barn, Rhody makes preparations for their wedding. During the season of hog killing, she and her grandmother are given the job of searching through vats of hogs' entrails for sweetbreads and other glands. It is a bloody and frightening business, and Rhody becomes sick. The grandmother enjoys the work and begins to use the wet mass of entrails to philosophize on the lack of glamour and significance in human life. "I reckon," she says, "you think Kirk Brown made the moon. I can show you Kirk in this tub here, right under my fist.... See, here. You'll hear 'im sing and talk sweet right outen this tub. I had my hand on 'im just a little while ago." The grandmother's sordid view of human relationships is supported when Rhody visits a married sister with unwanted and unloved children. Nevertheless, Rhody signals her own growing maturity when she arrives home to find her family preparing for the wedding and realizes that she must come to her own conclusions about the worth of love and life.

Like that of most southern writers, Roberts's fiction is filled with a sense of the presence of the past. Despite its contrived plot, "Record at Oak Hill" (in *The Haunted Mirror*) successfully chronicles the importance of long-ago actions to present generations. Morna Trigg is an old woman whose father had fought as a Confederate during the Civil War. Her farm is now managed by her grand-nephew, Richard Dorsey, who one day by accident finds a dagger buried in the plaster chinking of an old log cabin on the place. He remembers that Morna had told of the hard years her father had endured following the war and of his hatred for a man named Buchman. He remembers she had said that Buchman was found dead of a dagger wound in his own garden and that his murder was never solved. Now the year is 1932, and times are again hard. Will Neal, Richard's brother-in-law who has lost his farm, remarks sarcastically that at least in those days a man could find "something firm to stick a sword into ... something to kill." Now there is only "high-priced machinery, low-priced wheat and tobacco," and frustration.

In her short fiction as well as in her novels, Elizabeth Madox Roberts recorded and interpreted life as she knew it with sensitivity and insight and in a poetic, sensuous prose. Her ancestors had been pioneers in the new land called Kentucky. In her emphasis on developing the inner lives of her characters, she was a pioneer in the Southern Renaissance, which produced such writers as William Faulkner, Thomas Wolfe, Robert Penn Warren, and Eudora Welty.

A conference celebrating the centenary of Roberts's birth was held in Springfield, Kentucky, in the fall of 1981. There critics and scholars reassessed her fiction and poetry and reasserted her significant contributions to twentieth-century American literature.

Biography:
Harry Modean Campbell and Ruel E. Foster, *Elizabeth Madox Roberts: American Novelist* (Norman: University of Oklahoma Press, 1956).

References:
J. Donald Adams, "Elizabeth Madox Roberts," *Virginia Quarterly Review*, 12 (January 1936): 80-90;
Alexander M. Buchan, "Elizabeth Madox Roberts," *Southwest Review*, 25 (July 1940): 463-481;
Lamar F. Janney, "Elizabeth Madox Roberts," *Sewanee Review*, 45 (October-December 1937): 388-410;
Grant C. Knight, "Bluegrass and Laurel: The Varieties of Kentucky Fiction," *Saturday Review of Literature*, 50 (6 January 1945): 12-13;
Frederick P. W. McDowell, *Elizabeth Madox Roberts* (New York: Twayne, 1963);
Shields McIlwaine, "America Makes the Poor-White a Cause and a Literary Vogue. Sensibility and Realism: Edith S. Kelley, Elizabeth Madox Roberts, and Paul Green," in his *The Southern Poor-White from Lubberland to Tobacco Road* (Norman: University of Oklahoma Press, 1939), pp. 199-217;
"Remembering Elizabeth Madox Roberts," special issue, *Southern Review*, 20 (Autumn 1984);
Blair H. Rouse, "Time and Place in Southern Fiction," in *Southern Renaissance: The Literature of the Modern South*, edited by Louis D. Rubin, Jr., and Robert D. Jacobs (Baltimore: Johns Hopkins Press, 1953), pp. 126-150;
Earl H. Rovit, *Herald to Chaos: The Novels of Elizabeth Madox Roberts* (Lexington: University Press of Kentucky, 1960);
Rovit, "Recurrent Symbols in the Novels of Elizabeth Madox Roberts," *Boston University Studies in English*, 2 (Spring 1956): 36-54;
Mark Van Doren, "Elizabeth Madox Roberts," *English Journal*, 21 (September 1932): 521-528;
Edward Wagenknecht, "The Inner Vision: Elizabeth Madox Roberts," in his *Cavalcade of the American Novel* (New York: Holt, 1952), pp. 389-396.

Papers:
The Library of Congress has the Elizabeth Madox Roberts papers.

J. D. Salinger

(1 January 1919 -   )

Philip Stevick
Temple University

See also the Salinger entry in *DLB 2: American Novelists Since World War II*.

BOOKS: *The Catcher in the Rye* (Boston: Little, Brown, 1951; London: Hamilton, 1951);

Nine Stories (Boston: Little, Brown, 1953); republished as *For Esmé—with Love and Squalor, and Other Stories* (London: Hamilton, 1953);

Franny and Zooey (Boston: Little, Brown, 1961; London: Heinemann, 1962);

Raise High the Roof Beam, Carpenters and Seymour: An Introduction (Boston: Little, Brown, 1963; London: Heinemann, 1963);

The Complete Uncollected Short Stories of J. D. Salinger, 2 volumes, unauthorized edition (Berkeley, Cal.?, 1974).

SELECTED PERIODICAL PUBLICATIONS: "The Young Folks," *Story*, 16 (March-April 1940): 26-30;

"Go See Eddie," *University of Kansas City Review*, 7 (December 1940): 121-124;

"The Long Debut of Lois Taggett," *Story*, 21 (September-October 1942): 28-34;

"The Varioni Brothers," *Saturday Evening Post*, 216 (17 July 1943): 12-13, 76-77;

"Both Parties Concerned," *Saturday Evening Post*, 216 (26 February 1944): 14, 47-48;

"Soft-Boiled Sergeant," *Saturday Evening Post*, 216 (15 April 1944): 18, 82, 84-85;

"Last Day of the Last Furlough," *Saturday Evening Post*, 216 (15 July 1944): 26-27, 61-62, 64;

"This Sandwich Has No Mayonnaise," *Esquire*, 25 (October 1945): 54-56, 147-149;

"I'm Crazy," *Collier's*, 116 (22 December 1945): 36, 48, 51;

"A Young Girl in 1941 with No Waist at All," *Mademoiselle*, 25 (May 1947): 222-223, 292-303;

"The Inverted Forest," *Cosmopolitan*, 123 (December 1947): 73-80, 85-86, 90, 92, 95-96, 98, 100, 102, 107, 109;

"A Girl I Knew," *Good Housekeeping*, 126 (February 1948): 37, 186, 188, 191-196;

J. D. Salinger (Gale International Portrait Gallery)

"Hapworth 16, 1924," *New Yorker*, 41 (19 June 1965): 32-113.

A few writers are so enveloped in their reputations that their work is virtually impossible to read without being distracted by their fame and their relation to the public. No one else has ever been known in quite the way that J. D. Salinger has—first as the creator of a voice and a consciousness in which a vast number of very different readers have recognized themselves, second as an elusive figure uneasy with his audience and distrustful of his public, and finally as a kind of living ghost, fiercely protective of his isolation. Having created a body of fiction in which the author invites the love of his readers, he has become, in biographer Ian Hamilton's phrase, "famous for not wanting to be famous." The mythic status of Salinger the man is so compelling that trying to look clearly at his fiction, as fiction, is difficult and complicated. Yet the effort justifies the difficulty: many of his stories are evocative period pieces, catching the spirit of that time in which he defined large areas of sensibility; and some of the stories transcend their historical interest, as luminous examples of the art of short fiction.

The biographical record is thin and not very helpful. Jerome David Salinger was born on 1 January 1919 in New York City, the second child of Sol and Miriam Jillich Salinger, his father Jewish, an importer of hams and cheeses, his mother gentile, Scotch-Irish. It is odd that, for a writer who so valued the sensibility of the child, Salinger has said so little about his own childhood. Something can be inferred from the family's addresses, which record an increasingly prosperous life, and from the New York of the time, in many ways an attractive place for a bright and observant child. He attended several New York public schools and in 1932 was enrolled in the McBurney School, on the upper West Side, where he seems to have been quiet, introspective, and academically mediocre. In 1934 Salinger's father enrolled him in Valley Forge Military Academy in Pennsylvania, from which he graduated two years later. Remembered as being sardonic and detached, Salinger was also apparently fond of certain aspects of the military experience. It formed the background of his one novel, *The Catcher in the Rye* (1951); and it was at Valley Forge that Salinger first began to think of himself as a writer.

In 1937 Salinger attended New York University briefly and traveled in Europe, writing continuously and sending his stories to various magazines. In 1938 he enrolled at Ursinus College, near Philadelphia, where he wrote a column for the college paper, but left after a semester. And in 1939 he signed up for a class in the short story at Columbia University, taught by Whit Burnet, editor, anthologist, nurturer of developing talent, and champion of the short story. This was the beginning of Salinger's long friendship and correspondence with Burnet, and the course also marked the start of a new stage in Salinger's growing sense of professionalism. In 1940 Salinger's first story, "The Young Folks," was published in Burnet's *Story* magazine (March-April), and

shortly afterward "Go See Eddie" appeared in the *University of Kansas City Review* (December 1940).

Usually a writer of quality will leave behind a few apprentice pieces, uncollected, but will gather as he goes most of his short fiction in hardback volumes. In the case of Salinger, however, twenty-three stories appeared before those collected in *Nine Stories* (1953), few of them reprinted anywhere and none reprinted in an authorized collection of Salinger's own work. Salinger has disavowed those early stories and, on one occasion, took legal steps to enjoin their unauthorized publication. A pirated, two-volume edition was, however, published in 1974, and Salinger sued the owners of the bookstores that sold it.

Few readers of his early work, looking at it through the perspective of the talent he later showed, have ever imagined that it should be honored, studied, and collected. For one thing, until Salinger's 1946 appearance in the *New Yorker*, his stories appeared in middle-range magazines—the *Saturday Evening Post*, *Mademoiselle*, *Good Housekeeping*, *Collier's*—that were known for decades as "the slicks." The fiction that appeared in their pages was, for the most part, undemanding, entertaining, and often formulaic—in a word, commercial. Salinger's stories are not exceptions. Moreover, his early stories are inevitably flawed, their structures puzzling or unrealized, and their tone not fully controlled. Still, they demonstrate the beginning of certain features of craft and vision that were to remain. One of those features is Salinger's placing at the center of his craft the power of voice.

From the start, events are not very important to Salinger: little happens in his stories. Although he has a sharp eye for detail, the background, setting, or locale seems to matter less than it does for almost any other American writer. Even character, as it is usually understood, seems not finally a major interest. What does interest Salinger is the human voice. Stories in which there are large proportions of dialogue are a tradition in American fiction. Mark Twain, Ring Lardner, and Ernest Hemingway wrote brilliant dialogue stories, and much of the commercial fiction surrounding early works by Salinger was heavy with dialogue. But in the case of Salinger, the art and centrality of voice mean something more than simply a preference for the rendering of talk. He had an uncanny knack for producing in print the effect of a character's

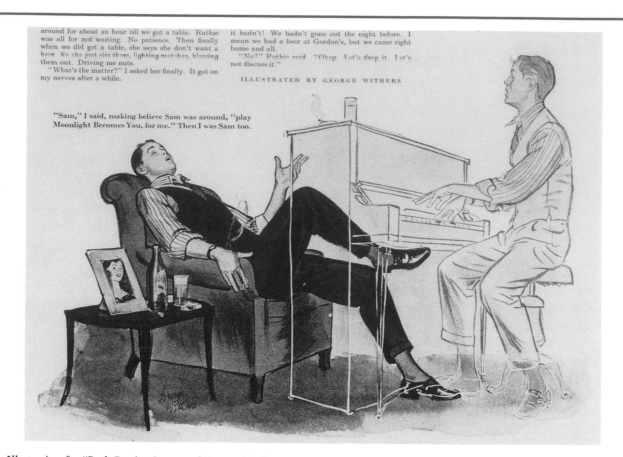

around for about an hour till we got a table. Ruthie was all for not waiting. No patience. Then finally when we did get a table, she says she don't want a beer. So she just sits there, lighting matches, blowing them out. Driving me nuts.

"What's the matter?" I asked her finally. It got on my nerves after a while.

it hadn't! We hadn't gone out the night before. I mean we had a beer at Gordon's, but we came right home and all.

"No?" Ruthie said. "Okay. Let's drop it. Let's not discuss it."

ILLUSTRATED BY GEORGE WITHERS

"Sam," I said, making believe Sam was around, "play Moonlight Becomes You, for me." Then I was Sam too.

Illustration for "Both Parties Concerned," one of Salinger's early stories in the Saturday Evening Post *(26 February 1944)*

unique speech, an effect so potent that readers, years after having read *The Catcher in the Rye*, can still "hear" Holden Caulfield speaking, when everything else in the experience of reading the novel has faded. The effect in the stories is smaller in scale than that in the novel but not different in kind. In "The Young Folks" the character Edna says: "I guess Doris *is* attractive to men. I don't know. I think I really liked her better though—her looks, I mean—when her hair was natural. I mean bleached hair—to me anyway—always looks sort of artificial when you see it in the light or something. I don't know. I may be wrong. Everybody does it, I guess." That striking insight into the way Edna would sound is the single feature that redeems an otherwise undistinguished story.

In addition to that remarkable empathy for the expressive power of speech rhythms, Salinger discovered a focus that was to continue through a large proportion of his fiction, namely the use of childhood, adolescence, or youth as both an object of interest in itself and as a thematic lever by means of which the nature of the wider world could be pried open. Sensitive and perceptive, Sal-

inger's younger characters are unable to prevail against the hypocrisy around them. Or, authentic and bright on the one hand, fatally naive on the other, they conspire in their own failure. Something of the energy and fascination with which the young Salinger regarded the child figure is suggested in "This Sandwich Has No Mayonnaise" (*Esquire*, October 1945), in which, six years before *The Catcher in the Rye* was published, Vincent Caulfield speaks of his brother Holden in a way that indicates the combination of brightness and vulnerability in Salinger's children: "He's only nineteen years old, my brother is, and the dope can't reduce a thing to a humor, kill it off with sarcasm, can't do anything but listen hectically to the maladjusted little apparatus he wears for a heart. My missing-in-action brother." Although some of the stories of the mid 1940s draw upon Salinger's military experience during World War II (he served in the Army Signal Corps and Counter-Intelligence Corps), it is to the image of innocence in a world of vulgarians that he returns again and again.

Salinger married a Frenchwoman named Sylvia (maiden name unknown) in September

1945, but the marriage was short-lived. They were divorced the following year.

In 1948 Salinger published three of the stories of his major phase, "A Perfect Day for Bananafish," "Uncle Wiggily in Connecticut," and "Just Before the War With the Eskimos," all in the *New Yorker*. Prior to those three stories, he had published just one story ("Slight Rebellion off Madison") in the *New Yorker* (21 December 1946); after 1948 he would publish only two stories elsewhere. He soon became "a *New Yorker* writer" and a friend of its major editorial figures; Salinger was honored by his presence in its elegant pages and by its high standards for fiction. Although he was suspect in some circles because of the arch and rarified tone the magazine seemed to foster, he was encouraged and challenged by the seriousness with which the readers of the *New Yorker* took its fiction. A few stories in the history of the *New Yorker* have seemed so powerful and so original that their appearance has constituted a cultural event. "A Perfect Day for Bananafish" (31 January 1948; collected in *Nine Stories*) is one of them.

The story opens with a sustained telephone conversation between Muriel Glass and her mother in which both reveal themselves to be shallow, materialistic, manipulative, and glib. References to Seymour, Muriel's husband, indicate that he has returned from the war, clearly damaged by the experience, and is eccentric at best, irresponsible at worst. But these observations come through the overheard words of Muriel and her mother, and the reader tends to discount them. Only two thirds of the way through does Salinger present Seymour—on the beach in an encounter with a very young girl, to whom he tells a strange parable about the self-destructive ways of the banana fish. Back at the hotel room, while Muriel is asleep, he takes a pistol from his luggage and fires "a bullet through his right temple."

It is a devastating ending for which the reader is totally unprepared. Yet after reading the story a second time, one sees that the suicide is meticulously prepared for. Seymour's instability is far more ominous than it seems at first, and the gulf between him (he reads Rainer Maria Rilke and T. S. Eliot and has a strongly spiritual dimension) and the meretricious Muriel is immense and obviously demoralizing. Other stories are finer artistic accomplishments, but no other story has drawn more commentary, much of it on the meaning of that odd banana-fish parable and the reasons for the suicide. Like other stories of

Salinger's, the most important moment is hauntingly plausible yet finally ambiguous.

American literature contains some distinguished examples of the short-story cycle, integrated collections of stories that circulate themes and motifs from story to story and that cohere, almost like chapters in a novel. "Bananafish" and the other works in *Nine Stories* may be seen as another example of such a form. Members of the Glass family appear several times. Even in stories very different from each other, aspects of technique and manner demonstrate a consistent sensibility. The same thematic oppositions run through story after story: a quick, precocious intelligence is opposed to a cynical, life-denying knowledge of all the wrong things; authenticity is opposed to the "phony"; often the insights of the young are opposed to the self-serving wisdom of the old—persistent patterns of vulnerability and psychic damage on the one hand, corruption and spiritual malaise on the other. Still, for all of their continuity, not much is gained by trying to see the stories as an integrated cycle, but they are, however they are viewed, a remarkable group of stories showing Salinger at the height of his power. And the best of them, by consensus, is "For Esmé—with Love and Squalor" (*New Yorker*, 8 April 1950).

The first half of the story places the narrator, an American serviceman during World War II, in England, observing and coming to know Esmé, an English girl, titled, attractive, courageous, and like so many of the young in Salinger's works, clever, sensitive, and verbal. Learning that the narrator is a writer, she expresses an interest in stories about "squalor." The narrator, amused by her, is also immensely charmed by her, and they part, he, presumably, for combat. The story then shifts its point of view to a third-person account of "Sergeant X," whom readers soon gather is the narrator of the first portion of the story, who is transformed by time and the trauma of the war, recovering in a military hospital. The sergeant moves through a series of encounters with some potent varieties of egotism and viciousness, all of which drive him further inward. But as the story nears its close, he receives a package, long delayed, containing the gift of her dead father's watch from Esmé, along with her wishes for his well-being. Damaged by the brutishness of experience, Sergeant X is redeemed by the gift, which is to say the love, of Esmé. It is a story of extraordinary economy and grace, and

I started running with my suitcases banging the devil out of my legs. I ran all the way to the Gate, stopped, got my breath, and ran across Route 202

Illustration by Leon Gregori for a story that features Holden Caulfield as its protagonist (Collier's, 22 December 1945)

the years since 1950 have not diminished its power.

Nine Stories appeared in 1953, two years after the appearance of *The Catcher in the Rye* had secured for Salinger a reputation and a readership unmatched by any other living writer at the time. In the six years following *Nine Stories*, Salinger published in magazines four works of fiction, later gathered into two volumes, *Franny and Zooey* (1961) followed by *Raise High the Roof Beam, Carpenters and Seymour: An Introduction* (1963). In each case, the first story is the shorter of the two, the latter being of novella length. And all four pursue the personalities and relationships of the Glass family, now Salinger's exclusive preoccupation. Two other aspects of these two volumes are immediately apparent. One is that Salinger's interest in Eastern religious philosophy in general, Zen Buddhism in particular, has extended and

deepened. A Zen koan, the most famous of them all, is the epigraph for *Nine Stories*: the master asks the novice to describe the sound of one hand clapping. And Eastern thought is alluded to often enough in *Nine Stories* to suggest that Salinger considered it an alternative to the superficiality and materialism of the world he portrays. By the time of the two later collections, the Zen interest has become central and pervasive.

What else is apparent is that, despite his continuing ease and grace with the colloquial, and his wit, ingenious detail, and verbal energy, something has begun to go slack in Salinger's sense of rhythm and form, so that the four fictions seem self-indulgent and needlessly expansive. Words like "interminable" began to appear in the reactions even of sympathetic critics. And Salinger's allocation of interest and admiration to the Glass family began, to more than a few readers, to

Featuring The Complete *Unconflected Short Stories*

THE LONG DEBUT OF LOIS TAGGETT
SLIGHT REBELLION OFF MADISON
THE HEART OF A BROKEN STORY
THE VARIONI BROTHERS
THE YOUNG FOLKS
THE HANG OF IT
GO SEE EDDIE
ELAINE
THIS SANDWICH HAS NO MAYONNAISE

I'M CRAZY
THE STRANGER
A BOY IN FRANCE
SOFT-BOILED SERGEANT
BOTH PARTIES CONCERNED
ONCE A WEEK WON'T KILL YOU
LAST DAY OF THE LAST FURLOUGH
PERSONAL NOTES ON AN INFANTRYMAN

Cover for volume 1 of the unauthorized collection of Salinger's early stories (1974), whose publication he fought vigorously in court and suppressed

seem narrow, private, and claustrophobic. Of these four fictions, "Franny" (*New Yorker*, 29 January 1955) is the most durable; its construction is tighter, its scale smaller than the others. Its energies are more convincing, presenting Franny Glass's situation as a bright, attractive twenty-one-year-old on a college weekend, in painful conflict with her sense of self and world—uneasy with the superficiality of her surroundings, its tangle of egos, and her profound wish for a spiritual dimension that would give her life a substance beyond all of the posturing, grasping, and self-assertion that threaten to engulf her.

In one of Seymour Glass's diary entries, in "Raise High the Roof Beam, Carpenters" (*New Yorker*, 19 November 1955), he writes, "I have scars on my hands from touching certain people." It is an arresting sentence, seeming to come from something essential to Salinger himself. In the winter of 1952-1953 Salinger had bought and moved into a primitive country house in Cornish,

New Hampshire. What began as a pastoral retreat became Salinger's permanent home. During his early years in Cornish, he married Claire Douglas on 17 February 1955 and eventually had two children, Margaret Ann and Matthew. (Salinger obtained a divorce in 1967.) In Cornish he gradually began to withdraw from his happy but limited involvement in the social life of the community. His extraordinary fame did not come immediately after *The Catcher in the Rye* and *Nine Stories*. But by 1956 he had clearly found the celebrity and the uninvited guests intrusive and repellent. There was one last story, "Hapworth 16, 1924" (*New Yorker*, 19 June 1965), and nothing more.

When *The Catcher in the Rye* began to garner the attention of critics and literary journalists, bringing also a serious consideration of Salinger's stories, the first reactions contained a remarkable amount of shock at their candor. That concern either to attack or defend Salinger's "vulgarity" may now seem a quaint and distant moralism, but it is not so bizarre as it might appear. Salinger's fiction *is* subversive and threatening; he had found his own, original way of undermining the pieties of the official culture. To the young characters in Salinger's fiction who contemplate joining the adult world, there is nothing to celebrate. After a few years, as Salinger's reputation became academically secure, the burgeoning body of criticism that addressed it took mostly a thematic tack, using such words as "innocence" and "alienation," seeking to find the center of the fiction in his images of loneliness and his portrayal of the desire for love. Many of those critical attempts to capture the essence in a sentence now seem either reductive or obvious. One that does not is the statement, in a 1958 study by Frederick L. Gwynn and Joseph L. Blotner, that Salinger is "probably the only American writer of fiction ever to express a devotional attitude toward religious experience by means of a consistently satiric style."

Not much is clear concerning the ultimate critical fate of Salinger's short stories, but this much is clear: they are especially expressive of an adversarial posture in the 1940s and 1950s, though it does not necessarily follow that they will seem increasingly dated. The best of the stories will likely continue to be regarded as classics of the genre, and their triumphs of art and spirit will continue to speak to an audience that can find, in Salinger's distinctive voice, a compelling vision of the self in the world.

Interview:

Shirley Blaney, "Twin State Telescope," *Claremont* [N.H.] *Daily Eagle*, 13 November 1953; reprinted in Edward Kosner, "The Private World of J. D. Salinger," *New York Post: Week-End Magazine*, 30 April 1961, p. 5; reprinted as "The Last Published Interview with J. D. Salinger," *Crawdaddy* (March 1975): 39.

Bibliographies:

Tom Davis, "J. D. Salinger: A Checklist," *Papers of the Bibliographical Society of America*, 53 (1959): 69-71;

Maurice Beebe and Jennifer Sperry, "Criticism of J. D. Salinger: A Selected Checklist," *Modern Fiction Studies*, 12 (Autumn 1966): 377-390;

George Bixby, "J. D. Salinger: A Bibliographical Checklist," *American Book Collector*, new series 2 (May-June 1981): 29-32;

Jack R. Sublette, *J. D. Salinger: An Annotated Bibliography, 1938-1981* (New York & London: Garland, 1984).

Biography:

Ian Hamilton, *In Search of J. D. Salinger* (New York: Random House, 1988).

References:

Everhard Alsen, *Salinger's Glass Stories as a Composite Novel* (Troy, N.Y.: Whitston, 1983);

S. I. Bellman, "New Light on Seymour's Suicide: Salinger's 'Hapworth 16, 1924,'" *Studies in Short Fiction*, 3 (1966): 348-351;

Harold Bloom, ed., *J. D. Salinger: Modern Critical Views* (New York: Chelsea, 1987);

Sally Bostwick, "Reality, Compassion, and Mysticism," *Midwest Review*, 5 (1963): 30-43;

James E. Bryan, "J. D. Salinger: The Fat Lady and the Chicken Sandwich," *College English*, 23 (December 1961): 226-229;

Bryan, "A Reading of Salinger's 'For Esmé—with Love and Squalor,'" *Criticism*, 9 (Summer 1967): 275-288;

Bryan, "A Reading of Salinger's 'Teddy,'" *American Literature*, 40 (November 1968): 352-369;

Brother Fidelian Burke, "Salinger's Esmé: Some Matters of Balance," *Modern Fiction Studies*, 12 (Autumn 1966): 341-347;

Richard Allan Davison, "Salinger Criticism and 'The Laughing Man': A Case of Arrested Development," *Studies in Short Fiction*, 18 (Winter 1981): 1-15;

Warren French, "The Age of Salinger," in *The Fifties: Fiction, Poetry, Drama*, edited by French (De Land, Fla.: Everett/Edwards, 1970), pp. 1-39;

French, *J. D. Salinger* (New York: Twayne, 1963; revised edition, Boston: G. K. Hall, 1976);

French, *J. D. Salinger, Revisited* (Boston: Twayne, 1988);

Bernice Goldstein and Sanford Goldstein, " 'Seymour: An Introduction'—Writing as Discovery," *Studies in Short Fiction*, 7 (Spring 1970): 248-256;

T. L. Gross, "J. D. Salinger: Suicide and Survival in the Modern World," *South Atlantic Quarterly*, 68 (1969): 452-462;

Henry Anatole Grunwald, ed., *Salinger: A Critical and Personal Portrait* (New York: Harper & Row, 1962);

Frederick L. Gwynn and Joseph L. Blotner, *The Fiction of J. D. Salinger* (Pittsburgh: University of Pittsburgh Press, 1958);

John V. Hagopian, " 'Pretty Mouth and Green My Eyes': Salinger's Paolo and Francesca in New York," *Modern Fiction Studies*, 12 (Autumn 1966): 349-354;

Kenneth Hamilton, "Hell in New York: J. D. Salinger's 'Pretty Mouth and Green My Eyes,'" *Dalhousie Review*, 47 (Autumn 1967): 394-399;

Hamilton, *Jerome David Salinger: A Critical Essay* (Grand Rapids, Mich.: Eerdmans, 1967);

John Hermann, "J. D. Salinger: Hello Hello Hello," *College English*, 22 (January 1961): 262-264;

Warren Hinckle and others, "A Symposium on J. D. Salinger," *Ramparts*, 1 (1962): 47-66;

Alfred Kazin, "J. D. Salinger: 'Everybody's Favorite,'" *Atlantic*, 208 (August 1961): 27-31;

Paul Kirschner, "Salinger and His Society: The Pattern of *Nine Stories*," *London Review*, 6 (Winter 1969-1970): 34-54;

Gary Lane, "Seymour's Suicide Again: A New Reading of J. D. Salinger's 'A Perfect Day for Bananafish,'" *Studies in Short Fiction*, 10 (Winter 1973): 27-33;

Jeremy Larner, "Salinger's Audience: An Explanation," *Partisan Review*, 29 (Fall 1962): 594-598;

James Lundquist, *J. D. Salinger* (New York: Ungar, 1979);

John O. Lyons, "The Romantic Style of Salinger's 'Seymour: An Introduction,'" *Wisconsin Studies in Contemporary Literature*, 4 (Winter 1963): 62-69;

Frank Metcalf, "The Suicide of Salinger's Seymour Glass," *Studies in Short Fiction*, 9 (1972): 136-144;

James E. Miller, Jr., *J. D. Salinger* (Minneapolis: University of Minnesota Press, 1965);

Laurence Perrine, "Teddy? Booper? Or Blooper?," *Studies in Short Fiction*, 4 (Spring 1967): 217-224;

Gerald Rosen, *Zen in the Art of J. D. Salinger* (Berkeley, Cal.: Creative Arts, 1977);

W. B. Stein, "Salinger's 'Teddy': Tat TvaM Asi or That Thou Art," *Arizona Quarterly*, 29 (1974): 253-265;

Terry Teachout, "Salinger Then and Now," *Commentary*, 84 (September 1987): 61-64;

John Wenke, "Sergeant X, Esmé, and the Meaning of Words," *Studies in Short Fiction*, 18 (Summer 1981): 251-259.

Papers:
There are two substantial collections of Salinger's correspondence: at the Harry Ransom Humanities Research Center, University of Texas at Austin, and at the Firestone Library, Princeton University.

Irwin Shaw
(27 February 1913 - 16 May 1984)

James R. Giles
Northern Illinois University

See also the Shaw entries in *DLB 6: American Novelists Since World War II* and *DLB Yearbook: 1984*.

BOOKS: *Bury the Dead* (New York: Random House, 1936);

The Gentle People: A Brooklyn Fable (New York: Random House, 1939); adapted as a play (New York: Dramatists Play Service, 1939; revised, 1939);

Sailor Off the Bremen, and Other Stories (New York: Random House, 1939; London: Cape, 1940);

Welcome to the City, and Other Stories (New York: Random House, 1942);

Sons and Soldiers: A Play in Three Acts (New York: Random House, 1944);

Act of Faith, and Other Stories (New York: Random House, 1946);

The Assassin: A Play in Three Acts (New York: Random House, 1946);

The Survivors: Play in Three Acts, by Shaw and Peter Viertel (New York: Dramatists Play Service, 1948);

The Young Lions (New York: Random House, 1948; London: Cape, 1949);

Mixed Company: Collected Short Stories (New York: Random House, 1950; London: Cape, 1952);

Report on Israel, by Shaw and Robert Capa (New York: Simon & Schuster, 1950);

The Troubled Air (New York: Random House, 1951; London: Cape, 1951);

Lucy Crown (New York: Random House, 1956; London: Cape, 1956);

Tip on a Dead Jockey, and Other Stories (New York: Random House, 1957; London: Cape, 1957);

Two Weeks in Another Town (New York: Random House, 1960; London: Cape, 1960);

Children From Their Games: A Play in Two Acts (New York: French, 1962);

In the French Style (New York: MacFadden-Bartell, 1963);

In the Company of Dolphins (New York: Geis/Random House, 1964);

Love on a Dark Street, and Other Stories (New York: Delacorte, 1965; London: Cape, 1965);

Voices of a Summer Day (New York: Dial, 1965; London: Weidenfeld & Nicolson, 1965);

Retreat, and Other Stories (London: New English Library, 1970);

Irwin Shaw in 1983 on his balcony in Klosters, Switzerland (photograph by Francine Schoeller)

Rich Man, Poor Man (New York: Delacorte, 1970; London: Weidenfeld & Nicolson, 1970);

Whispers in Bedlam: Three Novellas (London: Weidenfeld & Nicolson, 1972);

Evening in Byzantium (New York: Delacorte, 1973; London: Weidenfeld & Nicolson, 1973);

God Was Here but He Left Early: Short Fiction (New York: Arbor House, 1973; London: Pan, 1977);

Nightwork (New York: Delacorte, 1975; London: Weidenfeld & Nicolson, 1975);

Beggarman, Thief (New York: Delacorte, 1977; London: Weidenfeld & Nicolson, 1977);

Paris! Paris!, by Shaw and Ronald Searle (New York: Harcourt Brace Jovanovich, 1977; London: Weidenfeld & Nicolson, 1977);

The Top of the Hill (New York: Delacorte, 1979);

Bread Upon the Waters (New York: Delacorte, 1981; Leicester, U.K.: Charnwood, 1982);

Acceptable Losses (New York: Arbor House, 1982; Leicester, U.K.: Charnwood, 1984).

Collections: *Selected Short Stories*, with a preface by Shaw (New York: Modern Library, 1961);

Short Stories (New York: Random House, 1966);

Short Stories: Five Decades (New York: Delacorte, 1978; London: Cape, 1978);

Irwin Shaw: Four Complete Novels (New York: Avenel, 1981)—comprises *Rich Man, Poor Man; Beggarman, Thief; Nightwork;* and *Evening in Byzantium.*

PLAY PRODUCTIONS: *Bury the Dead*, New York, Ethel Barrymore Theatre, 18 April 1936;

Siege, New York, Longacre Theatre, 7 December 1937;

The Gentle People, New York, Belasco Theatre, 5 January 1939;

Quiet City, New York, Belasco Theatre, March 1939;

Retreat to Pleasure, New York, Belasco Theatre, 17 December 1940;

Sons and Soldiers, New York, Morosco Theatre, 4 May 1943;

The Assassin, New York, National Theatre, 17 October 1945;

The Survivors, by Shaw and Peter Viertel, New York, Playhouse Theatre, 19 January 1948;

Children From Their Games, New York, Morosco Theatre, 12 April 1963;

A Choice of Wars, Glasgow, Scotland, Glasgow Citizens Theatre, 1967.

MOTION PICTURES: *The Big Game*, screenplay, RKO, 1936;

Commandos Strike at Dawn, screenplay, Columbia, 1942;

The Hard Way, screenplay by Shaw, Daniel Fuchs, and Jerry Wald, Warner Bros., 1942;

Talk of the Town, screenplay by Shaw and Sidney Buchman, RKO, 1942;

Take One False Step, screenplay by Shaw, Chester Erskine, and David Shaw, Universal, 1949;

Easy Living, screenplay by Shaw and Charles Schnee, 1949;

I Want You, screenplay, RKO, 1951;

Act of Love, screenplay, United Artists, 1953;

Fire Down Below, screenplay, Columbia, 1957;

Desire Under the Elms, screenplay, Paramount, 1958;

This Angry Age, screenplay by Shaw and Rene Clement, Columbia, 1958;

The Big Gamble, screenplay, Fox, 1961;

In the French Style, screenplay, Columbia, 1963;

Survival 1967, screenplay, United Film, 1968.

Irwin Shaw is one of the most frequently anthologized twentieth-century American short-story writers. Over the years, such Shaw stories as "The Girls in Their Summer Dresses," "The Eighty-Yard Run," "Act of Faith," and "Main Currents of American Thought" have become staples of American short-story collections. Two of his World War II stories were O. Henry Memorial Award winners—"Walking Wounded" received the 1944 first prize, and the next year "Gunner's Passage" received the second prize. In a career that spanned almost half a century, Shaw published over eighty short stories; and the consistently high quality and thematic diversity of his work became especially evident in 1978, when sixty-three of his best were published in his *Short Stories: Five Decades*. While his initial recognition came in the 1930s as a proletariat protest writer, his best short fiction is in the tradition of existential modernism. He utilized the Jamesian "scenic" method and the technique of indirect and minimalist narration perfected by Ernest Hemingway, who was briefly his mentor, to create his own distinct brand of modernist short fiction. Frequently publishing in the *New Yorker* during the 1930s and 1940s, Shaw became known as one of the most influential *New Yorker* short-story writers. Still, the importance of Shaw's contribution to the twentieth-century American short story has been somewhat obscured by critical controversy concerning his other work, especially his novels. In addition, like F. Scott Fitzgerald, he was frequently condemned for the lavish nature of his life-style in Europe and America.

Shaw was born Irwin Gilbert Shamforoff in the South Bronx, New York, on 27 February 1913. His father was William Shamforoff, a Russian-Jewish immigrant, and his mother was Rose Tompkins Shamforoff, an American-born daughter of a Lithuanian Jewish family. When the future novelist, short-story writer, and playwright was seven, the Shamforoff family moved to Brooklyn, where he enjoyed, until the age of fourteen, a secure and happy childhood. His father changed the name Shamforoff to Shaw in 1923 and began, with his two brothers (Irwin's uncles), a real-estate brokerage company that same year. By 1928 the business was facing bankruptcy and never recovered, closing down completely in 1932. William Shaw, the once-ambitious immigrant, was never again able to support his family, though he tried his hand at door-to-door selling of housewares.

Still, in 1929, at the age of sixteen, Irwin Shamforoff (he had retained the name in high school) was able to enter Brooklyn College, as

Irwin Shaw. In his freshman year he failed calculus and was asked to leave in the middle of the term. After a brief period of disgrace, he returned to school, played on the Brooklyn College football team, wrote for the college literary magazine and the student newspaper, and graduated with a B.A. in 1934.

However, life was hardly promising for a new college graduate in the heart of the Depression, especially one who needed to support his family; and, after graduation, Shaw worked at several part-time jobs, including a brief stint in semiprofessional football. His first break came in 1934 when he landed a job writing radio serials— "Dick Tracy" and then "The Gumps." Shaw recognized that his writing for radio was hackwork and devoted what time he could spare to an experimental, one-act, antiwar play called *Bury the Dead*. In April 1936 the play was produced in New York by an Off-Broadway company. The overwhelming critical reception was an unexpected and welcome surprise. The review in *Theatre Arts* was typical of the enthusiasm with which *Bury the Dead* was received: "Irwin Shaw, catapulted into the forefront of young playwrights by the one-act tragedy—his first produced play—has written . . . a shrewd theater piece and fiery protest against war." Offers to write for Hollywood soon followed, and Shaw was never again plagued by financial problems. Three years after the successful production of *Bury the Dead, The Gentle People*, a realistic "fable" celebrating the courage of the American common man and his determination to resist Fascist oppression, was made into a play and produced by the legendary Group Theatre at the Belasco; Shaw was subsequently praised, along with Clifford Odets, as one of America's important new radical playwrights. Also in 1939 his first collection, *Sailor Off the Bremen, and Other Stories*, appeared to favorable reviews. The volume's title story, in which a small group of leftists take brutal revenge against a sadistic Nazi named Lueger, who has beaten and mutilated one of their associates before the story opens, cemented Shaw's growing reputation as a writer of angry social protest.

Despite several more attempts, Shaw had no more major success in the theater after *The Gentle People*, and in 1948 he published his first novel, *The Young Lions*, an ambitious and panoramic fictional treatment of World War II. *The Young Lions* was widely praised as one of the most important American war novels; subsequently Shaw largely abandoned the theater in order to write novels.

The Brooklyn College Warriors, 1930; Shaw is standing, second from right (Brooklyn College, Library Special Collections). Shaw based his well-known story "The Eighty-Yard Run" on his football experiences.

His second novel, *The Troubled Air* (1951), which recounts the hysteria of McCarthy-inspired blacklisting in the radio industry, demonstrated that he had not abandoned his commitment to social protest.

Thus, as the 1950s began, Shaw's critical standing as an important American writer seemed secure. The 1950s, however, saw the beginning of a steady deterioration of his reputation. In 1951 Shaw moved to Paris and began a twenty-five-year voluntary exile in Europe; as a result, he was condemned by several critics for abandoning his American roots. In that same year John W. Aldridge, in his influential critical study, *After the Lost Generation*, denounced *The Young Lions* as "a system of carefully contained parallels, near-parallels, and pseudo parallels" that give only an "appearance of unity." *The Young Lions* was a superficial novel, Aldridge concluded, and Shaw was a superficial novelist. Even more devastating to the writer's reputation was Leslie A. Fiedler's 1956 attack, "Irwin Shaw: Adultery, the Last Politics." Fiedler remembered his passionate excitement at seeing the Off-Broadway production of *Bury the Dead* but then, focusing upon Shaw's 1956 novel, *Lucy Crown*, charged him with having compromised his talent and abandoned his commitment to the masses in order to produce a commercially successful "half-art." Shaw published ten novels after *The Troubled Air*, but none was seriously regarded by the critical establishment. His two epics of the Jordache family, *Rich Man, Poor Man* (1970) and *Beggarman, Thief* (1977), were made into highly successful television miniseries, though, and brought the writer the greatest popular success of his career.

Therefore, Shaw, originally hailed as a revolutionary force in the American theater, then praised as the author of one of the major World War II novels, died in 1984 largely regarded as a writer of superficial best-sellers. Still, there was one important constant in his career. He never stopped writing his masterfully crafted short stories, publishing several collections, including *Sailor Off the Bremen, Welcome to the City* (1942), *Act of Faith* (1946), *Mixed Company* (1950), *Tip on a Dead Jockey* (1957), *Love on a Dark Street* (1965), and *God Was Here but He Left Early* (1973). Even when his novels were being largely dismissed by the critics, his stories were generally praised for their craftsmanship and narrative power. Even so, it was the short fiction he produced before his 1951 move to Paris that aroused the greatest admiration. Reviewing *Mixed Company* in 1950, William Peden wrote in the *Saturday Review:* "Like Dickens, Mr. Shaw has created, prodigally,

Shaw with the cast of Bury the Dead, *which was produced in April 1936 and became his first major success (Brooklyn College, Library Special Collections)*

a crowded gallery of memorable people. Like Dickens, too, he handles scenes superbly. . . ." A year later, also in the *Saturday Review*, Lionel Trilling interrupted his review of *The Troubled Air* to praise Shaw's short fiction: "nothing Mr. Shaw might write could be wholly lacking in interest of one kind or another. For one thing, he always *does* observe and always *does* feel, and even when he is facile in observation and sentiment he is not insincere." Trilling concludes by describing Shaw as the "moral" spokesman for "the gentle people," the American common men and women.

Trilling is correct, but Shaw's American stories exhibit a wider range of theme and social setting than is apparent from the comment. Not surprisingly he did publish proletarian protest stories in the 1930s, at least two of which obviously utilize the experiences of the writer and his family. Perhaps Shaw's most effective social protest story is "Second Mortgage" (*New Republic*, 3 November 1937; in *Sailor Off the Bremen*). An extremely brief tale, it is narrated by a seventeen-year-old boy whose unemployed father is literally hiding inside his home from potential bill collectors. Having been warned that "strangers are never friends at the doors of the poor," the narra-

tor, nevertheless, allows in Mrs. Shapiro, who holds a second mortgage on his family's home. Mrs. Shapiro, it turns out, is every bit as much a victim of the corrupt and bankrupt economy as the narrator's parents. She once ran a vegetable store; but, when her husband became terminally ill, she sold the store and, on the advice of a banker named Mayer, invested all her money in worthless second mortgages. Now she prowls the streets, futilely trying to collect on her investments from people like the narrator's family, who cannot even pay their first mortgages. The weak father, touched by her story, promises her that he'll have something to give her "next Sunday." His wife, more realistic and exasperated by her husband's weakness, then explodes with the truth: "We have no money and we're not going to have any! We expect to be thrown out of this house any day now! We can't give you a penny, Mrs. Shapiro!" But touched by the pathetic Mrs. Shapiro's despair, the mother then offers her some tea before she leaves. Much of the power of "Second Mortgage" comes from the fact that all the story's characters are equally victims of a distant and incomprehensible socioeconomic system symbolized by Mayer, the banker who never physically appears in the story.

Even more obviously autobiographical is "Main Currents of American Thought" (*New Yorker*, 5 August 1939; in *Welcome to the City*). Its focal character is twenty-five-year-old Andrew, who supports his family by writing the radio serials "Dusty Blades" and "Ronnie Cook and His Friends." Shaw effectively utilizes ironic juxtaposition. As Andrew mentally composes wildly improbable episodes of "Dusty Blades," he reviews the painfully prosaic reality of his life as represented by his overdrawn checkbook: "His father's teeth—ninety dollars. The money it cost to keep a man going in his losing fight against age." He is further distracted by telephone reminders from his agent that he is behind schedule on "Dusty Blades" ("you're not writing for the *Atlantic Monthly*"), as well as remembered demands from his fiancée that he marry her or break off the relationship ("Martha's family was poor and getting no younger and finally there would be three families, with rent and clothes and doctors and funerals"). In addition, Andrew's mother is demanding fifty dollars for a new dress for his sister in the hope that the plain young woman may finally attract a man who will marry her; and Andrew hears through the window the sounds of the neighborhood baseball game. Finally the pressure is too much, and the frustrated young man verbally explodes to his mother: "Everybody comes to me! . . . Nobody leaves me alone! Not for a minute!" Instantly ashamed, he promises his mother the fifty dollars and retreats to join the baseball game outside. The story's last sentence effectively summarizes its ironic mode: "His arm hurt at the shoulder when he threw, and the boy playing second base called him Mister, which he wouldn't have done even last year, when Andrew was twenty-four." There is, of course, not a great deal of difference between twenty-four and twenty-five; but the passage of time reminds Andrew that his youth is rapidly evaporating, and he cannot find time to work on his serious play writing. One ironic implication of the title is that America does, in fact, prefer—and is certainly more willing to pay for—escapist fantasies, starring such characters as Dusty Blades and Ronnie Cook, rather than serious art. Andrew cannot escape from writing mindless escapism.

Fiedler's charge that Shaw, in the 1950s, began to betray his social and political convictions in order to focus on such commercial themes as adultery is a considerable oversimplifica-tion. Even in the 1930s and the 1940s Shaw did not, in his fiction, focus exclusively on social protest. Marital infidelity was a dominant theme in his stories from the beginning. In addition, he produced some stories celebrating the rich diversity of life in New York City, while in others he depicted the pain and turmoil of adolescence.

Troubled marriages are central in two of Shaw's most well-known and frequently anthologized stories: "The Eighty-Yard Run" (*Esquire*, January 1941; in *Welcome to the City*) and "The Girls in Their Summer Dresses" (*New Yorker*, 4 February 1939; in *Sailor Off the Bremen*). Both are masterful examples of modernist short fiction, and both treat the theme of the immaturity of the American male. The focal character in "The Eighty-Yard Run," Christian Darling, is a former college football player who cannot adjust to the pressures of both economic survival in the Great Depression and an increasingly troubled marriage. As the story opens, Darling, thirty-five and working as a traveling tailor's representative, has returned to the midwestern football field of his undergraduate days. There he mentally relives his moment of greatest glory, an eighty-yard run *in practice*, and the fame and romance of his college years. In fact Darling was never a star on the football team—he played the unglamorous position of blocking back for an All-American named Diederich. Still, he was a starter and, subsequently, a glamorous figure on campus. (Shaw was himself primarily a blocking back who rarely carried the ball during his Brooklyn College days.) In an extended flashback, Shaw recounts the fifteen years of Darling's life since college. After graduation he had married Louise Tucker, his college sweetheart, and for a while things were good between them, despite his occasional infidelities ("There'd been other women for him, but all casual and secret, more for curiosity's sake, and vanity . . .").

Darling's father-in-law, an ink manufacturer, gave him an undemanding job in New York City. But then came 1929 and the bankruptcy of Mr. Tucker, who committed suicide four years later. Lost and bewildered, Darling began to sit around the apartment and drink, while Louise began to discover herself and flourish. She got a job on "a woman's fashion magazine," studied the Impressionists and Postimpressionists, and became involved with the new leftist theater and New York leftist politics in general. A critical point in their marriage came when Darling refused to accompany Louise and a lawyer

Shaw and Ken Marthey in France, August 1944, during their service in an army film-producing unit (photograph by Philip Drell). Several of Shaw's stories, including "Act of Faith," take place during World War II.

for the longshoreman's union to a new play "by a guy named Odets," called *Waiting for Lefty* (1935). Gradually, reluctantly, Darling acknowledged to himself the failures of his marriage and his adult life: "He hadn't practiced for 1929 and New York City and a girl who would turn into a woman."

For its conclusion, the story returns to the present. Thinking he is unobserved, Darling, dressed in a business suit, reenacts his eighty-yard practice run. After crossing the goal line, he realizes that a boy and girl sitting together at the end of the field have been watching him. In embarrassment he tries to explain: "I—once I played here." As with many of Shaw's best stories, this ending effectively communicates the central themes of the story. Darling, the perennial boy-man (he dislikes the fact that Louise affectionately addresses him as "Baby"), has fled the baffling sophistication of New York City to return to what he remembers as the idyllic and pastoral Midwest of his youth. But the young couple lounging on the field painfully remind him that he is thirty-five and a failure in life and marriage. A mere change of geography cannot erase the past fifteen years—he is, in fact, no longer anyone's "darling."

"The Girls in Their Summer Dresses" is justifiably Shaw's most frequently reprinted story. It exemplifies the narrative indirection and minimalism most commonly associated with Hemingway. Shaw claimed to have written the story in one morning when he was twenty-five. Less than ten pages long, consisting almost entirely of dialogue, it is the kind of modernist story in which, on the surface, little seems to happen. It opens with an affluent and apparently happy New York couple, Michael and Frances, strolling down Fifth Avenue one morning and planning an idyllic afternoon together. Almost immediately, however, a tension in their marriage becomes evident—Michael stares at a pretty woman on the street. Initially Frances attempts to laugh off her husband's obsession with other women; but, when he looks longingly at another young woman, Frances can no longer repress her anger: "You always look at other women, . . . at every damn woman in the city of New York." She refuses to let up in her attack: "I feel rotten inside, in my stomach, when we pass a woman and you look at her and I see that look in your eye and that's the way you looked at me the first time, in Alice Maxwell's house. . . ." Attempting to release the tension that has suddenly arisen between them, the couple retreats to a bar.

The bar provides no relief, however, as Frances accuses her husband of wanting the other women, "Every one of them." Michael then attempts to explain his obsession as a harmless mid-life crisis—New York's never-ending parade of pretty "girls in their summer dresses" reminds him of when he was young and first seeing, and falling in love with, the city. Refusing to believe there is not more involved, Frances, now in tears, demands to know whether her husband would "like to be free" to "make a move someday." Abruptly Michael confesses that she is correct. Frances then stops crying and gets up to make a phone call. Watching her walk across the room, Michael thinks, "what a pretty girl, what nice legs."

As with most successful modernist fiction, the story is open to several interpretations. In *Understanding Fiction* (1943) Cleanth Brooks and Robert Penn Warren suggest one reading of the story: the irony of the story's ending conveys "a serious idea—the failure of love through the failure to recognize the beloved as a person, as more than a convenience." It is true that, in the last paragraph, Michael is finally able to respond to Frances by depersonalizing her, by reducing her to a pair of "nice legs." Other critics, emphasizing the fact that it is Frances who initiates and prolongs the quarrel, focus on her insecurity—they suggest that Michael's climactic confession of wanting "to be free" can be read as an expression of anger and frustration resulting from his wife's relentless probing. Indeed there is no way to be certain that he ever intends to leave Frances; he does, after all, depersonalize *all* attractive young women. Real involvement with one of "the girls in their summer dresses" might force him to confront more directly than he wants to the fact that he is overweight and is getting older. It has also been suggested that the story illustrates the concept of "the ritual quarrel." Occasionally in Shaw's work, married couples who no longer have anything to say to each other fall back on well-rehearsed quarrels in order to communicate, however ineffectually. Shaw himself said the story was "about a man who tells his wife that he's going to be unfaithful to her" (*Paris Review* inter-

view, Spring 1979). Critics looking for autobiographical overtones in the story emphasize the fact that the writer was frequently and publicly unfaithful to his wife, the former Marian Edwards, almost from the beginning of their marriage on 13 October 1939, shortly before "The Girls in Their Summer Dresses" was written. After thirty troubled years of marriage, Shaw's infidelities finally resulted in divorce in 1970. (The Shaws had one child, Adam, born in 1950.) Those who insist on looking for autobiographical overtones in the 1939 story read it as an ominous prophecy of the future.

However it is read, one must admire the sheer craft of "The Girls in Their Summer Dresses." Fundamentally it is the story of a troubled relationship of which only one climactic moment is overtly depicted. As in Hemingway's "Hills Like White Elephants" (*transition*, August 1927), everything leading up to the present story is only hinted at or ignored completely. Still, Michael and Frances emerge as very real characters, and the reader becomes intrigued by trying to uncover what is really happening between them. One of Shaw's earliest stories, it effectively refutes Fiedler's contention that, during the 1950s, Shaw discarded his social conscience in order to treat infidelity among the affluent classes.

Of course, in the late 1930s and very early 1940s, Shaw did write several stories warning against the implications for America of European Fascism and protesting against American anti-Semitism. Since Shaw was a Jewish-American writer, it was hardly surprising that he began to focus on these related concerns. "Weep in Years to Come" and "Sailor Off the Bremen" (both in Shaw's first collection) are among the best of his stories emphasizing the necessity of the United States quickly and forcibly stopping Hitler. While some critics openly wondered how the implications of these stories could be reconciled with the pacifism of *Bury the Dead*, it seems obvious that, between 1936 and 1939, Shaw became increasingly aware of the Nazi threat to world peace and human decency. He was, in fact, never a pacifist to the point of accepting the genocide of his people.

During the war Shaw served in a documentary-film-producing unit under the successful Hollywood film director George Stevens. This role spared him from personal involvement in combat, but he was present during or shortly after some of the most dramatic events of the war—the struggle for North Africa, the Nor-

Shaw with his wife, Marian Edwards Shaw, during a 1961 trip to Yugoslavia. They were divorced in 1970 but reconciled and remarried in 1982.

mandy invasion, and the liberation of Paris. Not surprisingly, then, his war stories do not focus directly on combat, but portray the loneliness, tension, and boredom of the noncombatant soldier or the courageous lives of those involved in the French Resistance Movement. The award-winning "Walking Wounded" (*New Yorker*, 13 May 1944; in *Act of Faith*), for example, describes the alienation of a British soldier, trapped in a desk job in Cairo, who attempts desperately and unsuccessfully to remember what his wife in England looks like.

The themes of war and American anti-Semitism effectively merge in the frequently anthologized "Act of Faith" (*New Yorker*, 2 February 1946). The title story in Shaw's 1946 collection, it depicts the friendship of three American soldiers: Seeger, Olson, and Welch. Of the three only Seeger is Jewish. In the story, the war has just ended, and the three are eagerly planning a trip to Paris the next day. They already have the passes but have no money to spend in the expensive French capital. Welch and Olson ask Seeger

to sell a German Luger, which he had taken from its previous owner, "an enormous SS major, in Coblenz." But before agreeing to sell the Luger, Seeger reads a letter he has just received from his father. The letter, in a desperate and angry tone, recounts the outbreak of a new and vicious anti-Semitism in the United States: "Wherever you go these days—restaurants, hotels, clubs, trains—you seem to hear talk about the Jews, mean, hateful, murderous talk. . . ." Anti-Semitism has destroyed Mr. Seeger's Thursday night poker game, which had been a regular event for over ten years. He says he has even come to dread seeing Jewish names on petitions for worthy, liberal causes, fearing that any public notice of Jewish-Americans will only intensify the rampant anti-Semitism. He concludes by saying that reading about the pain and suffering of European Jews now annoys him: "I feel they are boring the rest of the world with their problems, they are making demands upon the rest of the world by being killed, they are disturbing everyone by being hungry and asking for the return of their property. If we could all fall through the crust of the earth and vanish in one hour, with our heroes and poets and prophets and martyrs, perhaps we would be doing the memory of the Jewish race a service. . . ."

Seeger is shocked and angered by what he has read. He remembers how the Jews his unit liberated throughout the war expressed reverence and pride when seeing him among their rescuers. He also remembers that he had vowed to take the Luger "back with him to America, and plug it and keep it on his desk at home, as a kind of vague, half-understood sign to himself that justice had once been done and he had been its instrument." Now he wonders if he shouldn't take it home "not as a memento" but as a means of protection. He begins to remember all the episodes of anti-Semitism in the army, which he experienced or merely heard about but had previously repressed. But just as he is about to give in to bitterness and anger, Olson and Welch reappear to withdraw their request that he sell the Luger and to apologize indirectly for the way in which they pressured him. Seeger then thinks of the times during combat when his two friends literally saved his life. Abruptly he turns to them and asks, "Say, what do you guys think of the Jews?" and they lightly, but sensitively, dismiss the question. Seeger now realizes the full importance of his bond with Olson and Welch: "He would have to rely upon them, later on, out of uniform, on their native streets, more than he had ever relied on them on the bullet-swept street and in the dark minefield in France." All three of the main characters epitomize Shaw's concept of "the gentle people," the inherently decent Americans who will, when sufficiently challenged, actively stand up for justice and honor. The story concludes with Seeger's "act of faith"—he agrees to sell the Luger in order to finance the sojourn in Paris. "What could I use it for in America?" he asks.

"Act of Faith" is more forgiving than Shaw's earlier stories about anti-Semitism. It is also more direct in narrative technique than Shaw's short fiction normally is—he utilizes the device of Mr. Seeger's letter for some editorializing. Still, the effectiveness of "Act of Faith" lies mainly in its success in making Seeger's concluding gesture believable after the pain and horror of the father's letter. The story itself is an "act of faith," representing Shaw's affirmation of the inherent decency of the American common man.

Several critics saw a decline in the quality of Shaw's short fiction after his 1951 move to Paris.

The expatriate short stories were not criticized as harshly as were the expatriate novels—virtually everyone agreed that Shaw's craftsmanship was still evident in the short fiction. But the critical consensus was that Shaw had abandoned the moral concerns of his earlier work for a kind of superficial cynicism. This judgment was best expressed by Hubert Saal in a 1957 *Saturday Review* article about *Tip on a Dead Jockey, and Other Stories*. Saal lamented that this shift in Shaw's moral stance was especially regrettable because of the quality and importance of his work during the 1930s and early 1940s: "Did any writer of that prewar time have a better eye and ear for what went on around him? Shaw cared, and his characters cared about politics and injustice and loneliness and love and growing up and growing old. They (and clearly he) believed fiercely in what Faulkner was later to spell out: 'that man will not merely endure; he will prevail.' "

There is some validity in this charge of a shift in Shaw's moral vision after 1951; as Saal points out, the story "Tip on a Dead Jockey" (*New Yorker*, 6 May 1954) does convey a strong degree of cynicism and ethical compromise. Nevertheless, some of Shaw's post-1951 stories are among his best. Much of his expatriate short fiction, rather than abandoning ethical concerns, reveals new ones. In a few of these stories, he expresses anger and despair over the epidmic of McCarthyism in America—"Goldilocks at Graveside" (*Esquire*, January 1964; in *Love on a Dark Street*) is an especially effective protest against the McCarthyism hysteria. The political repression in America was, in fact, a major reason behind Shaw's voluntary exile. He was briefly blacklisted, largely because of *Bury the Dead* and his public support of the Loyalist cause during the Spanish Civil War. At no time was he allied with the American Communist party—he was also a supporter and admirer of Franklin Delano Roosevelt. Shaw's politics were comparable to John Steinbeck's, leftist but not Marxist.

Among the post-1951 stories, "Where All Things Wise and Fair Descend" (first published in *God Was Here but He Left Early*) is a lyrical, evocative study of the turmoil of adolescence. In it, a shy, socially and physically awkward young boy is torn between grief and jealousy when his brother, a popular college football star, is killed. This late story is at least as good, if not better, than Shaw's earlier evocations of male adolescence—such as "Strawberry Ice Cream Soda" and "Little Henry Irving" (both in *Sailor Off the*

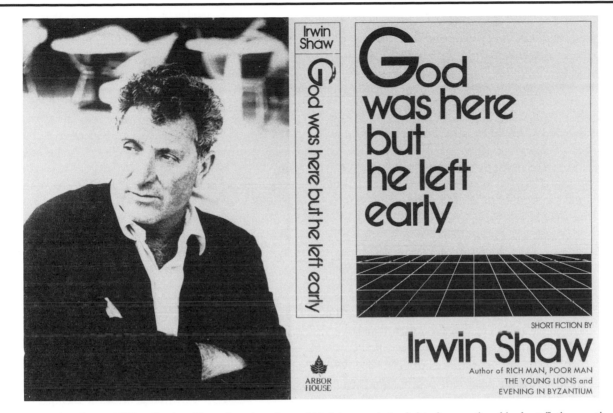

Dust jacket for Shaw's 1973 collection. Even though reviews of his later novels tended to be negative, his short fiction continued to be well received.

Bremen), and "Pattern of Love" (in *Welcome to the City*). But the most memorable group of Shaw's expatriate stories—"A Year to Learn the Language" and "The Man Who Married a French Wife" in *Love on a Dark Street*, and "Then We Were Three" and "Voyage Out, Voyage Home" in *Tip on a Dead Jockey*—are masterful variations on Henry James's "international theme." In them innocent Americans are changed by their encounters with sophisticated Europeans. "A Year to Learn the Language" (*Redbook*, November 1961) is perhaps the best of these. In this story nineteen-year-old Roberta James (one wonders if the character's last name is a form of acknowledgment and tribute on Shaw's part) travels from Chicago to Paris to study painting for twelve months. When the story opens, Roberta is involved in a nonsexual affair with a Frenchman named Guy, who claims to be twenty-one. Guy takes Roberta on his Vespa motorbike to an art gallery, where she hopes to exhibit some of her paintings. Initially prospects are not promising, as the gallery director, Monsieur Patrini, examines her watercolors, "frowning slightly, as though he were remembering a dish at lunch that hadn't quite agreed with him. . . ." But then a "man in a Homberg hat" mys-

teriously appears and expresses great admiration for Roberta's work. With an abrupt shift in mood, Patrini identifies the man as a baron, and the mysterious gentleman asks to take two of Roberta's paintings home to decide which one he wants to buy. After the titled gentleman leaves, Patrini advises Roberta that "the Baron has a famous collection, as you know."

That evening, after taking Roberta to a "needlessly bare and explicit film," Guy abruptly announces to her that "tonight we become lovers." But the innocent American girl, while tempted by Guy's demand, decides that sex with him must be postponed, at least until she knows the outcome of the baron's examination of her paintings. A few days later she hears from Patrini that the baron has decided to buy both her paintings and, furthermore, has invited her to a dinner that evening. Roberta decides she will go, even though it means canceling a date with Guy: "Artists must be ruthless, or they are not artists. Remember Gauguin. Remember Baudelaire."

At the baron's home Roberta initially feels that all her dreams are suddenly coming true. The nobleman tells her that he wants to show her something and takes her to a sitting room, where "on the wall opposite the fireplace were her two watercolors, handsomely framed, separated by a glorious pencil drawing by Matisse" and where "on another wall there was, indeed, a Soutine." The baron then gives her a check for 250 francs, the equivalent of five hundred American dollars. But when everyone is seated for dinner, Roberta gradually becomes aware that the atmosphere is less than idyllic. She is seated at the foot of the table and forced to listen to the right-wing opinions of several "tottering Gallic Babbitts" and their wives. When one woman says "she had heard from an American friend that President Kennedy has surrounded himself with Communists," Roberta loudly protests that is nonsense. No one listens to her, however. Gradually she realizes the true nature of the baron's interest in her and of his "collection" and thinks, "I know what *he's* after . . . and he's not going to get it."

Remembering Guy's true devotion to her, she leaves the table to call him to come get her. Looking at her paintings again, she also realizes the mediocrity of her talent: "[The paintings] looked pallid and ordinary and influenced by everybody." When Guy appears on his Vespa to rescue her, she informs the young Frenchman that she is now ready to go to bed with him. He then takes her to an inexpensive hotel because it is all he can afford; instead of romantic, their room turns out to be plain and uncomfortably cold. Further surprising her, Guy next insists that they undress separately without looking at each other. In bed with the lights out Guy despairingly confesses that he is a sixteen-year-old virgin, and the couple spends an innocent night together. Roberta awakens first the next morning, dresses hurriedly, and then awakens Guy. As he dresses this time, however, she watches "candidly" and then tells him that the previous night "was the most wonderful night of my life." "A Year to Learn the Language" is a flawless variation on James's "international theme." The innocent American girl is initially deceived about Guy's own innocence as well as by the baron's cynical sophistication. At the end of the story she is beginning to know and understand herself; Paris has accelerated her maturation process.

In 1976 Shaw returned from his voluntary exile abroad and, until his death in 1984, divided his time between Long Island's Hamptons and his beloved skiing village, Klosters, Switzerland. During these last years of his life he experienced a mixture of good and bad fortune. Because of

the television miniseries of his novels—*Rich Man, Poor Man; Beggarman, Thief;* and *Evening in Byzantium*—he enjoyed great popular success. He became reconciled with Marian and remarried her in 1982. Still, he was hurt by the consistently negative reviews of most of his post-1970 novels (though *Bread Upon the Waters*, published in 1981, was generally well received). Moreover, he discovered, after an operation in 1981, that he had cancer of the prostate and that there was no way of knowing whether the surgery had arrested the growth of the disease. Thus, during the last three years of his life, Shaw endured considerable physical pain, as well as mental torment. He and Marian kept the cancer a secret from their wide circle of celebrity friends until after the writer's death. Shaw generally succeeded in hiding his physical pain in public, and he continued his long-standing practice of giving support and advice to young writers. For example, he was especially generous to Kaylie Jones, the daughter of his old friend and fellow novelist James Jones, while she was working on her first novel, *As Soon As It Rains* (1986). Certainly one of the most gratifying experiences of Shaw's last years was the 1978 publication of *Short Stories: Five Decades*, which led critics to remember and recognize the rich diversity and craftsmanship of the short fiction of Irwin Shaw.

Interviews:

"The Art of Fiction, IV," *Paris Review*, 1 (1953): 27-49;

"The Art of Fiction, IV, Continued," *Paris Review*, 21 (Spring 1979): 248-262.

Biography:

Michael Shnayerson, *Irwin Shaw: A Biography* (New York: Putnam's, 1989).

References:

John W. Aldridge, *After the Lost Generation* (New York: Noonday, 1951), pp. 146-156;

Bergen Evans, "Irwin Shaw," *English Journal*, 40 (November 1951): 485-491;

Leslie A. Fiedler, "Irwin Shaw: Adultery, the Last Politics," *Commentary*, 22 (July 1956): 71-74;

James R. Giles, *Irwin Shaw* (Boston: Twayne, 1983);

Giles, "Irwin Shaw's Original Prologue to *The Young Lions*," *Resources for American Literary Study*, 11 (Spring 1981): 115-119;

William Peden, "Best of Irwin Shaw," *Saturday Review of Literature*, 33 (19 November 1950): 27-28;

Hubert Saal, "Disenchanted Men," *Saturday Review of Literature*, 40 (3 August 1957): 12-13;

William Startt, "Irwin Shaw: An Extended Talent," *Midwest Quarterly*, 2 (Summer 1961): 325-337;

Lionel Trilling, "Some Are Gentle, Some Are Not," *Saturday Review of Literature*, 34 (9 July 1951): 8-9;

Ross Wetzsteon, "Irwin Shaw: The Conflict Between Big Bucks and Good Books," *Saturday Review*, 8 (August 1981): 12-17.

Papers:

The manuscript of *The Young Lions* is at the Pierpont Morgan Library in New York City. Other Shaw papers, including his letters, are at Boston University and Brooklyn College.

Tess Slesinger

(16 July 1905 - 21 February 1945)

Kim Flachmann
California State University, Bakersfield

BOOKS: *The Unpossessed* (New York: Simon & Schuster, 1934; London: Barker, 1935);

Time: The Present, a Book of Short Stories (New York: Simon & Schuster, 1935; London: Barker, 1935); enlarged as *On Being Told That Her Second Husband Has Taken His First Lover, and Other Stories* (Chicago: Quadrangle, 1971).

SELECTED PERIODICAL PUBLICATIONS—
UNCOLLECTED:

FICTION

"Young Wife," *This Quarter*, 3 (April-June 1931): 698-708;

"Brother to the Happy," *Pagany*, 3 (January-March 1932): 77-82;

"Ben Grader Makes a Call," *Vanity Fair*, 42 (June 1934): 40, 70;

"The Old Lady Counts Her Injuries," *Vanity Fair*, 43 (October 1934): 23, 79;

"After the Cure," *Vanity Fair*, 43 (January 1935): 48, 65, 66;

"Mr. Palmer's Party," *New Yorker*, 11 (27 April 1935): 30-32;

"You Gi-i-ive Yourself or Drop the Handkerchief," *Vanity Fair*, 44 (May 1935): 41, 60b;

"The Best Things in Life Are Three," *Vanity Fair*, 44 (August 1935): 16, 52b;

Tess Slesinger in the late 1930s

"For Better, for Worse," *Delineator*, 128 (January 1936): 18-19.

NONFICTION

"The Lonelier Eve," *New Yorker*, 10 (28 April 1934): 32, 34;

"Memoirs of an Ex-Flapper," *Vanity Fair*, 43 (December 1934): 26-27, 74, 76;

"Hollywood Gallery," *Michigan Quarterly Review*, 18 (Summer 1979): 439-454.

MOTION PICTURES: *His Brother's Wife*, screenplay, M-G-M, 1936;

The Good Earth, adapted by Slesinger, M-G-M, 1937;

The Bride Wore Red, screenplay, M-G-M, 1937;

Girls' School, screenplay, Columbia, 1938;

Dance, Girl, Dance, screenplay by Slesinger and Frank Davis, RKO, 1940;

Remember the Day, screenplay, 20th Century-Fox, 1941;

Are Husbands Necessary?, screenplay, Paramount, 1942;

A Tree Grows in Brooklyn, adapted by Slesinger and Davis, 20th Century-Fox, 1945.

Since Tess Slesinger died relatively young (at thirty-nine), her literary production was sparse, and her reputation as a writer is based on only a few works, including one novel, entitled *The Unpossessed* (1934), one collection of short stories, nine uncollected stories, and eight screenplays. Though not very well known, her short fiction, a subtle blend of satire and gentility, deserves critical attention.

Slesinger was born into a Hungarian-Russian family on 16 July 1905 in New York City, where she grew up. She was educated at Ethical Culture Society School, Swarthmore College, and the Columbia School of Journalism, where she received her degree in 1925. In 1928 she married Columbia classmate Herbert Solow, a political journalist who circulated within a powerful group of New York Jewish intellectuals and who soon became assistant editor of the *Menorah Journal*.

Slesinger joined her husband's literary circle by transforming observations from her diary into stories. In March 1930 she published her first story, "Mother to Dinner," in the *Menorah Journal*. After divorcing Solow in 1932, Slesinger published a second story, "Missis Flinders," in *Story* magazine (December); two years later, this story was to become the last chapter of her novel. Shortly after this second publication, Slesinger was hired by New York's Briarcliff Manor, a private girls' school, to teach writing; this environment became the basis for a short story she wrote

in 1935, "The Answer on the Magnolia Tree" (first published in *Time: The Present*, 1935), for which she was paid twenty-five thousand dollars for screen rights in 1938. The film was titled *Girls' School*.

May 1934 marked the appearance of *The Unpossessed*, which was a critical success in New York. In its first month on the market, her novel went through four printings. John Chamberlain of the *New York Times* declared the work "quite simply and dogmatically, the best novel of contemporary New York City that we have read." Though the correspondences are far from exact, Slesinger relied heavily on the Jewish intellectuals in her life to create her characters. In these portrayals, she uses a mixture of sympathy and disdain to effect a final comment on her contemporaries, to whom the novel is dedicated. The fact that the chapters in this novel could work well individually testifies to Slesinger's natural propensity for creating short fiction.

Slesinger's only collection of short stories, published initially in 1935 as *Time: The Present*, without the story "A Life in the Day of a Writer" (*Story*, November 1935), is a group of her best works, set in the 1930s. Many of the stories appeared previously in *Scribner's*, *Story*, the *Forum*, *Vanity Fair*, *Redbook*, and the *American Mercury*. "A Life in the Day of a Writer" was also printed in Martha Foley's *Fifty Best American Short Stories, 1915-1965* and in Edward J. O'Brien's *The Best Short Stories, 1936*. After this story was added to her collection, the volume was republished by her second husband, Frank Davis, as *On Being Told That Her Second Husband Has Taken His First Lover, and Other Stories*.

Disagreement in the reviews of this collection when it first appeared ranged from Edith Walton's opinion in the *New York Times* that the stories were too "consciously clever" and overly sentimental to Whit Burnett's praise of the author (in *Story* magazine) as "a master of the tragic-comic situation in which her character is suspended at the moment where emotional feeling is checked by sophisticated and objective thinking." But the stories are generally accurate and surefooted, as they capture the essence of human growth and development at some of its most crucial stages. From fifteen to eighty-four pages long, these pieces are often third-person narratives that delve into the consciousness of their main characters in search of clear reasons and unspoken realities. Much of the emotional activity is rendered in a stream-of-consciousness fashion

Jobs in the Sky

A STORY

By Tess Slesinger

Iᴛ meant that you wanted to hold your job like no-body's business if you managed to get in ahead of Mr. Keasbey, whose name had been first in Mrs. Summers's section-book and the section-books of her predecessors for a noble fifteen years. Mr. Keasbey signed in daily at eight-forty (ten minutes before the deadline), and on the dot of eight-fifteen on pep-speech days (a good ten minutes before Mrs. Summers reluctantly counted you late)—and daily after removing the cover from his table of Important New Fiction and flicking his books with his private duster, stood with his fine white head bowed, waiting reproachfully like the best boy in the class. But on the day before Christmas, the Monday which was the last day of the Christmas rush, 1934, and the morning for which Mr. Mar-

Illustration for the March 1935 Scribner's Magazine *publication of a story collected in* Time: The Present *(1935)*

that makes the omniscience of the narrator powerful and serene at the same time. Knowing truths that others in the stories do not realize yet, the narrator essentially describes the characters coming to their individual revelations. The characters are crisp, precise versions of everyday people, though they successfully transcend the stereotypical. At her best Slesinger's descriptions of actions and thoughts thus become a series of perceptions of life delivered with insight and exactness.

Individually these vignettes help the reader visualize and understand single moments in human development; collectively they reveal human nature on a grand scale, as they move from adolescent crises (as in "The Answer on the Magnolia Tree") to the dilemmas connected with maturity and aging (as in "After the Party," first published in the collection). Within this framework the issue of personal identity becomes the focus of the author's study of human nature, as if it were the center of a wheel with several spokes leading to it.

Slesinger considers the problem of identity in each case as it relates to one other dominant theme. Beginning with her most fundamental concerns, Slesinger looks, for example, at struggles

for basic emotional survival in "After the Party" and "Jobs in the Sky" (*Scribner's*, March 1935). In the first case, Mrs. Helene Colborne, a wealthy resident of Gramercy Park, fights desperately for her survival after a nervous breakdown by giving parties for writers, which keeps her in touch with the world. "Jobs in the Sky," on the other hand, dramatizes the close connection between identity (and self-worth) and respectable jobs when two employees are delicately but emphatically fired from M and J Department Store on Christmas Eve.

Just as basic as survival is the question of sexual identity, which is the dominant focus in "Missis Flinders" and is a more subtle consideration in "Relax is All" (*Forum*, August 1933). As Margaret Flinders reminisces on the way home from Greenway Maternity Hospital in the first example, readers find that she has had an abortion for the sake of economic and intellectual freedom; now she is angry at her husband and questions both of their sexual identities. In "Relax is All" Ethel Blake, a businesswoman from New York, desperately trying to fit into a small group of horseback riders on an outing, cannot relax until she sexually conquers the haughtiest, most accomplished rider of the bunch, at which point she masters her own horse and gains new confidence and security.

Love is a secondary theme in many of Slesinger's short stories, but "On Being Told That Her Second Husband Has Taken His First Lover" (*Story*, April 1935) and "Mother to Dinner" focus on love more precisely than some of the others. In the first story, through a combination of dialogue and private thoughts, Slesinger explores the tenuousness and interdependence of the feelings of love and trust. In the second story the protagonist is trapped in the tension that exists between her mother and her husband until she becomes emotionally consumed by it.

Slesinger considers the relationship of self-definition and worth from a slightly different angle in "The Mouse-Trap" (previously unpublished) and "The Friedmans' Annie" (*Menorah Journal*, March 1931). The former is a satire about an advertising company whose highest executive operates exclusively on the power he derives from his position; though he is finally able to retain his discontented workers in the outer office (which he calls the "Mouse-Trap") by playing on their sympathies, he cannot overpower his secretary—physically or emotionally. In a slightly different fashion, Annie Schlemmer, the Friedmans' full-time housekeeper, is trying to discover her self-worth in "The Friedmans' Annie"; at the same time that she needs her independence from the Friedmans to achieve her own integrity, she strongly depends upon the household for her self-importance.

In a broader sense "The Times So Unsettled Are" (*Redbook*, March 1935) and "White on Black" (*American Mercury*, December 1930) consider finding one's identity through social amenities. The former studies the effects of love, death, and social unrest on an Austrian woman named Mariedel, who tries but tragically fails to find herself after losing her two brothers, her father, and her Socialist lover to politics and war. "White on Black" characterizes the potentially destructive effects of maturity and socialization on two black children, Paul and Elizabeth Wilson, and their classmates in an otherwise white junior high and high school.

Finally, on her most sophisticated level, Slesinger contemplates the paradox of self-definition in the last two stories in this collection (as it was published in 1971): "The Answer on the Magnolia Tree" and "A Life in the Day of a Writer." The first story concerns a search for iden-

Advertisement for Slesinger's only short-story collection (from Story, *July 1935)*

tity in a girls' boarding school. The longest in the collection, this story explores the suppressed desires that typify this particular age group. Through a transgression committed by one of the girls (staying out all night on the golf course with her date), readers become privy to a whole gamut of insoluble contradictions, revolving around the basic struggle between desire and restraint that defines these girls, and their repressed teachers, at this stage in their lives. "A Life in the Day of a Writer" considers identity through a writer's struggle with the forces of art versus life, sanity versus creativity, and reality versus imagination. The protagonist, Bertram Kyle, functions in a reverie that lets him transcend reality and, therefore, write; when this reverie is broken, he can no longer produce art.

At her worst Slesinger produced overwritten, tedious narratives with little depth in content or in character development. The import of "After the Party," for example, gets lost in petty descriptive details and uninteresting party plans. In contrast Slesinger's most successful stories are those that delve deeply into the souls of their main characters. In "On Being Told That Her Second Husband Has Taken His First Lover," for example, the main character is Cornelia North, whose sensitivities and inadequacies are revealed through carefully orchestrated dialogue and stream-of-consciousness narration delivered in the second person: "Time was when a thing like this was a shock that fell heavily in the pit of your stomach, and gave you indigestion all at once. But you can only feel a thing like this in its entirety the first time, after that it's a weaker repetition." The narrator conveniently becomes both Cornelia and Cornelia's other self, playing the role of admonisher and supporter simultaneously. She talks to herself and about herself, as in her longing at the end of the story for some sort of personal satisfaction and the return of her self-respect. In addition Slesinger's insights into human nature are clarified by a refined use of figurative language that slips coyly and naturally into the narrator's banter. The reader's understanding of this one incident in Cornelia's life is complete and profound because of the many levels on which the story functions.

In like manner Slesinger's artistry in "Mother to Dinner" surpasses that of some other stories because of her extraordinary character development. The story consists of eight sequential episodes that take place predominantly in Katherine Benjamin Jastrow's mind. Katherine has been married to Gerald Jastrow for eleven months and is consistently depressed by the tension between her husband and her mother. As she prepares for her mother and father to come to dinner on this particular day, she falls more deeply into a depression, which finally consumes her. The third-person, omniscient narrator regulates the timing of Katherine's decline with a series of introspective descriptions that reveal her emotional weakness in the face of this obsessive familial tension. Her identity is not strong enough to resolve the tension or keep it inside herself, so she becomes one with the literal and figurative storm that has been raging outside, as she is finally engulfed by the loneliness and meaninglessness that surround her.

Another successful story, "A Life in the Day of a Writer," recounts a single day in a writer's life. The interesting twist in the title suggests the irony with which the writer (Bertram Kyle) looks at life. The story functions on an increasingly frenzied level that will not release the reader from its overwhelming insanity until the end. The narrator's third-person, stream-of-consciousness technique dramatizes the writer's struggle to resolve the perpetual conflict he endures daily between art and life and between his own life and death: "he did not merely have to live with his life each day but he had to give birth to it over again every morning." He knows living is a poor substitute for art but a necessary prerequisite. He is caught up in the passionate whirlpool created by these two worlds, just as the reader is suspended by the language and momentum of the story itself.

Soon after the publication of her short-story collection, Slesinger moved to Hollywood to write movies for one thousand dollars per week. While living in California, she married producer-screenwriter Frank Davis, had two children (Peter and Jane), and wrote eight films that were produced. After coauthoring with Davis her last screenplay (*A Tree Grows in Brooklyn*, 1945), Slesinger planned to write a novel about Hollywood. Though she had not written any fiction since 1935, she maintained notebooks, which her son has kept, of ideas for future novels and stories. But cancer ended her life, on 21 February 1945, before she began this project.

Tess Slesinger's contribution to the genre of short fiction was not large in terms of volume, but her ability to dramatize everyday human feelings and actions with ingenuity and sincerity compensates for the scarcity of her work. The confidence with which she disassembles appearances as she reveals the tribulations of the human soul makes her work especially notable.

References:

Shirley Biagi, "Forgive Me For Dying," *Antioch Review*, 35 (Summer 1977): 224-236;

Janet Sharistanian, "Tess Slesinger's Hollywood Sketches," *Michigan Quarterly Review*, 18 (Summer 1979): 428-438;

Lionel Trilling, "Young in the Thirties," *Commentary* (May 1966): 43-51.

Jesse Stuart

(8 August 1906 - 17 February 1984)

H. Edward Richardson
University of Louisville

See also the Stuart entries in *DLB 9: American Novelists, 1910-1945; DLB 48: American Poets, 1880-1945;* and *DLB Yearbook: 1984.*

BOOKS: *Harvest of Youth* (Howe, Okla.: Scroll, 1930);

Man with a Bull-Tongue Plow (New York: Dutton, 1934; revised, 1959);

Head o' W-Hollow (New York: Dutton, 1936);

Beyond Dark Hills (New York: Dutton, 1938; London: Hutchinson, 1938);

Tim: A Story (Cincinnati: Little Man, 1939);

Trees of Heaven (New York: Dutton, 1940);

Men of the Mountains (New York: Dutton, 1941);

Taps for Private Tussie (New York: Books, Inc./Dutton, 1943); republished as *He'll Be Coming Down the Mountain* (London: Dobson, 1946);

Mongrel Mettle (New York: Books, Inc./Dutton, 1944);

Album of Destiny (New York: Dutton, 1944);

Foretaste of Glory (New York: Dutton, 1946);

Tales from the Plum Grove Hills (New York: Dutton, 1946);

The Thread That Runs So True (New York: Scribners, 1949);

Hie to the Hunters (New York: Whittlesey House, 1950);

Clearing in the Sky & Other Stories (New York: McGraw-Hill, 1950);

Kentucky Is My Land (New York: Dutton, 1952);

The Beatinest Boy (New York: Whittlesey House, 1953);

The Good Spirit of Laurel Ridge (New York: McGraw-Hill, 1953);

A Penny's Worth of Character (New York: Whittlesey House, 1954);

Red Mule (New York: Whittlesey House, 1955);

The Year of My Rebirth (New York: McGraw-Hill, 1956; London: Gollancz, 1958);

Plowshare in Heaven (New York: McGraw-Hill, 1958);

Huey, the Engineer (St. Helena, Cal.: Beard, 1960);

The Rightful Owner (New York: Whittlesey House, 1960);

God's Oddling: The Story of Mick Stuart, My Father (New York: McGraw-Hill, 1960);

Andy Finds a Way (New York: Whittlesey House, 1961);

Hold April: New Poems (New York: McGraw-Hill, 1962);

A Jesse Stuart Reader (New York: McGraw-Hill, 1963);

Save Every Lamb (New York: McGraw-Hill, 1964);

Daughter of the Legend (New York: McGraw-Hill, 1965);

A Jesse Stuart Harvest (New York: Dell, 1965);

My Land Has a Voice (New York: McGraw-Hill, 1966);

A Ride with Huey, the Engineer (New York: McGraw-Hill, 1966);

Mr. Gallion's School (New York: McGraw-Hill, 1967);

Come Gentle Spring (New York: McGraw-Hill, 1969);

Old Ben (New York: McGraw-Hill, 1970);

To Teach, To Love (New York: World, 1970);

Come Back to the Farm (New York: McGraw-Hill, 1971);

Autumn Lovesong: A Celebration of Love's Fulfillment (Kansas City, Mo.: Hallmark, 1971);

Come to My Tomorrowland (Nashville: Aurora, 1971);

Dawn of Remembered Spring (New York: McGraw-Hill, 1972);

The Land Beyond the River (New York: McGraw-Hill, 1973);

32 Votes Before Breakfast: Politics at the Grass Roots (New York: McGraw-Hill, 1974);

The World of Jesse Stuart: Selected Poems, edited by J. R. LeMaster (New York: McGraw-Hill, 1975);

My World (Lexington: University Press of Kentucky, 1975);

The Seasons of Jesse Stuart: An Autobiography in Po-

Jesse Stuart, 1971 (photograph by George Hoxie, F.P.S.A., Oxford, Ohio)

etry 1907-1976, selected by Wanda Hicks (Danbury, Conn.: Archer, 1976);

Honest Confession of a Literary Sin (Detroit: W-Hollow Books, 1977);

Dandelion on the Acropolis: A Journal of Greece (Danbury, Conn.: Archer, 1978);

The Kingdom Within: A Spiritual Autobiography (New York: McGraw-Hill, 1979);

Lost Sandstones and Lonely Skies, and Other Essays (Danbury, Conn.: Archer, 1979);

If I Were Seventeen Again, and Other Essays (Danbury, Conn.: Archer, 1980);

Land of the Honey-Colored Wind, edited by Jerry A. Herndon (Morehead, Ky.: Jesse Stuart Foundation, 1981);

Best-Loved Short Stories of Jesse Stuart, edited by H. Edward Richardson (New York: McGraw-Hill, 1982);

Cradle of the Copperheads (New York: McGraw-Hill, 1988).

SELECTED PERIODICAL PUBLICATIONS—
UNCOLLECTED:

"Kentucky Hill Dance," *New Republic*, 79 (16 May 1934): 15-16;

"My Land Has a Voice," *Arizona Quarterly*, 21 (Autumn 1964): 197-211;

"What Vanderbilt University Meant to Me," *Vanderbilt Alumnus*, 53 (November-December 1967): 21.

Jesse Stuart's first five collections of short stories (1936-1958), along with his other continuing literary production, set the pattern for his imaginary world with its distinctively real dimension, while he steadily worked out his vision and expanded his original design. He had no intention of becoming a part of any literary school or group, although the Fugitive-Agrarian writers had in his youth inspired him as much as Robert

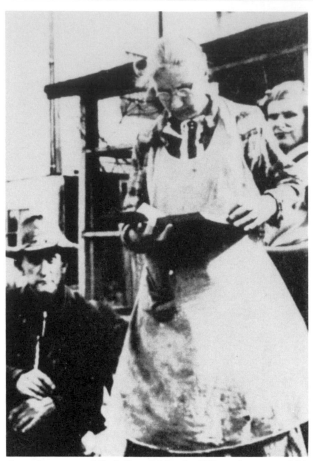

Stuart's parents, Mitchell and Martha Hilton Stuart, and his sister Glennis in 1932 (photograph by James Stuart; courtesy of the Jesse Stuart Foundation). Mrs. Stuart is reading aloud from the Bible.

Burns, Ralph Waldo Emerson, and Edgar Allan Poe earlier had in high school. Each writer, he believed, "had to build his mountain of thought and story-line, turning phrases into word-fabric, individually in his own choosing as Shakespeare, Chaucer, Dickens, Hardy, Yeats, Burns, T. S. Eliot, Twain, Emerson, Thoreau, Whitman, Hemingway, Faulkner, and others had done. In group agreement . . . there would be a danger of amalgamation to make a composite word-mountain. This idea formulated in my mind at Vanderbilt," he wrote in the *Vanderbilt Alumnus* (November-December 1967), "and for thirty-six years I have not deviated."

Stuart's first bibliographer, Hensley C. Woodbridge, in 1979 listed an astonishing 461 published short stories along with 55 books, nearly 2,000 poems, and 264 essays and articles. Of the remaining short-story collections that have appeared since *Plowshare in Heaven* in 1958, several have assembled fictional pieces by subject. *Dawn of Remembered Spring* (1972), for example,

unifies 15 stories and 11 poems dealing with snakes, and ranges thematically from the gruesome tale of the religiously fanatical Brother Fain Groan and his disciples who, in digging up Groan's wife to be "resurrected," encounter a nest of copperheads in the dark (in "Word and the Flesh," first published in *Head o' W-Hollow*, 1936), to the often-reprinted "Love" (*Story*, May-June 1940), selected by Edward J. O'Brien for his *Best Short Stories* (1941), and the title story, insightfully revealing something of the strange, many-leveled harmony existing between humankind and fellow creatures that live closest to the earth. With such stories, Stuart carved his literary niche as a local colorist who nonetheless voiced universal concerns in a strikingly original style.

Jesse Stuart was born in a log cabin about three miles south of the Ohio River town of Greenup, Kentucky, on top of a high hill overlooking W-Hollow to the north and the Plum Grove hills and Little Sandy River to the south. His father, Mitchell (Mick) Stuart, could not read and could barely write his name, while his mother, Martha (Sal) Hylton (sometimes Hilton) Stuart, had attended rural school through the fourth grade; but both parents championed education and encouraged their five children to go to school. Stuart grew up in W-Hollow on three different farms his father sharecropped until the family acquired a fifty-acre hill farm of their own, built a house, and moved there late in 1921, a year before Jesse entered high school. By his own account, he wrote his first story, "about the Easter rabbit laying eggs in the garden and covering them with straw," at the age of eight. Sometime during his freshman year, he purchased an orange-colored fountain pen, and in the early mornings before daylight, he went to the kitchen, built a fire in the wood range, and, as the kitchen warmed, sat on a woodbox close to the stove and read, studied, and wrote. His natural creative flair was fed by one teacher in particular, Mrs. Robert E. (Hattie) Hatton, who saw something in the boy, praised his work, and introduced him to the poetry of Burns, the Scottish plowboy with whom Stuart early identified.

The year before Stuart entered high school, he had by turns been a farm laborer, a concrete worker on the Greenup city streets, and a summer soldier in the Citizens Military Training Corps at Camp Knox, Kentucky. After graduating from Greenup High School in 1926, he worked with a carnival and struck steel at the American Rolling Mills at nearby Ashland, Ken-

Men o' the Mountain

by JESSE STUART

Illustration by David Hendrickson for the October 1936 Scribner's Magazine *publication of a story Stuart collected in* Men of the Mountains *(1941)*

tucky, to help pay his college expenses at Lincoln Memorial University in Harrogate, Tennessee. The first of his family to graduate from college, he returned to Greenup County to teach school in 1929. With borrowed money, he paid to have privately printed a volume of his poems, *Harvest of Youth,* in 1930. By 1932 he had completed two summer sessions at George Peabody College for Teachers and a year of graduate study at Vanderbilt University, where such teachers as Donald Davidson and Robert Penn Warren encouraged his creative endeavors. In 1934 he burst upon the national literary scene with the publication of 703 sonnetlike poems in *Man with a Bull-Tongue Plow,* which evoked from Mark Van Doren the observation that the young man was "a rare poet for these times" in that he was "both copious and comprehensible." Van Doren also made an often-quoted comparison, calling the Kentucky highland poet "a modern American Robert Burns" (*New York Herald Tribune Books,* 12 June 1934).

Stuart married fellow teacher Naomi Deane Norris of Greenup on 14 October 1939. Their only child, Jessica Jane (later Juergensmeyer),

was born on 20 August 1942 and was also to become a writer.

Just before Stuart had returned to W-Hollow from Vanderbilt in 1932, Davidson advised him, "Jesse, go back to your country . . . and write of your people. Don't change and follow the moods of these times. Be your honest self. Go back to your country, as William Butler Yeats is writing of his native Ireland. Your country is your material." Finding his native ground to be all Davidson said it would be, Stuart commenced one of the most prolific American literary careers of the twentieth century. By midcentury he had published four books of poetry, four collections of short stories, four novels, and two autobiographical prose works, an average of nearly a book a year, in addition to dozens of periodical publications of poems, short stories, and essays. During these years he was also a teacher and a superintendent and principal of schools. He lived in W-Hollow and his native Greenup County except for a year abroad in Scotland, England, and Europe (1937-1938), and service from 1943 to 1946 in the U.S. Naval Reserve in the Great Lakes and Washington, D.C.; he attained the rank of lieutenant (junior grade).

In November 1934 *Poetry*, edited by Harriet Monroe, awarded Stuart the Jeanette Sewal Davis Prize for his group of poems "Young Kentucky," published in the journal in May of that year, honorable mention going to Ezra Pound, William Carlos Williams, John Gould Fletcher, and Paul Engle. In 1937 he was awarded a John Simon Guggenheim Literary Award Fellowship, and in 1941 he received the Academy of Arts and Science Award for his short-story collection *Men of the Mountains*. His 1943 novel, *Taps for Private Tussie*, a Book-of-the-Month Club selection, received the Thomas Jefferson Southern Memorial Award that year, and in 1944 the novel's movie rights were sold to Metro-Goldwyn-Mayer, reportedly for fifty thousand dollars. In 1946 critic Henry Seidel Canby selected *Man with a Bull-Tongue Plow* as one of the "100 Best Books in America." Stuart's autobiographical *The Thread That Runs So True* (1949), a kind of educational hegira, was singled out by the National Education Association as "The Most Important Book of 1949." In 1954 he was honored by the Kentucky legislature as poet laureate of that state. Stuart received the *Lyric Magazine* prize for poetry in 1957, and in 1961 he was awarded the Fellowship of the Academy of American Poets, worth five thousand dollars. In 1962 Stuart was a U.S. representative at the Asian Writers Conference, and in 1962-1963 he made a seven-month lecture tour throughout the Middle and Far East, including Egypt, Greece, Lebanon, Iran, West Pakistan, Bangladesh, the Philippines, Taiwan, and Korea, for the United States Information Service. James Woodress in his *American Fiction: 1900-1950* (1974) included Stuart as one of the forty-four "most significant producers of fiction during the first half of the twentieth century."

As early as the 1930s, Stuart had begun to purchase and add parcels of land to the original Stuart homestead, until his holdings eventually accumulated to nearly one thousand acres. He explained that he had purchased the land from "old neighbors and friends of my parents and . . . tried to keep the land as they wanted it kept after they left it. . . . I bought it because my parents had rented and lived on these different farms and always felt so deeply for this land. . . ." Not surprisingly, the wellspring of Stuart's poetic and fictional world is W-Hollow, which takes its name from its shape and lies only two miles south of the Ohio River, over a bony ridge of hills, the "dark hills" of his literature.

Although "Battle Keaton Dies" (*Story*, July 1935) is frequently mentioned as Stuart's first published story, two naturalistic sketches, "Mountain Poorhouse" and "Kentucky Hill Dance," appeared the previous year in the *New Republic*. "Battle Keaton Dies" and "Mountain Poorhouse" are included in his first collection, *Head o' W-Hollow* (1936). The title story (*Yale Review*, September 1935) commences: "You can take any road you please. You can go take the way a crow flies or the way the wind blows. And you can follow your nose. But the road that leads you to W-Hollow is a wagon road, the first three miles of it. For the rest, it's a cow path, a goat path, a rabbit path, a fox path, a mule path. . . . The road is the color of a sand rock, a pied copperhead turned on its back in the sun."

This collection produced a critical stir. The response of the reviewer for *Time* (4 May 1936) was fairly typical, pronouncing the stories "partly funny, partly serious, in the main tantalizingly good . . . written in racy Kentucky dialect, with a wild-eyed, straightforward outrageousness that reminded readers more than once of Erskine Caldwell, at times of the ingenuous slyness of Chekhov." Lewis Gannet, reviewing for the *New York Herald Tribune* (16 April 1936), observed in these stories "the music of the American tongue. . . . Jesse Stuart is an authentic writer, worth a hundred slicker city products. He startled the slow New York publishing world. . . ." When the book was reprinted forty-three years later (in 1979), Robert Penn Warren, remarking on Stuart's gift of observation, lyricism, and humor, wrote in his foreword about one of Stuart's "pervasive effects— one of the most difficult effects for a writer to achieve . . . the sense of language speaking off the page, and that is a gift Jesse has, a gift based on years of astute listening and watching. It is a gift that goes far toward creating a world."

Stuart's second collection, the prize-winning *Men of the Mountains*, demonstrates the author's absorption with animate existence and his thorough knowledge of his W-Hollow world. In the first story, "Men o' the Mountain" (*Scribner's*, October 1936), even the heat of a July day is not left to generalities but is "hot as a roasted potato," and the dust rises like "white soup-beans." Wind moves in "dry burning sheets," and nature possesses emotion as well as a voice: cornstalks are "crying for water . . . whispering—to the hot wind." Lyricism and nostalgia characterize "New Ground Corn"

(*American Prefaces*, February 1940) and "This Is the Place" (*Esquire*, December 1936). Of the first, Edgar Lee Masters wrote Stuart in 1941, "I read . . . your story . . . and it is a marvel. It's beyond praise. . . ." Authenticity of dialogue in "One of God's Oddlings" (*Esquire*, March 1937) deepens the feeling of oneness with the earth, a prevailing theme in many of Stuart's works. Working close to the land, almost ritualistically the farmer in the story chews and smokes its tobacco ("the fragrant weed") and drinks its liquid corn until his eyes have "a faraway eagle look in them." Never is the hill farmer closer to his religion than when his shoes are in the dust. He is like a clod of earth into which God breathed life "as wind is breathed into the mule through his dry dusty nostrils . . . and he becomes a mirey beast." With the vital, lusty, and outrageous comedy of such "told stories" as "Hair" (*American Mercury*, July 1936), Stuart often juxtaposes the theme of death, as in the longest piece here, "Betwixt Life and Death" (*Esquire*, September 1939), in which frenzied parties on Friday nights center about a corpse held through winter in a garret, until "the wild roses begin to bloom in the fence rows" and relatives can return from the distant West to attend the funeral. At first blush such a work may seem to contradict reviewer Milton Rugoff's observation that there is in Stuart little of "the rawness of the Southern etchings of Erskine Caldwell nor the horrifying decadence of Faulkner." Indeed, he continues, "Next to Caldwell, Stuart seems lyrical and classic and next to Faulkner, wholesome and conventional" (*New York Herald Tribune*, 16 March 1941). Yet, with few exceptions, Stuart's stories are thematically more varied and of a more durable texture than Caldwell's, and they are more impromptu and less obfuscating, more gentle with humor if less Gothic, and invariably more natural and innocent than Faulkner's.

Honors for his stories came early and frequently for Stuart. Biographer Everetta Love Blair notes that, beginning in 1936, editor Edward J. O'Brien and his successors Martha Foley and Whit Burnett selected approximately seventy Stuart stories for inclusion in the *Best American Short Stories* series and other such collections. In the *New Mexico Quarterly* of August 1937, the "Contributors" section noted that Stuart was then "the most widely acclaimed short story writer in the United States," and W. S. Wabnitz observed that Stuart was one of the major new voices, innovative with such devices as informal commentary rather than the more traditional plotted action,

Stuart and his wife, Naomi Norris Stuart, circa 1940, outside Portsmouth (Ohio) High School, where he had taught English during the 1938-1939 school year

writing with a kind of exuberance or "rhapsody"; moreover, Stuart answered the current "plea for sincerity" in storytelling.

Stuart's third collection, *Tales from the Plum Grove Hills* (1946), includes such autobiographical stories of his youth as "The Storm," "Brothers," "Nest Egg," "Spring Victory," and "Dawn of Remembered Spring." "Whose Land Is This?" (*Esquire*, September 1942) features one of Stuart's memorable and recurring characters, gravedigger and handyman Uglybird Skinner, who knows every inch of the land and "has a deed for it recorded in his heart." Among the mellow comic pieces of the collection are two others originally published in *Esquire*, the uproarious tall tale "Rain in Tanyard Hollow" (April 1941) and the Chaucerian-toned story "Death Has Two Good Eyes" (December 1942). Stuart's masterly "Another April" (*Harper's*, August 1942) possesses a power to reveal an essential meaning of life, initiated by the commonplace coming together of a boy, his mother, his grandpa, and an ancient turtle with "1847" carved into its shell; their meeting illuminates a sustaining bond between nature and humankind. Concerning this opening story, Donald Davidson wrote Stuart on 15 October 1946, " 'Another April' is unbeatable. You have wrought better than you may realize in that story. It belongs at the top." Davidson later selected the story as an object lesson for stylistic illustration in his widely known text *American Composition and Rhetoric* (1953).

Clearing in the Sky (1950), Stuart's fourth collection, recapitulates the author's love of the W-Hollow land and, typically, focuses on family members, neighbors, and childhood friends in several of the stories, most memorably his father in the title story (*Household*, March 1949). The aging man, though recently stricken with heart disease and dangerously weak, defies doctor's orders not to climb a steep hill and does so secretly and repeatedly in order to clear a spot of new ground and make his garden; for, as he explains to his son when discovered, "This is the real land. It's the land that God left. I had to come back and dig in it. I had to smell it, sift it through my fingers again. And I wanted to taste yams, tomatoes, and potatoes grown in this land."

Plowshare in Heaven, which followed *Clearing in the Sky*, is an especially strong collection, exploring clannish mountain fanaticism and brutality in "Zeke Hammertight" (*New Mexico Quarterly Review*, August 1937); presenting a starkly naturalistic, frenetically paced treatment of an early-twentieth-century hanging in "Sunday Afternoon Hanging" (*Esquire*, April 1937); and including a factually based tale of the death of a prodigious mountain moonshiner and the puzzling logistical problems created by her burial, in "Sylvania Is Dead" (*Commonweal*, 30 October 1942), a piece later incorporated into Stuart's mythic novel *Daughter of the Legend* (1965). The collection also includes the hilarious shenanigans of the previously unpublished "Love in the Spring" (also in *Come Gentle Spring*, 1969). In requesting the story for *This Is My Best in the Third Quarter of the Century* (1970), Whit Burnett wrote Stuart on 23 May 1969 that the tale would "stand out like a jewel for its humor, universality and its bounce and rhythm . . . humor that is honest to God humor. . . ." A deep poetic vein runs through Stuart's "Walk in the Moon Shadows" (*Southwest Review*, Summer 1955), another "told tale" of obvious autobiographical significance, in which a small boy narrator, Shan, and his sister accom-

pany their mother through a magic April night to a long-abandoned hill cabin. There, as they wait in the cool, lonesome silence for what they may see and hear, the reader gradually perceives, as does Shan, that these strange goings-on have as much to do with imminent new life as with fear, superstition, and what may live from the vanished past.

My Land Has a Voice (1966) is perhaps the broadest in thematic range of the collections, at once innovative and representative. The lead story, "Corbie," flies in the face of traditional rules of literary unity, telescoping years into pages and months into sentences, yet the dialogue is as effective as it is lean. In rendering the tragedy of his pitiable little protagonist, who is mentally afflicted, Stuart also creates something of an Aristotelian paradox—a hero who is not heroic. In doing so Stuart succeeds in illuminating a profile of human compassion in a new way, and the effect is one of artistic purity. Ironically American magazine taboos resulted in the initial publication of this story in the *Philippines Free Press* (14 December 1963). Typically, the stories in the collection reflect a wide range of themes: the paradox of the old ways defeating the new as nature wins over the machine in "Red Mule and the Changing World" (*Chicago Magazine*, February 1956); the dignity of work, sweat, and honesty, demonstrably taught, with a gooseneck hoe, to a son by his fifty-year-old mother in "A Mother's Place Is with Her Son" (*Forum*, Spring 1964); a poor boy's love for his dog, her astonishing fecundity even in senility, and her loyalty that ceases only with death in "Lady" (*Progressive Farmer*, December 1943)—a story counterpointing the wisdom learned from the dog Friday in "Hand That Fed Him" (previously unpublished), in which Friday bites the hand of his master Shan, Stuart's alter ego in many stories of his youth. Humor proliferates in "Both Barrels" (*Esquire*, December 1964), a remarkably sustained monologue of a steel-muscled young man who seems to be a composite of Johnny Appleseed, John Henry, and a mythic faun, a youth who quits work in May to come home to lie beneath his favorite apple tree and hear "a tuneless song of the lazy spring wind." This child of the mountains philosophizes, "I laid on my back on the grass and looked up, because I have never seen much looking down. So it pays to look up and not down."

In addition to "Corbie" the most powerful of these slices of mountain life deal with submerged horror and superstition ("Yoked for

Life," *University Review*, Summer 1964); simple honesty and touching naiveté in the circumstances of pathetic isolation ("Beyond the News in Still Hollow," *Esquire*, December 1943); a young mother's instinct triumphing over jealousy and adultery in "April" (*Minnesota Review*, Spring 1964); the strange mingling of humor, fatalism, and fear in "As a Man Thinketh" (*Esquire*, October 1955); and the absorbing nostalgia for life and transcendent faith in "Here" (*University of Kansas City Review*, Summer 1958), a haunting story characterized by an apparently disembodied protagonist who himself is a kind of penumbra in the bright Plum Grove world through which he moves. The story anticipates Stuart's narrative technique in *The Kingdom Within: A Spiritual Autobiography* (1979), in which the protagonist, writer Shan Powderjay, finds himself attending his own funeral and observing a whole trainload of his characters ("brain children") taking that long walk to the summit of Plum Grove churchyard.

Relatively recent short-story collections by Stuart are *Land of the Honey-Colored Wind* (1981) and *Best-Loved Short Stories of Jesse Stuart* (1982), which has an introduction by Robert Penn Warren. The latter collection contains for the first time Stuart's most widely reprinted short story, "Split Cherry Tree," originally published in *Esquire* (January 1939) and since having had more than thirty reprints, including French and Israeli editions. In addition his works have been translated into Danish, Telegu, Bengali, German, Japanese, Arabic, Czechoslovakian, Norwegian, Spanish, Swedish, Dutch, Italian, Chinese, Polish, Russian, and Egyptian. In all his story collections, as well as in his poetry, novels, autobiographical prose works, and essays, Stuart did not deviate from his fundamental purpose declared in *Man with a Bull-Tongue Plow*:

> Spring in Kentucky hills and I shall be
> A free soil-man to walk beneath the trees
> And listen to the wind among the leaves—
> And count the stars and do as I damn please.

Underlining Stuart's declaration of self-assertion, Warren wrote (in his 1982 introduction), "He is unique. Totally himself. And unforgettable." Hal Borland wrote in the *New York Times Book Review* (6 November 1966): "The technique is Jesse Stuart himself, and so are the attitudes. And fashions never bothered him. He had something to say, and he has said it steadily . . . and if it seems to be about hill-country Kentuckians who live and love and fight and grieve and laugh, make no mistake—it is also about you and me, wherever we live. That is the triumph of Jesse Stuart."

Stuart suffered a serious stroke in 1978 and died in 1984. A teacher as well as a short-story writer, a farmer and conservationist as well as a poet, he identified profoundly with his land and declared a kinship with it in his frequent assertion that he was a "brother to the tree." Concerning his region and his feeling toward it, in an award-winning essay in the *Arizona Quarterly* (Autumn 1964), he spoke of "a valley where the land and everything thereon has become a part of me, where all men, bloodkin or not, are brothers. I cannot leave my land of four distinct seasons where life is never monotonous. . . . Where is there the sound of . . . the soft slither on the green grass and on the leaves, and the sounds of the winds in the tiger lilies, meadow grass, tobacco leaves, and the blades of corn? These are their voices telling me to stay. These are my invisible kin and non-kin in our world we have forever owned with deeds in our hearts. I will never leave here. I have learned where I belong. And from this heavenly prison of a Hills and Hollow Farm there is no escape. Like the spider's strong gossamer threads, anchored to the weed and flower to secure his food, make him a home, where he has dreams, a country and clime . . . maybe these same invisible gossamer strands of love have tied each of us to our valley forever."

This widely known Appalachian literary figure's work has so far resisted any definitive placement into the ever-shifting scope of American letters; but if theses and biocritical studies are accurate measures, since 1950 scholarly interest in his work has steadily increased. Among the most useful and significant is Ruel E. Foster's biocritical work *Jesse Stuart* (1968), a study both imaginative and discerning, in which Foster underlines at the outset of his chapter on the short story what he perceives to be among Stuart's major literary achievements: "When the definitive history of the American short story is written Jesse Stuart's name may well be near the top of the list of the best writers in this genre." Further, "He has created a *place* and wedged it everlastingly in the imagination of America."

Interview:

H. Edward Richardson, "*Men of the Mountains*: An Interview with Jesse Stuart," *Adena*, 4 (Spring 1979): 7-23.

Bibliographies:

Hensley C. Woodbridge, *Jesse and Jane Stuart: A Bibliography* (Murray, Ky.: Murray State University, 1979);

J. R. LeMaster, *Jesse Stuart: A Reference Guide* (Boston: G. K. Hall, 1979).

Biographies:

Everetta Love Blair, *Jesse Stuart: His Life and Works* (Columbia: University of South Carolina Press, 1967);

H. Edward Richardson, *Jesse: The Biography of an American Writer, Jesse Hilton Stuart* (New York, St. Louis, San Francisco, Toronto, Hamburg & Mexico: McGraw-Hill, 1984).

References:

Mary Washington Clarke, *Jesse Stuart's Kentucky* (New York: McGraw-Hill, 1967);

Ruel E. Foster, *Jesse Stuart* (New York: Twayne, 1968);

J. R. LeMaster, *Jesse Stuart: Kentucky's Chronicler-Poet* (Memphis: Memphis State University Press, 1980);

LeMaster, ed., *Jesse Stuart: Selected Criticism* (St. Petersburg, Fla.: Valkyrie, 1978);

LeMaster and Clarke, eds., *Jesse Stuart: Essays on His Work* (Lexington: University Press of Kentucky, 1977);

Lee Pennington, *The Dark Hills of Jesse Stuart* (Cincinnati: Harvest, 1967);

Dick Perry, *Reflections of Jesse Stuart* (New York: McGraw-Hill, 1971);

John Howard Spurlock, *He Sings for Us: A Sociolinguistic Analysis of the Appalachian Subculture and of Jesse Stuart as a Major American Author* (Lanham, Md.: University Press of America, 1980);

W. S. Wabnitz, "Jesse Stuart and the Old and New in Short Stories," *New Mexico Quarterly Review*, 7 (August 1937): 183-188.

Papers:

Stuart's manuscripts, scrapbooks, many periodical publications, and other materials are located chiefly at Murray State University in the Jesse Stuart Collection. A large collection is also available at the Patterson Rare Book Room, University of Louisville. Other smaller but useful collections have been acquired by the University of Kentucky; Morehead State University, Morehead, Kentucky; Lincoln Memorial University, Harrogate, Tennessee; the University of Chicago; and the Wisconsin Historical Society at Madison.

Ruth Suckow

(6 August 1892 - 23 January 1960)

Barbara A. White
University of New Hampshire

See also the Suckow entry in *DLB 9: American Novelists, 1910-1945.*

BOOKS: *Country People* (New York: Knopf, 1924; London: Cape, 1926);

The Odyssey of a Nice Girl (New York: Knopf, 1925; London: Cape, 1926);

Iowa Interiors (New York: Knopf, 1926); republished as *People and Houses* (London: Cape, 1927);

The Bonney Family (New York: Knopf, 1928: London: Cape, 1928);

Cora (New York: Knopf, 1929; London: Knopf, 1929);

The Kramer Girls (New York: Knopf, 1930);

Children and Older People (New York: Knopf, 1931);

The Folks (New York: Farrar & Rinehart, 1934);

Carry-Over (New York: Farrar & Rinehart, 1936);

New Hope (New York & Toronto: Farrar & Rinehart, 1942);

A Memoir (New York: Rinehart, 1952);

Some Others and Myself: Seven Stories and a Memoir (New York: Rinehart, 1952);

The John Wood Case (New York: Viking, 1959);

A Ruth Suckow Omnibus (Iowa City: University of Iowa Press, 1988).

SELECTED PERIODICAL PUBLICATIONS—
UNCOLLECTED: "An Old Woman in a Garden: Poems," *Touchstone*, 3 (August 1918): 391-392;

"Song in October," *Midland*, 4 (September-October 1918): 216;

"By Hill and Dale," *Poetry*, 18 (June 1921): 142-143;

"The Best of the Lot," *Smart Set*, 69 (November 1922): 5-36;

"Other People's Ambitions," *Smart Set*, 70 (March 1923): 5-38;

"A Part of the Institution," *Smart Set*, 72 (October 1923): 11-53;

"Literary Soubrettes," *Bookman*, 63 (July 1926): 517-521;

Ruth Suckow (University of Iowa Archives)

"Iowa," *American Mercury*, 9 (September 1926): 39-45;

"Elsie Dinsmore: A Study in Perfection," *Bookman*, 66 (October 1927): 126-133;

"A German Grandfather," *American Mercury*, 12 (November 1927): 280-284;

"The Short Story," *Saturday Review of Literature* (19 November 1927): 317-318;

"I Could Write If Only—," *Outlook*, 148 (21 March 1928): 461-463;

"Visiting," *Pictorial Review*, 30 (July 1929): 17-19;

"Homecoming," *Good Housekeeping*, 89 (August 1929): 54-57;

"The Folk Idea in American Life," *Scribner's Magazine*, 88 (September 1930): 245-255;

"Three, Counting the Cat," *Good Housekeeping*, 93 (September 1931): 30-33;

"Middle Western Literature," *English Journal*, 21 (March 1932): 175-182;

"The Crick," *Good Housekeeping*, 100 (February 1935): 32-35;

"Hollywood Gods and Goddesses," *Harper's*, 173 (July 1936): 189-200;

"What Have I," *Harper's*, 178 (January 1939): 126-137;

"An Almost Lost American Classic," *College English*, 14 (March 1953): 315-325;

"Friends and Fiction," *Friends Intelligencer*, 112 (12 February 1955): 90-92;

"The Surprising Anthony Trollope," *Georgia Review*, 12 (Winter 1958): 388-395.

At the height of her career in the 1920s and early 1930s Ruth Suckow was one of America's leading novelists and short-story writers. Her realistic fiction, set in her native Iowa, received high praise from writers such as Sinclair Lewis and Robert Frost. Critics likened Suckow to Anton Chekhov; in the *American Mercury* (November 1926) H. L. Mencken called her "the most remarkable woman now writing short stories in the Republic." By the time of her death in 1960 Suckow had been labeled as a "Midwestern regionalist." Today her work is practically unknown.

Ruth Suckow was born in Hawarden, Iowa, the second daughter of Anna Kluckholn Suckow and William John Suckow, who was a Congregational minister. In her autobiographical essay "A Memoir" (in *Some Others and Myself*, 1952), Suckow recalls that she began writing as a child, basing her style on the "purity and economy" of her father's sermons. Since her father changed pastorates frequently during her childhood, Ruth lived in Iowa towns of various sizes. Like Sarah Orne Jewett before her, she also gained an intimate knowledge of country life and landscape as she accompanied her father on his rural rounds.

Suckow attended Grinnell College, the Curry School of Expression in Boston, and the University of Denver, where she earned her A.B. (1917) and A.M. (1918) in English. She taught there as a graduate assistant and wrote a thesis on female novelists. Suckow decided on a writing career and, in preparation for supporting herself, studied beekeeping with a Denver woman in 1919. For the next five years Suckow ran an apiary in Iowa while establishing herself as a writer. Her first short stories appeared in *Midland*, a University of Iowa journal; its editor knew Mencken, who became her patron. He published sixteen of

her stories in the magazines he edited during the 1920s—*Smart Set* and the *American Mercury*.

Suckow's first published story, "Uprooted" (*Midland*, February 1921; collected in *Iowa Interiors*, 1926), contains all the elements that would be constants in her work: the setting is Iowa, the subject the family, and the method a quiet realism in which plot and incident are subordinated to character and atmosphere. Little "happens" in the story. Three married offspring and their spouses meet secretly in their parents' parlor to decide the fate of the old couple. Sam, the most prosperous son, succeeds in "uprooting" his parents and foisting responsibility for their care on the sibling who is "the poorest and had the least to say." As in most of Suckow's fiction the situation is commonplace, and the details that reveal character and build a sense of place are ordinary and familiar. Something homely, the parlor furniture, carries symbolic meaning. Sam feels uncomfortable in the stiff, old-fashioned chairs with bumpy springs. He hurries through the family conclave because "visions of a large leather chair at home, in which the hollows were his own, filled him with home-sickness." Ironically Sam cannot understand his parents' reluctance to leave their home— "It was strange how people seemed to take root in a place."

"Four Generations" (*American Mercury*, January 1924; in *Iowa Interiors*) concerns another family gathering, in which four generations are having their photograph taken. The story is static and much like a photograph itself, as each character is captured with the accuracy of a camera. Suckow conceived of art as pictorial rather than dramatic; it "catches in a frame what would otherwise be lost" ("Middle Western Literature," *English Journal*, March 1932). "Four Generations" explores Suckow's characteristic theme of social transition resulting in the "generation gap." While the family members pretend to enjoy the occasion, they really feel isolated and unable to communicate. Grandpa, an immigrant farmer, struggles for something to say to his son, a successful banker and "town man" who now seems a stranger; the son is bewildered by his educated daughter's aloofness; the daughter scorns the "grossness" of Iowa culture and longs for her adopted New England. Only Grandpa and his tiny great-granddaughter achieve a momentary closeness.

Suckow once said of her early stories: "Their purpose was frequently mistaken for an 'indictment' of American rural and small town life,

Suckow with her husband, Ferner Nuhn, in Santa Fe soon after their 11 March 1929 marriage (from the Bookman, *November 1929)*

particularly in the Middlewest, or for a sort of exposition on the general futility of human existence" ("Comments and Addenda," in *Carry-Over*, 1936). Inevitably, Mencken, Lewis, and other debunkers of Main Street (small-town life) saw only certain aspects of Suckow's fiction—the narrowness and hypocrisy of many of her characters and the mindless restraints of the farm/village/ town bourgeois family. But Suckow was not the typical "revolt from the village" writer of the 1920s. She was always a balanced observer, no more satirist than sentimentalist. If she presented much that is indictable, she also recorded the more attractive elements of rural and village life.

In one of her best stories, "Golden Wedding" (*American Mercury*, February 1925; in *Iowa Interiors*), an old couple live such a drab existence that they doubt the worth of their fifty years of marriage and hard work. However, Suckow describes the anniversary celebration organized by their children as a bright, festive, and charming occasion; it produces a sense of exaltation that lightens the couple's bitterness. In "A Rural Community" (1922; also in *Iowa Interiors*) Ralph Chapin, a prominent journalist and world traveler, visits his hometown of Walnut. His relatives act like "yokels." Although he "tried to give them some idea of what was going on in the world," they are unable to grasp anything beyond their limited sphere. Yet Ralph appreciates his family's simplicity; he begins to "be glad of their slow voices, their odd turns of speech, their rustic air. Those things suggested the deep stabilities of country life—the slow, inevitable progression of the seasons, the nearness to earth and sky and weather, the unchanging processes of birth and death. . . ." Ralph comes to Walnut feeling superior and leaves quieted and steadied.

Suckow's *Iowa Interiors* received favorable, often enthusiastic reviews. It was hard to answer Mencken's rhetorical question, "Who has ever published a better first book of short stories?" (*American Mercury*, November 1926). But once she had established her literary reputation, Suckow never again concentrated on the short story. She sold her apiary, moved to New York, and devoted herself to writing novels, completing five by the end of the decade. On 11 March 1929 Suckow married Ferner Nuhn, another writer from Iowa, and in that same year began work on her longest and most complex novel, *The Folks* (1934). With its depth of characterization and panoramic view of social change, it was the high point of Suckow's career. Thereafter she produced nothing comparable, although she continued to write until her death.

Suckow did not abandon the short story entirely after the success of *Iowa Interiors*; she published about twenty-five more stories, the bulk of which are collected in *Children and Older People* (1931) and *Some Others and Myself*. As a short-story writer Suckow failed to develop and improve in the way she did as a novelist. Yet, even if she never surpassed the achievement of her first collection, she produced some stories that stand up well in comparison. Suckow continued to write persuasively of old people and children, and she explored in greater depth a theme suggested in *Iowa Interiors* and major in her novels—the conflict between an individual's urge for self-development and small-town family traditions. The individual is more often female than male because Suckow saw the conflict as especially severe for women.

Most wives in Suckow's fiction have lost their personal identity in marriage. They often feel, like Winifred in "What Have I?" (*Harper's*, January 1939), that they are "only part of the surroundings" and "had got helplessly into some gigantic trap." In "The Resurrection" (*Midland*, June 1921; in *Iowa Interiors*) a woman's family "had never thought of her as a person in herself. She had been Mother, and, then, Grandma." Unmarried women may be even more restricted; several Suckow stories, most effectively "Mrs. Vogel and Ollie" (first published in *Some Others and Myself*), present women who have spent their lives at home serving a parent. One of Suckow's most memorable single women appears in "A Great Mollie" (first published by *Harper's Monthly* in April 1929 as "Strong As a Man"; revised and collected as "A Great Mollie" in *Children and Older People*). The vital, adventuresome Mollie drives her old Ford around the countryside, as she supposedly sells underwear but more often helps her clients with everything from housework to farm machinery. Although Mollie dreams of traveling to Chicago to open a business, Suckow makes it clear that she will not be able to withstand the objections of her family. Some critics have concluded from this story that Suckow believed "women's place is in the home." On the contrary, Suckow was an outspoken feminist both in her life and in her writings. She portrays realistically and convincingly the obstacles to women striking out for themselves—the almost universal assumption that it is a woman's duty to sacrifice herself for her family, and the enormous guilt and loss of reputation women must endure if they refuse.

Suckow contrasts the implications of male and female roles in "The Man of the Family" (*American Mercury*, December 1926; in *Children and Older People*) and "A Start in Life" (*American Mercury*, September 1924; in *Iowa Interiors*). Gerald and Daisy, the fatherless adolescents in these companion stories, begin in the same position; though reluctant to give up play and school, they are obliged to go to work. Gerald's first day as a drugstore clerk brings him, in his view, ample compensation. When he comes home from work, he claims to be "man of the house now" and dominates his mother and sisters, even turn-

Ruth Suckow, circa 1941

ing away his mother's prospective suitor. Daisy, in accordance with her gender, is transferred from one family to another, where she will live as hired help. Her pride in earning money is soon dashed when her employers teach her her "place." Whereas she had been "boss" of her siblings, she must now "obey" everyone, even the youngest children. Gerald's new responsibility brings him power and self-esteem, while Daisy's leads to reduced status and humiliation.

Suckow's feminism must be considered in accounting for the dramatic fall in her literary reputation. In the 1920s and 1930s feminism was more acceptable than it would be in the next two decades, just as the regional emphasis was then a plus and later a minus. Suckow recognized the dangers of being known as a regionalist, saying of herself, "The writer has always believed that the matter of locality has been overemphasized in estimations of her fiction. . . . If the stories did not throw a shadow beyond locality, she would never have gone to the trouble of writing them" ("Comments and Addenda," in *Carry-Over*). But more harmful to her reputation than either the matter of locality or a feminist worldview was Suckow's "feminine" choice of material and approach; she wrote of matters traditionally more important to women than to men. From the beginning many reviewers tempered their praise by complaining that Suckow was too domestic, too focused on the family and household affairs. They often found the homely domestic details either boring or embarrassing. Leedice McAnelly Kissane notes that a male reader judged one of Suckow's novels (*The Odyssey of a Nice Girl*, 1925) so "intrinsically feminine" that he exclaimed: "A man really ought not to be reading it!" (*Ruth Suckow*, 1969).

If a family reunion were considered as interesting as a bear hunt, if Iowa were as good a setting as New York, if household interiors could be as symbolic as big fish, Suckow's literary standing would be much higher. Still, the charge that her work is boring cannot be entirely dismissed. Paradoxically Suckow's most important contribution to the novel and short story is also her greatest weakness. Her skill at creating a sense of everyday reality often doubles back on itself: the characters seem dull in their very ordinariness, the lifelike details pall, and the quiet tone becomes monotonous. It is probably because of this blandness that many critics have preferred Suckow's short stories, in their brevity and sharper focus, to her novels. On the other hand, the novels offer the greater depth of characterization one would expect, plus a much broader range of characters and themes. Whether Ruth Suckow is foremost a short-story writer or a novelist comes down to a matter of taste, but without question her fiction should be better known and more highly regarded.

References:

Clarence A. Andrews, Introduction to *A Ruth Suckow Omnibus* (Iowa City: University of Iowa Press, 1988);

Andrews, *A Literary History of Iowa* (Iowa City: University of Iowa Press, 1972), pp. 79-101;

Joseph Baker, "Regionalism in the Middle West," *American Review*, 4 (November 1934-March 1935): 603-614;

Aimée Buchanan, "A Walk in the Mountains," *Southwest Review*, 46 (Summer 1961): 231-243;

Mary Jean De Marr, "Ruth Suckow's Iowa 'Nice Girls,'" *Midamerica*, 8 (1986): 69-83;

John T. Frederick, "Ruth Suckow and the Middle Western Literary Movement," *English Journal*, 20 (January 1931): 1-8;

Abigail Ann Hamblen, *Ruth Suckow* (Boise, Idaho: Boise State University, 1978);

Hamblen, "Ruth Suckow and Thomas Wolfe: A Study in Similarity," *Forum* (Houston), 3 (Winter 1962): 27-31;

Margaret Matlack Kiesel, "Iowans in the Arts: Ruth Suckow in the Twenties," *Annals of Iowa* (Spring 1980): 259-287;

Kiesel, "Ruth Suckow's Grinnell," *Grinnell Magazine*, 8 (November-December 1975): 7-10;

Leedice McAnelly Kissane, "D. H. Lawrence, Ruth Suckow, and 'Modern Marriage,'" *Rendezvous*, 4 (1969): 39-45;

Kissane, *Ruth Suckow* (New York: Twayne, 1969);

Abigail Ann Martin, "*The Folks*: Anatomy of Rural Life and Shifting Values," *North Dakota Quarterly*, 53 (Fall 1985): 173-179;

Lois B. Muehl, "Ruth Suckow's Art of Fiction," *Books at Iowa*, 13 (November 1970): 3-12;

Ferner Nuhn, "The Orchard Apiary: Ruth Suckow in Earlville," *Iowan*, 20 (Summer 1972): 21-24, 54;

Fritz Oehlschlaeger, "The Art of Ruth Suckow's 'A Start in Life,'" *Western American Literature*, 15 (Fall 1980): 177-186;

Oehlschlaeger, "A Book of Resolutions: Ruth Suckow's *Some Others and Myself*," *Western American Literature*, 21 (Summer 1986): 111-121;

Margaret Stewart Omrcanin, *Ruth Suckow: A Critical Study of Her Fiction* (Philadelphia: Dorrance, 1972);

Frank Paluka, "Ruth Suckow: A Calendar of Letters," *Books at Iowa*, 1 (October 1964): 34-40; 2 (April 1965): 31-40

Barbara A. White, "Nice Girls and Their Folks: The Adolescent and the Family in Ruth Suckow's Fiction," in her *Growing Up Female: Adolescent Girlhood in American Fiction* (Westport, Conn: Greenwood, 1985), pp. 65-88.

Papers:

The University of Iowa Library, Iowa City, has drafts of several short stories and articles, manuscripts of *The Bonney Family* and *The John Wood Case*, and a collection of correspondence, including letters from John Cowper Powys and Dorothy Richardson, as well as several unpublished reminiscences of Ruth Suckow and a copy of W. J. Suckow's unpublished memoirs. Mementos, pictures, and newspaper clippings are in the public library in Earlville, Iowa.

Booth Tarkington

(29 July 1869 - 19 May 1946)

James Woodress
University of California, Davis

See also the Tarkington entry in *DLB 9: American Novelists, 1910-1945.*

BOOKS: *The Gentleman from Indiana* (New York: Doubleday & McClure, 1899; London: Richards, 1900);

Monsieur Beaucaire (New York: McClure, Phillips, 1900; London: Murray, 1901);

The Two Vanrevels (New York: McClure, Phillips, 1902; London: Richards, 1902);

Cherry (New York & London: Harper, 1903);

In the Arena (New York: McClure, Phillips, 1905; London: Murray, 1905);

The Beautiful Lady (New York: McClure, Phillips, 1905; London: Murray, 1905);

The Conquest of Canaan (New York & London: Harper, 1905; London: Hodder & Stoughton, 1917);

His Own People (New York: Doubleday, Page, 1907; London: Murray, 1907);

The Guests of Quesnay (New York: McClure, 1908; London: Heinemann, 1908);

The Man From Home, by Tarkington and Harry Leon Wilson (New York & London: Harper, 1908);

Beasley's Christmas Party (New York & London: Harper, 1909);

Beauty and the Jacobin (New York & London: Harper, 1912);

The Flirt (Garden City, N.Y.: Doubleday, Page, 1913; London: Hodder & Stoughton, 1913);

Penrod (Garden City, N.Y.: Doubleday, Page, 1914; London: Hodder & Stoughton, 1914);

The Turmoil (New York & London: Harper, 1915; London: Hodder & Stoughton, 1915);

Seventeen (New York & London: Harper, 1916; London: Hodder & Stoughton, 1916);

Penrod and Sam (Garden City, N.Y.: Doubleday, Page, 1916; London: Hodder & Stoughton, 1917);

Harlequin and Columbine and Other Stories (Garden

Booth Tarkington (Gale International Portrait Gallery)

City, N.Y.: Doubleday, Page, 1918);

The Magnificent Ambersons (Garden City, N.Y.: Doubleday, Page, 1918; London: Hodder & Stoughton, 1918);

Ramsey Milholland (Garden City, N.Y.: Doubleday, Page, 1919; London: Hodder & Stoughton, 1919);

The Gibson Upright by Tarkington and Wilson (Garden City, N.Y.: Doubleday, Page, 1919);

Alice Adams (Garden City, N.Y. & Toronto: Doubleday, Page, 1921; London: Hodder & Stoughton, 1921);

Clarence: A Comedy in Four Acts (New York & London: French, 1921);

The Country Cousin: A Comedy in Four Acts, by Tarkington and Julian Street (New York & London: French, 1921);

The Intimate Strangers: A Comedy in Three Acts (New York & London: French, 1921);

The Ghost Story: A One Act Play for Persons of No Great Age (Cincinnati: Kidd, 1922);

Gentle Julia (Garden City, N.Y. & Toronto: Doubleday, Page, 1922; London: Hodder & Stoughton, 1922);

The Wren: A Comedy in Three Acts (New York & London: French, 1922);

The Trysting Place: A Farce in One Act (Cincinnati: Kidd, 1923);

The Fascinating Stranger and Other Stories (Garden City, N.Y.: Doubleday, Page, 1923; London: Brown, 1923);

The Midlander (Garden City, N.Y.: Doubleday, Page, 1924; London: Heinemann, 1924);

Tweedles: A Comedy, by Tarkington and Wilson (New York & London: French, 1924);

Women (Garden City, N.Y.: Doubleday, Page, 1925; London: Heinemann, 1926);

Bimbo, The Pirate: A Comedy (New York & London: Appleton, 1926);

Looking Forward and Others (Garden City, N.Y.: Doubleday, Page, 1926; London: Heinemann, 1927);

Growth (Garden City, N.Y.: Doubleday, Page, 1927; London: Heinemann, 1927);

The Plutocrat (Garden City, N.Y.: Doubleday, Page, 1927; London: Heinemann, 1927);

The Travelers (New York & London: Appleton, 1927);

Station YYYY (New York & London: Appleton, 1927);

Claire Ambler (Garden City, N.Y.: Doubleday, Doran, 1928; London: Heinemann, 1928);

The World Does Move (Garden City, N.Y.: Doubleday, Doran, 1928; London: Heinemann, 1929);

Young Mrs. Greeley (Garden City, N.Y.: Doubleday, Doran, 1929; London: Heinemann, 1929);

Penrod Jashber (Garden City, N.Y.: Doubleday, Doran, 1929; London: Heinemann, 1929);

Mirthful Haven (Garden City, N.Y.: Doubleday, Doran, 1930; London: Heinemann, 1931);

How's Your Health?, by Tarkington and Wilson (New York, Los Angeles & London: French, 1930);

Mary's Neck (Garden City, N.Y.: Doubleday, Doran, 1932; London: Heinemann, 1932);

Walton Mally (Garden City, N.Y.: Doubleday, Doran, 1932; London: Heinemann, 1933);

Presenting Lily Mars (Garden City, N.Y.: Doubleday, Doran, 1933; London: Heinemann, 1934);

Little Orvie (Garden City, N.Y.: Doubleday, Doran, 1934; London: Heinemann, 1935);

Mister Antonio (New York, Los Angeles, London & Toronto: French, 1935);

Mr. White, The Red Barn, Hell and Bridgewater (Garden City, N.Y.: Doubleday, Doran, 1935; London: Heinemann, 1937);

The Lorenzo Bunch (Garden City, N.Y.: Doubleday, Doran, 1936; London: Heinemann, 1936);

Rumbin Galleries (Garden City, N.Y.: Doubleday, Doran, 1937; London: Heinemann, 1938);

Some Old Portraits (New York: Doubleday, Doran, 1939);

The Heritage of Hatcher Ide (New York: Doubleday, Doran, 1941; London: Heinemann, 1941);

The Fighting Littles (Garden City, N.Y.: Doubleday, Doran, 1941; London: Heinemann, 1942);

Kate Fennigate (Garden City, N.Y.: Doubleday, Doran, 1943; London: Hammond, Hammond, 1946);

Image of Josephine (Garden City, N.Y.: Doubleday, Doran, 1945; London: Hammond, Hammond, 1946);

The Show Piece (Garden City, N.Y.: Doubleday, 1947; London: Hammond, Hammond, 1951);

Your Amiable Uncle (Indianapolis & New York: Bobbs, Merrill, 1949).

Collections:

The Works of Booth Tarkington, Autograph Edition, 27 volumes (Garden City, N.Y.: Doubleday, Page Doubleday, Doran, 1918-1932);

The Works of Booth Tarkington, Seawood Edition, 27 volumes (Garden City, N.Y.: Doubleday, Page Doubleday, Doran, 1922-1932);

Penrod, His Complete Story (Garden City, N.Y.: Doubleday, Doran, 1931)—comprises *Penrod, Penrod and Sam*, and *Penrod Jashber*.

PLAY PRODUCTIONS: *Monsieur Beaucaire*, Philadelphia, Garrick Theater, 7 October 1901;

The Man from Home, Chicago, Studebaker Theater, 29 September 1907;

Foreign Exchange, Chicago, Grand Opera House, 19 September 1909;

Your Humble Servant, Indianapolis, English's Theater, 18 October 1909;

Springtime, New York, Liberty Theater, 19 October 1909;

Drawing by Tarkington of his well-known character Penrod and his dog, Duke (from Barton Currie, Booth Tarkington: A Bibliography, *1932)*

Cameo Kirby, New York, Hackett Theater, 20 December 1909;

Getting a Polish, New York, Wallack's Theater, 7 November 1910;

The Ohio Lady, Columbus, Ohio, Hartman Theater, 24 January 1916;

The Gibson Upright, Indianapolis, Murat Theater, 14 July 1919;

Up from Nowhere, New York, Comedy Theater, 8 September 1919;

Clarence, New York, Hudson Theater, 20 September 1919;

Poldekin, New York, Park Theater, 9 September 1920;

The Wren, New York, Gaiety Theater, 10 October 1921;

The Intimate Strangers, New York, Henry Miller's Theater, 7 November 1921;

Rose Briar, New York, Empire Theater, 25 December 1922;

Tweedles, New York, Frazer Theater, 13 August 1923;

Magnolia, New York, Liberty Theater, 27 August 1923;

How's Your Health?, New York, Vanderbilt Theater, 26 November 1929;

Colonel Satan, New York, Fulton Theater, 10 January 1931.

Booth Tarkington, whose literary career spanned nearly five decades at the beginning of the twentieth century, was a popular and successful writer of fiction, long and short, and a playwright of some importance. Although he had more talent than most of his contemporaries, his work never quite achieved major significance, and he had to be content with a large rather than a discriminating audience. Despite his popular appeal, however, his work had importance for students of American literature, for he was a shrewd observer of people and manners, of social mobility, and of cultural conflict. He was an excellent craftsman, a witty and charming writer whose works are enjoyable if seldom profound.

Once his literary apprenticeship ended and he published his first novel, *The Gentleman from Indiana* (1899), he became the darling of the large-circulation magazines. He wrote with such facility that, from then until his death, he turned out 171 stories, 9 nouvelles, 21 novels, and 19 full-length plays (including dramatizations of two of his own works), plus movie scenarios, one-act plays, and radio dramas. His work was a regular staple of the *Saturday Evening Post, Redbook,* the *Ladies Home Companion, Cosmopolitan,* and other popular publications. It might be said that he was a victim of his own success, but he was a hardworking writer who took his profession seriously. Yet there is little questioning of values and no tragic vision in his work, and his popularity rested on an accommodation with the world he observed. There is much amused detachment, irony, and a first-rate comic sense in his work, but literary historians and critics have not been kind to his reputation.

Classifying Tarkington's stories presents something of a problem. Of the 117 stories that were reprinted in book form after first appearing in magazines, 81 were gathered into books that can be considered either story collections or novels. The three Penrod books are examples of a loose fictional structure in which all the stories deal with the same characters but have no significant, progressive plot development and were originally written as separate stories. The same is true of *Gentle Julia* (1922), *Women* (1925), and *Little Orvie* (1934). In some instances, however, Tarkington added unpublished material when he turned a story sequence into a book. Examples of this procedure are found in *Mary's Neck* (1932), *Rumbin Galleries* (1937), and *The Fighting Littles* (1941). Only five of the volumes in Tarkington's canon gather together unrelated stories.

Born in Indianapolis on 29 July 1869, the son of Elizabeth (Booth) and John Tarkington, who was a lawyer, Tarkington grew up in a typical middle-class professional family. The Indiana capital was simply a large country town in 1869 but grew during Tarkington's lifetime to be a thriving industrial and commercial city. He began high school in Indianapolis, attended Phillips Exeter Academy for two years, spent one year at Purdue, then transferred as a special student to Princeton. During his two years there he tried his hand at writing for undergraduate publications and wrote for and acted with the Dramatic Association, which changed its name to the Triangle Club during the year he was president. He left Princeton without taking a degree, returned to Indianapolis, and for the next five years tried unsuccessfully to become a professional writer. Tarkington turned out stories with great industry and collected many rejection slips; he also wrote for and played in amateur theatricals and began a novel. Some of his stories saw print in local publications, but the eastern magazines wanted none of him until Doubleday and McClure published his first novel.

Tarkington's first important short fiction was *Monsieur Beaucaire* (serialized in *McClure's* in 1899; separately published in 1900), a work of nouvelle length that he had written during the 1890s in his apprentice period. It belongs to the genre of costume romance popular in that era and had a long and successful development as book, play, movie, and anthology selection. After S. S. McClure had accepted Tarkington's first novel as a serial, he immediately had asked for more of his work and scheduled *Monsieur Beaucaire* for publication in *McClure's* as soon as *The Gentleman from Indiana* concluded. The nouvelle is a young man's tale, written, as Tarkington later said, "in the fashion of the time" when "a romanticism somewhat sentimental" was in vogue ("As I Seem to Me," *Saturday Evening Post*, 23 August 1941). The story is set in Bath, En-

Tarkington at three, during a visit with his uncle Newton Booth, then governor of California

gland, in the eighteenth century, during the era of Beau Nash, and describes the adventures of the duke of Orleans, disguised as a barber, among the English nobility at that famous spa. How the young Frenchman exposes the duplicity and baseness of the duke of Winterset and the snobbery of the beauty of Bath, Lady Mary Carlisle, provides the plot. The story has had many admirers over the years, one of whom was the hard-bitten Damon Runyon, who wrote in 1937: "*Monsieur Beaucaire* is ever green. It is a little literary cameo, and we read it over at least once a year" (*Indianapolis Star*, 7 August). Tarkington made the story into a play for Richard Mansfield (1901), and in its movie avatars it was a vehicle for both Rudolph Valentino and Bob Hope.

Monsieur Beaucaire is not typical of the bulk of Tarkington's short fiction, which falls usually into the mode of genteel realism as practiced by William Dean Howells, one of the authors Tarkington most admired. Tarkington began working the realistic vein after a brief foray into Indiana politics. He ran for the state legislature in

1902, was elected, and served one term. He learned a lot about politics in his role as legislator, but the literary harvest was more significant. *In the Arena* (1905) is a collection of six stories that make good use of his political experience. The tales still have interest as fictional treatments of the same material that the muckraking journalists of that period were exposing in their books and articles. One such story is "Boss Gorgett" (*Everybody's Magazine*, December 1903), a tale of machine politics in a mayoralty campaign in which a reform candidate is outmaneuvered by a wily four-term mayor. Another is "The Aliens" (*McClure's*, February 1904), concerning "politics in a tough district," a story in which Tarkington observes ward heeling at its slimiest. An innocent immigrant, Pietro Tobigli, loyal to his precinct boss, is betrayed by him in a sellout to the opposing party and dies as a result of the double cross. This little tragedy, which is a fair specimen of literary naturalism, is considerably grimmer than most of Tarkington's fiction. More in the usual Tarkington vein is "Mrs. Protheroe" (*McClure's*, February 1905), an entertaining story about the successful efforts of a female lobbyist (the secret owner of the ball park) to legalize Sunday baseball—an issue that actually was before the Indiana legislature during Tarkington's term. "The Need of Money" (*McClure's*, November 1904) is the story of a simpleminded country legislator who sells out to the railroad lobby without realizing that he has been bribed. *In the Arena* drew admiration from Theodore Roosevelt, who summoned Tarkington to the White House for lunch and to discuss Hoosier politics. Tarkington was astonished to find that the president had read and liked his tales.

After finishing his term in the legislature and writing the stories of *In the Arena*, Tarkington took his parents and his wife, the former Louisa Fletcher, whom he had married in 1902, on a grand tour of Europe. From this travel experience came Tarkington's first use of international themes in his fiction and drama, a two-part serial in *Harper's* (December 1904 and January 1905) called *The Beautiful Lady* (separately published later in 1905). Although Tarkington admired the realistic use that Howells and Henry James, another of his idols, made of international themes in their fiction, his story is more romance than realism. But the story was concocted in the manner of James from the germ of an idea: the bizarre sight of a man sitting in a Paris cafe with a theater ad painted on his shaven skull. To explain

this situation, Tarkington devised a complicated story in which an impoverished Neapolitan gentleman saves "the beautiful lady," who sympathizes with his plight, from a rascally half-brother and a disastrous marriage. Tarkington in this tale was still in his overplotting youth.

His next story, however, was a serious, less elaborate study of a smug, naive American who is victimized by two con artists in Rome. Written in Paris after Tarkington and his wife had returned to Europe to live, *His Own People* (separately published in 1907) is a tale that *Harper's* had asked for but turned down on moral grounds (a kiss the editors thought indecent). Tarkington subsequently sold the story to the *Saturday Evening Post* (where it appeared on 24 and 31 August 1907) and thereby began a long association with George Horace Lorrimer, who ultimately published more of his fiction than any other editor. *His Own People* is the tale of Robert Russ Mellon, a callow midwestern youth who accumulates a bit of money and goes to Rome on a holiday. The story opens in the new Excelsior Hotel, where Mellon is surrounded by the brilliant cosmopolitan society with which he longs to associate. He is dazzled by a French countess who turns out to be the partner of two professional cardsharpers. The young man is properly fleeced at a poker party in the countess's apartment.

After a decade of expatriation punctuated by frequent returns to the United States to oversee production of his plays, Tarkington's marriage foundered and he became a heavy drinker. He was divorced in 1911, swore off liquor two months later, and at the end of the year married Susanah Robinson. After he pulled himself together, he returned to his desk and wrote one of his best stories, "Mary Smith" (*Saturday Evening Post*, 17 August 1912; in *Harlequin and Columbine and Other Stories*, 1918). This is the tale of a midwestern youth who falls for a girl he meets on the train as he returns home from college at Christmas. Panic-stricken that he will never see her again, he begs for her address, as the porter picks up his luggage and the train slows down for his station. She gives him her address in a sealed envelope, which he opens on the platform as the train starts up. All the slip of paper says, though, is "Mary Smith, Chicago, Ill."

From this fresh start Tarkington went on to mine his richest creative vein in the Penrod stories, which with the addition of one or two novels may be his strongest claim to a permanent place in American literary history. By this time he was

Tarkington at thirteen with his grandfather and father (Joseph and John S. Tarkington); and during the late 1890s with his mother, Elizabeth Booth Tarkington, and nephew John Jameson

happily remarried and settled in Indianapolis, where his sister's three boys were growing up. The Penrod stories, realistic boyhood tales in the tradition of Mark Twain's *Tom Sawyer* (1876), are fashioned from Tarkington's own memories of his childhood in Indianapolis and his observations of his nephews. The stories began with "Penrod and the Pageant" in *Everybody's Magazine* (June 1913) and were an instant success. Four different magazines competed for Penrod stories, and Tarkington wrote a friend, Julian Street, at this time: "My prices astonish me. . . . I'm rather sorry for the magazines that pay 'em" (9 September 1914; quoted in James Woodress's *Booth Tarkington*, 1955).

Tarkington was in full mastery of his craft when he wrote these stories. His style is supple, articulate, and witty, and the tales entertain children and delight adults. He dropped his earlier elaborate plotting for the deft and subtle management of detail. Young readers vicariously enjoy Penrod's adventures, while the adults take pleasure in Penrod's "*suffering and* his mental processes, not what happens to him," as Tarkington put it (quoted by Woodress in *Booth Tarkington*). There are traces of the tall tale in the stories, but in essence they are everyday incidents in which style and arrangement of detail are everything. The successive stories about Penrod's secret authorship of "Harold Ramorez the Roadagent or Wild Life among the Rocky Mts." and the humiliating actualities of the pageant of the round table show juxtapositions that produce humorous irony; equally effective is the linking of Penrod's schoolroom daydreams with the realities of arithmetic.

The series of Penrod stories grew and grew until Tarkington eventually made three books of them: *Penrod* (1914), *Penrod and Sam* (1916), and *Penrod Jashber* (1929). Thirty-two stories went into these volumes; the first book was dedicated to his nephews, the second to Susanah, his second wife. The entire series had begun with her challenge to him to write a realistic boy's story when he had objected to the unreality of an English novel of life at Harrow, which she had been reading. The Penrod books, which were gathered into *Penrod: His Complete Story* (1931), sold a half-million copies during Tarkington's lifetime and have never stopped selling since his death.

Between *Penrod* and *Penrod and Sam*, Tarkington turned to the subject matter of "Mary Smith," that is, young love, and wrote the stories that were collected in *Seventeen* (1916). These tales deal with the trials of adolescence of Willie Baxter, a youth growing up in a midwestern city. He falls in love with an insufferable young woman, Lola Pratt, who has come to visit a friend. Again it is the skillful handling of detail that gives the stories their appeal, and the plot is fashioned from commonplace incidents. Anyone who remembers his own adolescence can empathize with Willie, but the stories are dated and seem today like period pieces. The world of adolescence simply has changed too much since 1916, but these stories in their book form were among Tarkington's most successful productions, selling some eight hundred thousand copies and providing material for a stage version, a musical comedy, and a movie.

Tarkington's longtime interest in the theater had fictional by-products: two nouvelles, three stories, and a novel, published over a thirty-year span of his career. "Harlequin and Columbine" (*Metropolitan*, September-November 1914; in *Harlequin and Columbine and Other Stories*) is a nouvelle, written after Tarkington's early playwriting years, which creates vividly the New York theater in the era before World War I. It deals with the trials of a young playwright during the production of his first play, as the actor-manager (who might have been drawn from Mansfield, John Drew, or John Barrymore, all of whom Tarkington knew) changes scenes, alters lines, and revises the stage business. The stories "The Property Man," "Francine," and " 'Thea Zell" and the second nouvelle, "The Divine Evadne," never were collected in book form, but " 'Thea Zell" (*Red Book*, April 1925), which appeared in *The World's Best Short Stories in 1926*, is a superb tale that should be better known. It is a brilliant characterization of a woman of meager talent whose stage ambitions bring her a lifetime of misery. She leaves her husband to go on the stage, struggles desperately to succeed in a highly competitive business, and is last seen as she returns to her hometown to play a bit part with a third-rate stock company.

In *Seventeen* Tarkington had created a tomboyish younger sister Jane, who makes life miserable for Willie Baxter. This character was so successful that Tarkington revived her as Florence Atwater in a series of stories that became the novel *Gentle Julia*. It is primarily upper-middle-class, urban-domestic comedy, of which Tarkington was a master. Thirteen-year-old Florence is the deus ex machina of the novel, which also is populated with Florence's Aunt Julia, a ravishing

Self-caricature by Tarkington in a letter replying to his father's request that he return to Indianapolis after ten weeks in New York
(from James Woodress, Booth Tarkington, *1955)*

belle who lives across the street and is perpetually besieged by males. Tarkington understood girls as well as boys and, in depicting the activities of Florence, her cousin Herbert, and his buddy Henry, handles successfully the emotional and mental lag between the sexes at the age of thirteen.

Although domestic comedy looms large in Tarkington's short fiction, occasionally he was prompted to serious social comment. *The Fascinating Stranger and Other Stories* (1923) contains two tales of this sort: "Jeannette" (*Redbook,* May 1921) and "The One-Hundred Dollar Bill" (*McCall's,* January 1923). In the former, Tarkington projects his own negative attitudes toward the Jazz Age in the character of Charley Blake, who first becomes deranged after his sister takes him to the Folies-Bergère in Paris, and then again after psychiatric treatment and a return home to the ca-

cophony of the music and the intimacy of the "toddle" at a party given by his niece Jeannette, a bobbed-haired "flapper." In the latter story (reprinted in the *O. Henry Prize Stories of 1923*) an uncontrollable chain of circumstances ruins a poor bill collector, who is goaded into gambling away his employer's money by a rival for his wife's affections. As he goes home after losing the money, he sees a monkey on a stick in a shop window and realizes he is a similar toy in the hands of fate. When Tarkington's story materials demanded naturalism, he could be a pessimistic determinist.

Returning to the urban, middle-class, domestic scene in the mid 1920s, Tarkington wrote another story cycle that became *Women.* By this time he had moved out of the central city to the suburban fringe of Indianapolis. He was interested in the daytime female world of suburbia, and as a

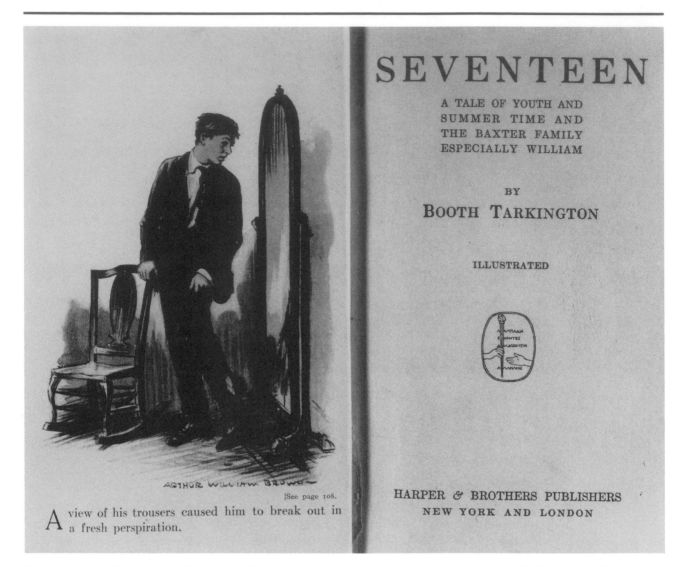

SEVENTEEN

A TALE OF YOUTH AND
SUMMER TIME AND
THE BAXTER FAMILY
ESPECIALLY WILLIAM

BY

BOOTH TARKINGTON

ILLUSTRATED

HARPER & BROTHERS PUBLISHERS
NEW YORK AND LONDON

[See page 108.

A view of his trousers caused him to break out in a fresh perspiration.

Frontispiece and title page for Tarkington's 1916 book of interrelated stories about the adolescent Willie Baxter. The book was adapted as a play, a musical, and a film.

male who was home while other males toiled in the heart of the city, he observed the daytime society made up of wives, teas, domestic servants, luncheons, children, literary clubs, and Amazon warfare of a highly sophisticated type. This is the subject matter of *Women*, and as in Tarkington's later manner, plot is foresworn for a great deal of carefully managed detail and good characterization. There are nine entertaining stories in this collection, and all show that the author understands female psychology as well as child and adolescent psychology.

From his early manhood Tarkington had been spending his summers in Maine, and after his second marriage, he bought property at Kennebunkport, where he built a summer home. It was inevitable that a novelist of manners would

sooner or later make use of the clash in values and life-styles of the natives and the summer folk. While *Mirthful Haven* (1930) is a serious novel using this material, Tarkington turned the lighter side of the matter into stories that became *Mary's Neck*. These ten stories had appeared in four different magazines and, when published in book form, were distributed by the Book-of-the-Month Club. The material of the tales is drawn from the aimless amusements of the summer colony, particularly the Massey family from Illinois, who are summering at Mary's Neck (Tarkington's fictional name for Kennebunkport) for the first time. The Masseys, tenderfeet when they deal with the natives, are victimized by the sellers of goods and services. Their two eligible daughters are constantly besieged by fatuous males, much to the disgust of Mr. Massey, who wishes he were back in Logansville, Illinois. There are some amusing local characters, particularly Ananias P. Sweetmus, a garrulous, self-satisfied chucklehead, who does not have enough sense not to kick a skunk right in front of the fresh-air intake of the Masseys' house. His monologues bore everyone but the reader.

The Great Depression had little effect on Tarkington's ability to sell his fiction, and he continued to live in his customary affluent manner. As a sensitive human being, however, he was concerned with economic problems and attempted solutions; yet he never had any sympathy with the New Deal, and his solution to hard times was always personal, never collective. He focused his attention on young people who had grown up during the prosperous 1920s and, between 1932 and 1934, wrote two nouvelles, a one-act play, and a full-length novel on the problems of the Depression. The nouvelles, "Pretty Twenty" (*McCall's*, October 1932) and "Rennie Peddigoe" (*Woman's Home Companion*, December 1934- April 1935), both deal with young lovers, from formerly wealthy families, who elope and start life from scratch, in the first instance returning to the land and in the other entering high-school teaching. Tarkington must have realized, though, that these two stories really had small relevance for the Depression, and he never reprinted either of them in book form.

His own large amount of purchasing power during the 1930s enabled him to indulge in his long-standing hobby of art collecting. Because of depressed prices in the art market, he was able to acquire a sizable quantity of the work of the old masters, and his experiences collecting art led to his use of the art world in fiction. Another story cycle, this one focusing on an art dealer named Rumbin, provided sixteen stories for the *Saturday Evening Post* between 1936 and 1945, six of which were gathered into *Rumbin Galleries*. This is one of Tarkington's most amusing collections, for he had gathered many anecdotes of the art market from Abris and David Silberman, New York dealers, both of whom had devoted a great deal of time and talent to selling him pictures. Both brothers figured in Tarkington's portrait of Mr. Rumbin, but especially David, who was fat and spoke a gorgeous broken English.

Before writing *Rumbin Galleries*, however, Tarkington had returned to the subject in which he long had specialized, stories of children. During the early 1930s he found himself surrounded

Tarkington in his study at Seawood, his summer home in Kennebunkport, Maine

by great-nephews and nieces, all around the age of seven. Their activities were as absorbing as those of his own nephews had been a generation earlier. Never having written about children of seven, he tried it and found it congenial. The result was another series (twelve stories) for the *Saturday Evening Post* that were collected as *Little Orvie*. Penrod had been eleven, Willie Baxter seventeen, and in this collection, Tarkington wanted to study, as he said, "the age of seven and its adjacencies, reaching out, too, for some slight exhibition of the relationship between a child of that age and his parents, and also striving to know something of his viewpoint concerning his contemporaries, household pets, worldly distinctions and importances" (quoted by Woodress in *Booth Tarkington*). This age, he thought, was another of the key years of childhood.

Tarkington's last story sequence, *The Fighting Littles*, returned to the urban Midwest for its setting, but it is rather tired Tarkington, and while there are some funny episodes in the tales, one has the feeling that Tarkington has done it all better before. The characters are fifteen-year-old Filmer; his eighteen-year-old sister Goody; her harebrained suitors; Ripley Little, the most irrascible man in town; and cousin Olita, who acts as housekeeper. The character of Ripley provided a safety valve for Tarkington through which he could abuse the New Deal, but Ripley is a ridiculous character, a caricature of the rabid anti-New Dealer.

There seems little likelihood that Tarkington's work will undergo any great future revival of interest. His reputation has settled him in a minor position among writers of the first half of the twentieth century. Yet he was a writer of charm and intelligence, and much of his work is fun to read. A few of his stories, such as the Penrod tales, will likely continue to interest readers because of Tarkington's wit, humor, style, and use of realistic detail. He captured the essence of unchanging childhood in unforgettable scenes and memorable characters. A few of his novels, such as the *Growth* trilogy (1927) and especially *Alice Adams* (1921), also will serve to keep his memory alive; they are works of lasting value in their authentic recreation of a time in America's past and in their statements of social significance.

Letters:

On Plays, Playwrights, and Playgoers: Selections from Letters of Booth Tarkington to George C. Tyler and John Peter Toohey, 1918-1925, edited by Alan S. Downer (Princeton: Princeton University Press, 1959).

Bibliographies:

Barton Currie, *Booth Tarkington: A Bibliography* (Garden City, N.Y.: Doubleday, Doran, 1932);

Dorothy Ritter Russo and Thelma L. Sullivan, *A Bibliography of Booth Tarkington, 1869-1946* (Indianapolis: Indiana Historical Society, 1949).

Biographies:

James Woodress, *Booth Tarkington: Gentleman from Indiana* (Philadelphia: Lippincott, 1955);

Susanah Mayberry, *My Amiable Uncle: Recollections about Booth Tarkington* (West Lafayette, Ind.: Purdue University Press, 1983).

References:

Keith J. Fennimore, *Booth Tarkington* (New York: Twayne, 1974);

A. A. Hamblen, "Booth Tarkington's Classic of Adolescence," *Southern Humanities Review*, 3 (Summer 1969): 225-231;

Winfield Townley Scott, "Tarkington and the 1920s," *American Scholar*, 26 (Spring 1957): 181-194;

John D. Seelye, "That Marvelous Boy—Penrod Once Again," *Virginia Quarterly Review*, 37 (Autumn 1961): 591-604;

James Woodress, "The Tarkington Papers," *Princeton University Library Chronicle*, 16 (Winter 1955): 45-53.

Papers:

Princeton University Library is the repository for a large collection of Tarkington's papers, including manuscripts, correspondence to and from Tarkington, scrapbooks, photographs, periodicals, books and ephemera.

Benedict Thielen
(29 April 1903 - 26 September 1965)

Eric W. Carlson
University of Connecticut

BOOKS: *Deep Streets* (Indianapolis: Bobbs-Merrill, 1932; London: Methuen, 1934);

Women in the Sun (Indianapolis: Bobbs-Merrill, 1933; London: Methuen, 1935);

Dinosaur Tracks and Other Stories (London: Secker & Warburg, 1937);

Stevie (New York: Dial, 1941);

The Lost Men (New York & London: Appleton-Century, 1946);

Friday at Noon (New York: Holt, 1947).

OTHER: "The Thunderstorm," in *The Best Short Stories: 1939*, edited by Edward J. O'Brien (Boston: Houghton Mifflin, 1939), pp. 283-291;

"Silver Virgin," in *O. Henry Memorial Award Prize Stories of 1939*, edited by Harry Hansen (New York: Doubleday, Doran, 1939), pp. 237-254;

"Night and the Lost Armies," in *The Best Short Stories: 1940*, edited by O'Brien (Boston: Houghton Mifflin, 1940), pp. 450-458;

"This Is My Own, My Native Land," in *High Lights in American Literature*, edited by Ola P. Srygley, O. V. Betts, M. M. Allison, and B. F. Fronabarger (Dallas: Banks Upshaw, 1940), pp. 673-682;

"The Psychologist," in *The Best Short Stories: 1941*, edited by O'Brien (Boston: Houghton Mifflin, 1941), pp. 319-331;

"Dawn Gun," in *Modern Reading, Number Seven*, edited by Reginald Moore (London: Gardner, Darton, 1943), pp. 52-64;

"The Empty Sky," in *O. Henry Memorial Award Prize Stories of 1946*, edited by Herschel Brickell (Garden City, N.Y.: Doubleday, 1946), pp. 259-271;

"Old Boy—New Boy," in *Prize Stories of 1947: The O. Henry Awards*, edited by Brickell (Garden City, N.Y.: Doubleday, 1947), pp. 246-256.

SELECTED PERIODICAL PUBLICATIONS—
UNCOLLECTED: "The Golden Land," *Esquire*, 6 (October 1936): 40-41, 171;

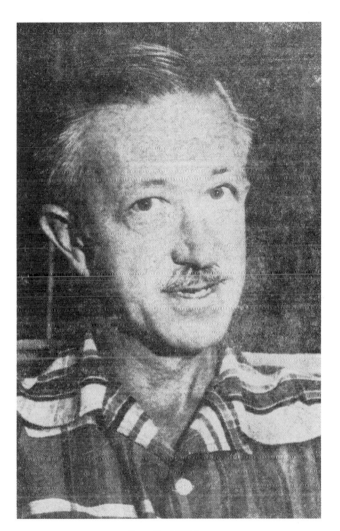

Benedict Thielen

"Man About Town," *Harper's Bazaar*, 70 (October 1936): 98-99, 140, 142, 144;

"Forever Cherished," *Esquire*, 6 (November 1936): 101, 235-237;

"Till Death Us Do Part," *American Mercury*, 39 (November 1936): 321-328;

"Peacock in the Snow," *Atlantic Monthly*, 158 (December 1936): 696-704;

"Haunted House," *John o' London's Weekly*, 36 (29 January 1937): 725-726;

"The Reluctant Fate," *Harper's Bazaar*, 71 (May 1937): 107, 143, 150;

"I Believe," *Harper's Magazine*, 175 (August 1937): 294-298;

"Polite Comedy," *Harper's Bazaar*, 71 (September 1937): 79, 153-155;

"Warrior's Return," *Esquire*, 8 (November 1937): 44-45, 191-192;

"A Victorian Room," *Harper's Bazaar*, 71 (December 1937): 94-95, 140, 142;

"The Globe," *Harper's Magazine*, 176 (January 1938): 124-128;

"A Ship at Anchor," *John o' London's Weekly*, 38 (4 February 1938): 749-750;

"Blossoms for My Bride," *Scribner's Magazine*, 103 (March 1938): 43-45;

"The Dark Continent," *London Mercury*, 39 (November 1938): 18-27;

"Arrival in Paradise," *John o' London's Weekly*, 40 (30 December 1938): 525-527;

"A New Hat," *Harper's Bazaar*, 73 (January 1939): 49, 112, 114;

"A House by the Sea," *Yale Review*, 28 (Spring 1939): 521-529;

"In the Year of Our Lord," *Esquire*, 11 (April 1939): 60-61, 104, 106;

"Fountain of Youth," *Esquire*, 11 (May 1939): 46-47, 163-164;

"Eyes That Have Seen Another Land," *Atlantic Monthly*, 164 (July 1939): 63-68;

"Flying Horses," *New Yorker*, 15 (12 August 1939): 15-17;

"Man Is a Hawk," *University Review*, 6 (October 1939): 5-13;

"A Voice of Our Time," *University Review*, 6 (March 1940): 149-158;

"Family Tradition," *John o' London's Weekly*, 43 (28 June 1940): 361-362;

"A Man and His Son," *American Prefaces*, 6 (Autumn 1940): 51-60;

"I'll Tell You the Story of a Brave Engineer," *Yale Review*, 30 (Winter 1941): 325-334;

"Lesson of a Cockfight," *Esquire*, 17 (January 1942): 61, 143, 145;

"Homeward Bound," *Harper's Bazaar*, 79 (October 1945): 132, 192, 194, 196-200;

"U.S.N. (Retired)," *Collier's*, 116 (29 December 1945): 20, 39-40;

"It's All Over Now," *Town & Country*, 100 (November 1946): 122, 240-241;

"We Prefer Florence," *New Yorker*, 24 (1 May 1948): 28-33;

"Nature Study," *Town & Country*, 114 (August 1950): 63, 99-101;

"The Perfect Day," *Harper's Bazaar*, 85 (August 1952): 122, 176, 178-181;

"Go Kiss Him If You Dare," *Collier's*, 121 (21 February 1953): 17, 44, 46-48;

"Lady on a Reef," *American Legion Magazine*, 54 (February 1953): 15-17, 43-44;

"Violence on Riverside Drive," *New Yorker*, 32 (24 March 1956): 81-88, 93-95.

Benedict Thielen's short fiction is distinguished from run-of-the-mill stories by its tone of authenticity (the "authority" of the narrator); superb craftsmanship, especially in the realistic dialogue and deft sense of metaphor, motif, and counterpoint; economic use of setting; sensitive and vivid descriptions of nature; diversity of subject, theme, and character; a penchant for the serio-comic; and freedom from strained effects or fine writing for its own sake. The reader of a Thielen story never needs to question the accuracy or authenticity of the dialogue—whether that of the crude Stevie or the European Karvalishes, whether spoken in French, German, Italian, Spanish, or regional American—or to wonder about the details of places, restaurants, dinners, wines, or the flora and fauna of the seashore and the tropics. Giving shape and unity to the stories are keen psychological insights and a well-defined philosophical perspective. Among the authors Thielen studied and admired were F. Scott Fitzgerald, Joseph Conrad, Thomas Mann, Anton Chekhov, Fyodor Dostoyevski, Gustave Flaubert, Henry David Thoreau, John Dewey, Virginia Woolf, Katherine Mansfield, Henry James, and Ernest Hemingway.

Thielen's strong awareness of his Austrian and German heritage and of European culture in general is reflected in his fiction in the contrasts between European and American values. Thielen was born in Newark, New Jersey, on 29 April 1903 to Henry J. Thielen, who had emigrated from Germany to the United States at about age twenty and eventually became a banker in New York City, and Theodora Prieth Thielen, whose father, Benedict, was a South Tyrolean who took part in a student rebellion in 1848. Benedict Prieth was imprisoned in Salzburg for a year but then escaped. An idealist and admirer of American democracy, he made his way to the United States and settled in Newark, where he founded a newspaper. He died in 1879. The Thielens lived with his widow, Grandmother Prieth, and young Benedict attended local schools, then matriculated at Princeton at age sixteen. His mother died in 1923; five years later, after a long illness, his father returned to Germany and died soon afterward.

Among the Thielen relations in New York City was the very wealthy Uncle Lo (Lothar Faber, of the U.S. branch of the noted German pencil-manufacturing family, who had married Theodora Prieth's sister Anna). Thielen moved in with his uncle and lived there during his senior and graduate years at Princeton. Faber had settled on Riverside Drive and become the head of an eccentric extended family that is vividly and humorously depicted in Thielen's story "Violence on Riverside Drive" (*New Yorker*, 24 March 1956). Except for the names, Thielen claimed this family portrait was based on fact. Although he said he had never written much autobiography, many of his stories reflect his experiences with people and places, both in life and in his reading, which was extensive and varied. To Thielen, Flaubert's view seemed a sound description of his own writing: "I recollected, I imagined, I combined."

After earning his B.A. in 1923, Thielen went on to graduate school at Princeton, receiving his M.A. after only a year, then setting out "to see the great world that lay beyond the golf links," as he later noted in conversation. He spent a year and a half in Paris, then five years intermittently in southern France, England, Italy, Germany, Belgium, Switzerland, Austria, Greece, and Yugoslavia. On 20 July 1930 he married painter Virginia Berresford, and from December 1932 to October 1940 they lived in New York City. Thereafter they resided in Key West and Martha's Vineyard. Thielen also traveled extensively in the West Indies, Central America, and the American West, especially California, Utah, and Arizona. But he was never able to live for long out of sight of the sea, "the most beautiful, clean, fresh element in creation," as he once referred to it in conversation. In the spring of 1949, after more than eighteen years of marriage, he and Virginia were divorced. Thielen married Helen Close on 9 July 1949. Her son from an earlier marriage, Charles Close, became his stepson; Thielen had no children of his own.

After 1940, in his career as a professional writer in Chilmark on Martha's Vineyard and in Key West, Thielen maintained a disciplined schedule of work from 9 to 11:30 A.M. and, after lunch and usually a swim, from 2 to 4:30 P.M., extending his writing hours when special needs dictated. For privacy he worked alone at his typewriter in a small shack separate from the main house at Chilmark and in an attic on Caroline Street, away from his hundred-year-old Dey Street house in Key West. His island residences enabled him to enjoy his hobbies of scuba diving and marine biology, especially conchology, as well as to absorb the spirit of the place: "In Key West we live by the fish wharves surrounded by Life (drunken sponge fishermen), Philosophy (John Dewey) and Art (Doris Lee and Arnold Blanch)" ("Lesson of a Cockfight," *Esquire*, January 1942). Of Chilmark he noted in his journal for 1935 that "the beauty and perfection of this spot seem to me to increase daily, and I want to seize every moment of it and squeeze every drop from these midsummer days. . . . There is a quality about this place that makes me think of the music of Bach or Beethoven . . . of the loftiness and purity such as is found only in [their] music . . . "

Thielen's thoughts on the artist's creative self-absorption and imaginative identification with nature and other people were crystallized by his reading of the letters of Flaubert and the diaries of Woolf. In "Advice to a Girl About to Marry a Writer" (*Harper's*, September 1955) Thielen says that although "the writer reacts to everything with emotion" out of "an intense need of it, he must defend himself against it [and] must submerge and look up through the cool depths" until he achieves the discipline and clarity of aesthetic distance. The writer is "the sensitive man . . . the man who understands . . . actually a very self-less man." Like an ascetic, "the writer faces a daily torment as keen in its way as any endured by holy men in the desert." And yet there are moments of joy that compare to the rapture of love. But then "his task returns and plucks him by the sleeve. The elusive words, the jumbled sentences, the cloudy pictures, the muffled voices begin to form and fade and form again." Beyond this daily torment and struggle of the creative writer, Thielen recognized the importance of perspective—the writer's attitude toward life, his values, and his artistic methods.

Thielen's career as an author falls into three periods: his long apprenticeship from 1924 to 1931; his fiction-publishing years, 1931 to 1956; and the period of his nonfiction writing (including travel pieces) for *Holiday* magazine, 1957 to 1965. In his third phase, he kept writing short stories, which remain unpublished and are on file at Princeton University Library (Manuscript Division). From the beginning, Thielen's stories

THEY had the tank filled and a quart of oil put in the motor and the man was just taking his wallet out of his pocket when the girl said:

"Oh, why don't we get something to eat while we're here? Don't you feel hungry?"

The man frowned and looked back down the road.

"That fellow'll pass us if we do," he said.

"Oh, well . . ."

"Well, you know what a time I had to pass him." He turned to the storekeeper standing by the red gasoline pump. "One of those regular road hogs. Never give you an inch of room if they can help it."

Illustration for the September 1934 Scribner's Magazine *publication of the comic story Thielen chose to end his first collection,* Dinosaur Tracks and Other Stories *(1937)*

appeared in the quality magazines: the *New Yorker, Harper's Bazaar, Scribner's, Town and Country, Esquire, Atlantic Monthly, Harper's Magazine, Yale Review, London Mercury*, and *John o' London's Weekly*, among others. That he was widely known and read is also clear from his having nine of his stories chosen for anthologies of the "best" or "prize" stories (three of which were later published in his own collections), and two chosen for modern-literature anthologies.

During his early apprentice years abroad, Thielen composed short stories and several novels (unpublished) prior to his first published novel, *Deep Streets* (1932), which is a series of related tragedies caused by the frustrating conditions and false values of city life, as reflected in characters representative of vain, self-deluded, indifferent, "independent," lonely, and trapped lives. In France, Thielen could live within his means and "work without being considered a social parasite by the Right Thinkers." There, too, he soaked up the atmosphere of the vineyards for his second published novel, *Women in the Sun* (1933). Critics praised it for its lively, natural dialogue, its genuine feeling for nature and music,

and its sardonic treatment of the futility of attempting to escape from the urban to the primitive in nature. In contrast to the realistic dialogue, the impressionistic use of occasional short sentences and simple syntax effectively convey changes of mood.

In 1937 Thielen selected seventeen stories, eleven of them unpublished elsewhere, for *Dinosaur Tracks and Other Stories*. Two comedies of the American West, "Dinosaur Tracks" and "Souvenir of Arizona," begin and end this collection. Most impressive are "Lieutenant Pearson" and "The Bells of Victory," with its ironic contrast of the well-fed boxing fans and journalists with Kid Meyer, the young boxer who never recovers from a knockout blow in the ring. "Auction" and "Young Country" also stand out as characteristic of Thielen's best work, as do "Prelude to Matrimony," "Afternoon of a Faun," and "Spanish Dancers."

Some years later Thielen exploited what he called his "low-comedy phase" in *Stevie* (1941), his major work in the Ring Lardner/S. J. Perelman tradition of satiric comedy. "Not that I think any the less of [the book] for that, because to be humorous is as important (if not more so) as being serious. It is dangerous to be only one or the other." The "honest businessman" Stevie, the narrator Joe, and their wives are depicted in eleven comic situations, largely through self-revealing dialogue. As a caricature of the ignorant, noisy, crude egoist, Stevie becomes the chief target of the author's double-edged humor and satire. But it is a gentle humor. To those readers who might be irritated by such "perfectly dreadful people," Thielen explained in his introduction to the book that such an attitude was "difficult . . . to understand." He wrote that he was "interested in the Higher Things" and listened "enraptured to the music of Beethoven and Mozart. . . . But I also like swing music, and boxing, and burlesque. . . . Stevie and his pals are, it seems to me, the corned-beef-and-cabbage, the beer, the weeds, the burlesque shows of this existence, and as such I like them and like to report their doings. . . ."

What had been a parallel, symbolic relationship between nature and man's inner feelings in *Women in the Sun* reappears with increased power and subtlety in *The Lost Men* (1946), the story of three World War I veterans on Labor Day 1935, when a violent hurricane swept across Lower Matecumbe in the Florida Keys, wiping out many residents and 272 of the 385 veterans living there. Begun in 1941, and interrupted by Thielen's service in the U.S. Navy (1942-1944), this novel was not finished until October 1945.

In *Friday at Noon* (1947) Thielen employed an even more complex structure of subjective interrelationships among characters, each with distinct personal drives and associations, and each seen through the eyes and minds of the others as well, after the manner of Woolf's *The Waves* (1931). As in *The Lost Men* Thielen here makes effective use of leitmotifs, symbolism, contrast of the subjective and the objective, past and present, interacting characters, and the subtle revelation of mood and motive.

Among Thielen's unpublished papers are notes for a long essay called "The Short Story as an Art Form." Here he distinguishes "art" from "technique," the latter being restricted to those mechanical devices by which it is assumed that "so complex a thing as the short story can be reduced to the level of a recipe for making fudge. . . . After all the analyzing and classifying and labeling of the resultant debris by the teacher of Technique, there is something that defies analysis. That something is the art or soul of the work—an imponderable without which no successful story can be written." To justify his own analyses, Thielen explains that they were made after, not before, the stories were written; they show the form the story *took*—the elements or "points" through which the curve was drawn. These details are the pictures in the mind that come from the unconscious and make up the story. Being "passionately fond of music," Thielen conceived his novels and stories as having a musical feeling underlying their structure, just as a sonata has an "apparently fixed yet immensely flexible form—exposition, development, recapitulation, and coda." The closer to the condition of music, the greater is the story, the poem, or the painting. Whereas inorganic form is conscious and structural, organic form is living, natural, and implicit in the story itself, producing a curve or shape that is never quite the same from story to story, or author to author. The story is a collection of preparatory details with an organic, dynamic life of its own, for the purpose of creating suspense and direction or forward movement. The action may take place in the present, the past, or the future, or in any combination of these. It may indicate the future as it must arise out of what happened in the past: "In fact, it is just this quality of the action of a story continuing in the mind after one has finished reading it that makes it live . . . in the mind with a life of its own."

As examples of the "curve" or pattern of significant details, three stories stand out. The best of these is "Peacock in the Snow" (*Atlantic Monthly*, December 1936), the story of two university-laboratory scientists visiting Henry, their friend and colleague just returned to town with his southern bride, Rosamond. The subtle use of contrasting leitmotifs (counterpoint) shows the values of the men—their preoccupation with logic, science, fact, and precision; their satisfaction with black-white effects (the Cape Cod house, the snow, the dark tree branches, and the night sky); their acceptance of the "cold" climate and house, and their preference for Bach—in contrast to Rosamond's need for emotional self-realization, as suggested by her love of vivid colors (the peacock colors of her gown, the flowers on the mantelpiece), her warm mouth and soft voice, her unusual name, her piano composition, and her sensitivity to cold. The steadily rising action of this counterpoint reaches a climax when Henry remarks, "Why, I never knew you wrote any music yourself, Rosamond," and Rosamond

Blossoms

For My Bride... BENEDICT THIELEN

Illustration by Norman Reeves for one of Thielen's uncollected stories (Scribner's Magazine, March 1938). One of his psychological studies, it tells of a widower who has just married his former mistress.

replies, "There are some things that even you don't know about me, darling." To Henry's friend Paul her music sounds "crazy"; to the other scientist, the unnamed narrator, it has a strange appeal that he cannot articulate. They smugly agree, though, that Rosamond will have to "adapt herself" to their climate, internal as well as external, and then they take refuge in their lab until 3 A.M. "I don't know why we did," remarks the narrator.

In the second example, "Forever Cherished" (*Esquire*, November 1936), Fred, the narrator, unlike the observer/narrator in "Peacock in the Snow," is at the center of the action. The central theme, which runs through the story, focuses on "this thing" Fred has on his mind—having to tell Eddie about his affair with Phyllis, Eddie's wife. But when Fred remembers Eddie's heroism in saving his life in battle and realizes how desperate is Eddie's hope that Phyllis still cares for him, he decides he cannot tell Eddie the truth. At this point, the climax of the story, it becomes evident that Eddie is blind, which adds poignancy to the ending. Thus the past (Eddie's self-sacrifice and

blindness) is shown as capable of influencing the present (the narrator's mental state).

In the third example, "Till Death Us Do Part" (*American Mercury*, November 1936) the rising curve revealing the main character's past is followed by a flat passage of ordinary talk between him, his former wife, and others. Then, in the latter half, three memory segments appear—one of the couple's life in France, another of their home and children, and a third of their separation; as these memories impinge on the narrator's present consciousness, he realizes his present and future fate as a lonely man-about-town ("all this, here on this street, present, now").

Thielen also viewed the short story in terms of its significance, that is, as "a part of the whole body of the author's work, or as a part of contemporary thought, or of some contemporary trend or movement, or the influence of that work on others." Taken as a whole, Thielen's seventy short stories (plus a score that remain unpublished) represent a wide range of subjects and themes. Among these are several on war as a self-defeating experience for the individual and as a tragedy for warring nations. The most effective example is "Night and the Lost Armies" (*Atlantic Monthly*, December 1939; in *The Best Short Stories: 1940*), which attempts to dramatize the horror and tragedy of war by depicting the wounded, dying, and dead soldiers of a retreating army, which, as the story progresses, symbolically encompasses an increasing number of "lost" armies. Interspersed are alternating passages reminiscent of the normal family life of these men before the war began. The stark contrast of this contrapuntal method, expressed in a rhythmic, musical, impressionistic style, builds to a climax: "The murmur of their voices rose with the rising day, subdued at first, then louder, swelling more deeply, rising into the sky, filling it, the voices of the living and of the dying, and, echoing back from the earth and the sea, the voices of the hundred-million-throated dead."

In two other stories war is the reality that determines the fate of an idealist. The young newspaper reporter Johnny in "I Believe" (*Harper's Magazine*, August 1937) has the vital faith and commitment that drive him into an active role for mankind—he rushes out to join the marching men in the street—a rebellious spark that is nearly smothered by the cynicism of some middle-aged journalists, whose capacity to believe in a cause has been repeatedly betrayed by the futility and hypocrisy of past wars. Counterpoint again effectively conveys these opposed attitudes, as it does in "In the Year of Our Lord" (*Esquire*, April 1939), in which three friends—French, German, and English—are together on a mountain-climbing outing. As they joke about each other's nationalistic traits and shortcomings, they express a deep faith in the growing acceptance of people without "all this narrow patriotic business." The next morning they rise early to view the *Alpengluehen*, which turns into a symbol: "For a time they said nothing, watching the changing light, the sky becoming a deeper blue and the snow on the mountains steadily whitening." When the German invites his friends to visit him in Germany the following summer, the present date, 28 June 1914, underlines for the reader the ironic futility of their plan.

Three other stories show the effects of war on the individual. In "Lieutenant Pearson" (*Atlantic Monthly*, July 1936; in *Dinosaur Tracks*) Frank Pearson dons his uniform for another Armistice Day parade. Having sensed that he is becoming encased in routine domestic activity, Frank rationalizes his image in uniform as the only valid recognition of himself as a person who *is* somebody. When his bungled speech brings him down to reality, he undergoes a pathetic ego deflation, honestly admitting the emptiness of being a mere pawn in the game of life, but also hungering for some meaningful enrichment in his life.

In "The Empty Sky" (*Yale Review*, Spring 1946; in *O. Henry Memorial Award Prize Stories of 1946*) George, just back from service in the air corps, awakens to "the ordered rhythm, the ebb and flow of daylight and dark, of all the days of the future." When his mother fusses over his health, his wound, and his medals, he begins to laugh, "laughing and suddenly seeing Andy, the gunner, laughing and laughing, and the ambulance carrying him off, the sound of his laughter still trailing behind it. . . ." Later he recalls vividly the faces of his crew members—so different from the faces and voices of those around him now—and Peggy smiling and wearing his fraternity pin. And when he hears a plane passing overhead, "he saw each man and all the men together. He heard the occasional crackle of their voices on the interphone, the jokes and the abuse, each man alone and each man bound by this slender thread to every other man, able to talk and knowing he would be understood. . . . For a time longer he sat at the window looking up at the empty sky. Then he went back to bed."

"A Man and His Son" (*American Prefaces*, Autumn 1940) tells the story of how a father anticipated that his son would, after college, enter the family business and eventually carry it on as his inheritance and responsibility. But when his son held long conversations with common workmen and, after a long trip around the country, announced that he was going to earn a living as a carpenter, the father considered the son a failure. During the war the son enlists in the ambulance corps to please his father. After the son's heroic death in saving a comrade, the father begins to hear and see his son, to believe that his son is back. Finally he imagines that his son comes to visit, and sees himself as having godlike powers: "I am the beginning and the end, and . . . at the sound of my voice the earth trembles and the shining of the stars is hidden from men's eyes." The interior monologue here takes psychological realism one step beyond "The Empty Sky" and "Lieutenant Pearson."

From 1936 to 1939 five of Thielen's stories pointed up the power of the past over the present. In these, psychological realism comes through dialogue rather than plot: the ghosts of the past are not easily laid to rest. In "Man About Town" (*Harper's Bazaar*, October 1936) the protagonist, Jerry, spends an evening in New York with four old friends, now married. Still a bachelor, he takes special satisfaction in his conversational wit, his knowledge of French wines and of the smart, amusing places (restaurants and bars) in town, and in being free from the trammels of marriage and domesticity. At 1:30 A.M., when his friends take sudden leave of him, his romantic illusions of being free and independent are shattered; his life seems empty.

In "Haunted House" (*John o' London's Weekly*, 29 January 1937) a bleak Victorian house becomes the symbolic equivalent of Edith's sacrificing love and marriage to live with her mother after her father's death. Now she hardly feels strong enough to marry her old love Charles, who has returned after thirty years abroad. "A Victorian Room" (*Harper's Bazaar*, December 1937) uses Victorian furnishings in a modern New York apartment to symbolize the early years of Maud and her brother, when they grew up in a small town among what now seem odd and provincial characters. But after her party, with "clever" guests who are actually the ultimate in arty pretentiousness, Maud looks out the window and sees nothing but blank, silent sky—her present lifestyle lacks all the natural values of her girlhood, when the sights and sounds of the changing seasons gave meaning to experience. The old-fashioned past, it turns out, is more real than the modern present. Similarly, in "Auction" (first published in *Dinosaur Tracks*) an old man remembers the quality of each piece—the Chinese vase, the Empire bookcase, the eighteenth-century Venetian bed, and the Prentiss portrait of his wife—as it is auctioned for a pittance compared to its real value.

In "The Thunderstorm" (*Story*, November-December 1938; in *The Best Short Stories: 1939*) a young wife, Margaret, jokingly at first, asks her husband about his former women friends, especially Phyllis, whose photograph she has seen. As an oncoming thunderstorm grows in intensity, her curiosity takes on a persistent, serious tone. Later, when the still rumbling thunder keeps the husband awake, "his mind felt wide open, with a strange sense of time, of all the time that there had been and all that there was to be, and the many nights of restless heat and storm that had lain over the earth in the past and many that were to come, and while she slept he listened for

each new distant roll of thunder and heard it as it came across the dark land toward their house."

Several of Thielen's stories explore the theme of matriarchal and patriarchal domination, countered by attempts to rebel against or escape from such domination. The dialogue between Mrs. Merkel and her married daughter, Charlotte, in "The Globe" (*Harper's Magazine*, January 1938), becomes the satiric setting for Mrs. Merkel's insidious undermining of Charlotte's faith in her husband and her support of his admirable interest in distant lands and other "global" realities. Here home, family, and maternity are turned into a matriarchal mystique that, in the words of Professor Edward A. Post, "debases man's tenderness as weakness, his respect as humiliation, and his hope as triviality; and with the whip of female verbal strategy in her hand [Mrs. Merkel] sees to it that man's dream is perpetually balked and frustrated" (unpublished comment, circa 1960).

In "Dawn Gun" (first published in *Modern Reading, Number Seven*, 1943) the independence of men and boys is constantly threatened by overprotective women. Uncle Willy's firing his cannon at dawn on July 4th and his colorful macho tales of Indian fighting and whaling underscore the virtues of the vital pioneer drive and independent spirit that are threatened by the "conditions" of life and the fears of women. This realization, along with the protagonist Neil's "sense of life, of fullness and completion" in the wild, untamed beauty of nature around him, make him feel "one of them" as he sits with the menfolk, mindful of the symbolic legacy of Uncle Willy.

In "Old Boy—New Boy" (*Town and Country*, August 1946; in *Prize Stories of 1947*) patriarchal pressure is the problem. Paul Carroll allows family and prep-school loyalty to overcome concern for his son's welfare and to sweep aside his son's deeper awareness that becoming a "new boy" at this academy will mean a denial of his own freedom and growth. "Nature Study," the latest of these stories (*Town and Country*, August 1950), is especially rich in the overtones of meaning resonating from significant motifs: the butterfly, the music, the geese, Mr. Allen and his guns, the story of Joe DiMaggio, and the boy Terry's mother's eyes. Terry, thirteen, feeling lonely and insignificant since his mother's remarriage, is confused not only by the strange music played by Paul, his stepfather, but also by the disapproval of hunting by his mother and Paul, in contrast to his neighbor Mr. Allen's love of guns and hunting. However, when his mother says, "There are all sorts of ways of being brave. . . . And there are all sorts of ways of being a man," and walks away, Terry becomes aware of her inner strength and serenity.

Bravery translates into stoical acceptance of the inevitable in "I'll Tell You the Story of a Brave Engineer" (*Yale Review*, Winter 1941). In mid-life Ed Roberts remembers his father as a train engineer and his own career as a bridge engineer—during those years when "there was always new land for more trains and new rivers and hills for more bridges. . . ." And he remembers "a song of building and of man's struggle with the earth, of arches of steel thrown into space. . . ." But now he experiences fear as being "a slow and slowly dawning creeping in the mind . . . from the endless identical days—the days that do not need you or your work." As he watches a building being demolished, his son Ted's eyes are lifted to a plane in the sky— "unhampered, free, not even bound by lines of rails on land, not even dependent on a bridge." "That's what I want to do. Fly a plane like that," the boy says.

Conflicts of cultural values, as well as conflicts between generations, figure in Thielen's stories that draw upon his extensive knowledge of differences between American and European character. In "We Prefer Florence" (*New Yorker*, May 1948) the Crosbys have as dinner guests Mr. and Mrs. Karvalish from Hungary (or possibly Romania—it is not specified), who turn out to be cultural snobs of a vulgar, ignorant, greedy sort, leaving Eleanor Crosby feeling far less anxious about her capacity as a hostess. By the end of the evening she realizes that her romantic memories of a baron she once met in Florence (triggered by Mr. Karvalish's cologne, slick hair, and suggestive advances) are false, and "only this was real— this room, these dishes, and this laughter." Much of the humor derives from the guests' mangling of English. "This is My Own, My Native Land" (*Harper's Magazine*, April 1937; in *High Lights in American Literature*, 1940) dramatizes the serious and regrettable conflict of ethnic differences between a family and community of Portuguese fishermen, on the one hand, and the native-American-Yankee middle class on the other, during the Feast of the Holy Ghost at a New England fishing port. Rose Oliver (Olivera) is caught between her Portuguese origins and customs (the annual procession with the silver crown, followed by the auction, food, and wine) and the town's prohibition

of dancing on Sunday, its disapproval of the procession, and its money standard of value, as represented by Nat, Rose's American fiancé. Become conscious of her cultural heritage, Rose identifies with it, fully, for the first time.

Among his international stories "The Dark Continent" (*London Mercury*, November 1938) seems influenced by Conrad's "Heart of Darkness" (1899). Archer, the narrator, journeys out of primitive Africa across the African land and jungle up through western Europe—Greece, Italy, and Austria—and from there to the coast, where he travels by ship to the United States. Each vignette or scene alternates with a philosophical interior monologue, adding depth and significance. The European cultural heritage of classical beauty and tranquillity, represented by Greek and Italian art, the brotherly feeling toward strangers experienced in the Tyrol—these and other rediscoveries are welcome changes from the savage jungle dances. But when the dull rhythms of the Nazi troops on maneuvers in Austria blend with the faster rhythm of the train, Archer is glad to be moving westward toward freedom. Aboard ship he hears in the rhythm of the steel propeller the "wild and savage dancing, advancing, receding, *one*-two-three-four, in endless repetition, in the darkness from which we were born, in the darkness to which we seek to return."

Two stories deal more directly with colonialism. In "Arrival in Paradise" (*John o' London's Weekly*, 30 December 1938) a young American couple arrive at an unnamed tropical country and are greeted with curiosity and enthusiasm by Americans already there as representatives of Royal Dutch and other corporations. The newly arrived wife, Lucy, is soon introduced not only to exotic flowers, birds, food, and weather but also to the empty lives of the colonials, whose chief time killers are bridge, golf, dancing, and drinking at the club. Though she intends to learn to play bridge, she notices that the neighbor's phonograph plays incessantly, and into her mind come nostalgic memories of Indian Pipe, Bouncing Bet, pipsissewa, bittersweet, lady's slipper, and other familiar flowers at home.

The other indictment of colonialism is ironically entitled "Polite Comedy" (*Harper's Bazaar*, September 1937). Here, as in E. M. Forster's *Passage to India* (1924), the British officials are seen as living empty lives: polo and tea, tennis and tea, or else pig-sticking, hunting, with drinks afterward, and endless talk of these every afternoon

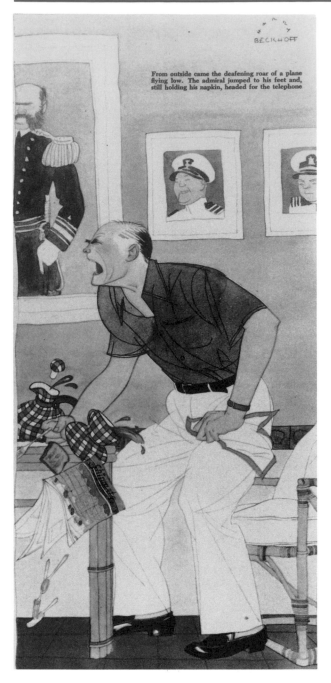

From outside came the deafening roar of a plane flying low. The admiral jumped to his feet and, still holding his napkin, headed for the telephone

Illustration by Harry Beckhoff for "U.S.N. (Retired)," one of Thielen's domestic comedies (Collier's, 29 December 1945). The story is about a sixty-five-year-old rear admiral who finds it difficult to adjust to civilian life.

and evening. And "the women playing bridge together alone [seem] weary of each other's faces." When Iris, the main character, first met Ronny, she was able to talk about other things—until her husband, Guy, one of the British officials, senses her new interest; pretending to leave the region of Simla, he returns and finds Iris alone with a cobra only a few feet away, "a swift and accurate in-

strument of death." Tempted by this ultimate solution to her dilemma, Iris feels a "profound calm" but is saved by Guy's shot from the window; Guy has never carried a revolver before. This story employs an effective counterpoint of dialogue (Iris talking to her sister Elinor) and interior monologue (Iris's thoughts of what really happened, which cannot be told, in contrast to Elinor's romantic notions of India). As often happens in Thielen's stories, here descriptive details are woven into meaningful motifs. The cobra, especially, adds not only suspense but symbolizes Guy's real character. After hearing about the snake, Tom, Elinor's husband, remarks, "You must forget about it, Iris. That's the only thing to do when you've had a terrible experience like that: just don't think about it."

Among favorite targets of Thielen's satiric comedy are certain American tourists who, gullible and greedy, waste their money on fake art and cheap souvenirs or dutifully tramp through the galleries without understanding what they see. "An Old Palace" (in *Dinosaur Tracks*) and "Tourist Home" (in *Stevie*) are good examples. In "Silver Virgin" (*Harper's Magazine*, February 1939; in *O. Henry Memorial Award Prize Stories of 1939*), the best of these satires, the Wrights, an American family touring southern France, stop at a walled town, where Mrs. Wright and the daughter shop and look at antiques, which are really fakes, and then visit the church to see the silver virgin. Meanwhile, Mr. Wright goes his own way, down a country road, until he is invited to stop at a house for water and wine. Feeling at home, he lingers over the wine and conversation, learning that the silver virgin is another fake and experiencing a new feeling of peace and contentment: "The earth was small and round and quiet. . . . A place like this was sheltered and warm and still. . . ." An added enjoyment for the reader is Thielen's play on French words in the conversations between Wright, the chauffeur, and the farmer.

Thielen's psychological studies of character, on the other hand, are serious and reflective, dramatizing forms of escape from life's stresses or demands. In "Warrior's Return" (*Esquire*, November 1937) Mr. Fletcher, the owner of a declining clock and jewelry business, is depressed by the changing tastes of customers who prefer the new chromium over the sterling. When he falls ill and is brought to the hospital, he welcomes "an untroubled peace and a freedom from responsibility" and follows closely each step in the stages of his pain and treatment until he finally loses consciousness before the operation, drifting into "tenderness, and the timeless center of time, defeating forever the coldness of winter and death, to warmth and the glowing center of life, alone, safe, locked deeply, rocked gently in the immemorial slumber of the deep core of the universe." Later when he "returned from the battlefield, wounded but heroic, he, the warrior with death, rested in victory," cradled in the arms of a grateful world (in his hospital bed), from warm day to warm night, until, when he is about to be released from the hospital, "the voices of the city, harsh and strident, beat like fists against the window pane . . . outside the window life, the undefeated, cried out. He shrank back, listening."

This kind of momentary encounter with the deeper self is not found in "Man Is a Hawk" (*University Review*, October 1939), which presents the mind of Phil, a businessman who admires and has assisted his younger brother Ashley, the "poet," in building a comfortable house. Still Ashley hankers for the freedom of the hawk, freedom from family and domestic ties, even though it becomes increasingly clear that he lacks the commitment and the talent to work at being a real poet. His whole life is a dependence on and a borrowing from others—a fact that Phil ironically fails to see; Phil has given up the pleasures of travel and the arts in order to support Ashley.

"The Psychologist" (*Yale Review*, Winter 1940; in *The Best Short Stories: 1941*) is among the most subtle and ironic of Thielen's stories of self-delusion; here, too, the narrator thinks he is being generous and helpful, when in fact his plan for a vacation escape from the city for his wife and himself simply underscores his lack of awareness that his wife has found her own escape from utter loneliness on Saturday afternoons. She has come to acknowledge and enjoy each of the passing street singers and musicians, none of whom he tolerates; he is also opposed to improved housing for the natives in the West Indies ("You put bathtubs in their houses, and they use them to store coal in. They like living the way they do"). Most ironic of all, he has completely missed any insight into his wife's state of mind, despite his claim to being able to analyze her thoughts.

Attempted escapes from dull reality take many forms in Thielen's fiction. In "The Perfect Day" (*Harper's Bazaar*, August 1952) a harried housewife, mother of two teenagers, rather self-consciously buys a new bathing suit and goes for a morning swim alone, enjoying the sun, the water, and especially the tranquillity of it all. On her return she feels surrounded "by an indefinite but heavy atmosphere of grievance" as her son and daughter complain about their lunch. When her tired husband comments favorably on her bathing suit, she realizes that her life with him means more than her "perfect day" alone at the beach. An earlier story, "A New Hat" (*Harper's Bazaar*, January 1939), is parallel in theme and situation: Mrs. Abbott, shopping for a hat with her married daughter, Louise, after some uncertainty, decides on one of the new-style "silly" hats. When Mr. Abbott likes the hat, she feels aglow inside, "because we're old. . . . I'm old," that is, free from the worries that trouble Louise.

In two stories, Thielen touched on the fine line between the psychopathic and the normal. "Lesson of a Cockfight" (*Esquire*, January 1942) opens with a pair of dancers quarreling over the loss of their performance engagement. The man, Roy, takes his female partner, Lucille, to a cockfight to show her how he would use it as the basis for a new routine; she would dance the part of the defeated cock. Given his deadly jealousy, his final gesture of putting his hands on her throat is an ominous sign. In "Young Country" (first published in *Dinosaur Tracks*) the locale is a clean, attractive tourist camp out West, where Mr. Fisher, his wife and two young daughters stop. A handsome, neatly dressed, smooth-talking young man named Ferris offers to go for ice cream with Winny, one of the daughters, but just then a posse appears looking for Ferris as the murderer of a young girl whose body has just been found—"the white thin body of the child lying torn . . . like a dead rabbit . . . in the awakening spring woods, among the frail new flowers, in the virgin land. . . ."

Two of Thielen's most moving narratives draw their power from the deep relationship of the human and the elemental in nature. The autobiographical "A House by the Sea" (*Yale Review*, Spring 1939) is Thielen's most memorable, graphic, and lyrical account of how a hurricane engulfed Thielen, his wife, Virginia, and their Jamaican cook on 21 September 1938 at Chilmark, when their new house was swept a half mile inland by the powerful winds and waves. The first ominous sign is the strange feeling of the wind, which increases with a "nervous insistence" during the day, until by afternoon yellow flecks of dirty foam blow over the sand dunes, followed by trickles of water gradually widening and deepening. When the residents finally leave the house for higher ground, the waves of ocean water come in so fast they have to swim for their lives; though Thielen, a strong swimmer, tries to hold on to Josephine, the cook, who could not swim, he loses his grip on her wrist when he is forced underwater to remove his boots and sweater. In the "eerie sur-realist dream quality" of it all, there is this image: "The poor frightened black face rises, then disappears in the gray whirling water. Above it a blue felt hat with a green feather pointing upward." Exhausted in their struggle, Thielen and his wife nevertheless manage to reach the hillside, where the next morning they find the house intact, though cracked, and the five men who built it are ready to restore it. Thielen's conclusion: above the sea there is still the land you love and the people on it—"They are close to each other in their bravery and their suffering, and you yourself are closer to them than you have ever been before."

"Eyes That Have Seen Another Land" (*Atlantic Monthly*, July 1939) is a subtler account of a man's profound experience with nature as he travels to join his wife and bring her back from a sanatorium located in a western desert. There the sun and air are so hot and dry, and the sand so fine—the kind used in an hourglass—that his watch and taxi fail to function. On the return journey he draws the train-window curtain to shut out this land of death and silence. Because of the understated natural details, the larger significance, the symbolic dimension, may not be apparent on first reading.

"A Voice of Our Time" (*University Review*, March 1940) is a partially autobiographical account of Thielen's meeting with his idol F. Scott Fitzgerald on the Riviera. The narrator, Bob, as Thielen was called by his family and friends, mindful of Matt Wayne's (Fitzgerald's) early success as a writer, is deeply distressed to find him in poor health and an alcoholic as well. Beyond a momentary pity, Bob concludes, "I felt envy, and the same kind of awe that I always used to feel when I was with him . . . no matter what he was like now he had once had a voice. It was a voice that had once been raised in song. It was a bell that had once rung out. And it was better to be a

cracked bell than to be mere metal, lying forever silent and uncast in the earth."

Even more so than Fitzgerald, Thielen was "a voice of his time" in the rich variety of his characters and themes—young and old; rich, poor, and middle-class; innocent and sophisticated; submissive and domineering; babbits and barons; unemployed war veterans and engineers; mothers, fathers, and sons; war heroes and war victims; the self-deluded "psychologist" husband; the "polite comedy" of a dead marriage; calculating European snobbery; ethnic vs. native American attitudes; human brotherhood vs. war; the simple beauty of the land vs. fake tourist souvenirs; life close to nature vs. citified high society; and comradeship as a natural, instinctive fellowship of men and women. Thielen's neo-naturalism and demo-epic perspective links him with Thoreau and Steinbeck, whose work he admired. His fiction was enriched by his knowledge of foreign languages—French, German, Spanish, and Italian; his literary studies at Princeton; his lifelong reading in classical, romantic, and modern literature and, to a lesser degree, philosophy; and his wide circle of friends—Perelman, Hendrik Van Loon, Henry Hough, Gregory Mason (war correspondent, anthropologist, novelist), Max Eastman, Thomas Hart Benton, Roger Stanton, Edward A. Post, Richard Curle (Conrad scholar), John Hersey, and many others. His voluminous journals (1920s to 1965) and letters, some of them among the Benedict Thielen Papers at Princeton, further represent the wide range of human values that inform Thielen's fiction.

References:

Eric W. Carlson, "Benedict Thielen: An Introduction and a Check List," *Princeton University Library Chronicle*, 13 (Spring 1952): 143-155;

Harry R. Warfel, *American Novelists of Today* (Westport, Conn.: Greenwood, 1972), p. 423.

Papers:

Princeton University Library's Manuscript Division has all the Thielen papers, including the manuscripts of *Deep Streets, Women in the Sun, The Lost Men,* and *Friday at Noon*; most of the stories, published and unpublished; and working drafts.

James Thurber

(8 December 1894 - 2 November 1961)

Steven H. Gale
Kentucky State University

See also the Thurber entries in *DLB 4: American Writers in Paris, 1920-1939; DLB 11: American Humorists, 1800-1950;* and *DLB 22: American Writers for Children, 1900-1960.*

BOOKS: *Is Sex Necessary? or, Why You Feel the Way You Do,* by Thurber and E. B. White (New York & London: Harper, 1929; London: Heinemann, 1930);

The Owl in the Attic and Other Perplexities (New York & London: Harper, 1931);

The Seal in the Bedroom & Other Predicaments (New York & London: Harper, 1932; London: Hamilton, 1951);

My Life and Hard Times (New York & London: Harper, 1933; London: Penguin/Hamilton, 1948);

The Middle-Aged Man on the Flying Trapeze (New York & London: Harper, 1935; London: Hamilton, 1935);

Let Your Mind Alone! And Other More or Less Inspirational Pieces (New York & London: Harper, 1937; London: Hamilton, 1937);

Cream of Thurber (London: Hamilton, 1939);

The Last Flower: A Parable in Pictures (New York & London: Harper, 1939; London: Hamilton, 1939);

The Male Animal: A Play, by Thurber and Elliott Nugent (New York: Random House, 1940; London: Hamilton, 1950);

Fables for Our Time, and Famous Poems Illustrated (New York & London: Harper, 1940; London: Hamilton, 1940);

My World—and Welcome to It (New York: Harcourt, Brace, 1942; London: Hamilton, 1942);

Many Moons (New York: Harcourt, Brace, 1943; London: Hamilton, 1944);

Thurber's Men, Women, and Dogs (New York: Harcourt, Brace, 1943; London: Hamilton, 1944);

The Great Quillow (New York: Harcourt, Brace, 1944);

The Thurber Carnival (New York & London: Harper, 1945; London: Hamilton, 1945);

The White Deer (New York: Harcourt, Brace, 1945; London: Hamilton, 1946);

The Beast in Me and Other Animals (New York: Harcourt, Brace, 1948; London: Hamilton, 1949);

The 13 Clocks (New York: Simon & Schuster, 1950; London: Hamilton, 1951);

The Thurber Album (New York: Simon & Schuster, 1952; London: Hamilton, 1952);

319

Thurber Country (New York: Simon & Schuster, 1953; London: Hamilton, 1953);

Thurber's Dogs (New York: Simon & Schuster, 1955; London: Hamilton, 1955);

A Thurber Garland (London: Hamilton, 1955);

Further Fables for Our Time (New York: Simon & Schuster, 1956; London: Hamilton, 1956);

The Wonderful O (New York: Simon & Schuster, 1957; London: Hamilton, 1958);

Alarms and Diversions (New York: Harper, 1957; London: Hamilton, 1957);

The Years with Ross (Boston: Little, Brown, 1959; London: Hamilton, 1959);

Lanterns & Lances (New York: Harper, 1961; London: Hamilton, 1961);

Credos and Curios (New York: Harper & Row, 1962; London: Hamilton, 1962);

A Thurber Carnival (New York, Hollywood, London & Toronto: French, 1962);

Vintage Thurber, 2 volumes (London: Hamilton, 1963);

Thurber & Company (New York: Harper & Row, 1966; London: Hamilton, 1967);

The Little Girl and the Wolf; and, The Unicorn in the Garden (San Diego: Reader's Theatre Script Service, 1982);

92 Stories (New York: Avenel, 1985).

Collections: *The Works of James Thurber* (New York: Longmeadow, 1986);

Collecting Himself, edited by Michael J. Rosen (New York: Harper & Row, 1989).

PLAY PRODUCTIONS: *The Male Animal*, by Thurber and Elliott Nugent, New York, Cort Theatre, 9 January 1940;

A Thurber Carnival, Columbus, Ohio, Hartman Theater, 7 January 1960; New York, ANTA Theatre, 26 February 1960.

Next to Mark Twain, James Thurber is the most critically acclaimed humorist in American literary history. Like Twain he first established his reputation as a journalist. By the time he died, he was recognized as one of the world's paramount short-story writers and a major stylist. Historically Thurber follows the traditional horse-sense humorists, and he is clearly related to the nineteenth- and early-twentieth-century journalistic humorists and literary comedians, such as Twain, George H. Derby (who wrote "A New System of English Grammar," collected in his *Phoenixiana* in 1856), Robert Henry Newell, Charles Farrar Browne, David Ross Locke, Henry W. Shaw, Charles H. Smith, Edgar Wilson Nye,

George Ade (the author of a series of fables in slang), Finley Peter Dunne, Ambrose Bierce, and Ring Lardner, among others. Thurber's "Little Man" character draws from the work of Robert Benchley, and perhaps later from that of S. J. Perelman, but Thurber is at the beginning of this tradition, and ultimately his refinements make the character uniquely and identifiably his own creation. It is no coincidence that in the public mind Thurber is identified with the *New Yorker* and that that journal is the most successful humor magazine in American history. The *New Yorker* turned out to be the perfect vehicle for publishing the versatile Thurber's work. While he did publish elsewhere, he was fortunate that the magazine came along when it did, for the approach to humor instituted in it brought about a revolution in American humor, and Thurber matched the developing style perfectly. At the same time, Thurber's impact on the *New Yorker* was monumental.

Born in Columbus, Ohio, on 8 December 1894, James Grover Thurber was Charles and Mary Fisher Thurber's second son. Charles Thurber, a native of Indiana, had hoped to be an actor or a lawyer, but spent his life in various appointed positions he received on the basis of his political connections. Never truly successful, he was to provide one of the models for his son's literary creation, the "Little Man." On the other hand, Mame, as Mary Thurber was nicknamed, was a strong-willed woman from an influential Ohio family, and no doubt she served as a prototype for the Thurber woman. While Thurber's father was victimized by mechanical gadgets, his mother took control of people and things and ordered the lives of those around her.

The family moved to Washington, D.C., in 1901, then returned to Columbus two years later. Thurber's life in the midwestern atmosphere of Columbus greatly influenced his values and perceptions of the world around him, something that he readily admitted.

Thurber was popular enough as a youngster that he was elected president of his high-school senior class. Furthermore, despite taking the difficult Latin curriculum, he graduated with honors. Thurber began his writing career by working on the high-school newspaper; after entering Ohio State University in 1913, he worked on the university's literary and humor magazines, the *Ohio State Lantern* and the *Sun-Dial*. While his writing was influenced by the popular culture of his day—including comic strips, movies, and dime

The Thurber family in 1915: William, James, and Mary (Mame) Fisher Thurber (standing);
Robert and Charles Thurber (seated)

novels—he also enjoyed the work of O. Henry and Robert O. Ryer, editorialist for the *Ohio State Journal*. Among the major events in Thurber's college experience was his experiencing, in English professor Joseph Taylor's class, the literature of Willa Cather, Joseph Conrad, and especially Henry James. He also met Elliott Nugent, with whom he would coauthor the popular Broadway play *The Male Animal* (1940). Still, things went so badly in general that Thurber dropped out for a year (1914-1915) without informing his parents. Nugent helped him become socially acceptable by getting him into the Phi Kappa Psi fraternity. But Thurber left Ohio State in 1918 without graduating, even though he was elected to the Sphinx, the senior honor society; as he explains in "University Days" (originally titled "College Days," *New Yorker*, 23 September 1933; collected in *The Thurber Carnival*, 1945), he could never

pass a required botany class because of an eye injury suffered as a child in Washington, when he and his older brother, William, were playing William Tell in the backyard of the family home. The arrow that hit one of his eyes most likely contributed to his almost total blindness by 1951, and he notes in "Draft Board Nights" (*New Yorker*, 30 September 1933; collected in *My Life and Hard Times*, 1933) that the injury also kept him out of the military.

Thurber's first job after college was as a code clerk for the U.S. State Department in Washington and then in the U.S. Embassy in Paris. Upon returning to Columbus in 1920, he became a reporter on the *Columbus Dispatch*, under city editor Norman Kuehner, and also wrote librettos for Ohio State University musicals. On 20 May 1922 Thurber married Althea Adams, who, like his mother, typified many of the traits of his female characters—overbearing, domineering, secure, aggressive women. James and Althea eventually had one child, Rosemary, born on 7 October 1931. In the meantime, at his wife's urging, Thurber decided to try his hand at free-lance writing, and during the summer of 1924, while they were living in a cottage in the Adirondack Mountains, he wrote "Josephine Has Her Day." A short story about a bull terrier, the piece appeared in the *Kansas City Star Sunday Magazine* on 14 March 1926 (collected in *Thurber's Dogs*, 1955) and was the first fiction for which he was paid.

Before its publication the Thurbers had moved to Normandy, France, where he attempted, unsuccessfully, to write a novel. In September 1925 Thurber took a position as rewrite man for the Paris edition of the *Chicago Tribune;* three months later he was made the coeditor of the newspaper's Riviera edition. He returned to New York early the following June and became a reporter for the *New York Evening Post.* Still, he continued to write humorous fiction.

Thurber records in *The Years with Ross* (1959) that he first heard of the newly inaugurated *New Yorker* magazine in November 1925, when he read in the *Paris Herald* about the flap created among New York City's high society by a piece written by Ellin Mackay. Back in New York, he began sending short pieces to the *New Yorker.* Although he says in *The Years with Ross* that they "came back so fast I began to believe the *New Yorker* must have a rejection machine," he did sell one submission to the magazine, "Villanelle of Horatio Street, Manhattan," a poem published in the 26 February 1927 issue. Finally, though, Thurber's wife convinced him that the problem with his prose writing was that he labored over it too long. As he explains, he took appropriate steps: "I grimly set the alarm clock to ring in forty-five minutes and began writing a piece about a little man going round and round and round in a revolving door, attracting crowds and the police, setting a world's record for this endurance event, winning fame and fortune. This burlesque of Channel swimming and the like ran to fewer than a thousand words, and was instantly bought by the *New Yorker.* For the first time out of twenty tries I got a check instead of a rejection slip."

"An American Romance," the 426-word result of Thurber's forty-five-minute exercise, appeared in the *New Yorker* on 5 March 1927. Unless the reader is aware of the author's description of the piece as a "burlesque of Channel swimming and the like," it is not likely that

such a connection would be made. Significantly the story contains several elements that were to become characteristics of Thurber's writing. Foremost of these is the main character, identified simply as "the little man." While Thurber's man differs from those of his predecessors, as envisioned in the works of Benchley, Perelman, and others, the hero of this story is clearly one of the genus. A meek, physically small man, he is badly dressed and has just experienced a "distressing scene" with his wife. He remains silent, going around in circles, while department-store management and a policeman try to bully him and while a "specialist" tries to analyze him to determine "if he had ever been in a cyclone and if he had ever had a severe shock while out walking." The little man persists in revolving for a total of four hours, at the end of which he receives $45,000 from a "big chewing gum magnate from the West" and more than $100,000 worth of vaudeville and motion-picture offers. His explanation for accomplishing the feat is a cliché: "I did it for the wife and children."

The fact that Thurber wrote "An American Romance" at one short sitting was an anomaly. Normally he spent enormous amounts of time perfecting his writing; many works remained unfinished for years. To some extent the writer's commitment of time to his work helps to explain his success. Thurber's style is, of course, his trademark. It is, above all, readable. Perhaps because his pieces are short they hold the reader's attention. Thurber made several attempts to write a satiric novel, one of which ("The Spoodle") resulted in his spending a thousand hours on a twenty-thousand-word book that went through twenty to thirty rewrites over a period of two years, yet was never published; he did not complete a novel because it seemed apparent that he could not sustain a reader's interest over such a length. Thurber was meticulous and precise in word choice, and as a result his prose flows. It is relaxed and subtle, not at all harsh and haranguing. In addition, his remarkable memory allowed him to recall conversations exactly and thus realistically, and his attention to detail gave his stories a further solid, realistic feel. As was true of other practitioners of basically journalistic humor, Thurber's writing is paradoxical in that it contains the oral quality of the best yarn spinners of the nineteenth century while simultaneously reflecting an appreciation for the way words appear on the printed page. The leisurely storytelling may be traced back to Henry James, whose

Thurber with his first wife, Althea Adams Thurber, soon after their 20 May 1922 wedding; they were divorced in May 1935.

work admittedly influenced his style, though Thurber also claimed he had to overcome that influence. Thurber's love of the physical appearance of printed words is evident in *The Wonderful O* (1957), for example, when he notes that the word "reason" is six-sevenths of the word "treason." Elsewhere he commented, "I liked the shape of words and phrases, and I liked clean copy. I never turned in a page with a single mistake on it. I always copied it over. Naturally, when you copy you make changes and you improve your copy" (in an interview with John Ferris, *Columbus Citizen*, 8 November 1953; collected in *Conversations with James Thurber*, 1989).

Ironically, even though Thurber had a great deal of difficulty in placing his first piece with the *New Yorker*, the range of his contributions to the journal is considerable, and he quickly became a staffer. In all he is credited with 365 signed "casuals" (the term applied by edi-

tor Harold W. Ross to the journal's shorter prose pieces), as well as poetry, parodies, fiction, half a dozen factual pieces, drawings, several photographs, and two profiles. Included in this mélange were "Famous Poems Illustrated," "Fables for Our Times," "Where Are They Now" (a seventeen-segment series in the mid 1930s reporting on famous people from the past, such as Gertrude Ederly and Virginia O'Hanlan, and appearing under the pen name Jared Manley), "Onward and Upward with the Arts" (a six-part series dealing primarily with the role of soap operas in American society), and fifteen essays on "The Tennis Courts," signed "Foot Fault," "T.J.G.," or "Footfault." "Our Pet Department," a parody of advice columns, appeared in seven installments in 1930 and followed a typical question/answer format, accompanied by a drawing (the series was reprinted in *The Owl in the Attic and Other Perplexities*, 1931).

In February 1927 Thurber became a *New Yorker* staff member. On board the *Leviathan* on the way to France several years earlier, he had met E. B. "Andy" White's sister. White was in charge of the magazine's most important department, "The Talk of the Town," and he agreed to introduce Thurber to Ross, who thought that White and Thurber were old friends. Thurber and White collaborated on *Is Sex Necessary?* (1929), but in the meantime, Ross, a former newspaperman, was impressed by Thurber's experience with newspapers and with the *Christian Science Monitor* and hired him as the journal's managing editor. It took Thurber some time to demonstrate that he neither desired to be nor was capable of being a managing editor. Since several people, including Dorothy Parker, had told Ross that Thurber was a writer, Ross reassigned his former executive to that position.

Ross's predilection for clarity, correctness, and detail was legendary, and his admiration for H. W. Fowler's *Dictionary of Modern English Usage* (1926) was the source of inspiration for Thurber's amusing series of parodies, "Our Own Modern English Usage," which ran in nine installments between 5 January and 21 December 1929 (collected in *The Owl in the Attic*) and considered the use of *who* and *whom, only, whether, which,* the perfect infinitive, exclamation points and colons, the subjunctive mood, adverbs, and the split infinitive. The treatment of this last subject is particularly humorous. The essay begins, "Word has somehow got around that a split infinitive is always wrong. This is a piece with the sentimental and outworn notion that it is always wrong to strike a lady," and contains sage observations, such as: "It is all but impossible to sit quietly by when someone is throwing salad plates."

In 1931 Thurber published *The Owl in the Attic*, a collection of some of his best *New Yorker* pieces. This volume, which includes eight stories and more than forty drawings based on the author's unhappy married life—featuring John Monroe as the protagonist—established Thurber's reputation as a writer and artist.

Thurber remained a staff member of the *New Yorker* only until 1933, but he continued his mutually beneficial association with the magazine until shortly before his death nearly thirty years later. Ross and Thurber felt great affection for one another, and it is clear that Ross's tutelage was a major factor in developing Thurber's precise style.

The other primary influence on Thurber's style was White. No longer under the time pressures of newspaper writing, Thurber could take advantage of White's guidance while writing segments of "The Talk of the Town." A simpler style emerged. As he admitted in a *Newsweek* interview (published posthumously on 13 November 1961), "After the seven years I spent in newspaper writing, it was more E. B. White who taught me about writing, how to clear up sloppy journalese. He was a strong influence, and for a long time in the beginning I thought he might be too much of one. But at least he got me away from a rather curious style I was starting to perfect—tight journalese laced with heavy doses of Henry James."

Over the years Thurber's fiction paralleled to some degree the events in his life. Most of his contributions to the *New Yorker* were published in the 1930s, and most of the earlier pieces were more lighthearted and innocent than those that were written during his marital difficulties with Althea (whom he divorced in May 1935 to marry Helen Wismer less than a month later, on 25 June); during social upheavals such as World War II and the McCarthy era (against which he spoke out on many occasions); and particularly during the bleak periods of physical illness and, in spite of numerous operations, the advancing blindness that led to his emotional breakdown as well. By 1951 he would be virtually sightless. The fiction that was produced during Thurber's black periods is terrifying, bitter, cold, and harsh. Closely aligned with the side of Thurber that delighted in cruel practical jokes and the misery of others, many pieces, such as "The Cane in the Corridor" (*New Yorker*, 2 January 1943; collected in *The Thurber Carnival*), a Poesque tale of a hospital visitor, cannot be classified as humorous by any definition.

However, Thurber's best humor is unsurpassed, and he wrote fine humorous fiction throughout his career. One of his earlier *New Yorker* stories is also one of his best—"The Night the Bed Fell," from the summer 1933 series "My Life and Hard Times" (published as a book later that year). Part of the semiautobiographical, semifictional genre in which Thurber excelled, "The Night the Bed Fell" (8 July) describes a hilarious sequence of events and misunderstandings that purportedly took place one evening during his childhood in Columbus. The humor builds as each event compounds what has gone before, and the events come faster and faster as the account pro-

James and Helen Wismer Thurber at the Algonquin in New York, 1938; they were married on 25 June 1935.

ceeds. Only the "Vegetable Man" sequence in W. C. Fields's film *It's a Gift* (1934) compares in the building of incidents to a comic climax.

"The Night the Bell Fell" and Thurber's tales that resemble it convey a sense of nostalgia, as the author reminisces about family life in a quieter, simpler, purer time and place. The incidents are recounted calmly, but a sense of immediacy, of actually being present and observing the action, is pervasive. The tone is that of fond remembrance, even when the happenings portrayed caused discomfort when they occurred, as when the commander of the Ohio State University ROTC berated Thurber for being "the main trouble with this university!" The persona adopted by Thurber as narrator reflects the tone and themes of these pieces, too. It is not quite the Little Man, but there is a kinship. The narrator is typically somewhat heroic and at the same time the butt of the humor. He is not the cowed individual of many of Thurber's other pieces; he is comparatively bright and competent. Perhaps this is because the narrator is closer to the real Thurber, who was fairly unflappable; perhaps it is because the memoirs seldom dwell on the battle of the sexes, and there is no overpowering female figure to contrast with the narrator, to expose the depths of his inadequacies, and to revel in his awareness of his failings.

Theoretically, humor serves a social function by exposing a society's foibles to the members of that society so that the existence of these faults can be recognized and corrected. In "The Case for Comedy," an article published in the *Atlantic Monthly* (November 1960; collected in *Lanterns & Lances*, 1961), Thurber declares: "The decline of humor and comedy in our time has a multiplicity of causes, a principal one being the ideological beating they have taken from both the intellectual left and the political right." As a result, he says, "only tragedy is [considered] serious and has importance." But, "the truth is that comedy is just as important, and often more serious in its approach to truth, and, what few writers seem to realize or to admit, usually more difficult to write."

Thurber touched upon all aspects of society in his fiction—including language, love, art, and war. He tended to be more politically oriented than most of his humorist contemporaries, but his favorite topic was the exploitation and mistreatment of the Little Man by women, creatures that he posited may have diverged from man's evolutionary path and thus actually belong to another race (a theme explored in Norris W. Yates's *The American Humorist*, 1964). The exploits of Thurber's Mr. and Mrs. Monroe are representative. Machines also are a source of the Little Man's downfall. Many of the incidents depicted in his short stories and cartoons are observed by dogs: independent, objective observers who see through pretense and bravado to vulnerability, yet who wisely seldom offer comments.

"The Secret Life of Walter Mitty" (18 March 1939; in *My World—and Welcome to It*, 1942) is one of the best-known and most popular short stories in world literature. When it was printed it aroused more reaction than anything else ever published in the *New Yorker*. The tale is a classic fantasy in which the Little Man/husband escapes from the realities of his mundane world by imagining himself performing heroic deeds in a variety of romantic situations—as a fighter pilot, for instance—with the action accompanied by a "pocketa-pocketa-pocketa" sound. In the *Paris Review* interview with George Plimpton and Max Steele (Fall 1955), Thurber said he was trying to "treat the remarkable as commonplace" in this piece. This approach to his material, and its obverse, is at the center of a great deal of his humor.

Throughout his writing career, Thurber was concerned about the misfit in society. Normally his misfits are presented as simple, sensitive, imaginative men caught in a mundane world that they do not completely understand and over which they have little or no control. Most often the world is too caught up in its own concerns to have much patience with such men, or to recognize their nature. Instead, it merely steamrolls over them. By extension, in examining the place of the imaginative Little Man in society, Thurber is metaphorically considering the conflict between an artist and his society. Another extension of this concept appears in the relationship between men and women that figures so prominently in his stories. In "The Secret Life of Walter Mitty" these concerns come together as forces that, consciously or unconsciously, exert pressure on Mitty to make him conform to their images of a solid, no-nonsense member of society and a manageable spouse.

The theme of overcoming a humdrum everyday life by opposing it with a fantasy life is developed from the opening lines of the story, as Walter Mitty is found at the controls of a storm-tossed seaplane. Reality soon intrudes, though, and the heroic image is replaced by a description of Mitty driving his wife to her regular visit with the hairdresser. Adventurous segments alternate throughout the tale of the couple's trip to town: Mitty's fantasy about being a skilled surgeon taking command in a life-and-death situation dissolves when he is confronted by a parking lot attendant who clearly is capable of managing Mitty's car better than he himself can. As the story progresses, Mitty also imagines himself in the role of the world's greatest pistol shot, a bomber pilot on a mission over enemy territory, an army captain about to lead his men into combat, and a proud, disdainful figure facing a firing squad. In his daydreams, Mitty is a heroic, skillful, commanding character, while in the real world he is subject to defeat in the conflicts with his wife and his society. In his imagination he takes on the characteristics that he would like to embody. This is a juvenile trait, but one that is defensive and necessary for his mental health.

Mrs. Mitty represents the devouring force of domesticity; she brooks no heated passions or heroics that might endanger her comfortable home and life-style. In some ways, then, the male and female in Thurber's writing reverse literary stereotypes and include some of the characteristics exemplified in the heroes and heroines of William Faulkner's novels and the dramas of George Bernard Shaw; but Mitty, Mr. Monroe, and the other Thurber Little Men, who cannot remove snow chains from their car tires and who suffer because of their overbearing wives, do not have the strength of the Shavian life force to drive them to true antihero status. Instead, and ironically, they defeat their unimaginative wives and restrictive society by exercising their imaginations.

Helen Wismer, Thurber's second wife, was a magazine editor who had graduated from Mount Holyoke and was not a prototypical Thurber woman; their marriage lasted until his death. Soon after they married in 1935, the couple moved from New York to Connecticut, where, between trips to Europe, the author composed several more of his most noteworthy short stories.

Thurber sometimes combined fiction and nonfiction to create what amounted to a new literary genre. The development of the concept of the "casual" at the *New Yorker* undoubtedly contributed to this form. The relatively light tone, combined with a focus on familiar, everyday occurrences, was well matched with his personality. The casual was also conducive to the technique of starting with an actual event in the writer's past and then branching off into fiction, extending the plot in order to carry a theme to an unlikely conclusion. Thurber was a master at casting such premises in a purely fictive mode as well.

The shock of recognition that readers experience with Thurber's work clearly relates to the strong popular appeal of both his fiction and his nonfiction. The audience shares the thoughts, concerns, and even many of the experiences embodied in his characters and the circumstances in which they are placed, and the seriousness of the situation is alleviated by Thurber's humorous approach to his material. This makes the shock of recognition pleasurable, too, thereby enhancing the appeal.

The relationship between his fiction and essays is further informed by the fact that the story is generally presented from a purportedly objective third-person point of view, as though the writer is engaged in straightforward, simple reportage. Because he was usually dealing with a common experience, one that his audience would find particularly familiar, all that Thurber had to do was to establish a pattern; he did not need to expand the plot very far. The fantasy tone of the tale is offset to some extent by the inclusion of specific unifying details, such as the appearance of a Webley-Vickers automatic pistol in two of Mitty's dream sequences. The use of such details is realistic in two ways. First, dreams frequently include elements that are incorporated from outside the dreamer (the ring of a telephone, for instance). Second, the details tie Mitty to reality, as when the use of the word "cur" in one imaginative segment suddenly propels Mitty back into reality, and he remembers the item that he had not yet bought—puppy biscuits.

Not all reactions to "The Secret Life of Walter Mitty" were positive. Charles Yale Harrison wrote Thurber a letter suggesting that the story had been inspired by his own novel *Meet Me on the Barricades* (1938). Harrison believed that Thurber had read his book, been the victim of a "psy-

chological deep freeze," and unconsciously plagiarized the work. Through attorneys for the *New Yorker* Thurber replied that he had been in Europe when Harrison's book was published and had read neither the novel nor any reviews of it. Moreover, Thurber had used a similar title previously ("The Private Life of Mr. Bidwell," 28 January 1933), and it was pointed out that he had also written stories about daydreamers before, "Mr. Pendly and the Poindexter" (27 February 1932) being a prime example. Ultimately, the charge was dropped.

The subject of language fascinated Thurber throughout his career, and several writings in his canon focus on it. Along with "The Secret Life of Walter Mitty," among the other pieces in *My World—and Welcome to It* one of the best known is "What Do You Mean It *Was* Brillig?" (*New Yorker*, 7 January 1939). The writer's allusion to Lewis Carroll's "Jabberwocky" in his title is appropriate, for in the essay he describes how a failure to communicate with his maid, Della, was brought about by dialectical differences. Taken aback by her announcement that someone was there with the "reeves"—which the narrator determined could be strings of onions, administrative officers, pens for cattle, poultry, or pigs, or females of the common European sandpiper—it was some time before he realized that "reeves" was how she pronounced the word "wreaths," as in Christmas wreaths.

Another publication in 1939, *The Last Flower*, came to be Thurber's favorite of his own books. White, in his 1961 *New Yorker* tribute (cowritten with William Shawn), said that it was also the work he most liked by his late friend and colleague. A parable in pictures with minimal text, the tale is about the cyclical nature of human destruction through warfare and the rejuvenation symbolized by the lone flower that survives the devastation.

By 1941 it was obvious that Thurber had to undergo a series of operations on his eye. Five times that year he underwent surgery for a cataract, glaucoma, and iritis. His suffering was compounded by the death of his father-in-law and the diagnosis of his mother's cancer that same year. Thurber became increasingly unpleasant, to the point that some of his friends and coworkers avoided him. This darkening mood was apparent in his writing, notably in "The Whip-Poor-Will," a 9 August 1941 *New Yorker* story (in *My World—and Welcome to It*) in which Mr. Kinstrey's insomnia drives him to multiple murders and suicide.

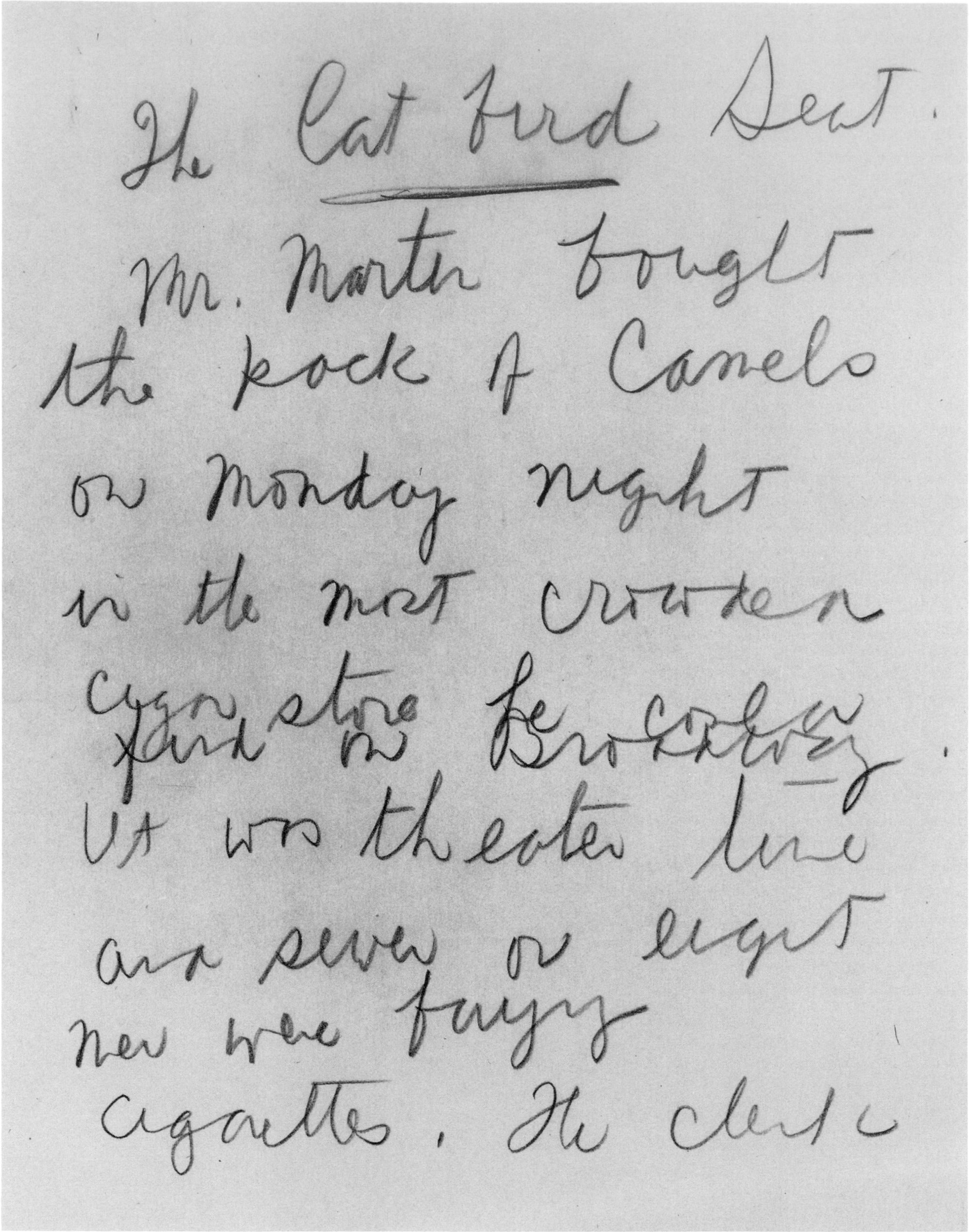

The Cat Bird Seat.

Mr. Martin bought the pack of Camels on Monday night in the most crowded cigar store on Broadway. It was theater time and seven or eight men were buying cigarettes. The clerk

Page of the manuscript for one of Thurber's best-known stories, first published in the New Yorker *(14 November 1942). Erwin Martin, the protagonist, is one of Thurber's "Little Men," reminiscent of Walter Mitty (Ohio State University Libraries; by permission of Rosemary A. Thurber).*

Some scholars see Kinstrey's plight as a reflection of Thurber's physical and mental condition. Fortunately the publication of *The Thurber Carnival* in 1945 demonstrated his emotional improvement. The book's reception must have aided his recovery further, for critics such as Malcolm Cowley praised the collection, and the public reaction was equally satisfying: 50,000 copies of the first edition sold, and the Book-of-the-Month Club edition accounted for an additional 375,000 sales. In the next few years Thurber would write several children's books and adult romances.

As Thurber's career evolved, his penchant for rewriting remained constant. Occasionally pieces such as "File and Forget" (*New Yorker*, 8 January 1949; in *Thurber Country*, 1953) were mostly dashed off in the course of one afternoon. However, in his interview with Plimpton and Steele, he explained that "File and Forget" came easily "because it was a series of letters just as one would ordinarily dictate." Even so, the last letter took him a week—"It was the end of the piece and I had to fuss over it." He also recounted how his wife, Helen, took a look at a first version of something he had written and said, " 'Goddamn it, Thurber, that's high school stuff.' I have to tell her to wait until the seventh draft, it'll work out all right. I don't know why that should be so, that the first or second draft of everything I write reads as if it was turned out by a charwoman." It took Thurber about eight weeks and fifteen complete rewrites before he was satisfied with "The Secret Life of Walter Mitty," which is approximately four thousand words long.

There are two reasons for Thurber's rewrites. First, as reported by Robert E. Morseberger, he said, "the whole purpose is to sketch out proportions. I rarely have a very clear idea of where I'm going when I start. Just people and/ or a situation. Then I fool around—writing and rewriting—until the stuff jells." Second, Thurber's "constant attempt," as he told Plimpton and Steele, is "to make the finished version smooth, to make it seem effortless.... With humor you have to look out for traps. You're likely to be very gleeful with what you've first put down, and you think it's fine, very funny. One reason you go over and over it is to make the piece sound less as if you were having a lot of fun with it yourself. You try to play it down."

As he grew increasingly blind, Thurber relied on a secretary to do the transcribing of his work. By the time he became effectively blind, he was so skilled at rewriting and his memory was so accurate that he could compose a two-thousand-word story in his mind at night and then edit it as he dictated it to his secretary the next morning. Thus, the loss of his sight obviously had little effect on his writing ability, though with his diminishing vision there does seem to have been a parallel reduction in the number of visual images incorporated in his stories.

Many critics have discussed Thurber's style and themes. Richard C. Tobias, for example, has written about his use of comic masks, in his first efforts, to explore common twentieth-century American subjects, how he uses conventional social and literary types later, and how he develops old comic plots in new ways. Like his colleagues White and Perelman, Thurber loved language— the way it sounds and the way it is used to mean something. His style depends on his precise usage, and much of his humor is based on an application of the literal meaning of words. Some of the techniques Thurber employed include puns, artistic allusions, and an exquisite sense of timing. He also utilized both hyperbole and understatement, frequently emphasizing a point by juxtaposing these devices. He was fond of reversal and other ironic forms, too.

Typically Thurber's setting, circumstances, and characters are normal, conventional, middle-class, and American. Among his greatest talents was the ability to take these elements and to emphasize one or two minor details in his descriptions to create an indelible image of the situation.

Thurber told Plimpton and Steele that "the act of writing is something the writer dreads or actually likes, and I actually like it. Even rewriting's fun." Moreover, in "The Case for Comedy" he concluded, "As brevity is the soul of wit, form, it seems to me, is the heart of humor and the salvation of comedy." He had no trouble following his editor Ross's admonition to "Use the rapier, not the bludgeon." In "Preface to a Life," which was added to the book version of *My Life and Hard Times*, Thurber described himself as a typical professional writer of light pieces running from a thousand to two thousand words and said, "The notion that such persons are gay of heart and carefree is curiously untrue. They lead, as a matter of fact, an existence of jumpiness and apprehension. They sit on the edge of the chair of Literature. In the house of Life they have the feeling that they have never taken off their overcoats. Afraid of losing themselves in the larger flight of the two-volume novel, or even the one-volume novel, they stick to short accounts of their misadventures because they never get so deep into them but that they feel they can get out. This type of writing is not a joyous form of self-expression but the manifestation of a twitchiness at once cosmic and mundane."

It is obvious that Thurber embraced what has come to be called the "*New Yorker* style": correct, clean, urbane, and witty. In his editorial functions he helped impose this style on other contributors—writers and cartoonists alike—a task that he recounts in *The Years with Ross*. Brendan Gill, another *New Yorker* staff member, in his *Here at The New Yorker* (1975), claims that Thurber and White were "invaluable": "Between them, they had done more than anybody else to set the tone of *The New Yorker*."

During the thirty-four years of his association with the *New Yorker*, which was essentially his whole writing career, both Thurber and the journal profited. Over this period he honed his style, a style that coincided with, exemplified, and helped establish the magazine's characteristic style. He was encouraged to write humor about what has been described as the line of tension where order and chaos meet, producing some of the finest humorous prose in his country's history. He likewise was instrumental in developing the notable tenor of one of America's preeminent journals. Ultimately, perhaps, the relationship between Thurber and the *New Yorker* is best summarized by the author's contention, stated in a letter to Ross: "*The New Yorker* is the only magazine for which a man can write with dignity and tranquility."

Regarding his drawings, Thurber did not consider himself an artist, because he drew his cartoons for relaxation and did them too fast for them to be called art. Still, his 307 drawings, most of which were cartoons, brought him almost as much fame as his prose did and, in those cases in which he illustrated his own volumes, are an integral part of his prose works. His first attempts to place his artwork in the *New Yorker*, though, were as inauspicious as his efforts with his short stories had been. In fact, the first Thurber line drawing to be formally submitted to the *New Yorker* was not even submitted by its creator; White had long been an admirer of Thurber's sketches, and, unbeknownst to his colleague, White presented the art staff with a picture of a seal looking at some black dots in a barren landscape and announcing, "Hm, explorers!" Thurber had drawn the sketch in 1929, and White had inked it in. Some months later Harper's pub-

lished Thurber and White's collaboration, *Is Sex Necessary?*, complete with Thurber's illustrations, which White had collected and insisted on having included. After the book became a best-seller, Ross agreed to publish Thurber's cartoons, which became extraordinarily popular. Many reflected the view of life that occupied Thurber's attention in his prose (White, in his introduction to *The Owl in the Attic*, identified Thurber's two major themes as the "melancholy of sex" and the "implausibility of animals"). One of the best known of his *New Yorker* cartoons is a rendering, published on 30 January 1932 (collected in *The Seal in the Bedroom*, 1932), of a man and a woman in bed, with a seal looking over the headboard behind them. The woman is saying: "All Right, Have It your Way—You Heard a Seal Bark!"

Thurber's whimsy comes through in a cartoon in which a startled man in the witness chair next to the judge's bench is confronted by an attorney pointing at a kangaroo and exclaiming, "Perhaps *this* will refresh your memory!" (in *Thurber's Men, Women, and Dogs*, 1943). In a drawing exposing what Thurber calls the war between men and women, a man is depicted sitting at a table with a heavyset woman who glares at him while a younger woman sitting across from him presses his foot with hers; the caption, spoken by his heavyset companion, is "Well, what's come over *you* suddenly?" (in *The Seal in the Bedroom*). Elsewhere, a wife, lying on a divan and speaking on the telephone while her husband watches from a nearby chair, demands, "Well, if I called the wrong number, why did you answer the phone?" And, if man cannot understand woman's logic, neither does he understand her relationship to the universe or her emotions and sensitivity. For instance, in one cartoon a couple is about to be engulfed by a giant, surrounded by black and speeding toward them from space, as the man says, "You and your premonitions!" In another drawing a woman in bed snarls, "Well, it makes a difference to *me!*" at a man standing nearby who is dressed in a pajama top decorated with spots, while the pajama bottoms that he wears have a striped pattern (all in *Thurber's Men, Women, and Dogs*).

Thurber's forte was the combination of imaginative concepts, insights, and approaches to life expressed in strikingly clear images that depend on a careful manipulation of words. Because his writing appeared in magazines, his style is journalistic in nature—that is, it is most effective when he captures and condenses the essence of a

"*Perhaps this will refresh your memory.*"

"*Well, if I called the wrong number, why did you answer the phone?*"

Two of the cartoons collected in Thurber's Men, Women, and Dogs *(copyright 1943 by James Thurber; copyright 1971 by Helen Thurber and Rosemary A. Thurber; published by Harcourt Brace Jovanovich, Inc.)*

thought within the limits imposed by the short-story format. Because of his immense popularity, it is no surprise that there would be attempts to transpose his work to the movie screen and to television, but as might be expected, the very elements that characterize his writing work against a successful translation of that work into other media. His most famous creation, Walter Mitty, appeared in the Samuel Goldwyn film *The Secret Life of Walter Mitty* (directed by Norman Z. McLeod and starring Danny Kaye) in 1947, but the result is only moderately effective—although a radio version featuring Benchley as Mitty was well received. Thurber had been a member of the Strollers, the university's theatrical group, while an undergraduate at Ohio State, and when he returned to Columbus in 1920, he was involved in writing, acting, and producing productions for the Scarlet Mask Club. It may be that this early dramatic experience had something to do with his play *The Male Animal* being a Broadway hit, and possibly because he had been working in a visual medium to begin with, the 1942 Warner Bros. screen adaptation (directed by coauthor Elliott Nugent and starring Henry Fonda, Olivia de Havilland, and Jack Carson) is entertaining and was well received. A second cinematic treatment of the same play, the mediocre musical titled *She's Working Her Way Through College*, directed by H. Bruce Humberstone and starring Virginia Mayo and Ronald Reagan, was released by Warner Bros. in 1952. In February 1960 the revue *A Thurber Carnival*, with Burgess Meredith directing, arrived on Broadway. Thurber was awarded the Antoinette Perry Special Award (the "Tony") for his writing. He even acted in the "File and Forget" sketch for 88 of its 243 performances. On the other hand, the 1969 television series based on *My World—and Welcome to It*, starring William Windom, albeit occasionally amusing, confirmed that the humor in Thurber's sketches could not be sustained indefinitely, since the original context was neither intended nor designed to be stretched.

The last Thurber casual to appear in the *New Yorker* was "The Manic in the Moon" (19 August 1961). Less than three months after this publication the author was dead, having suffered a stroke in New York on 4 October and then dying of pneumonia on 2 November. His body was returned to Columbus for burial.

When he died, Thurber's works had been collected in more than twenty volumes and trans-

lated into at least twenty-two languages, two of his plays had appeared on Broadway (and been adapted for the movies), and he had written the important and entertaining nonfiction study of the *New Yorker* entitled *The Years with Ross*. In 1951 T. S. Eliot commented about Thurber's writing, "It is a form of humor which is also a way of saying something serious. There is a criticism of life at the bottom of it. It is serious and even somber. Unlike so much humor, it is not merely a criticism of manners—that is, of the superficial aspects of society at a given moment—but something more profound. His writings and also his illustrations are capable of surviving the immediate environment and time out of which they spring. To some extent they will be a document of the age they belong to" (quoted by Joel Sayre in his "Priceless Gift of Laughter," *Time*, 9 July 1951). This assessment of Thurber's art corresponds with his own artistic theories.

The numerous awards that Thurber received are a measure of both his abilities and his popularity. His first award was a Library Association Prize for best juvenile picture book, awarded for *Many Moons* in 1943. The Ohioana juvenile book medal for *The White Deer* (published in 1945) followed three years later. Then came the Laughing Lions of Columbia University Award for Humor (1949); honorary doctorates from Kenyon College (1950), Williams College (1951), and Yale University (1953); the Sesquicentennial Career Medal of the Martha Kinney Cooper Ohioana Library Association (1953); the American Cartoonists' Society T-Square Award (1956); the American Library Association's Library and Justice Award (1957) for *Further Fables for Our Time* (1956); and a Certificate of Award from the Ohio State University Class of 1916 for "Meritorious Service to Humanity and Our Alma Mater" (1961). It is noteworthy that the humorist declined one honor. Ohio State University offered him an honorary doctorate in 1951, but he refused it on the grounds that his alma mater's trustees were antithetical to academic freedom. A special house has been set aside in Columbus, Ohio, to hold materials related to Thurber's writing, and a writer-in-residence program has been established there in his name. Thurber and his writing were immensely popular during his lifetime, and these last honors, along with the continuing publication of collections of his work, are evidence that this popularity continues.

The Thurbers backstage at the ANTA Theatre in fall 1960, during the New York production of A Thurber Carnival. *Thurber acted in eighty-eight performances and won a Tony award for his writing.*

Letters:

Selected Letters of James Thurber, edited by Helen Thurber and Edward Weeks (Boston: Little, Brown, 1981; Harmondsworth, U.K.: Penguin, 1982).

Interviews:

Harvey Breit, "Mr. Thurber Observes a Serene Birthday," *New York Times Magazine*, 4 December 1949, p. 17;

George Plimpton and Max Steele, "The Art of Fiction: James Thurber," *Paris Review*, 10 (Fall 1955): 35-49; reprinted in *Writers at Work: The Paris Review Interviews*, edited by Malcolm Cowley (New York: Viking-Compas, 1959);

Alistair Cooke, "James Thurber: In Conversation with Alistair Cooke," *Atlantic*, 198 (August 1956): 36-40;

"Jim," *Newsweek*, 58 (13 November 1961): 35-36;

Conversations with James Thurber, edited by Thomas Fensch (Jackson: University Press of Mississippi, 1989).

Bibliography:

Edwin T. Bowden, *James Thurber: A Bibliography* (Columbus: Ohio State University Press, 1968).

Biographies:

Charles S. Holmes, *The Clocks of Columbus: The Literary Career of James Thurber* (New York: Atheneum, 1972);

Burton Bernstein, *Thurber: A Biography* (New York: Dodd, Mead, 1975; London: Gollancz, 1975).

References:

Walter Blair, *Horse Sense in American Humor* (Chicago: University of Chicago Press, 1943), pp. 283-294, 297, 311, 324-325;

Blair and Hamlin Hill, *America's Humor: from Poor Richard to Doonesbury* (New York: Oxford, 1978), pp. 437-459;

Max Eastman, *The Enjoyment of Laughter* (New York: Simon & Schuster, 1936);

Steven H. Gale, "James Thurber," in *Popular World Fiction, 1900-Present*, volume 1, edited by Walton Beacham and Suzanne Niemeyer

(Washington, D.C.: Research Publishing, 1987), pp. 1524-1599;

Gale, "*The New Yorker*," in *American Comic Journals*, edited by David E. E. Sloane (Westport, Conn.: Greenwood, 1987), pp. 179-191;

Gale, "Thurber of *The New Yorker*," *Studies in American Humor*, 3 (Spring 1984): 11-23;

Brendan Gill, *Here at The New Yorker* (London: Joseph, 1975);

Charles S. Holmes, ed., *Thurber: A Collection of Critical Essays* (Englewood Cliffs, N.J.: Prentice-Hall, 1974);

Catherine McGehee Kenney, *Thurber's Anatomy of Confusion* (Hamden, Conn.: Shoe String Press, 1984);

Lost Generation Journal, special Thurber issue, 3, edited by Tom Wood (Winter 1975);

Robert E. Morseberger, *James Thurber* (New York: Twayne, 1964);

William F. Nelson, "James Thurber," in *Encyclopedia of American Humorists*, edited by Gale (New York: Garland, 1988), pp. 445-451;

Joel Sayre, "Priceless Gift of Laughter," *Time*, 58 (9 July 1951): 88-94;

William Shawn and E. B. White, "James Thurber," *New Yorker*, 37 (11 November 1961): 247;

William L. Shirer, *20th Century Journey, A Memoir of a Life and the Times: The Start 1904-1930* (New York: Simon & Schuster, 1976), pp. 217-233, 260, 270-273, 279, 293;

Richard C. Tobias, *The Art of James Thurber* (Athens: Ohio University Press, 1969);

W. J. Weatherby, "A Man of Words," *Manchester Guardian Weekly* (9 February 1961): 13;

Norris W. Yates, *The American Humorist: Conscience of the Twentieth Century* (Ames: Iowa State University Press, 1964), pp. 275-298.

Papers:

Most of Thurber's papers, from 1940 on, are in the Thurber Collection at the Ohio State University Library, Columbus, Ohio. Minor holdings and Thurberiana are at the Thurber House and the Martha Kinney Cooper Ohioana Library, both in Columbus, and some papers relating to *The Years with Ross* are in the Yale University Library.

Eudora Welty

(13 April 1909 -   )

Michael Kreyling
Vanderbilt University

See also the Welty entries in *DLB 2: American Novelists Since World War II* and *DLB Yearbook: 1987*.

BOOKS: *A Curtain of Green* (Garden City, N.Y.: Doubleday, Doran, 1941; London: Lane, 1943);

The Robber Bridegroom (Garden City, N.Y.: Doubleday, Doran, 1942; London: Lane/Bodley Head, 1944);

The Wide Net, and Other Stories (New York: Harcourt, Brace, 1943; London: Lane/Bodley Head, 1945);

Delta Wedding (New York: Harcourt, Brace, 1946; London: Bodley Head, 1947);

Music from Spain (Greenville, Miss.: Levee, 1948);

The Golden Apples (New York: Harcourt, Brace, 1949; London: Bodley Head, 1950);

Short Stories (New York: Harcourt, Brace, 1950);

The Ponder Heart (New York: Harcourt, Brace, 1954; London: Hamilton, 1954);

The Bride of the Innisfallen, and Other Stories (New York: Harcourt, Brace, 1955; London: Hamilton, 1955);

The Shoe Bird (New York: Harcourt, Brace & World, 1964);

Thirteen Stories, selected by Ruth M. Vande Kieft (New York: Harcourt, Brace & World, 1965);

Losing Battles (New York: Random House, 1970; London: Virago, 1982);

One Time, One Place: Mississippi in the Depression; A Snapshot Album (New York: Random House, 1971);

The Optimist's Daughter (New York: Random House, 1972);

Fairy Tale of the Natchez Trace (Jackson: Mississippi Historical Society, 1975);

The Eye of the Story: Selected Essays and Reviews (New York: Random House, 1978);

Women!! Make Turban in Own Home! (Winston-Salem: Palaemon, 1979);

Acrobats in a Park (Northridge, Cal.: Lord John, 1980);

Bye-bye Brevoort (Jackson, Miss.: New Stage Theatre/Palaemon, 1980);

Moon Lake and Other Stories (Franklin Center, Pa.: Franklin Library, 1980);

White Fruitcake (New York: Albondocani, 1980);

Miracles of Perception (Charlottesville, Va.: The Library, 1980);

The Collected Stories of Eudora Welty (New York: Harcourt Brace Jovanovich, 1980; London: Boyars, 1981);

One Writer's Beginnings (Cambridge, Mass.: Harvard University Press, 1984);

The Little Store (Newton, Iowa: Tamazunchale, 1985);

Eudora Welty Photographs (Jackson: University Press of Mississippi, 1989).

RECORDING: *Eudora Welty Reads Her Stories Powerhouse and Petrified Man*, Caedmon, TC 1626, 1979.

Eudora Welty's achievement in the short-story genre is primarily in the area of form. Several other writers could be said to have introduced the subject matter of the South to the American short story in the twentieth century. In fact, to look at Welty's short stories solely through the lens of subject matter dangerously limits any sense of her art; her reviewers, especially those writing about the first two collections, have frequently made that unfortunate mistake. Welty has from the outset of her writing career insisted on a unique form for the short story. She has not always indulged in critical explanations of that form, but one can see from careful readings its principal elements. The strong and consistent desire for revelations in the instant, rather than disclosure piecemeal over time (plot), is central to Welty's practice in the short story. She is not, for example, like Thomas Wolfe, for whom the only distinction between novel and short story seemed to be simply length. What New Criticism has called the moment of revelation can be adapted to Welty's stories, for denouement occurs in the

Eudora Welty

psyche of a character, not in history and incident.

Welty made frequent use of the tension between the demands of rational, social existence and the possibilities of the imagination—the nontallying "validities" of everyday life and the story. She also made increasingly multifarious use of allusion (biblical, literary, mythological, and psychological) to show how art is the vision of nodes or crossings of these lines of meaning. *The Golden Apples* (1949), for example, is the perfect monument to that end and is her best collection. Her style in general continues to be influential and often praised.

Welty was born in Jackson, Mississippi, on 13 April 1909, the first child and only daughter of Christian and Chestina Andrews Welty. The writer was named for her maternal grandmother, Eudora Carden Andrews; the Andrews clan, a large and boisterous bunch, lived in West Virginia. Christian Welty, an Ohioan, had met the only daughter of the Andrews clan there, courted her, and married her. The couple moved to Jackson, the small-town capital of Mississippi, where Mr. Welty went to work for the

Lamar Life Insurance Company. He eventually rose to the level of vice-president by the time of his early death in 1931. The surviving Welty family—the widow, daughter, and two sons— never moved from Jackson.

When Welty successfully placed her first short story in a literary journal—"Death of a Traveling Salesman" in *Manuscript* (Athens, Ohio) in the spring of 1936—she had just turned twenty-five. She had attended Mississippi State College for Women in Columbus (1925-1927), the University of Wisconsin-Madison (1927-1929)—where she earned her B.A.—and the Columbia University School of Business (1930-1931). She might have stayed in New York after attending Columbia, for the world of the theaters and galleries appealed to her, but the Great Depression and her father's sudden illness and death from leukemia summoned her back to Mississippi.

Reading and writing were a major part of her childhood and education. Her memoir of the years of childhood and young adulthood, *One Writer's Beginnings* (1984), is replete with reminiscences of library trips, books read, stories heard, and family voices reading and talking. It is not surprising, then, that as a girl Welty placed her writing in the children's magazine *St. Nicholas*, that she later wrote for her high-school paper, and that she wrote verse, satirical essays, and sketches (as fellow Mississippian William Faulkner had done) for college magazines. Her years in Madison steered her literary education in more canonical directions; there she was schooled in art history and English literature, with a special emphasis on the poetry of W. B. Yeats.

Her year at Columbia opened up the worlds of the Broadway stage, the museums, the art galleries, and the movies. There has always been, in Welty's fiction, an important visual facet. Graphic arts vied with the literary for her time and talent. Also important are the conflict and tension between her home in Mississippi and the wide outer world that Welty knew as a student and frequent traveler. Two of the biggest mistakes readers make is assuming that her writing is southern local color only and that as an artist she is more primitive than modern.

Back in Mississippi in the 1930s Welty worked as an advertising writer for the radio station owned by her father's insurance company, contributed society features to the *Memphis Commercial Appeal*, and wrote reports and publicity for local projects of the Works Progress Administration. The latter job got her out into the state with a camera as well as a notebook; she was exposed to sounds and scenes and people that accumulated in her imagination like a writer's capital.

Her photographic images have been published in several places, the most notable of which are *One Time, One Place: Mississippi in the Depression* (1971) and *Eudora Welty Photographs* (1989). The greater number of her images are scenes of rural and small-town Mississippi, including buildings, gatherings of people, and individual portraits. There are relatively few landscapes. Most of the photographs, dating from the early 1930s, were snapped on Welty's frequent WPA trips around the state to county fairs, market days, and Fourth of July celebrations. They provide an interesting and useful documentary introduction to the subject matter of some of her early fiction.

When Welty began to write short stories in the early 1930s she thought of the fiction and the photographs as parts of the same ensemble or exhibition. As a writer she did not have as an exclusive medium the printed text. She had her photography, too. Before a single short story was accepted for publication, Welty was circulating

among the New York publishing houses a manuscript composed of short stories and photos: "Black Saturday." This manuscript was eventually dismantled, most of its contents being published in other collections. Somewhat like Julia Peterkin and Doris Ulmann's *Roll, Jordan, Roll* (1932), Welty's first manuscript exhibited fiction and photography in the same gallery. "Black Saturday" was never published; most editors considered Peterkin and Ulmann's book enough on the subject.

Welty also kept several short stories in the mail to literary journals and quarterlies—the low-circulation, often university-related "little magazines" of the decade. In *Manuscript*, published by sculptor John Rood and his wife, Katherine, Welty had her first success. In March 1936 the Roods accepted two stories from Welty after rejecting an earlier submission. "Death of a Traveling Salesman" was scheduled for immediate publication (in the May-June issue); "Magic" was held for later in the year (September-October). Also in 1936 another story, "The Doll," was published in the *Tanager* (June), the campus literary magazine of Grinnell College (Iowa). Neither magazine paid contributors.

"Magic" and "The Doll" have not been saved among Welty's collected stories; comparing them to "Death of a Traveling Salesman" (collected in *A Curtain of Green*, 1941), one can imagine the author's reasons for saving the one and discarding the other two. But they have something to tell about the early short-story practices of Welty. "The Doll," earlier in composition, is quite short (under two thousand words) and a little obvious in its meaning. It is narrated through the point of view of Marie, a young, engaged woman to whom the nature of love and experience is still veiled by the glitter of the engagement ring she continually contrives to display to herself and anyone else nearby. Her fiancé, Charles, unexpectedly appears on the street, and Marie is shocked by the object-ness of him, going through the motions of his life as if she did not exist. There is a glimmer of an echo of Nathaniel Hawthorne's "Wakefield" (in *Twice-Told Tales*, 1837) in this scene of "The Doll."

Welty works out a fairly complicated (for such a brief story) psychological undercurrent by means of a rag doll that Marie carries with her as a sort of extension of her own vulnerable personality. When her own psychological security seems in jeopardy from the obliviousness of Charles, she clutches the doll to reassure herself that she

Welty's parents, Chestina Andrews Welty and Christian Webb Welty, in Jackson, Mississippi, 1927
(photograph copyright 1989 by Eudora Welty)

is still the center of caring attention. The young woman's idea of love is stalled somewhere in a Hollywood version of hothouse passion with a soundtrack: "He [Charles] turned her by the shoulders so that she was looking up at him. His face was in the dark, part of the still leaves. His body in white was like a shaft being sunk into her stupid brain. She stopped crying finally. Stretching her arms up to his head she pulled herself up and caught her lips to his in a kiss the end of which she dreaded more than she could bear."

It is tempting to predict that, with no intervention, this writer is destined for the pulp racks at the local supermarket. But Welty's imagination complicates the story. After the kiss the lovers are interrupted by the sirens of a fire brigade rushing to a burning house. Charles and Marie impulsively follow, and the story reaches its dramatic and psychological climax as they watch the fire consume a small house, in the window of which, "standing with stick arms raised like a doll, [was]

a woman waiting to be rescued." The lovers embrace with a "throbbing" intensity, and Marie "lay in sudden exhaustion against Charles . . . feeling dead and tender toward him."

In "The Doll" the young Welty tests some of the techniques that, in her later short fiction, won her the reputation of a master of the genre. The stunning ambiguity of the final lines of the story, in which Marie feels both dead and tender toward her lover, points to future stories in which ambivalence and ambiguity are used as powerful devices.

"Magic" continues these themes and techniques, but it is a more polished story than "The Doll." In it Welty tries to capture a kind of ethnic dialogue ("Wipe that smile offa ya face, you always smilin', people think you crazy") and a more detailed material ethos than in "The Doll." "Magic" is almost aggressively realistic in the style of the 1930s, as defined by such writers as Erskine Caldwell and John Steinbeck: "Ralph had scrubbed his red bumpy face into complete sullenness. He wore a pair of dark green trousers with darker green bulges below the knees, and a brown coat and shirt, with a grey bow tie on an elastic at his collar. His raked hair was wet. He stood with his hands fumbling over the knots in the weakened coil-spring on the screen door, and he looked from Myrtle's smile to the wall where there was nailed a Coca Cola sign in the shape of a bottle with a thermometer in it." In hindsight one is tempted to guess that, in a story like "Magic," the young Welty saw a path toward southern realistic writing—gritty, a little hard-boiled—the ground that Caldwell had written about and that Margaret Bourke-White had photographed.

But "Magic" does not find its denouement in realistic forces and historical resolutions. Ralph is a Western Union courier, his bicycle his steed, and Myrtle is the mortal he has enthralled. Their rendezvous takes place in the local cemetery; the narrative picks up their postcoital dialogue. "If you don't like it, shut up. . . . I know plenty of women that do," says the ragged Mercury. "We've been layin' here on a grave," says the nymph, whose lips are so stiff with the rigor mortis of love that she can hardly articulate the words. Like the carbuncular young man and the solitary typist of T. S. Eliot's *The Waste Land* (1922), Welty's couple find no erotic release from the anomie of their lives. For Myrtle, however, there is an added moment not allowed Eliot's typist. A stranger passing by the graveyard peers in, a witness to dishonor: "He was a man with a black felt hat and he was laughing without making a sound, thrusting his black hole of a mouth outward at her like a funnel. That had been it. It was over. That thing." Myrtle screams and flees from Ralph. The deserted god "strode" away from the site of his conquest to a pool hall, there to stand tall and assured among his male compatriots.

"Magic" seems to map out the early stages of a route toward a modernist short-story technique following Eliot and James Joyce: a mythological underplot floating the central theme of modern malaise, the failure of love; a strong focus on two central characters in the throes of exploring the nature of love; a psychologically charged element of the exploration lurking beneath the woman's search and retreat; allusions to mythological figures and situations broadening the field of reference; and images from the history of Western art enriching the story by adding a visual intertext (the man with the mouth like a funnel is recruited from a medieval allegory by Hieronymus Bosch).

Neither "The Doll" nor "Magic" brought Welty to the attention of a national reading audience. "Death of a Traveling Salesman" did that, just as John Rood had foretold in his letter of acceptance. Quickly after the spring 1936 issue of *Manuscript* had been distributed, letters came to Welty from New York publishing houses praising the story and asking about the possible existence of a novel. Inquiries were full of praise for what the editors considered regional realism and the vividness of character and situation; they all suspected that a novel could not be far behind. The author, however, was dedicated to the short story and responded to each inquiry with an offer to send a volume of stories. There were no takers.

With so much of Welty's writing career in perspective now, it is relatively easy to see where some original readers went off the path with "Death of a Traveling Salesman." The story deceptively presents a realistic facade. When the central character, itinerant shoe salesman R. J. Bowman—recovering from influenza and still subject to hallucinations (like Katherine Anne Porter's Miranda)—first sees the woman whose cabin he approaches after his car tumbles into a ravine, he *thinks* he sees a Margaret Bourke-White image, a hard-edged and indomitably real presence: "She had been cleaning the lamp, and held it, half blackened, half clean, in front of her. He saw her with the dark passage behind her. She was a big woman with a weather-beaten but unwrinkled face; her lips were held tightly together, and her eyes looked with a curious dulled brightness into his. He looked at her shoes, which were like bundles."

The photographic image (in which the oxymoron "dulled brightness" might make sense) is deceptive because Bowman is not a reliable camera. His senses being attenuated by influenza, he is no more than half-conscious at any moment. The story is the better for the protagonist's infirmity, for it turns realistic moments, like Sonny's bringing home a blazing stick for the hearth, into a moment full of allusive power: "After they had waited a while, Bowman looked out the window and saw a light moving over the hill. It spread itself out like a little fan. It zig-zagged along the field, darting and swift, not like Sonny at all. . . . Soon enough, Sonny staggered in, holding a burning stick behind him in tongs, fire flowing in his wake, blazing light into the corners of the room."

The allusions to Prometheus gently impinge upon the story; between the local color of Mississippi place names, gravel roads, and speech idiom and the wake of fire there is a strong tension that supports the story. One could argue that, sustained over the course of a novel, the tension would go flat, become mechanical, and break altogether. No one made this critical argument to Welty in the 1930s; she did not make it to herself. She knew only that her gift was for the short story, and requests for a novel grated upon her ears.

After the success of "Magic" and "Death of a Traveling Salesman" in *Manuscript*, editors of other publications seemed to look with more favor on stories Welty sent them. "Lily Daw and the Three Ladies" (collected in *A Curtain of Green*) was taken by *Prairie Schooner* in late 1936 (appearing in the Winter 1937 issue). After turning down "Flowers for Marjorie" and "Petrified Man" early in 1937, Robert Penn Warren and Cleanth Brooks at the *Southern Review* accepted "A Piece of News" and "A Memory." Later they were to change their editorial minds on "Petrified Man." (All four are also in *A Curtain of Green*.) Welty, discouraged at the story's repeated failure, had destroyed her only copy and had to rewrite it from memory. "Petrified Man" was published in the *Southern Review* in spring 1939.

Welty's publishing success in the 1930s came in quarterlies and journals sustained usually on modest budgets from which contributors were seldom paid. *Southern Review* did pay (by the word); although Welty's stories there did not make her rich, they did provide a more or less steady ground for remuneration.

But Welty wanted to try her skill in the large, national, and more lucrative market of the "slicks." The slicks, so called because of the coated paper on which they printed text, photographs, and ads, were the Fort Knox for short-story writers. *Saturday Evening Post, Collier's, Good Housekeeping, Harper's Bazaar, Mademoiselle*, and others often paid several hundred dollars or as much as a few thousand for a story. Tales abound of F. Scott Fitzgerald selling a short story to one of the slicks for one or two thousand dollars, then spending the cash before dawn the next day. A frugal short-story writer could live well on the income from two or three stories sold at these prices. Welty wanted to give it a try.

To that end, when Diarmuid Russell, one of the founders of a new literary agency (Russell & Volkening, Inc.), wrote to offer his services in the late spring of 1940, Welty accepted. Russell had been recommended by her editor-apparent at Doubleday, Doran—John Woodburn—who had taken a collection of Welty's stories off to New York with him after a scouting trip through the South. He had had little luck in persuading his house to publish the stories; he thought the agent could be of help. Moreover, Russell was the son of AE (George William Russell), the poet, painter, editor, and friend of Yeats. Welty knew AE's work, as well as Yeats's; such had been her reading for much of her two years at the University of Wisconsin. The query letter from Diarmuid Russell did not seem to be an accident, but rather a stroke of literary providence.

Russell's plan was to continue to urge the stories upon periodical editors, with the immediate goal of breaking into the national magazines. With such visibility, Welty's chances at a publishing house were greater. Russell reasoned that a string of national story publications would persuade a publishing house to forego the reigning prejudice against books of short stories by "unknown" writers. It took Russell six months, until December 1940, to sell a story to a national magazine; but then he sold two: *Atlantic Monthly* bought "Powerhouse" and "A Worn Path" (both collected in *A Curtain of Green*). *Atlantic Monthly* did not then pay as much as the other slicks: only about two hundred dollars per story. But along with *Harper's Magazine*, *Atlantic Monthly* was one of the most prestigious of the national magazines, one of the oldest, and one of the best edited (by Edward Weeks). Russell and Welty were reconciled to the cash shortfall.

It would not be accurate to say that from December 1940 onward Welty's literary fortune and reputation were made. Individual stories were still rejected (the *New Yorker* held out until the early 1950s). It is safe to say, however, that Welty has never been out of print since the publication of *A Curtain of Green*, the collection of seventeen stories that Doubleday, Doran finally published in 1941 in a first printing of twenty-five hundred copies at a price of $2.50 each, about a year after *Atlantic Monthly* broke the national publishing impasse by purchasing "Powerhouse" and "A Worn Path."

Most of the seventeen stories are among those that Welty herself, in retrospective interviews, has called "easy" and scarcely revised. Subsequent stories, as a rule, were more difficult for her. With the exception of "A Worn Path"— written after the collection was effectively com-

Welty with friends—Hubert Creekmore, Margaret Harmon, and Nash K. Burger—in Brown's Wells, Mississippi, circa 1930s
(photograph copyright 1989 by Eudora Welty)

plete but squeezed in late because it had won the O. Henry second prize in 1941—all the early stories more or less follow the lines of artistic development adumbrated in the three stories already discussed.

Katherine Anne Porter drew attention to "Petrified Man" and "Why I Live at the P.O." (*Atlantic Monthly*, April 1941) in her introduction to the book; these are stories highly seasoned with the familiar local-color grotesque. Other critics, however, have pointed out the classical mythology in the former (derived from the myth of Medusa), and feminist critics have noted that both stories are funny at the expense of some assumptions about gender roles that readers tend to leave unexamined. "The Whistle" (*Prairie Schooner*, Fall 1938) is an anomalous story in the Welty canon in that it is realistic, almost without modifying devices. "A Memory" (*Southern Review*, Autumn 1937) has been frequently interpreted as a story following the formation of the artist's mind in youth. "Lily Daw and the Three Ladies," "Clytie" (*Southern Review*, Summer 1941), and

"Old Mr. Marblehall" (*Southern Review*, Autumn 1938—as "Old Mr. Grenada") can be read as stories about the frustrations, social and psychological, of small-town life: they follow in the vein of Sherwood Anderson's *Winesburg, Ohio* (1919).

In other words Welty's achievement in the first collection of short stories was that of a diverse talent interested in various forms and modes for the short story. One of those directions deserves a bit more discussion: her literary modernism. One story crucial in this respect is "The Hitch-Hikers" (*Southern Review*, Autumn 1939). Tom Harris, the protagonist, is one of several itinerant people in these early stories. Harris, with his nondescript name, is the archetypal wanderer, the modern soul searching in a darkened and desolate landscape for meaning, connection, renewal, and hope. He makes the apparently gratuitous decision to pick up two hitchhikers on a Mississippi road; one of the men carries a guitar and sings incessantly; the other, called Sobby, is morose and only uses his voice to complain. The situation of the prototypical modern drama, Samuel Beckett's *Waiting for Godot* (1954), lurks in the shadows of "The Hitch-Hikers."

Harris leaves the riders in his car while he goes into the Dulcie (Mississippi) Hotel to reserve a room for himself. When he returns, he finds Sobby in the custody of two strangers; the guitar player, still in the back seat, is bleeding profusely from a head wound. Sobby admits he did the deed: he just got tired of the singing. Harris looks into the car at the dying man: "It was the man with the guitar. The little ceiling light had been turned on. With blood streaming from his broken head, he was slumped down upon the guitar, his legs bowed around it, his arms at either side, his whole body limp in the posture of a bare-back rider." Harris sees the injured man in the frame and in the pose of Pablo Picasso's *The Old Guitarist*. Harris, the modern wanderer, faced with the brutality common to life, shows that his perceiving faculties operate with a sort of buffer that guards him from naked contact with the world. The harshness of the world is filtered through art, one of the most familiar and highly stylized motifs from the modern period. Elsewhere in the story Harris continues the cool, detached modern temper, fending off the ardent interests of two women and finally riding away from the complicated situation, away from violence, commitment, and desire.

Many of Welty's early stories run in this general modern pattern: a character of recognizable "modern temper" finds himself/herself in the immediate presence of unmitigated life. The challenge is how to meet life. The young, would-be artist in "A Memory" frames everything with her fingers before looking. Harris retreats. Bowman tries to pay, to reduce life to a money exchange. Some characters break through the impasse. Mrs. Larkin in "A Curtain of Green" (*Southern Review*, Autumn 1938) submits to life (succumbing to grief for her dead husband) in spite of her will to deny it; "Powerhouse" (*Atlantic Monthly*, June 1941) is the story of the reconciling of life with art in the performance of the central blues artist.

Welty's first collection of stories was both hurt and helped by Porter's introduction. Since Porter was considered at the time the foremost master of the short story in America, her endorsement of the young Welty's work could not but help its reception. Porter was known for tough insistence on the integrity of the short-story form: it was not a truncated novel but its own thing. She exemplified tireless precision in the craft of writing, formal subtlety, a certain political awareness (which Welty never desired to emulate), and high standards of quality over quantity. The introduction she wrote, however, had the unfortunate result of commanding too much attention for itself and correspondingly less for the stories themselves. Some reviewers read Welty's stories from perspectives set up by Porter in passages such as this: "She [Welty] began writing spontaneously when she was a child, being a born writer; she continued without any plan for a profession, without any particular encouragement, and, as it proved, not needing any. For a good number of years she believed she was going to be a painter, and painted quite earnestly while she wrote without much effort."

The image of the Mozartian prodigy, moving effortlessly from easel to typewriter, not only far from fact, was bound to cause cynicism in reviewers. Porter's praise concocted a Welty in just the image that would attract hostile attention from a northeastern, urban, working literary press skeptical of "born writers," especially born writers from the South. Porter makes a point of calling Welty a southern writer of a particularly genteel sort: Greek and Roman classics, Shakespeare, Milton, Dante, the French and English novelists of the eighteenth and nineteenth centuries, Tolstoy, Yeats, and Virginia Woolf are presented as a sort of humming fabric of Welty's household conversation. Such a mythologized typecasting of the southern writer was as liable to draw fire in 1940 as it is today.

When Porter turned her attention away from the writer to the stories of *A Curtain of Green*, she put down a track that too many early readers followed uncritically. Of "Why I Live at the P.O.," Porter wrote that the heroine was a "terrifying case of dementia praecox." "Petrified Man" she called "a fine clinical study of vulgarity—vulgarity absolute, chemically pure, exposed mercilessly to its final subhuman depths." Porter tended to constrict the focus to these stories and gave the impression that all seventeen are studies in the grotesque. With such broad brush strokes laid upon the stories, the finer points were naturally obscured.

It is understandable, then, that reviewers tended to see Porter's version of the stories, not the stories themselves. Rose Feld (*New York Herald Tribune Books*, 16 November 1941) wrote: "As a whole, 'A Curtain of Green' shows too great preoccupation with the abnormal and grotesque. Some day someone might explore this tendency of

Southern writers." The anonymous reviewer for *Time* (24 November 1941) also took Porter's gambit: "But like many Southern writers, she [Welty] has a strong taste for melodrama, and is preoccupied with the demented, the deformed, . . . the highly spiced." Welty was learning how difficult it could be for a writer who was both southern and devoted to the short story.

She persevered. Her next collection, *The Wide Net, and Other Stories* (1943), published in a first edition of twenty-five hundred copies by Harcourt, Brace (who had become her publishers in 1942), contains fewer (eight) but more complex stories. *The Wide Net* also represents Welty's attempt to go beyond the miscellany collection toward the portfolio or suite model—several works on the same theme. As suggested by her agent, Russell, the focus of *The Wide Net* was to be the Natchez Trace, the five-hundred-mile trail used by traders, pioneers, and Indians moving back and forth over the territory between Natchez, Mississippi, and Nashville from the 1790s through the early decades of the nineteenth century. The surveying of the historical route of the Trace—part of the federal funding that would lead to its establishment as a national park—had spurred interest in the mid 1930s. Robert Coates's *The Outlaw Years* (1930), a popular history of the bandits of the Trace, was a book both Welty and Russell admired. Welty, then, used the Natchez Trace as a guiding force and figure for the working of her imagination. "A Worn Path," her first published tale of the area, went into the earlier collection. "First Love" (*Harper's Bazaar*, February 1942), the first story undertaken with the conscious discipline of the Trace as the theme for a book, came next. Welty used a historical situation (the trial of Aaron Burr for treason in Natchez in 1811) as the grounding of the story but imagined a superstructure lightly tethered to historical fact. This fruitful give-and-take, the obligation to the factual nature of a place and its history versus the creative discretion of the writer's imagination, shapes each of the stories, with the exception of "The Purple Hat" (*Harper's Bazaar*, November 1941), a ghost story set in New Orleans.

The very first Natchez Trace story Welty wrote is *The Robber Bridegroom*, separately published in 1942 but in existence as a story in some form as early as the spring of 1940, the time that also marks the beginning of Welty's long partnership with Russell. A version of *The Robber Bridegroom* lay on his desk unpublished for two years, and while she waited for him to read it and see it

successfully into print, Welty wrote her second Natchez Trace story, "A Worn Path."

The first story in *The Wide Net* is "First Love." The story went through several versions, was in no way as easy as the earlier stories to write, and Russell had much to say about its obscurity and veiled pockets of meaning. "First Love" is the story of a deaf-mute, Joel Mayes, a boy who has seen his parents disappear on the Trace, swallowed up by the wilderness or perhaps captured by the Indians. He becomes a deaf-mute because of the traumatic experience and finds a place in Natchez as the boot boy of an inn where travelers come and go. One of those travelers is Aaron Burr, portrayed as a mysterious adventurer who continually gestures with his right hand to the West, "some extension to the West of the Natchez Trace," as if only Burr can imagine the Trace as a dream infinitely extendable in the human mind if not in actual space. Joel identifies with Burr, watches every gesture, and lives with every mood, even though Joel can neither hear him nor speak to him. Burr's trial for treason comes, and Burr eventually decamps, reading the handwriting on the wall. The center of the story, though, is not the fidelity of Welty's Burr to the historical figure (whatever one can reconstruct of him) but the realization of Joel that he himself is a particular human being, made up of his trauma and his deep sensitivity, a consciousness with a peculiar kind of sight. The realization begins when Joel wakes suddenly one evening and sees Burr and his coconspirator Harman Blennerhassett in the room where he sleeps: "[Joel] did not at once betray the violation that he felt. Instead, he simply sat, still bolt upright, and looked with the feasting the eyes do in secret—at their faces, the one eye of each that he could see, the cheeks, the half-hidden mouths—the faces each firelit, and strange with a common reminiscence or speculation. . . ."

Thus does Welty demonstrate her own certain sort of attention. She sees the world in a certain order, a certain composition of plane and light. There is secrecy and intrusion, for Joel—and Welty—begin to penetrate to the "reminiscence or speculation" concealed under the object's exterior.

The Natchez Trace stories turn on moments like this, and like the one in "A Still Moment" (*American Prefaces*, Spring 1942) when John James Audubon beholds the white heron in the company of evangelist Lorenzo Dow and murderer James Murrell. This scene has often been dis-

Dust jacket for the 1949 short-story collection that many consider Welty's best work

cussed; less often have readers realized that each of the stories in the collection harbors a similar moment. Many readers point to the passages in which Audubon's fierce attention "feasts" on the heron in the slow seconds before he shoots it. He sees it microscopically, with a vision no ordinary human can master: "Audubon's eyes embraced the object in the distance and he could see it as carefully as if he held it in his hand. It was a snowy heron alone out of its flock. He watched it steadily, in his care noting the exact inevitable things. When it feeds it muddies the water with its foot...." Like Joel Mayes, Audubon is an artist with his eyes. He might go for weeks in the Natchez wilderness without speaking to another human being. To him "the exact inevitable things" are the objects of love. No words intervene, as they do for Dow, who expresses love in sermons and in letters. No personal manias cloud Audubon's vision, as Murrell's vision is clouded by his criminal past and his crazy dream of an insurrection of slaves that he will lead. It is the clarity, silence, and inevitability of Audubon's artist's vision that commands Welty's attention.

Versions of this theme appear in each of the stories. The final one, "At the Landing" (*Tomorrow*, April 1943), incorporates both of the aspects of the Trace that the author used in focusing her imagination and craft: the grounding in geographical certitude and inevitability, and the metaphorical consideration of becoming a certain type of person: an artist and a writer. "At the Landing" carries an intriguingly ambivalent title, for landings can be both the beginnings and the ends of journeys. The ambivalence suits the character of Jenny Lockhart, the central character, for she finishes one journey (like Josie in "The Winds" she is leaving childhood for the beginning of maturity), under the influence of her grandfather in his house, and enters another form of domination by a man, Billy Floyd, a curious incarnation of the destructive and the liberating. Jenny lives at the terminus of the Trace, not far from Natchez but closer to the Mississippi River, in a dilapidated plantation house.

Jenny is locked, a bit like Joel, into a silent and unbreakable routine. Until her grandfather dies and a flood comes to erase the omnipotence of the house and the memory of her grandfather, Jenny scarcely has her own life. The flood and Floyd combine to rescue her from this isolation. In a crucial scene, Jenny tries to speak to Floyd to express her self, fledgling as she is: " 'I . . .' she began, and stopped. He scowled. She knew at once that there was nothing in her life past or even now in the flood that would make anything to tell. He already knew that he had saved her life, for that had taken up his time in the time of danger. Yet she might confess it. It came to her lips. He scowled on. . . . 'I . . .' She looked softly at him as if from a distance down a little road or a little tether he sent her on."

This moment on the brink of self-expression never goes to fulfillment, never to the completed sentence in the world. The words stay in Jenny's mind. She desires communication, the telling of the new between two. Floyd is not made the same way. Almost his next act is to "violate" Jenny; the world's form of communication (as Joel had learned when he forced his mouth into the loamy ground of the Trace to stifle a cry, as Audubon knew as he sighted on the heron and squeezed the trigger) is often violence.

The rape changes Jenny. She goes back to the house when the floodwaters recede and undertakes the Herculean task of cleaning the mud from everything. She cannot, however, clean Floyd from her mind as easily. Her thoughts dwell upon him; he gradually becomes the figure of love. A long passage describes Jenny's unspoken meditations: "Then the radiance [at the thought of Floyd in the world] touched at her heart and her brain, moving within her. Maybe some day she could become bright and shining all at once. . . . But now she was like a house with all its rooms dark from the beginning, and someone would have to go slowly from room to room, slowly and darkly, leaving each one lighted behind, before going to the next. It was not caution or distrust that was in herself, it was only a sense of journey, of something that might happen. She herself did not know what might lie ahead, she had never seen herself. She looked outward with the sense of rightful space and time within her, which must be traversed before she could be known at all. And what she would reveal in the end was not herself, but the way of the traveler."

One metaphorical pattern of language is clear in this passage: the journey. As the restless and the adventurous came up and down the Trace in search of new conditions in which to imagine their lives and fortunes, Jenny and her precursors in *The Wide Net* embark on journeys at the ends of which, at the various landings, wait new versions of themselves. Just as Jenny had never seen her self, she knew that confirmation of her being in the world would only come from another. Joel learned less painfully perhaps; Audubon, as the mature artist of the Natchez stories, knew the secret all along. Jenny learns it, in the rape by Floyd, and the violent penetration becomes the uneasy metaphor for the continuation of the traveling, the search. "At the Landing" ends with more sudden violence. Jenny looks for Floyd among some nomadic fishermen at the river. She is raped by these men, too, who commemorate their brutal deed by throwing their knives into a tree, which "bled" with each cut. Jenny listens to them with an enigmatic "original smile" on her face.

The Wide Net was a satisfying project for Welty. Each of the eight stories had been previously published in good magazines. With the exception of the individual story "The Purple Hat," they made an interesting ensemble, something like an exhibition, a model she had known from her own photography exhibit in 1936. Even so, reviewers were still not completely convinced of her abilities. The anonymous reviewer for *Time* was ambivalent: "These eight stories about the South present as perplexing and exasperating a mixture of good and bad as U.S. writing can

show. . . . At her best, 34-year-old Miss Welty runs a photofinish with the finest prose artists of her time and displays a delicateness of sensibility which borders at once on genius and indecency" (27 September 1943). Diana Trilling, writing in the *Nation* (2 October 1943), found the stories to manifest a surplus of style, "a heart for decay and an eye for the Gothic in detail." Reviewing continued to dwell upon the southernness of Welty's stories and only gradually caught on to the art of the short story that this author was developing. One important positive voice was Robert Penn Warren's in his influential essay "The Love and Separateness in Miss Welty," published in spring 1944 (*Kenyon Review*) and still worthwhile.

The short-story technique, for Welty, was both practice and theory, even though the early stories of *A Curtain of Green*, by the author's own admission, had not been heavily theorized, revised, or consciously shaped. Welty did not use a system or process for her stories and resisted writing criticism herself for fear the discipline would make her too conscious of her own creative technique. In 1943 she began reviewing books regularly for the *New York Times Book Review*, but book reviewing was a few steps short of outright literary criticism. Welty finally ventured into criticism in 1947 with her lecture/essay "The Reading and Writing of Short Stories" (*Atlantic Monthly*, February-March 1949; separately published in 1950 as *Short Stories*).

The summer of 1947 seemed auspicious. Welty's novel, *Delta Wedding* (1946), which had begun life as a short story, had had a successful serialization in the *Atlantic Monthly* and good sales as a novel. Her other titles were being republished in modest printings. Back-to-back O. Henry first prizes for "The Wide Net" (1942) and "Livvie" (1943), following her second prize for "A Worn Path" in 1941, had shored up her confidence and reputation. When the opportunity occurred to deliver a lecture at a writer's conference in Seattle in August, Welty took the occasion as her first voyage into literary criticism.

Welty wanted her lecture to be simple, not the arcane and specialized jargon of the private club of criticism. Her essay radiates a tone of clearing the air, setting limits to what criticism can teach about literature, and consolidating Welty's hard-won lessons in the writing and reading of short stories. As a general rule Welty the critic preferred to draw a line between the analytical (critical) and the synthetic (creative) faculties of the imagination. She did not, however, "deny the pow-

Dust jacket for the book version (1954) of a novella that was first published on 5 December 1953 in the New Yorker

ers and achievements of good criticism," perhaps because she herself was a card-carrying critic by virtue of her stint as a professional book reviewer. The distinction she strove for, then, lay between "blind . . . ingrown and tedious" story criticism and the kind that illuminated and revealed "large wholes and . . . subtle relationships." Welty would not grant that criticism, "or more strictly analysis," could reveal how a short story had been written nor recover the "passion" in the imagination of writer or reader. "The arrow of creation" flies only once per story (for the writer) and in only one direction (toward the reader). Analysis, unlike creation, could kill the story.

Even so, a writer of Welty's subtlety could suggest the trueness of the arrow's flight by reading her favorite authors' stories with the attention of an accomplished and passionate critic. D. H. Lawrence's "The Fox," Hemingway's "Indian Camp," Stephen Crane's "The Bride Comes to Yellow Sky," Katherine Mansfield's "Miss Brill" (perhaps a prompter for Welty's own "The Purple Hat"), and others received the separate tributes of well-honed literary attention, enough to illuminate the hearts of the stories but not so much as to cause them to shrivel up.

The only critic she felt comfortable in quoting was E. M. Forster, whose book *Aspects of the Novel* (1927) she admired as much as any book of literary criticism. Forster's style of criticism, and the nature of his fiction, helped Welty form her most important statement on the short story as a genre, and on her practice of it: "Which brings us to the interesting disparity between integrity—which emerges in a story as truth or validity—and plausibility. The validity of everyday life is notoriously dependent on certain things. The validity of a story—not quite so notoriously—depends on things of an entirely different order. There's no need to hedge about—the two validities conflict. That is, there was never any question of their tallying." The point is crucial for understanding Welty's approach to the short story. The story's "integrity" balances the novel's "plausibility"; instantaneous vision balances plot. Her earlier stories had moved between these poles. The stories of *The Wide Net* moved toward "integrity." In *The Golden Apples* Welty showed what she meant; the collection remains her masterpiece and one of the most significant works in the short-story genre.

The Golden Apples contains seven stories and is even more firmly and elaborately integrated than the stories of *The Wide Net*. Place is, once again, the keystone: the imagined town of Morgana, Mississippi, serves as the field for these stories of wandering and return. As in *The Wide Net*, journeying is the dynamic motif, with the sense of place the static one, but journeying in *The Golden Apples* is ramified into its many and various aspects. The central traveler of the stories, King MacLain, moves across geography, through time, in and out of mythological and realistic modes. He appears in one story under an alias. King is both character and archetype—plausible as character, integral as archetype: all the other characters derive identity, in some ways, from King.

The technical achievement of these stories, individually and as a collection, is the pinnacle of Welty's short-story art. Networks of mythological and literary allusion (the Irish symbology of Yeats, classical Greek, versions of Sir James Frazer's *Golden Bough* [1911-1915]) are densely interwoven into a collection of stories that outstrips many novels in artistic unity. The model of self-reinforcing, self-integrating pattern here is the modern symbolist poem—the work of literary art as object. Resolutions deferred in one story are disclosed in a later one; motives seemingly accidental to one story become central to another. Readers find themselves in a way reading the seven stories simultaneously, for later stories cast meaning back upon the earlier.

The best entry into the technical elegance and continuity of *The Golden Apples* is through the image of Benvenuto Cellini's *Perseus and the Head of Medusa* (1545-1554), another example of Welty's penchant for blending one art form into another. In the first story, "Shower of Gold" (*Atlantic*, May 1948), King's pose at one point resembles that of Perseus. Cellini's Perseus holds the severed head of Medusa aloft in his left hand. His right hand grips his short, heavy blade at hip-height, the point of the blade at a right angle to his torso. His right leg is straight, bearing all the weight, foot planted on the headless female body; his left leg is cocked, the foot poised on toes and just a little behind the right. Perseus is nude, his musculature carefully and sensuously defined to show his youth, masculinity, grace, and fitness. Like Donatello's *David*, Cellini's Perseus is coded both for sensuality and for violence—

supple flesh, sharp blade. He is well chosen. The narrator of "Shower of Gold" is Katie Rainey, who has heard the story from a local black man, Old Plez Morgan. Welty projects the Perseus figure into subsequent meaning: "So Plez says presently the familiar stranger [King] paused. It was in front of the MacLain's—and sunk his weight on one leg and just stood there, posey as statues, hand on his hip. Ha!" King, the wandering progenitor of *The Golden Apples*, is home for a fleeting visit. His pose signifies his relationship to the family situation he chooses to leave aside. Like Perseus he has severed his responsibility to the female-centered hearth. His attractiveness to women, however, is undiminished. Katie herself testifies to the attraction, and Mattie Will Sojourner, in "Sir Rabbit" (*Hudson Review*, Spring 1949), succumbs to King as well.

The Perseus figure returns overtly in "Moon Lake" (*Sewanee Review*, Summer 1949), a story in which three young girls, Jinny Stark, Nina Carmichael, and Easter (an orphan who is one of King's illegitimate children), explore mysteries of life and death, self-protection, and adult sexuality while at summer camp. The denouement centers upon the rescue of Easter from drowning by Loch Morrison, a Boy Scout kept nearby to watch over the girl campers. His artificial respiration administered to Easter in full view of campers and counselors appears simply violent to the young, and disturbingly like sexual violation to the older women. Easter is revived and Loch becomes a hero. Later that night, in his tent, sequestered from the campers, he is spied by Jinny and Nina: "He was naked and there was his little tickling thing hung on him like the last drop on the pitcher's lip. He ceased or exhausted study [of his sunburn] and came to the tent opening again and stood leaning on raised arm with his weight on one foot—just looking into the night, which was clamorous." Like King in the earlier story, Loch strikes the Perseus pose. The blade is reduced to "his little tickling thing" but is still threatening. The girls, sensing but not consciously aware of what they see, vow never to marry. The vow, as subsequent stories reveal, is broken, much to the misery of both.

The culmination of the Perseus pattern comes in the final story of the collection, "The Wanderers" (*Harper's Bazaar*, March 1949—as "The Hummingbirds"). Virgie Rainey, who has emerged as the female equivalent to the Perseus male myth, has returned to Morgana for the funeral of her mother, Katie, the narrator of the

Dust jacket for Welty's 1980 collection, her largest and most comprehensive

first story. Virgie has never been married, never been enthralled in the male trap of narcissism and hurt as presented in the stories, but she has had liaisons with men. She returns to Morgana as if to old choices and their consequences: talent misspent, world security still eluding her, her rootedness in her family and Morgana, and her potential for happiness, in question because of her singleness and refusal to settle in one place. All of the uncompleted meaning, though, is washed away as resolving rain begins to fall and memories rush to Virgie's consciousness: "Cutting off the Medusa's head was the heroic act, perhaps, that made visible a horror in life, that was at once the horror in love, Virgie thought—the separateness. She might have seen heroism prophetically when she was young and afraid of Miss Eckhart. She might be able to see it now prophetically, but she was never a prophet. Because Virgie saw things in their time, like hearing them— and perhaps because she must believe in the Medusa equally with Perseus—she saw the stroke of the sword in three moments, not one. In the three was the damnation—no, only the secret, unhurting because not caring in itself—beyond the beauty and the sword's stroke and the terror lay their existence in time—far out and endless, a constellation which the heart could read over many a night."

What Welty seeks, and succeeds in finding, in the narratives of *The Golden Apples* is a fiction technique, seated in the short story, that reveals instantaneously and wholly (not serially as in the plot of the novel) experience and its meaning in time. The culminating moment of "The Wanderers" does that. On the level of circumstances, Virgie remembers, in this climactic scene, a picture in Miss Eckhart's house (the MacLain house, now rented) that shows Cellini's Perseus and Medusa. But light striking the glass of the picture often obscures the image. The image of a framed picture invisible in the sun's glare is described near the beginning of "June Recital" (*Harper's Bazaar*, September 1947—as "Golden Apples"). The character who cannot see what is in the glass is, not surprisingly, Loch Morrison a few years before his heroics. Thus is the last story linked to story number two, and the two together into the whole. Carefully implanted motifs work in this way—surreptitiously, antichronologically—to shift this fiction out of plot and into instantaneous vision. Welty thought she had done something very good in *The Golden Apples*, and she had. Reviewers called her a master of the short story, and the public bought out three printings (more than twelve thousand copies) of the book in its first season.

Her fourth collection, *The Bride of the Innisfallen, and Other Stories* (1955), was greeted by more lukewarm reviews. The stories themselves are long, deeply encoded with the journey motif and the sexual stalemate, but without the so-called "objective correlative" of the Perseus and Medusa myth and painting or that of a single place. Readers felt less secure with these stories. That is understandable but regrettable. "The Burning" (*Harper's Bazaar*, March 1951), for which Welty won her second O. Henry second prize in 1951, is her only Civil War story and can be read as her homage to Faulknerian rhetoric and style. Such rhetoric, it turned out, did not suit her. "Kin" (*New Yorker*, 15 November 1952) is a return to the Delta material left over and unexplored in the writing of *Delta Wedding*. "The Bride of the Innisfallen" (*New Yorker*, 1 December 1951), largely written and revised at Bowen's Court, the Irish home of Elizabeth Bowen, is a story of intriguingly truncated events, repetitions, and of "sprung" narrative. These stories are challenges to readers; they anticipate postmodern and magic-realism narratives.

After *The Bride of the Innisfallen* a series of family demands, including the long illnesses of her mother and two brothers, kept Welty from completing many new stories for publication. In the heated aftermath of the assassination of Medgar Evers in 1963, she wrote, in one night, "Where Is the Voice Coming From?"—an imaginative reconstruction of the killing and the killer mentality that the *New Yorker* published immediately (6 July 1963), dismantling an issue already in the press in order to get the story into print. As a study of the mind in desperation, deracinated by hate, frustration, and despair, "Where Is the Voice Coming From?" (later included in *The Collected Stories*, 1980) is powerful. For her presentation of the single, flat-echoing, desperate voice, Welty seems to have retrieved something from an earlier, uncollected story, "Retreat" (*River*, March 1937). Something new has been added, though: the sinister power of television to dehumanize both assassin and victim. "Where Is The Voice Coming From?" is stitched together with allusions to television, to the remorseless power of the medium to bore into the mind with the good and the bad. The assassin murders his victim in a hallucinatory state, the events seeming to him to be captured on black and white film in soundless close-ups. And the flat image of the vic-

Welty with V. S. Pritchett in Savannah, 1985 (photograph copyright 1989 by Eudora Welty)

tim as previously seen on television by the murderer seems to allow him to believe that he shoots an image, not a man.

One additional short story, "The Demonstrators" (*New Yorker*, 26 November 1966; also in *The Collected Stories*), returns to the civil rights tumult of the 1960s. In this story—much longer and more complex than "Where Is the Voice Coming From?"—Welty explores the depth and recesses of race relations and the subtle maneuvers behind the overt lines of legislation by which we maintain cordons of difference. "The Demonstrators" bears close comparison with Faulkner's "Pantaloon in Black" (in *Go Down, Moses*, 1942), for both stories examine racial distinctions and myth as they are embedded deeply in social psychology. "The Demonstrators" won for Welty her third O. Henry first prize.

After a long sabbatical Eudora Welty returned to the public eye in 1970 with her most successful novel, *Losing Battles*. This was followed by *The Optimist's Daughter* (1972), another successful novel (seven printings), for which Welty was awarded the Pulitzer Prize for fiction in 1973. Her short stories have been continually in print from first publication, and in 1980 Harcourt Brace Jovanovich issued *The Collected Stories of Eudora Welty*, including the contents of each collection, plus the uncollected stories of the 1960s.

Perhaps Welty's most powerful contribution to the short-story genre is her involvement of the reader in the act of imaginative creation. Welty induces readers to make connections from reader to text, as the writer does from text to reader. For Welty, art is nothing if not communication.

Interviews:

Peggy Whitman Prenshaw, ed., *Conversations with Eudora Welty* (Jackson: University Press of Mississippi, 1984).

Bibliographies:

Noel Polk, "A Eudora Welty Checklist," *Mississippi Quarterly*, 26 (Fall 1973): 663-693;

Victor H. Thompson, *Eudora Welty: A Reference Guide* (Boston: G. K. Hall, 1976);

Suzanne Marrs, *The Welty Collection: A Guide* (Jackson: University Press of Mississippi, 1988).

References:

Alfred Appel, Jr., *A Season of Dreams: The Fiction of Eudora Welty* (Baton Rouge: Louisiana State University Press, 1965);

Harold Bloom, ed., *Modern Critical Views: Eudora Welty* (New York: Chelsea House, 1986);

J. A. Bryant, Jr., *Eudora Welty* (Minneapolis: University of Minnesota Press, 1968);

John F. Desmond, ed., *A Still Moment: Essays on the Art of Eudora Welty* (Metuchen, N.J.: Scarecrow, 1978);

Albert J. Devlin, *Eudora Welty's Chronicle: A Story of Mississippi Life* (Jackson: University Press of Mississippi, 1983);

Devlin, ed., *Welty: A Life in Literature* (Jackson: University Press of Mississippi, 1987);

Elizabeth Evans, *Eudora Welty* (New York: Ungar, 1981);

Ruth M. Vande Kieft, *Eudora Welty* (New York: Twayne, 1962; revised edition, Boston: G. K. Hall, 1987);

Michael Kreyling, *Eudora Welty's Achievement of Order* (Baton Rouge: Louisiana State University Press, 1980);

Carol S. Manning, *With Ears Opening Like Morning Glories: Eudora Welty and the Love of Storytelling* (Westport, Conn.: Greenwood, 1985);

Thomas L. McHaney, "Eudora Welty and the Multitudinous Golden Apples," *Mississippi Quarterly*, 26 (Fall 1973): 589-624;

Peggy W. Prenshaw, ed., *Eudora Welty: Critical Essays* (Jackson: University Press of Mississippi, 1979);

Claude Richard, ed., *Delta*, special Welty issue, 5 (November 1977);

Robert Penn Warren, "The Love and Separateness in Miss Welty," *Kenyon Review*, 6 (Spring 1944): 246-259;

Patricia S. Yaeger, " 'Because a Fire Was in My Head': Eudora Welty and the Dialogic Imagination," *PMLA*, 99 (October 1984): 955-973.

Glenway Wescott

(11 April 1901 - 22 February 1987)

Sy M. Kahn
University of the Pacific

See also the Wescott entries in *DLB 4: American Writers in Paris, 1920-1929* and *DLB 9: American Novelists, 1910-1945.*

BOOKS: *The Bitterns: A Book of Twelve Poems* (Evanston, Ill.: Wheeler, 1920);

The Apple of the Eye (New York: MacVeagh/Dial, 1924; London: Butterworth, 1926);

Natives of Rock: XX Poems· 1921-1922 (New York: Bianco, 1925);

Like A Lover (Macon, France: Wheeler, 1926);

The Grandmothers: A Family Portrait (New York & London: Harper, 1927); republished as *A Family Portrait* (London: Butterworth, 1927);

Good-Bye Wisconsin (New York & London: Harper, 1928; London: Cape, 1929);

The Babe's Bed (Paris: Harrison of Paris, 1930);

Fear and Trembling (New York & London: Harper, 1932);

A Calendar of Saints for Unbelievers (Paris: Harrison of Paris, 1932; New York & London: Harper, 1933);

The Pilgrim Hawk (New York & London: Harper, 1940; London: Hamilton, 1946);

Apartment in Athens (New York & London: Harper, 1945); republished as *Household in Athens* (London: Hamilton, 1945);

Images of Truth: Remembrances and Criticism (New York: Harper & Row, 1962; London: Hamilton, 1963).

OTHER: "The Dream of Audubon, Libretto of a Ballet in Three Scenes," in *The Best One-Act Plays of 1940*, edited by Margaret Mayorga (New York: Dodd, Mead, 1941), pp. 361-374;

The Maugham Reader, introduction by Wescott (Garden City, N.Y.: Doubleday, 1950);

Short Novels of Colette, introduction by Wescott (New York: Dial/Permanent Library, 1951);

12 Fables of Aesop, retold by Wescott (New York: Museum of Modern Art, 1954);

Hugh Ford, *Four Lives in Paris*, foreword by Wes-

Photograph by George Platt Lynes

Glenway Wescott

cott (San Francisco: North Point, 1987), pp. xvi-xxiii.

SELECTED PERIODICAL PUBLICATIONS—
UNCOLLECTED:
FICTION
"Hurt Feelings," *North American Review*, 234 (September 1932): 223-240;

"The Rescuer," *Life and Letters Today*, 15 (Autumn 1936): 150-156;

"The Sight of a Dead Body," *Signatures*, 1 (Autumn 1936): 135-138;

"Mr. Auerbach in Paris," *Harper's*, 184 (April 1942): 469-473;

"The Frenchman Six Foot Three," *Harper's*, 185 (July 1942): 131-140.

NONFICTION

"Alexander Blok," *Poetry*, 19 (December 1921): 149-151;

"The Two Dollar Novel," *New Republic*, 35 (4 July 1923): 158-159;

"The First Book of Mary Butts," *Dial*, 75 (September 1923): 282-284;

"Miss Roberts' First Novel," *Dial*, 82 (July 1927): 73-75;

"Elizabeth Madox Roberts: A Personal Note," *Bookman*, 71 (March 1930): 12-15;

"A Sentimental Contribution," *Hound and Horn*, 7 (April-June 1934): 523-534;

"The Moral of F. Scott Fitzgerald," *New Republic*, 104 (17 February 1941): 213-217;

"I Love New York," *Harper's Bazaar*, 77 (December 1943): 53, 55, 58, 104, 106, 108, 111;

"A Day in the Country," *Tomorrow*, 6 (July 1947): 35-37;

"A Succession of Poets," *Partisan Review*, 50, no. 3 (1983): 392-406.

Glenway Wescott earned a sustained literary reputation primarily for his short stories and novels written and published during the 1920s while he resided in France (particularly Villefranche, near Nice) and for his novella *The Pilgrim Hawk* (1940). He was one of the youngest of those American writers who made France their workshop after World War I and who, with the distance and objectivity that foreign residence provided, frequently analyzed and assessed their American backgrounds, culture, and experience. During the 1920s Wescott's reputation rivaled those of Ernest Hemingway and F. Scott Fitzgerald, also midwesterners and expatriates in France. When Wescott won the Harper Prize for his novel *The Grandmothers* in 1927, he elicited expectations among critics and writers that he would enjoy a major writing career. However, after 1930 Wescott published little fiction and none at all after 1945, when his last novel, *Apartment in Athens*, was published. Wescott's early promise did prove valid in *The Pilgrim Hawk*, widely praised as not only his best work but also one of the best examples of the novella written by an American.

Wescott was born on 11 April 1901 to Josephine Gordon Wescott and Bruce Peters Wescott, a farmer, and grew up in Wisconsin. He attended the University of Chicago and, in 1919, withdrew after less than two years, spending the next few years traveling in the United States and Europe. During this period he published imagist poems. In 1925 he settled in France for eight years, although he made occasional visits to his family in Wisconsin. He returned to the United States in 1933 and for the rest of his life resided either in New York City or in rural New Jersey. He never married. In 1945 he started to be more active as an essayist, critic, lecturer, and commentator on literary topics. In 1947 Wescott was elected to the National Institute of Arts and Letters, serving as its president from 1959 to 1962.

During his writing career Wescott worked in a variety of forms in addition to the novel, short story, and poetry. He wrote a libretto for a ballet (1940; published in 1941), a commentary on saints (1932), a reworking of Aesop's fables (1954), and several lyric essays, which were vehicles for highly personal commentary on books and writers. To these forms Wescott brought an elegant style and structure. All of his writing is characterized by a lyrical, highly cadenced prose, by inventive metaphors and images, and by rich symbolism. These radiated from a probing and speculative intelligence. Although Wescott wrote in various genres, the volume of work is slender in any category. He published only sixteen short stories, ten of which were written during the 1920s and collected in *Good-Bye Wisconsin* (1928). His story *The Babe's Bed* (1930) was published as a book in a small Paris edition. Of the remaining five stories, three were written and published during the 1930s and two in 1942. The collected short stories and *The Babe's Bed* are superior in craft to these later ones.

In the 1920s Wescott set his fiction in Wisconsin. Both his early novels, *The Apple of the Eye* (1924) and *The Grandmothers*, as well as *The Babe's Bed* and all the stories in *Good-Bye Wisconsin*, are set there. Although these works depict a state and region with which Wescott had various quarrels, it is clear that he was more concerned with rendering a state of mind than a state. Wisconsin is the arena but not the circumference of these novels and stories. They embrace more than a region; they comment on a culture as understood by one of its writers who has physically escaped its boundaries but not its psychological and emotional effects. In these works Wescott attempts to probe, understand, and resolve the problems of his youth, past, heritage, and family. In the mosaic of his long and short fiction, Wescott attempts to define his past, himself, and the tensions created by his expatriation but not freedom from all that Wisconsin symbolizes. Wisconsin is the Midwest, and the Midwest is a metaphor for America as understood by Wescott. In order to escape the judgments and narrow perspectives of a restrictive culture, as well as to gain the wider, more complex viewpoints of seasoned, sophisticated civilizations, Wescott felt it necessary to "backtrail" to the East and to Europe. Wescott employed the knowledge of art and life that France provided to render his family, local characters, and history, and by such exercises of memory and intuition he attempted to understand himself as man and artist.

Although his early stories are based on a Wisconsin mosaic, they are, of course, discreet literary works. Seven of the ten stories in *Good-Bye Wisconsin* had been published previously, between 1924 and 1928. Sy M. Kahn, William H. Rueckert, and Ira D. Johnson have all observed that Wescott seems to have worked best in short forms, especially illustrated by his superior 1940 novella, and that his novels of the 1920s are as much a composition of refracting segments as they are sustained narratives. Wescott's skill in short forms is also shown to good advantage in his collection of short stories.

Introduced by Wescott's essay concerning a visit to his native state, the stories in *Good-Bye Wisconsin* can be grouped around particular themes. The problems of flight and expatriation are explored in "The Runaways" (first published as "This Way Out" in *Collier's*, 4 July 1925), "The Sailor," and "The Whistling Swan." Two other stories, "The Dove Came Down" and "Prohibition," may be seen as his contrasting reactions to middle-class propriety and the constrictions and restrictions of midwestern Protestantism. Two others, "Adolescence" and "In a Thicket," explore the themes of awakening sensibility and approaching maturity. The remaining three, "The Wedding March," *Like a Lover* (first published separately in France in 1926), and "A Guilty Woman," explore the nature of love. As these groupings suggest, Wescott is only incidentally concerned with locale. Ultimately he is engaged by the emotional and psychological implications of suppression, flight, awakening, thwarted sexuality, guilt, violence, and the flowering, disappointments, and resolutions of love. These themes are in harmony with those explored in Wescott's two early novels.

Significantly, the first and final stories in *Good-Bye Wisconsin* deal with flight and expatriation, persistent themes in Wescott's life and fiction during the 1920s. Consequently, an examination of the three stories that explore these themes reveals how Wescott developed these ideas in this period, as well as something of his narrative techniques and strategies.

In "The Runaways," Amelia Fox and Nick Richter seek relief from their sluggish courtship, stale marriage, and drab lives. Having no money, they set fire to their house for the insurance. Because of their inept planning and fear, they lose their claim and end up in a dowdy boardinghouse where they meet two show women from a carnival. The women take Amelia and Nick to the "Gay Paree" show, which dazzles and beguiles them, but Nick ends up driving a van and Amelia cooking sausages. They learn that "romance is for those who see, never for those who do, and [is] underpaid as a profession." The story is an implied criticism of expatriation. "Gay Paree" is the reduced, shabby symbol of Paris itself and is a warning to dreamers that romantic destinations do not assure escape from drudgery, particularly for the inept and naive. This story is the least sophisticated of the three exploring the theme of expatriation. The symbols verge on cliché, and the story's point is blunted by being too heavily pressed. However, the suggestive detail, the symbolic gesture, and the unity of mood that Wescott used with increased skill in almost all the other stories in the collection are prefigured in this first one.

In "The Sailor" (previously unpublished) the nomadic Terrie returns from abroad, particularly France, to visit his brother in Wisconsin. Verbally stilted, Terrie cannot adequately relate the complications and essence of his foreign experience, especially his increased capacity to experience emotions—the result of a disappointing love affair. Although he has ambivalent feelings toward both Wisconsin and Europe, Terrie finds himself unable to remain in Wisconsin. Frustrated by "a brother who did not know enough about life to understand what he was talking about," Terrie yearns for the "sharp contrasts" and "distinct good and evil" of Europe, a place less dull though more dangerous than the tedious farm.

"The Whistling Swan" (*Bookman*, June 1928) offers the most complex evaluation of the problems of expatriation. Herbert Redd is a pianist and composer whose artistic life is at stake in his choice between Wisconsin and France. Like Terrie, Redd has lived in France, but unlike Terrie, he clearly understands the precise artistic and social advantages and disadvantages of life

Illustration by John Alan Maxwell for the magazine appearance of the story Wescott collected as "The Runaways" in
Goodbye Wisconsin *(1928)*

abroad. Wescott emphasizes the psychological implications of expatriation and raises the pitch of torment by subjecting an intelligent, introspective, and talented character to the conflicting impulses of renunciation or acceptance of Wisconsin. Redd's choice is complicated by the fact that his wealthy Chicago patrons, the Crawleys, disapprove of his "extravagances" and patronage by others. Further, a naive, youthful sweetheart, Muriel Pater, has been waiting for him in his home state. Redd becomes paralyzed by indecision between seeking new patronage and returning to France or marrying Muriel, making a life in Wisconsin, and eventually losing himself in a music school "in a swarm of mediocre youngsters." Torn between his desire for socially and artistically sophisticated Paris on the one hand, and on the other for the admiring, loving, but uncritical and innocent Muriel and the predictable small-

town life she represents, he mulls over his dilemma while walking in a Wisconsin wood. Startled by a large swan, he shoots it. With the falling of the bird, Redd's indecision vanishes. Wescott's skillful phrasing makes the downed bird externalize and dramatize Redd's decision to remain, teach in a small college, and marry. These sudden resolutions seem to assert themselves out of various and unchartable impulses, as Redd approaches the floundering bird: "In despair at dying, it whistled, whistled, and took its breath. Broken open, a heavy stream of music let out—but it was the opposite of music. Now husky, now crude, what were like dots of purity often, the rhythm of something torn."

Redd's reactions are swift and complex. He feels a "sick satisfaction, definite jealousy of the dead bird, an extreme feebleness, a great haste." The prevailing implication is that Redd has killed his own desire to fly and will be "almost content with his apparent loss." However, the end of the story, despite the symbolic swan and its song, remains ambiguous and elusive. There is no sense of victory or defeat in Redd's decision; it is immediately overshadowed by new complications. Out of the death of one way of life—expatriation, symbolized by the swan—have arisen, phoenixlike, new possibilities: to outmaneuver circumstances in Wisconsin through the creation of ideal music or to hold a "wholesome, personal peace." The swan itself emphasizes an ambiguity. Habitually silent, only in death does it jet its music. Was Redd's own "music" expended in the rhythm of his sobbing in the woods—a duet of death, lamenting both the swan and abandoned expatriate life—or was it the overture to either a richer expression or a contented silence? The ambiguity is natural, though. Any decision involves complications, possibilities, and risks.

As these three stories illustrate, the problem of expatriation has no easy solution—actually no solution at all. The rewards of flight and life abroad can be ambiguous and dubious. Disillusionment can displace innocence; new appetites can stimulate new hungers. There is no resolution, merely an exchange of values apt to leave one more restless than before. Individual decisions, if one is to judge by these stories, are not arrived at wisely or judiciously but through circumstances, moods, obscure collisions of ideas, and reactions in the back of one's mind. In any event the blessings of expatriation are mixed, the possible damnation subtle.

Whether Wescott is dealing with expatriates, love, the transition from innocence to maturity, or rebellion against stultifying and mundane circumstances, his short stories are rendered in lyrical prose with elegant nuances of mood. These stories are quite unlike those of Hemingway or Fitzgerald, though Wescott, in his own way, set a standard and demonstrated the poetic possibilities of the form. In Wescott's stories, the plot, narration, action, realistic detail, and dialogue are subordinate to evocation of mood and tone, suitable to the impressionistic nostalgia that characterizes his style in general, as each short story moves toward the revelations of a central truth.

As mentioned, during the 1930s Wescott published three short stories, and two more in 1942, his last published stories. All five were attempts by Wescott to break free of his Wisconsin material as well as his characteristic fictional style, toward which he was becoming increasingly distrust-

ful. During the late 1920s, and subsequently, Wescott felt the difficulty of rendering the "truth" of his perceptions through the strategies of fiction available to him. These strategies, Wescott felt, invited subjectivity rather than the truth of a subject and idea, a dilemma itself explored as a central theme in *The Babe's Bed*.

Wescott's attempts to work closer to the truth of his observations and insights resulted in a series of aborted novels during the 1930s. The three short stories he published during the decade, "Hurt Feelings," "The Rescuer," and "The Sight of a Dead Body," may be reductions or fragments of failed or incompleted novels; surely "Hurt Feelings" (*North American Review*, September 1932) derives from the abandoned novel "The Dream of Mrs. Cleveland." All three stories are examples of Wescott's attempt to fashion a fiction more satisfying to his aesthetic goals. "Hurt Feelings" revolves around the character of Mrs. Cleveland, who discovers the secret of her father's life as she is going through his papers while he is slowly dying. John Durn, her father, a self-made, immensely rich man, has been motivated by the "hurt" he suffered when his wife praised his partner, Gilson, as a better businessman and man than himself. Durn's jealous rage makes him vengeful the rest of his life against his partner, wife, daughter, son-in-law, and grandchild. Ignorant of Durn's animosity and the cause of his emotional failures, Gilson defends Durn to his daughter, Mrs. Cleveland. However, with the revelations Durn's papers supply, she realizes that her father has essentially thrown away his personal life and spoiled the lives of others to assuage his "hurt feelings." With this knowledge, Mrs. Cleveland plans to save her son and to effect a reconciliation between herself and her husband, whom her father had seen as a rival years before and sent away with a lifelong stipend.

What is new here is Wescott's attempt to break free from his midwestern settings and characters, from fictional masks for himself, and from the characteristic lyricism of his narrating voice. Further, the story is not drawn from family history, memories of his youth, or local legends, as were his earlier short stories and novels. "The Rescuer" (*Life and Letters Today*) and "The Sight of a Dead Body" (*Signatures*)—both published in autumn 1936—are also attempts to objectify external reality and provide aesthetic distance between the story and its informing voice and consciousness. However, in the two central figures of these latter stories, Martin Herz and Mi-

Wescott, circa 1927, the year before his only short-story collection was published

chael Byron, respectively, as well as in Mrs. Cleveland, Wescott did not completely succeed in developing new fictional voices, points of view, and techniques; at least he did not feel they were successful enough to pursue further.

The last short stories Wescott committed to print were "Mr. Auerbach in Paris" (April 1942) and "The Frenchman Six Foot Three" (July 1942), both in *Harper's*. These two stories may be taken as part of what Wescott called his "war work." This work began in 1932 with the publication of *Fear and Trembling*—a collection of impressionistic and sometimes mournful essays resulting from a trip through Europe—in which he hoped to alert American readers to the political realities of German nationalism, Nazism, and impending war. His "war work" was completed with *Apartment in Athens*, a popular novel dealing with the German occupation of Greece, particularly the billeting of a German officer in an Athenian household. Between these two books were the short stories of 1942, meant to be useful as explanations of ruthless German power victimizing a weaker but aesthetically and sagaciously more valuable France.

Both short stories employ Alwyn Tower as participating narrator, the fictional persona Wescott used in *The Grandmothers* and *The Pilgrim Hawk*. Each of these essaylike short stories was born of Wescott's conviction at the time that literary work should be relevant to a world at war, and each is meant to render truths central to an understanding of France and Nazi Germany. In "Mr. Auerbach in Paris" the title character is an aged German Jew who, while visiting Paris in 1923, voices his admiration for Germany to Tower, his youthful companion. Auerbach's literal shortsightedness and eventual blindness before his death symbolize Wescott's opinion of Auerbach's blind admiration of German nationalism, power, and efficiency. Because of its 1923 setting the story gains ironic force, given the experience of German power as well as the fate of European Jews by 1942. Although both the elderly Auerbach and youthful Tower admire Paris, Auerbach claims that Paris would be greater had Germany won it in World War I, because France "is a sensual, effeminate, idle, decadent nation," in contrast to the "virile" and "self-sacrificing" Germany. However, at the end of the story, Tower offers the correcting view: without the humanizing influences and forces represented by French culture, "humankind would be cut in half " and life scarcely worth living.

In "The Frenchman Six Foot Three," set in 1938 but narrated from the perspective of 1942, Wescott arranges the details of the story so as to evoke an odd, tragic atmosphere presaging the defeat of France. Tower's friend, an outsized and effete Frenchman, ridiculous in a uniform several sizes too small for him, is about to embark on a fortnight's military service. Pathetically comic and fretful, he symbolizes a weak and unprepared France. The elegiac tone and tender concern that pervade the story betray Wescott's sentiments. He is like a lover defending a paramour whose weaknesses are somehow more endearing than her virtues. As Tower bids farewell to his departing friend, one senses that the departure is a prologue to defeat. This notion is confirmed when the French soldier returns from his brief duty and confides to Tower the weakness of the French military and the inadequacy of the Maginot Line. The truth must be told, the Frenchman insists, and America must be prepared to help. Tower is pressed to carry this message home. Less didactic than the previous story, or the war novel to follow, this story is meant to convey Wescott's ironic yet sympathetic perceptions of one particular Frenchman as a suggestive emblem of France's dilemma prior to her fall.

After 1942 Wescott published in a variety of forms other than the short story. Most frequently he resorted to the lyric essay, a form that liberated him from fictional narrators and points of view, from armature of plot, setting, and action, and from the burden of dialogue, never one of Wescott's writing strengths. The lyric essay permitted Wescott to exploit his talent for poetic, graceful prose—brilliant images and rich evocations of mood and feeling, which distinctively characterize all his writing. Although his works are limited in number in any one form, Wescott attained distinction whether in fiction, poetry, or essay—and even in his only libretto for a ballet, "The Dream of Audubon." In his sixteen short stories, especially those published from 1924 to 1928, Wescott demonstrated the poetic possibilities and dimensions of the form, and he sometimes attained and rendered the elusive truths he sought.

Bibliographies:

Sy M. Kahn, "Glenway Wescott: A Bibliography," *Bulletin of Bibliography*, 22 (September-November 1958): 156-160;

Kahn, "Glenway Wescott," in *A Bibliographical Guide to Midwestern Literature*, edited by Gerald Nemanic (Iowa City: University of Iowa Press, 1981), pp. 348-350.

Biographies:

Sy M. Kahn, "Glenway Wescott: A Critical and Biographical Study," Ph.D. dissertation, University of Wisconsin, 1957;

Bruce Brawer, "Glenway Wescott, 1901-1987," *New Criterion*, 5 (May 1987): 36-45.

References:

Ira D. Johnson, *Glenway Wescott: The Paradox of Voice* (Port Washington, N.Y. & London: Kennikat, 1971);

Sy M. Kahn, "Glenway Wescott: The Artist at Work," *Papers on English Language and Literature*, 1 (Summer 1965): 250-258;

Kahn, "Glenway Wescott's Variations on the Waste Land Image," in *The Twenties: Fiction, Poetry, Drama*, edited by Warren French (De Land, Fla.: Everett/Edwards, 1975), pp. 171-179;

Patrick R. Quinn, "The Case History of Glenway Wescott," *Frontier and Midland*, 19 (1938-1939): 11-16;

Jerry Rosco, "An American Feud, Wescott and Hemingway," *Lost Generation Journal*, 9 (Spring-Summer 1989): 28-29;

Rosco, "An American Treasure: Glenway Wescott's *The Pilgrim Hawk*," *Literary Review*, 31 (Winter 1988): 133-142;

William H. Rueckert, *Glenway Wescott* (New York: Twayne, 1965);

C. E. Schorer, "The Maturing of Glenway Wescott," *College English*, 18 (March 1957): 320-326;

Morton D. Zabel, "The Whisper of the Devil," in his *Craft and Character in Modern Fiction* (New York: Viking, 1957), pp. 304-308.

Papers:

Original manuscripts of Wescott's works are collected at the New York City Public Library. An archive of his unpublished manuscripts and letters is at Yale University.

Ben Ames Williams
(7 March 1889 - 4 February 1953)

Philip Stevick
Temple University

BOOKS: *All the Brothers Were Valiant* (New York: Macmillan, 1919; London: Mills & Boon, 1920);

The Sea Bride (New York: Macmillan, 1919; London: Mills & Boon, 1920);

The Great Accident (New York: Macmillan, 1920; London: Mills & Boon, 1920);

Evered (New York: Dutton, 1921; London: Mills & Boon, 1921);

Black Pawl (New York: Dutton, 1922; London: Mills & Boon, 1922);

Thrifty Stock, and Other Stories (New York: Dutton, 1923);

Sangsue (London: Mills & Boon, 1923);

Audacity (New York: Dutton, 1924);

The Whaler (Garden City, N.Y.: Garden City Publishing, 1924);

The Rational Hind (New York: Dutton, 1925; London: Mills & Boon, 1925);

The Silver Forest (New York: Dutton, 1926; London: Mills & Boon, 1927);

Immortal Longings (New York: Dutton, 1927);

Splendor (New York: Dutton, 1927; London: Mills & Boon, 1928);

The Dreadful Night (New York: Dutton, 1928; London: Paul, 1928);

Death on Scurvy Street (New York: Dutton, 1929); republished as *The Bellmer Mystery* (London: Paul, 1930);

Touchstone (New York: Dutton, 1930; London: Paul, 1930);

Great Oaks (New York: Dutton, 1930; London: Paul, 1931);

An End to Mirth (New York: Dutton, 1931);

Pirate's Purchase (New York: Dutton, 1931);

Honeyflow (New York: Dutton, 1932);

Money Musk (New York: Dutton, 1932); republished as *Lady in Peril* (New York: Popular Library, 1948);

Pascal's Mill (New York: Dutton, 1933);

Mischief (New York: Dutton, 1933);

Hostile Valley (New York: Dutton, 1934); republished as *Valley Vixen* (New York: Avon, 1948);

Ben Ames Williams, circa 1933

Small Town Girl (New York: Dutton, 1935);

Charles Bismark Ames: In Memoriam (Greenwich, Conn.: Conde Nast, 1936);

Crucible (Boston: Houghton Mifflin, 1937);

The Strumpet Sea (Boston: Houghton Mifflin, 1938); republished as *Once Aboard the Whaler* (London: Hale, 1939);

Thread of Scarlet (Boston: Houghton Mifflin, 1939; London: Hale, 1940);

The Happy End (New York: Derrydale, 1939);

Come Spring (Boston: Houghton Mifflin, 1940);

The Strange Woman (Boston: Houghton Mifflin, 1941);

Deep Waters (Chicago: Western Newspaper Union, 1942);

Time of Peace: September 26, 1930 - December 7, 1941 (Boston: Houghton Mifflin, 1942);

Leave Her to Heaven (Boston: Houghton Mifflin, 1944; London: Hale, 1946);

It's a Free Country (Boston: Houghton Mifflin, 1945);

House Divided (Boston: Houghton Mifflin, 1947);

Fraternity Village (Boston: Houghton Mifflin, 1949);

Owen Glen (Boston: Houghton Mifflin, 1950);

The Unconquered (Boston: Houghton Mifflin, 1953).

OTHER: "They Grind Exceeding Small," in *O. Henry Memorial Award Prize Stories*, edited by Blanche Colton Williams (Garden City, N.Y.: Doubleday, Page, 1919), pp. 42-55;

A. L. McCorrison, *Letters from Fraternity*, edited by Williams (New York: Dutton, 1931);

Amateurs at War; the American Soldier in Action, edited by Williams (Boston: Houghton Mifflin, 1943);

Mary Boykin Chesnut, *A Diary from Dixie*, edited by Williams (Boston: Houghton Mifflin, 1949).

SELECTED PERIODICAL PUBLICATIONS—
UNCOLLECTED:
FICTION

"The Wings of Lias," *Smith's Magazine*, 21 (July 1915): 641-652;

"Deep Stuff," *Popular Magazine*, 37 (23 August 1915): 201-207;

"Worth a Leg," *All-Story Weekly*, 60 (29 July 1916): 736-744;

"The Mate of the Susie Oakes," *Saturday Evening Post*, 189 (14 April 1917): 71, 75, 79, 82;

"The Squealer," *Collier's*, 59 (1 September 1917): 15-17, 24, 26;

"Steve Scaevola," *Saturday Evening Post*, 190 (24 November 1917): 13-15, 37-38, 40;

"A Charge to Keep," *Country Gentleman*, 83 (26 January 1918): 6; (2 February 1918): 20; (16 February 1918): 18; (23 February 1918): 17;

"The Ninth Part of a Hair," *Saturday Evening Post*, 191 (7 June 1919): 18-19, 54, 56, 59, 61;

"Not a Drum Was Heard," *Collier's*, 65 (12 June 1920): 5-7, 32;

"The Gem of the Collection," *Munsey's*, 72 (February 1921): 77-88;

"Jeshurun Waxed Fat," *Century*, 102 (September 1921): 723-730;

"The Man Who Lied," *Collier's*, 69 (15 April 1922): 7-8, 21;

"One Crowded Hour," *Saturday Evening Post*, 194 (6 May 1922): 5-7, 134, 136-138;

"A Threefold Cord," *Saturday Evening Post*, 195 (19 May 1923): 10, 107, 110;

"Fox Bog," *Saturday Evening Post*, 196 (1 September 1923): 8-9, 108, 113;

"The Wine of Violence," *Ladies' Home Journal*, 41 (May 1924): 28;

"Valor," *Saturday Evening Post*, 197 (30 August 1924): 5, 40, 42, 44;

"The Missing Attribute," *Saturday Evening Post*, 197 (18 October 1924): 8-9, 101-102, 104;

"The Ancient Landmark," *Saturday Evening Post*, 197 (27 December 1924): 3-5, 60, 62, 65-66, 71-72;

"The Palsied Eld," *Saturday Evening Post*, 197 (21 February 1925): 20-21, 52, 57;

"The Silver Sword," *Saturday Evening Post*, 197 (30 May 1925): 3-4, 73-74, 76, 78, 80, 83 (6 June 1925): 36-40, 142, 145-146, 148, 151;

"Scapegoat," *Saturday Evening Post*, 198 (7 November 1925): 10-11, 66, 71-72;

"Stave Stuff," *Saturday Evening Post*, 198 (19 December 1925): 8-9, 138, 140;

"The Nurse," *Harper's*, 152 (April 1926): 549-557;

"The Body Blow," *Saturday Evening Post*, 198 (1 May 1926): 24-25, 134, 139;

"More Precious Than Rubies," *Saturday Evening Post*, 199 (29 January 1927): 10-11, 157-158, 162;

"Old Loving-Kindness," *Saturday Evening Post*, 199 (2 April 1927): 18-19, 66, 71;

"A Tangled Web," *Saturday Evening Post*, 199 (30 April 1927): 10-11, 58, 63;

"A Net of Circumstances," *Saturday Evening Post*, 199 (28 May 1927): 3-5, 105-106; (4 June 1927): 40-42, 93, 95, 98, 103;

"Red Hair," *Collier's*, 80 (2 July 1927): 13;

"A Case in Point," *Saturday Evening Post*, 200 (30 July 1927): 20-21, 102, 105, 107, 109-110;

"As a Man Speaketh," *Saturday Evening Post*, 200 (17 September 1927): 30-31, 156, 161-162;

"Habit," *Collier's*, 80 (1 October 1927): 11;

"The Uses of Inquiry," *Saturday Evening Post*, 200 (22 October 1927): 3-5, 156, 158, 161, 163; (29 October 1927): 20-21, 54, 56, 59, 61; (5 November 1927): 38-40, 92, 94, 99, 102;

"The Good Girl," *Saturday Evening Post*, 200 (18 February 1928): 10-11, 126, 128, 131;

"General Delivery," *Saturday Evening Post*, 200 (31 March 1928): 12-13, 58, 63, 65-66;

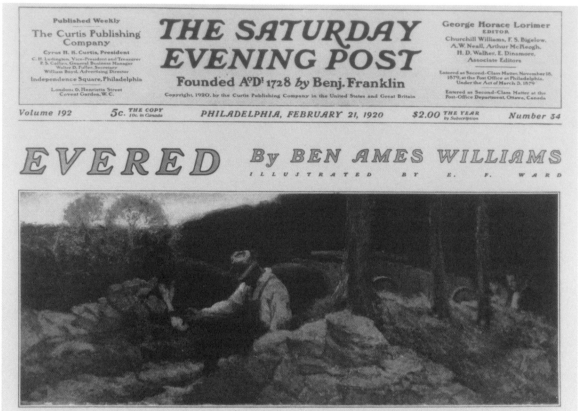

Illustration for the first installment of a long story serialized in the Saturday Evening Post *(21 February - 6 March 1920) and published as a book (1921). It was one of thirty-five serials Williams placed in the* Post, *the magazine in which most of his short fiction appeared.*

"The Premeditated Prodigal," *Saturday Evening Post*, 200 (23 June 1928): 35-38, 134;

"The Rich Man's City," *Saturday Evening Post*, 201 (29 September 1928): 20-21, 83, 86, 91;

"Merrymeeting," *Saturday Evening Post*, 201 (12 January 1929): 28-30, 116, 118, 121;

"Cinderella by Request," *Saturday Evening Post*, 201 (13 April 1929): 10-11, 121, 124, 127;

"The Luck Cat," *Country Gentleman*, 94 (May 1929): 6;

"Tell It Not in Gath," *Saturday Evening Post*, 201 (25 May 1929): 14-15, 151, 154, 157;

"Preferred Lies," *Saturday Evening Post*, 202 (3 August 1929): 12-13, 90, 93-94;

"Touch," *Saturday Evening Post*, 202 (9 November 1929): 20-21, 171, 173, 176;

"Creatures of the Night," *American*, 109 (February 1930): 32-35, 97-100;

"The Arduous Art," *Saturday Evening Post*, 202 (3 May 1930): 6-7, 191, 193-194, 197;

"Lets and Hindrances," *Saturday Evening Post*, 202 (14 June 1930): 10-11, 164-166, 170;

"The Lie with Circumstance," *Saturday Evening Post*, 203 (2 August 1930): 35-36, 38, 40;

"Isaiah," *Saturday Evening Post*, 203 (13 June 1931): 16-17, 134-136;

"The Shape of Fear," *Saturday Evening Post*, 204 (22 August 1931): 8-9, 44-47;

"Whenas In Silks," *Saturday Evening Post*, 205 (31 December 1932): 10-11, 33-34;

"Adventure's End," *Saturday Evening Post*, 206 (5 August 1933): 5-7; (12 August 1933): 21; (19 August 1933): 20-21;

"Balance All," *Saturday Evening Post*, 206 (24 February 1934): 14-15, 66-67, 69;

"A Bit of Gallantry," *Saturday Evening Post*, 206 (9 June 1934): 18-19, 128, 130, 132;

"The Idolater," *Saturday Evening Post*, 207 (11 May 1935): 42, 75-76, 78, 81;

"His Public," *Saturday Evening Post*, 208 (26 October 1935): 14-15, 57, 59;

"As Big a Fool . . . ," *Liberty*, 13 (18 April 1936): 46-50;

"The Outsider," *Saturday Evening Post*, 209 (11 July 1936): 14-15, 42, 45, 48;

"A Matter of Timing," *Collier's*, 98 (19 December 1936): 14-15, 28;

"The High Heart," *Saturday Evening Post*, 210 (25 December 1937): 18-19, 42-45;

"Dan'l Come to Judgment," *Saturday Evening Post*, 210 (9 April 1938): 10-11, 106-110;

"Day of Rest," *Saturday Evening Post*, 211 (29 April 1939): 18-19, 77, 80-82.

NONFICTION

"How to Recognize a Short Story," *Writer*, 41 (April 1929): 102-103;

"The Short Short Story," *Writer*, 46 (November 1934): 389-391;

"Thinking Up a Story," *Writer*, 49 (June 1936): 14;

"The Happy Ending," *Writer*, 54 (October 1940): 291-292;

"Ben Ames Williams Discusses His Work," *Philadelphia Record, Spring Books Supplement* (30 March 1941): 8;

"Fiction's Fourth Dimension," *Saturday Review of Literature*, 31 (16 October 1948): 8-9, 32-33.

Ben Ames Williams's accounts of himself are so charmingly self-deprecatory that others, writing about him, tend to echo the tone. He never thought of himself as a natural writer or an enduring one and always emphasized both his doggedness as a writer and his fondness for simple pleasures—family, bridge, travel, and the outdoors. Consequently words such as "uncomplicated" and "amiable" recur in reviews of his work, words which are at once true and unfortunate, obscuring his achievement and craft. He was not only one of the best-known writers of his time, he was also very good at what he did. Working within the limits of magazine fiction in his short stories, he was a master of its formulas. Yet he strained against those limits quite unselfconsciously, producing a body of stories that extended the contours of the magazine fiction of his time; his stories are subtle, sharply observed, graceful, and seemingly effortless, tending again and again toward the sketch rather than the plotted story and creating an ethic and a sense of place that is often pastoral and atavistic but by no means facile and superficial. Apparently innocent of the art fiction of his time, he wrote, nonetheless, a body of stories with their own implicit claim to seriousness.

Williams was born in Macon, Mississippi, on 7 March 1889. His grandfather had emigrated from Wales about 1835, settling in rural southern Ohio, where his father, Daniel Webster Williams, was born in 1862. Educated at Ohio University in Athens, Daniel Williams there met Sarah Mar-

shall Ames, whom he married in 1887. After their marriage, Ben Ames Williams's parents lived briefly in Macon, moving to Jackson, Ohio, when he was a few months old. Later Williams would recall his early childhood with fondness, remembering especially the mutual interest of parents and child in the world of books and, as he grew older, his involvement—as printer's devil, typesetter, pressman, and sometimes reporter—with the *Jackson Standard Journal*, which his father owned and edited. Williams attended grammar school and a year of high school in Jackson, studied with a tutor for a year in Cardiff, Wales, where his father was U.S. consul, and then entered Dartmouth, graduating in 1910.

In the fall of that year, he began as a reporter for the *Boston American* and soon wrote his first short story, which was rejected. Thus began his long and frustrating apprenticeship, during which he wrote over eighty stories, attempting various permutations of style and plot, emulating Robert Louis Stevenson, Guy de Maupassant, Rudyard Kipling, O. Henry, Honoré de Balzac, and Bret Harte, even laboriously translating from the French Georges Polti's plot manual *Thirty-Six Dramatic Situations* (originally published in 1895). Finally, after four years, Charles Agnew MacLean, the general editor for Street and Smith magazines, accepted "The Wings of Lias," which he published in *Smith's Magazine* (July 1915). Meanwhile, in September 1912, Williams had married Florence Talpey, daughter of an English mother and a Yankee sea captain, graduate of Wellesley, and devoted believer in his potential talent. They eventually had two sons and a daughter: Roger, Ben, and Penelope.

In the two years following his first acceptance, the proportion of rejected stories far outweighed the published ones. Yet Williams's work had begun to appear regularly in such pulps as *Smith's, Popular Magazine, All-Story Weekly*, and *American Boy*. And he had begun to attract the respectful notice of the editors. Within two years of his first publication, two events permanently altered the nature of his career. First, he had a story accepted by the *Saturday Evening Post* ("The Mate of the Susie Oakes," 14 April 1917). It proved to be the first of some 135 stories of his (along with thirty-five serials and seven articles) published by the *Post* over twenty-four years, and it marked his transition from the pulps to the well-respected, mass-circulation magazines. Second, he resigned from the *American*, becoming a full-time professional writer and living in Chestnut

Florence Talpey Williams with the Williams children at their home in Chestnut Hill, Massachusetts, circa 1933

Hill, Massachusetts. As he put it himself, "since then except for three months in the Fox lot in Hollywood I have never drawn a salary."

By 1919 he had achieved the success for which he had worked so long. Four stories and one eight-part serial appeared in the *Saturday Evening Post*. Other publications in which his work appeared for that year read like a roster of the "slicks" of the period: *American, Munsey's, Collier's, Blue Book, People's Home Journal,* and *Redbook*. That year there were twenty stories in magazines, conversions of several serials into books and movies, and the selection of two of his stories of 1919 for inclusion in several anthologies.

Although he became identified in later years with rural Maine because so many of his stories were set there, his settings and themes were from the start quite various. What unites the early stories is his common concern with story values, the rhythms and energies of an efficient plot. Williams seems never to have thought of his

transition from the pulps to the slicks as a liberation into the possibility of a wider range of forms. But that was the effect, since publication in magazines such as the *Saturday Evening Post* permitted him a greater length, if he so chose, with the possibility of serialization over several issues, and it afforded him the luxury of a more sophisticated audience, with a consequent relaxation of the compulsions of plot and a richer play of character and place.

"They Grind Exceeding Small" (*Saturday Evening Post*, 13 September 1919) shows the effects of such a transition. The story's plot, surprising at the end, has a "turn" in the O. Henry manner, is somewhat mechanical in its irony, and conveys a morality that can only seem facile to a reader now. But the story grows, develops, and gathers force in a manner so leisurely and lyrical that no editor of the pulps would have tolerated it. The story opens with a persuasive sense of winter landscape and the culture of the far North. The central character appears, laconic and coarse, so that he seems a feature of that frozen world, as Williams develops, meanwhile, an ironic narrator who is at once of the world he describes and apart from it. Williams's instinct for small, expressive gestures is as infallible as his ear for the nuances of colloquial speech. And so as the story draws to a close, the working out of the plot seems less important than the integration of personality and setting. In 1919 Blanche Colton Williams edited the first of many annual collections called *O. Henry Memorial Award Prize Stories*. "They Grind Exceeding Small" was one of the fifteen stories selected, and with good reason. It is an artful, knowing story, displaying the maturity of craft that Williams had attained in the little-more-than-four years of his career as a published short-story writer.

In the twenty years following, the range of Williams's publications was extraordinary—they appeared in *Country Gentleman* and *Snappy Stories*, *Cosmopolitan* and *Railroad Man's Weekly*, *Liberty* and *Elks Magazine*. But it was the *Saturday Evening Post* that dominated his career. Although he never had a contract, it was his custom to submit his stories to the *Post* first. And it was in his alternating success and failure in pleasing the two dominant editors of the *Post*, George Horace Lorimer and Thomas B. Costain, that Williams charted his own career.

In 1918 Williams had chanced to vacation in Searsmont, a rural town in Maine, where he eventually bought Hardscrabble, a summer home, and where he met a local farmer, A. L. McCorrison, with whom he formed a friendship that lasted until the latter's death in 1931. The two hunted, fished, and tramped the woods but most of all exchanged stories. It was through McCorrison that Williams began to know the past of the region and the special quality of life there. Writing in 1924, Williams recalled the way in which his growing affection for rural Maine had come to provide a basis for much of his fiction: "Four or five years ago I came to believe that a background familiar to the reader makes a story richer; with this in mind I began to center many tales in a single locality." (McCorrison himself was the model for the character Chet McAusland in many of the tales.) Thus began Williams's long series of some 125 stories set in the fictional town of Fraternity, the first of which ("Another Man's Poison") was published in *Collier's* on 6 December 1919 and many of which were published in the *Saturday Evening Post*. Twelve of the stories, includ-

ing "Another Man's Poison," were collected in *Fraternity Village* (1949). Although the social and geographical microcosm of Fraternity came to have a considerable appeal for Lorimer and the readers of the *Post*, Williams's tales tended to be leisurely, long on details of character and locale, and short on plot. Lorimer often resisted, but he often accepted them, too. In his introduction to *Fraternity Village*, Williams recalled such interactions with Lorimer: "During the years when *The Post* was a regular purchaser, Mr. Lorimer once suggested that I inject more plot into the Fraternity stories. I told him I preferred to write what I chose, and that he was free to buy what he chose. After that conversation he continued to buy stories of character—and to reject stories so full of plot that it spilled out of every paragraph." It was the Fraternity stories upon which Williams's contemporary fame came to rest; and insofar as he is remembered now, it is likely to be for those stories.

"The Eftest Way" (*Saturday Evening Post*, 6 November 1926; in *Fraternity Village*) shows the full range of Williams's craft. The story opens with a witty and affectionate description of the wisdom and convictions of Chet McAusland: "One learns that if Chet says a thing is true he but means that it was, on one occasion which he witnessed, true; it is hard to convince him that the times may change." For three pages, Williams spins anecdotal variations on the peculiar sagacity and dislocated time sense of Chet. "This introduction," Williams writes, "is devious and wandering and with no point at all, but many of Chet's tales are of this fashion." Of course, Williams, seeming rather apologetically to report Chet's habit of mind, has mimed his rural, discursive manner, adopted his rhythms, and gotten inside his way of organizing the world. The story turns to Uncle Joe, an old friend of Chet's, now dead, and again the mind of Chet governs the form, as the story moves through anecdotes of Joe as drinker, cardplayer, hunter, fisherman, and consumer of his wife's incomparable cooking. By now ten pages have passed and nothing has "happened," except that the narrative has transported readers into a mental landscape dominated by certain deeply felt pleasures, almost randomly assembled, and devoid of the purposeful "linearity" attractive to readers of the *Saturday Evening Post*. At this point Chet mentions, without much emphasis, Uncle Joe's expectation that he himself would die, naturally and happily, while hunting. After a passage on the infirmities that eventually overtook Uncle

Illustration by F. R. Gruger for the first part of one of Williams's last stories, later collected in Fraternity Village *(1949). After the publication of* Come Spring *in 1940, he devoted his writing time almost exclusively to work on novels.*

Joe, Chet and Williams come to "the ending of the tale," an amusing transition since up to that point there has been no "tale" at all. The last pages move effortlessly between the narrator's description of Chet and Uncle Joe hunting and Chet's own words, evoking an idyll. There is the hunt, done in loving detail; the two hunters separate; there are two shots from the direction Uncle Joe has walked; and Chet discovers Uncle Joe dead of natural causes, having just killed two birds. The appeal of the story for its audience is obvious: it renders a simpler world than almost any reader was likely to know, developing with great tenderness the bonds between man and earth, and man and man. The integrity of the story is less obvious but no less striking; it consists of Williams's discovery of the discursive, associative form that expresses superbly the imagination of his central character.

In 1926 Williams published twenty-one stories in the *Saturday Evening Post* and a handful of stories elsewhere. By the 1930s, however, his position as a writer of short fiction had diminished, partly because the world around him had changed and partly because he chose to withdraw gradually from the marketplace of magazine fiction. As the country sank into the Depression, the size of the *Post* was reduced to roughly a third of its size a decade before. It published less of everything, including fiction, a practice followed by all the large-circulation magazines.

Meanwhile, the editors, and presumably the public, had developed a taste for shorter and shorter fiction, "short shorts," as *Collier's* began to call them. "Stories are becoming shorter and shorter as the big weeklies more and more imitate the picture magazines," as Williams told Robert Van Gelder. "They'll all be down to one word on a page one of these days." Williams's stories were often rejected during the 1930s, and when they were accepted it was often with the provision that they be radically cut.

Looking back on that period, Williams several times reflected on the dangers to his talent in continuing to confine his imagination to the limits of the magazine story and on the seductions of easy money from Hollywood. He had had several lucrative movie adaptations. His imagination grew more expansive and he wished to try new directions, which necessarily meant, for him, fiction of novel length. So at the end of the 1930s he set out to do what he had not done before, namely to write a book. Always before, his books had been conversions of magazine stories or serials into book form. But in 1940 he published *Come Spring*, a novel of domestic life during the Revolutionary War, set in Maine.

In the remaining years of his career, there were nonfiction pieces for the magazines but very few stories. Instead Williams gave his energy in the last thirteen years of his life to novels, of which the best known are *The Strange Woman* (1941), *Leave Her to Heaven* (1944), *House Divided* (1947), and *Owen Glen* (1950). *House Divided* was his most sustained labor, a huge novel of some fifteen hundred pages, meticulously researched and intended to show the relationship between the events of the Civil War and their effects on a representative cast of characters. *Leave Her to Heaven* was his most widely read novel, a best-seller for many weeks, translated into Spanish, Portuguese, German, French, Czech, Norwegian, and Hebrew. Still at the peak of his career, just having finished *The Unconquered* (1953), a sequel to *House Divided*, Williams died of a heart attack during a curling match at Brookline, Massachusetts, on 4 February 1953.

Williams's stories are not likely to be anthologized again or widely read. Their style and structure must seem out of touch with what readers now take to be the possibilities of short fiction. He began his career, after all, in the age of O. Henry. He took as his models the great nineteenth-century realists—Maupassant, Stevenson, Balzac, and Tolstoy. And for all of the pres-sures of a difficult environment and the conflicts of strong personalities that his stories portray, his fiction still represents the bouyant, life-embracing view of experience that was his in life. Yet a reader of Williams's fiction now would be likely to feel the energies of style and craft that made Lorimer accept his "sketches" in spite of himself. The best of the stories create a myth of the human spirit in a difficult world; they are pastoral but strenuous, at once hedonistic and rigorously moral, and carry conviction even now.

Interview:

Robert Van Gelder, *Writers and Writing* (New York: Scribners, 1946), pp. 339-342.

Bibliographies:

Richard Cary, "Ben Ames Williams in Books," *Colby Library Quarterly*, 6 (September 1963): 293-302;

Cary, "Ben Ames Williams in Periodicals and Newspapers," *Colby Library Quarterly*, 9 (September 1972): 599-615;

Cary, "Ben Ames Williams in the *Saturday Evening Post*," *Colby Library Quarterly*, 10 (December 1973): 223-230.

Biographies:

Florence Talpey Williams, "About Ben Ames Williams," *Colby Library Quarterly*, 6 (September 1963): 263-277;

Richard Cary, "Ben Ames Williams and Robert H. Davis: The Seedling in the Sun," *Colby Library Quarterly*, 6 (September 1963): 302-327;

Ben Ames Williams, Jr., "House United," *Colby Library Quarterly*, 10 (December 1973): 179-189;

Cary, "Ben Ames Williams and the *Saturday Evening Post*," *Colby Library Quarterly*, 10 (December 1973): 190-222.

Reference:

Joseph B. Yokelson, "Ben Ames Williams: Pastoral Moralist," *Colby Library Quarterly*, 6 (September 1963): 278-292.

Papers:

A substantial collection of Williams's manuscripts, correspondence, journals, and memorabilia is housed at the Colby College Library, Waterville, Maine. Lesser collections of Williams material are in the Dartmouth College Library and with the Ohioana Library Association in Columbus.

Thomas Wolfe
(3 October 1900 - 15 September 1938)

Ladell Payne
Randolph-Macon College

See also the Wolfe entries in *DLB 9: American Novelists, 1910-1945; DLB Documentary Series 2; and DLB Yearbook: 1985.*

BOOKS: *Look Homeward, Angel* (New York: Scribners, 1929; London: Heinemann, 1930);

Of Time and the River (New York: Scribners, 1935; London: Heinemann, 1935);

From Death to Morning (New York: Scribners, 1935; London: Heinemann, 1935);

The Story of a Novel (New York & London: Scribners, 1936; London: Heinemann, 1936);

The Web and the Rock (New York & London: Harper, 1939; London & Toronto: Heinemann, 1947);

You Can't Go Home Again (New York & London: Harper, 1940; London & Toronto: Heinemann, 1947);

The Hills Beyond (New York & London: Harper, 1941);

Gentlemen of the Press [play] (Chicago: Black Archer, 1942);

A Stone, A Leaf, A Door: Poems, edited by John S. Barnes (New York: Scribners, 1945);

Mannerhouse: A Play in a Prologue and Three Acts (New York: Harper, 1948; London: Heinemann, 1950); revised and edited by Louis D. Rubin, Jr., and John L. Idol, Jr. (Baton Rouge & London: Louisiana State University Press, 1985);

A Western Journal: A Daily Log of the Great Parks Trip (Pittsburgh: University of Pittsburgh Press, 1951);

The Short Novels of Thomas Wolfe, edited by C. Hugh Holman (New York: Scribners, 1961);

Thomas Wolfe's Purdue Speech: "Writing and Living," edited by William Braswell and Leslie A. Field (West Lafayette, Ind.: Purdue University Studies, 1964);

The Mountains [play], edited by Pat M. Ryan (Chapel Hill: University of North Carolina Press, 1970);

The Notebooks of Thomas Wolfe, 2 volumes, edited by Richard S. Kennedy and Paschal Reeves

North Carolina Collection, University of North Carolina Library

(Chapel Hill: University of North Carolina Press, 1970);

Welcome to Our City: A Play in Ten Scenes, edited by Kennedy (Baton Rouge & London: Louisiana State University Press, 1983);

K-19: Salvaged Pieces, edited by Idol (Athens, Ohio & Columbia, S.C.: Thomas Wolfe Society/Bryan, 1983);

The Autobiography of an American Novelist, edited by Leslie Field (Cambridge, Mass. & London: Harvard University Press, 1983)—comprises original, uncut versions of *The Story of a Novel* and *Thomas Wolfe's Purdue Speech: "Writing and Living"*;

The Hound of Darkness, edited by Idol (Athens, Ohio: Thomas Wolfe Society, 1986);

The Complete Short Stories of Thomas Wolfe, edited by Francis E. Skipp (New York: Scribners, 1987).

Collections: *The Portable Thomas Wolfe*, edited by Maxwell Geismar (New York: Viking, 1946); republished as *Selections from the Works of Thomas Wolfe* (London: Heinemann, 1952);

The Thomas Wolfe Reader, edited by C. Hugh Holman (New York: Scribners, 1962);

OTHER: *The Return of Buck Gavin*, in *Carolina Folk-Plays*, edited by Frederick H. Koch (New York: Holt, 1924), pp. 31-44.

Best known for his four novels—*Look Homeward, Angel* (1929); *Of Time and The River* (1935); *The Web and The Rock* (1939); and *You Can't Go Home Again* (1940)—Thomas Wolfe was also the author of an impressive body of short fiction, published in collections including *From Death to Morning* (1935), *The Hills Beyond* (1941), *The Short Novels of Thomas Wolfe* (1961), and *The Complete Short Stories of Thomas Wolfe* (1987). Much of Wolfe's short fiction is of a piece with that published in longer form: it is autobiographical in nature and poetic in impulse, and it depicts Wolfe's vision of human isolation and estrangement. Unlike the longer fiction, the shorter works demonstrate Wolfe's increased ability in his later years to impose order and form upon his materials. Indeed, the artistic merit of some of his novellas exceeds that of any of the novels, with the possible exception of *Look Homeward, Angel*.

Thomas Clayton Wolfe was born on 3 October 1900 in Asheville, North Carolina; he was the youngest of William O. and Julia Elizabeth Westall Wolfe's seven children. Wolfe's father was a tombstone cutter from Pennsylvania. Wolfe was a precocious student and entered the University of North Carolina at Chapel Hill before his sixteenth birthday. After graduating in 1920, he studied play writing at Harvard University and earned his M.A. in 1922. Unsuccessful in adapting an early play (*Welcome to Our City*, published in 1983) for staging by the New York Theater Guild, he taught English at the Washington

Square College of New York University from 1924 to 1930. In 1925, aboard ship returning from the first of five formative trips to Europe, Wolfe met Aline Bernstein, a married woman almost two decades his senior, who helped support him and with whom he formed the most important romantic attachment of his life. In 1928 he attracted the notice of Maxwell Perkins, the Scribners editor, who gave him the guidance he needed to organize and sift the material for *Look Homeward, Angel*. He left Washington Square College in 1930, after receiving a Guggenheim Fellowship and breaking up with Bernstein.

From 1930 to 1933 Wolfe wrote compulsively and produced the more than one million words from which he and Perkins assembled *Of Time and The River*. Although Perkins did no writing, he advised, counseled, and suggested revisions to Wolfe over a nine-month period in 1934 but sent the manuscript to press without permission, while Wolfe was on vacation. After *Of Time and The River* appeared in 1935, the year which also saw *From Death to Morning*, Wolfe received the kind of fame and acclaim accorded few living writers. But he also was stung by the criticism that he was too wordy, too autobiographical, and too dependent upon Perkins. In December 1937 he signed with a new publisher, Harper, and acquired a new editor, Edward Aswell. In May 1938 Wolfe left two large packing cases full of manuscripts with Aswell in what he described (in a 6 May 1938 letter to Aswell) as "the same state of articulation" as *Of Time and The River* when he and Perkins began working on it. From this material, Aswell assembled Wolfe's posthumous novels, *The Web and The Rock* and *You Can't Go Home Again*, and a volume of short stories, *The Hills Beyond*. Aswell, unfortunately, was not as scrupulous as Perkins, either in restraining his own pen or in maintaining the integrity of Wolfe's intent in assembling the material.

In 1938, while on a tour of the western national parks, Wolfe contracted miliary tuberculosis of the brain. He died on 15 September. He had never married or fathered any children.

From Death to Morning, Wolfe's first collection, is made up of thirteen short pieces and a major novella, "The Web of Earth" (*Scribner's*, July 1932). The collection was published eight months after *Of Time and The River* in an attempt to capitalize on the success of that work. Some of the stories in *From Death to Morning* are related to the Altamont materials of *Look Homeward, Angel;* some to the New York-Europe materials in *Of*

Wolfe's parents, W. O. and Julia Westall Wolfe, in 1900 (North Carolina Collection, University of North Carolina Library)

Time and The River; and others to the Old Catawba-New York materials of *The Web and the Rock.* The collection is the only one of Wolfe's books not to sell out its first edition (of seventy-five hundred copies printed, some one thousand were remaindered in 1940).

Dedicated to the memory of his brother Ben, who died at twenty-six, "and to the proud and bitter briefness of his days," the book's thematic focus is man's loneliness and isolation in life and the finality of his death. Somewhat like the sketches in Sherwood Anderson's *Winesburg, Ohio* (1919), most of Wolfe's stories are connected by the presence of a figure who is clearly the Eugene Gant of his first two novels. The stories move in tone from the bleak resignation of "No Door" (*Scribner's,* June 1933) to the celebration of life implicit in the concluding novella. Significantly, however, both the opening and conclud-

ing stories evoke the image of ships in the harbor, which might, but do not, offer escape from drowning in life's ultimate meaninglessness.

"No Door" opens with the narrator's direct affirmation of his sense of isolation and his ironic wonder at the wealthy and socially prominent who romantically long for a life of solitude like the one he lives in grubby South Brooklyn. Like Gant in *Look Homeward, Angel,* looking for "a stone, a leaf, a door," the narrator has made his visit to a fashionable Fifth Avenue apartment to find "a word . . . a wall . . . a door that you can enter—that this man is going to tell you" and escape from his isolation. But there is no door, and "the old unsearchable mystery of time and the city returns to overwhelm your spirit with the horrible sensation of defeat and drowning." Moreover, there is no direct communication possible between him and his host, although both are on the same quest. The narrator cannot tell his host (or the reader) what his particular experience of life is like. "You cannot, nor ever recapture the feeling of mystery, exultancy, and wild sorrow that you felt then. . . . Instead you just tell him about the place you live in. . . ." It is from knowing in some detail about the nameless narrator's home and the people there and relating this knowledge to one's own experience that the reader and host, paradoxically enough, are able to gain some understanding of the narrator's sense of the universality of human isolation. After a series of such vignettes, Wolfe makes his despairing judgment: "we are lying there, blind atoms in our cellar-depths, gray voiceless atoms in the manswarm desolation of the earth, and our fame is lost, our names forgotten, our powers are wasting from us like mined earth, while we lie here at evening and the river flows . . . and dark time is feeding like a vulture on our entrails, and we know that we are lost, and cannot stir . . . and there are ships there! there are ships! . . . and Christ! we are all dying in the darkness! . . . And that is a moment of dark time, that is one of strange million-visaged time's dark faces."

"Death the Proud Brother" (*Scribner's*, June 1933) continues the themes of death and isolation. In a Whitmanesque affirmation of his knowledge of and spiritual identity with "the strange and lonely crowd of men who prowl the night," the nameless narrator affirms his identification with proud Death, his stern brother Loneliness, and their great sister Sleep. Alluding to biographical events depicted in *Look Homeward, Angel* and *Of Time and The River*, the narrator says, "I had watched my brother and my father die in the dark mid-watches of the night, and I had known and loved the figure of proud Death when he had come."

The narrator then describes four deaths in New York City, three of them violent: an Italian cart peddler is killed by a truck; a professional bum trips drunkenly over an iron beam and smashes his skull; and a worker is knocked off a steel beam by a white-hot rivet. In each instance the sky, the city, and even individual people are alien and indifferent toward the death of human beings who, like themselves, wish to live. Like Gant in *Look Homeward, Angel* the narrator thinks of "how our lives touch every other life that ever lived"; like Gant in *Of Time and The River* the narrator sees the "man-swarm" to which humans collectively belong. His vision is existential: man lives in a meaningless universe, isolated within him-

self, with only the dignity and pride of death itself in contrast to the indifference of human life.

Wolfe's final example in the story is of a man who dies naturally on a subway bench, a death that stuns and bewilders those who witness it. Yet this man has no real distinction. He is "the composite photograph of the man-swarm atom. . . . His only distinction was that there was nothing to distinguish him from a million other men." In short he represents all people. By implication his great dignity in death can be shared by all, in the face of indifference.

The story concludes with a Whitmanesque paean of praise to "proud Death, stern Loneliness, and Sleep." For Death opens the "dark door for us who never yet found doors to enter"; Loneliness brings strength, hope, triumphant joy, and confidence; Sleep finds people naked, alone, and united in the heart of night and darkness, where they are dying. It heals with "dark forgetfulness." It is, indeed, a desirable mid state between the isolation of life and the oblivion of death.

The relatively brief "The Face of the War" (*Modern Monthly*, June 1935), which follows "Death the Proud Brother," presents four episodes drawn from Wolfe's World War I experiences in Newport News, some of which are described in the closing chapters of *Look Homeward, Angel*. (Wolfe had loaded ammunition and other cargo on the docks during the summer of 1918.) And like the moments of *Look Homeward, Angel*, which are the "fruit of forty thousand years" and thus "a window on all time," these episodes "are four moments from the face of the war." The narrator's window on that time opens not on the glory and carnage of battle but rather on the dehumanizing effect the war has had on those who have stayed at home. A black man is brutally clubbed by a shabby southern white man in a display of racial hatred. Three boys on an innocent evening's walk are cursed and driven away from Langley Field by a soldier on guard who shows cowardly fear and hatred. The workers at Newport News "are the human cinders of the earth" as they stand in line waiting to have their lusts served by haggard, exhausted women—one of whom the narrator recognizes as a girl from a humble, decent family in North Carolina. She, her fellow prostitutes, and the workers all belong among the small, lonely, and forsaken men and women who have lived and walked as strangers. They are pathetic and worthy of compassion.

The final episode differs from the first three by suggesting that man's sense of humor,

Wolfe at eighteen, playing the lead role in his first play, The
Return of Buck Gavin, *produced by the Carolina
Playmakers at Chapel Hill on 14 and 15 March 1919
(North Carolina Collection, University of North
Carolina Library)*

his sense of the ridiculous, helps him cope with
the war's—and life's—frustration and despair. A
white first lieutenant is exasperated beyond measure by black enlisted men in his command who
cannot provide clean bills of health as they embark for Europe. The situation is resolved by an
on-the-spot physical examination accompanied by
great grins from the enlisted men, faint grins
from the medical officer, and somewhat more gentle cursing from the lieutenant. The war's face,
while brutal, corrosive, dehumanizing, frustrating, and cruel, can also evoke compassion and
humor—human qualities that cannot be destroyed utterly even by war.

Wolfe continues to develop variations on his
dominant themes. In "Only the Dead Know Brooklyn" (*New Yorker*, 15 June 1935) a Brooklyn native
tells of his encounter with a giant of a young
man, who, incomprehensibly, is trying to learn
the whole of Brooklyn. The young giant, obviously a Wolfean self-portrait (Wolfe was close to
six foot five), compulsively asks about and re-
peats the word "drowning," which recalls a passage from "No Door" in which the young narra-

tor remembers "the sensation of drowning in a
sea of horror, a sea of blind, dateless, and
immemorable time. There is no door."

"Dark in the Forest, Strange as Time" (*Scribner's*, November 1934) opens another window on
human experience. This time the episode is from
the Gant-in-Germany material in *Of Time and The
River*. As the young narrator leaves Munich by
train, he observes a mortally ill Jew saying a fond
farewell to his vital, sensuous wife. Then, out of
the dying man's sight, the woman is seen in a passionate embrace with a younger man. As the narrator and the old Jew travel together across Ba-
varia, their journey becomes an emblem of both
the journey of life and the journey of death. The
American listens to the Jew reflect on the passage
of his life from his youthful desire to have everything to his present knowledge that "vun life,
vun place, vun time," is all that any man has. As
the train approaches its destination, the youth discovers that the Jew is dead and wonders if it is
not better "in this great dream of time in which
we live" to know that "there will be silence for us
all and silence only, nothing but silence, at the
end?"

The title of "The Four Lost Men" (*Scribner's*,
February 1934) refers to the former presidents
James Garfield, Chester Arthur, Benjamin Harrison, and Rutherford B. Hayes, who are no
longer imaginable by the sixteen-year-old narrator as having ever known the hunger and yearning of youth. They are lost to the narrator as
vital figures of life and exist as "strange, lost, time-
far, dead Americans . . . remote, voiceless, and be-
whiskered faces. . . ."

"Gulliver" (*Scribner's*, June 1935), a story in
which excessive height is emblematic of "strangeness," celebrates the extent to which the over-
sized man "understands that world, in all the joy
and pain and strangeness of its incommunicable
loneliness." It also affirms "a belief in man's fundamental goodness, kindliness, and humanity."
This sense of there being something fundamentally positive about humankind is extended in
"The Bums at Sunset" (*Vanity Fair*, October
1935), when the leader among five vagabonds pro-
tects the youngest of the group from being bul-
lied and is rewarded with a package of cigarettes.
Although both the man and the boy must still
face "the wild, cruel and lonely distances of America" alone, they can share a moment of kindness
each to the other.

"One of the Girls in Our Party," "The Far
and the Near," "In the Park," and "The Men of

Old Catawba" differ from the other stories in the collection in that the Eugene Gant/Thomas Wolfe persona is absent. The protagonist of "One of the Girls" (*Scribner's*, January 1935) is a not-very-bright young woman from the Midwest who is touring Europe with a group of her fellow public-school teachers. The banality of her soul is suggested by her confused understanding of what she has seen and the high value she places on Holland's cleanliness and on the tour guide's witless sallies. "The Far and the Near" (*Cosmopolitan*, July 1935—as "Cottage by the Tracks") depicts the pathos of a railroad engineer who, after years of waving to two women who live near the railroad, is filled with "bitter loss and grief" when he finds them far different than what he had expected. "In the Park" (*Harper's Bazaar*, June 1935) introduces Esther Jack, the Aline Bernstein figure of *The Web and The Rock* and *You Can't Go Home Again*, remembering how as an eighteen-year-old girl she had wanted to communicate with her father and could not find the words she wanted. "The Men of Old Catawba"—a combination of "Old Catawba" (*Virginia Quarterly Review*, April 1935) and "Polyphemus" (*North American Review*, June 1935)—is a descriptive set piece that might well have been written to introduce the world of George Webber, Wolfe's alter ego in *The Web and the Rock* and *You Can't Go Home Again*. It is less a story than a Faulknerian attempt to suggest a land and the people who have lived on it over time. There is even the Faulkner-like sentiment that "the earth is never 'taken possession of': it possesses." But the essence of the sketch is entirely Wolfean: "The history of Old Catawba is the history of millions of men living alone in the wilderness, it is the history of millions of men who have lived their brief lives in silence upon the everlasting earth, who have listened to the earth and known her million tongues, whose lives were given to the earth, whose bones and flesh are recompacted with the earth, the immense and terrible earth that makes no answer."

"Circus at Dawn" (*Modern Monthly*, March 1935) returns to the Eugene Gant of *Look Homeward, Angel*, who with his stuttering, "whah-whah"-laughing brother Luke, watches the circus workers, performers, and animals as they get ready. Paradoxically, even though the lives of the circus performers are radically different from their own, a sense of familiarity and affectionate intimacy exists between the boys and the performers. The fact that the feeling exists suggests a fur-

ther movement away from the bleak isolation depicted in the opening stories.

Recognized as one of Wolfe's greatest artistic accomplishments, "The Web of Earth" (ninety-two pages) concludes *From Death to Morning*. Written to suggest the unrelated digressions of a garrulous old woman, this novella reveals the mind, character, and life—the very soul—of Wolfe's great character and narrator Eliza Gant, Eugene's mother. The apparent irrelevancies are tied together within the experience of Eliza, and by the end readers are likely to agree with her and her husband, W. O. Gant, that life is "pretty strange when you come to think of it." The story is set in Eugene's New York apartment at some time after W. O.'s death. Eliza is remembering the past: "the year that the locusts came," the strange voices she heard, and the people she knew. Before she can tell of this experience, Eliza must tell of earlier memories—the return of the men from the Civil War, the appearance of the Yankee villains, the death of her father, and most important of all, her life with her previously married, generally unfaithful, extravagant, hard-drinking, cancer-ridden husband from the time she first met him until the time of his fatal illness. The emphasis throughout is on the sheer vitality of this couple: the man who gets roaring drunk in the hospital and the woman who embodies "the power of Nature," who has borne with "no more trouble than the earth takes bearing corn, all of the children," who makes things grow by "touchin' them," and who affirms in the face of economic disaster that "we've got the earth. . . . We've always got the earth. We'll stand upon it and it will save us." When the message of the voices is finally understood to be a prophecy of the birth of the twins Grover Cleveland and Benjamin Harrison Gant, the reader realizes with Eliza that there is a pattern of meaning in life and shares with her and W. O. the sense that "it's pretty strange when you come to think of it. . . . By God it is." Wolfe's unstated view is that despite the isolation, death, cruelty, frustration, and even despair he depicts, it is far better to live than not. From the despair of meaningless death one can celebrate the morning and affirm the value of living.

From Death to Morning was not only the sole collection of Wolfe's shorter pieces published before 1940, it was also the last fiction of any sort he personally prepared for publication. Edward Aswell "edited" the posthumously published *The Web and The Rock* and *You Can't Go Home Again*. De-

Revised galley proof for "The Web of Earth," a long story first published in Scribner's Magazine *(July 1932), then collected in* From Death to Morning *in 1935 (Houghton Library, Harvard University; by permission of Paul Gitlin, Administrator of the Estate of Thomas Wolfe)*

spite a contract stipulating that "no changes, additions, or alterations in the title or text" could be made without Wolfe's written consent, Aswell extensively modified the raw materials upon which these works were based through silent cuts, transpositioning, and substantial original writing. *The Hills Beyond* was assembled by Aswell from leftovers from Wolfe's mass of manuscripts and from pieces previously published. It contains

short stories (six of these from the Eugene Gant material), sketches, a short play, part of an incomplete novel entitled "The Hills Beyond," and a note by Aswell giving a misleading account of his role in editing Wolfe's posthumous works. Lacking those elements which give *From Death to Morning* its Winesburg-like sense of order, *The Hills Beyond* is partially redeemed by having saved "The Lost Boy" and "Chickamauga" from oblivion.

"The Lost Boy" (*Redbook*, November 1937), the collection's opening story, is an account of Grover Cleveland Gant, Ben's twin brother, who died of typhoid at the St. Louis exposition in *Look Homeward, Angel*, just as Grover Cleveland Wolfe had done in actuality. Divided into four parts, which correspond to four different points of view, the story first presents Grover shortly before his mother takes him to St. Louis. A small boy with his canvas newspaper bag, he is passing along the square in his hometown and observing "the union of Forever and of Now." He does not feel lost because the square—which includes his father's shop—"was the center of the universe . . . the eternal place where all things came and passed, and yet abode forever and would never change." It is the place where the injustice of a stingy merchant who cheated him of three cents can be rectified by a strong, protective father.

But this child's world cannot last. In section 2 the narrative is told by Eliza Gant to her now-adult son Eugene some thirty years later. She recalls the death of Grover, whose birth is described in "The Web of Earth." Clearly her favorite, Grover "surpassed the whole crowd" of her children in intelligence, energy, and worth. And even though he is dead and "nothing is the same as it was," she remembers the lost Grover just the way he looked that morning on the train to St. Louis.

The third section gives an account by Helen, an older sister, who remembers the youthful Grover, the three-year-old Eugene, and the other children in St. Louis at the fair. Helen tells of Grover's sudden serious illness and sees in her own way (just as have Eliza and Grover in their sections) that life, the past, and our dreams somehow all get lost—that the reality of the past is further away and stranger than if it had happened in a dream.

The final section is Eugene's account of his return to St. Louis as an adult to find memories of his lost brother. He locates the street, the two corners, even the very house where they stayed and where Grover died. He wants to recapture the past. For a moment the years drop off, and he remembers the face of his older brother trying to teach him to say "Grover" in that same house so long ago. He leaves knowing he will never come back again. He also knows that "out of the enchanted wood, that thicket of man's memory . . . the quiet face of his friend and brother—poor child, life's stranger, and life's exile, lost like all of us . . . —the lost boy was gone forever, and would not return."

Skillfully crafted, "The Lost Boy" is Wolfe at his best as a short-story writer. It contains his characteristic themes, some of his strongest characterizations, and is both controlled and informed by the use of the four narrative points of view.

Other stories in the collection are less memorable. "No Cure For It" (previously unpublished) depicts a moment in the life of the Gants, a house call by Dr. McGuire caused by Eliza's concern that Eugene is growing too fast. Here there is no cure for life, time, and growth, just as in other works there is none for death and loss. Another moment is captured in *Gentlemen of the Press* (separately published in 1942). This dramatized sketch of city-room life, which rather melodramatically contrasts the trivia of provincial life before the United States entered World War I with the death of an American volunteer in France, gives further reason to be grateful that Wolfe abandoned drama for fiction. "A Kinsman of His Blood" (*Esquire*, June 1935—as "Arnold Pentland") is a sketch of Arnold, Eugene Gant's manic cousin who rejects and denies his family and abandons himself to loneliness and defeat. None of these narratives would likely attract a second reading were they not published in a collection by Wolfe.

On the other hand, "Chickamauga" (*Yale Review*, Winter 1938) certainly would. The narrator, ninety-five-year-old John Pentland, reminisces in 1937 to his great-nephew, Eugene Gant, about his experiences in the Civil War. He remembers not only his own particular story but also those of his friends and relatives. Over and over, he is struck by the strangeness of the way in which everything turned out. He focuses on what befell Jim Weaver, whose enlistment coincided with his chance meeting and prompt falling in love with Martha Pattern—an event which transformed Jim into a man possessed by one idea: to survive the war and marry Martha. Uncle John tells of early battles, the hell of Shiloh, and finally, Chickamauga, the bloodiest battle of the war, where Jim is killed. And readers vicariously experience the strangeness of life as Uncle John collects the personal effects of his friend, who wanted so desperately to live, and then returns home to marry Martha Pattern himself. As John says, it is "as strange as if it happened in a dream."

The last Eugene Gant story in the book, "The Return of the Prodigal" (previously unpublished), depicts a thirty-six-year-old Eugene and his return as a writer of some fame to Altamont after seven years away. He hears the voice of his brother Ben, who had died during the 1918 influenza epidemic, telling him that he can't go home again. Surrounded by "the weather of his youth," he is trapped by Eliza, who in her Molly Bloom–like monologue smothers him with the provincial values of Rotary and literary clubs and small-town politics.

"On Leprechauns" (also previously unpublished) is a satirical but not-very-funny piece on literary critics, the American reading public, and Irish writers. This and "Portrait of a Literary Critic" (*American Mercury*, April 1939) are part of Wolfe's revenge on those who took him to task for both his real and his perceived literary shortcomings.

"The Lion at Morning" (*Harper's Bazaar*, October 1941) presents James Wyman, Sr., who at age seventy-four remembers the strength he once had and at least for once rejects his present life of decaffeinated coffee, dry toast, and fruit juice. Although pleasant enough, "The Lion at Morning," like "On Leprechauns" and "Portrait of a Literary Critic," contains little of enduring value.

In "God's Lonely Man" (*American Mercury*, October 1941—as "The Anatomy of Loneliness") Wolfe describes in his own voice the personal loneliness and isolation he captured more effectively in works such as "The Lost Boy" and "The Web of Earth." As in "Death the Proud Brother," Wolfe ends with a prose poem in praise of loneliness, his "blood-brother" in life.

"The Hills Beyond" is a ten-chapter fragment of an uncompleted novel depicting the Joyners of Old Catawba, George Webber's maternal family. As presented by Aswell, the material moves from a broad picture of the European history of Old Catawba, beginning in 1593, through the arrival of the Joyners, to a description of various contemporary members of the Joyner clan. Like so much of the material in this collection, the fact that the narrative was published under Wolfe's name is its primary claim to serious continuing interest.

Wolfe at Central City, Colorado, 10 August 1935 (Thomas Wolfe Collection, Pack Memorial Public Library, Asheville)

It is difficult not to question Aswell's and Harper's motives in publishing *The Hills Beyond* as what was, apparently, to have been the final word from Wolfe. For some twenty years, until 1961, the collection *was* the final word. In that year C. Hugh Holman's *The Short Novels of Thomas Wolfe* was published by Charles Scribner's Sons and changed permanently any serious student's perception of Wolfe and his shorter fiction. Holman did not assemble new Wolfe materials. Instead he published five works originally written as novellas; but with one exception, their integrity of form had been lost in subsequent publication. The result of reading these works is to see Wolfe as a master of the novella.

The first is "A Portrait of Bascom Hawke" (*Scribner's*, January 1932). At the time it was written, Wolfe thought of it as a self-contained unit. When Max Perkins and he assembled *Of Time and The River*, however, Bascom Hawke was transformed into Bascom Pentland, and the novella was fragmented and scattered throughout the novel. "A Portrait of Bascom Hawke" is a sus-

tained, unified portrait of an old man's despair at and resignation to the passing of life and its ultimate meaninglessness.

"The Web of Earth" is this collection's second work. It is the only one of the works in Holman's collection that was readily available in its original form.

"No Door: A Story of Time and the Wanderer" was written in 1933 and was to have been published as a small book by Scribners in 1934. Instead it was published as two separate stories in *Scribner's Magazine*: "No Door" (July 1933) and "The House of Far and Near" (August 1934). The opening episode subsequently was published as "No Door" in *From Death to Morning*; the remainder appeared as fragments in *Of Time and The River* and *You Can't Go Home Again*. Holman's collection is the only place where "No Door" can be found in its original novella form.

"No Door: A Story of Time and the Wanderer" is a series of episodes in which the protagonist, a young American writer, first in New York and then in Europe, seeks an escape from his isolation and some meaning to life. The opening episode, here entitled "October: 1931," occurs in the apartment of a rich New Yorker and was discussed earlier as the opening story of *From Death to Morning*. The second, entitled "October: 1923," describes the narrator's attempt to escape his solitude and his wandering, through furious, voracious reading. It also contains the hymn to autumn, death, and October that constitutes one of the most splendid moments in *Of Time and The River*. The third section, "October: 1924," describes his search for escape and meaning during a period he spends living with a family in England. Although he lives with them, he cannot share the ruin and the unspoken disgrace of their life as a family.

The last section, "Late April: 1928," is again set in New York. The face of an unidentified man becomes for the narrator the "timeless image of fixity and judgment, the impartial, immutable censor of all the blind confusion and oblivion of a thousand city days, and of the tortured madness and unrest of my own life." In words unspoken, the face says, "Have patience and belief, for life is many days and all this present grief and madness of your life will pass away," and the changes of life exist within the changeless, enduring earth.

If there is no door, no escape, there is life and being. The effect of embodying the statement within this sustained novella rather than scattering it in bits and pieces through two novels and a fragment is to create a work that is unified in form and content. The effect is also to reduce the impression of excessive repetition.

The fourth story in Holman's collection is "I Have a Thing to Tell You," an account of an episode that Wolfe witnessed on the Berlin-to-Paris train in 1936, when a frightened Jewish traveler was taken away at the border by the Nazi authorities. Published in the *New Republic* in March 1937, the story resulted in his books' being banned in Germany. It is a moving, straightforward narrative that focuses on the people and the events of the story rather than on the narrator's sense of isolation, identity, longings, and wanderings. "I Have a Thing to Tell You" is admired even by those who generally do not find Wolfe to their taste. When Aswell later incorporated it into *You Can't Go Home Again*, he violated the spirit of the story by taking a passage out of context and using it to suggest that Wolfe had prophesied his impending death.

"The Party at Jack's" was published in *Scribner's Magazine* in May 1939, some eight months after Wolfe's death. It was expanded by Aswell and also incorporated within *You Can't Go Home Again*. As is the case with "I Have a Thing to Tell You," "The Party at Jack's" is much more objective in its form and focus than Wolfe's earlier works. Both stories represent a partial turning outward by Wolfe from the personal longings that people experience to the avoidable social evils that blight their lives. Jack's party occurs in a Manhattan apartment in a building disturbed from time to time by faint and distant tremors. In contrast to the reality of the Depression, the guests are entertained by Mr. Piggy Hartwell and his miniature circus made of wire figures. The performance is artificial and irrelevant, the guests the same, and the building continues to suffer from underground shakings.

Unlike Wolfe's earlier work, in which he would almost certainly have commented on the isolation of man, the bitter briefness of his days, and the meaninglessness of his life, Wolfe allows the events to speak for themselves. Because he trusts his reader to see all of this without being told, Wolfe can devote himself to underscoring the social criticism implied by the unidentified tremors below the structure in which the rich live and entertain themselves in Depression-era America. The result is a mature achievement.

Holman's presentation of these five novellas in their original form provides a portrait of an artist far different from that suggested by his longer works. Not only was he the creator of formless, sprawling novels, such as *Of Time and The River*, and repetitive short stories, he was the master of the long short story. Indeed, Holman's collection demonstrates that Wolfe's reputation for self-indulgent formlessness is as much the result of Aswell's need to create longer works that would sell and Perkins's sense that Wolfe needed a "major" work to establish his reputation as they are of Wolfe's creative instincts. For there can be no doubt about the integrity and merit not only of these stories, but also of the collection *From Death to Morning*, "The Lost Boy," and "Chickamauga." With the exception of *Look Homeward, Angel*, Wolfe created nothing that truly rivals the excellence of his work in the shorter fictional forms.

In 1987, utilizing manuscript and typescript versions as well as published texts, Francis E. Skipp collected fifty-eight stories, essays, sketches, and prose poems, in order of publica-

Dust jacket for the posthumous collection edited by Edward Aswell (1941). It includes short stories, sketches, a one-act play, and ten chapters of an incomplete novel bearing the same title as the collection.

tion, under the title *The Complete Short Stories of Thomas Wolfe*. All except "The Spanish Letter" had been previously published, but only twenty-three had been previously collected. Skipp's book offers a kaleidoscope of Wolfe's characteristic concerns: the autobiographical people and events; the themes of human isolation, loneliness, and incommunicability; the strangeness of time; the need for certainty in the midst of change; and the importance of coincidence and chance.

None of the newly collected works adds significantly to Wolfe's reputation and achievement as a writer. Few would have been deemed worthy of collecting for publication on the basis of their intrinsic merit. Even so, this collection, combined with Holman's *The Short Novels of Thomas Wolfe*, preserves Wolfe's shorter fiction as completely as we are apt to have it, and that is a valuable service.

Letters:

Thomas Wolfe's Letters to His Mother, Julia Elizabeth Wolfe, edited by John Skally Terry (New York: Scribners, 1943); revised as *The Letters of Thomas Wolfe to His Mother*, edited by C. Hugh Holman and Sue Fields Ross (Chapel Hill: University of North Carolina Press, 1968);

The Correspondence of Thomas Wolfe and Homer Andrew Watt, edited by Oscar Cargill and Thomas Clark Pollock (New York: New York University Press / London: Cumberlege/ Oxford University Press, 1954);

The Letters of Thomas Wolfe, edited by Elizabeth Nowell (New York: Scribners, 1956); abridged as *Selected Letters of Thomas Wolfe* (London: Heinemann, 1958);

Beyond Love and Loyalty: The Letters of Thomas Wolfe and Elizabeth Nowell, edited by Richard S. Kennedy (Chapel Hill & London: University of North Carolina Press, 1983);

My Other Loneliness: Letters of Thomas Wolfe and Aline Bernstein, edited by Suzanne Stutman (Chapel Hill & London: University of North Carolina Press, 1983);

Holding On For Heaven: The Cables and Postcards of Thomas Wolfe and Aline Bernstein, edited by

Stutman (Athens, Ohio: Thomas Wolfe Society, 1985).

Interviews:

Thomas Wolfe Interviewed, edited by Aldo P. Magi and Richard Walser (Baton Rouge & London: Louisiana State University Press, 1985).

Bibliographies:

George R. Preston, Jr., *Thomas Wolfe: A Bibliography* (New York: Boesen, 1943);

C. Hugh Holman, "Thomas Wolfe: A Bibliographical Study," *Texas Studies in Literature and Language*, 1 (Autumn 1959), 425-445;

Elmer D. Johnson, *Of Time and Thomas Wolfe: A Bibliography with a Character Index of His Works* (New York: Scarecrow, 1959);

Maurice Beebe and Leslie A. Field, "Criticism of Thomas Wolfe: A Selected Checklist," *Modern Fiction Studies*, XI (Autumn 1965);

Elmer D. Johnson, *Thomas Wolfe: A Checklist* (Kent, Ohio: Kent State University Press, 1970);

John S. Phillipson, *Thomas Wolfe: A Reference Guide* (Boston: G. K. Hall, 1977);

Carol Johnston, *Thomas Wolfe: A Descriptive Bibliography* (Pittsburgh: University of Pittsburgh Press, 1987).

Biographies:

Agatha Boyd Adams, *Thomas Wolfe: Carolina Student* (Chapel Hill: University of North Carolina Press, 1950);

Thomas Clark Pollock and Oscar Cargill, eds., *Thomas Wolfe at Washington Square* (New York: New York University Press, 1954);

Elizabeth Nowell, *Thomas Wolfe: A Biography* (Garden City, N.Y.: Doubleday, 1960);

Mabel Wolfe Wheaton and Legette Blythe, *Thomas Wolfe and His Family* (Garden City, N.Y.: Doubleday, 1961);

Andrew Turnbull, *Thomas Wolfe* (New York: Scribners, 1967);

Neal F. Austin, *A Biography of Thomas Wolfe* (Austin: Beachman, 1968);

Richard Walser, *Thomas Wolfe, Undergraduate* (Durham: Duke University Press, 1977);

David Herbert Donald, *Look Homeward: A Life of Thomas Wolfe* (Boston: Little, Brown, 1987).

References:

A. Scott Berg, *Max Perkins: Editor of Genius* (New York: Dutton, 1978);

Elizabeth Evans, *Thomas Wolfe* (New York: Ungar, 1984);

Leslie A. Field, *Thomas Wolfe and His Editors* (Norman: University of Oklahoma Press, 1987);

Field, ed., *Thomas Wolfe: Three Decades of Criticism* (New York: New York University Press, 1968);

Leo Gurko, *Thomas Wolfe: Beyond the Romantic Ego* (New York: Crowell, 1975);

C. Hugh Holman, *The Loneliness at the Core: Studies in Thomas Wolfe* (Baton Rouge: Louisiana State University Press, 1975);

Holman, *Thomas Wolfe* (Minneapolis: University of Minnesota Press, 1960);

Holman, ed., *The World of Thomas Wolfe* (New York: Scribners, 1962);

John Lane Idol, Jr., *A Thomas Wolfe Companion* (New York & London: Greenwood, 1987);

Pamela Hansford Johnson, *Hungry Gulliver* (New York: Scribners, 1948); republished as *The Art of Thomas Wolfe* (New York: Scribners, 1963);

Richard S. Kennedy, *The Window of Memory: The Literary Career of Thomas Wolfe* (Chapel Hill: University of North Carolina, 1962);

Carole Klein, *Aline* (New York: Harper & Row, 1979);

Bruce R. McElderry, Jr., *Thomas Wolfe* (New York: Twayne, 1964);

Herbert J. Muller, *Thomas Wolfe* (Norfolk: New Directions, 1947);

Hayden Norwood, *The Marble Man's Wife* (New York: Scribners, 1947);

Ladell Payne, *Thomas Wolfe* (Austin: Steck-Vaughn, 1969);

Paschal Reeves, ed., *Studies in Look Homeward, Angel* (Columbus: Merrill, 1970);

Reeves, *Thomas Wolfe's Albatross* (Athens: University of Georgia Press, 1968);

Reeves, ed., *Thomas Wolfe and the Glass of Time* (Athens: University of Georgia Press, 1971);

Reeves, ed., *Thomas Wolfe: The Critical Reception* (New York: Lewis, 1974);

Louis D. Rubin, Jr., *Thomas Wolfe: The Weather of His Youth* (Baton Rouge: Louisiana State University Press, 1955);

Rubin, ed., *Thomas Wolfe: A Collection of Critical Essays* (Englewood Cliffs, N.J.: Prentice-Hall, 1973);

Fritz Heinrich Ryssel, *Thomas Wolfe* (New York: Ungar, 1972);

William U. Snyder, *Thomas Wolfe: Ulysses and Narcissus* (Athens: Ohio University Press, 1971);

Richard Steele, *Thomas Wolfe: A Study in Psychoanalytic Literary Criticism* (Philadelphia: Dorrance, 1976);

Richard Walser, *Thomas Wolfe: An Introduction and Interpretation* (New York: Barnes & Noble, 1961);

Walser, ed., *The Enigma of Thomas Wolfe* (Cambridge: Harvard University Press, 1953);

Floyd C. Watkins, *Thomas Wolfe's Characters* (Norman: University of Oklahoma Press, 1957);

John Hall Wheelock, ed., *Editor to Author: The Letters of Maxwell E. Perkins* (New York: Scribners, 1950).

Papers:

Major collections of manuscripts and Wolfe materials are in the William B. Wisdom Collection in the Houghton Library, Harvard University; the Wilson Library of the University of North Carolina at Chapel Hill; the Braden-Hatchett Thomas Wolfe Collection at Memphis State University; the Sarah Graham Kenan Library of St. Mary's College, Raleigh, North Carolina; and the Pack Memorial Library, Asheville, North Carolina.

Richard Wright

(4 September 1908 - 28 November 1960)

Yoshinobu Hakutani
Kent State University

See also the Wright entries in *DLB 76: Afro-American Writers, 1940-1955* and *DLB Documentary Series 2*.

BOOKS: *Uncle Tom's Children: Four Novellas* (New York & London: Harper, 1938; London: Gollancz, 1939); enlarged as *Uncle Tom's Children: Five Long Stories* (New York & London: Harper, 1940; London: Gollancz, 1940);

Native Son (New York & London: Harper, 1940; London: Gollancz, 1940);

How "Bigger" Was Born (New York: Harper, 1940);

Native Son (The Biography of a Young American): A Play in Ten Scenes, by Wright and Paul Green (New York & London: Harper, 1941); revised by Green, in *Black Drama, An Anthology*, edited by William Brasmer and Dominick Consola (Columbus, Ohio: Merrill, 1970), pp. 70-178;

Twelve Million Black Voices: A Folk History of the Negro in the United States (New York: Viking, 1941; London: Drummond, 1947);

Black Boy: A Record of Childhood and Youth (New York & London: Harper, 1945; London: Gollancz, 1945);

The Outsider (New York: Harper, 1953; London & Sydney: Angus & Robertson, 1953);

Savage Holiday (New York: Avon, 1954);

Black Power: A Record of Reactions in a Land of Pathos (New York: Harper, 1954; revised edition, London: Dobson, 1956);

Bandoeng, 1,500,000,000 d'hommes, translated by Hélène Claireau (Paris: Calmann-Lévy, 1955); English version published as *The Color Curtain: A Report on the Bandung Conference* (Cleveland & New York: World, 1956; London: Dobson, 1956);

Pagan Spain: A Report of a Journey into the Past (New York: Harper, 1956; London: Bodley Head, 1960);

White Man, Listen! (Garden City, N.Y.: Doubleday, 1957);

The Long Dream (Garden City, N.Y.: Doubleday, 1958; London & Sydney: Angus & Robertson, 1960);

Eight Men (Cleveland & New York: World, 1960);

Richard Wright

Lawd Today (New York: Walker, 1963; London: Blond, 1965);

American Hunger (New York: Harper & Row, 1977; London: Gollancz, 1978);

Richard Wright Reader, edited by Ellen Wright and Michel Fabre (New York: Harper & Row, 1978).

PLAY PRODUCTIONS: *Native Son*, by Wright and Paul Green, New York, St. James Theatre, 24 March 1941;

Daddy Goodness, by Wright and Louis Sapin, New York, St. Mark's Playhouse, 4 June 1968.

MOTION PICTURE: *Native Son*, screenplay by Wright, Classic Films, 1951.

Richard Wright was a preeminent African-American writer whose influence on the course of American literature has been widely recognized. As Irving Howe has said, "The day *Native Son* appeared, American culture was changed forever." The importance of Wright's works, beginning with *Uncle Tom's Children* (1938; enlarged, 1940), comes not so much from his technique

and style but from the particular impact his ideas and attitudes have made on American life. His early critics' consideration was that of race. They were unanimous in the view that if Wright had not been black his work would not have been so significant. As his vision of the world extended beyond the United States, his quest for solutions expanded from problems of race to those of politics and economics in the emerging Third World. Finally, his long exile in France gave his national and international concerns a universal dimension. Wright's development was marked by an ability to respond to the currents of the social and intellectual history of his time.

Wright was born on 4 September 1908 near Natchez, Mississippi, to an illiterate sharecropper, Nathaniel Wright, and a well-educated black woman, Ella Wilson Wright. When Wright was six, his family moved to Memphis in search of employment, but his father left the family for another woman. After several more moves to various places, in 1918 his mother fell ill, and the family moved to Jackson, Mississippi, to live with Ella's mother, a fanatic Seventh Day Adventist. The harsh religious code Wright's grandmother imposed on him is well portrayed in the first volume of his autobiography, *Black Boy: A Record of Childhood and Youth* (1945). At twelve Wright was enrolled in a Seventh Day Adventist school near Jackson, and later he attended public schools in the city for a few years. In Spring 1924 the *Southern Register*, a local black newspaper, printed a short story, "The Voodoo of Hell's Half-Acre," his first attempt at writing. No complete version is known to exist.

From 1925 to 1927 Wright worked at a few menial jobs in Jackson and Memphis. In Memphis he began reading literature, especially the works of H. L. Mencken, Theodore Dreiser, and Sinclair Lewis. In *Black Boy* Wright tells how he was inspired by Dreiser's *Sister Carrie* (1900) and *Jennie Gerhardt* (1911): "It would have been impossible for me to have told anyone what I derived from these novels, for it was nothing less than a sense of life itself. All my life had shaped me for the realism, the naturalism of the modern novels, and I could not read enough of them."

In 1927 Wright traveled to Chicago and obtained a position as a post-office clerk. As the Depression hit, he lost the position, but the relief office gave him several temporary jobs, including work with the Federal Negro Theatre and later the Illinois Writers' Project. In April 1931 his first major short story, "Superstition," was published by *Abbott's Monthly*. The following year he attended meetings sponsored by the John Reed Club in Chicago, a leftist literary group, and became a member of the Communist party. Before moving to New York in 1937, he had written poems, short stories, and essays, many of which appeared in leftist periodicals.

In New York, Wright became the Harlem editor of the *Daily Worker*, a Communist newspaper, and helped edit *New Challenge*, a short-lived literary magazine. In 1938 four of his stories were collected and published as *Uncle Tom's Children* and won a literary prize from *Story* magazine. The following year he was awarded a Guggenheim Fellowship to complete his first novel, *Native Son* (1940). In August 1939 he married his first wife, Dhimah Rose Meadman, a white dancer. The couple soon separated, however. The year 1940 brought him fame and financial success: the Book-of-the Month Club chose *Native Son* as its March selection, and an enlarged edition of *Uncle Tom's Children* was published.

On 12 March 1941, after divorcing Rose, Wright married his second wife, Ellen Poplar, a white member of the Communist party, from Brooklyn. In the same year, he published *Twelve Million Black Voices*, the first of a series of nonfiction books on racial issues. His first child, Julia, was born in 1942. By the end of 1944 he had broken with the Communist party, as indicated in his *Atlantic Monthly* (August-September 1944) article "I Tried to Be a Communist" (incorporated into *American Hunger*, the second volume of his autobiography, published in 1977). His novella "The Man Who Lived Underground" was included in *Cross-Section* (1944), an anthology edited by Edwin Seaver (and later collected in Wright's *Eight Men*, 1960). *Black Boy*, published in 1945, captured wide publicity and was a Book-of-the-Month Club selection.

From after World War II until his death in 1960, although he traveled often, Wright became a permanent voluntary exile in Paris. He and his family became French citizens in 1947 and eventually bought a farm in Ailly, which they maintained along with a Paris apartment. Before the publication of his second novel, *The Outsider* (1953), no new books of his had come out since 1945, but he cherished his Parisian life, associating with French and African writers and intellectuals. His second daughter, Rachel, was born in 1949. In 1954 he published a minor novel, *Savage Holiday*. He also continued to travel in Africa, Europe, and Asia, which led him to write several

Margaret Bolden Wilson, Wright's fanatically religious grandmother, with whom he lived as a youth in Jackson, Mississippi. She branded all fiction as work of the devil.

nonfiction books: *Black Power: A Record of Reactions in a Land of Pathos* (1954); *Pagan Spain* (1956); *The Color Curtain: A Report on the Bandung Conference* (1956; first published in French, 1955); and *White Man, Listen!* (1957). Wright's last years were plagued by illness (amoebic dysentery) and financial hardship. He tried his hand at writing English haiku, four thousand of them, most of which were not published. He also tried to write a novel, "Island of Hallucination," which was never fully published (part of it—"Five Episodes"—was anthologized by Herbert Hill in *Soon, One Morning*, 1963). Wright did publish another novel, *The Long Dream* (1958), but it was doomed by adverse criticism. Nevertheless, he was successful in preparing another collection of short stories, *Eight Men*, published posthumously. Wright died in Paris at age fifty-two. A few years later *Lawd Today* (1963) was published; he had begun this short novel in 1936.

Wright was a remarkably resilient thinker and writer. His successes are beyond dispute, his failures understandable. He has fascinated not only literary critics, but also philosophers, psychologists, sociologists, and historians. Though many of his works failed to satisfy the rigid standards of New Criticism, his evolution as a writer has excited readers the world over. Biographer Michel Fabre speculates that toward the end of his life Wright "was once again going through a period of ideological change which, had its course been completed, might have caused him to start writing in a new vein. It is highly probable that the civil rights and Black Power movements would have given him a second wind, had he lived another five years."

The enlarged (1940) version of *Uncle Tom's Children*, Wright's first book, consists of five stories about the lives of black people in the deep South. These stories prefigure the theme, structure, and ideology of his later fiction. Wright seems to imply here, as he does in his other fiction, that American social conditions are directly responsible for the degradation of black people. Recent criticism, however, has modified this interpretation, suggesting that Wright went beyond naturalism. The pessimistic determinism often associated with naturalism taught the young Wright the meaning of racial oppression. A victim of oppression himself, Wright directed his energy toward rebellion. While he escaped the pessimistic outlook of naturalism, his respect for that philosophy helped him develop his own individualism and endow his characters with self awareness. Only vaguely are the black characters in *Uncle Tom's Children* conscious of their racially oppressive environment, but they willfully seek freedom and self-determination.

"Big Boy Leaves Home" (anthologized in *The New Caravan*, 1936), the first story in Wright's collection, features a young boy's escape from his violent southern community. Four innocent, happy-go-lucky black boys are discovered naked by a white woman while they are swimming in a pond on a white man's premises. When she screams, her male companion without warning begins shooting and kills two of the boys. Big Boy manages to overcome the white man and accidentally kills him. Now the two surviving boys must take flight; Bobo is captured, but Big Boy reaches home and is told by church leaders to hide in a kiln until dawn, when a truck will come by to take him to Chicago. While hiding, he poignantly watches Bobo lynched and burned. Witnessing such an event gives Big Boy not only a feeling of terror and hatred but a sense of self-awareness and maturity. Although the events take place in less than twenty-four hours, the story is divided into five parts that correspond to the crucial stages in Big Boy's development from innocence, through violence, suffering, and terror, to freedom.

"Down by the Riverside" (previously unpublished), the next story in *Uncle Tom's Children*, dramatizes the tragic death of Brother Mann, who steals a boat during a Mississippi flood to take his pregnant wife to a hospital for the child's delivery. On Mann's way to the hospital he is discovered by the owner of the boat who tries to shoot him, but Mann, in self-defense, kills the owner. When Mann reaches the hospital, he finds his wife is dead. Later he is asked by the town authorities to join their rescue work for stranded citizens. The first house to which he is sent, with a black companion, both of them on another boat, happens to be that of the owner of the stolen boat, whose family recognizes Mann. Although he considers killing them, he changes his mind and rescues them. Once the boat safely reaches the hills, they tell the white authorities that Mann is a murderer. As Mann flees down the riverside, he is shot to death. The story is filled with coincidental events that foreshadow Mann's doom. In contrast with "Big Boy Leaves Home," this story suggests the futility of a man struggling against the elements of chance and fate that undermine his perseverance and will to survive.

The plot of "Long Black Song" (also previously unpublished) is less complicated than the other stories. A white phonograph salesman seduces a black farmer's wife, Sarah, while her husband, Silas, is away during the day. When Silas returns home, he discovers her infidelity and fumes over it. The next day the salesman comes back, with another white man waiting in the car. Sarah leaves the house with her child to warn the salesman of Silas's presence. Silas then exchanges gunfire with the men, killing one of them. Later white lynchers arrive and set fire to the house with Silas inside. The story is told from Sarah's point of view. On the one hand, Sarah, unconcerned with the materialistic strivings of men, is trying to recapture the memories of a past love; on the other, Silas is trying to realize his dream of owning a farm. Both dreams, however, come to naught in the face of a caste system that allows for the exploitation of others. The success of the story lies in the noble victory of Silas, who realizes at his death that his wife's disloyalty to him has been permitted by the white bourgeois code to which he had so easily acquiesced. When white men sexually exploited black women other than

Wright's second wife, Ellen Poplar Wright, with their children, Julia and Rachel, at the Wrights' farm in Ailly, near Paris, circa 1956

his own wife, Silas did not think about it seriously.

The last two stories in *Uncle Tom's Children* deal with the Communist ideology as it affects the black communities of the South. "Fire and Cloud" (*Story*, March 1936) takes place during the Depression and presents a black minister trusted by both blacks and whites. His dilemma is whether to dissuade his congregation from demonstrating for the food they need, or to support the march at the risk of violence. While many of the elders in his church cannot break with their traditional faith in passive resistance, the Reverend Mr. Taylor can change and does opt for solidarity and militancy. Similarly, "Bright and Morning Star" (*New Masses*, 10 May 1938)—the story added to the collection in 1940—deals with the change of attitude a black woman takes toward Christianity. Aunt Sue, the mother of two revolutionary black youths, is accustomed to the attitude of forbearance preached by black church leaders, but now that she is awakened by the

"bright and morning star" of Communism, she becomes a martyr instead of a victim of white power. When she is summoned by the white authorities to claim the body of her murdered son, she shoots the official dead before she is killed.

The initial critical reception of *Uncle Tom's Children* in 1938 was generally favorable. James T. Farrell, appreciative of Wright's direct and realistic style, remarked in the *Partisan Review* (May 1938) that the book serves as an exemplary refutation for those who wished to write "such fancy nonsense about fables and allegories." In response to those critics who wanted Wright to pace more steadily in his narrative and delve more deeply into his material, Farrell argued that Wright effectively employs simple dialogue "as a means of carrying on his narrative, as a medium for poetic and lyrical effects, and as an instrument of characterization." Most reviewers, both black and white, praised Wright's first work without reservation; all respected him for breaking away from stereotypes. Malcolm Cowley found the stories "heartening, as evidence of a vigorous new talent, and terrifying as the expression of a racial hatred that has never ceased to grow and gets no chance to die" (*New Republic*, 6 April 1938). Cowley considered legitimate the Communist aim to unite black and white and regarded racial violence in the South as inevitable. Many critics were also impressed by Wright's language and art, especially his use of black dialect. Robert Van Gelder compared him to Ernest Hemingway (*New York Times Book Review*, 13 April 1938); Allen Maxwell likened his style to John Steinbeck's (*Southwest Review*, April 1938).

Some readers were antagonistic to Wright's racial views. As if in return for Wright's unfavorable review of her novel *Their Eyes Were Watching God* (*New Masses*, 5 October 1937), Zora Neale Hurston categorized *Uncle Tom's Children* as a chronicle of hatred with no act of understanding and sympathy (*Saturday Review*, 2 April 1938). She opposed Wright's politics, too, arguing that his stories fail to touch the fundamental truths of black life.

The earliest extended critical analysis of Wright's short fiction was by Edwin Berry Burgum (in the *Quarterly Review of Literature*, Spring 1944), who confirms Wright's skill in structuring the stories in the form of modern tragedy. the hero's individualism collides with the external forces of society. For example, Wright skillfully illustrates a black man's rebellion against society in the heroism of Silas, the protagonist in "Long Black Song." Burgum also finds Wright's style extremely congenial to his material, claiming that his style in the short stories was influenced by Hemingway: both writers use short sentences to describe surface activities; but whereas Hemingway disguises the confusions beneath the surface, Wright clarifies them.

Later estimates of the book concur with Burgum's. Edward Margolies, in *The Art of Richard Wright* (1969), observes that one of the successes of *Uncle Tom's Children* is Wright's use of Marxism for didactic purposes. Portraying conflicts that are true to the facts of life in the South, his stories usually succeed by their integration of plot, imagery, character, and theme. Wright also renders his stories sometimes in biblical terms. The Reverend Mr. Taylor and Aunt Sue, for example, arrive at their moments of truth through Communistic or Christian ideals, but also as a result of "their peculiar Negro folk mysticism." The sweep and magnitude of Wright's stories are, Margolies observes, "suf-

fused with the author's impassioned convictions about the dignity of man." Dignity, as Blyden Jackson, an eminent black critic, suggests, is a central issue in "Big Boy Leaves Home," as it is in Wright's fiction in general. He explains in *Southern Literary Journal* (Spring 1971) that "Big Boy Leaves Home," instead of showing the quality of a black man's will to survive oppression, presents the lynching of Bobo as "the ultimate indignity that can be inflicted upon an individual."

Eight Men, the other volume of Wright's short fiction, comprises seven short stories and one novella, published in various periods of his career. "The Man Who Saw the Flood" (*New Masses*, 24 August 1937—as "Silt") and "The Man Who Was Almost a Man" (*Harper's Bazaar*, January 1940—as "Almos' a Man"), both written in the 1930s, reflect the hard times black farmers faced in the South. The first story portrays a family of three stranded by a flood and then threatened by a white store owner because of their overdue debt; the second deals with the initiation of a black boy whose family all work for Hawkins, a prosperous southern farmer. Dave, the sixteen-year-old black boy, learns the meaning of white oppression the hard way: when he realizes his dream of owning a gun, a symbol of self-respect and power for him, but accidentally kills Hawkins's mule, he is forced to pay for it by working two full years. Rather than accepting this unjust punishment, he jumps on a train that will carry him North.

The stories Wright wrote in the 1940s, in contrast with those of the 1930s, have an urban setting in common. "The Man Who Went to Chicago" (anthologized as "Early Days in Chicago" in *Cross Section*, 1945) is based on Wright's own experience: he was employed first in a Jewish delicatessen—where he saw a woman cook spit in the food she prepared—and later in a hospital, where he observed a scientifically unreliable experiment being conducted in the name of science. "The Man Who Killed a Shadow" (originally published in French in *Les Lettres Françaises*, 4 October 1946) treats the psychology of fear in a black man. Saul Saunders, encountering in a library a white seductress who falsely "cries rape," kills her for fear of being discovered.

"The Man Who Lived Underground" (a short version of which appeared in *Accent*, Spring 1942) is an allegory of any man, black or white, who feels an innate, inescapable sense of guilt. Fred Daniels, a black man falsely accused of murdering a white woman, hides in a sewer and wit-

Richard Wright

nesses various aboveground activities: a church service, a business transaction, and a suicide resulting from the false accusation of a crime. In the course of his underground life, Daniels comes to realize, as "the man who went to Chicago" does, that much of life is chaotic and meaningless. When he finally emerges from underground to relate this revelation to the police, he learns that they have caught a white man who was the woman's murderer and that he is exonerated. But Daniels declares that he himself is guilty for the sake of all humanity. He then takes the police down the sewer to show where he had lived. One of them, tired of hearing his strange testimony, kills him, saying, "You've got to shoot his kind. They'd wreck things."

Wright's short stories from the 1950s focus attention on white men rather than black men in dealing with racial issues. "Man of All Work" (written in 1957 but previously unpublished) describes an unhappily married white man, who is shocked after he makes amatory advances to a maid who turns out to be a black man in disguise. "Man, God Ain't like That" (also previously unpublished) portrays a white American painter, John, who adopts a native African boy, Babu, as his servant. Babu privately conducts a secret ritual of making sacrifices to his Ashanti ancestors but publically sings Christian hymns. Impressed by white civilization, he reasons that white men must have killed Christ to create such a civilization and that he must kill John, his master, whom he regards as a Christ figure. "Big Black Good Man" (published in French in *La Parisienne*, January-February 1958) treats humorously the inferiority complex of a Danish hotel clerk confronted by a huge black sailor who asks for a room, a bottle of whiskey, and a woman companion.

Eight Men received a decidedly less positive response from critics than *Uncle Tom's Children*. Saunders Redding, a distinguished black critic, dismissed *Eight Men* as the work of a declining author (*New York Herald Tribune Book Review*, 22 January 1961). Though all the stories in the collection indicated distress with Wright's rootlessness, Redding theorized that his long exile, somehow lightened "his anguish," which was "the living substance of his best books." For Redding, even the most impressive story, "The Man Who Lived Underground," seemed only "a first-class Gothic tale." In a similar vein, Richard Gilman (in *Commonweal*, April 1961) found the collection of stories inept, "dismayingly stale and dated." Wright's attempts at humor, tragedy, and pathos "all fail." *Eight Men*, however, pleased Irving Howe, Wright's consistent champion, for its signs of the author's continuous experimentation despite uneven results. Howe found in "Big Black Good Man" "a strong feeling for the compactness of the story as a form. . . . When the language is scraggly or leaden there is a sharply articulated pattern or event." In "The Man Who Lived Underground" Howe found not a congenial expression of existentialism, as other critics did, but an effective narrative rhythm, "a gift for shaping the links between sentences so as to create a chain of expectation" (*New Republic*, 13 February 1961).

Later critical estimates of *Eight Men* are more favorable. Even James Baldwin, who was critical of *Native Son*, considered the collection a reflection of Wright's authentic rage: "Wright's unrelentingly bleak landscape was not merely that of the Deep South, or of Chicago, but that of the world, of the human heart" (*Encounter*, April 1961). Recent criticism of *Eight Men* has concentrated on "The Man Who Lived Underground." David Bakish regards this novella as Wright's finest accomplishment because it is an intellectualized story based upon an authentic experience. Michel Fabre (in *The Unfinished Quest of Richard Wright*, 1973) testifies to the authenticity of the story, showing that it derives not from Fyodor Dostoyevski, but from an account in *True Detective* (August 1941) of Herbert C. Wright, a Los Angeles white man who lived underground and robbed businesses in 1931 and 1932. Fabre reads "The Man Who Lived Underground" as an "existential parable" that presents a humanist message: while an individual can impose masks upon himself, he "acquires his identity from other men."

There is a distinct change of tone in *Eight Men* in comparison with *Uncle Tom's Children*. The earlier racial hatred is replaced by racial understanding in a story such as "Big Black Good Man." Moreover, Daniels's adventures in "The Man Who Lived Underground" may suggest

Wright's own feelings after ten years in the Communist underground. In any event, Wright thrived on naturalism, for when he moved from his naturalistic style in *Uncle Tom's Children* to a more subtle technique in *Eight Men*, he was not as impressive a writer as he was in *Native Son* and *Black Boy*.

Wright's reputation as a major American author was firmly established by his early works: *Uncle Tom's Children*, *Native Son*, and *Black Boy*. His emergence as a black writer was a phenomenon, as *Black Boy* clearly demonstrates, for not only did he endure oppression and lack of freedom in the South and the North but he triumphed over them. His successful transformation of that experience into enduring art has been recognized by readers of different races. Before Wright, the African-American writer primarily addressed himself to the black audience. Had he written for a white audience, he would have been expected to present stereotyped pictures of black people. Exceptions such as W. E. B. Du Bois and Charles W. Chesnutt went largely unheeded, because blacks, as Wright said, "possessed deep-seated resistance against the Negro problem being presented, even verbally, in all its hideous dullness, in all the totality of its meaning." Therefore, it was somewhat miraculous that both black and white readers believed what they read in Wright's early works, in which he destroys the white myth of the patient, humorous, subservient black man.

Bibliographies:

Charles T. Davis and Michel Fabre, *Richard Wright: A Primary Bibliography* (Boston: G. K. Hall, 1982);

Keneth Kinnamon and others, *A Richard Wright Bibliography: Fifty Years of Criticism and Commentary: 1933-1982* (Westport, Conn.: Greenwood, 1988).

Biographies:

Constance Webb, *Richard Wright: A Biography* (New York: Putnam's, 1968);

John A. Williams and Dorothy Sterling, *The Most Native of Sons: A Biography of Richard Wright* (Garden City, N.Y.: Doubleday, 1970);

Michel Fabre, *The Unfinished Quest of Richard Wright* (New York: Morrow, 1973).

References:

Richard Abcarian, ed., *Richard Wright's Native*

Son: A Critical Handbook (Belmont, Cal.: Wadsworth, 1970);

David Bakish, *Richard Wright* (New York: Ungar, 1973);

James Baldwin, "Everybody's Protest Novel," in his *Notes of a Native Son* (Boston: Beacon, 1955), pp. 85-114;

Baldwin, "Richard Wright," *Encounter*, 16 (April 1961): 58-60;

Robert Bone, *Richard Wright* (Minneapolis: University of Minnesota Press, 1969);

Russell Carl Brignano, *Richard Wright: An Introduction to the Man and His Works* (Pittsburgh: University of Pittsburgh Press, 1970);

Ralph Ellison, "Richard Wright's Blues," in his *Shadow and Act* (New York: Random House, 1964), pp. 77-94;

Michel Fabre, *The World of Richard Wright* (Jackson: University Press of Mississippi, 1985);

Robert Felgar, *Richard Wright* (Boston: Twayne, 1980);

Addison Gayle, Jr., *Richard Wright—Ordeal of a Native Son* (Garden City, N.Y.: Doubleday, 1980);

Gayle, *The Way of the New World: The Black Novel in America* (New York: Anchor/Doubleday, 1975), pp. 165-182;

Yoshinobu Hakutani, ed., *Critical Essays on Richard Wright* (Boston: G. K. Hall, 1982);

Irving Howe, "Black Boys and Native Sons," in his *A World More Attractive* (New York: Horizon, 1963), pp. 98-110;

Joyce A. Joyce, *Richard Wright's Art of Tragedy* (Iowa City: University of Iowa Press, 1986);

Keneth Kinnamon, *The Emergence of Richard Wright* (Urbana: University of Illinois Press, 1972);

Edward Margolies, *The Art of Richard Wright* (Carbondale: Southern Illinois University Press, 1969);

Don McCall, *The Example of Richard Wright* (New York: Harcourt, Brace & World, 1969);

David Ray and Robert M. Farnsworth, eds., *Richard Wright: Impressions and Perspectives* (Ann Arbor: University of Michigan Press, 1973);

John M. Reilly, *Richard Wright: The Critical Reception* (New York: Franklin, 1978).

Papers:

The most extensive collection of Wright's papers is in the Richard Wright Archive in the Beinecke Rare Book and Manuscript Library, Yale University. One of the manuscripts of *Black Power* is at Northwestern University. Eighteen letters by Wright are held at the Kent State University Library. Eight of these letters were published (1968) in an unauthorized edition. Rare magazines and newspapers that contain some of Wright's work are housed in the Schomburg Collection of the New York Public Library, the American Library in Paris, and the Harvard University libraries.

Stark Young

(11 October 1881 - 6 January 1963)

Thomas W. Cutrer
Arizona State University West

See also the Young entry in *DLB 9: American Novelists, 1910-1945*.

BOOKS: *The Blind Man at the Window and Other Poems* (New York: Grafton, 1906);

Guenevere: A Play in Five Acts (New York: Grafton, 1906);

Addio, Madretta and Other Plays (Chicago: Sergel, 1912);

Three One Act Plays: Madretta, At the Shrine, Addio (Cincinnati: Kidd, 1921);

Queen of Sheba (New York: Theatre Arts, 1922);

The Flower in Drama (New York: Scribners, 1923; revised, 1955);

The Colonnade (New York: Theatre Arts, 1924; London: Benn, 1924);

The Three Fountains (New York: Scribners, 1924);

Glamour (New York & London: Scribners, 1925);

The Twilight Saint: Play in One Act (New York & London: French, 1925);

The Saint: A Play in Four Acts (New York: Boni & Liveright, 1925);

Sweet Times and The Blue Policeman (New York: Holt, 1925);

Encaustics (New York: New Republic, 1926);

Theatre Practice (New York, Chicago, Boston, Atlanta & San Francisco: Scribners, 1926);

Heaven Trees (New York: Scribners, 1926);

The Theater (New York: Doran, 1927);

The Torches Flare (New York: Scribners, 1928);

River House (New York: Scribners, 1929);

The Street of the Islands (New York: Scribners, 1930);

So Red the Rose (New York: Scribners, 1934; London: Cassell, 1935);

Feliciana (New York & London: Scribners, 1935);

Artemise; in Three Acts (Austin: Von Boeckmann-Jones, 1942);

Immortal Shadows (New York: Scribners, 1948);

The Pavilion: Of People and Time Remembered, of Stories and Places (New York: Scribners, 1951).

OTHER: William Makepeace Thackeray, *The English Humorists of the Eighteenth Century*, ed-

Ossip Garber

ited by Young (Boston, New York, Chicago & London: Ginn, 1911);

"Not in Memoriam, But in Defense," in *I'll Take My Stand: The South and the Agrarian Tradition by Twelve Southerners* (New York: Harper, 1930);

Southern Treasury of Life and Literature, edited by Young (New York, Chicago, Boston, San Francisco, Dallas & Atlanta: Scribners, 1937);

Sidney Carver, *Selected Poems*, preface by Young (New York & London: Scribners, 1947).

TRANSLATIONS: Jean François Regnard, *Le Legataire Universel, Bulletin of the University of Texas*, no. 259 (1912);

Anton Chekhov, *The Sea Gull* (New York & London: Scribners, 1939);

Chekhov, *The Three Sisters* (New York, Los Angeles & London: French, 1941);

Chekhov, *The Cherry Orchard* (New York, Los Angeles & London: French, 1947);

Chekhov, *Uncle Vanya* (New York, Hollywood, London & Toronto: French, 1956).

Stark Young's worldview was the result of the blending of a perfectly provincial childhood and a remarkably cosmopolitan early manhood. His father, Alfred Alexander Young, was a Como, Mississippi, physician who had ridden with Gen. Nathan Bedford Forrest's Confederate cavalry during the Civil War and who would not allow his son art lessons for fear that he would become an "effeminate weakling, certainly of no credit to our class" (as Young recalls in *The Pavilion*, 1951). Young's mother, the former Mary Clark Starks, was a beautiful and accomplished Mississippi belle, whose delicate health and early death left a lifelong mark on her son's consciousness. Through his maternal grandmother, Caroline Charlotte McGehee, he came to know the vast clan of McGehee kin, who populate his novels and short stories, scarcely changed from real life or from the tales of them he heard as a boy. The South, he recalled, was a country peopled with ghosts, "warm, close, and human; the dead were often as present as the living," so quite naturally the family legends of Cousin Micajah, Miss Mary Cherry, and Cousin Lucy loomed large in his consciousness when, grown and living in New York, he turned his hand to fiction.

With his mother's death in 1890 the not-yet-nine-year-old Young moved into the Como home of his granduncle Hugh McGehee, where he lived until 1895, when his father married Lydia Lewis Walton, reunited his family, and moved to Oxford. There, the following year, fourteen-year-old Stark enrolled as a special student at the University of Mississippi, from which he graduated with honors in 1901. His education there, he insisted, "consisted not so much in what is usually called education and informed studies" as it did in personalities and the general principles that were accepted by his instructors, a good many of whom were men who "had come off penniless from the Civil War but were old school gentlemen." The greatest part of his undergraduate education, then, Young claims, was the ability "to recognize in a man the fine flower of the spirit."

His University of Mississippi credentials gained him entrance to graduate school at Columbia University, where he completed a master's degree in English in 1902. Young took with him to the North his native region's "grace of mind and regard for the sensibilities of others." At Columbia he learned the English and European poets, philology, and aesthetics, and spent his Saturdays at the Metropolitan Museum, so absorbed in the paintings and sculpture that his responses and technical perceptions became a habit of mind with him, "and certainly a passion."

The blending of the two cultures, North and South, was to be the hallmark of his career. Although he did not fail to appreciate New York, he was "not ready to abandon the heritage of his recollections before these new experiences; on the contrary, the two seemed to . . . feed and bless each other," creating the "doubleness of vision" that Allen Tate identified as the defining characteristic of the writers of the southern literary renaissance.

After leaving Columbia in 1902, Young served briefly as a reporter for the *Brooklyn Standard Union*, spent a winter in the mountains of North Carolina, and returned to Mississippi as an instructor at a military academy in the hamlet of Water Valley. After only a year he accepted an appointment to the English faculty at the University of Mississippi. In 1906 he published a volume of poetry, *The Blind Man at the Window*, and a verse play, *Guenevere*. The next year, his first of many trips to Italy broadened Young's cultural and intellectual horizons, and when in the fall of that year the University of Texas offered him a position, he resigned from Ole Miss to accept.

In Austin his academic promise, which had begun to blossom at Oxford, reached full bloom. There he edited William Makepeace Thackeray's *The English Humorists of the Eighteenth Century* (1911), translated Jean François Regnard's *Le Legataire Universel* (1912), and published *Addio, Madretta and Other Plays* (1912). In 1914 he wrote an unpublished novel, "The New Wing," and in 1915 he became the founding editor of the *Texas Review* (later named the *Southwest Review*). Despite this wide diversity of talents and interests, Young's energies became increasingly centered on his love of drama. Soon after arriving in Aus-

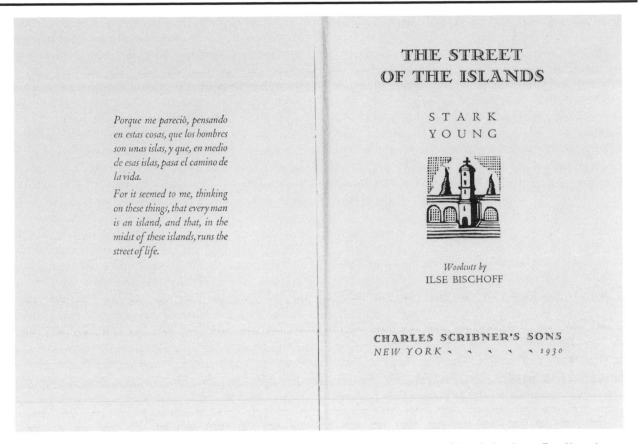

Porque me pareció, pensando
en estas cosas, que los hombres
son unas islas, y que, en medio
de esas islas, pasa el camino de
la vida.

For it seemed to me, thinking
on these things, that every man
is an island, and that, in the
midst of these islands, runs the
street of life.

THE STREET
OF THE ISLANDS

S T A R K
Y O U N G

Woodcuts by
ILSE BISCHOFF

CHARLES SCRIBNER'S SONS
NEW YORK ⟵ ⟵ ⟵ ⟵ 1930

Epigraph and title page for Young's first short-story collection, comprising stories and interludes that reflect Young's agrarian values

tin, he founded the influential Curtain Club, and with this catalyst, he mastered the arts of writing, directing, and designing sets and costumes for the theater.

Having established himself at the University of Texas as a distinguished southern man of letters, Young sought a larger role in the life of American theater. Thus when Amherst College in Massachusetts offered him a professorship in 1915, he accepted without hesitation. Although he never again lived in the South, the habits of mind formed in Mississippi and Texas had cast Young forever as a southerner and made the preservation of the fast-receding Old South value system the principle theme and impetus of all his fiction.

From his new stage at Amherst, Young burst upon the national community of letters with a succession of essays and reviews for the *Bookman, Nation, New Republic, North American Review,* and *Yale Review.* His new play, *At the Shrine,* was published in July 1919 in *Theatre Arts Magazine* (and collected in *Three One-Act Plays,* 1921). Despite these evidences of academic success and

an enthusiastic following of students, Young yearned to leave the teaching profession for a more active role as writer and critic. At the close of World War I he took a leave of absence from his teaching post to tour Spain and Italy, and, in 1920 he made up his mind to leave Amherst to pursue his literary ambitions. In the fall of 1921, at the age of forty, Young moved to New York to become a free-lance writer in the world of the arts.

Two factors made this a propitious time for Young to arrive on the New York artistic scene. First, the years in which Young was to review American theater, 1921 through 1943, proved to be its finest. Second, four magazines, the *New Republic* (where he became drama critic and member of the editorial board), *North American Review, Theatre Arts Magazine,* and *Vanity Fair,* were beginning to seek the thoughtful critical essays that Young considered to be the only truly valuable statements on the merit of a dramatic performance. Young contributed many such pieces, which were later collected by the legendary editor at Scribners, Maxwell Perkins, and published in *The Flower in Drama* (1923), *Glamour* (1925), and *Theatre Practice* (1926).

Soon after arriving in New York, Young became an editor of *Theatre Arts*, a monthly periodical that also published his plays *Queen of Sheba* (April 1922), *The Colonnade* (August 1924), and *Rose Windows* (October 1925), and his translation of Moliere's *George Dandin, or The Discomfited Husband* (September 1924). Young's four-act play *The Saint* was published by Boni and Liveright in 1925. During this period Young was also active as a director but abandoned this aspect of his career after 1924.

At the same time that he was establishing himself as America's most scholarly and aesthetically perceptive drama critic, Young began to dabble in satirical sketches and fictional portraits. These he contributed to the *New Republic* from time to time, and in 1926 he collected and published them as *Encaustics*. More serious work in fiction resulted in *Heaven Trees* (1926), Young's first published novel. He had probably begun work on the novel as early as his years at the University of Texas, and one of the chapters, "My Grandfather McGehee's Wedding," had been published as a short story by the *New Republic* in 1923. Like William Faulkner's *Go Down, Moses* (1942), *Heaven Trees* can be read as a collection of loosely related short stories and fictional sketches rather than as a novel. Unlike his fellow Mississippian, however, Young seeks to idealize plantation life in the decade prior to the Civil War by embuing it with all the qualities he found enduring and desirable in the southern way of life.

A second novel, completed in 1927 and published the following year, continues Young's interpretation of the southern experience. *The Torches Flare* is set in the years between 1850 and 1920 in Clearwater, Mississippi, a locale strongly reminiscent of Oxford. Much less idyllic in tone than *Heaven Trees*, *The Torches Flare* illustrates the physical and moral decay of the postbellum South and recapitulates its author's own plight, that of the artistically talented southerner who must leave his region in order to practice his art. A third novel, *River House* (1929), completes Young's trilogy of southern glory and decay. The plantation River House is a symbol for the region, once proud but now surrounded by the detritus of industrialized society and slowly rotting from within. Only a sense of honor, loyalty, and honesty, which Young sees as inherent in the southern culture, redeems River House and the family that owns it from total collapse.

Between the publications of *The Torches Flare* and *River House*, Young became one of the twelve southerners pledged to contribute essays to the agrarian manifesto, *I'll Take My Stand* (1930). Although others of the group, most notably Robert Penn Warren, Allen Tate, and John Crowe Ransom, have since risen above him in literary acclaim, Young was at the time the most notable of the twelve, and to him and his essay, "Not in Memoriam, But in Defense," fell the honor of the summation of the book's themes. Young's position was the one he had put forth in his trilogy of southern novels and the one that would sustain him through the remainder of his career in fiction: although many of the economic and social forms of the Old South were no longer viable or even desirable in the twentieth century, many of its merits yet lived and offered a guide out of the spiritual malaise of modern society. A strong tradition of humanistic values, he argued, a love of the land, family, religion, and the arts, was the proper answer to the question "What is the end of life?" and an antidote to the soul-destroying cult of materialism.

"Not in Memoriam, But in Defense" became in effect a thematic outline for Young's next and most popular novel, *So Red the Rose* (1934). While collecting material for this, his fullest and most definitive treatment of the southern tradition and value system, Young published his first volume of short stories, *The Street of the Islands* (1930). Set variously in Texas, Louisiana, Mississippi, New York, Spain, and Italy, these stories and interludes, although often different in subject matter from his novels, reflect their author's belief in the agrarian virtues of tradition, order, and family. These "prose pastels," as one reviewer called them, illustrate Young's credo that culture is "the sign and seal of a civilized society" and that the best lives are based upon "gentle feeling, on a formal code of behavior, on a certain vainglory of polish and grandiloquence, and on the life of the affections."

The most memorable of the stories in *The Street of the Islands* are "The Land of Juan de Dios" (*Scribner's*, June 1930), which is set in San Antonio in 1746 and portrays the reunion of a mother with her long-lost and much-beloved son; "Light on the Hills," the story of a Louisiana woman who had married poorly and died young but who still occupied a central position in the affections and tales of her grieving family; and "The Passionate Road," a complex story-within-a-story that explores the sometimes irrational

Illustration for the magazine publication of the story Young chose to open his second short-story collection, Feliciana *(1935)*

course of love and the often-too-heavy price lovers must pay.

In a perceptive and sympathetic review of *The Street of the Islands*, Ellen Glasgow praised the volume's delicate treatment of seemingly slight incidents that, taken in their proper context, speak volumes of meaning. This "perfect blending of style and material," she maintains, will directly transmit the author's impression to readers schooled in the plantation values and traditions. Outlanders may only sense a deeper meaning they may not fully comprehend due to their limited experience. This, she states admiringly, is "art that has roots" (*Saturday Review*, 27 September 1930).

For several years following the publication of *The Street of the Islands*, Young continued his agrarian crusade, making numerous trips into the Deep South and Texas in search of materials, and feuding with his more liberal colleagues at

the *New Republic* over that magazine's handling of the *Scottsboro* case. In 1934 his last, and by far his most successful, southern novel, *So Red the Rose*, was published. It quickly went through twenty printings and was made into a motion picture by Paramount. In order to capitalize on this notoriety, Scribners brought out Young's second collection of short stories, *Feliciana* (1935), and his anthology *Southern Treasury of Life and Literature* (1937).

Most of the stories in *Feliciana* are set on the same ground as *So Red the Rose*, the rich plantation country of Louisiana and Mississippi (although some take place in Texas and in Italy), and in much the same time frame, the decades bracketing the Civil War. As usual, the legends of the McGehee clan figure heavily in plot and theme. The lead story, for example, "Cousin Micajah" (*Saturday Evening Post*, 13 April 1935), is the tale of Micajah McGehee, who falls in love with Stella McNair, also the beloved of his brother Charles. Stella chooses Charles, and Micajah joins John C. Frémont's expedition to California, not to return until after her death. Only then does he make the trek back across the continent to live out his years on the family plantation. "I wrote that story over five times," Young said, "though its source is fact and has lain in my mind since I was a little boy. Cousin Micajah was dead long before I was born, but his life has always been with me."

Feliciana received almost four hundred notices, nearly all of them favorable. Most significant was that of Henry Steel Commager in *New York Herald Tribune Books* (28 July 1935). Commager recognized Young's talent for expressing universal themes with apparently trivial material. What is important in these stories, Commager wrote, is "never merely the incident but the things behind the incident, the gestures and the looks and the words that are not spoken." He also pointed out Young's thematic belief that "life, if it is to last, has a social scheme, has certain hard restrictions and finalities and orders, within which flourish all those affections, family loyalties, and uneventful times together that Southern people know the value of." Although Commager gives Young considerable credit as a stylist, remarking that the best of his stories are "eloquent with things that are not said; the echoes are heard in the music of the words," he takes Young's didactic stance somewhat to task, observing that even the best of his stories are "weighted down with moralizing." One of the few disapproving reviews came from Randall Jarrell in the *Southern Review* (Autumn 1935). The youthful Jarrell found Young to be "snobbish" and "sometimes sentimental." "At his best," however, Young was "decidedly worth reading," and Jarrell was especially keen on the story "Echoes at Livorno" (*Scribner's*, September 1934).

The material in *Feliciana* is admittedly uneven. Despite evidence of great care taken with such stories as "Cousin Micajah," "Echoes at Livorno," and "Shadows on Terrabonne," some of the stories and vignettes were obviously written in haste and largely as filler. In the wake of *So Red the Rose* magazines were offering Young from six hundred to two thousand dollars, three times the normal rates, for any short story. Since they were paying him more than anyone else then writing, Young took advantage of his popularity and slipped into print several stories and sketches well below the level of his best.

Stark Young

Feliciana was Young's last effort as a writer of fiction, and following its publication he returned his interest primarily to the stage. Translations of Anton Chekov's *The Sea Gull* (1939) and *The Three Sisters* (1941), and the writing of his own play "Belle Isle," later retitled *Artemise* (1942), occupied the greatest part of the period from 1938 to 1941.

Failure to find a producer for "Belle Isle" left Young severely depressed, and his work suffered as a consequence. At age sixty in 1941 Young saw his career reach its lowest ebb. As his work in the theater became less and less a joy to him, however, Young took up painting as an avocation and soon found that he had a genuine talent. Within two years of taking up the palette, he had exhibited his paintings at the Pennsylvania Academy of Fine Arts, the Whitney Museum, the Chicago Art Institute, and other prestigious galleries to very favorable critical notices.

In 1947 Young left the staff of the *New Republic*, and the following year he severed his connection with *Theatre Arts*. As a final bow to the theater, Young selected the best of his critical essays for an anthology, *Immortal Shadows* (1948), and then set to work on what was planned to be a two-volume autobiography. Extensive travel in the South and Europe for the next three years recalled scenes from his youth that found their way into his memoir *The Pavilion*. The second of the proposed volumes, which was to deal with his career in New York, was never written. Illness and advancing age sapped Young's energy and interest. He began some work translating plays and revising his earlier work, but in 1959 he suffered a debilitating stroke, from which he never fully recovered. Young died on 6 January 1963 and was buried among the graves of his kin at Como, Mississippi.

Stark Young will be remembered primarily as one of the few truly great American drama critics and, to a lesser degree, as the author of *So Red the Rose* and a contributor to *I'll Take My Stand*. Short-story writing was never the principal focus of his literary endeavors, and despite the obvious care he lavished on many of them—the artist's attention to detail, the striving for the precise word or phrase, and the acute sensitivity to each nuance of human emotion—the stories are little read today and are likely to cause the contemporary reader to feel, as did Jarrell, that Young is unduly patronizing and considers the rest of the world barbarian. Yet Young was able to capture and to hold bits of a fast-fading culture and to transmit what his friend and reviewer Glasgow called "the lovely memory of something I had known and lost and could never recover." Although his success as a writer of short fiction was not major, in several stories Young achieved his only stated goal, "to record or portray something of this thing as it passes near the horizon forever farther, rarer, more poignant" (*The Pavilion*).

Letters:

John Pilkington, ed., *Stark Young: A Life in the Arts: Letters, 1900-1962* (Baton Rouge: Louisiana State University Press, 1975).

Bibliography:

Bedford Thurman, "Stark Young: A Bibliography," Ph.D. dissertation, Cornell University, 1954.

Reference:

Robert Buffington, "Immortal Shadow," *Sewanee Review*, 85 (Summer 1977): 478-483.

Books for Further Reading

Aldridge, John W. *After the Lost Generation: A Critical Study of the Writers of Two Wars*. New York: McGraw-Hill, 1951.

Allen, Frederick Lewis. *The Big Change: America Transforms Itself, 1900-1950*. New York: Harper, 1952.

Allen, Walter. *The Short Story in English*. New York: Oxford University Press, 1981; Oxford: Clarendon Press, 1981.

Bates, H. E. *The Modern Short Story: A Critical Survey*. Boston: Writer, 1949; London: Nelson, 1948.

Bridgman, Richard. *The Colloquial Style in America*. New York: Oxford University Press, 1966.

Bryer, Jackson R., ed. *Sixteen Modern American Authors: A Survey of Research and Criticism*. New York: Norton, 1973.

Cowley, Malcolm. *Exile's Return: A Literary Odyssey of the 1920's*. New York: Viking, 1951.

Cowley, ed. *After the Genteel Tradition: American Writers 1910-1930*, revised edition. Carbondale: Southern Illinois University Press, 1964.

Friedman, Melvin. *Stream of Consciousness: A Study in Literary Method*. New Haven, Conn.: Yale University Press, 1955.

Grabo, Carl H. *The Art of the Short Story*. New York: Scribners, 1913.

Hicks, Granville. *The Great Tradition: An Interpretation of American Literature Since the Civil War*, revised edition. New York: Macmillan, 1968.

Hoffman, Charles Allen, and Carolyn Ulrich. *The Little Magazine: A History and a Bibliography*. Princeton: Princeton University Press, 1947.

Hoffman, Frederick J. *Freudianism and the Literary Mind*. Baton Rouge: Louisiana State University Press, 1945.

Kazin, Alfred. *On Native Grounds*. New York: Reynal & Hitchcock, 1942.

Kenner, Hugh. *A Homemade World: The American Modernist Writers*. New York: Knopf, 1974.

Madden, David. *Tough Guy Writers of the Thirties*. Carbondale & Edwardsville: Southern Illinois University Press, 1968.

Malin, Irvin, ed., *Psychoanalysis and American Fiction*. New York: Dutton, 1965.

May, Charles E., ed. *Short Story Theories*. Athens: Ohio University Press, 1976.

Mott, Frank Luther. *A History of American Magazines*, 5 volumes, Cambridge, Mass.: Harvard University Press, 1957.

O'Connor, Frank. *The Lonely Voice: A Study of the Short Story*. Cleveland: World Publishing, 1963.

O'Faolain, Sean. *The Short Story*. New York: Devin Adair, 1951.

Peden, William. *The American Short Story: Front Line in the National Defense of Literature*. Boston: Houghton Mifflin, 1964.

Peterson, Theodore. *Magazines in the Twentieth Century*. Urbana: University of Illinois Press, 1964.

Reid, Ian. *The Short Story*. London: Methuen, 1977.

Ross, Danforth. *The American Short Story*. Minneapolis: University of Minnesota Press, 1961.

Spiller, Robert E. *The Cycle of American Literature*. New York: Macmillan, 1955.

Stevick, Philip, ed. *The American Short Story, 1900-1945*. Boston: Twayne, 1984.

Swados, Harvey. *American Writers and the Great Depression*. Indianapolis: Bobbs-Merrill, 1966.

Thorp, Willard. *American Writing in the Twentieth Century*. Cambridge, Mass.: Harvard University Press, 1960.

Trilling, Lionel. *The Liberal Imagination: Essays on Literature and Society*. New York: Viking, 1950.

Voss, Arthur. *The American Short Story: A Critical Survey*. Norman: University of Oklahoma Press, 1973.

West, Ray B., Jr. *The Short Story in America: 1900-1950*. Chicago: Regnery, 1952.

Contributors

Susan F. Beegel .... *Nantucket, Massachusetts*
Robert H. Brinkmeyer, Jr. .... *University of Mississippi*
Eric W. Carlson .... *University of Connecticut*
Paul H. Carlton .... *Converse College*
Thomas W. Cutrer .... *Arizona State University West*
Bernard F. Engel .... *Michigan State University*
Kim Flachmann .... *California State University, Bakersfield*
Steven H. Gale .... *Kentucky State University*
James R. Giles .... *Northern Illinois University*
Joan Givner .... *University of Regina*
Yoshinobu Hakutani .... *Kent State University*
Wade Hall .... *Bellarmine College*
Sy M. Kahn .... *University of the Pacific*
Joseph Killorin .... *Tybee Island, Georgia*
Michael Kreyling .... *Vanderbilt University*
Victor Lasseter .... *California State University, Bakersfield*
J. P. Lovering .... *Canisius College*
Richard Messer .... *Bowling Green State University*
Robert W. Morrison .... *Montana State University*
Leonard Mustazza .... *Pennsylvania State University*
James O'Hara .... *Pennsylvania State University*
Paul A. Orlov .... *Pennsylvania State University*
Ladell Payne .... *Randolph-Macon College*
Vilma Raskin Potter .... *California State University, Los Angeles*
H. Edward Richardson .... *University of Louisville*
Joel Roache .... *University of Maryland Eastern Shore*
Kenneth A. Robb .... *Bowling Green State University*
Pat Salomon .... *Bowling Green State University*
Hans H. Skei .... *University of Oslo*
Philip Stevick .... *Temple University*
Joseph S. Tedesco .... *St. Bonaventure University*
Barbara A. White .... *University of New Hampshire*
James Woodress .... *University of California, Davis*
Laura M. Zaidman .... *University of South Carolina-Sumter*

397

Cumulative Index

Dictionary of Literary Biography, Volumes 1-102
Dictionary of Literary Biography Yearbook, 1980-1989
Dictionary of Literary Biography Documentary Series, Volumes 1-8

Cumulative Index

DLB before number: *Dictionary of Literary Biography,* Volumes 1-102
Y before number: *Dictionary of Literary Biography Yearbook,* 1980-1989
DS before number: *Dictionary of Literary Biography Documentary Series,* Volumes 1-8

D

E

G

H

I

J

K

L

N

O

S

U

V

W

Y

Z

(Continued from front endsheets)

80: *Restoration and Eighteenth-Century Dramatists,* First Series, edited by Paula R. Backscheider (1989)

81: *Austrian Fiction Writers, 1875-1913,* edited by James Hardin and Donald G. Daviau (1989)

82: *Chicano Writers,* First Series, edited by Francisco A. Lomelí and Carl R. Shirley (1989)

83: *French Novelists Since 1960,* edited by Catharine Savage Brosman (1989)

84: *Restoration and Eighteenth-Century Dramatists,* Second Series, edited by Paula R. Backscheider (1989)

85: *Austrian Fiction Writers After 1914,* edited by James Hardin and Donald G. Daviau (1989)

86: *American Short-Story Writers, 1910-1945,* First Series, edited by Bobby Ellen Kimbel (1989)

87: *British Mystery and Thriller Writers Since 1940,* First Series, edited by Bernard Benstock and Thomas F. Staley (1989)

88: *Canadian Writers, 1920-1959,* Second Series, edited by W. H. New (1989)

89: *Restoration and Eighteenth-Century Dramatists,* Third Series, edited by Paula R. Backscheider (1989)

90: *German Writers in the Age of Goethe, 1789-1832,* edited by James Hardin and Christoph E. Schweitzer (1989)

91: *American Magazine Journalists, 1900-1960,* First Series, edited by Sam G. Riley (1990)

92: *Canadian Writers, 1890-1920,* edited by W. H. New (1990)

93: *British Romantic Poets, 1789-1832,* First Series, edited by John R. Greenfield (1990)

94: *German Writers in the Age of Goethe: Sturm und Drang to Classicism,* edited by James Hardin and Christoph E. Schweitzer (1990)

95: *Eighteenth-Century British Poets,* First Series, edited by John Sitter (1990)

96: *British Romantic Poets, 1789-1832,* Second Series, edited by John R. Greenfield (1990)

97: *German Writers from the Enlightenment to Sturm und Drang, 1720-1764,* edited by James Hardin and Christoph E. Schweitzer (1990)

98: *Modern British Essayists,* First Series, edited by Robert Beum (1990)

99: *Canadian Writers Before 1890,* edited by W. H. New (1990)

100: *Modern British Essayists,* Second Series, edited by Robert Beum (1990)

101: *British Prose Writers, 1660-1800,* First Series, edited by Donald T. Siebert (1991)

102: *American Short-Story Writers, 1910-1945,* Second Series, edited by Bobby Ellen Kimbel (1991)

Documentary Series

1: *Sherwood Anderson, Willa Cather, John Dos Passos, Theodore Dreiser, F. Scott Fitzgerald, Ernest Hemingway, Sinclair Lewis,* edited by Margaret A. Van Antwerp (1982)

2: *James Gould Cozzens, James T. Farrell, William Faulkner, John O'Hara, John Steinbeck, Thomas Wolfe, Richard Wright,* edited by Margaret A. Van Antwerp (1982)

3: *Saul Bellow, Jack Kerouac, Norman Mailer, Vladimir Nabokov, John Updike, Kurt Vonnegut,* edited by Mary Bruccoli (1983)

4: *Tennessee Williams,* edited by Margaret A. Van Antwerp and Sally Johns (1984)

5: *American Transcendentalists,* edited by Joel Myerson (1988)

6: *Hardboiled Mystery Writers,* edited by Matthew J. Bruccoli and Richard Layman (1989)

7: *Modern American Poets,* edited by Karen L. Rood (1989)

8: *The Black Aesthetic Movement,* edited by Jeffrey Louis Decker (1991)

Yearbooks

1980, edited by Karen L. Rood, Jean W. Ross, and Richard Ziegfeld (1981)

1981, edited by Karen L. Rood, Jean W. Ross, and Richard Ziegfeld (1982)

1982, edited by Richard Ziegfeld; associate editors: Jean W. Ross and Lynne C. Zeigler (198?)

1983, edited by Mary Bruccoli and Jean W. Ross; associate editor: Richard Ziegfeld (1984)